Captain Hogan

Seaman, Merchant, Diplomat On Six Continents

Michael H. Styles

Chester,
Mary Lee said you
would read this!
Michael Styles

Six Continent Horizons
Fairfax Station, Virginia
http://SixContinents.home.att.net

Published by Six Continent Horizons
7004 Sylvan Glen Lane
Fairfax Station, VA 22039-1706
http://SixContinents.home.att.net

Copyright © 2003 by Michael H. Styles. All rights reserved.

Printed in the United States of America

Styles, Michael H.
    Captain Hogan: Sailor, Merchant, Diplomat on Six Continents
    ISBN 0-9744347-0-1 (pbk.: alk. paper)
    Library of Congress Control Number: 2003095952

To the fourth person
to be named after Michael Hogan

Michael Hogan Carver

Sacred to the Memory of
Michael Hogan
During many years a resident of this City:
Born at Stone Hall, in the County of Clare, Ireland.
September 29, A.D. 1766.
In early manhood a bold and successful navigator
and discoverer in seas then almost unknown:
In mature years a prosperous merchant.
The decline of life was not unmarked by vicissitudes of fortune:
But prosperity did not elate, nor could adversity subdue
his firm and constant spirit.
Each quarter of the Globe bore witness to his enterprise,
and its success.
Regretted by his friends, respected by his enemies.
A life of stainless integrity, closed at the City of Washington.
March 26, A.D. 1833. Ætatis 67.

—*Plaque at Grace Church, New York City*

I feel singularly about him. I like the Man, though
I think his abilities (which are excellent in my
opinion) have too much invention and dexterity in
them for a small place such as this, girt in by
restrictions, yet holding forth temptations for
enterprise. He has many friends, is of mild
manners, anxious to please and to oblige.

—*Lady Anne Barnard to Lord Melville*
Cape Town, May 14, 1800

Mr. Hogan was truly a high minded Irish
Gentleman, very honest and liberal in all his views,
and no one more hospitable. He was quick in
temper and easily excited, brave and chivalrous
perhaps to a fault.

—*Autobiography by Rear Admiral Charles Wilkes*

He was energetic, impulsive, generous, hopeful
and knew no such thought as fail—alas the issue!

—*Epitaph by William Hogan*

CONTENTS

Preface   ix
The Setting   1
1   In Service of His Majesty's Navy   4
2   India Voyages   27
3   New South Wales   52
4   Cape of Good Hope Under British Occupation   88
5   Cape of Good Hope, The Investigation   134
6   Cape of Good Hope Under Dutch Restoration   154
7   Fame and Fortune in New York   172
8   New Careers in Hogansburg and Havana   205
9   Agent for Commerce and Seamen, Valparaíso   238
10   American Consul, Valparaíso   289
11   Last Days, Washington, D.C.   338
Epilogue   354
Notes   357
Bibliography   423
Index of Names   428

ILLUSTRATIONS

Cover. Il Netunno, later *Marquis Cornwallis*, oil on canvass (58.42 x 41.275 cm), Author's Collection. Presumed copy of oil on board, original, signed and dated Balthasar Solvyns, 1793, in private collection.

Frontispiece. Michael Hogan, lithograph of Endicott, N.Y.

Figure 1. Track of *Marquis Cornwallis in* East Indies   73

Figure 2. View of Table Bay and Table Mountain, ca. 1800   89

Figure 3. Side view of Claremont, 1806   200

Figure 4. Claremont Hotel, ca. 1860   200

Figure 5: William Hogan home, Hogansburg   225

Figure 6. Hogan home, Valparaíso   283

Figure 7. Hogan's consular appointment   287

Figure 8. Map showing early Hogan voyages   341

PREFACE

This book had its origins over sixty years ago. Both sets of my grandparents lived in Falls Church, Virginia, near Washington, D.C. In the nineteen thirties and forties, when I was a lad, Falls Church was colloquially styled a village, with a main tree-lined street, a *corner* with its postoffice, drug store, hardware store and one gas pump, and The Falls Church, an Episcopal colonial-style brick edifice where George Washington is said to have prayed and Union soldiers stabled their horses.

At one end of Falls Church, my mother's parents, Grandad and Nannan, lived on a four-acre lot called Green Hill. I cannot now evoke its image without suffering pangs of nostalgia, for this is where I like to think I cut my teeth and learned what it means to be free, creative and open to the big outside world. In my child's eye, the house itself was huge: living room, library, dining room, sun room, kitchen with a coal burning range, pantry, screened porch, five bedrooms, two full bathrooms, maid's room, sleeping porch and a two-level attic. I could sleep in a Marine Corps tent (my grandfather was a retired Brigadier General in the Corps), play across dusty Sleepy Hollow Road in the Civil War trenches at Fort Buffalo, hike down that road to ford streams, prance barefoot on the grass, climb trees to box houses, play with outdoor dogs who chased rabbits, and do all manner of things that will never fade from memory. That my memories should be so strong may be unusual because I and my immediate family lived at Green Hill only during occasional summers and, in my case, for one year when I was sixteen. But that one year was memorable. After four years of schooling in Dublin, Ireland, during the first years of World War II, my parents sent my brother David and me to stay at Green Hill with our grandparents so that we could continue our education in American schools. But Nannan was ill in a rest home the whole year, so David and I kept house with Grandad, learning how to cook (not very well) and house clean (not very often), shedding our British accents, and becoming re-Americanized at a real high school.

In the middle of the village, my father's parents lived at Rose Garden. Their house was small, dark, Victorian and smelled of overcooked vegetables, mold and dust. My memories are all negative, from the horse-haired couch on which it was impossible to sit without sliding off to endless Sunday dinners at which we were told how skinny we looked and admonished to have "a little more." But above all is the recall of a huge, heavy painting hanging over that couch of a dark, dour, sullen man who I was told was my great great great grandfather, Michael Hogan, after whom I was named. Next to him hung a portrait of a fairly attractive woman whom I then thought was his wife (she was in fact a daughter, my great great grandmother).

The irony of my memories is that this book, which is both an obligation and a labor of love, owes everything to the Rose Garden clan. Unknown to me at the time, their attic was the repository for the letters, diaries, papers, memorabilia and artifacts of Michael Hogan and many of his descendants. It was not until I was in my forties that I developed a real interest in Michael Hogan. At that time, my Aunt Betty, my father's spinster sister, began unloading the wealth of her attic. Since most of it related to Michael Hogan, I was the main recipient, at least of record materials. It was always understood that I would preserve these records in some form for posterity, preferably as a book. Hence, the obligation to which I have referred.

I made some initial efforts to sort and catalog the materials, but somehow never had the time or determination to proceed further. It soon became easy to promise that the task would be undertaken when I retired, an event that occurred several years ago. Two things then became apparent. One was that there were large gaps in the papers in my possession, even during periods replete with letters. The other was that, as I tried to fill in the gaps through outside research, I found that several libraries, historical societies and archives around the world held a great deal of information about Michael Hogan.

These discoveries led to a decision that the book should not be a genealogy or even just a biography, but a work that might attract broad interest. To do this, I have undertaken a considerable amount of research into public records that mention Michael Hogan or address events and activities in which he participated, as well as research into the history at the time and the places on six continents where he lived.

While the resulting book may not reveal hitherto unknown historical facts or events, I have some hope that the context in which it is presented will contribute to comprehension of the era. If it also leads the reader to ponder the relevance of the past to the present, I will be more than pleased that I have gained a convert. But if nothing else, this book is a simple tale of Michael Hogan, based on my own research and ideas and on those old, musty records of the Rose Garden clan—may those now in their graves forgive me for my contrasting memories of wonderful Green Hill.

I must thank the many persons, some unknown, who helped me find information in the several libraries, archives and historical societies I have consulted in London, Sydney, Dublin, New York, Worcester, Philadelphia, Baltimore, Columbia, Charleston, Savannah and Washington. I am particularly indebted to Dee Nash of Grahamstown, South Africa, an author in her own right, who provided me with a wealth of material from the Capetown Archives, as well as many suggestions and comments on the several chapters that deal with Hogan's stay and business at Capetown. Special thanks also to Diane Lethcoe for editing the text for grammatical errors, style and clarity.

THE SETTING

> *It was the best of times, it was the worst of times, it was the age of wisdom, it was the age of foolishness, it was the epoch of belief, it was the epoch of incredulity, it was the season of Light, it was the season of Darkness, it was the spring of hope, it was the winter of despair, we had everything before us, we had nothing before us, we were all going direct to Heaven, we were all going direct the other way....*
>
> —Charles Dickens, *A Tale of Two Cities*

Dickens often-quoted introduction was intended to describe the climate surrounding the twenty year period before and during the French Revolution from 1775 to 1794, but it could equally have applied to all of the West (now sometimes called the Atlantic community) through 1815 when the Napoleonic Wars and the War of 1812 ended. The main events of this book take place during these periods and into the next fifteen years.

Every period of history is transitional in some sense because each event, idea or trend is merely a precursor of the next one. Nevertheless, a favorite pastime of historians is to develop theories showing why particular eras or series of events mark significant historic change, and no change has attracted more attention than the advent of the modern era, sometimes called the industrial revolution. Some say it began with the invention of the steam engine in 1764, others that the seeds were sown as far back as the fifteenth and sixteenth centuries with the Renaissance, printing press, Reformation, and discoveries of new lands in the Americas and new trade routes to the Orient. The industrial revolution has been viewed as causing one of the two great shifts in human development, the other being the agricultural revolution some 10,000 years ago from which cities, government, diverse societies and conquest came to dominate the world scene. These theories are all correct, and all equally wrong. Major historical changes may be marked by one or two principal events (such as peristroika and glasnost, the direct causes of the sudden collapse of the Soviet Union and its hegemony over Eastern Europe), but the conditions which make major changes inevitable are years in the making. It is in this sense that the author can claim that the half-century covered by the main events of this book—roughly 1780 to 1830—marks the transition to the modern era. The claim is not without some basis in fact. Before the period, there was no mechanized industrial production; afterwards almost all countries in the Western world had taken at least initial steps toward industrialization, expanding international trade and the spread of consumerism to a wider range of classes. Before, monarchies with varying forms of absolute power reigned; after, democratic (as well as socialist) ideas were changing almost all Western governments. Before, while Britain may have been a leading power, it was not supreme; after, it was well on the way to acquiring the largest empire ever known and other European countries were also joining in imperial conquest of colonies in Africa and Asia. Before, the United States was nothing more than an outpost; after, it was growing faster in population and territory than any other country. Before, dynastic and balance of power wars were endemic; after, there would be comparative peace in Europe for almost a century, to be broken by the greatest wars of annihilation of all times. The era also saw the increasing rise of the entrepreneur in all economic activities as the human catalyst that made innovation and risk taking possible, breaking the traditional ways of guilds and government-protected trade monopolies. An increasing number of these entrepreneurs were common men who rose above the class into which they had been born by amassing wealth which previously only the privileged enjoyed. This is not to say that the rags to riches phenomenon did not previously exist or that it reached its zenith during this period. Some people had been able to rise from the lower and middle classes before, and the sagas of great wealth (Vanderbilt, Rockefeller, Carnegie, Gates) did not come until the latter half of the twentieth century and into current times.

Because no one can fully understand the era in which he is living, it probably would not have occurred to the central figure of this book—Michael Hogan—that he was witnessing and participating in a special period in history or that the dichotomies so dramatically portrayed by Dickens, writing (it must be said) many years later with the benefit of hindsight, had any meaning for him. But he was not an idle, stay-at-home observer, as most of us are. From a very young age he roamed the seas of the world, visited distant lands, was directly affected by the wars of the era, emigrated to different locations several times due to international events, and saw the development of many newly independent countries. He lived and participated in two worlds—the West of his birth and upbringing and the mysterious Orient from which he made his fortune. (Like other orientalists of the time, he would have had little or no comprehension of the latter-day consequences arising from the racial, religious and other disparities of these two worlds). In his own way, though his name is in few history books and he can claim no historical role, he was a man of the world, as much in his own way as were such well-known heroes and villains as George Washington, Thomas Jefferson, Napoleon Bonaparte, Talleyrand, Wellington or King George III.

He was first and foremost an entrepreneur, along with many other of his time, who rose, if not from abject poverty, at least from less than privileged conditions, to wealth, even if in the end he lost most of it. In the process, he contributed to the unparalleled economic advancement that has taken place in the Western world over the past two hundred years, fueled by international trade, capital formation and eventually industrialization. His story is not one of lofty ideals or romantic notions, such as Robin Hood or Horatio Alger. Readers will form their own judgment of his activities and character, possibly not favorable, but they may want to note that he was not alone in things that he did or how he did them. His greatest transgression, by any standard, was involvement in the slave trade. Slavery and the slave trade did not end during Hogan's lifetime, but moral attitudes were changing, as is illustrated by the lengths to which Hogan went to hide his involvement in the trade. Despite the outward cloak of respectability men of the era tried to give to their activities, greed, fraud, influence peddling and other forms of vanity and deceit were endemic, as they still are. Man was and is an imperfect creature. This book tries to paint Michael Hogan and others as they really were, not as they liked to think of themselves, nor for that matter as historian revisionists would dictate. If it does nothing else, I hope it will demonstrate the pitfalls of too readily passing judgment on those long gone, lest future generations do the same to us.

ONE

IN SERVICE OF HIS MAJESTY'S NAVY

...his share of...fun and frolic and odd adventures.

—William Hogan about his father

On March 13, 1781, a British Navy squadron of five ships-of-the-line, the precursors of modern battleships, mounting a total of 288 guns, sailed from Spithead on a secret mission. The squadron was accompanied by nine smaller fighting ships, eight armed transports with 2,600 troops, twelve supply ships and fourteen East Indiamen. Its mission was to take the Cape of Good Hope from the Dutch and to reinforce British forces in India. However, the force was originally put together for a different purpose that tells much about British economic interests.

In the summer of 1780, Britain had been at war with its rebellious American colonies for five years, with their French ally for two years and with France's Bourbon ally Spain for one year. France and Spain had entered the war because they were unwilling to continue to accept the 1763 treaty ending the Seven Years War, known in the Americas as the French and Indian War. France had lost its outposts in Quebec, the Mississippi region and India, and Spain had lost Florida and failed to regain Gibraltar. The expanded war would be fought on the seas and at colonial outposts ranging from North America and the West Indies to the English Channel, the Mediterranean, India and the East Indies. By 1780 the American Colonists were at a low point in their quest for independence. George Washington's army had suffered through a winter worse than that at Valley Forge, Savannah and Charleston had fallen to Cornwallis, who was threatening the Carolinas and Virginia in a strategic move to isolate the main American forces in the New York area, and funds to prosecute the war were almost depleted. Although the French had promised much to their American ally, they had so far delivered little in either troops or naval support. Nevertheless, the British had been unable to win a decisive victory, in large part because they were forced to spread their naval strength among defense of the homeland against threatened invasion by French and Spanish forces, protection of Gibraltar and retention of their sugar interests in the West Indies. It was important to British strategy to neutralize Spain's participation in the war and persuade it not to act in concert with its Bourbon ally.

Spain was not then considered an inconsequential enemy although its power was waning. It held substantial portions of territory in the New World and Orient, and many still believed that the West Indies and Central and South America held more promise than the northern colonies. The West Indies provided sugar, while Spanish America still produced the gold used to decorate European edifices and the silver needed to finance Europe's trade imbalances with China.

It was in this context that the little known South Seas project was approved by the British Cabinet in August 1780. Its objective was to take over several Spanish ports and territories in Mexico, Peru and Chile in attacks mounted from India.[1] The British hoped that Spain would opt out of its alliance with France and seek a separate peace with Britain when its economic interests in the New World and Pacific were unexpectedly threatened. (If the tactic had succeeded, the British would then be fighting only France and the American Colonists, with possibly disastrous consequences for the latter.) There was also a British economic motive in the venture founded on the perhaps unrealistic belief that the East India Company, which had a government-granted monopoly on trade between Britain and the Orient, could directly control the silver trade routes in the Pacific to finance its imports from China. (Although not yet articulated, it would soon become British strategy to extend its trade interests around the globe by acquiring key outposts to protect vital sea lanes.) When the East India Company was asked to provide supporting supply and troop ships, it insisted that the Philippines and the Spice Islands, mostly under Spain's control, be added to or substituted for the Latin America conquests.

Prior to the formal adoption of the South Seas project, the British authorities had given tacit approval to one or more private plans to seize Spanish ships and property in South America. The possibility of this limited action remained in the minds of British adventurers for a number of years, as will be seen.[2]

Whatever the motive, the ambitious plan was superseded by events. On December 20, Britain declared war on the Netherlands which, despite a long-standing alliance, had been defying Britain's trade edicts and showing unmistakable signs of friendship with, and even recognition of, the nascent American Republic. Britain was now at war, not only with the American Colonists, but also with France, Spain and the Netherlands, as well as facing the belligerent although still neutral Northern Powers, principally Russia. Although the Netherlands posed little military or naval threat, its entry into the war added India and the East Indies as areas of concern to Britain's economic interests. The Dutch held the Cape of Good Hope, a vital stopping off place for vessels sailing between Europe and India and the East Indies, as well as the naval base of Trincomalee on Ceylon from which the French could mount operations against British East India Company centers in India. It was feared that the French would reinforce the Cape in order to support military and naval operations in the Indian Ocean and, in the process, interdict Britain's vital trade with the Orient. The South Seas adventure was therefore abandoned; instead, the British Cabinet a few days later decided to send a naval and army force to seize the Cape of Good Hope and afterwards reinforce bases in India. It was on this secret mission that the British naval squadron was engaged.

When a French spy in London easily discovered the British intention, a French squadron of five ships-of-the-line mounting 340 guns, one sloop, and eight merchantmen with 1,100 troops aboard was dispatched from Brest on March 22 with orders to get to the Cape of Good Hope first.

Both the British and French squadrons were parts of larger fleets being dispatched for major naval and ground operations. The total British fleet consisted of thirty-three ships-of-the-line on their way to resupply Gibraltar, reinforce British naval and army forces in North America, seize the Cape of Good Hope and reinforce India. The French and Spanish combined fleet consisted of twenty-six ships-of-the-line sailing with comparable, though opposite, objectives to seize Gibraltar, assist in defeating the British in the American Colonies, seize Jamaica and reinforce the Cape of Good Hope and India. The French North American fleet, commanded by Admiral de Grasse, would shortly defeat the British at the Battle of the Capes, thereby contributing to the victory of General Washington and French forces at Yorktown in October 1781.

If the main British fleet had received better intelligence and not been delayed off Ireland by unfavorable winds, it might well have met the French fleet leaving Brest encumbered by 156 transports and merchantmen, and would likely have won one of the major and most fateful sea battles of all time, ending hopes for American independence for some years to come. But the main bodies of the two fleets never did meet.

The British squadron destined for the Cape of Good Hope was commanded by George Johnstone on the flag ship H.M.S. *Romney*. The fifty-one year commodore had an undistinguished career in the British Navy and had served in several non-naval capacities, including governor of West Florida when the British acquired the territory after the Seven Years War in 1763, one of the commissioners in the ill-fated British attempt to negotiate with the American rebels in 1778 and a member of Parliament.[3]

Fourteen year-old Michael Hogan was among a crew of 350 men on board one of the other ships in the squadron, the 50-gun H.M.S. *Jupiter* commanded by forty-seven year old Captain Thomas Pasley. The lad came from County Clare in the western part of Ireland, one of the poorest areas of the country. Jet aircraft today land and take off on runways at Shannon Airport just a stone's throw from property where there was once an area known as Stonehall. It was there on September 29, 1766, that the future midshipman was born.[4]

Stonehall was a 330-acre townland divided into some fifteen plots of land leased to tenant farmers, as well as the name of the manor home and outlying utility and office buildings which together occupied eighty-three acres. The manor house was "narrow, two storied, five bay, gable-ended, with seven chimneys, over a cellar and facing south, with a central front door level with the ground." It stood on grounds at the end of a long tree-lined carriage driveway with a commanding view of the estuaries of the Shannon and Fergus rivers. All that remains today are a half-standing wall and stones lying on the ground. The Stonehall land was one of the properties of the famous O'Brien family of Ireland but was occupied by Fitzgeralds when Michael was born.[5]

Very little is known about the Hogan family. Michael's father was Cornelius; his mother's name is unrecorded. His grandfather on the Hogan side was Dennis who had a sister named Mary and his Hogan great grandfather was Maurice, all of whom were born and lived in County Clare. He had an elder brother Dennis, a younger brother Maurice and apparently no other siblings.[6] The Irish name Hogan, sometimes appearing in its patronymic form as O'Hogan, is said to come from the old family Ógan, meaning The Sincere, who were allegedly descended from Brian Boru, a legendary Irish hero of the eleventh century. (Many proud Irish like to claim they are descended from Brian Boru.) Fifty years later, Michael claimed that "the British Government, under which I was born in Ireland, [deprived] my ancestor of one of the best inheritances in that country (which ought to be mine [and is] now in the hands of a court favorite)."[7] He was probably simply passing on something he had heard as a child; in this case, the common story that the British had taken lands belonging to Catholic ancestors and awarded them to English Protestant settler families or to Irish royal families, such as the nearby O'Briens, who had become Protestant. But, of course, the Irish are wonderful story tellers, embellishment coming naturally.

Whatever the family background, Michael Hogan could not have become what he did if he had been raised in a poor, uneducated, sod peasants family. He may have attended a small school recorded in 1837 as being near Stonehall.[8] The Hogan home on one of the fifteen tenant farms may have been a typical stone building with thatched roof divided into a main living area and two or three adjacent bedrooms and with only a few windows. (Houses were taxed based on their number of windows.) The rich and fertile land in the Shannon area was suitable for both tillage and stock raising. Although the Hogans were Catholic— and generally Catholic Irish were given little opportunity by their English and Protestant masters and landlords to advance in the world—the family may not have been immediately affected by the oppressive English measures. "Many [of the English landlords in County Clare] had Irish blood running in their veins and were therefore somewhat more easily disposed toward their Catholic neighbors"[9] than elsewhere in Ireland.

The rumblings of discontent and revolt in Ireland were beginning but none of this was to affect the Hogan family. What did affect the family was the death in 1775 of Cornelius when his sons were still youngsters, Michael only nine years old. There would be little prospect for them if they all remained in Ireland. Dennis was eventually sent off to join the British Army and with luck to become an officer, not then considered to be a mark of particular distinction, and Maurice, born in the same year his father died, would become a farmer, first in County Clare and later in the New World.

Michael Hogan was slated for the sea. It was not an unusual choice: many Irishmen joined the British Army and Navy, particularly during the American Revolution when England sought recruits in Ireland; moreover, Stonehall was only a short walk from the estuary of the

Shannon River where large sailing ships up to 1,000 tons navigated to the Atlantic Ocean. The nearby towns of Limerick and Ennis were commercial and trading centers.

The minimum age in the British Navy for boys was twelve, but there were many cases of younger boys, even from distinguished families, being admitted on warships with false ages shown on the ship's register. There were no birth certificates and church records were often inaccurate. Michael's age was shown in British Navy rolls as twelve when he signed up, two years more than his real age of ten. There was nothing in any of this background which foretold that one of the Hogans would become a world traveler, successful merchant and diplomat.

He began his naval career as servant to an unknown lieutenant. Until 1794, officers were allowed to have servants attend to their needs, though they were expected to perform normal sea duties as well and in some respects were treated as naval cadets.[10] After four unrecorded years, he was taken on board the newly commissioned H.M.S. *Jupiter* on July 1, 1780.

At an age when today he might just be finishing junior high school, Michael must have been in youthful awe over the adventures and battles that awaited him on board the *Jupiter* on its secret mission. He was certainly not focusing on the fact that his future was inevitably being shaped by what he would learn in the British Navy, by the historical events which were ushering in the modern era and by his own personal character which would ultimately control his destiny. Instead he was to see at first hand how ships of the time sailed the oceans, faced dangers from storms and turbulent seas, prepared for battle, administered discipline and faced enemy vessels in hostile waters.

He was fortunate to be on board the *Jupiter,* for Captain Pasley was an able sea officer. His great great great grandson, who transcribed and published his private sea journals, said he was a "petulant but kindly man, conscious of himself without self-consciousness, and strutting a little for his own entertainment."[11]

The British squadron stopped at Porto Praya in the Cape Verde Islands, off the northwest coast of Africa, for water and supplies, the *Jupiter* arriving on April 12. The islands had been a colony of Portugal since 1462, a neutral in the war but then and since friendly to Britain. Although aware from French letters intercepted on the islands that the French naval force was on its way to the Cape of Good Hope, Commodore Johnstone unexplainably took no special precautions. On the preceding evening (Easter Sunday), Pasley wrote in his journal that he "dined on board the *Southampton* where was assembled all the ladies and gentlemen passengers in the *Valentine* and *Fortitude*.... The day was spend most agreeably—our entertainment excellent—and high good humor reigned throughout. There was in the evening a dance, which I (though Sunday) being old and foolish partook in and stayed till past midnight."

The ladies to which Pasley referred were the wives and fiancées of officers and East India Company officials on their way to or already in India, but sometimes women with less respectability were to be found on British Navy ships at sea, as well as in port, a practice technically against regulations but often condoned.[12] Of course, Michael and other lowly sailors did not participate in such festivities, though they may have found their own means to relieve the tension.

The next morning—Easter Monday, Pasley "expected...to spend another very agreeable day; but far other employment was struck early out for me. At ½ past nine in the morning the *Isis*, who had an outside berth, made the signal for a sail in the N.E. and repeated it ten times, upon which [Commodore Johnstone] immediately made the signal for every person to repair on board their respective ships, and soon after the signal to prepare for battle." The British fleet had been caught unaware with all ships anchored in the harbor and 1,500 men on shore when the French fleet, under the command of Admiral Pierre André de Suffren, was sighted. There was great confusion among the British forces; a colonel in charge of one of the British regiments had to swim to rejoin his ship. Pasley recorded that the "confident impetuosity of the French did not allow us to remain long in suspense, for at 35 minutes after ten [Suffren], in a ship of 74 guns..., hauled around the eastern point into the bay; he was followed by four more of the line close at his heels. He had a signal flying at his mizzen peek but no colors hoisted; however as soon as he could bring his battery to bear on our outside ships (regardless of the neutrality) he spread his ensign and began to engage. At 40 minutes past ten our Commodore threw out the signal for battle, when we began to return the compliment with more than equal spirit. Several of the French anchored, one of 74 [guns] (who we afterwards found was the *Annibal*) on our starboard quarter within pistol shot.... After an hour's warm action in this close and pointed situation, her mizzen mast was shot away altogether with her ensign staff, besides being on fire on her quarter deck for a considerable time, thus heartily drubbed she as well as their whole squadron cut their cable and put to sea....By noon the action was over...."

French mistakes had allowed Johnstone to avoid a humiliating defeat. Both sides suffered damage but there was no immediate victor.

Pasley could not speak "too highly of the intrepid and cool gallantry of my ship's company; the fire they kept up was past all conception—not one accident. Two particulars I cannot help mentioning: on the lower gun deck in the heat of action half a cartridge of powder was scattered when half a dozen fellows with all possible coolness gathered round and personally watered it to prevent accident; the other my Coxswain Harrison (who, poor fellow, is dangerously wounded in the hand) brought me one of the enemy's shot and requested my liberty to return it out of his gun—so reasonable a request I could not refuse." He also signaled out his "officers [who] behaved with equal spirit and judgment; even my Youngsters, Pulteney [Pasley's nephew], Charles and Norton, I had all under my eye on the quarter deck ready to fly at my command to any part of the ship with orders." He wrote: "Our damage is trifling—not one man killed, only two wounded and those not dangerously."

After the morning engagement Johnstone called his captains as well as General William Medows commander of the troops[13] to his ship and asked, "Shall we, Gentlemen, cut and follow our blow by giving them battle again before they recover from their drubbing." Pasley "most heartily" agreed, and although others demurred, Johnstone ordered his ships to cut or slip their cables and do battle again in the early afternoon. No shots were fired in three hours of fruitless maneuvering. Pasley, whose *Jupiter* was one of the few British warships that was in position to engage the French, remonstrated: "What a glorious opportunity was lost of destroying this squadron and immortalizing ourselves! If we had bore down to cut the three ships off astern of the disabled one, they must either have abandoned her or fought us three to five, which after the sample they had got in the morning they would not have been foolhardy enough to attempt." Pasley had come close to seizing the *Annibal*, but it escaped.

Several of the accompanying British Indiamen were damaged or captured by the French. One of them, the *Hinchinbrook*, was recaptured the next day by the *Jupiter*.

There were no further contacts between the two squadrons. Within a few days the senior officers were again enjoying their interludes of fun and games. Pasley, showing a proclivity for the ladies, wrote of an after-midnight party on another ship where he encountered two "Ladies, …the first a very pleasing well-bred girl that has been in the world; the last, pretty, but foolish, vain, silly and insipid. I was obliged to ask her lover to be of the party as I delight to see a pretty face clothed in smiles...."

Johnstone kept his fleet at Porto Praya for over two weeks repairing the damaged vessels and composing a despatch to London in which he rationalized his conduct and blamed others for the lack of decisive victory, principally Captain Sutton of the *Isis* whom he had placed under arrest. (Sutton was later exonerated.)[14] He had only kind words for Pasley who, he said, "had worked hard from the beginning of the business and had got a spring on his cable, by which effort every shot told from the *Jupiter*." He also reported that, in repairing the damaged vessels, he was "chiefly indebted to the indefatigable attention of Captain Pasley whose zeal in this, and every other occasion, I wish may be represented to His Majesty."

There was, of course, no specific mention of Michael Hogan in any of these accounts, but he at least had the satisfaction of being on board the one British ship in the squadron that inflicted serious damage on a French warship.

Johnstone thought, not without some reason, that Suffren would have to send the damaged *Annibal* to the West Indies or Brazil for repairs, for "in either case we shall have a great advantage by the preceding action."[15] But Suffren did neither. Towing the *Annibal* most of the way, he arrived at Simon's Bay in the Cape of Good Hope on June 21, landed troops under the command of an Irishman, Brigadier Thomas Conway, and secured the colony against attack.

The British squadron finally left Porto Praya on May 2, the *Jupiter* making a slight detour to view a small island called Trinidada which was to play a role during the return voyage to England. The squadron finally arrived in the vicinity of the Cape in early July. One of the British ships easily captured a Dutch merchantman, the *Held Wottemade*, on her way to Ceylon with £40,000 in bullion, from which Johnstone learned on May 9 that the French were already well entrenched, and that five Dutch East India Company vessels were at anchor at Saldanha Bay, considerably to the north of Cape Town. Johnstone was in a quandary. Seizing the Cape of Good Hope now might require another sea battle and certainly the landing of troops against what he thought might be significant French and Dutch forces. He initially announced he would attempt to capture the Cape, but Medows was hesitant to commit his troops and Johnstone was distracted by at least two other factors. One was the attraction of capturing the Dutch merchantmen at Saldanha Bay, and the other was visions of glory if he proceeded with the previously approved but abandoned plan to plunder Spanish ships and property along the South American coast. Pasley probably captured Johnstone's character best when he wrote: "So many schemes enter his head that they confound and confuse him. He wants decision in matters of consequence: every man he consults, but abides by no man's opinion." Johnstone's decision was to defer an attack on the Cape and instead capture the Dutch prizes with both naval forces and troops participating. Pasley was certain Medows had insisted on being involved only to share in the spoils; he wrote: "'Tis not long since Buenos Aires was styled by [Medows] a buccaneering party..., now he gives up the glory and honor of taking the Cape (which I by no means think impossible) to act a part in a paultry, shameful, sheep-steeling, marooning party on shore."

The British fleet, with the *Jupiter* included, entered Saldanha Bay at eight o'clock in the morning of July 21. Johnstone later reported that our "arrival was so unexpected, and our movements so rapid, by carrying every sail we could bear, [that] the Dutch had just time to cut their cables, to loose their fore-top sails, which were kept bent for this purpose, and to run their ships on shore and to set them on fire.... But our boats boarded them so quickly, and our people behaved so gallantly, that the flames in all of them were soon extinguished, except in the *Middelburg*; she burnt with incredible fury and, becoming light as she [was] consumed [by fire], she got afloat, when her masts tumbled and had nearly drifted on board two of the other prizes. However, by an exertion of the boats of the squadron, she was towed off, stern foremost.... The boats had not left the *Middelburg* ten minutes when she blew up...."

Michael witnessed all the activity; many years later he recalled that several colorfully garbed East Indies kings and princes were discovered on the Dutch ships. Johnstone's report, received in London on October 15, also recorded that "a boat was seen rowing to our ship [*Romney*], filled with peoples in the eastern garb, making humble signs of submission. They proved to be the Kings of Ternate and Tidore with the Princes of their respective families whom the Dutch East India Company had long confined on Isle Robben, with different malefactors, but had lately removed them from that island to Saldanha."[16]

The Dutch ships at Saldanha Bay, as well as the Kings and Princes of Ternate and Tidore imprisoned on Robben Island, had been sent there from the main anchorage at Table Bay when it was learned on May 12 that a British squadron was on its way to seize the Cape and that a French squadron was on its way to protect it from the British. The Dutch presumably thought the ships would not be discovered and could thus make their escape in the event the British did succeed in taking Cape Town along the shore of Table Bay.[17] The reason that the kings and princes were prisoners stems from the fact that the Dutch East India Company had encountered resistance from local Muslim sultans in the East Indies during its attempts over several centuries to establish control over a number of East Indies islands, including Ternate and Tidore in the Moluccas, and to monopolize the spice trade. The Company, which exercised administrative control at the Cape Colony, had imprisoned some of their leaders on Robben Island near Table Bay to prevent the spread of a feared Islamic *jihad*. The island continued to be used by the Dutch, later by the British and still later by South Africa to quarantine incoming vessels and isolate political prisoners, including Nelson Mandela.

After the Saldanha Bay captures, the debate among Johnstone's officers and with Medows continued over landing troops in the Cape Town area, which ships to send to India, returning the main fleet to England or resurrecting the Spanish plundering scheme by an adventure in South America. On the principal question of attempting to land troops, the die had already been cast by the mutual reluctance of Johnstone and Medows, despite their vows to the contrary, to engage either French land or naval forces. In the end, part of the fleet and all the troopships would proceed to India, several vessels would be sent on a South America venture, and the remainder of the fleet, including Johnstone himself, would return to England. First, however, the *Romney*, *Jupiter* and *Lark* cruised in the vicinity of the Cape of Good Hope hoping to find ships in a French convoy to seize. Finding none, and Johnstone being unwilling to get too close to the French warships in the area, the homeward bound contingent left the Cape area on August 6 for St. Helena.

One lesson young Hogan learned from the Saldanha Bay affair was that there could be a monetary advantage to being in the British Navy—the reward of prize money. All those on board Navy ships were eligible to share the profits from selling captured enemy prizes and their cargoes. Captains of British Navy ships were allocated a three-eighths share, lieutenants and other officers a two-eighths share, midshipmen and warrant officers a one-eighth share and all others a two-eighths share. It was this reward that made the British Navy much more attractive than the Army; some British Naval commanders became rich from seizing prizes, and there doubtless were cases where they avoided battling enemy men-of-war hoping instead to find and seize unprotected enemy merchant vessels.[18] There was another reason why enemy merchant ships were more attractive than warships—the latter did not usually carry valuable cargo that could be sold. In an attempt to counteract this tendency, the British Admiralty awarded prize bounty, sometimes called head bounty, usually £5 for each person on board a destroyed or captured enemy warship. Commodore Johnstone and the officers and crew of his fleet were ultimately denied any prize money when the British House of Lords ruled four years later that the seizures were not related to the objective of capturing the Cape of Good Hope.[19] The decision may have been influenced by the belief in official British quarters that Johnstone had bungled his mission, a conclusion shared by most historians. Although Hogan received no prize money, a teak chest of his that remained in the family for some years is said to have come from this venture.

A staunch proponent of the South America option was Captain Pasley. Thus it was that his ship, with Hogan aboard, as well as the frigate *Mercury* and the cutter *Rattlesnake*, separated from the returning fleet at St. Helena on September 25 with orders to land a settlement party at the previously reconnoitered Trinidada, a small island under nominal Portuguese control some 800 miles to the east of Rio de Janeiro, after which they were to cruise in the River Plate off Buenos Aires and capture enemy prizes. This small fleet was well equipped to settle a new territory. Captain Pasley recorded that "My *Jupiter* is at present a perfect Noah's Ark; bulls, cows, rams, ewes, ram goats, ewe goats, lambs and kids in variety—calves of both species, boar and sow pigs with old and young—turkeys, geese, ducks, fowls—singing birds of different kinds to turn loose—all kinds of trees to plant and grasses of every kind—seeds both Cape and European without number and without name—Water Cresses, Sorrel, Water Dock, Purclean, Will'd Mint, Time—and the Lord knows what. How my Commodore's scheme may be relished at home I know not."

On October 5, the ships reached Trinidada where a small contingent and all the flora and fauna that Pasley had described were put ashore. The *Rattlesnake* was wrecked on shoals. After a month waiting in vain for Johnstone's expected rendezvous, the *Jupiter* and *Mercury* proceeded to the River Plate where they found no opportunities for mischief. There were numerous problems on this voyage. On

November 6, two seamen were blown to bits from an accidental gun powder explosion. Michael Hogan may have been splinter wounded in this accident. Later On December 3, when some of the seamen refused to remain on deck during the entire time of their daily eight hour watches, Captain Pasley displayed one of them before the entire crew, gave a lengthy lecture on the wisdom of obeying orders, and administered a dozen lashes to the hapless seaman. Never shy about self-praise, Pasley recorded in his diary that half an hour later the seamen gathered before him to admit their error and promise to stay on deck during watches, and that then "one and all, [doffed] their caps, and gave me a voluntary three cheers."

A more serious problem was scurvy from which several men, including the surgeon, died. Seafarers knew that scurvy could be cured by an adequate diet of fresh fruit and vegetables, but there was no means then of keeping such victuals fresh on board ships which were often away from ports for weeks, even months, on end. (A Scottish doctor had discovered in 1753 that oranges and lemons could prevent scurvy, but it was not until 1795 that the Royal Navy ordered lemon, and later lime, juice to be issued to seamen. The broader discovery that lack of vitamin C was the cause of scurvy did not come until even later. The word *limey*, meaning an English sailor, is derived from this.) But in 1781, the only accepted solution was to get to port where the men could regain their health and strength from a diet of fresh food. Pasley was therefore most anxious to return to Trinidada as soon as possible.

The *Jupiter* finally arrived at Trinidada the day after Christmas to find that Johnstone, who was supposed to rendezvous with him there, had already left. Pasley saw that his main task was to get the sick men, of which there were some ninety (not including Michael), back to good health. There were delays in getting them on shore because of the high surf, but this was at last accomplished. The sick made rapid recovery, due in no small measure to the gardens of vegetables and herbs that Pasley had ordered the landing party to plant three months earlier. By the end of January, all ninety sick men had been reported healthy and rejoined the ship. Pasley left twenty-eight men and one woman on the island and sailed on January 31, 1782, for England. He arrived at Spithead off Portsmouth on March 9 where they would have heard of the defeat of Cornwallis at Yorktown the previous October. (Eleven days later, Lord North announced his Ministry's resignation, leading to the installation of an opposition government and the opening of peace overtures with America.) The contingent left at Trinidada stayed for a year when the British Cabinet decided it did not want to retain the island as a base.

About this time, Hogan's lieutenant master released him to become an able-bodied seaman. Within a few months, he was again promoted to become master-at-arms, a petty officer charged with the maintenance of order and discipline on board ship and the custody of prisoners. The experience would stand him in good stead when as an adult he had to contend with mutineers at gun point at several locations around the world.

Hogan remained on board the *Jupiter*, still under Pasley's command, when it became the temporary flag ship of Admiral Hugh Pigot who was to relieve Admiral Rodney at the Leeward Island station in the West Indies. Rodney had fallen into disfavor with the Admiralty, but just before Pigot was to sail, news was received that Rodney had defeated French Admiral de Grasse, the victor in the Battle of the Capes which preceded Washington's victory at Yorktown, at the decisive Saintes battle off Guadeloupe on April 9–12. Although the French would continue to have a presence in the West Indies (and still do to this day), this battle marked final British supremacy in that part of the world. Realizing that Rodney would now be a hero, the Admiralty sent a letter to Plymouth countermanding Pigot's orders, but the letter arrived twenty-four hours after Pigot had sailed on May 18, and a fast cutter sent to intercept the *Jupiter* failed to do so. Pigot arrived at Port Royal in Jamaica in July 10 and took over from Rodney.

The *Jupiter* left Jamaica on July 17 for New York City where it arrived with Pigot's fleet on September 3. Although the British had decided to end their attempt to hold onto their former colonies after the Yorktown debacle, they would not completely evacuate the city until November 1783. Hogan contracted measles while there and was temporarily left behind as an invalid when the main fleet returned to the West Indies in mid-October, but he still managed to have "his share of...fun and frolic and odd adventures." He left New York, probably in November with the remainder of the British naval forces under Admiral Samuel Hood, to rejoin his squadron in the West Indies.[20] He had a bout with yellow fever, which was widely prevalent in the West Indies, killing many seamen, but he did not suffer any serious consequences.

During his last few months in New York and over the next six months in the West Indies, Hogan might have met the irascible Prince William Henry, the third son of George III, who was assigned as a midshipman to the *Warwick* operating out of New York and later the *Barfleur* based at Jamaica during these periods.[21] Hogan later bragged to his family that he was on friendly terms with the Prince, who was just one year older than Hogan, but this is unlikely; they were on different ships and, in any event, royalty did not readily mix with commoners, even in the close quarters of British Navy vessels. A little known story about the Prince is that George Washington in March 1782 authorized a secret plan to kidnap him, as well as Admiral Digby, from the quarters of British General Clinton in New York City, cautioning however "against offering insult or indignity to...the Prince." The plan was abandoned when it was discovered that Clinton's quarters were heavily defended. The Prince, who was made Duke of Clarence in 1789, became King William IV in 1830 during the brief interregnum before Queen Victoria took over in 1837. During the King's brief reign, the American minister at London some fifty years later showed the King Washington's letter authorizing the kidnaping, to which the King is reported to have said, "I am obliged to General Washington for his humanity, but I'm damned glad I did not give him the opportunity of exercising it towards me."[22]

Hogan finally returned to England with the fleet in July 1783. By then the several peace treaties finally marking the end of the American Revolution and the war between Britain and France, Spain and the Netherlands had been signed and relative peace would return to Europe for ten years. The only clear winner of the multinational conflict, for it was truly that, was the newly independent United States. The patriotism of its leaders and citizens was important to the outcome, but in truth the victory was chiefly due to the wisdom of General Washington in fighting the British only when he had superiority, to the financial, army and naval support of the French, and to a subtle change in British colonial strategy that would henceforth look to the east rather than the west for a new empire. In short, holding on to the American colonies was no longer worth the cost, particularly in comparison with establishing British dominance in the West Indies. In the long run, the British were also winners. By acknowledging the independence of the United States and its free hand to territory south of the Great Lakes in return for American acceptance of Britain's claims to much of Canada, the British preempted French aspirations in the New World. They also assured a continuing market for British goods and investment. And, although the French had a marginal advantage in the naval and land battles fought late in the war in India, the British finally became masters of that subcontinent. As one author put it, "The struggle had opened in a grey dawn at Lexington; its last shot was fired eight years later on the other side of the world outside a dusty town in southern India."[23] Britain lost its American colonies but cemented its claim to India, while France, although on the winning side in assuring the independence of the United States, lost its toehold in the Americas and its claims in India and acquired massive war debts. Spain, which had indirectly helped the American cause by retaking Florida from the British and, with the French, threatening (though not carrying out) an invasion of England, was awarded the Louisiana territory and the return of Florida. Within forty years, Spain would lose almost all its territories in the New World. The Second British Empire, as one author has coined it, had begun.

On his return to England, Hogan wanted to become a full-fledged midshipman. British Navy vessels were manned by an assortment of men and boys of often sharply contrasting social backgrounds. Officers obtained their commissions by virtue of the social class into which they were born or by serving since boyhood as midshipmen on British Navy vessels where they were trained and educated in both general studies and seamanship. To become a midshipmen, a seaman first had to serve two years at sea after the age of thirteen. Midshipmen from privileged backgrounds were allowed on the quarter deck of ships, such as the future Admiral Horatio Nelson who first went to sea at age twelve, while the less fortunate were confined to the lower deck. In contrast, ordinary seamen were often rounded up, by press gangs if necessary, in Britain or on the high seas and forced to serve on British Navy ships. This practice of impressment, as it was called, was sanctioned by an Act of Parliament because, however much Britain's interests depended on a strong Royal Navy, the Parliament was parsimonious in appropriating adequate funds for personnel.[24]

Since Hogan was eligible at his true age sixteen (age eighteen on British Navy rolls), he obtained his appointment as midshipman. He had help from what he thought was a family connection.

Hogan had heard that his great aunt, Mary Hogan, was about to marry Charles O'Hara, a brigadier general in the British Army who had fought the American Colonists in the Revolutionary War. The British forces in America were commanded by Lord Charles Cornwallis, a remarkable man who had opposed British policy in America but who, compelled by a sense of duty, agreed to take the unwanted job.[25]

Cornwallis found much to admire in O'Hara and soon made him his second-in-command. They were more than fellow soldiers. Cornwallis wrote of personal matters in letters to *Dear Charles* (it was the British custom in correspondence to call all but the closest friends by their last names), and there is later evidence of their friendship when O'Hara substituted for Cornwallis during the surrender ceremony after the Yorktown battle to save him the embarrassment of conceding defeat. After the battle, O'Hara was an American prisoner of war until exchanged in February 1782, and in May he went with a British force to Jamaica where Hogan was also present aboard the *Jupiter*.

O'Hara sought out Hogan in Jamaica because of his acquaintance with Mary Hogan and promised he would help the young lad in his naval career. His appointment as midshipman was the first sign of help. Later, possibly through O'Hara's intercession, Cornwallis' brother offered Hogan command of a British Navy ship in India by. Just how much O'Hara and Cornwallis were responsible for these advancements is not certain, but Hogan was convinced of Cornwallis' interest and help. He showed his gratitude in later years by giving several of his enterprises the Cornwallis name. There is no evidence that Hogan ever met Cornwallis.

Hogan was mistaken, however, in believing that Charles O'Hara was to be the husband of his great aunt, Mary Hogan. That they had some sort of relationship is evident, but O'Hara never married anyone. He was one of several illegitimate children of James O'Hara, the second Baron Tyrawaley of County Mayo in Ireland, a soldier and diplomat who was considered "singularly licentious, even for the Courts of Russia and Portugal." (A contemporary reported that the father returned to England from Portugal, where Charles was born, "with three wives and fourteen children.") Charles O'Hara capped an active military career as governor of Gibraltar where he was known as "Old Cock of the Rock" and where his "lavish entertainment and agreeable companionship made him generally popular." He had a "double row of sausage curls that projected on either side of his toupee" and affected old-fashioned garb. At one time, he wanted to marry a Mary Berry, a writer of some renown, but she broke off the relationship after several years. She described him as "the most perfect specimen of a soldier and a courtier of the past age." When he died at age sixty-two, he left a large sum of money for two ladies at Gibraltar by whom he had families.[26] Whatever his relationship with Mary Hogan, it is easy to see why she may have been charmed by him.

IN SERVICE OF HIS MAJESTY'S NAVY

During his some thirteen years in the British Navy, Midshipman Hogan may have received little education in the liberal arts, as did those who were sent to prestigious schools in England, but he learned much more about the practical aspects of sailing, business, trading and the realities of the world than his seemingly better-situated brethren. He was growing up in an age in which discoveries, inventions and societal pressures would irrevocably and ever more rapidly change the nature of the world.

Europe's seagoing trade with the Orient had its origins in 1498 when the Portuguese Vasco da Gama had discovered the long sea route around Africa's Cape of Good Hope to India. Ever since then European vessels had been bringing whatever they could sell to India, the East Indies and China in order to obtain the silk, porcelain, spices, sugar, tea and even the piece goods made with cheap Indian labor that were increasingly in demand in Europe. The Chinese, however, did not want European goods, which is why as much as half the silver mined in the Americas eventually found its way into Chinese coffers to pay for Europe's unfavorable balance of payments. This basic trading problem was exacerbated when the demand for Chinese tea in England increased dramatically from 1784 onwards because of the reduction in the level of duty levied by Britain on its importation. The situation was inflamed by a number of incidents in which, to the British mind, the Chinese had mistreated British citizens and ships in Canton. The foreign community there was in fear for its safety, and there were calls in England for the Crown to take steps not only to protect its citizens and shipping but also to convince the Chinese that they should buy British goods in return for the tea that was in so much demand in England. The problem was more than a mere imbalance of trade. England had developed its own textile manufacturing industry, based initially on water power and then toward the end of the eighteenth century on the newly invented steam engine, which was fast becoming competitive with Indian-made textiles, and it wanted to sell these products throughout the Orient. The ramifications of these developments would influence Hogan's career.

The English East India Company, known familiarly as the John Company, had held a government-granted monopoly for almost two hundred years for all British trade to and from the Orient. It had become so powerful that it was sometimes referred to as the *Honourable Company*. By 1795, as many as fifty large merchant vessels, called Indiamen and Chinamen, were sailing from England every season to carry whatever goods of British manufacture India and China would buy and to bring back products from the Orient. The roundtrip voyages sometimes took over a year, mostly because the ships were built to carry as much cargo as possible, rather than for speed. Faster ships could make a one-way trip in a little over three months.[27]

The international scene was also undergoing revolutionary changes. The Americans had already won their freedom and, although it was a different sort of revolution, the entrenched monarchial system of government in France would soon be overthrown, at least temporarily, carrying with it eventual nationalistic changes elsewhere. There were pressures in other countries, particularly Britain, for social change caused by increased economic activity and wealth, resulting expansion in populations and, despite growth in the merchant or middle class, the ever increasing distance between the rich and powerful and the poor. Traditional alliances were changing, and Atlantic Europe was growing apart from Central and Eastern Europe in its economic, social and political values. The Western world was also soon to experience the Napoleonic Wars, the first true world war, although it was not called that.

Midshipman Hogan no more understood that these basic forces were changing the world than any current observer can know of his own era. But he had ample opportunity to develop his knowledge of, and interest in, merchant trading. And, although class barriers would prevent him from having personal relationships with the titled and privileged aboard navy ships, their presence must have been a factor in his drive to succeed and in the ease with which he was able to deal with those better born. His life of adventure in the British Navy instilled in him the drive and ambition that would earn him a fortune. But this drive and ambition would in the end lead to his financial downfall and make him into a bitter old man.

There is no record of what Hogan did for a three-year period after his return to England in July 1783 at age sixteen. He could have continued to serve on Royal Navy ships, but because England was at peace, many seamen were discharged and those holding rank were often placed on inactive duty, and thus half-pay. Maximum regular pay for a midshipman was two pounds, five shillings a month (some ten U.S. dollars), which today seems a trifling amount, even for a young man, but in the late eighteenth century it was more than many laborers or farmers could earn. (Officers, of course, earned more; for example, many captains earned £28 a month while on active duty.) Nevertheless it was accepted, and even expected, that officers and midshipmen not from wealthy families would find other sources of remuneration during peacetime.[28]

Thus it was that, at age nineteen, Hogan signed on with the 765-ton East India Company ship *Pigot* (Captain George Ballantyne) when it sailed from England on March 26, 1786. Six months later the ship arrived at Canton, the only port at which the Chinese allowed European vessels to call. It was back in England on June 29, 1787, where Hogan was paid some £50 for his labors. He later told his children and grandchildren that he served as executive officer on the *Pigot* during the latter part of the voyage to China, "running from the South through Sunda Straits...to Canton," but official records list him only as "gunner." A year later, he was on the country ship *San Antonio* on a voyage "from [Canton] to Bombay, running from there to Singapore with the northwest monsoon, and then through the Straits of Malacca moving a traverse against the Bay of Bengal." He later claimed that he was commanding officer on this vessel. It is possible that Hogan was given some kind of command responsibility on these two vessels (young seafarers two centuries ago could hold command positions and Hogan was not lacking in experience after more than five years at sea), but it is more likely that he was exaggerating his youthful experiences to impress his children and grandchildren.[29]

He was in Bombay in May 1789 where he found employment with Robert Henshaw, who had come to India in 1764 as a twenty year-old youth and become one of Bombay's leading and most popular merchants, overseeing the construction at the Mazagon Docks of an 899-ton merchant ship to be called the *Bombay Anna* or, later, the *Anna*, a large ship by the standards of the day.[30] Indian Parsees had developed a shipbuilding industry in Bombay from about 1735. Ships built at Bombay, as well as Calcutta, were reputed to be superior in quality to those built in Britain because they were made of teak, not oak. Most of them were owned by private British traders in India and used to circumvent the East India Company's monopoly. Their construction was often overseen by British firms, the ships were usually given English names, and they were often manned by English officers.

India was not then a possession of the British Crown; that did not come until the mid-nineteenth century when Queen Victoria reigned. Instead, the East India Company wielded power and control over only parts of India from the three centers that it did govern—Bombay, Madras and Calcutta. It retained its own military establishment, composed mostly of Indian soldiers, made its own arrangements with the Indian Mogul and Hindu rulers and operated the civil government in these three areas. Englishmen could make fortunes in India through connivance with Indian princes and nawabs (from which the English corruption *nabob* developed) and lead luxurious lives surrounded by servants, lavish entertainment, racecourses and very little work to do. For a number of reasons, not the least of which was a reassessment of its colonial policies following the loss of its American colonies, the British Government in the early 1780s decided to complete the process that had been underway for some time of converting what was essentially a private trading enterprise when it was founded into an instrument of state policy. Among the steps taken was the dispatch of Lord Charles Cornwallis as governor general in 1786 with a mandate to impose reforms and assert British Government authority over the Honorable Company, while still respecting its trading and governance roles.

Lavish living was mostly confined to Calcutta, the headquarters of the East India Company in the Orient and its principal shipping and trading center, where intrigue, influence peddling, social snobbery and high-jinks living were rife. Bombay, which Charles II had acquired as a dowry from his intended Portuguese princess bride in 1661, was much smaller, although still large by European standards (estimates vary from 100,000 to 150,000 inhabitants), with a European population of less than one thousand, and had a decidedly Indian atmosphere tinted with Portuguese overtones. The town was on one of several islands separated from the mainland by narrow waterways, with a protected harbor that served as a base for British Navy and East India Company ships. Nearby on islands with names such as Salsette, Elephanta and Old Woman's stood ancient Hindu temples, caves and stone statues. One author wrote that, "In the eighteenth century, Bombay was the Cinderella of the English settlements in India, the unhealthiest, the poorest, and the most despised." It was certainly less colorful and exciting than Calcutta: another author said the British there "lived a dull and demoralized life.... Not for them were the rich pickings of Bengal or the plums of Arcot, but dull conversation at formal dinner parties where the guests invariably sat next to the same neighbors in an unyielding order of precedence."[31] Bombay, now known as Mumbai, is the bustling commercial and financial capital of India with 13 million residents—some rich, most very poor—crammed into an area two-thirds the size of New York City.

Histories of old Bombay tend to focus on the upper echelons of British society, the leading Indians and the vast number of poor. But there were British and natives who were comfortably situated without either a lineage or high social standing. Among these were the Richardsons, a family with a long history of merchant trading in England, Portugal and India. William Richardson, eldest of five children of Christopher Richardson of York, England, came to India in 1764[32] just after the end of the Seven Year's War when British merchants were being encouraged to settle there. He became a merchant trader and sea captain. One of his brothers, known as Christopher of Limehouse, engaged in trade with Baltic countries, Portugal and the West Indies, and another brother, Rowland, was a ship broker affiliated with Lloyds. Shortly after his arrival in Bombay, William Richardson married Anna Maria de Lacey of a Portuguese family that had resided in Bombay and Goa for many years. She was reputed to be a Parsee, although this is doubtful. Parsees are a religious sect descended from Persian refugees who had settled in the Bombay and Goa area of India in the seventh and eighth centuries to escape Mohammedan persecution of Zoroastrians, and they remained a distinct racial and religious group with little or no intermarriage with others. The term was often loosely and incorrectly applied to any Portuguese who had settled in India.

Richardson had four daughters. The two eldest, Jane and Frances, had been sent to England as young children, as was the custom, to stay with Richardson relatives living at Streatham, a small town half way between London and Croydon, and receive "the best English education" at Mrs. Ray's school at Russell House in Streatham Park, next door to Streatham Place, the home of Henry and Hester Thrale. Frances's son many years later recalled that "it was at Mr. Thrale's [that] Dr. Johnson was so constant a guest that my dear mother saw something of that lion of the day." Samuel Johnson and other social and intellectual figures of the day were frequent guests at the Thrales until Henry's death in 1781 when Frances would have been only ten years old. The Richardson girls returned to Bombay in 1786 when Jane was seventeen and Frances fifteen. Jane soon married a British Army officer, Captain Barnaby Boles, stationed in India.[33]

Three years later in 1789, Michael Hogan met and courted Frances Richardson. She was not a beauty, but she was from a respectable and cosmopolitan family. The choices for acceptable matches among residents of the British colony were limited. Perhaps the couple found commonality in their non-English backgrounds, for both could have been regarded privately, though never publicly, by the pure blooded English elite as a notch below full acceptability, Hogan for his Irishness, Frances for her Portuguese blood.

Hogan recorded in a long lost log called the Green Book that he "made an excursion" to Salsette Isle on October 16 and again over the weekend of November 28 and 29, that the "great Hindor festival, all holiday, except [for] Parsees" was on Sunday October 18, and the "Gentoo [a variant of Hindu] holiday, when none work," was on November 3. Frances may have been with him on these occasions.

Michael Hogan and Frances Richardson were married on Tuesday, December 15, 1789, at the home of her father, Captain William Richardson, with the chaplain of the British forces officiating and various dignitaries, staff and friends in attendance. Included was William Medows, commander of the British forces and governor at Bombay, who had come to India in 1782 after the Porto Praya battle in which Hogan also took part on the *Jupiter* over eight years earlier. His log reported the weather as being "very pleasant." Two days later, he was back at the shipyard where he "served sweetmeats to all the artificers employed, it being customary, and hoisted the Union Jack." Christmas day was "very pleasant, rather warm; a holiday to the men." He was barely twenty-three; Fanny, as he called her, was eighteen.

TWO

INDIA VOYAGES

I have probably my life to spend at sea.

—Michael Hogan to Captain Barnaby Boles

Now that he was married, Michael Hogan had to decide whether to make the Royal Navy his career or pursue another gainful occupation. Midshipmen could become lieutenants at age twenty after serving three years at sea and passing an oral examination. If they failed, or elected not to take the examination, they could remain in the Navy as oldster midshipmen.[1] It was a sought-after career, made famous by a long line of well known British naval heros. But there were some unpleasant facts behind the outward glamour. The Navy had acquired a reputation for inefficiency, intrigue and patronage; it was commonly accepted that the only way to advance was to have the right connections.

Hogan had not taken the lieutenant examination and had all but decided to make his living in commerce when an unexpected offer came to him. Commodore William Cornwallis, known among other sobriquets as Billy Blue, the younger brother of Lord Charles Cornwallis, had arrived at Calcutta on H.M.S. *Crown*, three months before Michael Hogan and Frances Richardson were married, in command of a squadron of British naval vessels to survey the coasts and islands of the Bay of Bengal and, in the process, extend Britain's presence in the area. Lord Cornwallis was also in India at the time as governor general (1786–1793). When Commodore Cornwallis visited Bombay in early 1790, Hogan looked him up and was offered command of one of Cornwallis's frigates. Forty-two years later, Hogan recounted to his son William that "Admiral Cornwallis, old Billy Blue as we used to call him for he was a gruff, surly, old fellow, sent for me and offered to make me a post captain. 'You shall have the [unnamed ship] now and in six weeks I will give you [another unnamed ship].' I thanked him, but said that I could not be appointed as I had to serve six weeks of my rating as a midshipman. 'Must not thank me,' he gruffly said, 'it is my brother [Lord Cornwallis, Governor General] orders, and you have been a rated midshipman two months in my books; so your time is out.' I was always a favorite of Lord Cornwallis, but don't know altogether why I was so, partly perhaps because he was very partial to General O'Hara, my grand uncle.... I again expressed my thanks but asked time to consider. 'Certainly,' said he, 'take a fortnight and then let me know.' I was then six weeks married and engaged in building, and part owner of, the *Bombay Anna*, a fine ship of 930 tons of which I was to have command. It is still in the Red Sea trade, built of teak, and [so] I determined to decline the offer, flattering as it was. To tell the truth, I was perhaps a little afraid of the old Blue who had already sent home three of his captains under arrest and afterwards broke them, and at the end of the fortnight, I told him how I was situated and declined the offer. 'You are right,' said he, 'if I [had a] son, I [would] rather make a cobbler of him than a sailor.'"

Hogan also recounted that "a school fellow of Fanny's named Charles Moorsom, then a second lieutenant in the Navy, had just come out [from England] and Fanny, desiring to serve him, asked me to say a word for him to the Admiral. This honor I could not do, but we spoke of it to [an unnamed person] who was always at our house and used to joke with the Admiral, which few could do, and he promised to mention it, which was done when opportunity offered. Old Gruff shook his head but said, 'I like that Fanny Hogan; she is a sensible young woman and, if she recommends him, I'll think about it.' In a short time, Moorsom was promoted and is now high up in the list of the old Admirals...."[2]

Hogan never learned that his great aunt Mary Hogan had not married Charles O'Hara. Whatever happened in this relationship, it was not one that caused O'Hara to renege on his promise to help Hogan's career through his friendship with Cornwallis.

Although he had turned aside a possibly illustrious career as a British naval officer in favor of a hopefully more lucrative career in commerce, Hogan told his brother-in-law, Captain Barnaby Boles, that "I have probably my life to spend at sea." He initially thought he would command the ship whose construction he had been employed to oversee at Bombay, the *Anna*, but he decided instead, perhaps guided by his father-in-law whose advice he could not afford to disregard at so early a stage in his new business life, that some practical experience in commerce would be desirable. On May 5, 1790, he sailed from Bombay on the *New Triumph* with his bride and Captain Richardson aboard. The ship's captain was Alexander Tennant with whom Hogan would become a business partner seven years later at another location. The ship stopped first at Tellicherry where Frances was left to visit her sister Jane and Captain Boles at Calicut. The *New Triumph* arrived at Calcutta on July 8 where it picked up a cargo of rice and then returned to Tellicherry in November to bring Frances back to Calcutta where Michael had decided to make their home and to try his hand at business ventures on his own.

Calcutta had supposedly been founded in about 1690 by a man named Job Charnock, but the area had been for many centuries a sprawl of living quarters and bazaars, some sixty miles up the Hugli river, inhabited by possibly as many as 600,000 persons of separate groups and castes and later by a few rich Indians attracted to the area to do business with the British. The foreign quarters were distinctly separate to the south where a small colony of Englishmen and other Europeans lived behind the walled Fort William and in "elegant garden houses surrounded by verdant grounds laid out in the English style" along the river.[3] The Europeans had servants, with names such as durwan (door keeper or porter), ayah (lady's maid), mussalchee (scullion), peon (messenger) and jemadar (guard), and could ride through the streets in their palanquin carried by several hircarrahs.

Michael took his first major business step, buying a ship then under construction for his own account from the eminent shipbuilding firm of Messrs Gillett Lambert & Ross & Company.[4] It was to be three-masted frigate, 104 feet long and 34 feet at the beam, with three decks, weighing 654 tons.[5] The largest ships being built at the time were in the 1,200-ton class designed for the China trade, but most ordinary merchant vessels were only in the 200-ton class. Many in the Calcutta trade were over 300 tons, though they could not exceed some 800 tons to navigate safely on the Hugli estuary to Calcutta. Hogan's ship was thus a large one and probably enjoyed the good reputation for quality that Calcutta-built ships then commanded.[6] He needed to borrow a considerable sum of money, about 120,000 rupees,[7] to make the purchase. He offered a quarter share to Pondoosett Tewajusett in Bombay, a quarter to his brother-in-law Boles (and any other Army officers who wanted to subscribe—several did), and a third quarter to his father-in-law, keeping the last quarter for himself. After some delay, principally because Boles needed to raise money to buy his share, the necessary money was advanced, including a 5,000 rupee investment by Messrs Forbes Sheppard & Company in Bombay. Some of the money was advanced in respondentia bonds, with the ship's cargo as security, and he may have obtained some short-term money from shroffs—Indian money lenders and bill exchangers. Hogan's main share must have come from profits he was able to make shipping goods, principally rice, from Calcutta to other ports in India and to the Persian Gulf on the American ship *Myrtle*, which he had chartered. He may also have been engaged in other shipping transactions from which he profited.

Hogan told others that he planned to ship rice from the granary centers around Calcutta to other parts of India where he would pick up cotton and opium for transport to China. Trade between India and China was known as the "country trade" to distinguish it from the Orient trade to and from Europe. He intended to command the new ship himself, leaving Frances at Calcutta.

Difficulties in implementing this plan arose when an embargo was imposed on the export of all grains from Bengal on October 10, 1791, because of a drought and potential famine in India.[8] Hogan's initial reaction was to abandon the China plan, to sail the vessel to Bombay early in 1792 and to make the family home there. He confided to Captain Boles: "I hope you will not think of selling your bungalow as there will be no necessity for it on account of your concern for me. When I come round, I shall be very glad to purchase it, if Mrs. Hogan will reconcile herself to living in the country in my absence. I never mean that she shall go to sea any more, as I intend to settle her in Bombay and make that her home. I was perfectly aware of Bengal being an improper place for her but, at that time, I could not well have acted otherwise. However, she finds it more pleasant now the time approaches for our leaving it." Frances, who had become pregnant in October, let it be known that she preferred to move to Bombay to live. She could not have thought that Bombay was physically more comfortable than Calcutta. Perhaps she simply felt more at home in the city where the British had an easy relationship with the Parsees, unlike the British in Calcutta who were developing unmistakable signs of racial consciousness.[9]

The new ship was launched on November 12, but the arrangements made for its use were quite different from Hogan's initial plans. He told others a few days before the launching that, due to "the embargo on grain and many indifferent prospects before ship holders in this country," he had given up plans to engage in the country trade and instead placed the ship under Genoese colors as *Il Netunno* and chartered it for three years to Messrs Robert Charnock & Company to sail on two voyages between India and Ostend in Belgium. At the same time, he announced he was giving up the idea of making Bombay the family home, electing London instead, at least for the time being. Explaining this decision to Boles he wrote: "Mrs. Hogan will have the opportunity of spending some time with her friends in England with which she is quite delighted, and as we leave this port at a good time of the year, early in January, the passage I doubt not will be pleasant in so capital a ship. Her accommodations will be far superior to any [East India] Company ship." He told Messrs Michell Amos & Bowden, a well-known merchant house at Madras, that " the workmen in general who have seen [the *Netunno*] allow her far to exceed any [that] Gillett built, and I will venture to say, far to exceed any foreign ship that ever left this country; nay, even [East India] Company ships will not bear a comparison as to strength and accommodation, which are but few, yet very large, plain but neat and everything adjoining to them to make a sea voyage comfortable. She is coppered to the bends and may be expected to sail exceeding fast, well-manned, and as well sound as any ship ever went to sea, all which with a new and compleat ship reduces the risk very considerably."

He also asked the Madras firm to find passengers to fill a roundhouse with five windows over the stern and three nine by twelve-foot cabins, each with a porthole, and he told an Armenian at Madras that the ship would have "good accommodations for Armenians or such people who may not come to my table."

Hogan was proud of his new ship. In 1793 while he was in Calcutta on his second voyage, he commissioned a painting of the *Netunno* by a Flemish artist named Balthazar Solvyns who lived in Calcutta for twelve years and produced many etchings portraying the people and life in Bengal. Several versions of the painting still exist.[10] Later, he procured two etchings of a wooden model of a sailing vessel that looked very much like his *Netunno*.[11]

A description of Oriental trading patterns is necessary to understand fully the situation that Hogan faced. The major item in Britain-Orient trade was the tea that came from China. The East India Company zealously kept this trade to itself, particularly after interlopers lost their competitive advantage with the drastic reduction in Britain's import duty on tea in 1784, but it still could not effect a payments balance without exporting specie because China prided itself on being self-sufficient in material goods. It would only authorize the importation of some mechanical curios from Europe and culinary, magical and medicinal items from Southeast Asia. The British solved the problem in two ways. First, toward the end of the century, China developed a need to import raw cotton, a need that would be met from India, mostly in the Bombay area. And secondly, factories were established in India to satisfy China's insatiable appetite for opium, a trade that was officially illegal in China but openly condoned. Because this solution did not satisfy British manufacturers, one last effort was made to induce the Chinese to "buy British" by sending a trade mission to Canton in 1793 led by Lord George Macartney who would later be posted as governor at the Cape of Good Hope, where Michael Hogan moved in 1798. When this mission failed, the British apparently felt relieved of any moral compulsion to ban the opium trade from India. In 1839 China finally cut off this trade, leading Britain to send warships to bombard Chinese towns, an act which led to the Opium Wars and the enforced establishment of Treaty Ports in China, the vestiges of which still cloud modern day China's relations with the West.

For a variety of reasons, including the vagaries of sailing ships, monsoons and trade winds, the East India Company found it expedient to allow independent traders in India to carry cotton and opium to China in their own ships on their own account or as freight on Company vessels. This move led to the strengthening of several prominent European agency houses, particularly in Calcutta,[12] and ultimately was one of the factors that undermined the Company's trading monopoly. The Company facilitated this trade by what was known as the China mode of remittance, a system under which merchants in India exporting to China could turn the proceeds of their sales into the Company's offices at Canton in return for bills of exchange redeemable in India or London, giving the Company the means to pay for its purchases of Chinese tea and giving merchants in India useable money. The Bengal government supported this system by advancing funds to finance the cost of procuring goods for export to China, with the promissory notes to be paid off only into the Canton Treasury. By the terms of one government offer, these funds seemed to be available only to the supercargoes of Company ships, but Hogan's correspondence shows they were also available to others, probably as secondary loans via agency houses, for he was himself in October 1791 hoping to acquire two lakhs (200,000 rupees) from the expected government offer.[13] The offer was announced on November 23,[14] by which time Hogan had decided on the Ostend venture, but still in December he reported that the China mode of remittance was "both precarious and disadvantageous," perhaps because he could not secure a secondary loan from an agency house on acceptable terms. In effect, both the Company and the Bengal government were controlling the amount of country trade with China they would allow to independent traders through manipulating the amount and terms of the China mode of remittance.

It was not so easy, however, for the Company to control what has aptly been called the free-lance trade between India and Europe,[15] much of it destined ultimately for Britain. This trade has been viewed simplistically by some historians as merely an evasion by interlopers of the East India Company's monopoly, but the truth is far more complex. Firstly, the evasions did not begin in the latter quarter of the eighteenth century, as some have suggested, but go back to the first years of the Company when its principal business was the spice trade from the East Indies, an indication that leakage always occurs when unnatural restraints are applied to any system. And secondly, the system was then very different from those we know today, possibly due to the fact that there was a very fuzzy line between the government and private sectors in Britain in the eighteenth and even nineteenth centuries. Technically, the structure of the British Government was close to what it is today; a body such as the East India Company would now be called a public corporation with its powers and authority regulated by government, but two hundred years ago it exercised quasi-governmental powers hand-in-hand with its government overseers—in the eyes of many, the Company *was* "government." Most historians do not distinguish whether actions or events were the result of company or of government decisions; the two were usually so inexorably linked that they were in reality the same thing. This inseparability inevitably fostered—there can be no other word for it—corruption. It was not unusual for Company officers also to hold government positions, nor was it unusual for government officers to hold positions or have a stake in commercial houses and affairs. Many of these situations would today be considered serious conflicts of interest meriting at least dismissal and possibly prosecution; in yesteryear they were accepted as part of the system, at least for as long as they were exercised with some discretion. It may have been true that gentlemen did not work for a living, but they found ways to maintain and supplement their wealth by delving into the lucrative world of commerce through friends and connections—and, if they held senior positions, by exercising their right to privilege and dispensing jobs.

The English East India Company, like its companion companies in the Netherlands and Denmark, owed its existence to the necessity of operating not only a trading system but also an administrative infrastructure (principally in India) to protect the trade. Over the years, as England's trading needs were being met outside of Company channels, gradually at first and then increasingly so, the Company's administrative role came to dominate its affairs. It was not only independent merchants who were taking advantage of this situation, but Company servants as well. The latter had always been allowed a portion of private trade on Company vessels—it was one of the privileges of the job—but their participation in non-Company trade went much further than that. Even senior directors had their hands in the outside business; some of them were hidden or sometimes active partners in agency houses that dealt in both Company and non-Company business, often with offices in both India and London, as well as in other European ports that were centers of the inaptly called clandestine trade. There are numerous examples of these arrangements.

The Company had no one but itself to blame for its declining role in the India trade. It had secured government approval of several requirements which it believed would protect its interests but which did the very opposite. One of these was that ships engaged by the Company had to sail under the British flag with British officers (the crew, however, need not be and often were not British). Enterprising Englishman found that one way to circumvent these restrictions was to have ships built at shipyards in India, registered under the flag of some country other than Britain and used in apparent trade between the Orient and ports in continental Europe. The two most popular ports were Copenhagen and Ostend. A commentator noted that "any ship in the Eastern trade, however mysterious its origin and whatever flag it might...be flying, was given facilities [at Ostend] with no questions asked."[16] This trade was organized by firms at these ports that were fronts for merchant houses in London. Robert Charnock, for example, the main partner in the company at Ostend that had chartered the *Netunno*, was an Englishman who lived alternately in Ostend and in Flushing in the Netherlands but owned a reputable merchant house in London.[17] He did business with an agent in London who had himself once been a Bombay merchant and who continued to have close trading and apparently financial ties with a prominent Calcutta agency houses.

While some of the goods imported from India were sold on the European continent, and thus were not in contravention of the East India Company's monopoly, a large portion of goods found their way back to Britain, either by transshipment or smuggling.

Among those who engaged in the free-lance trade between India and Europe while Hogan was in India was Sir Home Popham, at that time a lieutenant in the Royal Navy on a leave of absence. He had come to Calcutta in 1787 and engaged in at least two voyages to Ostend in 1788 and 1793. His stay in Calcutta would have overlapped with that of Hogan from April 1791 until early 1792. Unlike Hogan, whose evasion of the East India Company monopoly was never discovered, the ship on Popham's last commercial voyage was seized by British authorities. There is no record that they met or had any business dealings at this time, but they surely must have known one another in the closely knit British community.[18] They would meet again—and this time have a business relationship (that went sour)—nine years later in Cape Town when Popham had become a rear admiral.

Another popular method of circumventing the Company's rules was to ship goods from India (and sometimes China) to Europe on American ships with an ostensible stop at an American port, a practice which Britain unintentionally fostered by liberalizing trade relations with the United States in the Jay Treaty of 1794. American ships, as well as other non-Company ships, were being built to sail faster than the cumbersome and broad-beamed Indiamen and Chinamen vessels which had been able to lumber along because there was little competition; they were also able to turn around at ports much more quickly than the Company's vessels.[19] It has been estimated that by 1799 American and other non-British traders were carrying at least half of the India goods moving to Europe.[20] Slowly but surely the forces of free trade were bringing the East India Company's trade monopoly to an end.

The question arises why the Company was unable—or unwilling—to reverse the erosion of its trading position. As will be seen, there were forces in the Company—called the old shipping interests—who fought to keep all Orient trade in the Company's hands. They occasionally tried to enforce the ban on Company servants engaging in the outside trade or to insist that free traders must be licensed by the Company, but these measures were usually ineffectual and short-lived. (Beginning in 1793, the Company set aside an annual tonnage that private traders could carry on Company ships, an amount that was woefully short of the demand.) The conclusion is inescapable that the old shipping interests were more interested in keeping all trade, even the non-Company trade—in their personal hands than in preserving the sanctity of the Company's monopoly. One reason they might have had for taking this position was that those who had made their fortunes in India, whether Company servants or independent traders, found it increasingly difficult to repatriate their profits to England because the Company would not sell bills of exchange for this purpose. They found ingenious ways to do so; one of them was the non-Company trade. Another possible reason why the Company did not fight effectively to maintain its trade monopoly might have been its interest—like any bureaucracy—in maintaining its administrative functions in India that provided income to so many of its servants, as well as the opportunity for favored access to trade, however the latter was conducted.

Once the comparatively risk-free plan of engaging in the China trade was no longer immediately feasible, Hogan had every reason to join the ranks of free-lance traders with Europe. His decision to do so, however, could not have taken place suddenly in the three weeks between October 16, 1791, when he was still talking of the China plan, and November 8, when he announced the Ostend plan. He must have already given advance thought and planning to the alternative. The earliest item in the surviving collection of Hogan memorabilia is a letter dated June 13, 1791, to Robert Charnock at Ostend that refers to the Tellicherry rice transaction that took place in November 1790, a full year before Hogan told others that he had decided to drop the China option and engage in the Ostend trade instead. Perhaps his father-in-law, William Richardson, who was either an independent free trader or one licensed by the Company (he was definitely not a Company servant), introduced Hogan to Charnock and the Ostend connection. Hogan may also have been induced to consider the Ostend plan because the potential profits from this business were enormous. One estimate is that the average cargo from India unloaded at Ostend was worth £50,000;[21] another is that profit margins at continental ports were at least two or three times what could be expect in the legitimate Indian trade to London,[22] so that with only a few voyages an entrepreneur could make what was then a fortune. These numbers are probably exaggerated—certainly Hogan did not realize profits in this order of magnitude—nor do they take into account the risk of being seized by pirates in the Indian Ocean (or during war by the enemy), the high cost of insurance, high interest rates in India, the possibility of being subject to interference at the instigation of the East India Company (though this seems seldom to have been done effectively), or the fact that profits had to be shared among ship owner, charterer, agents, supercargoes and others.

On January 30, 1792, Michael and Frances Hogan, as well as the ailing Captain William Richardson and his wife, sailed from Calcutta on the *Netunno*. The ship stopped at Gangam (now Chatrapur), Madras, Vizagapatnam (now Vishakhapatnam) and Pondicherry on the Coromandel Coast (the east coast of India) to take on freight and passengers, finally leaving Pondicherry on March 11 loaded with saltpeter, sugar, coffee and coarse goods. One of the passengers was a Mr. Cooper, an East India Company official. The captain was a Genoese named Angelo Borgo; Hogan was aboard as supercargo for Messrs Robert Charnock & Company. Before leaving Pondicherry, Hogan had a scare when the Bengal government threatened to hold the *Netunno* as British property, which of course it really was.[23] The threat arose because the government had learned just after the *Netunno* left Calcutta that the Court of Directors of the East India Company in London had issued a proclamation the previous June imposing severe penalties on any person, including Company officials, found to be engaged in "illicit and unlawful trade...carried on between Europe and India by British subjects under the false colors and passes of foreign nations."[24] Nothing came of the threat to Hogan, nor apparently did the East India Company attempt to enforce its edict strenuously.

Hogan told a correspondent that the *Netunno* "stops at no port whatever and sails very fast" and later claimed the voyage took only three months and fourteen days. The elapsed time was closer to three months and twenty-one days, still a speedy trip by the standards of those days, and the ship did stop at St. Helena on May 18 and probably also dropped anchor, as did almost all ships sailing westward, at the Cape of Good Hope before that. Hogan's enthusiasm for a quick voyage was based on more than good business practice. On leaving Pondicherry, he said "we may first give the late glorious news in Europe." The "glorious news," contained in the March 1 issue of the *Madras Courier*, a copy of which was in Hogan's hands, was that a preliminary peace treaty had been concluded between the British in India and Tippoo Sultan following the latter's decisive defeat by Lord Cornwallis and General Robert Abercromby in the Third Mysore War, thereby destroying the prestige of the Mysore dynasty and paving the way for complete British control over all of India, although that would not come until the next century.

The *Netunno* would probably have stopped at St. Helena in any event, but Hogan may have wanted to find out whether any other vessel was ahead of him in delivering the news to England and, if not, to assure that he would at least be the first to apprize the main British outpost on the trade route from the Orient. The Governor, Robert Brooke, forwarded an extract from the *Madras Courier* to the Court of Directors of the East India Company on a French vessel and also gave Hogan a letter of introduction to the Company in case he should arrive first. Not to be outdone by a French ship, Hogan disembarked his passenger, Mr. Cooper, at Havre de Grace on June 30 so that he could get to London with the news on a packet boat without having to wait for the *Netunno* to unload its cargo at Ostend. Cooper delivered Hogan's covering letter, Governor Brooke's letter and the *Madras Courier* to the Company on July 2. The three texts, including Hogan's brief letter, were printed in *The Times* the next day as London rejoiced at the "glorious news." One British spokesman said that Lord Cornwallis "had made the British name loved and revered in India."[25]

After unloading cargo at Ostend, the *Netunno* sailed for England. Hogan found temporary quarters at Covent Gardens in London where Frances gave birth to their first child, William, on July 17. The saucy—and fictitious—Fanny in the once scandalous book *Fanny Hill* lodged in Covent Gardens, widely known for its crime and bawdiness.[26] The Hogans would not have wanted to tarry long in that area.

Michael Hogan had been in England while in the British Navy, but only at naval bases, such as Plymouth and Portsmouth, and he had in mind returning with his family to the only home he really knew—India. But while his ship was still chartered out, he had to put up with London, then the largest city in the Western world with a population of some 860,000, with its pea soup fog and the foul air that Hogan detested. (The pea soup fog was caused by the noxious fumes from burning soft coal clinging to fog droplets which could hang over parts of England for days; the foul air came from the filth and stench of London's streets.) By the standards of its day, however, London was a modern city. Its main thoroughfares had been paved, foot pavements added, trash and garbage collected in some areas, the water supply improved, sewers installed, oil street lights erected and some of the worst of the decrepit edifices torn down. London was still a hodgepodge of houses and mansions where the wealthy lived, interspersed with many more shabbily built houses, hovels and shacks where everyone else lived. The worst parts of London were still in the alleys, lanes, rookeries and courtyards built in labyrinth manner (where the poor and destitute tried to survive) behind otherwise respectable houses to evade London's various building restrictions. These places now harbor some of the fashionable houses of London. The dockside areas of Limehouse and Bermondsey, where Hogan would have had to conduct some of his business and where the merchant house of Christopher Richardson of Limehouse was located, were full of thieves, fences and prostitutes and "honeycombed with places of bad character."[27]

The Hogans procured a house at No. 2 Christopher Street on rectangular Finsbury Square, possibly on the recommendation of Robert Charnock whose wife lived there.[28] The Square was the centerpiece of a well-ordered residential suburb laid out in the years 1777–1792 that became the fashionable area for the medical profession before it migrated to Harley Street at the end of the next century. Nearby stood the Bethlem Royal Hospital built in 1675 to incarcerate lunatics. Like most such institutions of that day, it offered virtually no treatment for the mentally ill. For many years, Londoners came to Bethlem, nicknamed Bedlam (from which the word *bedlam* is derived), to gawk at the helpless, confined inmates—it was one of the sights of London.[29] Hogan refurbished the house with curtains and draperies and new materials for the kitchen, nursery and fireplace. (Finsbury Park, as it is now called, has been in the news since the September 11, 2001, terrorist attack as the site of a mosque that espouses Islamic extremism and may shelter terrorists.) Captain William Richardson had decided finally to retire from the sea and commercial affairs; he built a house at Gainford on the Tees in Durham County, which the Hogan family visited from time to time.

The early 1790s were fateful years. Europe was waking up to the fact that the revolution that had taken place in Paris in 1789 might presage more than just a domestic squabble. The Jacobins had seized power, King Louis XVI made a prisoner, the Republic declared and the Reign of Terror instituted within three months after the Hogans arrived in London. Possibly believing war would bring new territory and therefore sources for additional taxation and economic exploitation to relieve its crumbling treasury, partly the result of its aid to the Americans during its revolutionary war, France had already gone to war with Austria and Prussia and was demanding that the Netherlands stop favoring Britain in the all-important trade centered on the Scheldt

River. Although Britain prided itself that it had already had its Glorious Revolution (in 1688), there was widespread belief among the upper classes that the French version, coming so soon after the disastrous American Revolution, endangered the established—and comfortable— order of government and society. Trials for treason had become a daily occurrence. By the end of the year it was commonly assumed that Britain also would soon be at war with France, the only question being who would declare war first. With the country in the midst of an economic recession, fearful of the impact of the Jacobins and of treasonous acts by its own citizens, weary of yet another war with France, and anxious to return to better times, Britain was in no mood for what was to become a titanic struggle lasting almost a quarter of a century.

In January 1793, Louis XVI was beheaded (Marie Antoinette lost hers the following October), and on February 1 France declared war on Great Britain and the Netherlands, the news reaching London eight days later. Unaware of the full significance of these events, Michael Hogan began the return voyage of the *Netunno* to India on the evening of February 16, passing Lands End three days later. He had probably read in London newspapers that Lt. General Charles O'Hara, his presumed great uncle-in-law, was also sailing from England on almost the same day to take up his new post as lieutenant governor at Gibraltar, but he did not meet O'Hara at this time (or any other later time) for he might then have learned the truth about the absence of a marriage with Mary Hogan.[30]

The *Netunno* was still under charter to Messrs Robert Charnock & Company of Ostend but now under command of a different Genoese, George B. Corvetto.[31] Hogan had, however, retained the firm of David Scott & Company of London as his personal agent, and this firm may also have been acting for other principals.[32] Before leaving India on the previous voyage, Hogan had secured advance commitments from several merchant houses to buy £12,000 worth of European goods. The ship was therefore heavily loaded, principally with European-made piece goods for sale in India as well as the Cape of Good Hope, and he had every reason to expect that this venture would turn out profitably. Also on board were personal items that William Richardson was sending to his daughter and son-in-law, Jane and Barnaby Boles, and "a parcel of newspapers and the latest popular pamphlets" and some "new-fashioned Parisian ornaments...of bracelets, necklace and earrings" that a friend was sending for William Hickey and his "favorite native woman" in Calcutta.[33]

The first part of the voyage was not without danger. On February 23, 1793, while in the Bay of Biscay, the main mast came close to breaking. The ship was "then so far to the westward owing to a smart gale from SSE and SSW that I was under apprehension we should have been obliged to bear away for Ireland. However, the wind became so moderate that I was able to secure [the mast] tolerably well." But after crossing the equator March 18, "we have been very unfortunate in our winds. Though we were not farther than 30° West longitude, the SE trade winds failed us entirely, finding them [feeble] and very light, which retarded our passage wonderfully...."

The *Netunno* finally arrived at the Cape of Good Hope on April 29. Once again, Hogan was the bearer of news, this time of the war with France, but it is likely that the Dutch colony had already heard this news. Due to a local shortage of money, he had to offer his goods at below cost, taking in only £800.

Hogan's main concern during his brief stay at the Cape was to repair the faulty main mast. Thanks to " light winds and calms," he wrote, he was "able to make [the mast] sufficiently strong to carry us I hope safely to Bengal where it must be shifted." He also needed to replace "a few additional hands in lieu of those that we lost at Margate," the infamous British prison in which some of Hogan's sailors may have been incarcerated. He noted: "I really believe we have as many languages on board as there are letters of the alphabet.... I had only 20 Lascars, 5 Chinamen, 2 Seacannies [steersmen] and 8 Europeans to bring her this far, all of whom behaved very well. The Lascars particularly could work the Europeans to death in either hot or cold climate. I have now had a trial of both and should ever prefer Blackies...." His reference to lascars—or Blackies—meant dark-complexioned sailors of Asian or African origin. They occupied an ambiguous status common in the Indian Ocean area, being half-slave, half-freemen.[34]

On the voyage between the Cape and Madras, an incident occurred in which Hogan thought Captain Corvetto improperly attempted to prevent several of the British officers from quelling a near mutiny of non-English sailors. Recalling he had just told Messrs Robert Charnock & Company that the captain was behaving "very well" and concerned that his principals might blame him, Hogan on June 17 wrote a long letter to Captain Corvetto when the vessel was just south of Ceylon reprimanding him and in the process improperly asserting his dominance over the Captain in matters of ship safety.

He was in Madras a week later where he sold a third of the European goods, invoiced at £18,000, for a 47 to 50 percent profit. The remaining two-thirds he sold in Calcutta when he arrived there a month later at a 54 percent profit. He found that European articles were "much in demand [except for] shoes, boots, hats and broad clothes," but he was only able to sell fifty-three of the 155 barrels of Peter Blackwell beer and had difficulty in selling some cherry brandy. These goods were offered for sale in Calcutta by Messrs Davidson & Maxwell & Company in an advertisement that appeared in the *Calcutta Gazette* on August 8 headed "Fresh Europe Goods." The long list of articles for sale, which also included goods imported on a Genoese sister ship, *Il Triomfo*, reads like a combined advertisement of grocery, liquor, hardware, sports, clothing, shoe, stationery and drug stores and gives a colorful picture of habits and life styles two hundred years ago, at least in British India. Among the goods listed were:

Claret, pale ale, porter, brandy and gin; Westphalia and York hams; pickled foods; raisins, nuts, milk chocolate, dried fruits and Gloucester, Berkley and Pine cheeses; plates, glasses, mirrors (called looking glasses); dinner sets (called Queen's ware); tools, fencing foils, shooting tackle, rifles, pistols, gunpowder and toys; iron ham boilers, fish kettles, sugar boxes, steam pea boilers, tea kettles, rat and mouse traps and other tin and ironware; assorted medicines; colors for drawing, hair pencils and lead pencils; gold vellum strap epaulets, scarlet and gold sword knots and silk sashes; cloths, cashmeres (called cassimeres), quilting, satinet, flannel and buttons; gold earrings and necklaces, ivory tooth-pick cases, silver shoe buckles and smelling bottles; violet hair powder from Smyth, Marchelle powder, lavender water, essence of peppermint, Windsor soap, tooth powder and brushes, razors and Arquebusade water; telescopes, boat compasses and brass index quadrants; Dutch quills, ink powder, pounce [a fine powder once used to prevent ink from spreading], blotting paper, India rubber, foolscap and message cards; Norway doe breeches, drab leather waistcoats, Venetian beaver and ladies' Woodstock wash habits; military cocked hats with cockades, bands, buttons and loop, round hats bound with silk and leathered with silk bands and buckles and latest fashion hats for ladies elegantly trimmed; hosiery, boots, shoes, saddlery and even paints, tar and copper nails for ships.

The advertisement ended with an inducement: "D. and M. take the liberty of recommending the present opportunity to the gentlemen of the Army...of ordering their supplies from the above instruments, as it may be reasonably supposed that the Honorable Company's ships, having sailed very late in a fleet and with convoy, will not reach Bengal for some considerable time, and they may therefore be now furnished with almost every article they can want." D. and M. even offered to dispatch boats to "the upper stations" at their own expense to effect delivery of any sales made.[35]

Prospect for similar profits on the return voyage would not be as good. Hogan could not procure saltpeter because the government had embargoed its export,[36] and the East India Company had taken all the limited supply. He canvassed merchant houses in India, including the firms of John Forbes & Company, Fairlie Reid & Company and John Ferguson & Company,[37] to interest them in shipping pepper, indigo, cotton or sugar to Europe, pointing out that the eighteen East India Company ships sailing westbound that season were already booked, that no other ships would call at Madras before the next season, and that it would be safe to ship on a neutral vessel in time of war.[38] There was general concern over the state of markets in Europe because of the war but, because it took many months for news to get from one place on the globe to another, even overland or by fast ship, accurate and current information was not available. When buying goods in India, information on the state of the European markets was often at least three months old and it would be another four months before the goods would be unloaded and sold in Europe. Reflecting unusual pessimism, Hogan wrote to a partner that he had seen "a letter...giving the most discouraging accounts of the markets [in England] I ever saw in my life. Everything [is] a drag and no sale for anything but sugar and indigo and that declining fast. No money, no credit, trade at a perfect standstill, and a general discontent throughout the great City of London."

These practical problems were particularly on Hogan's mind over goods he and a partner were buying for their own account on speculation. On his voyage from Tellicherry to Calcutta in 1790, he had met Nathaniel Sharpe who held out that he could procure raw materials from Rungapore (now Rangpur) without going through the traditional middlemen. Hogan had signed agreements with Sharpe promising to advance money for Sharpe to buy sugar and raw silk, with the net profits from their sale in Europe split 50-50. When Hogan received reports that the European market for silk was plunging, he asked Sharpe to curtail his purchases, but it was too late; the raw silk had already been bought. To add to their woes, the silk arrived dockside "very indifferently packed." Hogan told Sharpe, "[I] am sure you could not have seen it sent away in such a state but must have trusted to the report of sircars [Hindu overseer] both as to quantity and packing, for the muster you sent me is 30% better than the silk in the bales, having had occasion to open one to repack it, as also to double ginny and rope the whole."

There were other balls that Hogan also had to juggle. He had managed to pay back Pondoosett Tewajusett's quarter share in the ship building venture, but he still had to settle with Captain Boles and his father-in-law. The latter could be put off until he returned to London, but Boles politely insisted that he wanted to see a return on his money. While he was at Madras, Hogan wrote to Boles offering a choice of a refund of the money he and another officer had put up at 15 percent interest or they could take their one-quarter share of any net profit from the venture, which Hogan clearly implied might be very small or even, after he had paid all expenses, non-existent. Boles accepted the first alternative, much to Hogan's relief. When this matter was finally wound up, Hogan told Boles: "I would further recommend that you never hold any concern in ship or ships. You can lend your money, taking care to divide your risks and always insuring to the full amount, for a trade that will not bear the premium of insurance is not worth carrying on." Hogan could well have followed that advice himself in later years.

Hogan stayed in Calcutta over four months while he sought business for the return voyage. He encountered difficulties in finding shippers willing to accept the high freight rates then being asked. He initially quoted £25 a ton but had to accept £16 for one-third of the ship's cargo space, with the remainder filled with goods purchased on account of his principals or on his own account. Through an agent at Madras, he made arrangements with a Colonel Bruce to rent the roundhouse and the adjoining cabin to carry the colonel, his family, four servants and baggage back to England, though not until he had reduced his asking price to £1,080. The colonel wanted to leave in October, but Hogan persuaded him that, "by leaving [your coast] in the latter end of December or first of January, we will I trust have a [safe] passage and a quick one, and get to England about the first of May, whereas were we to sail in October we might expect a tedious winter passage and arrive in the piercing cold month of March." Learning that the colonel was ailing, he also promised that "I have belonging to the ship a very experienced good surgeon with everything in that hire that can be of use." Normally, ships sailing westward from Calcutta left before September when storms and heavy weather became prevalent in the Bay of Bengal, but private traders often found it advantageous to be out of synch with the East India Company ships. Hogan was finally able to sail from Calcutta on December 14, carrying raw silk, sugar and indigo. On this occasion, there was no threat that his vessel might be seized for carrying illicit cargo to Europe in contravention of the East India Company's monopoly, possibly because there was no certain way to establish that departing ships might be engaged in such practices, even though they were required to submit a "full and true manifest of the export cargo" before they could obtain port clearance from the Calcutta Customs Master.[39] It is interesting to note, however, that both paintings of the *Netunno* that Hogan commissioned at this time show the ship flying the red ensign of a British merchant vessel, not the colors of Genoa, perhaps to avoid any hint of illicit trade.

After stopping briefly at Madras, the *Netunno* anchored at Tranquebar, a Danish enclave on the east coast, to pick up Colonel Bruce's party of four, as well as a Mrs. Mair, a Captain Maxwell and his seven children, all accompanied by servants. Hogan reported to Messrs Fairlie Reid & Company at Calcutta that "many who wished much to go fell back in consequence of the very bad state of the Colonel's health, his life being despaired of by all the faculty. However, we shall I hope be comfortable and make a good passage, the ship being in excellent trim drawing 18 feet water only and 900 tons of goods on board. The passengers having all crowded down to this place, I was prevailed on to come to take them on board [rather than at Madras], which was much against my inclination. Everything is now perfectly clear and ready, and we are beginning to heave up our anchor for Europe." He lamented that the "cash I expect to receive here falls short for two reasons: first, the passengers being fewer [than I expected]; secondly, some making their payment at home."

Although the European war had so far little affected India, Hogan seems to have had some concern for his safety, for he left with Messrs Fairlie Reid & Company at Calcutta "a large packet of papers sealed which I request you will open in case you have certain accounts of any accident having happened to me, such as death, capture or detention by Foreign Powers or shipwreck; it contains papers that require your attention and management on the account of my family in case either of the foregoing circumstances should take place."[40] In addition to insuring the ship and its cargo to Ostend, or Hamburg in case Ostend had been overrun by the French, he also left instructions for the continued payment of premiums on life insurance for himself and Frances in the *lottery tontine*, an annuity system under which the surviving subscribers receive the deceased's benefits.[41]

The *Netunno* was at the Cape of Good Hope on February 20 and St. Helena March 15, where Hogan was probably told that, so far as was known, Ostend was still in friendly hands. But the transmission of news being what it was, he could not be certain of his reception on entering the port. In preparation for the worst, he intended to identify his ship before anchoring so that no time would be wasted in arranging to unload cargo. Before leaving India, he had written to Messrs Robert Charnock & Company: "The ship will draw 19 feet water, therefore prepare accordingly. We shall hoist a red flag at the fore top gallant…as soon as we get sight of your steeple, and when we see it off the deck I shall fire two guns, one 15 minutes after the other." The *Netunno* arrived at Ostend at noon on May 29 to find the port was threatened but not yet occupied by the French. Just five weeks later, the French were in control of the port. Lord Cornwallis arrived at Ostend while Hogan was there, on his way to join the Prussian Army on the Rhine, but they did not meet.[42]

Although the goods aboard the ship were unloaded at Ostend, an earlier letter Hogan had written to Messrs Robert Charnock & Company from Calcutta hinted that the final destination might be otherwise: "Let me have letters from you in the Downs laying in the hands of the English Company's agents there and at Mr. Harvey's Ship Inn, Dover, with your advice on what is best to be done. I know the orders this vessel is under from the American freighters. Therefore, curtail my letters without going to particulars." While at Ostend, he also wrote a letter to Messrs David Scott & Company at London establishing that this merchant house had a central role in the *Netunno* venture and, in particular, that it was acting as agent for the British firm of Messrs Campbell & Company of Ratcliffe which had 993 bags of sugar on board, presumably destined for England. The significance of this letter, and of many subsequent business dealings between Hogan and Messrs David Scott & Company was that David Scott, who began his business life as a free merchant in Bombay in 1763 and in 1786 established his agency house in London, was a senior director in the East India Company and a champion of giving non-Company ships a greater role in the Orient trade than the old shipping interests in the Company wanted. Scott believed that not only the Company's interest but those of Britain as well were being weakened by the protectionist schemes the Company had adopted over the years and that trying to stop the clandestine trade served only to enhance it. As early as 1787, a year after he left Bombay, he had proposed that the

Company surrender the trade from England to India and from India to China to private merchants,[43] a position that was accepted in so far as India-China trade was concerned and that made possible the voyage of the country ship *San Antonio* between Bombay and Canton in 1788 with Hogan on board. "Leave the clandestine trade alone," he wrote in 1796; and later: "My opinion on this is decided. Whether this monopoly is for the good or the contrary of the Company's commerce, it should be abolished. If the Company cannot carry on trade without a monopoly, they should leave it." The battle within the Company on this issue was of long-standing, and for a while Scott and his followers had some success in turning the Company's policies around. But the opposition was strong and ruthless. Shortly after Hogan's return to England, Scott's detractors accused him of using his East India Company position to favor his private agency business. He denied this and was found innocent, but he resigned his position in Scott & Company, turning it over nominally to his young son. Scott was charged on several occasions over the years with a number of indiscretions involving his private business activities and was on each occasion found innocent. But his efforts were ultimately in vain; the old shipping interests forced Scott to resign in 1802.[44] Nevertheless, the East India Company gradually declined into oblivion, first losing its India monopoly in 1813, its China monopoly in 1834 and its role in operating the India civil government in 1857, when the British Government completed the process of taking over the governance of India from the Company, which was dissolved a year later. The result of the loss of its India monopoly was a trebling in trade and a dramatic reduction in freight rates from the £40 a ton once paid to the Company to £10 a ton paid to private traders in 1830.[45]

While Scott was a true reformer, the policies he advocated as director in the East India Company lent support to the agency house which continued to bear his imprint. There is little question that he was one of the leading, if not the leading, merchant playing both sides of the Orient trade—participating in both the East India Company and free-lance trades. His association with Hogan is itself evidence of this, but there are numerous other connections. Throughout his London business career, he maintained close contact with British agency houses in India, including his original Bombay partners, James Tate and Alexander Adamson, and with William Fairlie who also served as Hogan's principal agent in Calcutta for many years. James Sibbald, who with William Lennox was supposedly running the London firm when Scott bowed out, was his brother-in-law and another former British merchant in Bombay.[46]

The letter that Hogan wrote to the Scott firm from Ostend in June 1794 is the first direct evidence of his association with that firm, but he certainly already knew who Scott was and may have had an earlier relationship. A letter that Hogan wrote a year earlier to a firm in Bombay referred to "a receipt from Messrs [Joseph & Louis] Baretto & Company of Calcutta for a respondentia bond running on a Portuguese ship to Mozambique...the amount...to be paid to the Governor there who was to remit it to Mr. De Souza of Bombay...." The transaction in question probably went back to the time that Hogan was first in Calcutta in 1790 and 1791. There were many De Souzas in Bombay; one of them was a partner of Tate & Adamson, a firm in which David Scott had been a partner when he was a Bombay merchant and with which he continued to do business from London.[47] Hogan himself would later have a close relationship with Adamson. The Barrettos were also well known to Scott.[48]

The letter mentioning De Souza may also indicate that Hogan had another venture underway in addition to those involving the *Netunno* and, earlier, the *Myrtle*. While he may not have been an active participant in this otherwise unexplained transaction, the main direct trade from Africa to India at that time was slaves from Mozambique and Madagascar, carried on both Portuguese and British ships to Goa and Bombay. The indirect African slave trade to Asia via Arabia and the Persian Gulf had been underway for many centuries. Most of the black slaves in India were domestic servants, manual laborers and soldiers, rather than agricultural workers as in the Western Hemisphere, and in Bombay were generally accorded better treatment than elsewhere in India. Slavery was legal in India (although subject to some restrictions) until 1834, when it has been estimated there were close to one million black Africans in the country.[49] It would not have been unnatural, therefore, for Hogan to have been involved in the slave trade at this early point in his career; later, he would become a direct participant on a much larger scale.

Hogan presumably cared nothing for either the economic theory, morality or politics of what he was doing. He probably never heard of Adam Smith's *Wealth of Nations* written in 1776, the grandfather of modern economic theory. His immediate interest on returning home was to sell the sugar and silk that he and Nathaniel Sharpe had procured on speculation, as well as a bale of white muslin handkerchiefs (large cloths used as neck scarves and bundle wrappers) on his own account. The *Netunno* did not tarry long at Ostend; the ship with Hogan on board was back in England sometime in June. Hogan returned to the continent in September, this time at Flushing in the Netherlands. He may have been there on the *Netunno* (which by this time, as will be seen, might have been registered under British flag as the *Marquis Cornwallis*) as part of an effort, assisted by British Navy vessels, to carry British citizens and French and Dutch émigrés back to England following the failure of Britain and its allies to stem the steady march of French troops and Dutch sympathizers through the Netherlands. Robert Charnock may have been one of his return passengers. His main purpose, however, was to secure the safety of the goods that he had unloaded at Ostend three months earlier. The sugar and handkerchiefs, which were on his own account, had been sold without difficulty, but the silk owned jointly with Nathaniel Sharpe was a different matter. Either because their goods hit the market at the wrong time or because some of the silk had been damaged, they were not to benefit from the increased demand for Indian silk and piece goods on the continent that had resulted from war devastation and a change in dress fashions.[50] While at Flushing, Hogan shipped the silk on the *Eliza* to Hamburg where he asked his agent, Messrs Parish & Company, to do all they could to sell the silk in Europe. Later, he tried to have the unsold silk shipped to England, even though he reported that "the price of that article is much reduced here in consequence of the large quantity in the [East India] Company's sales," but this effort encountered one bottleneck after another. Eventually, the silk was all sold, but although Hogan and his partner must have at least recovered their costs, put at 43,985 Zealand florins (roughly £3,500), they did not garner the huge profits they had expected.

He also asked his agent at Hamburg to provide a Mrs. Harwand, "whose sufferings have been great," and her four children with sufficient funds to make their escape from Basel, Switzerland, to England, presumably because France was then making threatening gestures toward Switzerland, but the lady managed to get to England with her children in April 1795 without Hogan's help.[51]

While Hogan had been at Calcutta in 1793, he had made detailed plans for a third voyage from India to Ostend. He even entertained the notion that Frances and their first born (William) could accompany him. These plans were dropped for several reasons. The most immediate was that Frances gave birth to a daughter, who was to be called Fanny, on March 6, 1795. Thereafter, the Hogans acted as though London would be their home for some time. They bought new Brussels carpets, added garden gates and repainted their house on Finsbury Square.

It must also have become evident to Hogan that there were other obstacles to undertaking another voyage to India. When war broke out in early 1793, the British expected it to be of short duration and, indeed, victory appeared to be in sight when in August the French naval base at Toulon turned against the Revolution and invited in Allied forces. But in December, a young French artillery officer named Napoleon Bonaparte made a name for himself and rekindled the French war effort by retaking the port from its British occupiers, who happened to include Lt. General Charles O'Hara who had been wounded and taken prisoner by the French. By January 1795, the Netherlands and Belgium had been completely overrun by the French, and the Prince of Orange had fled to London to be befriended by Britain. Dutch patriots sympathetic with revolutionary France established the Batavian Republic, which became an ally of France. In April Prussia withdrew from the Allied side and three months later Spain also made peace with France. Although led by one of Britain's great Prime Ministers, William Pitt (The Younger), the country seemed to be in a sorry state. Domestic prices were rising, there were protests and bread riots in London, the Irish problem again commanded attention, and there were intermittent fears of a French invasion. Moreover, this new war was turning into a different kind of conflict from those in the past; France was now not only an aggressive neighbor threatening the balance of power on the continent, as well as an invasion of England, but also its seemingly never-ending excesses of revolutionary spirit, which might otherwise have found support among Englishmen, were being perceived as an ideological menace, not unlike that later posed, though at the opposite end of the political scale, by Hitler.

Of more immediate concern to Hogan was the fact that British-registered vessels engaged in the Orient trade were increasingly at risk because of the presence of French privateers in the Indian Ocean, as well as in the waters near Britain. The risk could be avoided only with the protection provided by British Navy convoys, which was available only to East India Company ships or private British vessels sailing under government auspices or under contract with the Company. Hogan's choices were thus limited to doing business for the Company or with the British Government—or of finding some other career. He could not even consider the latter. Even with the help of powerful agency houses, such as Messrs David Scott & Company in London and its allied agencies in India, the earlier, seemingly unlimited opportunities for entrepreneurs to prosper in international trade were becoming more difficult to realize.

Fortunately, Hogan was now free to use his ship for new purposes. The charter on the *Netunno* had ended; he had renamed the ship the *Marquis Cornwallis*, another indication of his attachment to Cornwallis, cemented no doubt by the circumstance of their frequently being in the same place at the same time, and registered it on September 23 under British flag.[52] In October, after his return from Flushing, he offered to undertake four, six or more India voyages for the East India Company. His application emphasized the best features of the ship: "She is coppered fore and aft to the bends and shall be fitted under the inspection of your officers with the number of anchors and cables required and a sufficient quantity of stores and she shall mount 14 guns, six-pounders, with the quantity of ammunition required and be navigated with seven men and one boy to every one hundred tons of her chartered tonnage."

When he was initially turned down, he offered the vessel as a man-of-war to the Navy Board in February 1795 but was again unsuccessful. He finally found clients for a roundtrip voyage in March. Under contract with the Transport Board, the *Marquis Cornwallis* would carry Irish convicts from Ireland to New South Wales. On the return voyage, he would pick up cargo in China and India under contract with the East India Company. The voyage, as well as political developments, would change his career forever.

THREE

NEW SOUTH WALES

...the worst of all human beings—Irish convicts.

—Hogan to British Navy Commissioners

The eastern reaches of the continent of Australia were unknown to Europeans before Captain James Cook entered Botany Bay—near present day Sydney—in 1770 on the *Endeavour*, after first touching at Tahiti and New Zealand on a westerly sailing. He and James Banks, a noted naturalist, brought back reports of aborigine natives, odd flora and fauna and a desolate, bleak land. But the new territory was still thought of as a mysterious region on the opposite side of the globe, almost as though it were on a different planet, unworthy of being populated. It was not until after the American Revolution that British government planners turned their attention to the new continent.

British jails and hulk prison ships had been overflowing with convicted criminals for well over a century. Most of these criminals were poor people who had committed sometimes the most petty of crimes but who were nevertheless convicted and sentenced to long jail terms. It was commonly accepted in Britain that the large and growing class of poor people presented a serious threat to society because they turned to crime rather than labor to support themselves, and that the only solution was wholesale incarceration or transporting them elsewhere. Ever since the early seventeenth century, Britain had managed to keep its jails from overflowing by sending convicted felons to Jamaica and Barbados and as many as 50,000 to the American colonies. But the American Revolution, as well as the economic preference for black slaves from Africa to work as laborers, dimmed hope that the Americas could continue to serve as a useful dumping ground. Another territory had to be found.

After considering several areas, such as Gibraltar and parts of West Africa, Botany Bay in New South Wales was selected in 1786. Strategic considerations may have played a role in the decision. Despite their losses in India during the War of American Independence, the French had not given up their interest in the East. There was also some expectation, although little hard evidence, that Australia might be a plentiful source of pine and flax used for masts, spars and sails, the supply of which from Russia was threatened by shifting alliances in the 1780s among the major powers of Europe. This expectation proved to be false. The overriding reason may simply have been that Australia was far enough away that no convict would ever find his or her way back to Britain. Whatever the reasons for the decision, it was a momentous one because it led to the inhabitation and establishment of large new territories and was a forerunner of other, major population movements from Europe, mostly to the New World.

The first convoy of eleven vessels carrying English convicts arrived at Botany Bay in 1788 after a harrowing 252-day journey, the first visit by outsiders in eighteen years. They were the first of many ships which brought over 150,000 convicts to Australia over the next eighty years. Most scholars question whether transportation, as it was called, either solved or ameliorated Britain's problem with its poor and their perceived bent toward crime.[1]

Michael Hogan's offer to transport convicts to New South Wales was well-timed. The British zeal to purify their ranks extended to Ireland whose inhabitants were becoming increasingly rebellious. He was to be paid some £10,000 to transport poor Irish men and women convicted of one crime or another to New South Wales on the *Marquis Cornwallis*.[2] On its return voyage, the ship would carry cargo from China or India under contract with the East India Company.

The vessel left Portsmouth on June 8, 1795, after taking on board thirty soldiers to act as guards of an expected 200 convicts. Also on board was Hogan's brother-in-law, William Richardson.[3] The *Marquis Cornwallis* was already a little late, for the Transport Board had told the Admiralty on May 15 that, "It is…indispensably necessary, in order that this transport may secure her passage to China, from whence she is chartered to receive freight from the East India Company, that she should arrive by the 1st of June at Cork, and proceed thence as speedily as possible." The secretary for colonial affairs, the Duke of Portland, had also requested the Admiralty to provide a convoy for the vessel from Cork to an area near the Canary Islands. The request for convoy was approved on May 18 with the notation, "Their Lordships have taken measures for convoying her to Cork and will give directions to Admiral Kingmill [at Cove] to provide for her escort to such a distance as may place her in a state of safety."[4]

On arrival at Cove, the port for Cork in Ireland, Captain Hogan found that he was to take on board an additional twenty-four female convicts for whom he had to purchase supplies out of his own funds. This was not the end of his problems. While still in port, one of the soldiers, Bryan O'Donald, after "damning the King and saying he would not serve his Majesty," refused to stand guard as sentry. He was tried at a general court martial on August 5, presided over by an British Army commander, found guilty and given a sentence of 800 lashes, "this sentence to be put into execution tomorrow morning before 10 o'clock and to receive such part of the punishment as M. Hogan, the owner of the *Marquis Cornwallis*, shall think proper, the remainder of the 800 lashes to be given to the said Bryan O'Donald should he behave bad on his passage, and if he acts like a good soldier, M. Hogan will please to remit the remainder after what he receives tomorrow." Hogan remitted all but 150 of the lashes. Flogging was then standard practice on ships at sea.

At the very last moment, an additional nine male Irish convicts were brought aboard to make a total of 241 of whom 168 were males and 73 females. With the ship's crew and the soldiers acting as guards, there were 328 persons on board. The ship also carried 136,376 pounds of beef and pork and a one-year's supply of clothing being sent by the government to the inhabitants of New South Wales, as well as goods that Hogan expected to sell on his own account.

Concerned on the eve of sailing from Cove that he had left Frances short of cash, Hogan wrote his London agent: "I have written to Mrs. Hogan and told her you would pay her all the money of mine you may have after paying the bills I have drawn on you, which I request you will [do], and that you will receive it from the Board as soon as possible. On your receiving my certificate from Botany Bay, you will reserve in your own hands £1,400 of the money due on them and pay the rest to Mrs. Hogan." He was anxious to get underway after what must have seemed an interminable wait, for he also told his agent, "The signal is out for sailing and I assure you I never saw one that I am more happy to attend to."

The *Marquis Cornwallis* was finally underway at 6 p.m. on August 9, a month behind schedule. Captain Hogan reported the "ship was very full of rats." But rats were the least of the captain's problems on this long voyage.

Even before embarking from Portsmouth, there was a report that the guard detachment was mutinous and that the worst among them was a Sergeant Ellis. It was also known that several of the male convicts were Defenders, a loosely knit group of Catholic rebels against British rule in Ireland. *The Times* of London reported that "seventy [of the convicts] were Defenders [and that] just before [the *Marquis Cornwallis*] sailed, six of the same descriptions...were brought [to Cork] and shipped off with the *hopeful*[*sic*] cargo."[5] The reference to the "hopeful cargo" might today be interpreted as a sarcastic comment, but it probably then reflected a belief that criminals deserved the hard life they would face but might thereby redeem themselves. The *Marquis Cornwallis* was the first of many ships that would carry Irish political prisoners to Australia.

After a month at sea on September 9, two of the convicts sent a note to Captain Hogan asking to see him in private. The ship was near the equator in the vicinity of the Cape Verde Islands, its British Navy escort having just departed, the very islands where the youthful Hogan had participated in a naval battle fourteen years earlier. The meeting took place the next morning in the presence of William Richardson. The prisoners "informed me," Hogan later recorded, "that a conspiracy was formed by the convicts and soldiers to get possession of the arms and the ship and that I was the first person to be put to death, and that Sgt. Ellis and a few of the soldiers were at the head of this plot. They also informed me that the sergeant was to furnish the convicts with knives for the purpose of making saws to cut off their irons, and that the convicts were to send the sergeant money to purchase the knives, and that they and he corresponded regularly, and the notes which passed between them (after being read) were thrown overboard, and at daylight some morning they were to rush on deck in a body when the boys were let up to clear the buckets."

Hogan continued that this report "gave me some concern and additional caution, and induced me to request Ensign [John] Brabyn (the commanding officer of the troops) to fall his men in and muster their kits, and on examining the sergeant's first we found six knives upon him, all new and large but one. Last night he went to Ensign Brabyn and got two knives from him, saying he had not one to cut his victuals, but to our great surprise we found him possessed of six, for (I am sure) the worst of purposes."

It was also discovered that Ellis had spiked the touchholes of six muskets and disabled two pistols so that these weapons could not be used by the guards against the convicts. Having disarmed the presumed perpetrator and warned loyal members of the guard detachment against possible surprise attack, Captain Hogan thought the mutiny plan had been thwarted. But Sergeant Ellis was not finished. "On the 12th, at 8 p.m.," Hogan's report continues, "the gunner came to me in my cabin and informed me that last night between half-past 10 and 11 o'clock, being in the lee waist, he heard the sergeant make use of mutinous and inflammatory language to the soldiers, addressing himself mostly to the sentinels on the fore hatchway [the prison door]. He compared the situation of the soldiers to the convicts, saying they were worse off, for that some of the convicts were transported only for seven years, and that they were for life, and that they were damned fools to be sold."

Although Hogan was captain of the vessel, the guards were subject to the authority of their commanding officer, Ensign John Brabyn, and the latter was yet unwilling to arrest Sergeant Ellis, perhaps fearing the whole detachment might rebel. Hogan could do nothing but post additional guards. But the next day, a convict named Patrick Hines, a "man who I had good character of and had reason to form a good opinion of from his general conduct since he came on board," substantiated the earlier disclosure of a mutiny plot between Ellis and the convicts. Hogan instructed Hines to return to the prison and obtain further information from the ringleaders "by pretending to be hearty in their desperate cause."

The full plot, as it was later pieced together, was for prisoners to seize Hogan when he was making his twice weekly inspection of the prison accompanied by several ship's officers and one of the two surgeons on board. They were all "to be put to death by their own swords." Ellis and his fellow conspirators among the guards were to attack the remaining officers on deck, hand out arms to convicts as they escaped from their prison below, and once in control of the ship sail her to South America. It was also alleged that "some of the women were concerned in the conspiracy, their part being to convey knives to the men, and to put pounded glass into the messes of the ship's company."

Captain Hogan forced the issue upon the reluctant Ensign Brabyn on the 15th by assembling Brabyn, his fellow ensign, William Moore, and the ship's officers and crew to demand an indictment of the perpetrators of the plot. The assembled lot readily gave their unanimous consent. There was later dispute whether the order to punish the mutineers was given by John Brabyn, who had authority at least over his own soldiers, or by Captain Hogan, who had ultimate authority for the safety of the ship. Forty to fifty of the convicts were flogged and six of the women prisoners punished. The severest punishment was meted out to two soldiers: Sergeant Ellis's head was shaved, he was handcuffed, thumb-screwed and leg-bolted to one of his supporters, Private Lawrence Gaffney, and both were put in the ship's prison among the convicts.

On September 22, the convicts strangled one of the informers and attempted to force their way upon deck. One of the ship's officers later said that "Capt. Hogan rushed down the fore hatchway, followed by Mr. Richardson and three more of the officers and myself, armed with a pair of pistols and cutlass, where began a scene which was not by any means pleasant. We stuck together in the hatchway and discharged our pistols amongst them that were most desperate who, seeing their comrades drop in several places, soon felt a damp upon their spirits. Their courage failed them, and they called out for quarter. I broke my cutlass in the affray but met with no accident myself."

Seven of the convicts later died of wounds. Sergeant Ellis died on the 24th. There were no reported attempts of mutiny thereafter.[6]

Hogan was aware before sailing from Ireland that an initial British naval force commanded by Commodore John Blankett, with accompanying troops under Major General Sir James Henry Craig, had sailed at the end of February to take the Cape of Good Hope from the newly established Batavian Republic, and that the main naval force, commanded by Rear Admiral Sir George Keith Elphinstone, had sailed early in April. The British Cabinet had decided to take this step in January only after the Netherlands had been overrun by French troops and the Batavian Republic established. Before then, the Cape Colony had been considered a safe port for British ships because the Netherlands, after being an enemy when Able Bodied Seaman Hogan participated in the sea battle of Porto Praya, was now again an ally based on the Anglo-Dutch mutual assistance treaty of 1788. It was thus felt sufficient only to offer assistance to the Dutch in holding the Colony against an expected French seizure attempt. An agency of the East India Company had even been established at Cape Town in 1794 to facilitate the passage and supplying of Company ships. Although the views of British officials were not always unanimous on the question and changed over time, the prevailing view in 1795 and for some years thereafter was that the Cape should not become a permanent British colony. This central thought was well captured when Sir Francis Baring, Chairman of the East India Company, wrote to Secretary of State for War and Colonies Henry Dundas on January 12, 1795, urging prompt action to seize the Cape: "The importance of the Cape with regard to ourselves consists more from the detriment which would result to us if it was in the hands of France, than from any advantage we can possibly derive from it as a Colony. It commands a passage to and from India as effectually as Gibraltar doth the Mediterranean, and it serves as a granary for the Isles of France [in the Indian Ocean]; whilst it furnishes no produce whatsoever for Europe, and the expense of supporting the place must be considerable."[7] The corollary to this position was that the British occupation should cease and Dutch sovereignty restored when the war ended, assuming that the Batavian Republic would be among the vanquished.

When Elphinstone's fleet arrived in June, the local Dutch authorities were unwilling to submit peaceably when shown a British-instigated letter from the exiled Prince of Orange addressed to the Dutch authorities at the Cape asking them to place themselves under British protection. Among other things, the Prince's letter said he was "solemnly assured on the part of His Britannic Majesty that the [Colony] shall be restored in full sovereignty and use to Their High Mightinesses as soon as ever it shall please God to restore my afflicted County the blessings of independence and of its ancient and established form of Government."[8] There were several sharp skirmishes, but after Commodore Blankett arrived in August on H.M.S. *America* with several other ships, and Major General Sir Alured Clarke in September landed additional troops from India, the Dutch, having no real choice, finally capitulated on the 16th.[9]

After stopping at St. Helena on October 23, where Hogan would have learned that the Cape of Good Hope was now in British hands, the *Marquis Cornwallis* arrived at Cape Town on November 24 to find General Craig in charge, Elphinstone and Clarke having departed for India nine days earlier. (Word of the successful capture of the Cape did not reach London, however, until November.)[10] Hogan sold some goods at Cape Town and, with the proceeds and money borrowed from John Pringle, the East India Company's agent at Cape Town, bought clothing, wine and spirits for sale in New South Wales where he expected to make "at least a 100 percent yield." Somewhat hypocritically, he wrote to his London agent, Messrs David Scott & Company, to "[keep] this to yourself; you know I would not on any consideration trade while in government service."

Hogan must have reported to his London agent that he successfully dealt with the attempted mutiny on his vessel, but his papers are completely silent on the matter. Based on how he later dealt with another matter that certainly impugned his character, the likelihood is that he destroyed all papers mentioning the mutiny, in the apparent belief that the insurrection was a "black mark" on his character.

On this occasion, his stay at the Cape of Good Hope was "considerable owing chiefly to a stormy S.E. wind which blew for eight days so hard that all the ships in the Bay rode with their anchors ahead and no communication with the shore during that time. We are, however, the better for it, having all my people well refreshed and in good health and shall sail the moment the land wind comes off, with little doubt of getting to China as early as the Bombay ships. The most disagreeable thing is having to make an eastern passage out and home, but when I engaged to carry such a cargo as I have now, particularly my own countrymen, I conceive I had no right either to expect pleasure or comfort, and I have entirely reconciled myself to the want of both [on] this passage."

He also humorously noted that, "My stock [of people] are increasing in number for last night one of Dublin dames was brought by the lee and introduced a son of Mars."

The reference to an "eastern passage home" apparently meant he intended to return to England from China across the Pacific and via South America, a sailing course that was not unknown but was unusual. However, in the end his ship did not go to China.

Commenting on British governance, Hogan noted that "Admiral Elphinstone left the *America* (Commander Blankett) with the *Ruby*, of 64 guns each, here and proceeded himself about a month ago, they say, to Madras but more likely Batavia."[11] He also noticed that the "Army and Navy agree but indifferently, as [is] common on joint services where captures are in question and that causes such jealousy (every department using its own prerogatives) that the merchant, whether foreign or domestic, is the greatest sufferer."

The only change he noticed from Dutch governance was "a total prohibition of all imports or exports in any other ships but English, so that a foreign ship [i.e. not English] can benefit nothing by coming here for other than [to] get water and mutton, which is 2 [pence] per pound." The prohibition on neutral ships engaging in trade at the Cape of Good Hope had been imposed the previous month because, as Admiral Elphinstone reported to London, "if they are allowed to ship grain or wine, they uniformly pretend to be forced into the French islands [principally Île de France] by bad weather or cruizers, and there load with English prize goods, or take commissions to capture British vessels. Tranquebar has seventy ships belonging to it, notwithstanding the whole [Danish] settlement [in India] is not worth five thousand pounds."[12] The local British military commander found he could not apply the prohibition uniformly due to a combination of circumstances. The Colony was woefully short of various supplies; the cargoes of the East India Company ships that had called at the Cape were destined for the Orient or the home country, not for the Colony; no other British merchant ships had called at the Cape since its capture before the *Marquis Cornwallis* arrived;[13] only neutral vessels, principally American and Danish, had been willing to sell their cargoes at the Cape; and they had demanded to be paid in produce because there was a severe shortage of hard currency. Navy Commander Blankett remonstrated against General Craig on several occasions for allowing neutral vessels to load produce which he suspected was destined for Île de France,[14] a stance he could readily take because he had no responsibility, as did Craig, for the welfare of the population. Hogan was equally disenchanted with Blankett, writing that he was " a violent...man, ...determined to be trouble to all ships under a neutral flag and thinks he has a right to send them all to London for the inspection of [their papers], even I [on my] last voyage and knowing what I do now, I would give this place a wide berth while he commanded afloat." Apparently, Blankett had threatened to send the *Netunno* to London as a contraband runner during one of the ship's earlier calls at the Cape Colony. Craig was instructed a year later by the War Office to abandon the prohibition on neutral trading, but the Colony's problems in this area continued, as will be seen.[15] The jealousy between the Army and Navy over captures was caused by disagreement over who should share in the spoils. Elphinstone was eventually awarded £64,000 in prize money, General Craig and his Army officers receiving considerably less.[16]

Hogan's letter to Scott also predicted, correctly as it turned out, that the Colony would be faced with a surfeit of supplies because "every person here has been recommending to their friends at home to speculate in goods to this market."

After a twenty-five day sojourn at the Cape of Good Hope, the *Marquis Cornwallis* sailed on a direct track across the Indian Ocean and around the southern coast of Australia to Port Jackson, a voyage that took two months.

Long sea voyages in the last half of the eighteenth century were in constant danger of shipwreck, storm, attack by enemy naval vessels or privateers and illness. The British Navy assumed that one man in thirty would die of disease or accident on a sea voyage and that one man in six was always ill.[17] Few ships had naval surgeons aboard, although this deficiency was slowly being corrected. Even though there were two surgeons aboard his ship, one appointed by the government to look after the convicts and soldiers and the other to care for the ship's company, four men died of illness during the voyage, in addition to the seven who died from wounds in the gun battle of September 22.

Conditions aboard ships sailing to faraway ports, even in the late eighteenth century, would be considered atrocious by any modern standard. Although intended to satisfy the Transport Board that the prisoners had been adequately fed and to obtain reimbursement for expenses at the close of the voyage, a careful reading of the Certificate of Victualling executed by the government's surgeon on board, Matthew Austin, shows he only said that the convicts had "fresh provisions" served while the ship was in port, not while at sea. The certificate also noted that vinegar supplied by Hogan was used "in sprinkling the prison beams and carlines, washing the prisoners' berths, and giving them to drink."[18]

In a later letter to The Honorable Commissioners for Victualling His Majesty's Navy petitioning for reimbursement of the additional expenses he had incurred, Hogan alluded to the problem of getting provisions out of the hold and on deck where they could be aired or overhauled. "Indeed, the hatches were often left open longer in bad weather than I could have wished, but unavoidably so, for the immense quantities of water and provisions constantly wanted much regularly was not to be attained." Perhaps the worst condition was "the slop made by dirty women and filthy men [that] rendered it almost impossible to have a sail dried or provisions looked at." None of this was made any easier by the "forty days strong-blowing West Wind from the Cape of Good Hope to Van Diemen's Land."

Never one to refrain from hyperbole in pleading his case or defending a deficiency, Hogan ended his letter by saying that "on due consideration of these circumstances, which are facts that were I on my death bed I would willingly make oath to, I am led to hope you will be pleased to order these articles put to my credit and my accounts settled that I may get paid for what I well earned...in performing 7 months of the most disagreeable service that ever man was engaged on, carrying the worst of all orders of human beings, Irish convicts. I beg leave at the same time to assure you that no man living could have paid more attention to the provisions and everything belonging to Government than I did on board that ship, and that, as she was my own property and my character as well as interest at stake, I felt it both my duty and inclination to do so."

Life aboard Captain Hogan's ship was hardly the worst among the convict voyages to Australia, however; most of the earlier and some of the later voyages were much worse.

On February 11, 1796, six months after sailing from Ireland, the *Marquis Cornwallis* arrived at Port Jackson, the port for Sydney, where the prisoners were put ashore and placed in the hands of the local authorities. Some of the convicts who had been punished were not fully recovered and were sent to the hospital.

Under British law, offenses committed on board British ships on the high seas were subject to trial or review by Admiralty Courts. Governor John Hunter reported to London that "a daring and dangerous insurrection has been reported to have been planned by the convicts, aided by some other disaffected people [on the *Marquis Cornwallis*]," but he said he was at a loss to know how to proceed judicially.[19] A Vice Admiralty Court had not yet been established in Australia. Hogan applied to the governor to conduct an official inquiry because he did not want to stay in New South Wales while the question of the governor's legal authority was debated with London and because he wanted to be cleared of any possible charges against him. Hunter directed that such an inquiry be held, after which he would address the judicial issue.

The inquiry was held on March 21 before the Judge Advocate, David Collins, and the Acting Chief Surgeon, William Balmain. Gaffney and several other soldiers testified that, although they were not part of the plot, Hogan had grossly mistreated them, but Ensigns Brabyn and Moore, other soldiers, the two surgeons on board and two ship's officers all confirmed the plot and testified that Hogan had acted properly throughout the affair. Collins and Balmain reported to Governor Hunter on April 30 that "we have no difficulty in saying we think Mr. Hogan, situated as he found himself with a dangerous conspiracy in his ship on the point of breaking out and headed by some of the most daring and desperate offenders that the jails of Ireland could produce, could scarcely have acted otherwise than he did, and we are of the opinion that nothing but the steps he took ensured the safety of the ship and the preservation of the lives of all on board." The report also said that "it does not appear to us that there was any improper interference with the military guard on board on the part of Mr. Hogan."[20]

Governor Hunter immediately wrote to the Duke of Portland apprizing him that "upon arrival of the ship *Marquis Cornwallis* in this port, I received information...from Mr. Michael Hogan, her commander, that a very desperate plan had been laid by the convicts, and was in considerable preparation, for seizing the ship and murdering the officers and ship's company during her passage to this country.... I directed such enquiry to be made into this affair as might enable me to lay the whole of this horrid transaction in as clear a light as possible before your Grace, which shall be done by the first opportunity after the departure of the above ship. All I can at present observe upon it is that the steps which were taken by Captain Hogan...appear to me to have been the only means which could have been used to save the ship and their own lives."[21]

Hunter did not forward the official report of the inquiry to London until September 5,[22] long after Hogan had left New South Wales. Much later the Duke of Portland in a letter to Hunter acknowledged receipt of the report without comment.[23] Nothing more was heard of the matter.

There was, however, less than perfect harmony among the ship's officers. Matthew Austin, the Government's surgeon on board the *Marquis Cornwallis*, who testified in support of Hogan in the mutiny plot, had earlier charged Hogan, the other surgeon (John Hogan, apparently no relation) and the pilot who came on board at Port Jackson with assault, for what is not disclosed. The Court acquitted John Hogan and the pilot but fined Michael Hogan £50.[24]

It had been eight years since the first convict ships had arrived. The Colony had survived near starvation and was becoming self-supporting, due in large measure to the work of the officers and men of the New South Wales Corps, each of whom could be awarded twenty-five acres of free land for the asking. Officers could obtain 100-acre lots, together with ten convicts who were, in effect, used as slave labor to serve the colony, including the cultivation of farm lands in the Hawkesbury River area north of Sydney. During his brief stay in New South Wales, Hogan acquired a plot of land previously known as Woodhay which he called Cornwallis Place (or Estate) after his favorite nobleman with the intention of raising livestock and growing grain. The plot consisted of 400 acres purchased from Lieutenant Abbott and 30 acres from Samuel Jackson, Abbott having bought a number of the 25 and 100-acre lots previously awarded to New South Wales Corps members to make up the 400-acre parcel. Later in April 1797, Hogan's farm supervisor purchased an additional 30-acre lot called the Rowan Farm. Both were on the Hawkesbury River slightly to the north of a settlement later named Windsor.[25]

Governor Hunter cited Hogan's farming plans when he wrote to Under Secretary for Colonial Affairs King to encourage the Government to send some settlers, rather than only convicts, to the new British Colony. He noted that Captain Hogan, "having purchased a farm which was partly cleared… has left several people upon it from his own ship, and a few of the convicts he brought out he has taken off the hands of the public, and seems determined to make his farm productive. He has left some live stock, tools of every kind and, in short, promises fair to [become] really a respectable farmer. It could have been well for this colony could we have early had fifty or a hundred such settlers, but many of those who have been permitted to fix [here] are truly worthless characters, and very few sent out by permission of the Government are likely to benefit the settlement. They seem, most of them, disposed to speculate in some way of no great advantage to the colony. I wish they were in their own country again."

In the same letter, sent with seven other government dispatches on the *Marquis Cornwallis* when it returned to England, Hunter promoted Hogan as " a man of property and good connections [who had] mentioned to me that he liked the country and climate, and had some intention of making proposals to Government to be permitted to establish a store here for the supplying with of every article which may be wanted either the settlement at large or individuals." Hunter lent his support to such a venture because he "long wished that some steps could be taken…to [suppress] effectually that shameful imposition which has so long distressed poor individuals who pay for every little article [at] the most unjust and unreasonable prices." The governor also believed that such a store would be "a means of introducing the manufactures of our own country in greater abundance into this settlement, and thereby lessen the speculations of foreigners and adventures from the East Indies."

Putting in a good word for Hogan in London, Hunter closed by saying that, " if his proposals were attended with moderation in point of profit, I thought it probable Government might listen to him."[26]

Cornwallis Place was to become a weight around Hogan's neck over his lifetime and, seventy years later, an inheritance problem for his children and grandchildren. Expecting to reap profits from livestock and grain, Hogan had arranged for two convicts on the *Marquis Cornwallis*, John Riley and Philip Tully, to be assigned to work the farm, and he signed an agreement with an unscrupulous and almost illiterate ex-convict named Mark Flood to manage the farm.[27] Flood managed to avoid paying Hogan whatever profits the farm earned and to run up considerable debts by one subterfuge or another, aided and abetted by one John Stogdell, who acted in a similar capacity for a fellow landowner, John Palmer. Realizing Flood needed to be supervised, Hogan sought the intercession of John Macarthur who later became wealthy when he introduced Europe to wool from Merino sheep. The cause of the farm's problems was not wholly attributable to his tenant farmers; there were many crop failures in New South Wales during the early years of the Colony, and in May 1799 there was a disastrous flood on lands near the Hawkesbury River. Nor was the farm always a loss; in 1805 Governor King reported to London that Cornwallis Farm "has been very successfully and advantageously cropped on account of Government since the year 1800."[28]

While Hogan was still in New South Wales, Governor Hunter granted him a six-acre plot on the "eastern side of Sydney Cove," a possession Hogan apparently forgot about for over thirty years.[29] In 1830, he asked his land agent in Sydney to obtain an "authenticated copy of a grant made to me by Governor Hunter of the point of land below the governor's garden called Bennselou's [sic] Point. It was in the month of April or May 1796 and regularly recorded.... I think it measured about 9 acres." The correct name of the area was probably Bennelong Point, near what is now Government Wharf and the site of the famed Sydney Opera House.[30]

Hogan's plans for a retail store at the Colony were not all conjectural, as Governor Hunter implied. He had brought with him dry goods, wine and spirits, and he was allowed to open a shop on shore to sell these articles to the inhabitants. Although by 1796 a half dozen or so ships would arrive every year from England and India bringing basic supplies, the inhabitants still looked forward to each arrival to bring news and what were considered luxury goods, such as clothing and liquor. Hogan would not be so fortunate in avoiding Government control when he tried to do the same thing on nearby Norfolk Island. His concept of commercial establishments to supply British Government settlements around the world, although hardly original, would later blossom at another British colony.

Hogan told at least one person that he intended to take up residence in New South Wales some time in the future.[31] Although his talk about this may simply have been intended to please those who stayed behind, whether willingly or not, it is enticing to speculate that he might have had the most personal of reasons for later returning to the colony. Just two weeks before Hogan left Sydney, a thirty-one year old woman convict named Ann Ryan, who had come there on the vessel, gave birth to a daughter. She named her Mary Hogan and listed Michael Hogan as the father.[32]

It is possible that Ann Ryan named Hogan as the father out of some spite (perhaps she was one of the mutineers who "put pounded glass into the messes of the ship's company") or to avoid the onus of the daughter's having a convict as her father, but there is no good reason to doubt the claim. It had become common practice for officers and even crew on board ships with unattached women, particularly prisoners and others in subservient positions, to acquire their services for personal comfort and, inevitably, for sexual purposes. The women could be easily lured with promises of extra rations, time outside the prison hold or other comforts. Hogan had already been away from home two months when his union with Ann Ryan would have taken place, before the mutiny attempt surfaced in mid-September. It is possible that the report of women conspirators among the prisoners came from Ann Ryan herself. She might even have been genuinely pleased to be selected, not by some crew member, but the captain himself, as well as happy to escape from the dreadful conditions in the prison hold.

Hogan must have known that Ann Ryan was pregnant because she was already in her seventh month when she arrived at the Colony. Whether he knew of the birth of Mary before he left Sydney cannot be known, but it is equally difficult to conclude that he was both unaware of his parenthood and totally uncaring. Perhaps, after all, he did seriously consider returning later to address the issue of his illegitimate child.

Even if he was unaware of his daughter while he was in Sydney, he would have later been told of Mary Hogan's existence by one of the several persons with whom he maintained a correspondence at Sydney for many years. One such person could have been John Macarthur. Another might have been Captain David Collins, the judge advocate in New South Wales, who on his return voyage to England on the *Britannia* wrote enigmatically in a letter left for Hogan at Cape Town in March 1797 and received by him there a month later: "If a certain acquaintance of mine is with you, a certain acquaintance of mine desires to be kindly remembered to her. I do the same." Many years later, Hogan's grandson, who had reason to look into his grandfather's activities in New South Wales, wrote in pencil on this letter that the two phrases "a certain acquaintance" meant in each case "a woman." Collins was traveling with "my little family," consisting of Nancy (or Ann) Yates and her two illegitimate children sired by Collins in Sydney. Like Hogan, Collins had left a wife in London. His "remembrance" might have some perfectly innocent explanation, but the only one that seems to fit is that Collins was relaying greetings from his Nancy to Hogan's Ann, with whom Collins could have been "acquainted" and who he perhaps had some reason to believe was with Hogan in England, though why he might have thought so defies explanation.[33] Another person who might have told Hogan was Philip Gidley King, governor of Norfolk Island, as will be seen in the next chapter.

It had been Hogan's intention to sail the *Marquis Cornwallis* to China by a new route through the East Indies, but he gave up this plan due to the lateness of the season. Instead, he would go to Bengal to pick up freight for England under his contract with the East India Company. Perhaps concerned that the Company would fault him for this decision and wanting advice on the dangers of sailing close to the coast of Java, now in the hands of the Batavian Republic and an ally of enemy France, he consulted with Governor Hunter who reported to the Transport Board that "Captain Hogan, commanding the transport ship, the *Marquis Cornwallis*, having consulted me relative to his route from this country to India and having observed by his charterparty that he is engaged by the East India Company to proceed from hence either to China or Bengal, I did not hesitate a moment to assure him that

I considered his season to China as past and that it was my opinion he should endeavor to fulfill that part of his engagement which left it in his power to proceed to Bengal, as the season for that voyage was now in its commencement...." Hunter left it to Hogan to decide whether to take a course to the south or north of Batavia (now Java) because "we are uncertain in this time of war what the fate of Batavia. may be...."[34] In the end, Hogan chose the northern route.

The *Marquis Cornwallis* left Sydney on May 15, 1796, after a three-month stay in New South Wales. There were several paying passengers on board. One was seven year old Edward Macarthur, the eldest son of John Macarthur, who was being "packed off to school" in England, "without a tear," according to his mother.[35] Another was an ex-convict family.[36] Six days later, the ship stopped at Norfolk Island, one thousand miles off the east coast of Australia, also the dumping ground for the "worst of worst" convicted felons, in order, according to Hogan, "to oblige the Government by landing dispatches and a few bad characters." The bad characters were four convicts; also on board were two women convicts who had permission to join their husbands on Norfolk Island.[37] But Hogan had another purpose in stopping there. Before sailing, he had sent a servant to the island with a letter for Lt. Governor Philip Gidley King proposing that he be allowed to sell dry goods, brandy, rum and whisky at the commissary store on the island. The dry goods were sorely needed; Norfolk Island had been without such supplies for four years.[38] The common man's drink, rum, then commanded a major role in the economy and social life of New South Wales; for many, particularly the convicts and freed laborers, access to liquor was considered as important as food and shelter. Laborers sometimes asked that their wages be paid in spirits, and freed farmers sometimes committed future harvests against present delivery of rum.[39] Every ship that arrived at Port Jackson would have rum and wine aboard, and the sellers of these goods could easily make money. Although the drinking was portrayed in Britain as evil incarnate, such as in Hogarth's paintings and drawings of besotted men and women in debaucherous state, the sale and consumption of rum was not considered to be an evil or social disgrace among those in the Colony.

The governor allowed the sale of Captain Hogan's dry goods, but initially refused the retail sale of spirits. After pleading the expenses he had incurred and the fact that the spirits had already been landed on the island, Hogan lowered his price slightly to 15 shillings a gallon, "not charging more than 20 shillings retail." The governor again refused but said "it may be in my power to relieve you in some measure from your personal embarrassment [having already unloaded the spirits] if you will state to me the lowest price you will take for it, to be paid, if I approve of the price, in bills on His Majesty's Treasury on sixty days sight." Concluding, he said, "I think it necessary to say that I am informed that the price paid by Governor Hunter to you was only six shillings per gallon for the spirits and wines." Hogan could not accept the rebuke, though he may have wondered if it were not King who would make the profit instead of him. He acknowledged the price paid to Governor Hunter but noted he had already sold some of the spirits and wine at Port Jackson for 10 and 15 shillings per gallon. Nevertheless, Hogan relented on the price question, telling King that: "The losses I've met with and the great expense attending the ship during her stay in the spring under a heavy press of sail to prevent being blown off by the strong gales that now prevail will, I hope, if taken into your consideration, justify me in the addition of two shillings six pence per gallon upon the prices paid by Governor Hunter, [that is] to say, 8s/6p per gallon for the whole of what I have." Perhaps as another factor for King to consider, he added that "among the wines which is Cape Madeira there is one port which may be found useful for the hospital and for which I paid 10 shillings per gallon to an American ship at Port Jackson."

King accepted the offer, taking pains to say that it will be " much more profitable...for the Publick Service and the interest of the industrious individuals that [the spirits] should be in the hands of Government in preference to any set of individuals, who would not fail to make an improper use of it." King, who also purchased two tons of sugar from Hogan, felt it necessary to defend his purchase of the wine and spirits in a lengthy letter to the Secretary of the Treasury in which, among other things, he said that "for the last three years few articles of use [or] comfort have been sent from Port Jackson to this place and those which some individuals have been fortunate to receive have retailed at an advance of 500 and sometimes 1,000 percent above the extravagant price paid for these articles at Port Jackson. By this extortion, the return of the industrious settler's labors have been totally insufficient to supply himself with scarce an article of use or comfort beyond the produce of his ground which has always been a great discouragement.... The price that I have given for [the wine and spirits] will in great measure be done away by the prices I have directed the Commissary to dispose of them at, in exchange for fresh pork and wheat" After noting that Governor Hunter in New South Wales, had purchased a quantity of spirits "for the purpose of giving a proportion to those whom he may think proper on publick occasion," King felt justified in reserving "123 gallons for that purpose which will last more than a year." By this, King meant that the reserve would be for the use of government officials and "the industrious settler and other private cultivators." He had no "doubt of its increasing that revived spirit of industry which I am sorry to say that till of late much pain has been taken to repress and discourage."[40]

It will be noted that Hogan still made a 42 percent profit on the wine and spirits, but in obtaining only 8/6 per gallon he did not do as well as one report that rum could be sold for 30 shillings a gallon.[41] He received a Treasury bill of exchange for £1,025-10-6 for the 2,413 gallons of wine and spirits purchased by King. As for the 3,200 pounds of clothing he landed, King reported that, "The quantity of clothing and other articles of equal use and comfort that have been sold here by the Master of the *Cornwallis* has relieved the wants of many industrious individuals, and the quantity of these articles he has left behind for sale will make the present scarcity of clothing in the publick stores less felt than it otherwise would have been."[42] Hogan received £419-4-6 for the goods sold before he left and appointed William Neate Chapman, storekeeper at Phillipsburg, as his agent to sell the remaining 1,200 pounds of goods, giving him a five percent commission for goods sold wholesale and ten percent for those sold retail.[43]

Because of his concern to be sailing alone in waters where attack from many quarters was possible, and not being able to count on convoy protection until he reached India, Hogan persuaded Governor Hunter before leaving Port Jackson to write to King: "As Captain Hogan of the *Marquis Cornwallis* does not think his ship in the present uncertain state of the war in India sufficiently armed, he is very desirous of having four of the *Sirius*' 6-pounders. If he can get them on board, I have no objection to his being supplied with them and a few shott."[44] Governor King obliged by supplying Hogan's ship with four guns taken from the *Sirius*, a Government supply vessel that had foundered at Norfolk Island, and 140 rounds of shot. Hogan was also given 84 yards of canvas and 20 fathoms of two-inch rope made from the flax plant found on Norfolk Island which he was to make into a main royal sail for delivery to the Admiralty in England with his remarks on the sail's wearing qualities, it then being thought that the flax found on Norfolk Island might make superior sails for the British Navy.[45] Lastly, Governor

King gave Hogan three boxes containing seeds and pine tree and Norfolk flax plants, together with a letter of introduction to the naturalist, Joseph Banks, to whom Hogan was to deliver the items.[46] Captain Hogan sailed from Norfolk Island on June 18.[47] He now had on board another seven-year-old passenger, Norfolk King, one of two illegitimate sons of the governor, the other named Sydney, both born before Anna Josepha King joined her husband on Norfolk Island in 1791. Their mother was an English convict transported on the First Fleet who, according to an eye witness, was seduced by King with promises of comfortable treatment, even freedom. There is ample evidence that Mrs. King was aware that her husband was the boy's father.[48] That all this could happen with hardly an eyebrow raised, at least a visible one, speaks volumes of the mores of the time. Illegitimate children were common among both the poor and the advantaged. They were often raised alongside legitimate children in a family atmosphere, and moral disapprobation was not yet generally attached to the male's role in such procreation, even by disillusioned but compliant wives.

He plotted his course from Norfolk Island to India to take him northwest through the Coral and Solomon Seas; northwest along the northern coast of New Guinea; through Dampiers Strait (northwest tip of New Guinea) and Pitts Passage (now the Ceram Sea); southwest through the narrow Straits of Bocton (between the small islands now called Muna and Buton in the southeast corner of Celebes); then south through the narrow Straits of Selayar (southmost tip of Celebes) and the Straits of Sape (between the Indonesian islands of Sumbraw and Flores); and then along the southern coast of Java to the Indian Ocean and a direct course for Ceylon, Madras and finally Calcutta where he would pick up cargo for England (Figure 1, page 73). He wrote that he decided to take this course, which was similar in most respects to the one recommended by Governor Hunter, to avoid the Java Sea between Java and Borneo with its storybook marauders and pirates, not to mention possible French or Dutch naval vessels and privateers. Even so, before leaving Port Jackson, Hogan was ready for assault: "I fear nothing under a heavy frigate. I mount 16 good guns with 70 sizeable fellows to stand by me and by God she shall never go while there is a cartridge of powder on board." The passage to India through waters in the East Indies that were not yet fully known to Western sailors was difficult, as evidenced by notations that appear on the several charts he used showing safe tracks through coral reefs, sand bars and often narrow straits that required steadfast navigation and sailing skills.[49]

Writing from Madras in early September, he said that forwarding the Treasury bills received from Governor King to safe hands "has in some degree eased my mind as it divides my risk and makes me of less value to a Frenchman should we meet one of superior force. While at Norfolk Isle, I borrowed of the Government there four six-pounder guns with 160 shot and increased my crew to 100 men fearing Dutch cruisers among the Molucca Isles. I came through the [Molucca Islands] and afterwards through the Straits of Sappy [to] 11° South. Never saw a vessel till I arrived off Madras hills when I fell in with the *Dublin* and the other ships who are safe arrived."

The *Marquis Cornwallis* was never in any real danger from French or Dutch naval vessels on its voyage through the East Indies to Madras, but the situation could have been quite different if a French naval force of six frigates under Rear Admiral Sercey had decided to raid British shipping off Madras and Calcutta during August and September instead of sailing directly across the Bay of Bengal from Ceylon toward Penang on the Malay Peninsula. Both British Navy forces responsible for the protection of India, one under Elphinstone stationed at the Cape of Good Hope and the other under Rainier based at Madras, were elsewhere at the time, leaving the Bay of Bengal unprotected against enemy marauders if any had known of the British naval absence. As it was, Sercey did not know of this British weakness, and fortunately for Hogan, the westbound track of the *Marquis Cornwallis* was some thousand miles to the south of Sercey's eastbound track. If Hogan had instead sailed north of Java and through the Strait of Malacca, he might well have become a French prize.[50] Although he was, in fact, out of danger, he did not know this when informed at Madras that the French fleet had sailed to the east in mid-August. He wrote to his Calcutta agent that, "though I dare say we shall do our utmost in case of being attacked, there is little prospect of success if we should meet the six French frigates mounting 20 guns. I have 100 men in very good discipline."

The *Marquis Cornwallis* left Madras on September 12 in company with the East India Company ships *Europa* and *Fort William* under the overall command of Commodore George Simson on the latter vessel. Hogan was not impressed with Simson. In a letter to Messrs David Scott & Company upon his arrival on September 24 at Hugli River downstream from Calcutta, Hogan reported that "Commodore Simpson

Figure 1. Partial track of *Marquis Cornwallis* through East Indies 1796. Author's Collection

[*sic*], who from ignorance of [the Bay of Bengal], stupidity or obstinacy,...led us to the eastward on the Coast of Aracan [Burma] and Chittagong [east of Calcutta], and made a foul wind of a strong fair one, by which we tore our ship's sails to pieces and with much difficulty got in on the 24th. I ran up the Eastern Channel and got a pilot in Sugar Roads. [If we] had come from Madras singly, I would be moored under fours at Calcutta on the 20th, and I have now to thank Mr. Simpson's bad management for a great loss of time, large expenses, much wear and tear, and loss of three anchors, and no prospects of getting up [river to Calcutta] before the full moon on the 15th [of October]. Should he be our Commodore home, I shall write to insure all my freight and cover my premiums."[51]

He also told Scott that "I never gave three cheers at the head of my ship's company with more pleasure that I did in Madras Roads on hearing of the downfall of the old shipping interest in Leadenhall Street." Leadenhall Street was the headquarters of the East India Company in London. Hogan's reference to it shows that he was aware of the battle being waged in London between the old shipping interests and those, such as David Scott, who wanted internal reform and increased opportunities for private traders. In March, the old shipping interests were unable to thwart the adoption by the General Court of the Company of measures designed to enlarge the circle of shipowners who could trade with the Orient.[52]

Navigating up the Hugli River to Calcutta was sometimes difficult. Hogan reported that the "freshes [floodwaters from monsoon rains, rushing to the sea] are so very strong in the river that I do not think it safe to quit her till she gets up [river] and, though I have been eleven days in the river, I have not yet seen our friends at Calcutta." When finally moored, he forwarded the seeds for Joseph Banks by another vessel and told him that, unfortunately, the pine and flax plants had decayed due to water damage and the extreme heat in the round house, which he said was seldom under 85° and often 95°.[53] During his three month stay at Calcutta, he had little to do but load cargo and wait for convoy protection. The latter need was occasioned by the continued concern over enemy attacks at sea.

He reported at the end of November that, "There is also certain accounts arrived this day by a ship that is come in from the eastward that the French frigate *Sybelle* [was] sunk after the action with the *Victorious* and that four large ships were seen going round Achim Head [north end of Sumatra] even after the French squadron sailed from

Mergui [northwest coast of Malay Peninsula, now in Burma], supposed to be bound to Batavia, a place which I wish Sir George would think of. He might take it in two days, bring away the ships and treasure and lay the town under a contribution or destroy its works."
Hogan's report that the *Sybelle* had been sunk was in error. The correct French name was *Cybèle*, one of the six ships in Sercey's squadron which, after taking several British prizes in the roads at Achin Head on September 1, had encountered the 74-gun British ships *Arrogant* and *Victorious* off Sumatra on the 9th, when Hogan was safely at Madras. The engagement between the better armed British ships and the smaller but more numerous French frigates was indecisive. No ships were sunk, the British probably escaping serious damage only because Sercey was under orders to avoid fighting and attack commerce instead.[54]

French corsairs were more daring than Sercey's squadron. While the *Marquis Cornwallis* was still moored at Calcutta on December 21, a twenty-gun French corsair entered Balasore Roads, just south of the Hugli River, where she easily captured three British schooners whose captains believed the French vessel was either British or neutral. One of the British vessels was recaptured, but the other two and the French privateer made their way safely to Île de France.[55] Fortunately, the *Marquis Cornwallis* encountered no French privateers on its return voyage to England.

She sailed from Calcutta at two p.m. on January 8, 1797, in company with six East India Company ships and at least 30 passengers on board: six army officers, a civilian and "a number of children," including the Macarthur and King boys.[56] Hogan was in Madras six days until February 1, two of the six accompanying ships having not yet arrived, the other four going separately to Ceylon. He reached the Cape of Good Hope on April 12 where he learned that a Dutch fleet had anchored in Saldanha Bay in August of the previous year intending to retake the Colony but readily surrendering when Vice Admiral Elphinstone, who had returned from India on obtaining intelligence of the Dutch intentions, confronted the fleet in the bay and General Craig threatened from the land.[57] Hogan would have found that Major General Francis Dundas, nephew of Secretary of State for War and Colonies Henry Dundas, had arrived two months before his arrival to take charge of the Colony pending the arrival of a civilian governor capable of addressing the many problems of governance that could not be resolved on strictly military grounds.

Hogan stayed at the Cape for only sixteen days, time he must have used to survey business prospects and become reacquainted with John Pringle. It was here that he received the previously-noted letter from David Collins with its enigmatic references to "certain acquaintances."

After stopping at St. Helena, Hogan was back in England on July 24 where he delivered his cargo to the East India Company warehouse, Edward Macarthur to his uncle in Devonshire and Norfolk King to his adopted grandmother.[58] Hogan's ship was the first of the East India Company fleet to return that season, beating some others by a few days, a circumstance that he used to advantage by sending a letter to the Court of Directors giving the names of the ships en route but not yet arrived that was dutifully printed in *The Times*.[59]

After more than a two-year absence, Hogan found an England beset by problems both at home and abroad. The war with France and its allies posed a new menace. Not only had Napoleon been successful in his attacks on Austria and Italy, but he had been appointed to command forces for the invasion of England. Britain's allies—Austria, Russia and Prussia—had made peace with France. Spain had reentered the war, this time as a French ally. British sailors had mutinied against the vaunted Royal Navy at its home port at Spithead. Economic conditions domestically were worse than when Hogan left the country two years earlier. Largely in response to fears of an imminent French invasion, there had been a drain on financial resources that had led the Bank of England to suspend payments in specie in February.[60]

Like many people before and since, Hogan's life and career had been largely determined by chance: he went to sea because that is where his family decided he should go; he found himself in Bombay because a ship had left him there; he had learned from others how to evade the monopoly of the East India Company; and he had taken Irish convicts to New South Wales because he had an available ship at the particular time the Government needed transport. But he must have realized, as others do, that there comes a time when a person has to try to control his destiny.

During his two-year voyage, he had ample time to ponder his future and many opportunities to make instructive observations. No doubt one of his thoughts was that continuing to command ships on long voyages, while exciting and adventuresome for a young man, was not a career for a family man. Moreover, he had tasted the reward that money brings to personal comfort and stature and wanted more. The two Indian voyages had been profitable and the journey to New South Wales would bring further cash into his accounts. Others might have been tempted to retire to the life of a gentleman, but this would have been totally out of character for Hogan. He would continue to do what he knew best—shipping and international trading— but this time on a grander scale. What particular line of this business should he choose and where should he settle? The latter question may have been the easier one to answer. Although he had once thought his future lay in India, this no longer seemed attractive. The shipping trade there was now a dangerous business not only to and from Europe, which seemed to be coming increasing under French control, but even locally within the Orient. The war with France was now being fought not only in Europe but also on sea lanes stretching from the West to the East Indies. He did not think much of London itself; not only was it an unpleasant place in which to live but it might be difficult to compete with the long-established merchant houses there, many with better connections than Hogan could hope to obtain.

Hogan's choice for a new location was the Cape of Good Hope which he had reason to believe offered a good prospect for successful business and profits. The *Marquis Cornwallis* had been one of the first private British ships to call at Cape Town some two months after the Dutch surrendered, and Hogan had also stopped there on his way back to England. He had talked with Pringle and probably other British officials, as well as with British merchants such as Alexander Tennant who had come to the Cape since its seizure. He had known Tennant when he commanded the *New Triumph* on Hogan's voyage from Bombay to Calcutta six years earlier. Pringle himself indicated he could be helpful to Hogan as a business partner, or at least so Hogan thought.

British merchants in London surely must have known that the Colony would probably be returned to the Dutch when the war was over and that the English East India Company would in the meantime retain its monopoly over trade between the Cape and the Orient. Hogan certainly knew this when he said in a letter written in August, "Our holding the Cape is yet a matter of great uncertainty." Why then did Hogan—and other British merchants—chose to reside at the Cape in the face of clear evidence that their stay would probably be temporary and possibly even of short duration? There is no certain answer to this question, but such evidence as exists, as well as common sense, suggest that there were two reasons. One was that British merchants were encouraged to do so by government officials who held out vague promises of government backing and profits. Some steps in this direction were taken, notably displacing the *VOC* (the acronym for the Dutch East India Company)[61] with the English East India Company and giving the latter a central role in keeping the Colony supplied with imported goods and foodstuffs. Another step, taken late in 1796, was to allow duty free imports from Britain and all British possessions, while goods of friendly nations could be admitted by paying uniform tariffs, thus countermanding the earlier prohibition on the importation of all foreign goods.[62]

The other more obvious reason for the influx of British merchants was the expectation of profits, a motive which surely attracted adventuresome spirits having few other choices. Hogan would have been especially attracted, not just because he was adventuresome, but also because he was ideally suited by experience and training to enter into the kind of business at the Cape for which there would be a demand during wartime. One of these activities was privateering—the lawful seizure and sale of enemy merchant vessels and their cargo—for which the Cape was to become a focal point. Although Hogan did not like to do business with government, another possible activity was to supply British Navy and East India Company ships at the Cape and British forces in India and elsewhere. Lastly, not so far away was the new colony in New South Wales which offered opportunities not only for trade but also as a source of cheap convict labor to man privateer vessels. Hogan had become intimately familiar with all these areas during the past seven years.

He may also have been personally signaled out to pursue these ventures at the Cape. There is no written evidence of this, but it is easy to imagine the possibility—if one can escape from the bane of historians that nothing is reportable unless recorded in writing. Hogan's main agent in London was the firm owned by David Scott, who was close to Henry Dundas, Secretary of State for War and Colonies, who in turn was the guiding force behind the shipping and colonial policies of William Pitt the Younger. When British Navy ships first arrived at the Cape of Good to seize the Colony in 1795, letters from Scott were delivered on shore to the Dutch governor and to Colonel Robert Jacob Gordon, a Dutchman sympathetic to the British, and replies from them were sent to Scott in London. The fact that Scott's letters commanded this attention from the British invading forces shows that he was considered an important person in the affairs of the Colony.[63] Scott and Dundas met frequently with Pitt at his country place at Wimbledon.

Policies and plans were undoubtedly discussed when these three met, either among themselves or with other principal merchants and officials in London. Hogan could well have attended one of these meetings—at a coffee house where businessmen met both socially and to transact business, at a salon or at an organized meeting designed to brief merchants on the state of the war. He was in London from June 1794 to June of the next year and from July to November 1797. Even as early as June 1974, there could have been a conversation about the increasing possibility that the British might have to seize the Cape of Good Hope and a discussion of the consequences, including the fact that the government did not want the colony to be a financial drain and the consequent need for British merchants to provide the means to keep the colony supplied without excessive recourse to the British Treasury. Later, the conversation might well have dwelled on the desirability of merchants assisting the British Navy in seizing enemy prize vessels from bases at the Cape. In such a conversation with others, Scott could well have pointed to Hogan as an ideal candidate for such a job.[64] Though not confirmation of this conjecture, Hogan did carry with him to the Cape of Good Hope a letter addressed to the Earl of Macartney, the governor of the Colony, in which Dundas advised that he had given "permission to the bearer, Mr. Michael Hogan, to settle at the Cape of Good Hope as a Merchant and to take with him Frances Hogan, his wife, and Peter Thomas Richardson, his clerk."[65] Archival records do not record that other letters of this nature were written.

Whatever his reason for moving to the Cape of Good Hope, Hogan made the decision before his return to London in July of 1797. He clothed his new venture in an aura of secrecy, as though he were on a special mission. His letters also spoke of partners, either to participate in joint ventures or share in the rewards. He was in communication with several Londoners about these ventures. Shortly after his return to England, Hogan wrote to John Pringle at the Cape that "a large cargo…goes out with me and family on the *Anna* of Bengal, Captain [Mungo] Gilmore. I have great hopes it will be such as will suit the settlement and command an advance on costs. Therefore, …do what you can to convince the county people [sic] and those that supply them retail that a valuable cargo of useful articles [is] on its way. It may be from £20,000 to £30,000. Think of securing as many good bills as you can recommend and have an eye to a house with warehouses in a good situation for business. I have explained fully our intentions to our friend, Messrs David Scott & Company, whose wish to promote our mutual interests is beyond my power to communicate to you by letter. When we meet you will understand it fully and be able to determine. Our holding the Cape is yet a matter of great uncertainty and your being entitled to half pay after the War is a thing determined against you. Therefore, you have nothing to expect but what you can make in office and, while in such, your name cannot appear in business. Keep your ideas private till I see you. You must not give up your situation. It would be against the opinion of all your friends and your own interest...."

A little later, Hogan wrote from Portsmouth to a Dr. Cleland, who may have been a neighbor of his on Finsbury Square,[66] that "I shall, on my arrival [at the Cape] and arrangements made, furnish you with particulars and always give you the best information of state of market. Pringle and myself will undoubtedly be as one from his official capacity. His name cannot be in the publick firm of a house. We are also likely to have a very clever fellow Mr. Ross, the Buxy [sic] gentleman, a partner. This to yourself. They are both men of ability, integrity, good property and excellent connections.... You had better send your instructions to me and Pringle jointly till you get our joint letters."

But before pursing his new venture, there were several business matters that required his attention. One was that he still owed his father-in-law a substantial amount of money for his one-quarter interest in the *Marquis Cornwallis*. While William Richardson must have wanted to help his offspring and their spouses gain an economic foothold, parents who are not wealthy are not generally prepared to make substantial gifts to family members. While still at Calcutta, Hogan had told Messrs David Scott & Company that, "should the old gentleman call at your House, you will oblige me by assuring him that he may rest perfectly at ease as to the safety of my debt to him, as discharging it will be my first object after my arrival in London." He finally came to grips with the problem when he wrote to his father-in-law from London on August 15 offering to give him stock in lieu of paying off the bond. After pleading his difficult circumstances, including inability to redeem some £13,000 in Treasury bills, he said that he had "made arrangements that will enable me to put you in possession of stock [which] were yesterday as low as 52." He added that "no one thinks of stocks being lower.... All I wish is to set your mind at ease as far as I am concerned for I have lately learned from experience that the health of the body is the happiness of the mind."

The identity of the "stock" that Hogan proposed to exchange for the bond is not known,[67] but Richardson presumably accepted the offer since there is no further mention of the matter. Whatever the legal technicalities may have been, it appears that William Richardson acquired an interest in the ship, possibly a controlling interest. (Hogan's reference to his difficulty in redeeming Treasury bills may sound like an excuse, but in fact the British Treasury was delaying payments at that time.)[68]

The voyage to New South Wales had been a financial success, but Hogan had difficulty collecting all the money not already paid to him by the Navy and Transport Board. He was still trying to get full reimbursement months later on the eve of sailing to the Cape of Good Hope. In addition to the principal payment under the government contract, he sought payment for "six hogsheads of my own vinegar being expended for the use of the convicts [which] cost me in Cork…£28-7-0." The final accounting for £1,448-3-4 did not take place until November 1800.[69]

He would not be content simply to move himself and his family to the Cape of Good Hope by whatever means were available in order to begin a new business career there. He still had the *Marquis Cornwallis* at his disposal but did not want to use the vessel to transport himself to the Cape. Instead, the ship would carry freight to the Cape of Good Hope and cattle from the Cape to New South Wales. Because it was already six years old and needed some refitting, he held open the option of selling it, either in England or in India after its cattle voyage, and he wanted at least 10,000 guineas for the sale. The alternative was to obtain freight on the return voyage, either from China or India, under contract with the East India Company. He held these interrelated options open until final decisions were made.

The centerpiece of the plan was the cattle to be shipped to New South Wales, an idea he developed while he was still at Port Jackson. In September, he put the proposal to carry cattle to New South Wales and return freight from China to the secretary for home and colonial affairs, the Duke of Portland, who was also responsible for Irish affairs. He said: "My object is not to gain from Government; should it tend to promote the publick good it will be sufficient recompense for any personal trouble I may have in it; but should your Grace be pleased to approve, I shall hope that you will direct a letter to be written from your office to the Court of Directors of the East India Company, stating that the ship *Marquis Cornwallis*, of six hundred and fifty-four tons register, is employed by Government on particular service from the Cape of Good Hope to New South Wales, and request them to give her a cargo home from China on the same terms as the *Barwell*, which is employed by the Transport Board to carry out convicts [with] £1,000 [paid] in advance."[70]

Whether it was because the Duke of Portland was considered to be sympathetic with the Irish and Catholics or Hogan's proposal was a worthy one, the Duke immediately gave his support to the carrying of cattle from the Cape of Good Hope to New South Wales. The Transport Commissioners on September 26 advised that, "upon the whole, [we] are inclined to believe that the price and freight of £35 per head for cattle from the Cape of Good Hope, and actually delivered at New South Wales, is not unreasonable."[71]

But approval of the cattle plan did not automatically lead to approval of the other parts of the scheme—government freight to the Cape and either return freight under contract with the Company from China or India or sale of the vessel in India. Each element was contingent on the other, and the culprit in each case preventing an outcome to Hogan's liking was the East India Company.

The Transport Board was apparently ready to give freight to the Cape if the East India Company approved. Hogan applied to the Company for this permission, as well as for return freight from the Orient. Probably due to the fact that the old shipping interests had recently been successful in thwarting use of non-Company vessels to carry freight, even when under contract to the Company, Hogan was turned down on the return freight. He then asked for and obtained permission (it is not clear why permission was necessary) to sell the ship in India. The Company apparently did not object to freight for the Cape, but may have been responsible for inducing officials at the Transport Board to offer only £5 a ton. Hogan was furious. On the verge of leaving for the Cape of Good Hope, he wrote on November 1 to William Lennox, a senior partner with Messrs David Scott & Company, explaining how he had been ill-treated not only by the East India Company but also by the Transport Board. He was first "sorry and surprised Mr. [James] Duncan should think or say that I intended to [charter] the [*Marquis Cornwallis*] to government to the Cape for £5 per ton when they were not able to procure a [East India] Company cargo home for her. At the time when the Directors refused the letter from the Treasury, I acquainted the [Transport] Board with it. The members then sitting...expressed their surprise and offered me £7 per ton for what the ship would carry on condition that I would take it without their having any trouble with the Court of Directors [of the East India Company]. In consequence of that offer, application was made to the Directors for leave to let the whole ship proceed from New South Wales to Bengal to be sold. That being granted, I offered at the Transport Board by letter written by Mr. Lackland to close with the Board for £7 per ton and continue on with the cattle to New South Wales, as agreed on by the Duke of Portland. The corner of the letter was turned down, and written on it by one of the members, the service was countermanded. Mr. Whitehead brought it down to me and the disappointment, in addition to the many I had already experienced, added to the trouble and large expense I had been at, rather got the better of me. Mr. Whitehead saw the correspondence and Mr. Duncan has copies of the whole."

To underscore his determination, Hogan said, "I have too high an opinion of the honor and justice of the members of the Transport Board to think that, after my sacrificing my interest so much as to get permission from the Company to let the ship proceed to be sold in India, that they would retract from their original promise and intention. I have never varied in anything I offered or promised them and I hope that they, either as a body or individually, are incapable of acting as the Court of Directors have done to me. My wish was to meet their ideas in every respect."

Knowing that supplying the colony at New South Wales with cattle commanded government support, Hogan boldly threatened to withdraw the cattle offer: "Should government think that I am likely to make money by sending cattle from the Cape to Port Jackson, I by leave do decline that part of the contract. I will agree to the ship carrying their cargo to the Cape at £7 per ton for all that she can stow and safely carry and only require from them an official letter to deliver to the governor of New South Wales as a cover to her going there empty on her way to India. I never meant to take advantage of Government and I think Mr. Duncan must mistake the business. The idea of my offering to carry cattle was to strengthen the claim for freight home."

Hogan then laid out his "final"offer: "The true meaning of the original contract was in the [Transport] Board making good their promise that the ship should carry a cargo to the Cape at £7 per ton (I think she would take 850 [tons]), two-thirds of that freight to be paid on her arrival in the Downs, with demurrage as then stated, and the remainder on vouchers coming from the Cape of the cargo being delivered, thirty-five pounds per head to be paid for the cattle landed alive at New South Wales on the governor's receipt for them being produced at the Secretary [of] State's office. One thousand pounds of this amount to be paid in London in advance on signing the agreement for which ample security was to be given. Government are not sufficiently aware of the advantage this country will derive from having cattle sent to that Colony and, as that is the case, I wish to leave the matter open to them. It is known to many that I have been at large expense in fitting the ship for the voyage and, as I would be too great a sufferer by deviating in the smallest degree from the above mode of chartering the ship, let me enjoin you rather to let her remain idle at Deptford than engage her for such a voyage in any other way or for less than £7 out."

James Duncan, who was a ship and insurance broker responsible for concluding the necessary contracts, received an even more blunt letter from Hogan complaining about how he had "been infamously used by the Court of Directors" and how "I cannot suffer myself to be a dupe to all brands and all parties." He said he had requested "Lennox to consult you on this subject, trusting that you will do the most in your power to promote the welfare of that unfortunate ship and convince the Board that their following the footsteps of the Court of Directors will in no degree serve government nor add respectability to them individually or personally."

Hogan's hardline bargaining won the day. Three days after he sent these letters and just before he sailed for the Cape of Good Hope, a charterparty contract was signed by the Commissioners of the Transport Office and James Duncan on behalf of owners of *Marquis Cornwallis* to carry 800 tons of flour to the Cape of Good Hope at the price demanded by Hogan—£7 per ton. The ship would be captained at Hogan's request by Charles Munn and on board would be a young protégée of his from Limerick, Thomas Studdent, acting as second mate, another young man (not a relative) named William Hogan acting as fourth mate, and Mrs. Hogan's horse.

Before leaving England, Hogan made last minute arrangements involving members of his extended family and apprentices he had taken under his wing. It was difficult for young men to find honorable employment without the help of friends. Typically, Hogan would help the lads through school and then employ them aboard his ships or at his counting house. Thomas Studdent had sailed with him since the first voyage of the *Netunno* to India in 1792. These relationships did not always go smoothly. The William Hogan who joined Studdent on the *Marquis Cornwallis* on its first New South Wales voyage in 1795 became ill on its second voyage, acted oddly on his arrival at Port Jackson, ran off to join Mark Flood on Cornwallis Place and had to be forced back on the ship before it left port.

But it is the help Hogan tried to provide to his relatives that deserves attention. His elder brother, Dennis, although holding a commission in the British Army as captain, was a neer-do-well who could not, or more likely would not, find useful employment and was often in poor health. Hogan supported him with twenty guineas a year and also financed the education of his four motherless sons, Cornelius, John, Owen and Michael, at a school in Thirsk, Yorkshire, at a cost of seventy-two guineas a year. Before leaving for the Cape, Hogan wrote to the schoolmaster, the Reverend Daniel Addison, asking that he "extend [his] kindness to them as orphans who have no friend but myself, ...for [in] their first appearance to strangers and in a strange country, ...they may appear to you an awkward charge." Hogan counseled that "writing, arithmetic, merchant accounting and bookkeeping, French, Latin and dancing are what I would wish those young boys to be made as perfect in as possible, and should any of them incline to the sea, which is the line I have spent twenty one years in, I would wish him to be made perfect in navigation."

Up to mid-October there was concern that British ships would be in danger from a Dutch fleet in the Netherlands that had been poised for several months to take offensive action, possibly in support of a rumored French invasion of Ireland. (A small French force landed in County Mayo during the summer of 1798 in a belated and unsuccessful attempt to support the Great Irish Rebellion of that year.) Finally on the 14th news was received that Admiral Adam Duncan had soundly defeated the Dutch fleet off the English coast near the small village Camperdown, a victory that was particularly a cause for celebration after the disastrous naval mutinies during the summer. With the Dutch naval threat removed, Hogan made elaborate arrangements to transport himself and family to the Cape of Good Hope as part of a convoy of several ships.

He would sail with his wife, two children, William and Fanny, servants and merchandise valued at £31,000 on the *Bombay Anna*, with Captain

Mungo Gilmore at the helm, the same ship whose construction Hogan had supervised at Bombay in 1789. William, then five years old, later recalled that she had a "bay window standing out over the water." The *Anna* (Hogan always used its short name) was under contract to the East India Company, as were the other three ships in the convoy, *Surat Castle*, *Carron* and *Belvedere*, each also carrying private investments. Hogan had a stake in the cargo of the *Surat Castle* (Captain Isbister). There was a sixth vessel in the convoy, the newly-built, sixty-ton, six-gun schooner *Harbinger* that Hogan had just procured.[72] On October 23, he instructed the ship's captain, Morton Chapman, to proceed to Portsmouth to join the convoy for the Cape. All six vessels were to be escorted by the frigate *Niger* (Captain Griffiths) as far as Madeira.[73]

Finally, after waiting two weeks at Portsmouth for favorable winds, the convoy sailed on November 6. Hogan had instructed Captain Chapman to keep company with the *Anna* and *Surat Castle* and to come within hailing distance should he display his "private signal—a Dutch jack at the mizzen peak." Chapman was also given sailing directions for the Cape of Good Hope should he become separated from the other ships, a caution that proved necessary when the *Harbinger* parted company in the Bay of Biscay. Separately, Hogan shipped goods destined for the Cape on board another vessel, the *Barwell*, which sailed a week later carrying convicts to New South Wales with a stop at the Cape.

The air of secrecy surrounding Hogan's plans continued when he wrote to Pringle from Madeira, where many ships stopped to pick up its famous wine: "I have on board this ship a cargo of amount £31,000. There are, however, some obstacles in the way of its success for we have in the fleet two small ships...for your market and the *Belvedere* has a large private investment besides her cargo for Government. This, and the quantities of goods that have gone out in the last fleet, will I fear overdo your market. There are also considerable speculations taking place in England, chiefly in consequence of Lord Duncan's victory [over the Dutch fleet at Camperdown] which strengthens the general opinion that we shall retain the Cape. Of these [speculators], however, many will come to our own management."

His letter to Pringle again mentioned Ross as a partner. The "clever" Mr. Ross was undoubtedly Hercules Ross, under colonial secretary at Cape Town, who might have been recommended to Hogan by David Scott, another hint that Hogan's venture was backed by London mercantile interests.[74] He said that Ross "would be to our advantage in Europe on account of his good mercantile connections, and his knowledge of business is good, though he cannot act publicly while in Government service." Hogan reemphasized that "I, with all the first merchants in London, am fully of opinion that much business will be done at the Cape, and I have every reason to expect we shall have a large share of it."

The letter asked Pringle to "look for a proper house for us. It should be large, in the best situation for business with warehouses and if possible near the Parade to save wagon hire up the hill.... We will want a good wagon with strong horses, etc. for the conveyance of goods which I have reason to believe will be constantly going through our hands in great quantities. I have on board a neat curricle [a two-wheeled chariot drawn by two horses] for you and one for myself, each very compleat. Will thank you to look for a pair of safe curricle horses, if possible as strong as your own.... We have plenty of good furniture for any house at the Cape."

Finally, on leaving St. Helena on December 7, Hogan reported: "We are now past everything that I conceive dangerous, and [Rear] Admiral [Sir Hugh Cloberry] Christian has promised me to have ships cruising to the westward of the Cape to receive us."[75]

FOUR

CAPE OF GOOD HOPE
UNDER BRITISH OCCUPATION

The colonial necessity for [slaves] will continue to [increase] while the Colony increases in population and trade, two objects devoutly to be wished for, and earnestly hoped will succeed under the administration of Your Excellency's humane and indulgent Government.

—Hogan to Governor Yonge

Michael Hogan, his wife Frances, five-year old son William and two-year old daughter Fanny arrived at the Cape of Good Hope on February 4, 1798, and remained for six years. He became one of the leading merchants at the Colony and acquired a fortune. He also engaged in a fraudulent business scheme from which he escaped probable prosecution due only to the vagaries of international politics.

When the Hogan family arrived, the Cape of Good Hope had been in British hands for two and a half years and the European war was in its fifth year. Lord George Macartney (the same one who failed to obtain a Chinese promise to buy British goods in 1793) had arrived to become governor just a week after Hogan had left the Colony on his voyage home to England from New South Wales. Major General Francis Dundas, nephew of Henry Dundas, was in charge of the British land forces, and Rear Admiral Sir Hugh Cloberry Christian, soon to be replaced on his death by Vice Admiral Sir Roger Curtis, had just arrived to command the British naval forces. Macartney left the Colony nine months after Hogan's arrival, concerned over his advancing years and gout, leaving Dundas in charge as acting governor until a replacement arrived a year later.

From the time that Vasco da Gama discovered the African sea route to India in 1498, the Cape of Good Hope had been a natural stopping place for ships to replenish their water supply and provisions, repair damage and provide rest and rehabilitation to seamen. It was not until 1652, however, that a colony was established at Cape Town by the Dutch East India Company as part of the effort by the major European trading nations to protect their sea lanes to the Orient. Almost all vessels sailing between Europe and the Orient around the southern tip of Africa stopped at the Cape, although by the turn of the eighteenth century many ships made the voyage without calling at any port.

The fact that more vessels stopped at the Cape on their homeward passage than their passage eastbound meant that the Colony often received news from India more frequently than from Europe, which undoubtedly added to the sense of isolation that the inhabitants must have felt. Both the Dutch and British tended to treat the Cape of Good hope as a part of the Orient, tied more to India and the East Indies than to the home country. Many of the customs adopted by the white population at the Cape were imported from India; one unfortunate one being the developing racial consciousness of the British in India.

The business and trading center of the Colony was Cape Town, situated on the Atlantic side near the southern tip of Africa on the shores of Table Bay whose large anchorage facing to the north was preferred during the summer months from September to May (the seasons being reversed in the southern hemisphere) because it was then free from fierce northwesterly gales. Cape Town's prominent feature to its immediate west was Table Mountain, a massive rock formation, sometimes topped with a "table cloth" cloud. To its south was Signal Hill where a canon announced vessel arrivals. The other main anchorage was Simon's Bay to the south, with its small Simon's Town, in twenty-mile wide False Bay. It was the preferred anchorage from June to September when it was sheltered from the gales that plagued Table Bay. To the north of Cape Town were Saldanha Bay and St. Helena Bay; there were also several small ports and bays to the east, but these were used only for coastal shipping. During the British occupation, slightly over 1,000 merchant vessels touched at the Cape, 573 of them English, 215 American, 134 Danish and 56 prizes.[1]

Figure 2. View of Table Bay and Table Mountain, ca. 1800

Climate and living conditions in the Cape Colony were both favorable. Average temperatures, 55°F in winter and 70°F in summer, were close to ideal, even though frequent strong winds (keeping Cape Town free of the pollution Hogan so disliked in London), heavy winter rains and sudden temperature changes reduced the comfort level. The town was well-laid out and attractive. Its prominent features were the 100-year old Castle, a fort-like, pentagonal structure which housed government offices, officials and some troops; the adjacent Grand Parade which, as its name implies, was an open parade ground; and the nearby, extensive Company Gardens in which vegetables were grown. The Gardens were also the site of Government House which was used as the residence of governors during the British occupation. "Streets were straight, many lined with oak trees, the gardens of their flat-roofed houses irrigated by sparkling funnels of water. The surface was apt to be rough and stony, deep in clinging mud during the winter and, in the dry summer months, covered with a mantle of fine red dust."[2] A contemporary wrote that "the houses are almost all of stone and equally clean; they are white or yellow washed and from their cleanliness and the mildness of the climate have all the appearance of being but newly built. The inside is generally paved with flagstone."[3]

Cape Town, the only populous urban center, was cosmopolitan in nature because that was where British officials and most Dutch, British and other European merchants resided and because it had a steady stream of visiting sailors, merchants, officials and travelers. A ship's captain stopping at Cape Town in 1800 reported that: "The inhabitants are composed of adventurers from every part of the northern world and every circle of the German Empire."[4] At dinners, it was not uncommon to hear four or five European languages spoken. After the British arrived, a newspaper was established and at least one coffee house, called the Commercial Coffee House, was opened.[5] A Turf Club was established in 1796 by British Army officers; it sponsored spring and autumn horse races at which the purses were expressed in pagodas, an Indian coin worth about eight shillings, indicating that the impetus for horse racing probably came from the British colony at Calcutta.[6] Cape Town's first theater, supported by subscribers, was built while Hogan was there (now St. Stephen's Church). There was also a subscribers' concert held every so often at the Burgher Senate House.[7] There was social intercourse between the British and Dutch merchants and officials in Cape Town, though the relationship was sometimes strained. Contemporary English writers describing the Colony invariably referred to the portliness and lack of sophistication of Dutch women. Some of the British merchants, government officials and military and naval officers came as bachelors or did not bring their wives, which led to some marriages with Dutch women and to widespread affairs with Dutch mistresses and illegitimate children. Lady Anne Barnard, wife of the Colonial Secretary Andrew Barnard, recounts in her diary numerous instances of such liaisons, including those by commanding generals and admirals. Her attitude was not one of moralistic disapproval, but of sophisticated acceptance of the ways of men and women. The sexual mores at the Cape in fact bear some similarity to the often licentious behavior of high society in England during the Regency period. The ratio of men to women at Cape Town in 1797 was said to be 3:1.8.[8] Not unexpectedly in this milieu, the Colony had more than its share of persons of dubious background and character.

When the British occupation began, there were about 61,000 persons living at the Cape of Good Hope, consisting of 20,000 whites of European origin, 16,000 free persons of black or mixed race in service to Europeans, including the indigenous Khoikhoi and San (incorrectly called Hottentots and Bushmen, and known jointly as Khoisan), and 25,000 slaves of every shade of skin, from light brown to dark ebony. Cape Town had about 5,000 whites and twice that many non-whites, most of whom were slaves. Most of the white population living in the countryside were of Dutch or French origin, highly stratified, non-egalitarian in their social order and heavily dependent on slavery to support farming.

The British rulers made an attempt to get along with the preponderant Dutch population by leaving intact most of their domestic institutions of government, but their efforts were thwarted by the split between those who still supported the deposed House of Orange, who were sympathetic with the British, and those who leaned toward the Jacobins in the new Batavian Republican and therefore opposed British rule. The British also encountered difficulty in keeping peace on the eastern frontier between expansionist-minded, individualistic, God-fearing, trekboer farmers and the Khoikhoi and Xhosa blacks who had been resisting the expansion at Fish River since 1770. There had already been two frontier wars. A third, which began in 1800 during Hogan's stay, threatened Cape Town's meat supply.

There were no direct restrictions on Dutch or other non-British merchants from conducting business at the Cape, so long as they subscribed to the oath of allegiance required of all residents, which most did. Nevertheless, most of the import trade and commercial transactions involving prize ships and their cargoes were conducted by British merchants, no doubt because "they had the commercial and financial connections in England and with British officials at the Cape that the older Cape merchants lacked." Dutch merchants and a few from other countries were engaged primarily in domestic transactions and apparently also played a role in reselling goods originally imported or procured by British merchants. The principal British merchants at Cape Town were Alexander Farquhar, Michael Hogan, John Murray, John and Alexander Robertson, Alexander Tennant, William Venables and Alexander Walker. Isaac Strombom was a prominent merchant of Danish origin, and leading Dutch merchants included Hogan's neighbors Pieter Laurens Cloete and Cornelius Cruyagen.[9] Among the richest men in the Colony was Willem Stephanus Van Ryneveld who held the position of fiscal, the Colony's chief law officer.[10]

There was increased economic activity at the Cape during the British occupation, but the Colony did not prove to be as promising a center for British merchants as had been initially thought. Although the war provided business opportunities for some, such as those engaged in privateering, the unsettled state of the international scene and the constant threat of unfavorable developments arising from the war were not conducive to normal commerce. There were a number of scares when it was thought the Colony was to be invaded or otherwise harassed by Dutch or French forces. The Colony also supplied troops and provisions for various military ventures against the French in the Middle East and Orient, thus depleting its means of defense. To add to the Colony's woes, French privateers continued to harass shipping from Île de France in the Indian Ocean.

Another factor that upset initially high business expectations was that there was an increasingly severe shortage of money that could be sent home to Britain or used to buy imported products. Prices increased rapidly and the exchange rate became progressively worse.

There was also the question of the role that the East India Company would play. The Colony had been seized in large part to protect the Company's shipping, and there appears to have been an unwritten understanding that, as a consequence, the Company should be responsible for keeping residents supplied with food and other essentials. But at the Company's headquarters in London and its stations in India, the needs of the Cape of Good Hope were given low priority because of the Company's perception that the Colony was only an appendage of India, its occupation made necessary only to protect the Orient trade centered in India. The British government in December 1796 confirmed the Company's monopoly position for all goods traded between the Colony and the East and included in its instructions to Macartney an order to enforce this policy. But Macartney had to tell Henry Dundas soon after his arrival that, because supplies and produce were not arriving, he was "compelled to deviate from [the Company's monopoly] sometimes, till proper steps are taken by the East India Company to render a deviation inexcusable." As with Generals Craig and Dundas before him, he said he had been forced to accept supplies from Danish ships coming from Batavia which, he thought, were probably really Dutch or possibly even English "though artfully covered."[11] The first supplies from India finally arrived in November, but were still not enough.[12] Nor was the Colony initially supplied with articles of European manufacture adequate to its needs. Finally in January 1798, Macartney was told by London that, while the East India Company accepted responsibility for supplying the Colony with goods from the East, it was reluctant to supply European goods. Thus, the instruction continued, "there is every reason to expect that in the progress of time, and as the extent and nature of your wants become better known, the spirit of private adventure will induce merchants to supply the market of the Cape with every article of European produce in a proportion adequate to the demands of the settlement."[13] The goods that Hogan brought on the *Anna* and *Surat Castle* thus came at a favorable moment. It was not until September, seven months after Hogan's arrival, that the Colony received its first major shipment of European articles organized by the government in London.[14] Part of the problem was that, if the Colony were forced to rely on actions initiated in India or England, it took a minimum of six months and as much as a year between the time an import need was expressed and its fulfillment. By the time the response had become well-organized, the Colony was likely to be overstocked, which was what happened by the end of 1798[15] and would happen in the next cycle. Aside from poor planning, the two main causes of the *feast or famine* phenomenon at the Colony were the deep-seated concern with the contraband trade, which motivated several actions designed to forestall private merchants from using the Colony as a re-export entrepôt, and the fact that the East India Company's agent at the Cape, John Pringle, aggressively attempted to assert a complete monopoly over the Eastern trade, so much so that the Honorable Company came to be looked upon "with undisguised hostility by the embryo mercantile community of Cape Town who regarded it as a major barrier to the genuine commercial freedom promised in 1795."[16]

These strains were not felt all at once, so that at the beginning of his stay at the Cape, Hogan would have been confident of the future.

His first responsibility on arrival was to find lodging for his family. He bought a residence at No. 2 Bergstraat and established a business office at No. 29 Heerengracht in Cape Town. These streets are now known as St. George's Mall and Adderley Street. His neighbors on Bergstraat included Cloete at No. 7, Tennant at No. 16 and Cruywagen at No. 18, with all three of whom he developed business relationships.[17] He also bought three other pieces of property for his warehouse and possibly homes for his employees.[18] An 1800 tax census shows that he had thirty-one slaves, fourteen horses and seven oxen. Three more children were born to Frances Hogan: Harriet on April 10, 1799, John in November 1800 and Sophia on March 9, 1802. John died in infancy.[19] When William was ten, he was sent back to England to attend school in London.

Hogan would soon begin business ventures in two new areas, but his first business task was to arrange for cattle to be shipped on the *Marquis Cornwallis* to Port Jackson under contract with the Transport Board. The vessel finally arrived at the Cape on May 1 and spent almost two months procuring and loading the cattle and other goods before sailing on June 26. It arrived four months later at Port Jackson where 158 cows and 20 bulls were landed, as well as brandy, wine and miscellaneous goods procured at the Cape[20] and some cows and mares Hogan sent to his Cornwallis farm. Governor Hunter reported "there are a few [cattle] rather weakly, but in general they are in as good health as any I have seen landed [at Port Jackson] after a voyage of such extent and will be a vast acquisition to the Colony." (Hogan was paid £37 a head for the cattle, but future business for him and others in cattle exports ended in 1800 when New South Wales decided to increase its stock by breeding and even sought an export market.)[21] Hogan later received a lengthy account of the difficulties his agent at Port Jackson, John Macarthur, had experienced in obtaining satisfaction from Mark Flood, the man Hogan had left in charge of his Cornwallis Place in 1796, principally involving Flood's refusal to accept instructions from Macarthur or to pay him moneys earned from growing wheat and raising livestock. Flood was a troublemaker, repeatedly in court over threatened or actual assaults and non-payment of debts, but part of the recurring difficulty was Hogan's poorly framed powers of attorney and instructions to Flood, Macarthur and others. At one point, Macarthur sought to have Flood dismissed as manager of the farm, but the Civil Court of Indicature denied the request, stating it could not "consider [Macarthur] or any other person or persons as agents to Captain Hogan, no paper having been produced to this Court which they think of sufficient weight to induce them to set aside the agreement entered into between Captain Hogan and Mark Flood...." After reporting that Flood had assaulted a servant of Charles Munn, captain of the *Marquis Cornwallis,* and threatened to murder him, Macarthur in exasperation told Hogan, "I declare to God I believe the fellow is mad." The *Marquis Cornwallis* left Port Jackson on December 3. Contrary to Hogan's expectation when he was fighting with the Transport Board and East India Company a year earlier over how to package the ship's voyage, he did not sell his favorite ship in Bengal. Instead, the *Marquis Cornwallis* continued to trade between India and England, now apparently under the complete control of the Richardsons.

Hogan used other ships to trade with New South Wales where he thought, based on his experience there, a good market would develop and where his land interests continued to require attention. An early venture was to export candles and tallow purchased from the Spanish prize *La Union* to New South Wales in May 1798.[22] Beginning a practice of naming ships he had purchased after his children, he shipped Cape wine and brandy to Port Jackson on the *Young William* in October 1799.[23] He well knew the high demand for spirits in New South Wales, and he may have been particularly persuaded by the report he had received from Macarthur of the high prices obtained for wine and brandy imported the previous year at Port Jackson on the convict ship *Barwell*.[24] These were only a few of the vessels on which he shipped goods to New South Wales.

There would be many other normal business activities for Hogan, most stemming from the Colony's dearth of foodstuffs, timber and ship supplies and the need for sea transportation to import these supplies and to ferry troops and military supplies. One early example was a government-approved procurement of a cargo of tickwood [teakwood] from Pegu in what is now Myanmar (Burma), as well as two tons of beeswax and bags of rice from India.[25]

While these normal business activities provided needed income, Hogan had come to the Gape of Good Hope primarily in expectation of profits from privateering. But his first major venture would be in another area—the slave trade.

Slavery, in one form or another, has been practiced since antiquity, reflecting the centuries-old hierarchal system of society, with masters at the top and slaves at the bottom. The longest lasting and most extensive slaving has been of Africans. Most of them, an estimated eighteen million, were delivered to southern Europe and the Middle East in the Islamic trans-Sahara and Indian Ocean slave trade over fourteen centuries; another eleven million were shipped in the transatlantic trade, principally to Brazil and the Caribbean islands and in smaller numbers to the American colonies and southern states, from the time of Columbus until about 1870. Opposition to African slavery did not develop until the second half of the eighteenth century, and it was then directed as much against the slave trade and the treatment of slaves as the practice itself. The principal outcry began in England. There were only a handful of black slaves in the country, mostly domestic servants, but its merchants profited enormously from the slave trade. British ships had entered the trans-Atlantic trade in large numbers in the eighteenth century; about one-half the slaves shipped annually from West Africa to the Americas were transported in British bottoms. A British court ruling in 1772 effectively declared slavery in the home country illegal, but Britain did not prohibit the international trade in slaves until 1808, nor the practice of slavery in its colonies until 1834. American Quakers also initiated opposition to the slave trade and slavery itself prior to the Revolution. Individual states abolished the foreign importation of slaves in the years after the Revolution, except for South Carolina which opened its ports briefly from 1804 through 1807, but slaves were still imported clandestinely in the South, even after the Congress imposed a federal ban effective in 1808. As is well-known, slavery was not abolished throughout the United States until the Thirteenth Amendment to the Constitution in 1866 which followed Lincoln's Emancipation Proclamation freeing slaves only in the Confederate States. Brazil was the last New World country to abolish slavery in 1888. It was not until after World War II that there was a universal condemnation of slavery in the United Nations Universal Declaration of Human Rights. There are occasional reports that slavery is still practiced in parts of Africa and Asia.

Neither the institution of slavery nor trade in slaves was unlawful at the Cape of Good Hope while Hogan was there. While there were occasional outbursts of opposition by some officials and citizens and the abolition movement in Britain was growing rapidly, virtually all well-to-do people, both British and Dutch, owned slaves. The largest slaveholder at the turn of the century was the Cloete family with 114 slaves on six farms. Many families, however, had only one or two slaves and there were few farms with many slaves.[26] In Cape Town, slaves were used mostly for domestic tasks or hired out as artisans. In the countryside, where they were most numerous, they were used by settlers in agriculture.

Slaves were not indigenous to the Cape Colony. Native Africans were available to be hired by farmer settlers for labor, but they were often reluctant to enter service for little or no wages and, as a consequence, some were forced to serve under slave-like conditions. Slaves had been imported since the early days of the Dutch presence to provide cheap labor, mostly from Dahomey and Angola on the west coast of Africa and, later, from Mozambique, Madagascar and Zanzibar. Most Dutch East India Company slaves came from southern India, Ceylon and what is now Indonesia. When the slave trade was finally abolished by the British in 1808, their population in the Colony had increased from 25,000 in 1798 to nearly 30,000.[27] There was also trade in slaves from the east coast of Africa around the Cape of Good Hope to Rio de Janeiro and Montevideo on the east coast of South America, almost all in Portuguese ships. This "black ivory" trade increased significantly in the nineteenth century due to the growing effectiveness of restrictions on the traditional west coast trade; American ships also began to participate, carrying slaves to Southern American states (often clandestinely), Havana and South America.[28] These ships sometimes stopped at the Cape of Good hope in the hope that local buyers might be found that would make the long passage to the Americas unnecessary. Another reason for stopping there, apparently innocently, was that Portuguese traders, unlike British merchants in Britain engaged in their infamous triangular trade, did not have as ready access in South America to the goods that African chiefs wanted, and were therefore often ready to sell their slaves at Cape Town for hard money which could be used to acquire goods necessary for future slave acquisitions. Because there was as yet little competition for slaves from Mozambique, they were also cheaper than those from West Africa.[29] Whatever the source of slaves, it was necessary to obtain government permission to import them at the Cape and pay the import duty under penalty of heavy fines.

While by the end of the eighteenth century a growing number of people found the slave trade (and to a lesser extent even slavery itself) morally reprehensible, it continued to flourish. A number of reasons can be assigned for this apparent inconsistency, such as the lure of profits, the excuse that "everyone does it," and the perceived economic necessity for low-cost and compliant labor. Many merchants throughout Europe and the Americas engaged in the commerce, some of them well-known for their charity and support of noble causes. Although governments were by now less involved in the trade than in previous times, licenses, taxes and fees were still demanded in some quarters for the privilege of slaving. But these rationalizations could not have survived outright moral condemnation. The fact is that the condemnation was muted by the belief among many that black Africans were basically inferior to whites. From this, apologists would say that Africans were better off in the Christian and civilized countries of the west than in "barbaric" Africa.

Pressure to allow the importation of additional slaves after the British occupation came as early as January 1797 when General Craig, noting that none had been imported since 1793, informed London that, "Upon representation from the magistrates in the name of the inhabitants and from my own knowledge of the real state of the Colony in this respect, 1 have been induced…to give leave to a Portuguese vessel from Mozambique to dispose of her cargo of 350 slaves, which sold at a price beyond what was ever known before."[30] (The British authorities were not themselves adverse to using slaves, as demonstrated by the fact that the British Army commandeered 534 former VOC slaves for hard labor in 1795.)[31] After Macartney arrived several months later, the Burgher Senate asked him on least two occasions to allow slaves to be imported. He rejected both requests, the last a few days after Hogan's arrival.[32] But Macartney had not, in fact, denied all the requests he received. He allowed Isaac Strombom to bring in 150 slaves from Mozambique on the *Good Hope* early in 1798. One estimate is that, from the beginning of the British occupation to mid-1798, when Hogan became active in the slave trade, 605 slaves had been imported.[33]

Hogan's full involvement in the slave trade at the Cape of Good Hope and later the United States is known only because of archival records. As with the mutiny on the *Marquis Cornwallis*, he must have thought that retaining papers detailing his involvement in slave transactions would cast a "black mark" on his character. One curious exception is a lengthy document that he titled "Communications made to the Secret Committee at the Cape of Good Hope relative to Sir George Yonge," containing his 1801–02 testimony and evidence in the matter of slave imports, the final outcome of which is addressed in the next chapter. Perhaps he could not bear to destroy a specially prepared legal document, or more likely he thought the document reflected unfavorably on the governor and his aides, not on him.

Shortly after arrival at Cape Town, Hogan joined with Tennant in doing business as Messrs Tennant & Hogan and, for a while, with Donald Trail in Messrs Hogan & Trail. These partnerships were more than coincidental. Hogan was already acquainted with Tennant, a Scotsman who had come to the Cape as a respectable merchant in 1796 and soon became involved in slave trading.[34] Trail, also a Scotsman, had been Master of the *Neptune* on which thirty-one percent of the convicts aboard died during the ship's 1790 voyage to New South Wales. There was an uproar over the high mortality rate when he returned to England which led to charges being placed against him and a confederate for murdering the Portuguese cook on the ship, but both were acquitted. Trail came to the Cape with the British occupying forces in 1795. Hogan could well have met Trail either in London when preparing for his own voyage to New South Wales on the *Marquis Cornwallis* or at Cape Town while on his way to Sydney. Trail was appointed Master Attendant in charge of the Navy Office at Simon's Bay "where he proved himself a great rogue in his profiteering in the victualing [of British Navy ships], particularly with vegetables." He was relieved of that job shortly after Hogan arrived and returned to England in 1799.[35] Hogan had business relations with him up to at least 1804, as will be seen.

The early attempts of Tennant and Trail to obtain permission to import slaves from Mozambique were rebuffed by a combination of Macartney's resistance and the fact they had to charter the ship intended for the mission to the British Navy.[36] Finally, in May Macartney relented, at least in part. Noting that "Mr. Hogan, Mr. Strombom, Mr. Roos and Mr. Tennant applied some time since for leave to send for slaves," he announced that, "if they can agree among themselves, I shall allow one ship to go to the West Coast of Africa, to Angola Congo, or to Calabar in the bite [sic] of Benin to bring 400 slaves, of which one-fourth are to be females." Hogan and Tennant agreed to undertake the venture but only after saying they could not "but regret the communication with Mozambique and Madagascar being prohibited, from which alone some solid advantages may be expected in that very necessary article of commerce."[37] Hogan sent his schooner, the *Harbinger*, to the Coast of Guinea on November 25 to fulfill the license.[38] Macartney's reason for not allowing the slaves to come from Mozambique is not recorded, but it may well have been based on documents captured the previous year on the *Diana*, a prize of the British Navy, which purported to contain a secret plan "for vessels to sail from Mozambique under the Danish and Portuguese flags, with a sufficient number of slaves on board to disarm suspicion. They were to put into Table Bay, pretending to be bound for Brazil, and were then under some excuse to sell the slaves and purchase as great a quantity of provisions as possible, with which they were to make their way as speedily as practicable to Mauritius. If by any chance they could not sell the slaves or obtain food supplies in the Cape of Good Hope, they were to proceed to Rio de Janeiro and get what they could there."[39]

This was only one of the several subterfuges that officials at the Cape thought were practiced by the French or neutrals, particularly Danes and Americans.

Whether Macartney had specific grounds for being suspicious of the Hogan/Tennant interest in slaves from Mozambique cannot be known with certainty, but it is of interest to note that appended to an earlier list of questions that Macartney had drawn up regarding Tennant's proposed slave venture involving Mozambique was the following: "When leave was given [to Tennant] to export flour [to Mozambique], no reason of state was then known against [the transaction], but when evidence appeared that it was intended for the supply of our enemies, it was in consequence interdicted and the less Mr. Tennant says upon this subject will be the wisest course for him and his partners."[40] Hogan would shortly have reason to wish he had known of Macartney's suspicions, for he was himself to enter upon a venture which might evoke comparison with the secret plan to keep Île de France supplied by resorting to trickery at the Cape. But this would come later.

On January 27 of the following year, the Portuguese ship *Joaquim* arrived at Table Bay with 422 slaves from Mozambique who were placed in quarantine on Robben Island in Table Bay. The *Harbinger* had not yet returned from its mission to the west coast of Africa. After claiming that this mission had failed, Hogan and Tennant asked Acting Governor

Dundas for permission to land and sell the *Joaquim* slaves. The Dutch Burgher Senate had on February 25 requested that Dundas allow the importation of 1,000 slaves annually.[41] Perhaps not wishing to appear negative to this request, Dundas told Messrs Hogan & Tennant on March 2 that he would allow the importation and sale. At the same time, he annulled the previous license to import 400 slaves from the West Coast of Africa and said he would "not allow any more slaves to be imported from any quarter till I have the opinion of His Majesty's Ministers upon a subject of such national importance."[42] The slaves were landed on March 10 at the end of their six-week quarantine and 381 of them sold by auction. The other forty-one slaves were apparently sold privately, an action that would later lead to a complaint against Hogan.

Dundas promptly wrote to London for guidance on the slave import question. He first absolved himself of blame by noting that he had "been prevailed upon to give permission to Messrs Hogan and Tennant [to import] four hundred [*sic*] Negro slaves, it having been represented to me by the Burgher Senate that slaves are wanted in the Colony...and as I was more easily induced to consent...from the consideration that the late Governor Macartney had already granted them his permission to import four hundred slaves from the west coast of Africa." Dundas then posed the question: "As I consider the importation of slaves to be a matter of some delicacy as well as perhaps of extreme national importance, it would be very convenient for me to possess particular instructions upon that head, having every day applications made to me for leave to import slaves into this Colony, that traffic have attended with great profits, but I have hitherto resisted every application and shall continue to do so until I am favored with your particular orders and directions relative to that subject."[43]

Hogan apparently knew that the *Harbinger* mission would not prove to be a complete failure because, just after obtaining Dundas's approval to land the 422 slaves from the *Joaquim*, he asked that the annulment of the *Harbinger* license not preclude landing up to forty slaves that might yet arrive on the vessel.[44] Three months later on June 13 the *Harbinger* arrived with thirty-nine male and eight female slaves from the West Coast. Dundas reluctantly gave Hogan permission to land and sell these slaves as well, but only after noting that he was "satisfied you were induced to dispatch that vessel to the West Coast of Africa for a cargo of slaves in consequence of having obtained the sanction of the late governor...for that purpose...."[45]

Perhaps sensing at some point that government permission to import slaves would prove increasingly difficult, maybe impossible, to obtain, Hogan set in motion a scheme that resulted in slaves being allowed to be landed at the Cape Colony on the grounds that they had been on board enemy ships seized by his privateers. It cannot be known with certainty that Hogan concocted this scheme with foreknowledge of the result, but all signs point in that direction.[46]

Hogan had met Captain David Smart of the merchant vessel *Bombay Castle* within two months of his arrival at Cape Town. The extent of their early relationship is unknown.[47] In March 1799 he made him captain of the 90-ton *Collector*. She left Table Bay on the thirteenth with letters of marque authorizing the seizure of French and Spanish ships. Hogan owned two-thirds of the vessel; Captain David Smart the other third.

The *Collector's* first purported prize was a small French ship, *La Rose,* which arrived at the Cape on November 10 with a prize crew and forty-eight male slaves who, it was deposed before the Vice Admiralty Court, were on board the French vessel when she was seized in the Seychelles Islands after the crew had abandoned her. The same explanation was given when *L'Africana* arrived on December 25 with twenty-six slaves. Based on this evidence, the Vice Admiralty Court promptly allowed both condemnations; the slaves were then sold for the benefit of Hogan.[48] The outcome of these ventures did not play out until March 1800.

Meanwhile, Hogan had finally begun to enter into legitimate privateering, which was his principal reason for moving to the Cape Colony and the activity that attracted London investors. Over the next four years he became the leading player at the Colony in this activity and profited greatly thereby. A privateer is an armed private vessel which has been issued letters of marque by the country in which the vessel is registered authorizing the seizure of enemy merchant and naval vessels and their cargos during time of war. Privateering was a perfectly lawful activity under British law and the laws of most other countries and had been so for centuries.[49] Most merchant vessels were routinely equipped with letters of marque in case an opportunity arose against a smaller and less well-defended enemy vessel. After seizure, a prize had to be condemned, in the British case by a Vice Admiralty Court, after which the vessel and its cargo could be sold and the proceeds divided up among the owner of the vessel and its captain and crew in accordance with agreements concluded among the parties. A Vice Admiralty Court had been established at the Cape of Good Hope in January 1797 with John Holland as presiding judge.

Hogan had procured the *Harbinger* while he was in London for the specific purpose of privateering, but while it was still on a slave mission, he needed an alternative. It would be the 131-ton *Harriet*, named after his newly born daughter, for which he obtained letters of marque to cruise against French, Spanish and Dutch vessels. She sailed from Table Bay under the command of William White on September 2, 1799.[50]

Twenty-six days later, she encountered a large Danish vessel at the southwest end of Mozambique channel, the 841-ton *Holger Danske*. The vessel was seized, a prize crew placed on board under the charge of Third Mate John Leadan and the ship returned to Table Bay, where it arrived on October 13. Just three days later, the Vice Admiralty Court ordered a condemnation hearing to be held in twenty days. At the end of this period—November 5—there was a fierce storm at Table Bay which forced several vessels on shore. Hogan later recorded that it was John Leaden's "courage and good conduct that we are indebted for all we are now receiving from the *Holger Danske*. On the night of the 5th November, when the *Sceptre* of 64-guns and six other ships went on shore in Table Bay, the Dutch or Danish Chief Mate of [the *Holger Danske*] took axes forward to cut the cables and sent men out to loose the fore stay sail ready for running on shore. Leaden with a brace of loaded pistols pointed at the Mate, threatened to blow his brains out if he or any of his men touched the cables or sails, and with his own people armed with the best weapons he could get, drove the officer and ship's people below. He continued armed all night with his twelve men, freshening hawser and taking care of the ship to the great admiration of all that heard of it next morning. It is his merit, not being a relation of mine, that claims this recommendation [for an extra share of the prize money] from me; were he a Turk, I should do him the same justice. A few pounds would be of great service to his poor parents, for he is dead."

The circumstances of the seizure of the *Holger Danske* and the subsequent actions of the various parties involved were mysterious from the beginning. Captain White later alleged that ship's papers established that the Danish ship was carrying a rich cargo of spices, coffee and goods taken on board in Batavia, an enemy territory. But Denmark was not then at war with Britain and technically Danish vessels were not covered by the *Harriet's* letters of marque. The subject of legitimate embargoes imposed by belligerents and seizures of neutral vessels violating their embargoes was complicated beyond belief, as any student of British seizures of American ships preceding the War of 1812 will know.[51] Britain believed it was entitled under international law to seize ships of neutral countries trading with the enemy. Denmark not only did not accept this interpretation but asserted its right under the doctrine of armed neutrality to defend its merchant ships. Denmark was also an irritant to Britain because it feared that Napoleon would persuade the Danes to become a French ally, a fear which later led Admiral Nelson to battle and defeat a Danish fleet off Copenhagen in April 1801.

The precise status of British orders-in-council affecting Danish vessels at the time of the seizure of the *Holger Danske* is unclear. It was well known at the Cape, however, that ships of neutral countries often traded with Britain's enemies. Danish and American ships, secretly bound for Île de France, sometimes stopped at the Cape, declaring they were destined for some other place, such as Tranquebar, a small Danish enclave in India, and some of them had been seized by the British Navy while in port. American ships were increasingly calling at Île de France, sometimes on their way to India, Batavia or China, to take advantage of the oriental goods seized by French privateers and sold there at prices substantially less than in Calcutta or Canton. An American consul had been appointed to the French island as early as 1794, after which American ship arrivals increased.[52] The Danish ship *Christianus Septimus* had been seized in June 1798 by the British Navy on arrival at the Cape Colony from Batavia and its cargo of coffee, sugar, pepper and arrack condemned by the Vice Admiralty Court, and then seized again on a subsequent arrival at the Cape in December 1799. (Hogan purchased the hull of the ship on August 3, 1800, for 3,975 rix dollars, apparently then holding a two-thirds share in the vessel.)[53]

Whatever legal justification Captain White had for seizing a Danish ship, he may have been told in advance by Hogan where and when the *Holger Danske* would be located and that he was to seize the vessel based on Hogan's knowledge that it had come from Batavia. White was probably not told why Hogan seemed to be so well informed.

During the preceding year (1798), Governor Macartney had received a copy of an intercepted letter written by the Dutch Committee for East Indian Trade at Amsterdam to its agents in India and Batavia stating that it had sold to Messrs Deconnick & Company of Copenhagen a quantity of goods of Batavian origin.[54] Macartney had more than a general acquaintanceship with Hogan; they both were members of the Court for the Suppression of Piracy (the other official members were Dundas, Judge Holland of the Vice Admiralty Court, Colonial Secretary Andrew Barnard, John Pringle and several Navy officers). This court held a trial at Cape Town from June 26 to July 6, 1795, of mutineers on an East India Company ship at just the time Macartney received his secret intelligence. It would have been natural for Macartney to give Hogan the intelligence about Deconnick's trading with the enemy activity. Four years later, a business confidant in London wrote to Hogan that "Deconnick & Company had represented to [their London agents, Messrs David Scott & Company] that, having appointed you their agent, they had written you particularly respecting [the *Holger Danske*] and were naturally enough astonished at what has since happened. Mr. [Innes] offered to procure me copies of the letters. I told him that I felt greatly obliged by his concern and the offer to produce the letters which I was bound to declare in the most solemn manner had never reached the Cape and as to the idea of your fitting out a privateer on purpose to take the *Holger Danske* it was too absurd to call for confutation."

It is easy to surmise that Hogan did, in fact, receive the letters from Deconnick about the *Holger Danske*, letters which presumably asked Hogan to act as agent for the ship at the Cape and which would have given its itinerary for this purpose. Hogan was not unknown to the Danish company; it had an office in London and had done business with him at its Hamburg office in 1795 in connection with a bond repayment. The well-known company could also have been recommended by Messrs David Scott & Company. Mr. Deconnick was described as "the most opulent merchant in Denmark."[55] Hogan could have decided to keep his receipt of the letters secret so that he could use his knowledge of the vessel's intentions and its itinerary to engage a vessel to perform the patriotic act of seizing the *Holger Danske* as a prize when the time was ripe. That time came just a year later when the Danish vessel was seized and brought back to the Cape.

Other mysterious elements of the *Holger Danske* saga are addressed later. In the meantime, the Danish ship was to play an indirect role in Hogan's slave business.

A month after the fierce storm at Table Bay, Sir George Yonge arrived to become governor. Although both Macartney and Dundas had allowed the importation of some slaves, they were both considered opposed to the trade and unlikely to grant further licenses. Yonge's official instructions contain no mention of the slave question, nor is there a record of any London reply to Dundas's request for guidance on the subject.[56] If Yonge had been given guidance in London, it was likely to have been to discourage the slave trade but to do whatever was necessary to keep the Colony supplied with local produce.

Governor Macartney had been chosen by Henry Dundas, but Yonge got his appointment because he was a favorite of King George III. He had been a member of Parliament, as well as a lord of the Admiralty and secretary of war, before he came to the Cape. He would not therefore have been unfamiliar with British policies and goals. But he was almost seventy years old when he arrived and singularly ill-equipped by temperament to assume the difficult task of governing the Colony. He was widely regarded as being more interested in the accouterments of his office and residence than in the welfare of the Colony.[57]

He soon let it be known that he did not necessarily share Macartney's views on any subject. Seeing an opportunity to pursue the slave import question again, Hogan raised the subject with Yonge in January 1800. Thus began an affair that led to several scandals, a subsequent official inquiry into the activities of Yonge and his immediate staff, and the discovery of information damaging not only to the governor and his immediate assistants but to Hogan as well. In testimony later given to an inquiry commission in 1801-02, Hogan claimed that Yonge "said he did not see [slave imports] in the same point of view with Lord Macartney, that what [Macartney] thought upon that subject or any other was of no consequence to him and that he would soon convince the Colony they now had a governor whose ambition it was to make trade flourish and not to cramp those under his protection, as was invariably the conduct of Lord Macartney in governing the place he had been at.... [F]inding the governor disposed to acquiesce, I set my claim for the importation of slaves in the strongest point I could and begged to know whether I might write him on the subject, to which he replied he was ready to attend to what I chose to write to him, that he had heard of me in England and would be glad to be intimately and secretly acquainted with me and desired I would speak to Blake."[58]

As requested, Hogan then met with the governor's private secretary, Richard Blake, who had come to the Colony with Yonge and whose wife was generally thought to be his niece.[59] Blake pointedly told Hogan that "nothing would be done or be allowed [in the slave trade] without...his participating in the profit." Hogan visited the governor again, hoping to get around Blake, but Yonge referred Hogan back to Blake. Meeting Blake in the hall after this second meeting, the latter said, "I told you nothing could be done without me." The two then bargained for Blake's share, Hogan offering one-quarter and Blake demanding one-half the profits. They eventually agreed on one-third for shipments totaling 600 slaves from Mozambique.

On January 27, 1800, Hogan formally sought Yonge's approval to import slaves in a lengthy letter that set forth the reasons why the importation would benefit the Colony, including the astonishing statement that farmers would treat slaves better than native Hottentots. There was not a word about their earlier private conversation or the profit sharing arrangement with Blake. Hogan also requested permission to export 12,000 Spanish dollars to buy the slaves, in return for which he would execute a bond to import 18,000 Spanish dollars within ten months. Permission was necessary because there had been a chronic shortage of this universally accepted specie coin at the Cape for many years.

Yonge granted permission for the slave imports on February 8, but only after justifying his action by claiming that, although he was "not inclined to encourage too much the increase of slaves in the Colony, [he was] perfectly aware of the necessity...for an additional number of laboring men and, though I would wish to see them all free men, yet, as I perceive, slaves in general meet with good usage and regulations will soon be made to regulate more favorably their treatment...."

He also approved the Spanish dollar transaction, but noted that: "No goods whatever will be allowed to depart in the vessel, except a small quantity of Cape wine which I would be glad to find its way to the countries that are in amity with us."

When Hogan received the governor's letter, the *Joaquim* was again at anchor in Table Bay with a cargo of 400 slaves from Mozambique allegedly bound to Brazil but, according to Hogan, to be sold at the Cape if permission could be obtained. By this time, Yonge had publicly announced that all applications to him should be submitted through Blake or one of his aides de camp,[60] so Hogan had a double reason for going to Blake to obtain permission to include these slaves as part of the number allowed by Yonge. Blake was willing, but this time he wanted not one-third of the profits but one-half which he would split with Major James Cockburn, the senior aide de camp to the governor.[61]

On February 15, Yonge formally approved importation of the slaves on the *Joaquim*. His letter was quite clear that these 400 slaves were "part of the number before granted"[62] but Hogan and Blake treated them as an additional number. The slaves were then sold for a net profit of some 36,000 rix dollars (a bare 90 rix for each slave, compared to the going sales rate of some 400 rix dollars) which Hogan dutifully split among the beneficiaries of the under-the-table deal.

While the slave business was underway, the social life of Michael and Frances Hogan blossomed. We owe it to Anne Barnard's diaries and letters for much of the information that is known about both social and official happenings at the Cape Colony during her stay there from 1797 to early 1802. When Macartney was governor, she served as his social hostess and, although she had to surrender that role when Yonge came, she continued to entertain often and widely and to soak up considerable information which would not otherwise have been recorded in official documents. Among the British merchants that supped at the Barnard's official residence in the Castle, and with whom she supped, were the Hogans. One of her first entries regarding Hogan is to note that she wanted to view the auction of the slaves from the *Joaquim* who were landed in March 1799. (She did not attend because of the proscription that then applied to women attending male-managed business affairs.)[63]

There was a pleasant interlude for the Hogans when Philip Gidley King, en route from England to become governor of New South Wales, and his wife Anna Josepha stayed with the Hogans during their 11-day sojourn in Cape Town. King had been lieutenant governor of Norfolk Island when he and Hogan had their set-to over the sale of wine and spirits two years earlier. Apparently with that now all forgotten, Anna Josepha wrote in her diary that on February 4 she and her husband "went on shore and spent all our time at Mr. Hogan who had been expecting us upwards of a year and half" and that "a large party dined at his house on that day."[64] Anne Barnard also had a dinner party for the Kings.[65] Many years later in another quarter of the globe, Hogan was to meet King's son, Commander Philip Parker King.

One has to wonder whether the subject of Hogan's illegitimate daughter Mary arose on any of these occasions. It is unlikely Hogan would have told King about Mary while he was at Norfolk Island in 1796; he may not even have known he had an illegitimate daughter at that time. But David Collins probably knew when in 1797 he left at Cape Town the ambiguous letter to Hogan cited in the previous chapter. The Kings were on the same ship between Australia and Cape Town as was Collins who, having his own illegitimate children, could readily have shared the Hogan-Ann Ryan gossip with Philip King who in turn could easily have told his wife, perhaps as a means of trying to excuse his own behavior by pointing out to her that he was not the only sexual transgressor among their peers. Did Anna King mention the matter to Frances Hogan? Realizing she might, did Hogan himself admit his indiscretion to Frances? It is impossible to know because, except for the pencil notations added by Hogan's grandson to Collins' 1797 letter that "a certain acquaintance" was "a woman," there is no mention whatsoever to the existence of Mary in any of the Hogan papers.

Before selling the slaves from the *Joaquim*, Hogan wanted to be certain that the East India Company did not consider slaves from the East as trade reserved for the Company. In the previous year, Acting Governor Dundas and Pringle had disputed a decision of the recently established Vice Admiralty Court allowing the local sale of a portion of the cargo of a Danish vessel chartered by Americans, the *Angelique*, which had been seized carrying piece goods from Madras to Manila. (Hogan had acted as agent for the Danish owner of that part of the cargo which was not of East Indies manufacture—brandy, soap and oil—and obtained Dundas' permission to sell this portion in April 1799.)[66] The dispute was temporarily settled when a judicial commission ruled that prize goods of Eastern origin could not be disposed of for local consumption. This ruling was later interpreted to mean that condemned prize articles of Eastern origin could be sold locally at public auction, provided the buyers gave security bonds that the goods would be exported to Britain. Exceptions could also be granted for perishable articles.[67] Hogan asked Pringle whether the slaves were included in the prohibition. Perhaps not wanting to be the cause of slaves being "exported to England" but reluctant to rule they were "perishable," Pringle reported to the East India Company in London on March 29 that he would not "intermeddle in the business, if [the Governor] thought fit to grant [import and sale] permission."[68]

The first hint that trouble was brewing in the slave transactions came when Hogan began unloading the slaves from the *Joaquim* in early March. On the seventh, the captains of several Royal Navy ships anchored at the Cape, including particularly Captain John Osborne of H.M.S. *Tremendous*, wrote to Collector of Customs John Hooke Green to inform him of their opinion that the Portuguese ship "cannot legally import slaves the produce of Mozambique into this Colony, such trade being prohibited by [English law]." The Navy officers threatened to seize the ship if a single slave was landed. Green wrote back the next day that he could do nothing because Yonge had granted permission for the importation.[69°] The captains were, strictly speaking, wrong in asserting that British law prohibited the importation of slaves into British possessions; the British prohibition on slave trade then applied only to the home country.

Rumors that Hogan and Blake had connived together were circulating among some government officials at least several days before March 7. Lady Anne Bernard reported that "it is generally believed here that Mr. Blake has accepted of a present from Mr. Hogan to procure him this [slave import] advantage." When she asked her husband Andrew if he believed this report, he responded that "Mr. Hogan was a likely man to offer a [bribe] where he expected to reap a greater in return" and that Hogan had told him that he had "reserved the choice of six good slaves...for him," an offer that Barnard refused. Barnard also told Lady Anne that, when he expressed his regret to Yonge that he had permitted the importation, "he never saw a man blush redder." Lady Anne also thought it must have been Hogan who initiated the douceur, as she called it.[70]

Undeterred by the rumors, Hogan proceeded to sell the slaves at several auctions in mid-March. As with the previous slave shipment on the *Joaquim*, only 321 of the slaves were sold in this manner, the other 70 apparently privately. Although unrelated to the Hogan-Blake connivance, these sales and previous ones led the fiscal to initiate a judicial investigation of a complaint that Hogan had sold slaves at auction at inflated prices and, in other cases, privately outside the auction. Hogan wrote to his presumed protector, Governor Yonge, denying that he had done anything wrong and indirectly asking Yonge to intercede to stop the inquiry. He provided information, based on Customs House records, showing that the prices he obtained, ranging from 346 to 485 rix dollars, were below those received by others. (An official British survey in 1798 showed that a male slave then commanded 400–500 rix dollars; a female slave 350–400.)[71] Maintaining a righteous air, Hogan told Yonge that, "as he was well-convinced that it is Your Excellency's wish to encourage and protect the fair trader, by which alone a Colony can flourish, I feel no apprehension from the disposition of the Chief Magistrate nor the jealousy of individual people who have not the means nor the ability to transact business in an open, fair and honorable manner".[72]

Shortly after receiving Hogan's letter, Yonge finally reported to Henry Dundas in London that he had "consented to the supply of slaves being compleated, which was begun before my arrival and I hope this will be sufficient for the present. I have however at the same time directed a revisal of the laws concerning their treatment, which in truth is in general not severe, and I hope by some improvement in these laws to render their situation nearly similar to husbandry laborers in England."[73]

The statement that he was merely completing a program begun by Macartney was patently misleading. Nor did Yonge try to enact laws to make slaves the equals of English farm laborers, which would have required outlawing their treatment as property. It was not the first disingenuous letter that Yonge would write.

While the Hogan-Blake connivance remained but a rumor, the matter of the slaves allegedly seized as prize by the *Collector* would threaten Hogan publically. The *Collector* had returned to Table Bay on February 10 with more slaves who, it was alleged, had been taken off a French brig, the 132-ton *L'Auguste*, captured in the Miranda River, Madagascar, after she had been run on shore and burned and the crew fled. There were allegedly 250 slaves on board when the ship was captured.[74] Some of the slaves had died on the voyage and others were sickly; the survivors were therefore held on board in quarantine for almost two months.

At some point, Captain Hans Laurens Smit and other officers of the *Holger Danske*, still lying at Table Bay, had made it known around Cape Town that two of the earlier French vessels claimed as prizes by Captain Smart, *La Rose* and *L'Africana*, had not been captured. Instead, they had witnessed Smart buy the French ships and the slaves in question at Mozambique.

The Port Captain, Donald Campbell, whose duties included oversight of vessels entering the port, brought the reports to the attention of Andrew Barnard in early April. Anne Barnard wrote of the "whispered" reports that Mr. Hogan had practiced "more tricks, more deceits" in order to get two cargoes of slaves taken by a his privateer landed at the Cape Colony. She also reported that Campbell had "plainly and boldly asserted that Hogan made no scruple of admitting that he had given a douceur [to] either the governor himself or Mr. Blake."[75]

Although Campbell delayed taking any formal action, he was being pressed to do so after being criticized by some British merchants "in a manner reflecting on [his] character." He therefore proceeded to take evidence from the Danish officers and some of the slaves, all of whom confirmed the reports of duplicity. He later averred that it was "his intention to bring the business forward by writing an official letter to the Governor, ...but [he had] his doubts...on account of Mr. Hogan's influence [at Government House], it might not be delivered to the Governor, ...for if Mr. Hogan was apprised by his friends there what was going forward, he would be enabled to take such steps and precautions as might effectually prevent and frustrate every attempt to get at the truth of the matter."

Campbell did, however, discuss the matter on several occasions with Andrew Barnard who had taken it upon himself "to keep all parties free from *Scrapes* or free from such dealings as must on discovery *injure themselves*." When he tried to persuade Hogan to be "cautious how he brought [the slaves] forward as prize property" if there was any evidence they were otherwise, Hogan "got into a very great rage...and boldly maintained his [version] to be true...." Barnard suggested that it might be Captain Smart who engineered the subterfuge, which Hogan vehemently denied. Barnard's last effort was to persuade Hogan to land the slaves for the benefit of their health but to delay selling them until he (Barnard) could look into the matter further, a suggestion that Hogan said was impossible because he could not continue to bear the heavy expense of keeping the slaves. Barnard was almost convinced that Hogan was telling the truth and that it was Captain Campbell who had been taken in.

Barnard finally "saw the duplicity of the transaction" when Campbell gave him the concrete evidence. Barnard nevertheless advised Campbell to let the Vice Admiralty Court decide the issue and allow the slaves to be sold "before he laid his objections before the governor or Fiscal." Campbell agreed but asked that, when the necessity of a letter to the governor arose, Barnard would deliver it to Yonge.[76]

The Vice Admiralty Court decided the issue on April 11 by condemning the cargo of slaves taken from *L'Auguste*, allowing the survivors, of which there were by then only 164, to be landed. Yonge approved their sale just three days later on the fourteenth in a letter signed by Blake and delivered directly to Collector of Customs Green. The next day Campbell delivered to Barnard his letter to the governor,[77] and at the same time privately advised Van Ryneveld what he had discovered. Van Ryneveld immediately sought an audience with Yonge who, when pressed, agreed on the same day that the fiscal should proceed in accordance with law.

The commissioners of the Court of Justice were immediately called to take evidence. In a letter sent to Yonge on the 16th, Hogan asked the governor to intercede. He described the charge that the slaves had been purchased as "a transaction so improbable in nature and so contrary to the concurrent and unimpeached testimony of the witnesses…that [he] had no difficulty in meeting such a question in any court whatever and with great confidence since the persons resorted to for the support of so scandalous a charge were daily and almost hourly privy to the proceedings had in the Vice Admiralty Court without ever having expressed the slightest objection thereto." He then invoked his family and his reputation as a merchant by calling the charge "of a magnitude seriously to affect his family and, what is still of greater importance to him, his character as a merchant and a man." Arguing that the Vice Admiralty Court had already decided the issue, he tried to impugn the adverse testimony of the captain and officers of the *Holger Danske* by observing that "the evidence to warrant the proceeding in another court is sought for amongst the master and mates of a ship taken under neutral colors by another privateer [*Harriet*] of [mine]."[78]

Sympathetic to Hogan's plea, Yonge tried once more to quash the proceedings. He told the fiscal that, "if he were in Mr. Hogan's place, he would not appear before, nor pay any regard to, the Court of Justice respecting the matter, after the case had been decided by [the Vice Admiralty Court]." The investigation nevertheless continued with damaging evidence produced, including the fact that the *Collector* came into Mozambique under the name of *Mountain* and that, at the same time it was being loaded with slaves, slaves were also being loaded on board the *Joaquirn*, the Portuguese vessel on which Hogan had in February landed 400 slaves at the Cape after paying off Blake and Cockburn. There were further mysteries: the witnesses who had earlier deposed that the slaves were from French prizes could not be found; and a second version of the logbook of the *Collector* was unearthed, the first one being patently fabricated. Smart was ordered arrested on April 21 and brought to trial, but he also had disappeared, leaving the Cape altogether. The Court of Justice declared Smart an outlaw and banished him from the Cape for life.

At the beginning of the trial, Hogan had appeared in Court and stated that he objected to the proceeding on the grounds that the cause had already been decided by the Vice Admiralty Court. The Court, quite properly, rejected this argument, at which point Hogan declared he would not appear further in Court. However, when the true logbook was discovered, Hogan presented a memorial to the Court in which he stated "that circumstances having now come to his knowledge which have raised some doubts in his mind of the legality of Smart's proceedings with regard to the slaves, and that he had reason to think the said Smart had deceived him; he requested to withdraw the objection he had made on a former day, stating that the exception he proposed would only render the legality of the cause more uncertain, and that should any fraud be discovered, the suspicion would fall upon him of being the author or at least of participating in the transaction; he therefore left the decision of the question in their hands."

Since illegality had been established, Van Ryneveld petitioned the Court to order Hogan to refund the value of the slaves sold by public auction and to impose a penalty of triple damages. The Court ordered the refund but did not impose the penalty because there "were not sufficient proofs to attach the criminality of the transaction to Mr. Hogan, whose property alone in this case would have suffered." Nothing was apparently done as a result of the investigation into the prices charged for his slaves.

It was in this posture that the *Collector* incident was temporarily closed. Hogan was not, however, unaffected emotionally by the incident. Anne Barnard noted she had observed Hogan's "extreme dejection" on one occasion and his "dejected eyes and conscious melancholy" on another, even though he had told her that "all his friends affect to be perfectly at ease now that it is incontestably proved that Mr. Smart alone was to blame." Lady Anne did not believe, however, that "so clever a man as Mr. Hogan could be ignorant of the activities of Captain Smart. She added, however, that "as every body wishes the man well, inspite of the duplicity of the act, we are all glad to see the affair blow over, and I am so amongst the rest tho' I think he is much too clever for a poor man or rather for any man who is not rich as to be independent of the gains which stratagems produce."[79] She made an equally friendly appraisal when she later wrote to Henry Dundas, as will be addressed in the next chapter.

Michael and Frances Hogan were certainly not the social equals of the Barnards or of other titled officials, but Lady Anne was conscious of the slights that the Hogans were occasionally subjected to and tried to rectify them. Well before Yonge arrived, she noted that "Mr. and Mrs. Hogan had taken pet" at receiving no invitation to one of her large parties. She added that Frances "is a woman of color and all women of that complexion are distrustful of neglect. Mr. Hogan knows the nature of the Cape Dutch to be so disposed to disdain any one in whose blood there was a drop of the Slave that he was almost afraid of bringing her here. She herself however [is] so well received by the English that she had nothing almost to suffer from the others, but the small want of attention or appearance of it is always on the point of mortifying her—and on this occasion did also." By referring to Frances as a "woman of color," she meant a person from India, although there is no evidence that Frances's mother was other than Portuguese in origin. Lady Anne rectified her staff's mistake by inviting the Hogans (and others) to dinner three nights later. On another occasion six months later, Anne Barnard recounted an incident where Frances had been walking contentedly with a group of English women when several of them suddenly left to meet a person they all knew, apparently slighting Frances when they did not extend an invitation to join them.[80] Lady Anne also observed that Frances was protective of her husband. At a large party celebrating the wedding of a Cloete family daughter six months after the *Collector* incident, many of the guests overindulged in their consumption of spirits. She observed that "Mr. Hogan's intoxication took the melancholy turn and from less to more he entered into discussion with me on his own precarious situation…. My Dear! said Mrs. Hogan, taking his hand and seeming to know what he had been saying. She added no words, but she grasped the hand she Held. Aye, replied he, if the last leaf in the book durst not turn over favorably it must be so. It froze me. I had seen and heard such hints [of remorse over lost abilities] before…."[81]

With the *Collector* incident behind him, nothing stood in the way of completing arrangements to import the remainder of the 600 slaves for which Yonge had granted permission or entering into other transactions involving Yonge and his henchmen. There would be an eight-month wait for more slave ships to arrive. Hogan reported in his memorial that "two Portuguese vessels [*St. Josea DeIndiana* (Captain M J. Pereira) and *Boa Caetana* (Captain J. Delesparado)] arrived [on December 18], one with one hundred and fifty and the other with seventy slaves which I purchased at a high price under the permission I had obtained."[82] Blake relayed the governor's permission to land the 220 slaves on the two vessels. Hogan was upset, however, that fifteen of them "were taken from me by an order of Mr. Blake to Mr. John Robertson who picked the best for Mr. Duckitt." William Duckitt had been sent to the Colony from England "to practice the English mode of farming" as a demonstration of efficient farming techniques for Boer farmers. He had arrived at Cape Town three months before the incident described by Hogan[83] and was later placed in charge of agricultural and meat production at the Colony. Hogan appealed to Yonge to reverse this decision but reported that "the only satisfaction I received was his telling me 'Duckitt must have them,' notwithstanding I had paid for the slaves."

Hogan's advertisement auctioning the slaves from the *Boa Caetana* referred to "125 men and boys and 25 young women; these slaves have had the small pox before they left Mozambique,"[84] by which he meant, as he had told Yonge, that the slaves had "been inoculated for the small pox at Mozambique." The centuries-old concern over smallpox had recently given way to optimism with the discovery that an inoculation of vaccine from cows provided immunity. Dr. Woody of Cape Town, who had gone to England to obtain information about the vaccine, returned later in 1801, presumably armed to inoculate the Colony's inhabitants.[85] Whether the vaccine was then available in Mozambique is unknown.

The last episode involving slaves authorized by Yonge concerned Hogan's brig, the *Fanny*, named after his eldest daughter, with Captain Archibald McKellar in command, which sailed to Mozambique on September 22.[86] It returned on January 29 with 180 male and 90 female slaves. The 270 slaves, who were again advertized as having "all had the small pox," were sold at public auctions beginning February 19.[87]

Hogan later testified in his memorial that, "as the expenses attending the [sale of all the slaves] were great, the advantages were not so considerable...." By this time, Hogan was not on "speaking terms" with Blake, so it was "Colonel Cockburn who day after day pressed for the money, and to finish finally and be done with them, being at the same time short of funds, Colonel Cockburn agreed to take my bond for £1,500... in full consideration of the one-third share of all the profit that he and Mr. Blake were to receive for the whole of the slaves imported under the governor's [license] exclusive of the cargo of the *Joaquim* for which they had already been paid."

Hogan may have kept some of the slaves from the foregoing shipments for his own household and business. Or he may have kept for his own use six slaves landed in an entirely separate transaction from the Spanish prize vessel *Santa Rosa*[88] just a few days before the investigation into the *Collector* incident began in April 1800. In any event, he must have acquired more than he needed, for a year later he advertized for the sale by public auction of "about 15 exceedingly good men slaves, two or three young boys and two girls, all of very good conduct, having been upwards of three years in his house."[89]

Hogan was not the only merchant at the Cape who sought permission to import slaves, nor the only one to offer Blake and Cockburn money for the privilege, but the evidence shows he was the major player in the slave trade at the Cape and the beneficiary of their perfidy. His memorial and other sources show that he imported 890 slaves under the permission granted by Yonge, including the 400 on the *Joaquim* in February 1800. If the 469 slaves imported by Hogan & Tennant in 1979 are included, the grand total is 1,359 to the end of 1802. One author has estimated that a total of about 2,000 slaves were imported during the British occupation,[90] the true number probably being higher. As will be seen in the next chapter. He imported 500 more slaves into the Colony during the Dutch restoration in 1803, and a large number were shipped from Mozambique to the New World, either directly or transshipped via the Cape.

Nor was slave trading the only area in which Hogan was involved with Yonge and his accomplices. He recounted to the official inquiry commission that he refused their offer to sell him the exclusive right to import timber. However, he said he had told Mr. Blake that, "if the governor chose to favor me amongst others, I should feel the obligation but I would in future only take my chances with the community. At this, Mr. Blake was much disappointed and no longer what he termed my friend, nor did I afterwards receive any notice from Sir George Yonge. Soon after, I perceived Mr. Blake had found no difficulty in making his timber arrangements."

When questioned further, Hogan testified that Blake asked him specifically "if in case the exclusive privilege should be given to him [Hogan], what share of the profits would he be willing to give up to him [Blake]." It was probably Hogan's refusal to give a cut to Blake that turned Blake against him.

Hogan already had a contract to supply lumber for the British troops at the Cape, but he needed specific permission to bring timber from Plettenberg (to the east of Cape Town) for this purpose. He told Blake that he wanted to see Yonge to discuss the matter, to which Blake said he would let the governor know. Suspecting that Blake might say something injurious to his case, Hogan stepped close behind him into the room, where he overheard Blake tell Yonge "to be firm in his determination and not to be shaken by any argument [Hogan] might make use of."[91] Hogan later learned that the license to import timber had been given to Messrs Walker & Robertson Company, for which these merchants later admitted to the Yonge investigating commission that "it was their intention to make [Blake] a *present* for his services in *facilitating* their concerns with Government [emphasis added]." Anne Barnard thought there was more to the relationship between Yonge and Messrs Walker & Robertson than a gratuity for Blake. In October 1800, she recorded that Walker & Robertson were the governor's "heirs apparent" to the benevolence that had previously been bestowed on Hogan.[92] In a subsequent letter, she called the company "Yonge's firm" and said that the *Lady Yonge*, allegedly owned by Walker & Robertson, "is supposed to be Sir George's own ship."[93] This ship (Captain Smith) sailed from Table Bay at the end of 1800 with letters of marque and returned in late April with 400,000 pounds of sorely needed rice, just in time to transport the soon to be disgraced governor back to England.[94] However, the Yonge investigating commission noted that the ship chartered by government to bring the timber from Plettenberg, the *Young Nicholas*, owned by Walker & Robertson, had been hired at an "exorbitant rate." Dundas later disapproved payment at this rate, apparently 7,200 rix dollars a month. Hogan then became the agent for the vessel, offering it to government in April 1801 to carry timber from Plettenberg at 3,546 rix dollars (then the equivalent of £591) monthly.[95]

Hogan's memorial does not refer to the permission he had been given by Dundas to import teakwood from Pegu. He had purchased a Prussian prize vessel seized by the British Navy, the *De Drie Broeders* (Three Brothers), which he renamed the *Sir George Yonge*, obviously to curry favor with the governor (and not to be outdone by Walker & Robertson's *Lady Yonge*—even though Yonge's wife was not with him at the Cape), and in May 1800 obtained Yonge's permission to send the vessel to India.[96] The ship was wrecked in bad weather on Mascall Island near Chittagong, east of Bengal, in 1801 after picking up its teakwood at Pegu, but Hogan was able to recover 120,000 rupees from insurance taken out on the cargo. He was only one of the share holders in the transaction;[97] the others are not recorded, but one wonders whether Yonge himself held an interest, just as he was suspected of owning part of the *Lady Yonge*.

Another of the governor's schemes was to control the production and sale of Gonstantia wine. To this end, he issued a proclamation on August 14, 1800, appointing Blake as Chief Taster and Examiner of All Wines and Brandies.[98] Hogan recorded in his memorial that "early in [August 1800], Blake...proposed that I should purchase the wine farm which was to be advertized immediately, stating that, as he was appointed wine taster, he could pass any sort of wine as good for the canteens, etc., and that we should hold it as a concern and divide the profits. I begged I would consider of it and give him an answer which I did, declining in total any thing to do with the wine or any concern whatever with him."

There was more. Hogan had been asked by Cockburn to submit a bid for supplying the Barracks Department with furniture, utensils and other items, but when he did so Cockburn demanded 20 percent of the contract price. Hogan said he could not possibly afford this because he had priced all the articles as low as possible. After obtaining Yonge's approval, Cockburn told Hogan to increase his prices by 10 percent and pay the additional amount to him, which Hogan did.[99]

Hogan was enmeshed with Yonge in many other ways during his brief stay as governor at the Cape, the full extent of which may never be known. An indication of the breadth of his involvement was the story of Hogan's 70-ton brig, the *Dispatch*. In a document executed later in an attempt to recover payment from government,[100] Hogan alleged that, in October 1800, Yonge asked if he had a vessel available to go to St. Helena to carry government despatches and a message from the inhabitants of the Cape to His Majesty the King; that Captain John Gouston Price Tucker, one of Yonge's two aides de camp, approached him saying he should get his vessel ready; that he did so; and that, relying on a Yonge proclamation that "all communications from either his private secretary [Blake] or two aides de camps [Cockburn and Tucker] were to be considered official," he believed he had an oral contract. He then went to Yonge to ask with whom he should conclude a charterparty agreement and what price he would be paid, "to which Sir George Yonge, then walking in the front veranda, replied in a hurry, 'pho, pho, you will be liberally paid for her!'" In a different document, Hogan recalled this incident in additional detail: "...Yonge desired through Captain Tucker I would go to the Government House to speak to me about a vessel which he ordered through the same aide de camp I would get ready to carry his despatches and he (Captain Tucker) to St. Helena. Some conversation took place at which Mr. Blake and I differed and then I told Colonel Cockburn that Mr. Blake would be the cause of Sir George Yonge's grey hairs going to the grave in disgrace. After this Mr. Blake left nothing undone to prejudice the Government against me."

Hogan probably did not know that his pointed remark about Yonge's going to the grave in disgrace was about to prove figuratively true. He did know that the message to King George III was intended to show the loyalty of the Colonists following an abortive assassination attempt on his life. But neither he nor anyone else would have known the true nature of the government despatches that Captain Tucker was to carry on the *Dispatch*.

Ever since his arrival, Yonge had been flooding London with reports of how well he was governing and how much others were interfering with his noble plans. His first officially recorded rebuke from London (for criticizing Macartney) would have been received in mid-1800, the next (for exceeding his authority) about October 1800. He had answered the first criticism by vigorously defending himself and adding further complaints against General Dundas, Macartney and others, but when the second rebuke arrived, he must have realized that he was in serious trouble at home. He wrote five letters all dated October 22 to Henry Dundas, four of them defending his action, the fifth dutifully reporting an illicit, but probably irrelevant, French trading scheme. It was these letters, not the message for the King, that Yonge was so anxious to get to London on Hogan's vessel.[101]

The *Dispatch* sailed from Table Bay on October 27[102] carrying Yonge's self-preservation pleas to be transferred at St. Helena to the first ship sailing for England, while the *Dispatch* was to proceed to Ascension and then return to the Cape. The ship's captain, Robert McCarthy, relying on the directions of Captain Tucker rather than his own navigational skills, missed St. Helena. After consulting Tucker, he decided to go to Rio de Janeiro, arriving there at the end of December. Tucker found passage to Lisbon on a Portuguese vessel, taking the despatches with him, after first selling "his cargo" at Rio and buying tobacco, hair powder and tallow to be shipped on the *Dispatch* for the Cape market. He did not return to the Cape.[103] McCarthy was in turn given despatches at Rio destined for the Cape and St. Helena by a Captain Heals of the *General Boyd* and left Rio on January 30, 1801. The *Cape Town Gazette* later reported that "the greatest distress prevailed...on the passage [from Rio de Janeiro] to St. Helena Bay, the crew subsisting part of the time on a composition of [Tucker's] hair powder and salt water."[104] The *Dispatch* finally reached Table Bay on April 7 where McCarthy gave the Cape despatches to

Hogan and the St. Helena ones to Pringle. Yonge then wrote a letter in his own hand to Barnard asking that, to set an example, "whatever penalty the law warrants may be levied" on McCarthy for violations of Colonial Regulations in not waiting for his ship to be cleared by the Harbor or Health Master and for not delivering his despatches to the Post Office.[105]

The details of this interesting story are less important than what it tells about Hogan's belief that he could obtain favorable treatment from unscrupulous government servants so long as understandings were kept private and informal. No sensible businessman would ever accept a government promise to pay without a written agreement, and Hogan certainly knew that. He undoubtedly expected that he could later work out a profitable arrangement both for himself and for Yonge and his assistants. He had been lured in the past by what he thought were special relationships and it would shortly happen again.

The questions of the seemingly minor infractions that led Yonge to rebuke the ship's captain and of Hogan's being paid for the use of his vessel on government service would be put aside because, in mid-April, just eight days after Yonge sent his personal note to Barnard, the governor received orders from London dated three months earlier advising that he had been replaced, that he was to return to England by the "first opportunity," and that he should transfer his responsibilities immediately to General Dundas as acting governor. (The intended replacement for Yonge never did arrive, events overtaking its necessity.) Yonge tried to delay his departure by various devices, none of which succeeded. He finally left the Colony with Mr. and Mrs. Blake on May 29, 1801, in virtual disgrace, traveling on the *Lady Yonge*, the ship Anne Barnard believed belonged to Yonge himself, as far as St. Helena.[106]

Yonge probably knew that the letters he had sent on the *Dispatch* could not have arrived in London before his dismissal order was signed, and he had known since at least February that a dismissal order was probable. As before, he had tried to head it off by sending more pleas to London, but they were too late.[107]

But before the Yonge saga was to be played out to its final conclusion, Hogan continued to have business that required attention. In an attempt to avoid abuse and excessive profits, commissioners had been appointed to regulate the import and consumption of grain which was often in short supply, particularly after the failure of the 1800–01 crops. Hogan was the recipient of several of these purchase contracts in early 1801: 200 tons of rice from India on the 280-ton *Fanny* (Captain George Thompson), not the same ship that procured Mozambique slaves for Hogan; rice, wheat or flour from Rio de Janeiro on the *Boa Caetana* which had brought slaves to the Colony for Hogan; and a major shipment of rice from Madras on the 1,200-ton *Matilda* (Captain James Sheen).[108] The latter business did not go smoothly. When the *Matilda* returned on November 2 with not only the contracted rice but also Indian piece goods, the latter were discovered to have not been declared at the Customs House. Pringle reported to the East India Company in London that the omission "has occasioned a serious discussion between Mr. Hogan...and the Customs House" which led to the imposition of a 4,000 rix dollar fine. There was also a complaint that there was much dust in the *Matilda's* rice.[109]

Throughout the period that Hogan was actively involved in the slave business, he continued to pursue his original objective of engaging in privateering. Shortly after his arrival at the Cape Colony, he had met John Black, purser on the *Lady Shore*, who had found his way to the Cape after he and other ship's officers had been turned adrift by mutineers. Black had become captain of the whaler *Indispensable* which in June 1798 transported to New South Wales the previously noted cargo that Hogan had purchased from the Spanish prize *La Union*.[110] When Black returned to Cape Town over a year later, Hogan sought him out to command the *Harbinger*. The Government had commissioned her for its own uses after her ill-fated return from Guinea in June 1799 with only a few slaves. Hogan finally obtained a release from government service and on February 26, 1800, just as the *Collector* incident was unfolding, concluded an Articles of Agreement with Black who, equipped with the necessary letters of marque, was to seize French and Spanish prizes off the Brazilian coast. The *Harbinger* returned to Table Bay on August 22,[111] its two small Spanish prizes, the 30-ton sloop *Nossa Senhora del Carmen* and the 70-ton brig *Nossa Senhora del Rosario* having arrived fifteen days earlier,[112] the sloop with 4,000 Spanish dollars aboard. The brig had encountered difficulties on its voyage from the River Plate. James Grant, captain of H.M.S. *Lady Nelson* reported that: "On coming within hail [on June 23], the prize master informed me that he had neither book nor chart on board and that he did not know where he was. He had suffered considerably in the heavy weather we had seen breakers in, and begged some canvas and twine to repair his sails, and a few other articles he stood in need of.... The brig was...laden with bees wax, hides, tallow and tobacco.... [On the 24th] our boat was hoisted out, and sent for the prize master, to whom I gave a chart of the Cape, and the harbors in its vicinity, ...some canvas, twine, tea, sugar, and rum, which his men, from being constantly wet, stood much in need of. He received these many expressions of thankfulness." In August, both vessels were condemned by the Vice Admiralty Court and sold with their cargoes. There may have been a third prize of the *Harbinger.* In October, the Vice Admiralty Court declined to condemn some tobacco allegedly taken by the *Harbinger* from a Spanish vessel which had been destroyed because the captors produced no evidence of the capture other than their own testimony.

Hogan had in mind another captain to continue privateering, but first he sent John Black on the *Harbinger* to New South Wales in November with a cargo of general merchandise, 2,800 gallons of spirits and 3,000 gallons of wine.[113] She arrived at Port Jackson in January 1801. On her passage, she sailed on a new route along the southern shore of Australia through Bass Strait and gained valuable navigational information. Harbinger Rock near King Island, between Victoria and Tasmania, was named after the ship. The authorities at New South Wales wanted additional navigational exploration, so they purchased the *Harbinger* for £700, one-half the sum Hogan had asked, and renamed her the *Norfolk.* Governor King, apparently not influenced by his friendship with Hogan, wrote that "the offer I made [Hogan] was...much less than her real value." However, the ship foundered in a storm before she could complete any further exploration.[114]

Hogan had been pleased with Captain White's performance in seizing the *Holger Danske* and dispatched him again on the *Harriet.* But this time the tables were turned. After capturing three small French prizes, the *Harriet* was herself captured by a French corsair and taken to Île de France in mid-1800. French corsairs were operating out of Île de France in force at this time; an American ship reported that nine of them were cruising and that in one ten-day period nearly thirty vessels had been captured.[115] The *Harriet* was later returned to Hogan, and White managed to make his way back to the Cape where Hogan put him in command of the *Chance,* a 178-ton French-built vessel mounting 16 guns and crewed by 50 men.[116] Letters of marque were granted and Articles of Agreement concluded between Hogan and White on February 12, 1801, calling for the *Chance* to engage in privateering against French and Spanish vessels and setting forth how any prize money was to be shared. After deducting all expenses, as well as a five percent commission reserved for Hogan, two-thirds of the net profits would go to Hogan, the remaining one-third to be divided among the captain and crew.

Hogan separately gave Captain White lengthy and detailed instructions. He was first to apply to the governor of New South Wales for "permission to engage a number of men as will complete your ship's company to eighty, or one hundred if you conceive you have room for such a number without endangering the health of your crew." He was then to proceed to the Spanish coast of South America and "obtain the best information possible of the trade of the enemy, the strength of their ports, the nature of the cargoes exported from each port, what ships are ready for sailing and what expected, when and from whence their vessels carry the treasure to Acapulco, their strength (not because I apprehend they are equal to you but that you may be well-prepared), what their route commonly is and where it is best to fall in with them. Being in possession of these particulars, I can only direct you to pursue such line of conduct as will appear most likely to ensure success in defeating the enemy by making reprisals of their ships and property when and where you can find them, …without going to objects which the spirit and honor of a British sailor ought to pass by, i.e., private small property of individuals."

Hogan described how White could approach Spanish vessels without identifying himself as a privateer:

> You should get close in with the coast of Chile… about Valdivia, range close inshore in the character of an American whaler to the northward as far as Valparaíso, examining every little port, of which there are many and some very rich trade carried on. Here you will not fail to fall in with small and perhaps some very large coasters, some of which you may make an object to send here. They will chiefly be laden with grain and provisions, but your great object will be information, charts, etc. All ships bound to Valparaíso from the northward invariably make the Isle of Juan Fernández, then steer in for the port. I believe it is an open roadstead. By disguising yourself properly, you may obtain every information by boats coming to you while under American colors. But [since] much caution is necessary, …show but few men and state as an excuse for being armed [that] France was at war with America and, when you left [the U.S.], you did not expect to round Cape Horn.

Hogan's reference to France being at war with America was not exaggerated. Jacobin France, with its attention focused on holding domestic power and fighting Britain, had been preying on American vessels, particularly in the West Indies and Indian Ocean, in an undeclared naval war in which there was little serious action but much concern among Americans. The Cape Colony was indirectly affected because some of French privateering in the Indian Ocean was directed at American ships. In March 1800, just as the *Collector* incident was unfolding, the American Navy frigate *Essex* had anchored for seventeen days in Table Bay on its way to the East Indies to escort American merchant vessels returning to the United States from Batavia and recapture American ships taken by French privateers in the Indian Ocean. The ship's captain, Edward Preble, was treated as an honored guest, being entertained by Governor Yonge, Vice Admiral Curtis, the Barnards, and several British Navy captains then in port.[117] (It would not be many years before naval courtesies gave way to battles between British and American Navy ships. Pringle for one was suspicious. Perhaps because the *Essex* was the first U. S. Navy ship to sail east of the Cape of Good Hope, he wrongly thought "its real intention [was] to examine the Islands of St. Paul (and others) on the coast of Sumatra, and in general to look for a proper place to form an Establishment.")[118] The mini-naval war with France had all but ended, but this was still unknown at the Cape. Hogan's suggested excuse for the *Chance's* being in South American waters under an American flag might therefore have been believed, although such an excuse was probably unnecessary—American whalers had been prevalent in the South Pacific for several years.

Privateering was dangerous to the participants and risky for the ship owner and investors. Although seamen were a rough lot, signing up on a privateer vessel meant they would likely have to engage in close combat with other armed ships where they might be killed, with no guarantee of success and only a future prospect of receiving prize money. Candidates for such jobs were bound to be those to whom violence was a way of life, which is probably why Hogan told White to seek crew members from among ex-convicts in New South Wales.[119] The business was risky because seizures often took place far away from home ports where the seamen and even the captain might decide they would be better off putting into some distant port, selling the cargo and the prize ship themselves, and running off with the proceeds, never to be seen again. There was little the investors could do about this risk because identification of culprits was virtually impossible, there being no fingerprinting, photography or identification numbers.

After signing up fifty crewmen, White left Table Bay on February 15, 1801.[120] He arrived at Port Jackson on April 13, where 480 gallons of spirits and a like quantity of wine were unloaded for sale to the settlers.[121] He turned these items over to John Black who was to remain in New South Wales for over a year disposing of the goods and spirits brought on both the *Harbinger* and *Chance*, some of which he consigned to Commissary John Palmer and Simeon Lord at Sydney, with another part sent to Norfolk Island. Black also spent some time trying to straighten out Hogan's affairs with Mark Flood and others concerning the Hawkesbury farm. Hogan expected Black to return to the Cape, bringing bills from the sale of the goods and spirits, but Black decided to stay in New South Wales where he had acquired some land in 1798.[122] Hogan was fortunate that all his wine and spirits were allowed to be landed for sale. During the fifteen months straddling the deliveries by Captains Black and White, sixty percent of the almost 90,000 gallons of wine and spirits brought into Port Jackson was turned away in an attempt to control liquor consumption in New South Wales.[123]

The *Chance* left Port Jackson in ballast for the coast of Peru after spending twelve days in port to add thirty-three additional crew members, probably former convicts who had been given their freedom. Four months later, after a fierce sea battle and an on-board man-to-man struggle, the much larger Spanish vessel *Amiable Maria* was captured near Lima, Peru, and a month after that the Spanish man-of-war *Limeno* was seized near Guayaquil, Ecuador, following another exchange of cannon fire. Captain White later reported the battles in a letter to Vice Admiral Curtis that was printed in *The Times* of London:[124]

Extract of letter from William White, commander of *Chance*, private ship of war fitted out at Cape of Good Hope to Vice Admiral Curtis.

At four p.m., on August 19 [1801], ...saw a large ship bearing down upon us. At nine brought her to close action, and engaged her within half pistol-shot for an hour and a half, but finding her metal much heavier than ours, and full of men, boarded her...and, after a desperate resistance of three-quarters of an hour, beat them off the upper deck; but they still defended from the cabin and lower deck with long pikes in a most gallant manner, till they had twenty-five men killed and twenty-eight wounded, of whom the captain was one. Getting final possession, she was so close to the island that with much difficulty we got her off shore.... She proved to be the new Spanish ship *Amiable Maria*, of about 600 tons, mounting fourteen guns, 18, 12 and 9-pounders, brass, and carrying 120 men, ...laden with corn, wine, bale goods, etc. On this occasion, I am much concerned to state Mr. Bennett, a very valuable and brave officer, was so dangerously wounded that he died three days after the action; the second and fourth mates, Marine officer, and two seamen badly wounded by pikes but since recovered. On the 20th, both ships being much disabled, and having more prisoners than crew, I stood close in and sent eighty-six on shore in the large ship's launch to Lima. We afterwards learned that seventeen of the wounded had died.

At 4 a.m. on September 24, standing in to cut out from the roads off [the island of] Puna in Guayaquil Bay, a ship I had information of, mounting twenty-two guns, fell in with a large Spanish brig, with a broad pendant at maintopmast-head. At five she commenced her fire on us, but she being at a distance to windward and desirous to bring her to close action, we received three broadsides before a shot was returned. At half-past five being yardarm and yardarm, commenced our fire with great effect and, after a very severe action of two hours and three-quarters, during the latter part of which she made every effort to get away, I had the honor to see the Spanish flag struck to the *Chance*. She proved to be the Spanish man-of-war brig *Limeno*, mounting eighteen long 6-pound guns, commanded by Commodore Don Philip de Martinez, the senior officer of the Spanish Marine on that coast, and manned with 140 men, sent from Guayaquil for the express purpose of taking the *Chance*, and then to proceed to the northward to take three English whalers laying in one of their ports. She had fourteen killed and seven wounded; the captain mortally wounded, who died two days after the action. The *Chance* had two men killed and one wounded, and had only fifty men at the commencement of the action; mounting sixteen guns, twelve and six-pounders.

White had put prize crews aboard both the *Limeno* and the *Amiable Maria* with instructions to sail the vessels to the Cape of Good Hope. The *Limeno* arrived safely on December 10th[125] and was condemned by the Vice Admiralty Court. White arrived in late January, surprised that the *Amiable Maria* had not yet reached the Cape; he thought it might have put into Sydney. Hogan had earlier told him: "Should you find it convenient to send any [prizes] to Port Jackson, I would recommend you to appoint Doctor John Harris and Mr. John Palmer the agents there, accountable to me for the proceeds of sales. But this is a matter that I would if possible wish you to avoid." Believing that the prize crew aboard the Spanish vessel might have taken this option for some reason, Hogan in April formally appointed Palmer and Harris, whom he had met while at Sydney in 1795, as his agents in New South Wales and gave them instructions for disposing of White's prize.[126] Hogan was not to learn of the true fate of the *Amiable Maria* until a year later.

The facts that Captain White reported his capture of the *Limeno* and *Amiable Maria* in a letter to Vice Admiral Curtis and that a leading British naval author writing in 1813[127] listed White's vessel as a "private ship of war" indicate not only that privateering was encouraged by the British authorities at the Cape of Good Hope but also that such private vessels were viewed as an extension of the British Navy.

Hogan appears to have engaged only the *Collector*, *Harriet*, *Harbinger* and *Chance* as active privateer ships on his own account, but he also acted as agent for owners of other active privateer vessels and for their prizes.[128] One was the *Salamander* (Captain Thomas Hopper), owned by a Mr. Mellish of London for whom Hogan acted as agent. This ship, described as a South Seas whaler, captured the *St. Josea Escabre*, a small Spanish vessel laden with beef, off the coast of Brazil on December 30 and the Spanish brigantine *St. Antonio de Ballena* off the coast of Patagonia the following February. The *Ballena* arrived at Table Bay in April and, with its cargo of bread and flour, was offered for sale by Hogan. The Corn Committee bought the bread and flour but initially refused to pay for them at their appraised values, which were less than the market prices claimed by Hogan. Hogan appealed this decision to Dundas who ordered the Commissioners on the Corn Committee to reconsider, which they refused to do.[129] Despite Hogan's efforts to obtain a better price, Mellish was not satisfied. Captain Hopper had convinced him that Hogan should have obtained the market price for the bread and flour. Hogan's personal agent in London was still arguing with Mellish on this point well into 1803, telling Hogan that he would "be glad to see all the *Ballena's* papers, however voluminous and the great the expense, that will serve to convince Mr. Mellish how little confidence he can place in the reports of her master regarding prizes."

Another aspect of Hogan's privateering-related activities was buying prize vessels or their cargos from others, sometimes in joint ventures with partners, and then reselling the ship or its cargoes or using the ship for his own purposes. Many of these prizes had been seized by British Navy ships and then sold with their cargoes to private buyers at the Cape, with the proceeds divided among the Navy claimants. The *De Drie Broeders* has already been mentioned. Another was the *Numero Seite*, a Spanish prize seized by a British Navy squadron off Île de France in 1800 and sold by Hogan for 22,461 rix dollars.[130] Others arose from a partnership arrangement with Donald Trail to purchase prize vessels for freighting or resale The first prize ship in the joint venture, the *Charlotte*, was sold at Calcutta in March 1799 for a profit of 30,000 sicca rupees. Another ship was the *Union*, one of several in which Hogan had an interest. The one in which Trail was also involved was probably a ship captured by Admiral Elphinstone's *Diomede* and acquired by Hogan in 1800.[131] In October he offered its cargo of "Carolina rice, in casks, cotton in bags, American staves, bullock's hides, fustick, deer skins, logwood, etc." for sale at his storehouse on Berg Street.[132] In December he felt obliged to have the *Union* inspected for seaworthiness because "some evil disposed person or persons [have] wantonly and without cause attempted to prevent the ship *Union*, belonging to me, from getting a freight to London by maliciously representing to those who had engaged to ship on her that she was unworthy of freight."[133] The *Union* was eventually sold on behalf of its several owners, each holding shares and receiving periodic distributions from Hogan and Trail. One of the owners was Bartholemew Cottam, Hogan's adversary as agent for claimants of cargo in the *Holger Danske* case. Hogan and Trail did not finally settle their accounts on the Union and *Charlotte* until 1804, long after Trail had left the Cape in 1799.

The war with France provided Hogan with other business opportunities. In 1798, the brash and confident, twenty-eight year old Napoleon Bonaparte, with his successes in Austria and Italy behind him and only Britain remaining as a viable enemy, eluded the British fleet in the Mediterranean and in July landed troops in Egypt.[134] The invasion was a carefully calculated strategy to threaten British interests in India and even Australia and thus cut off Britain's vital supply lines with these colonies. Moreover, French engineers were confident they could construct a canal connecting the Red Sea with the Mediterranean and thereby provide a direct sea passage between Europe, including French ports on the Mediterranean, and the Orient. If successful in either attempt, Britain would be left alone with no viable colonies in the East to supply its many needs. British possession of the Cape of Good Hope would become meaningless. The only real disadvantage to the scheme was that Napoleon could not take Egypt and invade England at the same time, but he had concluded, probably wisely, that an across-Channel invasion would be both costly and possibly unsuccessful. Nor did he think that Britain would seize the occasion of the French being occupied in Egypt to try any continental adventures of its own, a surmise that proved correct.

Napoleon and his generals achieved easy success in Egypt despite the difficulties of the desert terrain and non-existant local transport. The Ottoman rulers of Egypt relied on mamluk slaves for defense. They were a military oligarchy of white men raised to be warriors after being bought as children from impoverished peasant families in Georgia in the Caucasus. Their military feats and ferocity were legendary, but they were no match against the well-disciplined and much better armed French troops. The French easily took Alexandria and Cairo and were well on their way up the Nile when the British fleet in the Mediterranean under Rear Admiral Sir Horatio Nelson in August demolished most of the French fleet at anchor near Alexandria in the Battle of the Nile. Despite this naval victory and subsequent assistance provided to the mamluk warriors by Turkish troops, the French expanded their hold in Egypt and even advanced into Palestine. But in August 1799, Napoleon returned to France, leaving a hapless French general with vague but unfilled promises that help was on the way.

Although the French incursion in Egypt was a long way from the Cape of Good Hope, the potential risk to the Colony from a strong French presence in the East was not lost on its British residents. They responded in several ways. For example, a ship in which Hogan had a one-third interest, the *Hope* had been chartered by government to carry troops from the Colony to Madras in September 1798 in response to orders from London that the Colony send two regiments to reinforce the British presence in the event Napoleon might try to extend his Egyptian campaign to India.[135] Whether due to the India connection or to fear that the French were about to attack the Colony itself, a number of the British residents had sent a joint letter on January 5, 1799, to Acting Governor General Dundas offering their services. Hogan was one of the more than sixty signatories.[136]

Britain was more than a little alarmed by Napoleon's Egyptian excursion but was unwilling initially to commit anything more than Nelson's fleet to the battle, so concerned was it that Napoleon had returned to France to begin plans for an invasion of England. Steps were taken, however, to prevent any French incursion beyond Egypt by sending British Navy ships to blockade the Red Sea. It was felt that it was better to leave the French troops bottled up in Egypt than to evict them with the risk they might join other forces in Europe threatening England directly. This policy prevailed until October 1800 when Henry Dundas brought the Cabinet around to his point of view that the French must be evicted because otherwise France might remain in possession of Egypt, with its potential long-term threat to Britain's interests in the Orient, once peace came. The plan was to land troops in Egypt from the Mediterranean near Alexandria and from the Red Sea. In March 1801, British troops landed from the Mediterranean and forced the weakened, demoralized and sickly French troops to barricade themselves inside Alexandria.

Another force was secretly dispatched from England in December 1800 to land troops on the Red Sea coast of Egypt in support of another

CAPE OF GOOD HOPE, BRITISH OCCUPATION 131

contingent of ships and troops that was being sent from India. The British Navy fleet, consisting of five ships under the command of Captain Sir Home Riggs Popham on H.M.S. *Romney*, arrived at Table Bay on February 10. Their arrival had been predicted by the *Cape Town Gazette* as early as December 20 when it conjectured that "Manila might be the object of attack." Later, on March 7, the newspaper correctly conjectured that "the expedition is intended to join [British armed forces] in the Red Sea." The real intent could hardly have been withheld from the merchants at the Cape who were asked to provide supplies and support.

Hogan planned to use four ships in the Red Sea campaign, but only two of them completed their missions. They were the Spanish-built 203-ton *Regulus*, purchased after its arrival at Table Bay from Europe, and the 343-ton *Sea Nymph*, an American-built French prize seized by the Royal Navy near Île de France and then purchased by Hogan. With the help of his agent in Calcutta, Messrs Fairlie Gilmore & Company, he chartered the *Regulus* and *Sea Nymph* to government to carry troops and supplies from the Cape and Bengal to the Red Sea for the British Army and Navy. He placed Archibald McKellar (recently returned on the *Fanny* with its slaves from Mozambique) in command of the *Sea Nymph* and a man named J. Renton as captain of the *Regulus*.[137] Alexander Adamson, an associate of David Scott and Hogan's appointed agent in Bombay and the Malabar Coast of India, acted as supercargo on one of the ships and a young man named Scale was supercargo on the other.[138]

The two vessels that did not complete their missions were Hogan's *Fanny* and the *Montgomery*, the latter captured by the British Navy and then purchased by Hogan in 1801. The *Fanny* was to perform a commission received from Pringle on May 1 to carry wine and other supplies for the Red Sea expedition, but Pringle canceled the contract when the vessel was damaged on the banks of Lagullas during a local storm.[139] (The supplies were sent instead on the Hamburg ship *Adventura* in company with the East India Company ship *Tremendous*.) Hogan then sold the *Fanny* to Messrs Walker Robertson & Company for 3,500 rix dollars. This ship, in which John Elmslie seems to have had an interest, ran afoul of the British authorities in 1802 when it reportedly tried to smuggle goods obtained from Île de France at Mossel Bay and later was a total loss when it went on shore on Greenpoint near Cape Town in early 1803.[140] John Elmslie, a Scottish-born British citizen named in April 1801 as American consul at Cape Town, had been suspected of aiding American vessels to trade illicitly with Île de France.[141]

With regard to the *Montgomery*, Hogan had entered into a joint venture with Peter Thomas Richardson, his former clerk and probably a relation of his wife, who had joined a trading company at Madras, to use the vessel to ship goods valued at £12,300 from India to British forces in the Red Sea area. The venture reportedly failed because of "the effect of grog" on the supercargo, a man named Moore, or more likely because, by the time the *Montgomery* could have arrived late in 1801, most of the British forces had left the area.[142]

There was one additional arrangement that Hogan made that was to turn out sour—a private agreement directly with Popham to load additional supplies, including wine and brandy, on the *Regulus* and *Sea Nymph* to make the lives at sea of Popham and his senior officers more comfortable than they would otherwise have been. Although not part of the government contract, Hogan later tried to claim that Popham had obligated the Transport Board for the additional supplies. When advised that this argument was not legally supportable, he pursued the matter as a private debt of Popham. At one point, it was suggested that Lady Popham's furniture in London be seized to recover the debt, but Hogan graciously declined to be at odds with Popham's wife. In the end, it appears that Popham repaid most of the debt, except for two bills for £35 which Hogan was determined not to drop. In November 1802, he asked his agent in London to "have my demand made up with interest, presented to him the moment he lands in England by a lawyer and, if he refuses payment for one moment, that he will be lodged in gaol. It would be well to wait silently his arrival in London where spunging [*sic*] houses are at hand. [I trust] to your correctness and activity in punishing a man of his injustice and ingratitude." There was a sequel to this story. When Popham returned to England in 1803, he was charged by the Navy with padding his accounts for supplies, repairs and maintenance of his ships during and after the Red Sea campaign. The accusations made no mention of Hogan's possible involvement and, since two years later Popham was found innocent by Parliament after the Navy bungled its investigation, no firm conclusion can be drawn of the role Hogan may have played.[143]

Popham's main fleet left the Cape on March 1, 1801; two troopships and the *Sea Nymph* followed on March 30;[144] the *Regulus* sometime later. Altogether, the fleet carried 1,200 troops from the Cape Colony contingent.[145] Popham's fleet arrived in the Red Sea during the third week of May to find a contingent of Indian troops already there under the command of Major General David Baird. The troops were landed at Cossier on the Egyptian coast of the Red Sea,[146] marched northward along an ancient commercial route that had been used by the Romans to bring silk and spices from the Orient to Europe and arrived in Cairo on August 10, too late to take part in the campaign. Cairo had surrendered to British and friendly Turkish forces six weeks earlier and on September 2 the beleaguered French troops at Alexandria also surrendered. The French left Egypt completely by October 1801.

The Suez Canal was not dug: French engineers had erroneously reported that the Red Sea and the Mediterranean were at different levels. But the successful British campaign marked the beginning of a 150-year era during which Britain would maintain either a presence or active interest in the Near and Middle East.

As the Egyptian campaign came to a close, news was received at the Cape that would threaten forever to tarnish Michael Hogan.

FIVE

CAPE OF GOOD HOPE
THE INVESTIGATION

> *That Mr. Hogan was the person who planned and by means of his credit carried into execution... the whole of the illegal transaction..., the Commissioners cannot entertain a single doubt.*
>
> —Yonge Investigation Commission Report

In October 1801, General Dundas received an ominous letter dated five months earlier from Lord Robert Hobart, who had taken over Henry Dundas's ministry: "Accounts have reached me by different channels which, though of a private nature, are apparently entitled to the fullest credit, of a variety of abuses having taken place under the government of Sir George Yonge, tending to the injury and vexation of the inhabitants of the Colony, the prejudice of the interests of this country, and greatly affecting the honor and character of the British Government."

Dundas was told to institute an enquiry into five charges contained in an enclosed Minute against the governor, one of which involved "receiving from Mr. Hogan and appropriating to his own use a sum reputed to be £5,000 sterling for permission to import into the Cape 800 slaves." The Minute also included "two other transactions which [if true] involve in considerable guilt...those who were concerned in them." The first of these were "the captures made by the privateer the *Collector* [where] the guilt of all the parties directly or indirectly concerned in the illegal and piratical proceedings of this privateer is so enormous, the steps taken against her pretended prizes were so tardy and reluctant, that coupling these circumstances with that of none of the avowed delinquents having been prosecuted, it is impossible not to wish to see removed the suspicions that have in consequence arisen...."[1]

Yonge had, in large part, sealed his own fate by taking actions that could not but fail to be disapproved by London and by his persistent, almost paranoid, attacks against Macartney, General Dundas and anyone else whom he thought was standing in his way. The decisive factor may, however, have been letters written by Andrew Barnard to former Governor Macartney and by Lady Anne to Henry Dundas.[2] This is undoubtedly what Lord Hobart meant when he referred in his message to Dundas that: "Accounts have reached me by different channels which, though of a private nature, are apparently entitled to the fullest credit." The Barnards both had reason to dislike Yonge: Andrew because the governor had relieved him of responsibilities as colonial secretary that Macartney had willingly bestowed; and Lady Anne because Yonge had turned to Mrs. Blake to act as official hostess, a role she had gratefully assumed during Macartney's governance. Their letters recounted in detail the various misdeeds of Yonge. Hogan's involvement in the *Collector* incident and rumors of kickbacks to the governor's aides for allowing slave imports were also reported. Andrew Barnard characterized the *Collector* affair as "one of the most daring and barefaced acts of smuggling (not to call it a worse name) that ever was practiced upon the public." Lady Anne added further details: that Major Henry Erskine, an aide de camp and friend of the general, and his father-in-law, a wealthy Cape burgher named Arend de Waal, had shares in the *Collector,* and that Erskine's involvement "was the cause of Mr. Hogan's obtaining permission from the general to land slaves" on the first *Joaquim* venture in 1799. She also reported that "an exertion of power has lately been made in favor of a merchant [Yonge] is unconnected with, giving him not only liberty to import 1,600 [*sic*] slaves but to land here a supposed prize cargo (afterwards proved by Captain Campbell in the Court of Justice to be a smuggling transaction, not to use a harsher name to it, the slaves really having been purchased at Mozambique) that it is general believed that a *douceur* of no small magnitude was given to effect what, had it passed, would have put from ten to fifteen thousand pounds in the merchant's pocket whose privateer affected to have taken those slaves. You will naturally say how it happened that Mr. [Barnard], who knew how opposite it was to the ideas of government at home, ...he omitted to state its impropriety to the governor. Mr. Barnard actually did so, in the strongest terms—he also told the merchant he would oppose it—but found the governor deaf to all remonstrance or arguments, and as proof of his being anxious to avoid all further conversation or respectful opposition from Mr. Barnard, [Yonge] gave the order for the landing and selling of the slaves and all necessary arrangements himself, without bringing them through the [colonial] secretary's office as is customary."

Lady Anne's letter then identified the merchant as Hogan, but rather than castigating him on moral grounds, she told Dundas that the "present occasion calls on some little explanation of my ideas respecting [Mr. Hogan]. I feel singularly about him. I like the Man, though I think his abilities (which are excellent in my opinion) have too much invention and dexterity in them for a small place such as this, girt in by restrictions, yet holding forth temptations for enterprise, if the wheels which may counteract them can only be tied up from moving. I need not say more for I think you have here his character. He has many friends, is of mild manners, anxious to please and to oblige."

On October 24, Dundas formally appointed an investigation commission consisting of Brigadier General Thomas P. Vandeleur, John Pringle, Willem Stephanus Van Ryneveld (Fiscal), Edward Buckley (Civil Paymaster) and John Barrow (Auditor General) to ascertain the facts and, in the process, "observe an inviolable secrecy with respect to [the] proceedings."[3]

The commission began its activities on October 29 and completed its report in four and a half months in March 1802. Dundas sent it to London on April 5 without comment.[4] It found much to criticize in Yonge's improprieties during his eighteen-month stay at the Cape, including the payoffs that Blake and Cockburn demanded of Hogan for the slave imports and barracks contract; the wine and timber incidents; favored contracts given to Yonge's family and friends; the imposition of fees for clubs, public billiard tables and shooting game; the closing Cape Town's famous Company Gardens for the governor's personal use; and raising the duty on brandy. The commissioners reported that Hogan's "statement furnishes a painful and humiliating proof to what height of profligacy and depravity the persons immediately connected with the [governor] were carried when even to a stranger…they would have the audacity of proposing without shame or delicacy such disgraceful stipulations as appear upon the face of [the] statement." Hogan's statement is contained in one of the few document about slave imports that he did not destroy, the one entitled

"Communications made to the Secret Committee at the Cape of Good Hope relative to Sir George Yonge."

But the commission was not interested only in Yonge's duplicity or that of his henchmen, all of whom had long since left the Cape. It was the evidence collected and the conclusions drawn regarding Hogan's involvement in the *Collector* incident that was the most astounding and certainly the most damning to Hogan personally. Among the evidence collected was that Captain Smart had told Port Captain Campbell, after the true logbook had been discovered, that "Hogan had basely and falsely traduced his character, [and] he was determined to prove to the Court of Justice and to the world the villainy and the falsehood of Hogan, as [he] had not only been privy to the whole transaction...but had formed and arranged the whole plan"; that Hogan had been seen "in a very humiliating situation entreating [Smart] to abscond, otherwise the ruin of himself and his family would ensue"; that Hogan had told Smart, "How often must I tell you Smart that a still tongue makes a wise head"; that Tennant, Hogan's business partner, when asked by Smart what compensation he should demand from Hogan for absconding, suggested two thousand pounds, "which sum [Tennant] was further of opinion Hogan would not refuse him"; and, finally, that Hogan paid five or six thousand rix dollars to buy a small brig from the current owners of one of the two French prizes seized by the *Collector* on which Smart made his escape from the Cape. The commissioners ended with this unequivocal rebuke: "That Mr. Hogan was the person who planned and by means of his credit carried into execution through Smart the whole of the illegal transaction of his ship the *Collector*, the Commissioners cannot entertain a single doubt, but it does not appear from their enquiries that any other person was connected with him or had any interest in that ship, except the captain, officers and seamen, nor that any undue influence was used to attempt to bias the proceedings of the Court of Justice, though an attempt was certainly made to intimidate the Prosecutors and the Court from trying the cause."

The commissioners did not find Hogan at fault for the death of some of the slaves on board the ships that brought them to the Cape Colony, but this was small consolation. They did find that Hogan was the sole perpetrator, thus rejecting Anne Barnard's allegation that Major Erskine and Arend de Waal were involved as shareholders of the *Collector*. Nor did the commissioners consider Yonge's actions to be an attempt unduly to influence the Court of Justice.

Although Hogan had testified before the commission regarding his involvement with Yonge, Blake and Cockburn in the slave import business, he was apparently not asked to testify with regard to the *Collector* incident nor offered the opportunity to respond to the incriminating evidence that must have been supplied by Port Captain Campbell or other third parties. Hogan probably did not see the actual report and he may not have been aware of the rebuke against him, or at least of its severity. He may have assumed from the beginning of the inquiry that it was Yonge who was the target of the inquiry and that he was not in harm's way. After all, although the previous inquiry had ordered him to refund the money made from the public sale of slaves landed by the *Collector*, it had not found him criminally at fault. It would also have been in Hogan's character to assume that he would be found to be an innocent bystander. It is ironical that the crime for which he was found at fault had nothing to do with Yonge. When he initiated the fraudulent scheme by sending the *Collector* on its mission in March 1799, the license he had previously been given to import 400 slaves had just been canceled and Dundas advised that he was seeking the opinion of His Majesty's Minister upon "a subject of such national importance." He may have concluded that he was not going to receive any further official blessing to import slaves. The lure of huge profits from this activity must have been great, but he could not simply bring a vessel into port with slaves and hope to obtain permission to land them for sale. Such an act would not only have been perceived as defying Dundas but also might cast suspicion on him as a collaborator with the French in their reported scheme to bring slaves to the Cape under false colors in order to buy supplies for Île de France. By the time Governor Yonge arrived and he realized he could do business with him, the *Collector* plan was almost finished and it was, in any event, too late to stop the scheme. He could well have considered that he was merely trying to make a living despite official obstacles, not unlike the trading he did between India and Europe, in which he found willing collaborators in reputable quarters. "Why then," he might have said, "should I be pilloried when I acted on my own and harmed no person?"

An indication that Hogan believed the commission's report focused on Yonge and not on him can be found in the aftermath of the *Dispatch* affair. A month after the commission's report was sent to London, Hogan renewed his appeal to Dundas to be reimbursed for six months' use of the *Dispatch* commissioned by Yonge to carry his self-serving letters to London. It seems unlikely that he would have taken this action if he thought he was in disfavor with Dundas, who knew the content of the report. To the contrary, he might have believed the presumed condemnation of Yonge in the commission's report would have made Dundas more sympathetic to his plea. In any event, Hogan argued that, if the vessel had not been on government service, "he would have loaded her with merchandise, whereas on the contrary she had only barely enough to ballast her," and that "I must also take the liberty of stating that, between merchants, a single word is sufficiently binding for sums a thousand times the value of my demand, and that a denial of such engagement, which are everyday made, would be total ruin to the honor and credit of the person."[5] Dundas asked Hercules Ross, deputy colonial secretary, and William Parry Wallis, secretary to Vice Admiral Curtis, to look into the facts and submit a recommendation. Finding no written agreement but having "full confidence that the brig *Dispatch* was originally fitted out for [the] voyage with the express purpose of carrying Captain Tucker and the despatches of government to St. Helena," they recommended that Hogan be paid for three months use of the vessel—1,890 rix dollars, half the amount Hogan asked.[6]

While all this was happening, events in Europe were changing the international scene. In 1800, Pitt was replaced as prime minister by Henry Addington after incurring the disfavor of George III over his attempt to negotiate a union with Ireland. By then, Britain was once again without strong allies, all others having withdrawn or made their own peace arrangements with France. Addington had initiated peace negotiations, Britain's hand seemingly strengthened shortly thereafter by Nelson's defeat of the Danish fleet and final withdrawal of the French from Egypt. On October 1, 1801, preliminary articles toward a peace agreement were concluded. When the inhabitants at the Cape received this news in mid-December, their initial speculation was that Cape Town would become a free port.[7] The inhabitants did not learn until eight months later that the Treaty of Amiens, concluded on March 27, 1802, between Britain, on one side, and France, Spain and the Netherlands, on the other, would return the Cape of Good Hope to Dutch governance.

In the meantime, Hogan's business activities continued, unimpaired by either the Yonge investigation or the preliminary peace agreement. Even though by early 1802 Hogan could count dozens of seemingly successful business ventures during the previous four years involving not only slave trading and privateering but normal commercial transactions as well, the fortune he constantly sought was illusive. His immediate cause for concern was that he was in a net debit position with many individuals and agency houses. One reason was that he was not a well-organized businessman. Although he employed clerks to keep his books, a necessity when all letters and accounts had to be prepared by hand and even copies had to be painfully transcribed with quill and ink, and although he did business through established and well-known agencies at key locations in London, Calcutta, Bombay, Madras, Port Jackson, New York and elsewhere, most of the why's and wherefor's of his dealings were kept in his head. This may have been due to his personal character, but the more likely explanation is that he wanted to keep the details to himself because so many of his ventures required, or were thought to require, secrecy; if not that, they were often speculative in nature. He was a man who believed he could achieve any goal and whose experience at age thirty-five lent support to his belief.

He had several trusted clerks, notably Edward Lewis and Francis Fowkes. Fowkes had been a midshipman in the British Navy, serving in American waters about the same time as Hogan in 1782–83. He became a clerk in London, was sentenced for theft of a great coat and boots and transported to New South Wales on the first fleet in 1787. After serving a seven-year sentence, he acquired some land on the Hawkesbury River and must have met Hogan during his sojourn there in 1796. Fowkes went to the Cape in 1801, possibly at the request of Hogan who acted as his security.[8]

He found an overall business manager in a Scotsman at Cape Town named William Anderson, who would remain a faithful and loyal servant for some five years.[9] After clearing up Hogan's books at Cape Town as well as he could, Anderson realized that he would have to go to London to sort out credits and debits with the London agency houses. Shortly after Hogan's youngest daughter Sophia was born, he sailed from Simon's Bay on the *Friendship* (Captain Smith) on March 21, 1802, just a month after the Yonge investigation report was sent to London, with Hogan's ten year old son William and the cargo from the *Holger Danske* slated for sale in London. William was being sent back to England to attend school, as was then the custom. He was accompanied by a companion, but probably not the "little slave boy sent as a present" by his father from Madagascar in August 1799.[10] Although William's grandfather William Richardson had died in England three years earlier, and his grandmother Anna Maria had returned to India to live with her son, also a William, he would have other Richardsons to look after him.

Hogan had also established what he must have considered a trustworthy source for procuring slaves in Mozambique, a man named Joaquim do Rosário Monteiro, described as one of the "most substantial merchants" in Mozambique during the Napoleonic Wars, principally in the slave trade to Brazil.[11] The relationship probably went back to when Hogan first began slave trading with the *Joaquim* and *Collector* in 1799.[12] He would continue a close relationship with Monteiro for the remainder of his stay at the Cape Colony and probably thereafter.

With the Red Sea expedition finished, Hogan had the *Regulus* and *Sea Nymph* at his disposal toward the end of 1801. He had obtained letters of marque for both vessels[13] but decided instead to use them for different purposes, even though he could not have had much confidence in their captains, J. Renton and Archibald McKellar. One of them, probably Renton, had reportedly been "put in irons by Sir Home [Popham]" and both had been accused of being "blackguards and drunkards" while in the Red Sea. On its return voyage, the *Regulus* carried some cargo from the Red Sea area and picked up slaves, probably at Mozambique and probably with Monteiro's help. The ship returned to the Cape Colony on November 25, where its merchandise was offered for sale at auction on December 5,[14] and after loading Cape wine sailed via Ascension to the British Colony of Demerara (present day Guyana) in South America, where the slaves and wine were sold. Possibly because the local authorities might raise difficulties in unloading property clearly labeled "slaves," they had been listed in the ship's articles as seamen. One of them, named Remaldo, having a "certificate of baptism in his possession," had to be sent "home" after getting help from "some pretty pettifogging attorney." There were other difficulties with Captain Renton and with Hogan's agent on the ship, a man named King. The *Regulus* procured cargo in Jamaica and sailed for England where it arrived in July 1802 after an eleven week journey. Anderson thought at first he could obtain a contract from the Transport Board for the ship to carry supplies for British forces in the Mediterranean, but London shipping was then in oversupply due to decreased demand with the end of the war. Eventually, Anderson was forced to sell the *Regulus* for only £500.

The *Sea Nymph* on its return voyage stopped at Mozambique, according to the Portuguese governor "to save herself from some French privateers and to procure some succor she was in want of."[15] The vessel was there sold to Monteiro and given the Portuguese name *Ninfa do Mar,* which means "nymph of the sea." Two of the ship's officers later said that, "in consequence of the disasters which happened [to the *Sea Nymph*], it became necessary to sell her at [Mozambique] to save the owner (Mr. Hogan) from total loss, which must have been the case had not a sale of the ship been effected."[16] Although the details of what happened are not clear, it seems that Captain Archibald McKellar had something to do with deciding that the ship should be sold. It had apparently been reported to Hogan that McKellar had been killed, perhaps by a French privateer, but seven months later when another of his ships was at Mozambique he discovered that "Captain McKellar had preferred staying [at Mozambique] in the employ of a Portuguese. I learn he was too much ashamed to show his face here." Perhaps it had been reported that McKellar was dead in order to conceal his behavior from Hogan while he remained at Mozambique working for a Portuguese.[17]

Although Monteiro was clearly the new owner of the renamed *Ninfa do Mar,* Hogan wrote as though the *Sea Nymph* was still his, possibly indicating that he continued to have a financial interest in the ship's cargo. The *Ninfa do Mar* arrived at Cape Town on March 23, 1802, with upwards of 400 slaves destined for Rio de Janeiro.[18] Also on board was the retiring governor of Mozambique, Francesco Guedes de Carvalho Menezes, who on September 8 of the previous year had written a letter addressed to Yonge (not knowing he had left the Colony over three months earlier) stating that he proposed to touch at the Cape on his return to Lisbon to pay his compliments to the governor and "treat of some politic affairs concerning these two Governments."[19] What Acting Governor Dundas and the retired Portuguese governor had to say to one another when they met is not recorded. The Portuguese captain of the *Ninfa do Mar* asked for and obtained permission to land and sell forty of the slaves to defray port expenses, but was denied permission to sell an additional twelve for his own account.[20] Hogan sent instructions on the *Sea Nymph,* as he still called the ship, to two Portuguese merchants at Rio "to seize upon the person and property of [Antonio Janus] to enforce payment of his debt to me of 15,750 rix dollars with interest since November 1799," a debt that may have been incurred when the *Collector* was fraudulently shipping slaves from Mozambique to the Cape that year. The *Ninfa do Mar* returned to the Cape on January 28, 1803,[21] and continued to engage in the slave trade between Mozambique and South America for several years, but on these occasions clearly not in association with Hogan.

Hogan may or may not have been involved in the slave venture of the *Ninfa do Mar* in 1802, but he was certainly involved as an equal partner with Charles Joseph Guezzi in carrying 200 slaves from Mozambique to Montevideo during the same year on the Portuguese vessel *Louisa*. Guezzi had arrived at Cape Town on January 19, 1802, on board the Portuguese slave ship *Calypso*.[22] In a letter to Dundas requesting permission to land, Guezzi said he had practiced as a doctor in Mozambique for ten years and wished to sojourn for some months at the Cape to restore his health.[23] He carried a letter of recommendation from the new Mozambique Governor, General Izidro de Almeida Souza e Sa,[24] who had also addressed a letter to Yonge asking the governor "to deign lending all the aid and favor which [Domingos Joze Lopes, master and owner of the *Calypso*] may have occasion for, for the benefit of his commerce."[25] Acting on behalf of Guezzi, Hogan requested and obtained permission to land and sell twenty-five slaves from the *Calypso* to meet Guezzi's expenses on shore, as well as to bring on shore two Negroes and a mulatto as Guezzi's personal servants.[26] Dundas also gave Guezzi permission to export otherwise prohibited East Indies articles from the Colony to Brazil, saying he had "been induced in consideration of the particular circumstances of the case to shew his indulgence."[27] The main business of the ship, however, was the disposal of its slave cargo at the Cape Colony and here also Guezzi obtained a sympathetic response. On February 2, Dundas allowed the landing and sale of "300 slaves from the *Calypso*... because the speculation is shared between Walker & Robertson, who recently petitioned for and were refused permission to import a large number of slaves in accordance with a promise made to them by the late Governor [Yonge], and Mr. [George Frederik] Goetz to whom Government is indebted."[28] At the time Dundas granted this permission, the commission investigating Yonge had almost finished its deliberations. One has to wonder what persuaded Dundas to fulfill a promise made by the now discredited ex-governor or what service Goetz (a leading Dutch merchant at the Cape) had performed for which government was indebted. However, the important point for our story is that Hogan and Guezzi joined forces in promoting at least one recorded slave venture, that of the *Louisa* which stopped at the Cape Colony in May on its way from Mozambique to Montevideo. Two hundred slaves were sold there for 31,200 Spanish dollars, as well as the vessel itself.[29] A

Paul Roux was supercargo on the ship; when he returned to Cape Town on October 9, he handed Hogan a lump of pure gold weighing 46.95 ounces, received to settle a bill of exchange, for which he paid an additional 850 Spanish dollars for "the convenience of smuggling." Hogan sent it to Anderson in London via a returning British officer asking that Anderson "sell it immediately and, ...as I may be in receipt of gold and silver money from the same quarter, I wish to be informed particularly as to the value of bullion and all coins In London."[30]

During the first five months of 1802 alone, four ships had arrived at the Cape Colony from Mozambique, the *Joaquim*, *Calypso*, *Ninfa do Mar* and *Louisa*, carrying some 1,350 slaves, all but 340 of them transported to Rio de Janeiro and Montevideo. As will be seen, the Atlantic slave trade from the east coast of Africa, particularly to the east coast of South America, had become big business. After it was learned at the Cape that peace was to reign and the Colony returned to the Dutch, there would be other Hogan slave ventures involving Mozambique and both the Cape Colony and the Americas.

Hogan's business efforts were also focused on reaping the profits he expected from the seizure of the *Holger Danske*. It is impossible to piece together the full story because of the legal complexity of the case, the fact that insurance was involved and incomplete records.[31] The Vice Admiralty Court at the Cape decided that the vessel should be restored to its owners, Duntzfeldt & Company of Copenhagen. It was sold by auction at Simon's Bay on August 22, 1801, at its appraised value of 15,010 rix dollars to Messrs Walker Robertson & Company acting on behalf of William Lennox, a senior partner in Messrs David Scott & Company of London. The ship was renamed *Castle of Good Hope* and sent to Bengal (with letters of marque) to procure a cargo of rice destined for England.[32]

The facts surrounding disposition of the cargo on the vessel are anything but clear. The owners of the cargo, also Messrs Deconnick & Company of Copenhagen, acting through its newly named Cape Town agent, Bartholemew Cottam, acknowledged that goods had been boarded at Batavia but asserted that this portion had already been unloaded elsewhere. Cottam tried to influence the Vice Admiralty Court by introducing a letter from Deconnick's agent and correspondent in London, none other than the David Scott company, addressed to Cottam containing the following seemingly gratuitous remark: "They [David Scott Company] trust [recent political developments in the

Northern Confederacy] would operate in the mind of the [Vice Admiralty] Court and prevent any precipitous decision taking place relative to the cargo of the *Holger Danske*."[33] Hogan must have questioned in his mind whether the Scott company did not have a conflict of interest, representing both itself and the owner of the Danish ship's cargo, and he may even have wondered if the Scott company had played some role in the voyage of the *Holger Danske* itself because it had acted in other transactions as London agent for the ship's owners, Duntzfeldt & Company. These suspicions may not have had any basis in fact, but Hogan would later learn beyond a shadow of doubt that Lennox was masterminding an attempt to undermine his character.

In the end, the Vice Admiralty Court condemned the cargo and awarded it to the captors, that is, Captain White, Hogan and the other shareholders in the *Harriet* enterprise. But the Court ruled that the captors would have to remit to the owners of the cargo, from the proceeds of its sale, the cost of freighting the cargo from Batavia to the Cape. There was also on board a larger than usual consignment of goods belonging to its Captain Smit, described as the *Master's Private Adventure*, and this portion the Court condemned but restored to Smit. There is no record why the Court reached these varied decisions, which were rendered sometime before May. The owners of the ship's cargo (the claimants) filed a notice of intent to appeal against the award of the cargo to its captors, while the captors filed a similar notice against the award of freight cost to the claimants and the award of the Master's Private Adventure to Smit. Cottam acted as agent for the claimants in the former action, while Hogan acted as agent for the captors in the latter two actions. The appeals could only be pursued by filing the necessary law documents with the High Court of Admiralty in London.

Hogan requested permission from Dundas on November 5 to sell the cargo of the *Holger Danske* at the Cape "for export to London." The latter phrase was an euphemism for an argument Hogan later advanced in a deposition dated December 26 that, despite the ruling that goods imported from the East could not be sold for local consumption unless brought in by the East India Company or with its approval, he should be allowed to sell all the cargo at the Cape, there being no loss of foreign exchange since local buyers held their funds in Britain in any case. Both Hogan and Cottam were allowed to sell for local consumption those portions of cargo that had been damaged or were perishing in order to pay for some 25,000 rix dollars of warehousing and other local expenses. The sale took place at Simon's

Town on March 3, 1802, the items consisting of sugar and coffee, cloves, nutmegs, pepper, camphor, cotton yarn, indigo, sago, curcuma, cardamum and 30 leaguers of arrack. The rest of the cargo was shipped to London with Anderson on the *Friendship*, as has been noted.

Anderson reached London in early June. The investigation commission's report probably reached London about the same time. It was quickly buried. The British Government considered it expedient not to draw attention to Yonge's mismanagement of the Cape Colony under British rule when it was about to be restored to the Dutch. Moreover, it may have been thought to be imprudent publically to cast aspersions on Yonge, who continued to be a favorite of King George III. Neither Yonge, Blake nor Cockburn was ever charged with wrongdoing. Hogan was an unintended beneficiary of the decision not to make the report public, even though its nature was undoubtedly known to influential persons at the Cape and in London. Some historical reviews written years later characterize Hogan as notorious or infamous, and no doubt some thought ill of him at the time, but there is ample evidence that he continued to enjoy business and social standing during his remaining time in the Colony. Perhaps, after news of the peace negotiations was received, past questions of prestige and repute were put aside as all British residents faced in common an uncertain future.

On his arrival, Anderson told Hogan that his son William "is now in high health and spirits, very busy with the purchases for his sisters at the Cape," which turned out to be "some boxes full of toys." Hogan's brother, Captain Dennis Hogan, "offered his services to accompany William to St. Albans" school in Middlesbrough in York. William later recalled "the church roof being tumbled in, boxing, fencing and genteel card playing." After a year, he transferred to Harrow near London where he stayed for three years. Hogan continued to be plagued by his brother, nominally with the Dragoons, seemingly always malingering, whether in London, Yorkshire, or the sulfurous waters of Harrogate in Durham, and asking for money, such as £120 annually to care for William. At one point, Hogan warned Anderson "not [to] trust the key [to the wine cellar] to my brother least he should collect soldiers in way to dinner." Hogan also occasionally asked after his four nephews, whom he continued to support, including the youngest, another Michael Hogan.

Anderson's first letter to Hogan said he was "much harried." He was indeed harried for his main task was to untangle Hogan's accounts, principally with Messrs David Scott & Company which, Anderson learned, was in trouble. He had heard from a passing ship on his way to England of "the downfall of the great house [of David Scott] and the shocking fall of poor Mr. [Lennox]. He must have been a man of uncommon fine feelings to have taken this desperate resolution in so early a stage of their [word intentionally crossed out], at least when there might remain some hopes, with his ability, of supporting the [word intentionally crossed out]. But now I can form no idea in what situation their affairs may be on our arrival. A Committee of Inspection sworn to secrecy had declared the House solvent, and they had resumed payments, but the surviving members of the firm are not even known to, much less in the confidence of, their enormous India constituents. I do not see how it can exist twelve months longer. I was much pleased at receiving this intelligence so easily. I shall be better prepared to take such measures as this unexpected change may render proper."

It was undoubtedly Hogan who "intentionally crossed out" the two words to conceal the true nature of some venture, probably the one involving the *Holger Danske*. It would not be the first concealment involving the prize vessel.

Anderson found that the Scott company was not in as bad shape as he had first been led to believe. After concluding that he had forever lost his battle with the old shipping interests in the East India Company, David Scott, Senior, had resigned his directorship in September 1801 and returned as a partner in Messrs David Scott Junior & Company in April 1802. He later wrote that "the death of Mr. Lennox rendered it necessary for me, owing to my son's not being of age, to stand forward again as a merchant and establish the House anew under my own name."[34] Anderson reported that, when he held his first meeting with the House in June, "I met with a kind and rather flattering reception which was the more pleasing as it was so very unexpected. What a pity that Lennox should have hurried himself so precipitously into the other world as there does not appear to have been the smallest reason for so rash an action as far is regarded the solvency of the House…. I was introduced to all the new members and Mr. Scott who happened to be in the office. He made a number of kind inquiries about your family…. I can say nothing about your accounts with them until the next opportunity. They appear to me very indifferent now about this immense balance…."

But Anderson discovered two things which were disquieting. The most immediate was that William Lennox, who had died (Anderson implied by suicide) on February 14,[35] had made known in London his distaste for the conduct of Michael Hogan. Although the incident or incidents which led to this are not recorded, details of the *Collector* incident, as well as insinuations involving seizure of the *Holger Danske*, were more than likely circulating among the well-informed in London and may have been the cause of Lennox's verbal assault. They were probably also the cause of the Scott company's conflict of interest in appearing to support Deconnick & Company against Hogan's claims on the *Holger Danske*. It was on this occasion that Anderson wrote to Hogan that he had responded to the "[allegation] of your fitting out a privateer on purpose to take the *Holger Danske*, [that] it was too absurd to call for confutation." As for Lennox's general conduct, he told Hogan that "I observe what you say of [the firm's] infamous and unwarrantable conduct circulating the most mutinous reports to the prejudice of your credit and character, particularly Mr. [Lennox] who it seems was lately very lavish of personal abuse of you from sheer habit and never could mention your name without bursting out with most violent imprecations and the foulest calumnies. But the world, my friend, are now convinced that these were only the ravings of a madman whose conduct, in many instances previous to his death, his own friends lament bitterly should have even seen the light...."

Hogan himself was less certain that other members of the House were not also against him. He wrote to Anderson in the injured, and sometimes incomprehensible, terms to which anger so often led him, saying "I cannot consent to any compromise with people who have so much injured me as the House of D. Scott Junior & Company. No [bit of] slander puts the scourge equal to the one that is whipped and none so easy to punish as a person remote unsupported by any mercantile interest or connection to say one word in his defense but generally and slightly known. The tongue of slander when set going by the powerful influence of that House is too much to bear up against and, as the present firm have by their circular letter in my possession, taken upon themselves all the responsibility of the former, I shall take from them nothing short of what the law gives in the [*Holger Danske*] case, which I hope you will prosecute with vigor. In other respects, their senior [David Scott] shall answer to me...."

The remaining page or pages of this letter are missing; perhaps because they contain an explanation of Hogan's real involvement in the *Holger Danske* incident which he wanted to hide forever.

Anderson retained counsel and, with the help of David Ponterdant, did all he could to press for a favorable outcome. Ponterdant had been an officer in the Vice Admiralty Court at Cape Town but had been dismissed by Judge Holland in April 1800 and sent back to England after running afoul of British officials because of the role he played in the dispute whether the East India Company's monopoly extended to goods shipped to the Cape from the East. A Customs official, Henry James Jessup, and an Irish attorney named Peter Mosse had taken conflicting positions, and Ponterdant's attempt to conciliate the dispute was regarded as an unwarranted attempt to silence Jessup. Mosse and Ponterdant were declared *persona non grata* in the affair, which Anne Barnard described as a "strange higgledy-piggledy business"; she also thought the punishment unfair in the case of Ponterdant. Jessup was merely suspended from his position in the Customs House.[36]

Before Ponterdant became a Hogan confidante after Anderson's arrival in London, he had been one of the persons complaining to official London of Yonge's conduct at the Cape of Good Hope. He had also sought an appointment as British consul at Cape Town, now that the Colony was to be restored to the Dutch, a request that seems to have been disregarded.[37]

Anderson and Ponterdant were successful in instituting an appeal action on the freight issue by serving an unchallenged intention to do so on the claimants, but apparently did nothing to appeal the personal award to Smit. The appeals could not be pursued until officially notarized law documents had been received from the Cape, and for some reason Hogan did not send them until March 9, 1803; he did not even send a full set of copies of the Vice Admiralty Court documents prepared by notary public Thomas Wittenoon until July 1802, by which time counsel for the claimants had already been armed with their copies.

Anderson was not sanguine that Hogan would prevail on appeal. On June 27 he wrote: "The rage for condemnation in similar cases is not yet entirely subsided in this country, but when tranquility is restored in Europe and the utmost harmony prevails between us and the Northern Powers, the interference of their ministers will have greater weight and more delicacy observed throughout in all our arrangement with them." He was referring to the brief *detente* between Britain and Denmark, following the Battle of Copenhagen, that lasted until 1807. Anderson also reported to Hogan on July 28 that Mr. Innes of the Scott firm "observed that he was sorry the [cargo of the *Holger Danske*] should be burdened with further expense, as he was clear the *bona fides* belonged to those who claimed it." Aside from the legal maneuvering, the only action taken was the sale of the ship's cargo at a London auction on August 16 for £40,000, after payment of costs, with the funds placed in escrow pending the expected appeals.

However, the claimants did not formally press their appeal. Anderson was able to write to Hogan on January 8, 1803 (a letter not received until March 28): "...we have ascertained that, no appeal having ever been lodged here against the sentence pronounced at the Cape condemning the Joint Adventure of the Master as lawful prize to the *Harriet*, the proceeds...do therefore belong to the Captain [White, and of course Hogan]." But Anderson also had to tell Hogan that "The Master's [private] adventure is in the same situation with respect to the captors. It was restored [to Smit] and no appeal being lodged in time, the opportunity was lost before I arrived." He then added, "It runs in Mr. Ponterdant's head that there was some private agreement between yourself and the Master [Smit] which, if this [is the case], I am quite ignorant."

Because there is no record of a decision by the High Court of Admiralty on the remaining issue of the freight, and because Hogan was writing to Anderson as early as 1804 about a dispute with Captain White over his share of the prize money, it is likely that there was no effective appeal here either, which meant that all the original decisions of the Vice Admiralty Court remained unchanged.

That Hogan profited from the *Holger Danske* is certain. If the agreement among the shareholders in the *Harriet* enterprise was similar to the one he later executed for the *Chance's* venture off Peru, Hogan would have received two-thirds of the net profits, which would be about £20,000. But the full story, including several unanswered questions, must remain a mystery. Was there a secret, private arrangement between Hogan and Smit which persuaded Hogan not to press his appeal in this case? Why did six months pass from the time the *Holger Danske* was at Table Bay after being seized until the knowledge its captain and officers had about the illicit activities of the *Collector* come to official light? Why was William Lennox, Hogan's nemesis at Messrs David Scott & Company, the purchaser of the *Holger Danske*? Was Lennox acting behind David Scott's back in the whole affair? Was it even possible that the David Scott firm itself was involved, perhaps in trying to protect its reportedly illicit trading activities carried out through both the Deconnick and Duntzfeldt companies?[38]

One can also read between the lines of the letters Hogan and Anderson exchanged at this time to implicate several officers of the Vice Admiralty Court, including its Judge, John Holland, and its Marshal, George Rex. Officers of the court were paid very little and, except apparently for the presiding judge, were allowed to earn additional income from outside activities. George Rex, for example, who sired a large family without benefit of a recorded marriage, would not have been above accepting money for official favors. (He was thought for many years to be an illegitimate son of King George III, a rumor recently proven to be false.)[39] Although there is no direct evidence that court officers were improperly involved or benefitted on either side of the *Holger Danske* case, the unanswered questions and conundrums seem to point to further complicity somewhere.

Anderson's other disquieting discovery on arrival in London was that he could not pay off Hogan's various debit balances as they were falling due. He was principally in debt to Messrs David Scott & Company, but there were many other claimants, such as Mellish who wanted more from the *Salamander's* prizes than Hogan thought he was due. He was not only woefully short of cash but also having difficulty in receiving various amounts owed to him, such as some £5,360 from a Mr. William Kenyon of New York for spices shipped by Hogan from the Cape to Boston on the American ship *Lapwing* in December 1800;[40] £118 advanced by Hogan in the same month to pay expenses of the *Joseph Harvey* at the Cape, a brig owned by Robert Lenox of New York;[41] money owed by the Transport Board for the voyages of the *Sea Nymph* and *Regulus* in the Red Sea Expedition; settlement of several accounts involving the *Fanny's* voyage to India to procure rice in 1801;[42] insurance for damage done to the *Marquis Cornwallis* in the English Channel; and a number of other items. (Robert Lenox, no relation to the late William Lennox, was to be a central figure in Hogan's business affairs later in New York.) Anderson frequently remonstrated with Hogan to send him more cash and, above all, avoid speculative ventures. He was concerned that Hogan would never receive the full amount of some of the credits appearing on his accounts because of his penchant for relying on oral agreements, some of dubious character.

To add insult to injury, the usual temperate Anderson was furious when Hogan asked him to advance £2,500 to his brother Dennis for some unstated, but apparently nebulous, project. He accused Hogan of disregarding "the fairest jewel in a merchants cap, his credit and reputation. For instead of supporting that high respectability which the present posture of your efforts enable you to do, and which is especially necessary to extricate your character from foul calumny, you seem determined unnecessarily to involve your credit, render all my poor exertions of no avail and destroy the fondest wish of my heart."

Anderson was not without ideas for new Hogan ventures. He had become entranced with the then plentiful turtles on Ascension island on his way to England and had told Hogan: "I have often thought the *Harriet* schooner would make a good turtle ship, though rather small. When properly filled up, she would carry I suppose 150 or 200 turtles." Turtle dishes were then quite popular at the Cape of Good Hope. But instead Hogan chartered the vessel, which had been returned to him after being taken at Île de France, to government for 2,500 rix dollars in April to carry cargo to Algoa Bay on the east coast. While there in May, the vessel was driven on shore by a storm and damaged beyond repair. Its long boat was taken by H.M.S. *Penguin* for use by the garrison at Algoa Bay, for which Hogan later sought 340 rix dollars in reimbursement.[43]

Fortunately, the Scott house did not press for immediate payment; it did not even present a full accounting until the end of 1802 when a net debit of only some £4,000 was shown. By that time, Anderson had been able to raise enough in bills and cash to clear the account with Scott from transactions in London, from Hogan's agents in Calcutta and by retaining Robert Lenox in New York to force payment of Kenyon's debt. Nor was Hogan's reputation in London in as much disrepute as Anderson had thought. He wrote to Hogan in January 1803 that "the present members [of David Scott & Company]...have uniformly shown a wish of settling all your accounts amicably and, so far from discovering any symptoms of precipitate hurry, although the balance is still in their favor, I have never yet been asked when it was to be paid." Anderson could not refrain, however, from noting his own moderation toward the Scott firm and admonishing Hogan that "I should have been glad had the same moderation marked your own proceedings since I left the Cape."

Hogan had also become active in the retail business at Cape Town. Its merchants regularly offered goods they had imported or purchased from prize vessels for sale to the public. There were no retail stores as known today; merchants advertized in the *Cape Town Gazette and*

African Advertiser for public or private sale of goods or by auction, with sales taking place in their homes, storehouses or packhouses or sometimes at the Commercial Coffee House. Most auctions were conducted by Matthiessen, Vendue Master, who had purchased the right to this title and to receive auction commissions. Hogan's advertisements, offering a wide assortment of goods at his storehouses, appeared frequently.

For several months in 1801, he regularly sold goods on Tuesdays and Fridays of every week. A fire in his wool store on July 16 "fortunately," according to the *Gazette*, "was prevented from doing any considerable damage by the timely exertions of the inhabitants," and the regular Tuesday and Friday weekly auction sales were quickly resumed in a month.

Sometimes, he would have an entire ship's cargo to sell, such as that of the *Phœnix* advertized on August 14, 1802, listing names of products and measures no longer familiar to most people:

Irish mess beef and pork in tierces and barrels, of excellent quality. Salt cod and ling fish in good order. Irish and English butter in firkins. Brown stout porter and ale in hogsheads and half hogsheads. Port wine and sherry in six dozen chests. Ditto in pipes. 30 boxes of window glass, of sizes. 3 cases looking glasses. 1 case of cutlery of sorts. 7 cases of ladies and gentlemen's assorted hats. 2 chests and 1 bale of slops assorted. 1 chest of men's shoes. 1 trunk of gentlemen's fine shoes. 2 bales of Osnaburgs. 1 bale of white counterpanes and blankets. 2 bales of duffels and coarse broad cloths. 1 bale of fashionable waistcoat shapes. 8 cases and 2 casks of earthenware of sorts. 4 cases of paper hangings for rooms, of fashionable patterns. 3 cases with waggon harness for 24 horses compleat. 1 case with 3 hunting and 3 side saddles. 2 trunks of haberdashery. 2 cases of assorted stationary. 2 cases of pocket books, purses and sundries. 50 kegs of black varnish. 17 casks and cases of ships chandlery of all sorts. 11 cases and casks of tinware of sorts, pewter ware, japanned ware, and Britannia metal wares. 2 boxes of gold leaf. 12 cart wheels with iron axles. 2 chamber organs, with a quantity of music. 1 table clock. 1 gold repeater and 2 plain watches. A phaeton with harness, of the newest fashion.

Two days after this announcement, the *Gazette* reported that the Treaty of Amiens had been signed returning the Cape Colony to the Dutch, with no guarantee that Cape Town would be a free port.

SIX

CAPE OF GOOD HOPE UNDER DUTCH RESTORATION

> *I hope however to be with you before Christmas.*
> *I would sooner, but must go to Mozambique*
> *to recover what no one can do for me,*
> *for agents are unequal to the task of*
> *settling and recovering on a rogue.*
>
> —Hogan to William Anderson

Anderson was aware when he arrived in London that the Treaty of Amiens had been concluded and that the Cape of Good Hope would soon return to Dutch governance. But no one at the Cape yet knew this; they only knew that preliminary agreement had been reached to return the Colony to the Dutch. In a letter sent on July 7, Hogan told Anderson that the Colony was "without a line or any arrival from England, Bengal or Madras, and as you may conceive [we are] in the most anxious expectation. Property is of no use nor a bill of any sort to be had under 25 to 30 or 32% and that [only] as matter of great favor." Some of the Dutch merchants were already making plans to send ships to Île de France and Batavia, the reports of which alarmed Pringle greatly.[1] Finally, on August 12, 1802, an English frigate arrived with the news, which appeared in the *Cape Town Gazette* four days later, that the Treaty of Amiens had been signed returning the Cape Colony to the Dutch. The time for restoration was set at daybreak on January 1, just twenty weeks away. The British inhabitants were in a state of shock. They certainly knew that Britain had disclaimed an intention of keeping the Colony when it was seized from the Dutch seven years earlier, but they must have thought that this attitude had changed when British merchants were encouraged to reside at the Colony and when Governor Macartney had urged that the Colony remain a British possession after the war. They had thought the expected peace agreement would make Cape Town a free port. But the fact that peace had been restored or that the Netherlands, insofar as it was represented by the Prince of Orange in exile, was a nominal ally of Britain mattered little. To the local British residents and the anti-Jacobin Dutch, it was the Batavian Republic, allied with Jacobin France, that would govern at the Cape Colony. The treaty must have seemed doubly strange to Hogan, for the British negotiator was none other than his patron and presumed hero, Lord Charles Cornwallis. But, in a perverse sense, he might have viewed the news as a good omen, for it might mean that no action could now be taken against him as a result of the *Collector* affair.

Normally peace would be received as good news, but many of the British merchants at the Cape not only dreaded living under Dutch governance but also believed that business prospects at the Cape, so dependent on the war for the past six years, would now dry up. The British forces and many British merchants at the Cape therefore made plans to leave. Hogan, perhaps accustomed to dealing with a variety of different nationalities from his travels to many countries, did not act particularly concerned, though he had several reasons to be apprehensive. He would not receive his first letter from Anderson in London reporting on his several accounts until October 8. Moreover, he had complained in early July that, "I have been on my beam now with [gout] in both legs for twelve days," and it might still have been plaguing him.[2] But with everyone else he wanted to send his family back to England as soon as possible before leaving himself. He made arrangements for Frances and his three daughters to return to England on the East India Company ship *Tremendous*, taking with them "part of the [silver] plate and best of her linens," while he would remain a while to tend to remaining business. He told Anderson on October 11 that "God knows when or what sort of craft I may go home in. I am however using my best endeavors to get clear of what I have here and I doubt not of selling the house and stores to advantage as soon as the Dutch Government is established, for which I am heartily anxious, for the sooner we have a change the better."

Hogan also wrote that Admiral Sir Roger Curtis had "spent a week with us on the return of the squadron from Simon's Bay and was in better spirits than he had been for many months." Curtis had asked for the meeting on September 26, telling Hogan that he would like to journey to Cape Town "to ask a favor of you [and] solicit your assistance." Curtis's visit may have been purely social, or perhaps the admiral was seeking a private loan; Hogan was fond of helping out his Navy friends and fellow seamen. A more likely explanation is that Curtis wanted Hogan's advice on how to arrange for private ships to help transport some 7,000 troops and government servants to India or back to England, there being few troopships to effect the evacuation.

When Anderson received Hogan's letter, he replied that he was "sorry to observe that your attachment to your worthy naval friends is stronger that ever; while your obligations are less." Whether this speculation is true or not, Hogan secured a contract from Pringle in November to provide wine, vinegar, sails, awnings and cooking kettles for 930 troops being carried to Bengal on several ships, including the *Milford, Manhattan, Phœnix* and *President*.[3] Judging from how closely he reported the evacuation to Anderson, he may have been involved as a middleman in many other ways. He also told Anderson, after sending his trusted assistant Edward Lewis to Calcutta, that "you will hear from him on his arrival there and I hope to satisfaction. Such steps are very painful though very necessary." The nature of Lewis's activities in India is not known.

In the same October 11 letter, Hogan reported: "Since the [British] garrison was withdrawn from Algoa Bay, the Kaffirs [Xhosa acting as auxiliary police] have made rapid marches toward the Boers. In consequence, the troops have halted halfway from Graaf-Reinet. [The Kaffirs] swear they will leave no Boer in that country and that they value none but English soldiers. The Dutch troops must be active when they arrive to keep this country in indifferent order, for even the inhabitants of this town now begin to seriously regret the approaching change. The Dutch officers are to be billeted on them and 3 skillings a day is already established as the board and lodging money to be paid by people of their own country, which is not satisfactory. [The inhabitants] have, however, risen it to 4 rix dollars for the English as a mark of parting favor."

Hogan did not abandon business during his final months at the Cape of Good Hope, particularly his renewed interest in the slave trade. He had Captain William White in mind for another slave venture. White had returned to the Cape on January 21 following his successful privateering cruise off the west coast of South America, but there had been no news of the fate of his prize, the *Amiable Maria*. Much later Hogan learned that the vessel "came close in with this land in a strong

Southeaster.... She had a boisterous passage across [the Indian Ocean]; ill-managed, many of her crew died of the cold; she reached Walvis Bay where she anchored; Mr. Jordan and McPherson with the crew abandoned her; in about 15 days she parted, went on shore on the point of rocks and soon after to pieces. Jordan quarreled with the natives who speared and killed him, McPherson and two others. Some made their escape.... She was a very large and valuable ship and totally lost from misconduct. They were forever in a state of intoxication and Mr. Jordan was constantly asleep in his watch, which was the chief cause of their missing this Bay." The news had taken a year to reach him even though Walvis Bay is only 800 miles from Cape Town!

The ultimate disposition of the *Chance* after its arrival at Table Bay is unrecorded, but Hogan was entranced with White's prize, the *Limeno*, which had come into Table Bay the preceding December. He had first offered her for sale at public auction on January 5, describing the vessel as "built in Cartagena, Spain, for the King's service, about six years ago, had a complete repair at Guayaquil [Ecuador] in August last year, where she was new coppered, is an uncommon fast sailer, and a very beautiful and compleat vessel, about 360 tons measurement, well-calculated for any trade where despatch and a light draft of water [are] required."[4] Instead of selling the ship, however, he renamed her the *Felis Eugenia*, put her under Portuguese colors with a nominal Portuguese Captain, F.J. Costa, and at mid-year sent her with White in real command and a man named Rillas on board to procure slaves at Mozambique for shipment to Surinam. The ship would then sail to London with produce procured in the West Indies, just as the *Regulus* had done the previous year.[5]

The venture did not go smoothly. Hogan received word in October that "Mr. Rillas is safe at Mozambique, being picked off an island [i.e., captured] by a French brig and carried to the Mauritius. White made a passage of twelve days to [Mozambique] but struck on a rock that shivered his keel and obliged him to careen the ship to put on a new one." White told Hogan he still expected to get to the Cape in November with a cargo of slaves. But he did not put to sea until November 10 and even then he had not finally left Mozambique. The finale to this "great cruise," as Anderson called it, would be played out during the last days of 1802 and early the following year.

Hogan continued to talk of having to return to England because of the upcoming Dutch restoration, but he may have hoped that peace would allow him to stay at the Cape Colony for a further period of time. His seeming lack of real concern was misplaced because trouble was again brewing in Europe. The terms of the Amiens treaty were widely criticized in the British Parliament and elsewhere. English merchants were particularly upset that commercial rights to trade with the continent had not been restored by the treaty and that France had refused to do so in subsequent negotiations. It soon became apparent that Napoleon's cold war strategy was to close the continent to British shipping and trade and to continue his military and political encroachment not only in Europe but in the New World as well. (Even before the treaty had been signed, news had been received in London of Napoleon's acquisition of Louisiana from Spain.) The First Consul—he would be declared Emperor within a year—became so inflamed when an English newspaper criticized his behavior and actions that he demanded British censorship of its own press. In October, Anderson reflected on these events and the view of many Englishmen when he wrote in a letter to Hogan:

> Between this country and France there seems to exist the same animosity and hatred as during the War. Our Ministry [under Henry Addington] have discovered, from their first coming into power, the greatest weakness and imbecility and, unless speedily removed, Bonaparte will dictate the terms of the Commissariat [commercial] Treaty in the same stench as the Treaty of [Amiens]. So jealous he is of the introduction of British manufactures into his territories that the most positive orders have been spread to watch the frontiers with redoubled vigilance. No English newspapers are allowed to be read in France and it is rumored that a formal remonstration is to be made to our court against the freedoms of the British press. In short, so rapid and gigantic are the strides which the Chief Consul is making, gaining more by negotiation than even his boasted conquests in Italy, that unless he receives a timely check, we shall feel the same necessity with other defeated nations to bow the neck to his overgrown power. We shall certainly have a new Ministry after the meeting [of Parliament]. It is the only thing that can save the nation.

In the same letter, Anderson, after hoping "the voyage you have planned for White...will turn out advantageous, if he gets to his destination," said he was "amazed at the sum you are in advance to [Joaquim do Rosário] Monteiro & [Charles Joseph] Guezzi if you mean it exclusive of the old balance (which can hardly be the case). No wonder you should be short of cash, but I would earnestly recommend your avoiding an extension of joint concerns in that quarter, however advantageous they may appear and not in the least doubting the integrity of the parties as, on leaving the Cape, you may experience much difficulty in winding them up."

While still waiting for Captain White to arrive, the Portuguese ship *Serah* anchored at Table Bay during the closing days of December with a cargo of slaves from Mozambique. Dundas initially refused Hogan's request to land them for sale, but he gave authority to export them to "South America or the West Indies" after Hogan on December 30 stated that the slaves had been sent to him "in consequence of an offer made to me of payment of a large sum due me by persons belonging to the settlement of Mozambique."[6] There would be a later reference to this sum owed him by "a rogue" in Mozambique; it was probably Monteiro or possibly Guezzi.

The transfer of power at the Cape of Good Hope was to take place just two days later.[7] The Dutch Commissioner General, Jacobus Abraham de Mist, and a contingent of 1,300 Dutch troops under the command of Lieutenant General Jan Willem Janssens, who was to be governor, had arrived, and all but one company of British Grenadiers, as well as most of the British male civilian servants, women and children, had left by the end of the month for either England or India. But at noon on December 31, the British sloop *Imogene* arrived in Table Bay with a despatch for Dundas, recently promoted to lieutenant general, to delay the transfer and do everything possible to avoid irritating the Dutch officials. The order, dated October 17, was sent at the instigation of Pitt who, convinced that he alone could save Britain and expecting to be returned as prime minister, persuaded Addington's government to postpone the evacuation of the Cape Colony (as well as of Malta and Alexandria).[8] Anderson was apparently aware of the order to delay the transfer when he told Hogan in a letter sent in December that "I fear you will be in some measure disappointed [in leaving with the British forces] as none of your squadron can leave the Cape before February, if then, by reason of various circumstances which ere now you must be acquainted with."

Dundas acted quickly. After bringing 900 troops on shore from two vessels in Table Bay that were to sail the next morning to India, he told Janssens of his orders. Fortunately, because both were prudent men, a peaceful standoff was negotiated within several hours. British colors continued to fly from the Castle, the name for government headquarters. It was a tense period, however. Reflecting the probably held view that Britain had changed its mind about restoring the Colony to the Dutch and that war either had been resumed or shortly would be, Hogan wrote on January 14: "The report of a French squadron of seven sail-of-the-line alarmed us here very much. Since then, by comparing the logbook [of an American vessel] with the situation of some of the large Dutch ships that have arrived, we find it more than probable it was [the Dutch ships] that were seen. If otherwise, the Frenchmen must have touched on the Coast of Brazil. The necessary preparations are made here and, unless they arrive, there is no doubt of our holding the Colony in case of hostility against the force opposed to us, which in numbers are equal to ours, every day increasing by the arrival of [Dutch] troopships."

The "report of a French squadron" came originally from a British agent in Paris in November 1802 that Napoleon had new designs on India where, with the help of the Dutch at the Cape of Good Hope, he would "chase the English from Bengal." On this occasion, the ships were not French, but the report would shortly prove to be correct.[9]

Hogan's letter continued that Dundas's "proclamation of martial law [on January 2] staggers the whole of the inhabitants who have just found out that, the moment the government is changed, the first call on them will be 20% of their property, after which [a] very heavy quarterly tax is to be imposed on town and country. They are all shut up in their houses ever since this came out and the most profound silence observed." On January 21, he told Anderson: "You cannot conceive the anxious state we are in. Reports of war from every [ship] arrival and great prospects entertained of it at Île de France from whence privateers innumerable will be out at the first moment...."

While the standoff continued, Captain White and the *Felis Eugenia* finally arrived at Table Bay on January 16 with 400 male and 100 female slaves on board. Hogan was initially uncertain whether to send the slaves on to Montevideo or Havana. He wrote Anderson on January 22 that he was "greatly at a loss to know what is best to be done with the slave ship. In these perilous moments it is difficult to determine which way to turn and the property at risk is immense on which I am of opinion insurance could not be effected with a prospect of safety. If, however, I should change my mind in that subject and dispatch her to the River Plate or Havana, I will write to you to cover a considerable sum on her cargo which, if not very unsuccessful, is worth £25,000, but I am so unfortunate in everything that I am determined not to count upon her voyage. Poor White has had an arduous task and the worst is to come when the judgment of the head [*sic*] is to be put to the test.... I hope, however, the expedition will be productive, for it merits success."

But unlike the *Serah* venture just two weeks earlier, Dundas allowed these slaves to be landed and sold, perhaps because during the period of uncertainty about Dutch restoration he was willing to accede to Dutch desires to allow the importation of slaves. They were sold at several auctions during February and March.[10]

The interregnum lasted only seven weeks. On February 19 another British ship brought orders instructing Dundas to proceed with the transfer at once. (Pitt was again the instigator; he had changed his mind about holding the Colony when his expectation of becoming prime minister fell through.)[11] The next day, Sunday, the British guards at the Castle were replaced by Dutch guards, and on the morning of February 21, 1803, the Dutch flag was raised. The last British troops left in early March.

These events also determined what Hogan would do with the *Felis Eugenia*, which he had renamed the *Favorite*.[12] He secured a contract to carry British ordnance stores back to England. With William White in command, the *Favorite* sailed on March 4 "in company with the British squadron."[13] Hogan was now totally dissatisfied with White, the captain who had brought him three prize vessels, two shiploads of slaves and whom he once lauded on every occasion. He told Anderson: "The accident that ship met with by gross mismanagement in her navigation and obstinacy in her captain whose self-conceit is unbounded will put her to great expense in addition to what she has already cost me. I am therefore desirous that the moment she is discharged, you will pay every person now on board her what is due them which, will be very little, and make the best arrangements you can for...alterations and repairs." Hogan still thought highly of the *Favorite*, telling Anderson in June: "I am quite at a loss to know how to recommend employment for the *Favorite*. [I] must leave that point to your own judgment on the spot. Perhaps you could get her chartered for the Mediterranean or on some other route to employ her until my arrival. I had views this way for her but the state of the place has induced me to give it up. She is a ship I should wish to hold on account of her many good qualities." Instead, he was to see her again two years later in New York. He would also not be rid of White who two years later challenged the sufficiency of his share of prize money.

Neither Hogan nor his family left the Cape when the Dutch took over, as had been expected. There were several reasons. The *Tremendous* was not going back to England but to India. On January 14, Hogan had noted: "Nothing short of profound peace will send any of the squadron to Europe, so that my plan of sending Mrs. Hogan and the children home is much deranged. Were not little Sophia very ill of a cold and sore throat, I would try to prevail on [Mrs. Hogan] going home on the *Resolution*...that sails next week directly." But that plan also had to be deferred because, early in February, Frances Hogan had a life-threatening miscarriage. Hogan told Anderson on March 4 that "this is the thirtieth day with Mrs. Hogan in bed confined with the terrible effects of a miscarriage in which everything went wrong and, what is bad to state, those we have called doctors have not been able to administer the least relief; indeed, had not my opinion been confirmed before, the proof now before me is more than sufficient to be certain they know nothing. She is very low, though much better, for I had for two days almost given up all hopes of her recovery."

In another letter sent the same day, Hogan told Anderson that the "alteration in the destination of part of this squadron has induced me to purchase the *Carteret* in order to be sure of a passage for my family and self home.[14] She cost £2,200 in bills which I will try to make her earn before she proceeds northward. I hope however to be with you before Christmas. I would sooner, but must go to Mozambique to recover what no one can do for me, for agents are unequal to the task of settling and recovering on a rogue." The purpose of the intended trip to Mozambique would soon become clear.

He had, in the meantime, begun to sell off his personal and business properties in Cape Town. He placed an advertisement in the *Cape Town Gazette* on March 19 announcing a "public vendue [of] his dwelling house, with the stores and stables thereto annexed, together with his household furniture, plate, linen, etc., [as well as] his new store in Berg Street, wine vats, and other property in different parts of the Town." The advertisement was repeated on April 9, with the addition of slaves—"a cook, tailor, cooper, carpenter, houseman, stable hand and about a dozen strong warehousemen."

Finally, by April 17, Hogan was able to tell Anderson: "I am very happy to inform you that Mrs. Hogan is quite recovered of the illness with which she was so long and so dangerously confined, but cannot say when you will see her in London. She has written to William and

Miss Bean and desires I will request you will make William a present of something in her name for the good accounts she has had of him. Our little ones are all well but I have another attack of the gout which I hope will soon depart." Despite his depressed state, Hogan was selling his various properties at a profit. He reported to Anderson that "I have got clear of every thing, except the new wine stores and the old long wine store. I could also dispose of these, but judge them at present better property than paper money, of which I have one hundred and ten thousand rix dollars in [Vendue Master] Matthiessen's hands and my own, and see no channel by which I can remit any. I have been fortunate in selling my house to [Johannes Andries] Veyl, the butcher, for 80,000 [florin],[15] ...and our furniture has all gone off at vendue at about first cost covering 25 percent for remittances. I quit this house next week and go into Lauries which I have hired for five months! Exclusive of the wine stores and cash therein that will sell for about twenty-four thousand rix dollars, I have still on hand twenty prime slaves and other matters to the amount of full 12,000 rix [dollars], together with good [credits] outstanding of more than 8,000 rix [dollars], and how on earth to remit the one-half I know not, for Government draw no bills payable in this year and in the next the revenue will be ample for the expense of the Colony. No ships touching. Even the Danes have forbid their ships touching here, on account of the expense of the port."

He was considering where he should next settle. He noted it is "difficult and dangerous to propose any plan [lest] the next arrival may frustrate the whole of one's projects. I believe, after all, that some solid establishments in England would be most desirable, were not the climate so very hostile to us both. I have heard Liverpool is better than London. In the latter, I should be suffocated. Does Ireland promise anything? Leghorn is open and the advantage of Trieste and Venice would in my opinion render that a desirable plan to us. In war it would be better than in peace (of which I fear we are never to experience much). The climate is excellent, country plentiful and beautiful and I have always understood it to be a desirable situation for persons well-versed in shipping concerns in which I confess I feel more at home than in any other line."

Hogan told Anderson that "You can conceive nothing more dead than this place. All the Jacobins are appointed to office but the salaries are so small that it is merely name. Amongst others is Mr. Grand just arrived from Holland to be a member of Council." George Francis

Grand was a French-Swiss citizen formerly in the service of the English East India Company. Hogan was certain that Grand's presence was "a preliminary to a French Government here or that it is aimed at the [East India] Company's interests in India, for doubtless he is in the interest of [Napoleon] and has the ability to be a thorn in the side of the Company, in which service he was upwards of twenty years." In fact, he had been sent by the Dutch authorities in the Hague to Cape Town (where he had briefly resided in 1799) as a consultant to the Committee for Asiatic Possessions and Establishments, the remnant of the disbanded VOC. It had been Talleyrand who had instigated this move. In 1802 he had secretly married Grand's former wife, Catherine Werlée and thought that Grand's continuing presence in Paris could become embarrassing. De Mist, furious at being "surrounded by intrigue," managed to ignore Grand.[16] (Hogan was not sufficiently displeased with Grand, however, to refrain from selling him three tables for 280 rix dollars before he left the Cape.)

Hogan reported on other matters also: "Our friend Cloete is a member of the Board of Finance which ranks after the members of Council. Most of those that were employed by our Government are continued in some situation, except the Fiscal [Van Ryneveld] who holds no office. His own friend Vantertook destroyed his character in Holland. Most of the English have advertised to sell off and depart but very few of them will have anything to remit. Tennant's property is handed over to the Court of Justice for the benefit of his creditors, and some others that stood high will be little better...."

On a lighter note, Hogan wrote that, because the "rains set in early this month, ...the quantity of wine this year is more than was ever known before and will be very cheap, for...the [army] officers and soldiers like coffee better than wine...."

Hogan's fears about the French taking over were not without some foundation. The report of a French squadron coming to the Cape in January had proved to be false, but a French squadron would arrive later. An unidentified British resident wrote to London on May 14: "There are three French frigates and a seventy-four arrived at Simon's Bay with a general and troops for the Cape; the Dutch say for Pondicherry [India], but there seems to be only one opinion about that: everything is ordered for them in the name of the Batavian Republic. I am afraid all is not yet understood in Europe, for one of the Frigates on making the inner bay stood off again on not seeing the Dutch colors, which by some means had been neglected to be hoisted, and made a private signal from the outer bay to the hill which on being answered she stood up into Simon's Bay. However, all is quiet and it never required any gift of prophecy to foretell this would be the case."[17] The French squadron had secret orders to sail to India to prepare for the renewal of war which the French thought might begin by September 1804.[18]

In the end, despite fears such as those expressed by Hogan and the unidentified writer, neither the Asiatic Committee nor the French managed to exert any influence at the Cape during the three years of Batavian rule. The Dutch, however, did impose changes. One was the use of the Dutch language in all official notices and correspondence, as well as for the only newspaper, now called the *Kaapsche Courant*. They also tried to protect Dutch commerce by giving preferential treatment to trade with the Netherlands and its possessions and by prohibiting colonists from shipping goods to Europe except in Batavian bottoms or from buying foreign goods directly from foreign ships. The Asiatic Committee, as with the now defunct VOC, continued to maintain a commercial fleet and claimed a monopoly on tea, spices and opium trade from the East. (These economic restrictions could not be enforced because the Dutch Colony eventually had no recourse but to rely on neutral ships to meet its needs.) The economic system in the Colony was clearly less free than under British rule,[19] and equally the prospects for commerce did not appear good. One resident reported on April 11 that "the monied [Dutch] men are all preparing for evacuating the Colony."[20] There was no such exodus, but business conditions remained in a poor state during the Dutch restoration, despite attempts to institute reforms. One such attempt was a law promulgated on April 11, 1803, prohibiting the importation of slaves, to which, however, there were many exceptions. In 1803 alone, 306 slaves were imported under license,[21] not counting the 400 Hogan had landed from the *Felis Eugenia* during the interregnum.

But although Hogan saw no future for himself at the Cape—he called it "this declining Colony"—he did not send his family home by Christmas of 1803. In fact, he and his family did not finally leave the Cape Colony until over a year after the Dutch took over in 1803. As a practical matter, Hogan also had to linger in order to find some means of turning his fortune, for it had indeed become that, into foreign exchange or assets that could be taken out of the country and used at a new location. The usual medium for foreign exchange was government bills (akin to U.S. Treasury bills) denominated in pounds sterling, but when it was learned that the Colony would have to be turned over to the Dutch, the British authorities had no reason to raise money by selling bills. Even when sellers of foreign exchange could be found, the exchange rate was ruinous. Anderson had earlier expressed the hope that "Dutch Government will want all the money you can spare and give you a favorable exchange on Holland," but this was said before the war resumed. Since Hogan could not convert his rix dollars directly into useable foreign exchange, he did the next best thing, which was to buy local goods with the useless local currency to sell for useable currency at his next place of residence.

Hogan may also have thought that he could continue to conduct business under Dutch governance, it only being necessary to adjust his commercial activities to the changed circumstances. He was later reported to be on friendly terms with Governor Janssens, which may have given him a false sense of security.[22] Aside from selling his wine stores, furniture, residence, business office and other properties at the Cape, which were considerable, he again directed his attention to slaves at Mozambique where the man he called a "rogue," probably Monteiro or Guezzi, owed him money and to Mauritius where trade could now be conducted legally.

On June 1 he wrote to Anderson: "I am just on the eve of embarking in the Dutch ship *Maria* for Mozambique. On my return round Madagascar, it is intended to touch at [Mauritius] and, as there will be no time lost, I doubt not of being here again in the middle of September. What specie I can collect shall be sent to India if a safe opportunity offers."[23] He also cryptically told Anderson that Francis Fowkes, "being ready to embark the moment an opportunity offers by an English or Dutch ship, ...will explain to you the nature of the packets that you will receive in this conveyance."[24] The contents of the separate packets were not revealed. However, on August 30 Anderson procured transportation on the *Iris* (Captain Skinner) from London to New York. Did Fowkes carry a private message for Anderson that he should travel to New York? There is no record of when or how Fowkes left the Cape, but the timing would permit this conclusion. Anderson sailed on September 12 and arrived in New York on October 24.[25] During the following three weeks, he also visited Baltimore and Philadelphia.

The date of Hogan's return to Cape Town from his venture to Mozambique is also not recorded, but he was certainly there before the end of September when the inhabitants at Cape Town learned that

Britain had declared war on France over four months earlier on May 18, thus resuming a European-wide war that was to last another twelve years. The British action was courageous because the country could not be assured of allies, and its timing was fortunate because Napoleon had hoped for more time to gain territory without having to engage his main enemy.

The Netherlands was not a declared enemy of Britain and did not want to be an ally of France but, because virtually all its autonomy had been surrendered to, or seized by, France, it was for all practical purposes an enemy.[26] The immediate impact of the resumed war at the Cape Colony was to reduce British shipping to zero, the last English ship to call at the Cape being the *Calcutta* on August 12. Thereafter, with one exception, no English ships stopped at the Cape Colony during the three years of Dutch rule. Most of the Colony's outside contact was with Danish and American ships during this period.[27] There were other local impacts as well. In November, all British subjects were "requested" to sign an oath of allegiance to the Batavian Republic, not unlike the oath which Dutch subjects signed when the British arrived eight years earlier. Hogan and 146 other British subjects signed the oath, which was in Dutch.[28]

Not knowing that Anderson was by then in the United States, Hogan sent him another letter addressed to London on October 28 reporting that: "On the 8th instant, a Portuguese ship, the *Excellentissimo Augusta*, Captain Francisco Louis Madeiro, belonging to Mr. Antonio Arthur e Almeida of Mozambique, arrived here with a cargo consisting at bill of lading of 350 male and female slaves. Nineteen of the above number, being sickly, were landed the day before she sailed from Mozambique and twenty died on their passage to this port, being 28 days. The remainder 311 arrived in good condition, of which 17 were landed here under the permission of Government.... This cargo was sent here on Portuguese account to pay a debt that was due to me from persons at that place and by agreement they became my property and at my risk in twenty-four hours after the ship was moored in this Table Bay. When this agreement was made, [the resumption of] war was unexpected and the property was precarious by circumstances while laying here with a Dutch man-of-war and French privateer along side the ship.... The circumstances of the war and not knowing what Power or Island is neutral has determined my sending the ship the clearest route to lay off Charles Town Bar for orders where to proceed to a market... She sailed from this [port] on the 19th instant,[29] ...with 294 fine slaves on board as cargo, and I doubt not her Portuguese papers will be respected in other parts as much as they were here." Hogan described the *Excellentissimo Augusta* as "a very fine, fast-sailing, coppered ship and capitally manned; has two excellent English officers and chiefly English seamen."

The Dutch authorities interposed no objection to sending the 294 slaves to the New World, though the ship's papers showed their destination was to be Havana, not Charleston. Hogan had not previously mentioned the possibility of sending slaves to the United States. Havana, as well as Rio de Janeiro and Montevideo, were well-established markets for selling slaves. What changed his mind? The likely reason was the business relationship he had established with a man named Alexander McClure of the firm Alexander & John McClure of Charleston, an American citizen and joint owner of a vessel called *Horizon*. On November 7, while the *Horizon* was anchored at Table Bay, McClure appointed Hogan as his agent with full power of attorney.[30] Whether the *Horizon* was on slave mission on this occasion is unknown, but the ship was recorded as landing 243 slaves from Mozambique and a cargo of wine, brandy and spices at Charleston on July 10, 1804,[31] and as departing that port on December 4 for Zanzibar, another African east coast slave market.[32] McClure could have met Hogan at Mozambique—he certainly met him at Cape Town, and he could well have told him that there was a demand for slaves in the American South and that he could find a market for Hogan's slaves if his ship would check with his firm when it arrived off Charleston bar without entering the port. This would explain why Hogan instructed the captain of the *Excellentissimo Augusta* "to lay off Charles Town Bar for orders where to proceed to a market." McClure would not have known that the South Carolina legislature had passed a law opening that state's ports to slave imports effective January 1, 1804, but he would have regarded this as irrelevant because he knew, as did all Charleston merchants, that slaves could easily be landed clandestinely all along the southern coast. A ship's captain wrote in 1802 of leaving a shipment of slaves "on the beach northward of Charleston [where he later] found them all well, and much better than I expected, for the weather was very cold. They had no clothes, and no shelter except the sand hills and cedar trees, and no person to take care of them." He added: "I don't see that the trade stops much, for they come in town 2 or 3 hundred some nights."[33]

Exactly what happened is unrecorded, but the ship must have arrived off Charleston during the last days of 1803 and there been told by the

McClure firm to continue a few miles south and unload the slaves near Savannah, Georgia.[34] The ship is recorded as arriving at Savannah on January 7, 1804, with the ship's origin shown as Brazil.[35] Since slaves could not be imported legally into Georgia,[36] the ship must have unloaded its cargo somewhere along the coast or on one of the many offshore islands, perhaps directly on a plantation, and then entered the port of Savannah, declaring it had come from Brazil in order to prevent suspicion of its true cargo. The vessel was still in port on March 17.[37]

Whatever the facts, Hogan undoubtedly profited handsomely from the venture, contributing to his wealthy status on arrival in New York a few months later. His involvement with the slave trade did not end with the *Excellentissimo Augusta*.

The purpose of Anderson's visit to the United States is not recorded. Several letters he wrote to Hogan at the Cape from Baltimore and Philadelphia on November 14 have not survived. The letter written from Philadelphia was probably dispatched on the *Perseverance* whose supercargo, a Mr. Smith, carried a letter from Anderson introducing him to Hogan. On its arrival at Table Bay on January 28, the ship was recorded as bound to Batavia, which must have been its original intention. Another American ship, the *Silenius*, on its arrival on January 1 from the Netherlands, was also recorded as bound to Batavia. Neither vessel proceeded beyond the Cape; these vessels and three others (*Louisa* of Baltimore, *Juno* of Boston and *Surprize* of Philadelphia) were used instead to effect Hogan's departure from the Colony.[38] Thus, one possible explanation for Anderson's visit to the United States was that, knowing of Hogan's need for adequate transportation to export the goods he was acquiring to another country, the absence of British shipping, the risks of using enemy ships (French or Dutch), and the difficulty of contacting neutral Danish ships, he saw that the solution was to persuade American ships planning to call at the Cape Colony that the resumption of the war and the scarcity of supplies provided an opportunity to sell American goods and produce there and to pick up Hogan's acquired goods for some other destination. Although American vessels were regularly calling at the Cape Colony, most were destined to other markets, such as Île de France, India and Batavia, and would not be inclined to abort their missions unless primed in advance to the possibility of a market there and return freight.

Although it is difficult to believe that Anderson was so prescient as to predict Hogan's ultimate decision to move to the United States, he did, while he was there, set in motion at least one business venture for which an American vessel was to be used, one involving Robert Lenox who will appear again in the next chapter.

Just when Hogan made the decision to move to the United States is uncertain. He may have been considering this possibility since June when he sent his cryptic letter to Anderson, but news of the resumption of war must have been the determining factor. Although he probably could have found a way of getting himself and family back to England, the trip would have been laborious and possibly risky since no British ships would be available. He must have worried that the *Collector* affair, and even insinuations involving the *Holger Danske*, might tar him in London. Returning to Ireland as the prodigal son might have been romantic but was nevertheless foolhardy. The European continental locations he had earlier mentioned were now out of the question because they might well be in French hands or otherwise threatened by the war. Just as he had chosen the Cape of Good Hope as his base after the voyage to New South Wales, he now thought of places where his adventuresome spirit would find a welcome home. In this context, the choice of the United States was completely understandable. He may have been impressed by the aggressive commercial ideas of Americans, such as McClure, whom he was now meeting more frequently than before at Cape Town, as well as by the smaller, faster and economically efficient ships in which they sailed. He may also have known, or at least sensed, that more and more international trade was now being carried in American bottoms.

Through 1803 and early 1804, Hogan pursued his plan os using the large amount of cash he had at last been able to accumulate to buy goods for carriage to and sale in the United States. One source of funds came from selling to Cape residents the sugar he had procured on his voyage to Île de France on the *Maria*.[39] Among the major transactions was the purchase from the Dutch authorities of coffee, sugar and pepper valued at over 100,000 rix dollars. He had decided he could wait no longer. In January, he wrote to Anderson at London, where he would soon be: "I have engaged a passage for self and family on the American ship *Silenius*.... She is a very fine ship of 450 tons and she sails very fast.... A longer stay at this place is unnecessary while I apprehend that things cannot change for the better. Pray write me immediately and very fully to New York to care of Messrs Franklin Robertson & Company, owners of the ship I go in." On January 22 his chief assistant, Edward Lewis, sailed on the *Juno* (Captain Thomas

Clements) to Boston with a cargo of sixty-four tons of coffee, possibly obtained on the Île de France venture.[40] The next shipment was also coffee on the *Surprize* (Captain Richard Renshaw) which sailed about mid-February for Philadelphia. He engaged space on the *Perseverance* to carry more coffee and other goods and spices to Philadelphia and the *Louisa* (Captain Tillinghast) to carry 132 tons of unrecorded cargo to Baltimore. In his final letter to Anderson on February 23 he said, "I enter into no details. We are all well and everything so far has succeeded to my utmost wishes."

Some two weeks before this final letter, Governor Janssens had issued a proclamation ordering all British subjects to leave the Colony within two months and prohibiting other citizens from doing business with British subjects. Hogan had already made his plans to leave and thus had no cause to be concerned over the proclamation, but other British citizens were in a state of consternation because it was becoming increasingly difficult to find passage on departing ships, must less to find space to take their worldly possessions with them. Some left in panic but the proclamation was not strictly enforced and, although no one could have known it at the time, the British again took over the Cape of Good Hope in just two years.[41]

William Hogan later recorded that "on 8 March 1804, my father with my mother and three sisters and a retinue of nine servants bade farewell to the Cape of Good Hope, embarking for New York on board the American ship *Silenius*, Captain [Joseph King], chartered and freighted wholly by my father, as also were the bon ships *Perseverance*, *Louisa* and *Surprize*, their cargoes of Java coffee and spices almost exclusively embracing all the moveable and readily convertible property he had in six years gathered at the Cape, falling little short of half a million of dollars, exclusive of real estate there and in New South Wales and large values of then still open business in England and the East Indies. The *Silenius* entered New York harbor on the evening of the 3rd May 1804."

SEVEN

FAME AND FORTUNE IN NEW YORK

> ...[he] was a prince of a merchant. He kept his carriage, and was a fine old Irish gentleman, until about the close of the war with England [when he] failed but was not disheartened.
>
> —Scoville, *Old Merchants of New York City*

Michael Hogan was a man of unquestioned wealth when he arrived at New York. He would have created hardly a ripple had he returned to England, but he took New York by storm. New Yorkers were acquainted with merchants who had come to the United States from England, Ireland, Holland, other places in Europe or even the West Indies, but no one of means had ever come from the Cape of Good Hope and before that India. His misdeeds at Cape Town were probably unknown, but even if there were rumors they would count for little in the United States because they had been inflicted by and on Englishmen, not Americans. He no doubt encouraged others to believe the most romantic and adventuresome stories about him, and the appearance that he and his family and entourage presented was ideal material for fanciful tales. He was reputed to be rich, to have a dark-skinned Indian princess as a wife, to have traveled to far and mysterious corners of the globe, and to have engaged in many daring and risky adventures. Even sixty years later his reputation as one of the leading merchants of old New York was recalled in glowing, if not always accurate, terms:[1]

Michael Hogan...had only landed in the city a few months, but what attention he received from all the leading men of that day! Robert Lenox...sent an invitation to the distinguished stranger the second day of his arrival. He was such a man as did not arrive in the then small city of New York every day. Michael Hogan brought with him in solid gold sovereigns £400,000, equal to $2,000,000, and he had a wonderful history! What I would not give if I could write it all out! All those 160 Hogan families [in New York City in 1863], mostly Irish, are kith and kin of the great nabob, for such he was when he arrived here in 1804, with his dark Indian princess wife. Michael Hogan was born at Stone Hall, in the County Clare, Ireland, September 26th, 1766. So he was thirty-eight years old when he landed in New York, with his dark skinned lady and his fabulous amount gold. But what scenes he had been through in these eventful thirty-eight years! He had been a sailor; he had commanded ships bound to ports in every quarter of the world—in Asia, Africa, America, and Europe; he had been to North as well as South America; and he had voyaged to the West as well as to the East Indies; he had made successful voyages to the then almost unknown land of Australia. In the East Indies he had married a lady of great wealth. This was the story that was talked about when Captain Michael Hogan came here.

The amount of gold brought out by Mr. Hogan seems incredible. The sum may be exaggerated, and yet there is no doubt that he brought to this country immense wealth.... The larger part of his fortune was acquired in the East Indies, probably by his marriage.

He did an immense business, and was a man that commanded universal respect. At this time he gave the grandest dinners that ever were given in the city. They were attended by all the leading men, and by all the foreigners of distinction. Copenhagen Jackson, the celebrated British minister, used regularly to be there; and when his carriage drove down to No. 52 [Greenwich Street], with the grand turn out and the servants in livery, the boys of the vicinity used to congregate, and regard those things with wonder.

Mr. Hogan was one of the most delightful, as well as desirable of acquaintances. He spoke different languages. He could tell of almost unknown countries, and he was a perfect Irish host and gentleman.

The inaccuracies in this account are legion: Frances was not an Indian princess; Hogan had not traveled to South America (unless his Trinidada adventure in the British Navy is counted); his assets were not held in gold sovereigns nor was his wealth a dowry from his wife; he did not "regularly" entertain British Minister Jackson; and his true net worth was no where near two million dollars, which today would be equivalent to at least thirty million. But whether all the stories that have been recalled and written about him during the height of his prosperity are true is beside the point. Legends are often built on quicksand, and Hogan's was no exception. Having acquired financial wealth, which he later said amounted to $430,000 (about six and a half million dollars today, but the amount may not have represented *net* assets),[2] he would now seek a niche for himself and family as an honorable and esteemed citizen in the business community and in the society of the young but rapidly growing United States of America.

Hogan had visited New York twenty-two years earlier when he was only fifteen on board a British Navy ship during the closing years of the American Revolution. He regaled his family with stories of his adventures at that time, not all of which, as will be seen, were quite true. He would certainly have noticed that New York was now a vastly different place, though it would still bear little resemblance to the New York of today.

Its population was growing rapidly, from 60,000 inhabitants in 1800 to 95,000 by 1808, but the city was still concentrated within a two-mile area in the southernmost part of Manhattan Island. Even here there were still open areas, swamps and farms. Several of the main streets were cobble stoned and had sidewalks, but were reportedly not kept as clean as in some cities of Europe. Broadway was the finest and most frequented street; Wall Street was already the center for banking and the stock exchange; Greenwich Street, which had been partly constructed on reclaimed land, was a main residential street. Transportation was mostly by private means, although there was a stagecoach that operated five round trips a day between what is now Greenwich Village and the Wall Street area for twenty-five cents a trip. Ferries provided access to Manhattan Island across the Hudson and East Rivers. Water was supplied from either individual wells and pumps or a central well leading to a reservoir from which it flowed through underground pipes to pumps alongside some streets. The latter supply was not considered adequate or sanitary. There were no covered sewers until after 1819, no public gas lighting until after 1815 and no adequate or safe water supply until 1842. And there was as yet no indoor plumbing or stove heating. Infectious diseases, such as yellow fever and cholera, had been common in the 1790s and would recur. New York was, however, rapidly becoming the center of commerce and finance in the United States. By 1800, it had become the leading port in the United States, and its merchants, traders and financiers were ready to do business with all comers.[3]

The United States in 1800 was still largely confined to the eastern seaboard. Its population of a little more than five million was almost one-fifth Negro slaves, with only some one million males who could vote, and was predominantly rural. Only Boston, New York, Philadelphia, Baltimore and Charleston could claim city status. Visitors often commented on such negative characteristics of Americans as boorishness, boastfulness, bad manners, uncouth behavior and love of drink; they also regarded the United States as a weak, second class nation. Perhaps the country could boast few intellectual, cultural or social attainments, but the proportion of land-owners was higher than anywhere else, and Americans were learning to develop a new society based on liberty and the pursuit of happiness, even if the latter was usually translated as economic gain. They were a diverse lot, often thinking of themselves first as Virginians or New Yorkers or whatever state or locality they came from. In truth, one could wonder what held the country together, for the people in its various parts seemed to hold markedly different views from one another on how their newly created nation should be governed or, for that matter, where its future lay.

The industrial revolution, accompanied by waves of immigration, would make its full impact in the United States within several decades. The steam engine would soon propel paddle wheel vessels and steam locomotives were not many years away. There would eventually be well-known and regarded American writers, poets and artists. The young nation had obtained its freedom from Britain but saw enemies, real or imagined, at every crossroad. Even if the country wanted, it could not escape from becoming embroiled in the Napoleonic Wars. Both England and France interfered with American shipping and impressed American seamen and both posed occasional territorial threats from Canada, Mexico, Haiti or the Louisiana territory. Spain was a thorn in its side because it continued to hold Florida, which the United States coveted, and interfered with American shipping through New Orleans. The Federalists, who had been in power since Washington became president and whose standard bearer was Alexander Hamilton, believed in a strong federal executive and protection of property rights and feared mob rule. The Republicans, epitomized by Thomas Jefferson, believed they were the true inheritors of the Revolutionary War which had been fought to oppose strong central authority and achieve liberty and equality for all, as these terms were then understood. They portrayed Federalists as wanting to subject the country to a Northern plutocracy sympathetic to the British and to expand territory by military action, while the Federalists accused Republicans of wanting to destroy property rights and religion and make the United States a satellite of France. Fortunately for the country, extremists in neither faction prevailed. After Washington's presidency, John Adams wisely eschewed the more extreme demands of the Federalist radicals and steered a moderate course, though not without signing the infamous Alien and Sedition Acts. In 1801, after twelve years of Federalist rule, Republicans took over the presidency after a raucous campaign that far surpassed today's national elections for the venom of its mudslinging, first with Thomas Jefferson, then James Madison, James Monroe, and lastly

John Quincy Adams who in 1829 gave way to the populist Andrew Jackson. The Federalists never again came to power, but their political and intellectual philosophy provided food for thought and action by American leaders for many years to come. Although Jefferson spoke of the predominance of states rights over federal authority, even championing the concept that states could invalidate federal legislation considered unconstitutional, he and the fellow Republicans who followed him did not change the basic direction in which the Federalists had steered the country toward strong central authority and independence from foreign entanglements. Jefferson was also fortunate in foreign affairs when Louisiana fell into his hands with little diplomatic effort. The Louisiana Purchase ranks as one of the great milestones in American history for it ended the French threat, provided protection against England's gaining access to the vital Mississippi River basin, undermined Spain's territorial pretensions, and finally and most important of all left Americans free to expand to the West.

New England was the hotbed of Federalism. Its religious and political leaders believed that the Republicans under Jefferson stood for terror, atheism and free love. The Louisiana purchase, which swung the balance of political power to the Republicans and to the ascendancy of Virginia in national politics, was cause for talk in New England of separation from the federal government, newly established in Washington, D.C., and the formation of a Northern Confederacy. Alexander Hamilton would have nothing to do with the conspiracy, but Aaron Burr, Jefferson's outgoing vice president, disaffected by Jefferson's inattention and already showing signs of opportunism and adventurism, had been rumored to be a collaborator, although later evidence shows he was not. He ran for governor of New York, losing badly when Hamilton urged Federalists not to vote for him. Six weeks after the election, Burr and Hamilton engaged in an acrimonious letter exchange over an ambiguous slur by Hamilton. Possibly because the origins of their mutual dislike went back many years, neither was willing to back down. The inevitable result was a duel, the most famous in American history. On July 11, 1804, just two months after the Hogan family landed in New York, Hamilton died from Burr's bullet on the Palisades along the Hudson River. Burr fled, first to Philadelphia, then to a plantation in Georgia owned by a Major Pierce Butler, a later friend of Hogan, where he was given refuge for a month[4] and finally to the home of his daughter, Theodosia Burr Alston, in South Carolina, from whom Hogan later purchased some property and who was a friend of one

Natalie de Lage de Volude, the husband of Thomas Sumter, Jr., son of the illustrious Revolutionary general of the same name, who had a subsequent business dispute with Hogan.

When it became apparent Burr would not be arrested for killing Hamilton—dueling although illegal in some states was still an accepted means of settling questions of honor among gentlemen, he returned to Washington to assume his duties as president of the Senate during the waning days of his vice presidency in early 1805. It was about this time that Burr began plotting to establish an independent empire in Mexico free of Spanish rule and perhaps—this part was always vague and in the end unproven—to detach the Louisiana territory from the United States. Burr proceeded to the West where he unveiled one plan after another in an attempt to obtain financial and military support. Jefferson, now in his second term, chose at first to disregard the widespread reports of Burr's activities. Perhaps he was not adverse to privately sponsored sorties against Spanish lands as a means of applying pressure—from which he could later, if necessary, disassociate himself—in negotiations over territorial issues that had been underway with France and Spain ever since the Louisiana purchase. But in late 1806, when presented with hard evidence of Burr's plans and perhaps not wishing to displease Spain when there was reason to believe that the territorial negotiations concerning Louisiana and West Florida might achieve a successful outcome, he felt he could at last proceed against a man he disliked and distrusted. Burr was arrested on the charges of treason against the United States and of misdemeanor for plotting against Spain. The arresting officer was the father of a man who later married a Hogan granddaughter. During the search for Burr, one John Marsden Pintard, who was involved at the time with Hogan in a dubious business venture, was seized and questioned, possibly because he was acquainted with one of Burr's stepsons. Burr was brought to Richmond for trial. After several months of court proceedings that held the nation enthralled, Burr was acquitted of treason (and later of the misdemeanor charge) after Chief Justice John Marshall ruled that the key evidence upon which the treason charge was based could not be used for that purpose. Although Marshall was undoubtedly legally correct in his ruling, the bitter personal and political animosity that existed between him and Jefferson was certainly a factor. Although Hogan apparently never had any association or direct contact with Aaron Burr, his path crossed with those of several of the people mentioned above, and he was to become directly involved with a Burr stepson twenty years after the duel.[5]

The morning after arrival in New York harbor, the Hogan "family all landed in good health...and took possession of ample suites of rooms at Mechanic Hall (then new) on the upper corner of Park Place (then called Robinson Street) and Broadway." The eight servants in his entourage were presumably given a place to sleep and eat in separate quarters, it being the custom for servants regularly to travel with their masters but not share the same quarters. William later recorded their names as two servants, William Hayward and John William Reeder; five male slaves, Christian, Lodewick, Jack, Edmond and Charles; and one female slave, Vinissa,[6] ranging in age from fourteen to twenty-three. On the eve of leaving Cape Town, Hogan had each of them place his or her X to mark their acceptance of a written instrument in which they bound themselves for fourteen years as "apprentices" to Hogan and his family. They were to "do no damage to their said Master and Mistress and their children, nor see it to be done of others; ...they shall not waste the goods of their said Master or Mistress or their children, or lend them unlawfully to any; they shall not commit fornication nor contract matrimony within the said term; they shall not play cards or any other unlawful games whereby their said Master, his wife or children may have any loss; they shall not haunt taverns or playhouses, nor absent themselves from their Master's or Mistress's service unlawfully; but on the contrary in all things they shall behave themselves as faithful apprentices toward their aforesaid Master and Mistress and their children during the said term. And the said Michael Hogan, in consideration of their services...shall teach and instruct or cause to be taught and instructed his said apprentices in the same art of ways of servants by the best means that he can; finding [*sic*] to his said apprentices meat, drink, apparel, lodging and all other necessaries, according to the custom of servants during the said term."[7]

It is often supposed that slavery had been declared unlawful in all the Northern States shortly after the Revolution. While most of them did so, New York and New Jersey did not finally end slavery until the 1820s. The 1800 census recorded 36,505 Negroes in bondage in Northern States, most apparently living on farms. In New York City, 2,868 persons were listed as slaves, 3,499 as free non-whites, out of a total population of 60,489.[8] The State of New York had enacted laws in the 1780s outlawing the import and sale of slaves, but numerous attempts to abolish slavery itself failed until the turn of the century when Negro children born of slave mothers after July 4, 1799, were freed but would have to continue to serve their masters until they reached their twenty-eighths birthdays. (The legislators apparently selected Independence Day as the passage date to freedom—even if 28 years away—to show how patriotic they were—surely a cruel joke!) Finally in 1817 New York freed all slaves as of July 4, 1827. Prior to then, there were numerous evasions of the laws and several legal exceptions, such as an 1801 statute permitting slaves to be brought into the State by persons intending to reside permanently there and who had owned the slaves for at least one year prior to their importation.[9] Hogan could therefore legally bring his slaves into New York and keep them indentured to him but could never sell or transfer them (at least within the state), and he could disengage them only by setting them free or returning them to the Cape of Good Hope. The only information on what happened to the slaves is the recollection of a Hogan grandson that, "He freed them all after being a short time in New York. Some returned to the Cape but others remained with him as servants for years, as one was a nurse to my aunt [Sophia Hogan], then a child, she thinks about 1804."

Like many Northern and even Southern masters, Hogan may well have treated his slaves with care and compassion, but they would still have been regarded as slaves with no legal or social rights. Even the prohibition on their sale was circumvented by advertising for the sale of the "time of a Negro wench" or the "time of a healthy active Black boy."[10] Negroes who had been set free did have some legal rights in the North, such as the right to vote in some States (assuming they met property qualifications), and some even held office, but there was vast distinction between legal equality and political and social equality. The view that the Africans were inferior to whites was widely held in both the North and South, even among those who rose in pulpits and political podiums to speak of the horrors of slavery. Jefferson, the author of the ringing words of the Declaration of Independence that "all men are created equal," although urging a federal prohibition of slavery, wrote that Negroes were inferior to whites in body and mind. These attitudes were not confined to the United States, nor were Negroes the only disenfranchised lot. Women did not have the vote, nor did those with insufficient property—the poor, not to mention American Indians.

Hogan had a number of personal needs to fill in his newly adopted country. He ordered £400 worth of personal items from London for his wife Frances and wrote to William Anderson, now back in London, asking that he procure "a [curricle, a two wheeled chariot drawn by two horses abreast].... I mean it for the firm. Hire a pair of horses and use it for some time, then pack it well and ship it as your own second hand carriage to obviate a heavy duty of 25 percent here on new carriages."

Hogan also wrote Anderson that, "In lieu of taking a country house during the heat or sickness, I propose proceeding with my family up the North River to Albany, visit the Springs of Ballstown, Saratoga and the Lakes and see what we can with comfort of the interior to escape the heat of New York." He expected to be back in New York by October. At some point in 1804, possibly just after his summer sojourn (though the time could have been as late as 1805), he visited Philadelphia, living in a house on Chestnut Street purchased or rented from the naturalist Dr. Benjamin Smith Barton. His possible reason for going there will be covered later. His son William later said his father "did not like [Philadelphia]" and soon moved back to New York City where he rented a dry goods store at No. 225 Broadway, near where John Jacob Astor lived at the time and where Astor House was later built in 1834, with the family quarters above the store. He apparently used this place to store and sell his imported merchandise.

Hogan's family was growing up. William was still in England being educated at Harrow when the family arrived in New York. Hogan wrote to Anderson shortly after arrival in New York saying that "we are all delighted with the account you give of our doting boy. The desire of having him here is very great, but that must give way to the necessity of completing his education where he is. We are only at a loss how to dispose of him during holidays, as when you are gone the poor fellow will have no home and he will feel deserted.... I fear they are hammering Greek into his head. Any time at that is lost. Latin is the only one of the dead languages that can be of any use to him. The other branches of education are the most necessary but I suspect and fear much it is not the school for the merchant, which is the only line that William has a chance of being engaged in. Pray explain to the master my wish for his giving William as much of a mercantile education as can be consistent with the roles of the school. At the same time, I do not wish to cramp in any respect the turn William's genius may take."

A little later Hogan again pondered what to do with his son: "With respect to my boy, I am much divided and not easy in mind as to the example of extravagance before him. [I] suspect I shall be obliged to bring him nearer."

Hogan continued to take an interest in his four nephews in England and their wayward father, Dennis. In the same letter to Anderson in which Hogan worried about William, he suggested that "the third (Owen, I believe, by name) should be sent so as to arrive here in November.... I mean to bind him an apprentice in a good ship out of this port and serve him when he merits it.... I know of no profession to suit John. I would place him in a merchant's house for two or three years and, if he did not show parts, I would then give him a farm with a mill, etc., and push him on to make the most of what may be most congenial to a dull soul, the mother earth. I have some better expectations for my namesake [Michael] and request you will push his education to the utmost to make him complete for a counting house. If he was not as far advanced as you wish on coming away, place him at a good mercantile school and he may be sent a year here.... Their older brother Cornelius could also be employed to a better purpose but that can be thought of hereafter."

Whether any of the nephews came to the United States is unknown. Hogan had told Anderson he would be "happy if I could prevail on [my brother Dennis] to change his parchment for Guineas and quit a life that he has no interest in pursuing with a broken constitution and advanced years," but when he eventually heard from Dennis, it was to be informed of his debts. In response, Hogan told Anderson: "I have already...expressed my wish respecting your paying my brother £200 or as much as may discharge his debts. He must be of a poor profession that does not afford him sufficient to live on." Dennis was soon to accept his brother's advice, though perhaps not because he had decided to become a merchant, for which career and all others he was probably not suited. He resigned his British Army commission in 1805 and three years later published an eight-page polemic tract costing 2*s*/6*d* titled: "Brevet Major, Late a Captain in the 32nd Regiment of Infantry. An appeal to the public and a farewell address to the Army in which he resigned his commission in consequence of the treatment he experienced from the Duke of York and the system that prevails in the Army respecting promotions, etc."[11]

Before starting new business ventures, there were old ones Hogan had to settle. The *Juno*, which had been the first to sail from the Cape of Good Hope, arrived safely at Boston, but its cargo of coffee was damaged. Hogan's second vessel, the *Surprize*, had sailed from Table Bay for Philadelphia with Richard Renshaw in command, but it never reached port. A Philadelphia newspaper later printed an article datelined St. George, Bermuda, reporting that "on [May 5] some young men of this town, perceiving something floating at a considerable distance from the shore to the northeast of the island, put off in a boat and picked up a writing desk which was found to contain papers belonging to an American brig called the *Surprize* belonging to Richard Renshaw of Philadelphia, homeward bound from the Cape of Good Hope."[12]

Fortunately, Hogan had insured both the *Surprize* and the coffee on the *Juno*. Hogan's other two ships arrived safely with their cargoes intact. The *Perseverance*, which had left Table Bay in company with the *Silenius*, arrived at Philadelphia on the same day Hogan and family reached New York, its cargo of coffee consigned to Nixon, Walker & Company. On anchoring, Captain Williamson fired a salute, happy to be back in his home port after a five months' absence. The *Louisa* reached Baltimore on May 23.[13]

Hogan still had some unsettled accounts in England, but he wanted Anderson with him in New York to manage his new business affairs. He sent his assistant, Edward Lewis, to England to "wind up all my old business with people in England," including his troublesome accounts with Donald Trail and the shareholders in the *Charlotte* and *Union* ventures. There was also the question of what to do with the *Favorite*. Apparently referring to this ship, Hogan told Anderson: "With regard to the Spanish project, the success of it would so much depend on the captain's management on the Coast of Peru that, however good it may be, I must drop the idea altogether." He also told Anderson to abandon an undescribed "Baltic project." The Spanish project could have been a privateering venture, perhaps conceived while Hogan was still at the Cape Colony wondering how he could make maximum use of his resources in England, which he later realized would not play very well in his adopted country that felt increasingly threatened by England. He finally told Anderson that, if the *Favorite* could not be sold for £3,000, she should be filled with coal and sent to New York. Anderson did so and sailed on her to New York, arriving on February 27, 1805, carrying coals consigned to Robert Lenox, a sow and "two small pigs of very superior breed."[14]

Tracing Hogan's new business ventures is difficult, largely because of the dearth of both personal and public documents. But it is possible to surmise their nature and some details from such evidence as exists. The nature of his business ventures clearly changed. When he began his career in India, he was both planner and executioner, relying on others only for financial backing. In Cape Town, he was still project manager, sometimes with active or passive financial partners, but he relied on employees for execution. Now in the New World, he finally had the visible evidence of the wealth that had eluded him for ten years—the cash that came from selling the products he had brought from the Cape Colony and from settling his accounts in London, Calcutta, Bombay, Sydney and elsewhere. Approaching what was then an advanced age—he was thirty-eight—he wanted to reap the rewards of his labors, enjoy the good life and become socially prominent. No longer would he actively manage projects; he would instead become an adviser and investor, passing the burden of execution to others while he enjoyed the profits—the true mark of a gentleman. Although American merchants and seamen were well-acquainted with international trade, Hogan was uniquely suited to be an adviser for any transaction involving the Cape of Good Hope based on his knowledge of the Colony, of contacts there and in such places as Mozambique and of trading patterns in the Orient. He told Anderson he had "adopted economy as my motto, Robert Lenox [as] my pilot." Hogan's name does not appear in the public records of many of the ventures in which he was involved, and no longer would newspapers regularly carry his advertisements, as they did in Cape Town. (One of the few that did read: "13 pipes 4th proof Valentia brandy of superior flavor [and] 130 tons of fustic [pistachio nuts]."[15]) His new-found mode did not mean he would totally refrain from initiating new ventures and trying to steer them himself—how could he ever escape from his natural propensity to activism, experimentation and speculation. But it would be his transformation from active entrepreneur to mostly armchair adviser and investor that would be a chief cause of his eventual financial downfall.

The Robert Lenox mentioned, no relation to the deceased William Lennox of London who had maligned Hogan, played such a crucial role in Hogan's life that some attention to him is in order. Born in Scotland in 1760, he moved to New York where in 1783 he married a Rachel Carmer. His main business was trading, but he was also in insurance as a director of the Marine Insurance Company in 1802 and later, in 1809, as president of the Mutual Insurance Company. John Pintard, a well-known New York businessman, merchant trader, civic leader and friend of Hogan, was secretary of the latter company and later founder of the New York Historical Society. When Lenox died in 1839, he left considerable property to his wife and eight children. One of the children, James Lenox, was the founder of the Lenox Library in New York City which subsequently became the New York Public Library.[16] This was the same Robert Lenox with whom Anderson had communicated from London in 1802 trying to recover money owed Hogan for shipping spices to William Kenyon on the *Lapwing*; the same Robert Lenox who, in the previously-cited remembrance of an author, "sent an invitation to the distinguished stranger [Michael Hogan] the second day of his arrival [in New York]."

Hogan's new shipping ventures included trade with the West Indies and probably other areas, but most of them continued to be with the Cape of Good Hope. He had good reason for trading there. While the British had some difficulty in keeping the Colony supplied with essentials while they were in power, the Dutch had ready access to neither grain sources nor naval power and increasingly relied on neutral countries as sources of both supply and shipment. Almost all the ships that called at the Cape were either American or Danish; very few were Dutch and, of course, none were British before 1806.[17] American ships carrying such needed items as rice and lumber regularly called at the Cape, some of them picking up Mozambique slaves on the return voyage destined either for Charleston or the east coast of South America. Hogan may have received a first-hand report of conditions at the Cape Colony from Dutch Commissary General de Mist when he arrived at New York with his daughter on April 25, 1805, on his way back to the Netherlands, unable to find a ship that could take him there directly.[18]

Hogan was probably involved in many unrecorded shipping transactions with the Cape Colony as an adviser or commission agent. Only his major ventures are recalled here. The first, involving the American ship *Octavia*, had its beginning when Anderson, still in the United States late in 1803 or early 1804, arranged with Robert Lenox to have the ship pick up wine at Madeira on Hogan's account. After loading its wine, the *Octavia* sailed for London, leaving there on June 4 and arriving at New York on July 23, with its wine consigned to Lenox and Gilbert Robertson & Company.[19] The ultimate purpose of the venture was to carry a cargo of various goods to the Cape of Good Hope. Writing to Anderson shortly after his arrival and before the *Octavia* reached New York, Hogan said: "I cannot but approve of every part of [the content of your letters], particularly as far as regards your plan in the charge of B. Stout and your very wisely ordering him here [on the *Octavia*].... On his arrival here, he will take on board forty thousand dollars and proceed as originally intended in order to make the voyage of some magnitude, and as it will be put upon a new construction here to avoid all difficulty, so it shall be considered in our adopted establishment as the property of it. Our worthy friend Mr. Robert Lenox will put everything in proper train and manage the return sales... I only regret you did not go to a higher priced wine [from Madeira]; that which R. Lenox sent to Bengal last year cost £44 per pipe and sold for 440 [sicca rupees]. The profit on your purchase may however turn to better account, but much depends on the quantity gone out this season."

The B. Stout mentioned may have been Benjamin Stout, an adventurous American sea captain from Boston.[20] But Stout was not placed in command, nor was the vessel to be used "a new construction here." The ship was the *Octavia*; it sailed from New York harbor on September 8 with $40,000 worth of cargo and John Flagg in command. She was recorded as "bound for India" but the intention was to proceed no farther than the Cape, where she arrived on December 19.[21] Her cargo of Carolina rice, brandy, tobacco, sundry goods, India goods and earthenware were sold there by Cloete & Cruywagen during the three years 1804–1806, either by auction or privately, for some 92,000 rix dollars, of which at least 30,000 were on Lenox's account. The *Octavia* left the Cape on January 29 and arrived at New York on April 3 with coffee shown as consigned to Lenox.[22]

Hogan also had an interest in at least one other Cape shipping venture arranged before he arrived at New York, possibly when Alexander McClure was at Cape Town in November 1803. This was the American ship *Industry* (Captain Millrea) which sailed from Savannah in April 1804,[23] presumably with goods for sale at the Cape. The ship left the Cape on September 15, arriving at Charleston on November 7 with "Madeira wine, Constantia wine, Cape brandy, hyson tea, gunpowder, japan[ned] wood and femmabook red wood" shipped by Cloete & Cruywagen and consigned to Alexander & John McClure.[24] The ship then proceeded to New York where it arrived January 18[25] with Hogan's share of wine and brandy valued at 18,000 rix dollars.

An interesting sidelight, which points to another Hogan business venture involving the Cape, was that he shipped 10,000 Spanish silver dollars to Cape Town on the American ship *Ganges* (Captain John Phillips) which left Philadelphia on August 21, 1804,[26] and arrived at Table Bay on November 9[27] where Cloete & Cruywagen gave Hogan a credit of 20,000 rix dollars. Hogan could have sent this cash to pay off a debt at the Cape, but he could have done this from the cash he expected to develop from sale of the *Octavia's* cargo which had arrived at about the same time. He had, in any event, deposited 8,000 Spanish dollars with Cloete & Cruywagen when he left the Cape. The silver dollars were more than likely intended to finance some future venture. It also has to be wondered why the silver dollars were sent from Philadelphia, since they presumably could as easily have been procured in New York. One possibility is that Hogan was in Philadelphia at the time; another is that he had been given the silver dollars at Philadelphia to settle a debt, it not being economical to transport the silver dollars, which would have weighed some 600 pounds, to New York. The debt could have come from the *Perseverance* venture, but normal business transactions were usually settled in currency, such as U.S. dollars. Could the amount have come from the clandestine disposal of the slaves on the *Excellentissimo Augusta*, thus pointing to a Philadelphia middle man in this business? The question will be addressed subsequently.

American merchant ships were increasingly in evidence at ports around the world in the early 1800s. They owed their ability to do this in part because business for the ships of many European countries, England included, had been adversely affected ever since the French wars began in 1793. Registered American tonnage engaged in foreign trade increased from some 400,000 tons in 1792 to almost 670,000 tons in 1800 and close to a million tons by 1810. By some measures, the American merchant marine had become the second largest in the world; it was certainly perceived by England as a menace to its dominance of international trade and to the protected position of the East India Company. Unlike the large ships of the Honorable Company, the American merchantmen were small, sometimes only several hundred tons, but they were fast and efficient.

Commercial ships were not engaged only in the trade of goods and produce; they also reaped the harvest of the seas, principally whales and seals. Ships, many of them American, ranged into unknown waters to find sources for these mammals whose varied products found a ready market in many parts of the world, including China which valued seal skins. Hogan would have known of these activities, many of them conducted in virtual secrecy in order to preserve hunting grounds discovered by adventurous sailors, from his vantage point at the Cape of Good Hope. This may have been why he was in possession of an 1804 agreement among three other persons, behind which there was an unbelievable, but true, story. A 120-ton brig called the *Union*, owned by Fanning & Company of New York and commanded by Isaac Pendleton, had left New York in October 1802 on a sealing expedition to the South Seas. On one of the ship's several stays at Port Jackson, Pendleton, Simeon Lord and John Boston in July 1804 concluded a complex agreement under which Lord and Boston were to credit Pendleton with $18,000 for 12,000 seal skins already in Pendleton's possession, procure sandalwood in the Fiji Islands, and then sell the skins and sandalwood in Canton, the profits to be applied toward a subsequent South Seas shipping venture of the three partners. Lord was the merchant in Sydney previously known to Hogan when the wine and spirits from the *Harbinger* and *Chance* were sold in New South Wales in 1801. He was an ex-convict with a reputation for often shady deals. Boston was supercargo of the American ship *Fair American*, also in port. Precisely what motivated this agreement is unknown, although Governor Philip Gidley King (the same King who was in charge at Norfolk Island when Hogan sold his wine and spirits there in 1796 and whom, with his wife, the Hogans entertained at Cape Town in 1800) was certain it was one of the many plots of Sydney merchants and Americans to evade the monopoly of the East India Company. Pendleton and Boston were murdered by natives while they were on shore on the Island of Toongataboo, one of the Friendly Islands. The remainder of the crew escaped a similar fate only because a woman named Elizabeth Morey, who had been on an earlier ship seized by marauders, managed to warn them from a canoe on which natives were attempting to lure others ashore, escaping herself in the process by swimming to the ship. In a subsequent rescue mission, the *Union* was lost with most of its crew. Lord found himself in possession of 60,000 seal skins, comprising the 12,000 that Pendleton had brought to Port Jackson and another 48,000 obtained by crew members that had earlier been put on shore on another island to find seals. He shipped the skins to Canton, sold them in return for China goods which were sent to an undisclosed eastern American port and sold for a handsome profit.[28] Hogan was given or obtained a copy of the 1804 agreement, clearly after the episode had been concluded. There is no ready explanation why or how it came into his possession, but it may have arisen from the fact that Hogan had a financial interest, though it appears to have been small, in the sealing ventures of three other ships, two of which were the *Hope* (Captain Sheffield) and *Asenath* (Captain Tripp), both engaged by the Fanning company, which carried seal skins to Canton and stopped on several occasions at the Cape of Good Hope in 1805 and 1806. Cloete & Cruywagen at one point politely but pointedly pressed Hogan to remind Fanning & Company to meet their debt of 4,983 rix dollars, "as we have no doubt of your endeavoring to have this debt paid, as being only occasioned by giving credit to those gentlemen on account of your introduction, no doubt with your best intentions towards us."

Hogan may have entered into shipping ventures involving other areas of the world, but if so, they seem to have been small ventures. During 1804, he was approached to join in a shipping venture to China, which he declined, telling Anderson in October that, "Mr. Lewis has remained here some months in expectation of going supercargo of a ship to China proposed by Mr. Lenox. The gentlemen that intended the expedition have declined it unless I invested one half the funds, a thing foreign to my intentions or thoughts, however ready I may be to take a large proportion. The lessons I have had are sufficient to guard me against further loose concerns and I do not intend placing property in the power of Eastern Governors or people from whom I can expect no justice."

But Hogan may have had a part in a China venture involving a man named T. Lezar who in October 1807 wrote Hogan from Cape Town, "I beg leave to charge you with the receipt of my balance due to me by Messrs William Davy & Son of Philadelphia which at the receipt of this I am assured will be closed and as I made my arrangements with Mr. Cruywagen in consequence you will have the goodness to credit this gentleman for the sum you will receive." That the business had to do with China is revealed in a later letter of Anderson's: "I was never sanguine that Lezar's concern would have proved productive and mentioned that to Cloete and Cruywagen when they begged of me to write you a letter for Lezar because I did not suppose that Davy had given him the real invoice cost. However, without any charge of freight or insurance on the China cost, it ought to have netted him something beyond that, which it will not do it appears."

Sometime in 1805, probably late in the year, Hogan laid plans for a major shipping venture involving the Cape of Good Hope. Its full dimensions remain unknown, and it cannot be proven that Hogan was a party in all aspects of the venture. But there is ample circumstantial evidence that the ultimate purpose of the venture was to ship upwards of one thousand Negro slaves from Mozambique to someplace in the Southern United States, that Hogan was the guiding force behind the entire venture, and that a number of merchants in New York, Charleston and possibly Philadelphia had financial interests in the venture.

Hogan could have been led to such a venture by a several factors. He knew from first hand experience how and where to procure slaves on the east coast of Africa, an area that previously had been exploited mostly by Portuguese traders.[29] While most slave traders turned their attention to the area of Africa they knew best along the west coast, Hogan could draw attention to the advantages of procuring slaves from Mozambique. Not only were they cheaper, but the problem of how to profit on the voyage to Africa and to pay for the slaves could be solved by carrying goods from the United States to the Cape of Good Hope, now in need of goods and grains, with the proceeds of sales used to pay off Portuguese middlemen in Mozambique. He could also have seen that, while he might have been able to profit by engaging in the business on his own, he could do even better in a joint venture with other merchants and financiers who could put up the most important ingredient, money.

Hogan already knew Alexander McClure, and he was acquainted with or placed in touch with other Charleston merchants. One was John Mathias Ehrick.[30] Another was Adam Gilchrist in partnership with his brother Robert in New York.[31] And another was Francis Depau, a Frenchman who had married the daughter of Admiral De Grasse of Yorktown fame. He had come to Charleston from Haiti and later in New York founded the first Le Havre packet line.[32]

Hogan may also have received advice from Major Pierce Butler, a well-known slave holder in Georgia who resided in Philadelphia.[33] This may explain why Hogan lived in Philadelphia for a brief period in 1804 or 1805 on Chestnut Street. Butler also lived on Chestnut Street. He had been born in Ireland in 1744, came to the United States in 1765 as a major in the British Army, and in 1771 married a Mary Middleton who had inherited a fortune consisting of several plantations and hundreds of slaves in South Carolina. Just before the Revolution, Butler acquired valuable land on St. Simons Island in Georgia which he called Hampton Plantation, selling his British Army commission to acquire the funds to make the purchase, though it was not until after the South Carolina plantations had been ravaged and the war ended that he gave support to his adopted country. He was a South Carolina delegate to the Constitutional Convention, the first United States Senator from South Carolina, and in both cases a strong supporter of slavery. After his wife died, he moved to Philadelphia in 1793 where he resided and conducted business until his death in 1822. It was this Butler who gave sanctuary to Aaron Burr at Hampton Plantation after his fateful duel with Alexander Hamilton, possibly during the time Hogan was in Philadelphia.

As has already been seen, Hogan did not find the slave trade repugnant. He was in company with many supposedly respectable merchants. It is ironic that it was technology and economics that perpetuated the slave problem in the United States and led to the Civil War. The price of slaves in the United States had been declining before the 1790s because productivity in such labor-intensive industries as tobacco and cotton was still low. It was the invention of Eli Whitney's cotton gin in 1793 that dramatically increased the demand for—and the price—of slaves in the South because more cotton could then be produced to supply the voracious British and later American textile factories. Cotton production in the United States increased dramatically until, by 1860 just prior to the Civil War, almost three-quarters of the world's cotton was produced in the American South and Southwest.[34] Part of the demand for slaves had been met by illegal foreign imports, principally into South Carolina, which finally dropped all pretense of banning the practice when its legislature reopened South Carolina ports to the slave trade as of January 1, 1804. During the next four years until all foreign imports of slaves were finally prohibited by federal law, 39,075 slaves are recorded as being imported at Charleston, the true number undoubtedly being higher. If the declared nationality of the ships is to be believed, which is questionable, about half the slaves came on British-registered ships, and most of the remaining came on ships based at Northern ports.[35] Some of these slaves were re-exported to New Orleans and Georgia, including the ones that Hogan shipped on the *Excellentissimo Augusta*, where the demand was as strong as in South Carolina.[36] The profits from the trade can be judged by noting that the average cost of buying a slave in Africa was $25–30, while a prime field hand could be sold in Charleston for $500 in 1805.[37] The lure was irresistible. An author has written: "For the next four years Charleston was one of the great slaving ports of the world. It seemed that almost all the white population was infected with Negro fever. Everyone with sufficient capital dreamed of outfitting a ship for the Guinea trade, or at least of sending out a few hogshead of rum or tobacco as personal ventures, while poorer citizens shipped as sailors before the mast. From all the cotton states, planters flocked in to buy slaves in Charleston. Ship chandleries flourished as never before, and there was a new demand for chains, shackles, cheap cotton goods, and quarter-barrels of gunpowder suitable for the African trade."[38]

The apparent plan was to send two ships, the *Dolphin* and *Young Adam*, on two voyages from Charleston to Cape Town, where their cargoes would be sold, and then procure slaves at Mozambique for delivery and sale somewhere in the South. These plans must have been fairly far advanced when, on March 26, 1806, Hogan and other New Yorkers learned that Admiral Sir Home Riggs Popham, the one whom Hogan had accused of skulduggery in the Red Sea campaign several years previously, and General Sir David Baird had retaken the Cape of Good Hope for England in January with minimum resistance.[39]

There had been considerable debate within the British government whether the southern tip of Africa was either strategically or commercially important to England. The Pitt government, which had returned to power following the resumption of war with Napoleonic France in 1803, came down strongly in favor of retaking and keeping it in British hands. The decision was based on the conclusion that its retention in British hands was important to the security of India, but the occasion for the decision was the mistaken acceptance of rumors planted by the French that Napoleon intended to take India. Napoleon's real objective was the invasion of England, a hope dashed by Nelson's decisive defeat of French and Spanish fleets at Trafalgar in October.[40]

Hogan could not have been pleased with the news because the return of the Cape to British governance meant that the Colony would no longer look to neutral countries to supply its needs. Moreover, the British Navy had recently begun to increase its interference with American shipping, and might be more likely to do so when slaves were involved. It must have been for these reasons that Hogan, upon hearing of the British occupation, dispatched William Anderson to Charleston to sail on the *Young Adam* back to Cape Town, hoping that, as an Englishman and previous resident, he would be able to persuade the British authorities to accept the goods being sent and not interfere with the ultimate purpose of the venture. The *Young Adam* (Captain John William Haviland) left Charleston on May 9, 1806, with a cargo of rice, sugar, soap and candles. The *Dolphin* (Captain

Andrew Ross) carrying rice, coffee, tobacco, sugar and staves sailed the next day. The Charleston agent for the *Young Adam* was Adam Gilchrist, brother of Robert Gilchrist in New York, while the local agent for the *Dolphin* was Francis Depau. A Mr. Pintard had a $10,000 interest in the *Dolphin's* cargo and an unreported interest in that of the *Young Adam*; more about Pintard later.

The *Young Adam* arrived at Table Bay on August 18, the *Dolphin* a day later (having first moored at Simons Bay on August 12).[41] Anderson would have found that the Colony had already received several shipments of needed supplies from India and England and that one American ship, the *Augusta*, had arrived on May 31 with coffee, sugar and bale goods.[42] Nevertheless, permission was obtained to unload and sell the goods on both vessels. Anderson later reported to Hogan that, "I found it impossible to dispose of the [*Dolphin's*] coffee except at a great loss while the American's coffee [possibly a reference to the *Augusta*] mentioned in former letters was forced off by auction two days in the week and therefore, with the advice of Mr. Cloete, kept it up for a few months." Cloete & Cruywagen, whom Hogan had appointed to represent him before his departure from the Cape, acted as agent and security for the two vessels.[43] Anderson, who was granted permission in October to remain at the Colony, continued to act as Hogan's personal representative. David Ponterdant was also back in the picture, having returned to the Colony with the Vice Admiralty Court, but he had become a debtor to Hogan and was no longer a confidante.[44]

The *Young Adam* left Simons Bay for Mozambique on October 4 where it picked up a cargo of slaves and sailed westward.[45] The *Dolphin's* departure date from the Cape is not recorded in Cape archives, but other records show that a receipt was given to the vessel for slaves at Mozambique on November 4.[46] No record of where the slaves were delivered has been found, but the voyages must have been completed safely because it was later reported that both vessels were again expected to arrive at the Cape of Good Hope with slaves from Mozambique about the last of June 1807.[47] Again, no record of where the slaves were delivered has been found.[48] The number of slaves delivered is also unknown, but two vessels on two passages, each carrying 250 slaves per trip, would total upwards of one thousand persons.

The two vessels must have delivered the slaves either to Charleston, along the Georgia coast, as the *Excellentissimo Augusta* had done, or to South America. The United States destinations are the most likely.

Although the Charleston agents for both ships were also involved in trade other than slaves, Gilchrist's name appears as agent for one other slave ship arrival at Charleston in 1806, while Depau's name appears for six others in 1807.[49] The *Charleston Gazette* reported 56 ships arriving from Africa with slaves in 1807; Customs records show only 43 such arrivals, others having obviously evaded Customs control. In addition, 27 vessels leaving or bound to Charleston in the African trade were not reported as arriving at Charleston or clearing Customs, including both the *Young Adam* and *Dolphin*.[50] Even though the trade was now legal, ships continued to import slaves clandestinely, possibly so that the ultimate owners, many of whom were Northerners, would not be publicly associated with the slave trade.[51] It is possible that the ships went to some other American port, such as New Orleans where there was also a demand for slaves. Through a loophole in the territorial law, slaves were legally imported into Louisiana in 1806 and 1807; New Orleans was specifically named in a U.S. Senate report of 1807 as one of the ports receiving re-exported slaves from Charleston.[52]

The possibility that the slaves went to Rio de Janeiro or Montevideo cannot be excluded. The slave trade to the east coast of South America had flourished for a long time and was hardly affected by British and American attempts to stop the trade altogether. Using the false colors of such countries as Portugal, American ships among others continued to carry slaves from Africa, particularly Mozambique, to present-day Brazil and Uruguay. Four American vessels, all registered at Northern American ports and all coming from Mozambique (but not the *Young Adam* or *Dolphin*), were sighted at Montevideo on February 14, 1806.[53] The only other hint—second-hand at best—of Hogan's possible involvement in this trade is that on September 29, 1808, Anderson sailed on the British ship *La Jeune Laura* from the Cape to Rio de Janeiro where he would stay for a "short period." Anderson's plea that it was his health that lead to the journey[54] seems unlikely. Was his trip related to earlier deliveries of slaves by the *Dolphin* or *Young Adam* to Brazil? Did it presage new slave shipments? These possibilities can only be conjecture.

After 1807, American and British laws prohibited the slave trade. The British Navy vigorously enforced the prohibition; the meager American Navy did not. Despite these increased risks, contraband shipments, often under the flags of other nations, continued to the United States, particularly through Georgia and Louisiana, and even increased after the War of 1812. Plantation owners in the South also turned to internal migration to feed the increasing demand for slaves across the southeast as far as Texas. After about 1820 the nature of slavery in the South changed from a patriarchal institution to one on which the political, social and industrial survival of the South was believed to depend, a change in circumstance that was the underlying cause of the Civil War.[55]

Although British shipping once again became predominant at the Cape of Good Hope, American vessels led all other countries in calling at the Colony. In 1807, twenty-nine American ships stopped there and fourteen in 1808.[56] However, few of them actually unloaded cargo there. In an October 1807 letter to Hogan, Anderson noted that "we are at present without any American produce in the market and prices [are] high except for provisions and flour which will only answer in times of real scarcity. Lumber is much wanted and will continue now so until the regular intercourse is again opened when the market is easily glutted.... Tobacco and...staves are also in demand.... There is yet a large quantity of Indian rice in the Colony but there is no chance of more coming from that quarter and if Carolina rice could be sent out in rum puncheons, I think it might answer well.... Since [Governor] Lord Caledon's arrival, bills are continuing to rise. The present exchange is 35% for government bills. It is to be hoped the return of the squadron under [Rear] Admiral [Charles] Stirling will lower the exchange."

Anderson had also reported on two fisheries in which Anderson (financed by Hogan), J.F. Reitz and P.L. Cloete were partners:[57] "I have reason to hope that our fishery in False Bay will answer our expectation if we keep this Colony. We were not prepared in time this season and besides fell short of casks before it was completed. Consequently, we lost the opportunity of doing what we expected. All the oil we collected is not quite 150 tons.... Our expenses for the first year have been very great, having all the materials to provide besides the first cost of 15 boys which we were obliged to purchase at a very high rate. We have recently obtained a grant of two islands for seal fishing. Malagasen in False Bay [now known as Seal Island] and another island midway between [Cape] Hangklip and [Cape] Agulhas where our people are now successfully employed in killing seals. The scarcity of beaver fur hat-making has lately raised the price of fur skins salted in the London market, so as to make it an object if we can collect some thousand skins, besides giving employment to our boys in the summer season."

Anderson ended his letter by lamenting his lack of funds and professing injury at apparent rebukes from Hogan. Perhaps the longstanding amicable relations between Hogan and Anderson had come, or were coming, to an end. No further correspondence between the two has been found.

An interesting sidelight of Hogan's continuing business ties with the Cape of Good Hope involved wine. He had continued to ship Cape wine for sale in his new country, but Anderson had to tell Hogan that, "as to the wine [to be shipped on the *Young Adam*], I pledge you my honor I went into every wine store in town and could not get any wine near so good and not cheaper than that which I took of Mr. Cloete. The demand for wine at the time for Buenos Aires was very great." The reason for this state of affairs was that, after seizing the Cape, Popham had sailed to the River Plate with some of the troops that had captured the Cape and seized Buenos Aires for a brief but long enough period to increase the demand there for vaunted Cape wine. Popham was later reprimanded by a court-martial for taking this action without instructions, which was technically correct, but he had ample reason for taking the initiative. The Venezuelan patriot General Francesco de Miranda had been trying for several years to obtain British and American help in liberating South America from Spanish rule.[58] In December 1804, following meetings in London between Miranda and British officials, one of whom was Popham, the admiral had been ordered to accompany Miranda to South America to cooperate in his liberation plans in order to secure a favorable British position in trade. The project was suspended and Popham ordered instead to seize the Cape of Good Hope. But a year later, while his fleet lay idle and seemingly unthreatened at Table Bay, he decided to follow through with the suspended plan when told by an American slave trader that Montevideo and Buenos Aires were weakly defended and could easily be seized. When the news reached England, there was an enthusiastic public response and calls from commercial interests to use the opening to expand Britain's access to the South American market. Swept up in the tide, the government ordered reinforcements and even planned armed expeditions to Chile and Mexico—a clear throw back to the aborted South Seas project twenty-five years earlier. The plan was abandoned when it was learned that the British force in Buenos Aires had capitulated; instead, a force was sent to free the captured troops. It was only when the British government began to court Spain as an ally in its conflict with Napoleon that it decided to castigate Popham for his initiative.[59]

Hogan was involved in some manner in a venture with a Captain Coffin that ran into difficulty after the British retook the Cape of Good Hope. He was probably George Coffin of the American ship *Rolla* whom he had met just before he left the Cape Colony in 1804 when he bought 48 bottles of claret at the captain's auction. Sailing from New York, the *Rolla* arrived at Île de France on July 27, sailed for Calcutta, was back at the French island on December 31, just before Popham landed at Cape Town, and returned to New York on June 4, 1806, with sugar, piece goods, cotton, tallow and other goods consigned to the ship's owners, D. Ludlow.[60] Somewhere on this voyage, the *Rolla* was seized or at least boarded by a British Navy vessel, now actively patrolling the seas around the southern tip of Africa, presumably because of its trade at Île de France.[61] In October 1807, Cloete and Cruywagen wrote to Hogan: "We could not expect any complaints from the owners of Coffin's ship against us. A security of Rds 30,000 given by us proves our good intentions and the delay of sending us the necessary documents and papers brought us very near to the moment of being obliged to depose the whole amount of this sum. The papers lately received are unhappily much more against Coffin's interest than favorable and for this same reason we shall be unable to save the expense of the law suit for which, without them, we entertained great hopes. The lawyers and proctors promise now to finish the whole in the course of a few days by friendly arrangements."

By 1806 Hogan must have felt confident that he was not only wealthy but also financially secure. Most of his major shipping ventures were behind him, and the slave transactions seemed to promise even more in monetary reward. He now could afford to live the good life as a proper gentleman and perhaps even commit some of his money to speculation.

He wanted to find a place outside the city to house himself and his family during the summers when it was not only the heat but sickness that drove those who could afford it to country homes. He found the ideal location in 1806 when he was the successful bidder at $13,000 under a mortgage foreclosure for an estate along the Hudson River between 121st and 127th Streets in what was then called Manhattanville and is now Riverside Park in the Upper West Side of New York. One of the deed-holders who conveyed the property to Hogan was Aaron Burr's daughter, Theodosia Alston.[62] The area was then very much in the country. A stagecoach trip from downtown New York along old Bloomingdale Road took from early morning to mid-afternoon. The grounds, on a bluff overlooking the Hudson River, were near the site of the Battle of Haarlem Heights during the Revolution and were once suggested by George Washington as a suitable site for the nation's capitol. The area was becoming popular as a summer retreat; during 1807 more houses were built there than in any previous year.[63] There were two portions of the estate, each with its own mansion, the southernmost named Monte Alto and the northernmost, near what was then Bloomingdale Road and 125th Street, Claremont.[64] The original houses may have been built before Hogan's tenure, but he added a second story to Claremont and improved Monte Alto. Architectural drawings show them both to be substantial edifices: Claremont, a two-story, 5,000 square foot Georgian-style mansion (Figure 3, page 200); Monte Alto somewhat smaller but still grand in appearance.[65]

In May of the same year, Hogan moved his family briefly to Franklin Square. Finally, in 1807 he sold the dry goods store and moved his main residence to No. 52 Greenwich Street. His new business office, then called a "counting house," was nearby at No. 82 Washington Street. Claremont would be their summer home. Although the Hogans may also have occupied Monte Alto from time to time, it was generally leased out, as was Claremont later on.

Numerous legends, some partly true, surround the Claremont estate.[66] One is that Hogan named the mansion after Claremont, the royal residence of Prince William Henry, Duke of Clarence (later King William IV) who had been a fellow midshipman with Hogan in his Royal Navy days. Many years later a Hogan descendant claimed that the Prince visited Hogan in the United States, but this is not true; William Henry never returned to the United States after his visit to New York in 1782 during the Revolution while Hogan was also there.[67] The more likely explanation of the Claremont name is that it was derived from Hogan's birth place—County Clare in Ireland.

Another often-repeated legend is that the British minister to Washington, William James Jackson, viewed the maiden run of Robert Fulton's paddle wheel steamboat, the *Clermont*, on the Hudson on August 18, 1807, from the piazza on the lawn of the Claremont estate.[68] Hogan and his family may well have viewed the *Clermont's* maiden voyage, but Jackson could not have seen the event, which attracted little attention in New York at the time, because he did not arrive in the United States until two years later. He had been sent to replace David Montague Erskine who, in the opinion of the British Foreign Secretary Canning, had not been sufficiently diligent in following instructions to resolve growing Anglo-American disputes over shipping. Jackson, familiarly known as Copenhagen Jackson because of the role he played in the British kidnaping of the Danish fleet in that port in October 1807, was unpopular in Washington and was recalled a year after his arrival in 1810.[69] Before leaving, he visited New York where he found a sympathetic audience among Federalists and local merchants. Among those he met was Hogan, which is probably what the previously-cited author meant when he said that "Copenhagen Jackson, the celebrated British minister, used regularly to be [at No. 52 Greenwich Street]." In May Jackson and his family leased the Claremont estate, and it was there that he viewed the regular run of the steamer, an event which prompted him to report to London that "one of the curiosities that we daily see pass under our windows is the steamboat, a passage vessel with accommodations for nearly a hundred persons. It is moved by a steam-engine turning a wheel on either side of it, which acts like the main wheel of a mill, and propels the vessel against wind and tide at the rate of four miles an hour. As soon as it comes in sight there is a general rush of our household to watch and wonder till it disappears. They don't all know what to make of the unnatural monster that goes steadily careering on, with the wind directly in its teeth as often as not...."[70]

Another famous person who leased Claremont was Viscount Lord William Courtenay. He was the eldest son of Henry Reginald Courtenay, Earl of Devon, who was Bishop at Exter, and became the eleventh Earl of Devon in 1835. Before that, he had been a sometime assistant clerk of the British Parliament but had come to the United States because of "political troubles." An author described him as "a great lion of New York, for he was a handsome bachelor, with title, fortune and reputation—a combination of excellencies calculated to captivate the heart desires of the opposite sex."[71]

A tomb on the land contains the inscription: "Erected in the Memory of an Amiable Child, St. Claire Pollock, Died 15 July, 1797, in the Fifth Year of his Age." The child fell to his death on the rocks below Claremont, and it was his father (or possibly uncle), George Pollock, a previous owner of the land, who erected the tomb. This was apparently not known when newspaper accounts appeared a century later on the possible origin of the child. A Hogan descendant believed it was Hogan who erected the tomb at the grave site out of sympathy because his son William and the Pollock child were both born in 1792, but this seems unlikely.[72]

Hogan sold his interest in Claremont in 1812, but the estate continued to draw the attention of New Yorkers for many years. Two years before the Civil War, the mansion was moved and became an inn and public restaurant (Figure 4, page 200). In 1872, the property was acquired by the City of New York as part of Riverside Park. The Inn featured a garden with tables, two private dining rooms and a verandah which formed the main dining room.[73] President William McKinley lunched there in 1897 when he attended the dedication of Grant's Tomb, and next year Admiral Dewey partook of breakfast after his triumphant return to the United States from the Battle of Manila Bay. A 1937 menu for Claremont Inn offered afternoon tea and evening dancing, a luncheon for one dollar and imported Czechoslovak pilsner for 50 cents; the most expensive item was a filet mignon for $2.25. A 1939 guide book described the Inn as "a green-trimmed, white frame manor house..., attractive in summertime with dancing and outdoor service under colorful awnings."[74] The condition of the building and quality of its clientele deteriorated during and after World War II. Complaints by local Riverside residents of "sounds unholy" coming from late night revelry led to court-imposed curfews. On March 14, 1951, after the City had decided to raze the building for a playground, it was consumed by fire. Michael Hogan would have turned over in his grave if he had read the *New York Times* the next morning reporting that "Hogan lived [at Claremont] with an Indian princess, a scandalous matter to the local people." The *Times* was, however, both more accurate and generous in noting that Claremont was one of the three grand wooden structures built in the post-Revolution era and still standing in New York City, the others being Gracie Mansion and Hamilton Grange.[75] The only remaining evidence of Claremont is an historic marble tablet embedded in the ground several hundred feet north of Grant's Tomb where Riverside Drive briefly divides into two segments north of 122nd Street. The area retains the Claremont Hill name; a street one block to the east is still shown as Claremont Avenue.

It was also in 1806 that Hogan became a land speculator in central and northern New York State, possibly hoping to increase his fortune

Figure 3. Side view of Claremont, 1806. Author's Collection.

Figure 4. Claremont Hotel, ca. 1860, unknown artist. The Metropolitan Museum of Art, Edward W.C. Arnold Collection of New York Prints, Maps and Pictures; Bequest of Edward W.C. Arnold, 1954.

even more and minimizing the risk by limiting his investment. Land was indeed cheap, but its acquisition was as speculative as it can be today. As an alien, he needed and obtained permission from the State of New York to buy real estate.[76] His first venture was the purchase in 1806 of some 6,600 acres of land near Utica. In partnership with Cornelius Ray and William Bayard, both of New York, he also bought and leased land near Sackets Harbor on Lake Ontario.[77] Then in 1807 he bought on his own 10,168 acres in Franklin County near the Quebec border for $15,250, at only $1.50 an acre, from the estate of Alexander Macomb who had originally acquired the land as part of a much larger plot in 1787. Two years later, he bought 9,949 adjoining acres at $2 an acre from John McVickar, a fellow pewholder at St. Michael's Church. The acquired area comprises the present towns of Bombay, South Bombay and Fort Covington.[78]

Hogan's shipping activities came to a virtual halt about 1807. The one known exception took place in 1809 when he joined two merchants in Charleston to charter the American passenger vessel *Charleston Packet* to carry Thomas Sumter, Jr., his wife and four children (one of whom was born just four months before sailing), servants and belongings from New York to Rio de Janeiro where Sumter was to be American minister to the Portuguese Court. In 1787 at age nineteen, he had an affair with a young girl that led to two illegitimate children whom the Sumter family took in as their own. When Jefferson became president, Aaron Burr sponsored Thomas, Jr., to be secretary to the American Legation at Paris under Minister Livingston. In New York to arrange ocean passage, Thomas visited fellow South Carolinian Joseph Alston who had just married Theodosia Burr and there met the beautiful Nathalie de Lage de Volude, daughter of a French royalist who had been sent to the United States as a ten-year-old child in 1793 to escape revolutionary France, who was also seeking passage to return to France. They sailed together, fell in love on the voyage and were married in France shortly after arrival in 1802. Sumter had a falling out with Livingston and returned to Charleston in 1803 where, through his father's efforts, he became Lieutenant Governor of South Carolina for a while. He may have arranged for the sea transportation to Rio through one or more of the same merchants that Hogan used in sending the *Young Adam* and *Dolphin* to the Cape of Good Hope in 1806 and 1807; or it may have been Burr's stepson, John Bartow Prevost, or the earlier mentioned John Marsden Pintard, both of whom were acquainted with the Sumters, who put Sumter and Hogan in touch with one another. (Prevost met with the Sumters in Washington on their six-months overland trip from South Carolina to New York.)[79] The *Charleston Packet* was procured in the name of one of the partners, a Charleston merchant named Jacob R. Valk, because Hogan was not then a U.S. citizen. The other partner was John Mathias Ehrick, also a Charleston merchant who later moved to New York.

There were difficulties in making final arrangements and in boarding the passengers. The highlight of the voyage, however, was another demonstration of Thomas Sumter's penchant for amorous activity. Henry Hill (to be consul at Rio de Janeiro), his wife and an unnamed woman friend were also on board the *Charleston Packet*. Many years later, Hogan recalled that Mr. Hill had written from Rio asking that Hogan publish his letter reporting that a "quarrel in the ship arose out of Mr. Sumter's intrigue with the female companion of Mrs. Hill, out of whose bed she was dragged, preferring her to his own wife." Hogan declined Hill's request, though he had no reason to mollify Sumter who refused to pay the full bill for his transportation. The business issue was not settled until fifteen years later when Hogan was also in South America pursuing a new career.

The Hogan family was growing up. William, now fourteen, arrived from school in England on November 25, 1806, on the *Orb* after a 69-day journey and entered Columbia College a year later. Hogan arranged for his younger brother, Maurice, who had remained in Ireland as a farmer, to emigrate to the United States in 1808 with wife Mary and children. In 1810 they settled on a farm near Utica on some of the land purchased by Hogan. Maurice and his descendants continued to live on the farm until at least the turn of the twentieth century. The Michael Hogan family, clearly better educated and financially situated than that of Maurice Hogan, continued to emulate their father's interest in and concern for their cousins for many years, but it seems to have been an obligatory, not voluntary, relationship.

The Hogans had been born Catholic, and Maurice and his family remained practicing Catholics. Michael Hogan, however, appears to have acted as though he was a Protestant, if one can draw this conclusion from the fact that he was reported to have attended Anglican services in Cape Town.[80] Formal church affiliation was taken seriously among the upper social strata in places such as New York and Boston. There were Catholics, even Irish Catholics, who were respected New Yorkers. One author, apparently himself Irish, listed Michael Hogan as one of nine Irishmen "who shone in the brightest circles of the society of their day and whose names are interwoven with the City's history of the first quarter of the nineteenth century," but he believed it was nevertheless dangerous to avow oneself Catholic.[81] There was a stigma attached to being common Irish: they were considered to be uneducated and suitable only as servants or working men. Many of New York's elite had been Loyalist sympathizers during the Revolution, when the city was continuously under British occupation, and many of those who did not return to England or go to Canada, merchants in particular, were still Anglophiles and certainly Federalists. Whether it was because he wanted to be one of them or believed that abandoning the Catholicism of his birth was not a cardinal sin, Hogan declared himself an Episcopalian soon after arrival.

He probably first attended Trinity Church at Broadway and Wall Street, founded in 1697 and considered by Episcopalians to be the "Mother of Churches" in the United States. A neighbor of his at No. 46 Greenwich Street was the Reverend John Henry Hobart, assistant rector at Trinity in 1813 and rector and Episcopalian bishop of New York in 1816. Hogan is said to have contributed an article to the *Churchman's Magazine* founded by Dr. Hobart in 1805, but no evidence of this has been discovered. The report seems unlikely given the emphasis on religiosity in the publication.

In 1808 Grace Church was erected near Trinity at the corner of Rector Street and Broadway and came to be known as Manhattan's "high society church of fashion." Hogan was one of the original pew owners, holding No. 20 on the south side, for which he paid $460 and an annual rent of £5. His daughter Frances and son William were confirmed there on November 12, 1812. And it was there that William Hogan was given permission in 1834 to erect the marble plaque memorializing his father whose inscription appears in the frontispiece of this book. When Grace Church moved in 1844 to its present location on Broadway at East 10th Street, the plaque was moved also, appearing on the wall of the north aisle near the entrance.

Michael Hogan was one of the original vestryman and pew holders at St. Michael's Episcopal Church when it was consecrated in 1807 in the village of Bloomingdale at 99th Street, not far from the Claremont residence. It was a small church with only fifty-three pews, intended to accommodate the residents of the summer homes in that area. John Henry Hobart was the first rector. Hogan paid $10 and $18, respectively, for three-year leases of pews No. 9 and 31. The building was destroyed by fire in 1853. A second and larger edifice was erected which in turn was taken down in 1890 and a new and much larger St. Michael's built on the northwest corner of Amsterdam Avenue and West 99th Street. A photograph of a Hogan portrait once hung in the vestry room at St. Michael's, contributed by his granddaughter Harriet Rebecca Donnelly Geffekin. Both Grace and St. Michael's churches, as well as Trinity, still stand.[82]

The family's good fortunes would not last. By 1811 there were ominous rumblings that all was not well with Michael Hogan's dream of continued financial prosperity.

EIGHT

NEW CAREERS IN HOGANSBURG AND HAVANA

In former times, I managed my own affairs and managed them well, for nothing ever failed through my own hands. I now will do so again, and notwithstanding all that has befallen me here, which may to the illiberal give the stamp of incapacity or idleness, I hope to prove at least that the latter is not a part of my constitution. These I leave claim an exertion extraordinary— If I fail they are gone.

—Hogan to Olivers of Baltimore, 1819

Michael Hogan told many people over many years that he suffered a financial downfall shortly before the War of 1812 and that it was caused by the deeds of others. There is ample evidence that he was forced to sell many of his properties and to seek gainful employment. But he was never destitute. It was as much his pride that was hurt than his economic well being.

The most persistent explanation that Hogan gave of the cause of the downfall was the failure of a presumed friend or friends to make good on a debt or debts for which Hogan had agreed to stand as security. Thomas Butler, son of Major Pierce Butler, told him in 1815: "It is hard to be deprived of the fruits of so many years of honest industry by the villainy of witches who are more remorseless and dastardly by their acts of plunder than those miserable beings who expose themselves to the vengeance of the laws in their petty deprecations." Answering a letter from Hogan in 1817, Christopher Richardson & Sons in London sympathized: "We are sorry the transaction that has given you so much trouble and detained you sometime from pursuing your own concerns; and will assuredly hint to William [Richardson in Calcutta] your friendly recommendation to be cautious of trusting Americans." In a letter to

President Monroe in 1818 seeking federal employment, he felt compelled to say, even if elliptically: "In [commerce] I was one of the sufferers and my interest in the [state of New York] was necessarily sacrificed to make up my deficiencies in [commerce], by which all were paid principal and interest, perhaps the only instance of the kind in this state for the last ten years."[1]

The most specific allegation was recorded in the autobiography of Charles Wilkes, a famous American naval officer whom we shall meet later in this book. During his last weeks on earth, Hogan shared many of his life's successes and misfortunes with Wilkes, who was then a naval lieutenant stationed in Washington. Wilkes later wrote that Hogan "felt greatly the dishonesty and trickery of many he had dealings with, & often cautioned me to beware of certain individuals whom he represented as 'snakes in the grass.'... [When he arrived in New York,] he found himself an idle man with an independent fortune.... His funds, on arrival, had been placed in the hands of Robt Lenox.... This, as he often told me, was a most unfortunate step on his part and he soon found it so. The investment of his funds was very illy advised and resulted in loss to him; at the same time, they were used by [Lenox] to his great benefit and was the foundation of the immense fortune he left his family. Mr. Hogan's liberality and desire to serve his friends caused him to endorse for many whose failures brought heavy debts and obligations upon him.... During his stress of means he made application to Robt Lenox, whom his fortune and funds had so much benefitted, but in return he received a refusal of aid and felt it deeply."[2]

Hogan planted the same idea in the mind of his son William who recorded that the critical date was January 11, 1811, when "my father made his ill-advised and unfortunate assignment to Lenox, Stick & Wills for benefit of his condition, the results of which entirely destroyed his fortune." In a separate, mostly unreadable scribbled note, William referred to "Men of high standing, perhaps themselves misled by false estimates of the future," and "Other friends with possibly good intent, possibly not, took advantage of...used...security and endorsements...." Lenox was Robert Lenox, but Stick and Wills, possibly his partners, are unknown.

William's son, William, Jr., penned a brief note many years later that referred to a "Discovery through Mr. Evarts" that Hogan "went security for friends and became heavy losses. He had not been naturalized. Lenox a Scotsman, Depaw who built Bleeker Inn (or some of his family), Dickey, all owed him money."

Evarts was undoubtedly William Maxwell Evarts (1818–1901), a well-known New York attorney who held several high government positions, including secretary of state during the Rutherford B. Hayes administration, and may have been known to William, Jr., in Washington during the period when he was trying to find out more about his grandfather. The Depaw mentioned was certainly Francis Depau, the previously-mentioned Charleston and New York merchant, while Dickey was his friend Robert Dickey.

If the event mentioned by William Senior took place exactly on January 11, 1811, and on no later date, William Junior's reference to Hogan's not being naturalized would be correct because he did not become a U.S. citizen until fifteen days later,[3] but it is difficult to see why his citizenship had anything to do with his financial difficulties.

The information recorded by Wilkes and Hogan's son was imparted to them during the closing years of his life when he was bitter over other perceived slights to his honor and status. During this period, he methodically went through his papers, expunging incidents that might place him in an unfavorable light. Some of these were simply business arrangements that had turned out badly or where there may have been some dishonesty or subterfuge. But the ones that must have stuck in his craw were those involving slaves.

By the early 1830s the slavery issue had become a divisive issue in American politics. Many Americans north of the Mason & Dixon line had become vocal opponents of slavery and were not likely to harbor friendly feelings toward anyone who profited from the institution, even if this had taken place a number of years previously. Hogan would not have wanted his legacy to be clouded by any hints or evidence of his past involvement in this business, particularly after his arrival in the United States. His charges against Lenox and others over bad debts and investments, vented only later in his life, may have told only part of the story, for there is earlier evidence that it was the *Dolphin* and *Young Adam* slave ventures that caused the downfall.

One of Hogan's New York friends was John Pintard, several of whose letters to his daughter refer to "uncle Marsden." One in 1818 calls Hogan "uncle Marsden's friend"; another a year later says Hogan "has been materially injured by poor Uncle Marsden"; and an 1831 letter states "uncle Marsden introduced me to [Hogan's] acquaintance when Mr. H. was very rich, but unfortunate speculations dissipated his wealth...." Uncle Marsden was John Marsden Pintard, a cousin of John Pintard. After both of John's parents died when he was a young child, he was raised by his uncle Lewis Pintard, a major New York importer of wine from Madeira, whose own son was John Marsden. There is little information available about "uncle Marsden." He was American consul at Madeira from 1790 to 1803[4] and probably had a hand in his father's wine trade business while serving in that capacity. There are several clues that Hogan and John Marsden Pintard were business acquaintances as early as 1804. He was probably involved in the shipment of Madeira wine on the *Octavia* in that year. As previously noted, he was recorded in one source as the grantor, or possibly one of the grantors, of the Monte Alto estate to Hogan in 1806. He was in Savannah (and probably Charleston also) in March of that year where he advertized for the sale of pipes of Madeira wine imported on a vessel called *Minerva*.[5] This was less than two months before the *Dolphin* and *Young Adam* sailed from Charleston on their slave voyages. A Mr. Pintard is show in Hogan papers as having a financial interest of at least $10,000 in the cargo of the *Dolphin* and an unreported interest in the *Young Adam*. This must have been John Marsden Pintard, not his cousin John Pintard who latter acknowledged that he "was concerned in several [ships] with poor generous Marsden in the Madeira trade" and in another letter said that Hogan was "very friendly to me, but not in a pecuniary way."[6]

The mention of Francis Depau by William, Jr., also points to the slave ventures, for Depau was the Charleston agent for the *Dolphin*.

The strong possibility exists that something went wrong with the *Dolphin* and *Young Adam* ventures which either caused or contributed to Hogan's financial downfall. Possibly John Marsden Pintard did not contribute his full share of the venture capital; possibly a profitable market for the slaves could not be found (though this seems unlikely given the strong demand for slaves in the Southern United States); or possibly so many slaves died on the voyages that the expected profits did not materialize (this being a common occurrence). If there were such losses, they may not have been covered by insurance. That the situation did not reach a critical stage until four years later in January 1811 (if this date had a real bearing) can be explained by the possibility that promissory notes, mortgages or bonds might have then fallen due. Perhaps the instruments in default were the mortgages secured on the Claremont and Monte Alto estates in 1806 or on the New York tracts that he bought in 1807 and 1809 when he thought he could rely on his expected profits from the slave ventures to meet the mortgage or note payments. Claremont and Monte Alto and the New York tracts were, in fact, the first assets that Hogan liquidated; there is some evidence that one or more of them went under foreclosure.

It is conceivable that Robert Lenox, Robert Dickey, Francis Depau or even others were also investors in the slave ventures, thus making it possible for Hogan to single out the best known—Lenox—as the culprit and to divert attention from the slave venture by making only vague references to bad loans or investments. But there is absolutely no evidence of soured business relations with these persons at the time the incidents took place. In fact, Hogan maintained a close personal friendship with Dickey for many years. It was Dickey who later helped Hogan handle a law suit to collect Sumter's unpaid bill for the *Charleston Packet* voyage. The two families were obviously close. In August 1817, Frances Hogan wrote to her husband, then in Philadelphia, addressing him as "Dear Mr. H": "Fanny has just come in from Mrs. Dickey's looking much better. She has promised to go out again next week." And in an 1824 letter to Hogan, Dickey said, "Mrs. D received Mrs. Hogan's letter...and she would at this time write to her but that she is on a visit to her sister Grace at Philadelphia, having left us a week since. The papers [being sent] you will inform you what is going on in this country and I must refer to the letters of your female friends for the changes and domestic news occurring here. Be pleased to remember me kindly to Mrs. Hogan and your daughters...."

Moreover, if the causal instrument had been a bad debt or investment unconnected with an odious transaction (slavery), there should have been law suits or evidence that the offending parties had also lost money. But Hogan sued no one, and there is no evidence that Lenox or Depau, or even Dickey, were ever in serious financial straits; Lenox and Depau both left substantial fortunes to their heirs.

While the evidence points to the slave venture as the cause of Hogan's financial downfall, the probable underlying truth is that he brought these problems on himself. He may have failed to recognize that amassing wealth at the Cape of Good Hope by being daring and aggressive was not the same thing as retaining and expanding that wealth in the burgeoning United States. While it was certainly true that opportunity beckoned in the New World, the resulting fierce competition produced many failures that elicited little sympathy from either government or fellow businessmen. Successful entrepreneurs had to be bold, for certain, but they also had to be careful, a difficult combination of qualities for any man to acquire. Perhaps convinced that he was now part of the monied establishment in New York, Hogan might have neglected to be careful enough about protecting his ventures. Or perhaps he simply could not be something he was not—a careful, analytical, conservative businessman. When the possibility of daring new ventures and new profits arose, he could not resist, any more than anyone can deny his or her true nature.

The War of 1812 had nothing to do with Hogan's declining fortune, nor would it prevent him from trying to recoup his losses by selling some of his properties or even from entering into new land transactions. But that war and the related twenty-three years of the European wars, both culminating in 1815, marked dramatic changes not only in world affairs but also in those of the United States. Before then, the young republic struggled with its role as an independent country, fearing Britain in almost paranoid fashion, uncertain how to relate to a presumably republican France suddenly turned uncooperative and even bellicose, fumbling over territorial issues because of Spain's continuing though diminished role in the New World, and still tied to the apron strings of European politics. It wanted desperately to avoid becoming involved in the European war, or even being affected by its consequences. It could achieve the former simply by remaining neutral (as long as no European power interfered militarily in the United States), but it could not avoid the war's consequences because from about 1804 its shipping was affected by conflicting British and French orders intended to blockade the other country, its seamen were being impressed by British Navy vessels, and there were perceived territorial threats from Britain and France and territorial claims against Spain. Thomas Jefferson, who abhorred war and the use of physical power, soon found he could not depend on the goodwill of European countries to continue to accept American commerce and territorial claims without taking firm action. In a misguided attempt either to remove the maritime issue as a cause of war or to coerce Britain into changing its policies, he persuaded the Congress in December 1807 to enact an embargo on all American ships sailing to any foreign port and, in a separate action, a prohibition on many imports and exports. The embargos seriously injured American shipping and the economy and did nothing either to ease tensions with Britain, bring about a change in its policies or cause France to throw even a token of support to its former ally. At first opposed only by shipowners and merchants, the embargo was finally unpopular with virtually all Americans; it was suspended after being in effect some fifteen months in March 1809, three days before James Madison became president.

Viewed rationally and in hindsight, the War of 1812 should never have occurred, but in the climate of the time it was an inevitable war, caused more by emotions on both sides of the Atlantic than by rigorous analysis of international power politics. British seizures of American vessels and their cargoes adversely affected individual merchants and shipowners, but American shipping as a whole benefitted when it filled vacuums left by the merchant marines of European countries. The seizures disadvantaged the South and West because of the decline in exports of agricultural and staple products, but it was the impressment of seamen on American ships, which arguably had a negligible effect on commerce, that infuriated the country. Many of the seamen on American ships were British subjects trying to escape the horrors of impressment; some had legitimately become naturalized Americans, others held false papers and some were plainly still British subjects. Britain asserted that it was entitled to board American ships and take any seamen born in Britain or its possessions, but Americans believed they had gained their freedom from Britain precisely so that those who wanted to become citizens of the new country could do so without interference from any foreign power, regardless of where they were born. Nor were Americans affected in quite the same way when France, after 1807, seized just as many American ships or lied when it assured American diplomats that its equally obnoxious "continental system" decrees (intended to prevent British trade with the rest of Europe) had been revoked for American ships. The Federalists accused Jefferson, Madison and fellow Republicans of favoring France over England, but the country as a whole found that the culprit was Britain. In short, many Americans still hated—and feared—England. It is for this reason that the War of 1812 is sometimes called the Second American Revolution.

The immediate cause of British policies affecting the United States was based on hate and fear, just as was the reverse in the United States: hate because the United States dared to continue to trade with Britain's arch enemy and its anointed emperor Napoleon, the scourge of Europe, against whom Britain had often stood alone; and fear because American ships were threatening Britain's predominant role in world shipping, the favored position of its East India Company and the interests of British shippers in the West Indies trade. Only a handful of Englishmen correctly saw that the United States had to export goods and agricultural products—and its shipping services—if British manufactured goods were to continue to enjoy an expanding market in the United States. Even after Britain clearly ruled the seas following the Battle of Trafalgar in 1805, it showed little disposition to resolve the disputes by diplomatic means. Britain, as well as France, was also distracted from listening with sufficient attentiveness to what the Americans were telling them—that war was becoming inevitable—in Britain's case by its conviction that any and all measures were justified by the war with Napoleon and its belief that the United States was a weakling, posing no military or naval menace; in the French case because Napoleon, whose focus was on his two arch enemies—England and Russia, ultimately saw nothing to be gained from cooperation with the United States after selling the Louisiana territory, although he could not resist occasionally dangling inducements before American diplomats.

There were war hawks in Congress and elsewhere who wanted a battle with Britain and sometimes Spain for quite different reasons—ejecting the British from Canada and the Spanish from Florida. The United States had finally acquired West Florida in 1810 and 1812, but some were looking for an excuse to seize the remainder of Florida, and others had their eye on Canada, using as an excuse alleged British sponsorship of Indian forays against American frontiersmen in the Northwest and Mississippi valley. The latter contributed to the emotional climate that led to the war.

Events came to a head in June 1812, when Madison, responding to the war hawks and probably having no other realistic choice, asked for a declaration of war against Britain, which Congress readily granted on June 18. On the previous day, Britain had revoked its obnoxious decrees and two days later Napoleon, unable to invade England but believing that defeating the eastern menace would permit him to concentrate on England, began his fateful march to Moscow with an army of 600,000 men. It is tempting to conjecture that war might have been avoided if these intentions had been known in Washington in the final weeks before war was declared, but this would have been unlikely, even if rationality had prevailed. The revocation of the British decrees was conditional, and no one could have foreseen that Napoleon's Russian debacle (only 40,000 French troops returned alive) would at last rouse the rest of Europe to bring the emperor to his knees.

The country was ill-prepared for war. Although its naval and privateering victories over British ships are legendary, the United States lost most of the land battles, the federal treasury became bankrupt, and Madison's administration virtually ceased to operate during the last year of the war. The war was particularly unpopular with New York citizens and merchants. A contemporary wrote: "The coffee houses were almost empty; the streets near the water side were almost deserted; the grass had begun to grow upon the wharves."[7] Henry Adams in his *History of the United States* summed up the mood of the country when he wrote, "Many nations have gone to war in pure gayety of heart; but perhaps the United States was first to force themselves into a war they dreaded, in the hope that the war itself might create the spirit they lacked."

Hogan was not much affected by the war because he had no trading or shipping ventures underway that might have been adversely affected. There is a cryptic reference in a letter Hogan later wrote to President Monroe to "the plan I had submitted to Commodore Stephen Decatur [during] the war" which, he claimed, "had [it] been followed, the burden of that contest would bear altogether on our enemy."[8] Just what this plan was is no where to be found. Toward the end of 1814, when it was feared that New York would be invaded by the British, Decatur was placed in charge of the naval defense of the city. When his squadron—the *President, Peacock* and *Hornet*—attempted in January to evade British war vessels blockading the port, the American ships had the worst of the engagement. Possibly Hogan, ever the seaman, gave Decatur some advice that the noted Commodore did not follow, making it possible for Hogan to make his unprovable claim. Decatur later did try to help Hogan obtain a government appointment.

The despair which many Americans had felt for almost three years finally came to an end in February 1815. There was first the news of Andrew Jackson's decisive defeat of the British at the Battle of New Orleans which preserved the Southwest for the United States against Spanish claims and possible British interference. And then, only several days later, came news of the conclusion of the Treaty of Ghent on December 24 which ended the war by restoring the *status quo ante*, the shipping and seamen issues having been mooted by Napoleon's apparent defeat, and by leaving boundary issues to be resolved later. Quickly forgotten was the fact that, except for New Orleans and a few isolated land and naval engagements, American forces had been badly beaten in battle and much of Washington, including the new White House and partly finished Capitol building, burned to the ground by British forces under Rear Admiral Sir George Cockburn. There was instead universal rejoicing—a collective sigh of relief. The "era of good feeling" was to begin. The country could now get on with the business of developing its vast potential without having to look over its shoulder at what Europe was doing. For almost a century, with a few minor exceptions, the United States would steer its own course, at last freed from its bondage to Europe.

The country's new purpose was aided by equally dramatic changing circumstances in Europe. In 1814, Napoleon had abdicated and fled to Elba, apparently bringing the European war to an end, and in the process making peace with the United States possible. But Napoleon escaped from Elba and returned in triumph to Paris. He was soon decisively defeated at Waterloo and banished to St. Helena. Europe at last was at peace. The comprehensive Peace of Vienna heralded a century of largely successful attempts to maintain the balance of power in Europe without continent-wide wars and to concentrate instead on economic and social advancement.

In the United States the government was once more able to operate, albeit from time to time in faltering style; the federal deficit disappeared almost overnight; prices of export goods, mostly agricultural, increased, while prices of imports, mostly British manufactured goods, dropped; and general economic conditions improved markedly. Trade with Britain grew faster than ever before. Another result of the war was that the United States could expand to the west, and to a lesser extent to the south, without the threat of foreign-inspired opposition. Although the main influx would not come until later, immigration from Europe increased dramatically. No passport, visa or health certificate was required; an immigrant could simply get off a ship in the United States and disappear into the new society. There were many causes for the beginning flow of immigrants, such as declining death rates, growing populations and severe food shortages in Europe, the increasing ease of travel and the lure of a boundless new country. Another was the desire to escape from onerous income and other taxes imposed by many European countries. In contrast, about the only taxes collected in the United States were property and excise taxes and import duties, and in the former case they were quite low.

Hogan's attempts to recoup his losses began just before the War of 1812 and continued thereafter. He first sold the 20,117 acres comprising the Macomb township that he had acquired in 1807 and 1809 to John and Robert Oliver of Baltimore. The Oliver brothers were prominent merchants in Baltimore.[9] Michael Hogan formed a lasting personal and business friendship with them that would continue throughout his life.

Hogan had called the area Bombay, after the Indian city where his wife, Frances, was born and where they were married. He was fond of naming his ships and residences after his family and close friends. However, the present-day town of Bombay was not officially created until after Hogan's death when William persuaded the local officials at Fort Covington to name part of that township Bombay.[10]

He was also able—or perhaps forced would be a better description —to augment his dwindling assets by selling the Manhattanville properties, first Monte Alto, sold in 1811 to a Jacob Mark, and then in March 1812 Claremont, deeded to trustees for the benefit of his creditors. Joseph Bonaparte, the elder brother of Napoleon Bonaparte who had him installed as King of Spain only to be dethroned when Napoleon's fortunes waned, resided at Claremont at some point after Hogan's ownership terminated. He had come to the United States in August 1815 to find a place where his banished brother might someday come "that might even arise to be a New France." Joseph acquired sizable lands in northern New York but abandoned any idea of living there himself or of obtaining his brother's release from confinement at St. Helena. He settled instead in Philadelphia where he sired several illegitimate children by a young woman named Annette Savage.[11] In 1821 Joel Post became the owner of Claremont.

In order to find more affordable housing, the Hogan family moved in 1815 from No. 52 to No. 29 and later to No. 33 Greenwich Street.

Beginning in 1814, he tried to sell the 6,600 acres he owned near Utica. Writing to the Olivers in Baltimore, he noted the "disposition of your friends to invest money in real estate in this state" and offered "as good land as any in our State in a solid block only six miles from Utica" for $8 an acre. The Olivers quickly found a potential buyer, a Mr. Craig, who was willing to pay $7 an acre, an offer that Hogan said he would accept if paid in cash. But Craig did not buy the property. Hogan advertised for its sale in Philadelphia's *Evening Post* early in 1816. He also tried to interest Thomas Butler's father, his old acquaintance Major Pierce Butler, to buy the property, offering it for $60,000, considerably more than he was willing to settle with Craig, but this gentleman finally told Hogan in August 1817 that "it is not convenient to me at this time to make the purchase."

Hogan tried to raise money by mortgaging the York House in Utica which had been built in 1797 and served for many years as a hotel and meeting place in Utica itself.[12] The Second Bank of the United States had just been formed and by January 1817 had opened for business. Hogan hoped the BUS, as it was called, would loan him the money. He sought help from both Major Butler, who had become one of the directors of the new bank, and the Olivers. He tried to entice the latter by giving them the inside information why some directors had been chosen, and others not, at the board meeting in November 1816. Among other things, he reported that Robert Dickey, who had been a protégée of the Olivers, had not been chosen, and that "[John] Astor has carried all before him."[13] But he was pinning his main hopes on Butler through whom he had applied for a $42,000 mortgage. Butler wrote in February 1817 that "I am apprehensive [the directors] may think the sum of $42,000 too near the value of the land." The BUS would not even consider the application. In April, Butler told Hogan that a "large majority [of the Board of Directors] declined taking mortgages of real estate, nor would they discount a note unless two of the parties resided in [Philadelphia].... It would have afforded me great gratification to have been useful on this to you interesting occasion. When [DeWitt] Clinton desired you not to sell your lands, it would have been friendly if he, knowing your situation, had pointed out a means whereby you could be enabled to keep them."

It was the Olivers who finally gave Hogan a mortgage on the York House and also purchased the 6,600 acres of land. It was about this time that Hogan petitioned the United States Congress for "indemnification and accretion for damages because of use and occupation of valuable house belonging to him in Utica by detachment of U. S. troops [during the War of 1812] on their march from Buffalo to Sackets Harbor."[14] In a law passed by the Congress on March 3, 1819, settling a number of war claims, the secretary of the treasury was directed to settle Hogan's claim "for damage done to his house in Utica by a detachment of troops of the United States...quartered there in February [1813]" in the amount of $1,813.[15] The house was apparently York House.

The Hogan children were becoming young adults. William had graduated from Columbia College in July 1811 at age nineteen with first honors in classical studies and delivered the Latin salutatory at commencement exercises. His intention was to become a lawyer; he studied law under John Wells, a noted New York attorney,[16] and was accepted as a New York Supreme Court clerk. This intention was interrupted when he held a military staff position during the early months of the War of 1812 and when in May 1813 he sailed to Europe on the *Minerva* for a three-year visit which his father hoped would educate him in commercial affairs. He was concerned that William would be distracted by other inducements. In a letter of introduction written to Alexander von Pfister, a New Yorker, then in Cadiz, Hogan requested " your kind advice to him, should he remain any time in your city. You are aware of all my fears for youth when in a place such as Cadiz without friends to caution them against the various inducements held forth by custom, which then may not be thought vicious, yet in our view terribly so. My dependence, however, on this young man is such that he will see them in their proper light and avoid all such, which his friends will always recommend." William did not deliver the letter because, as he noted, "I already personally knew Mr. von Pfister in New York and had not so good an opinion of him as a mentor as my dear father seems to have entertained." William visited Portugal, England, Germany, Holland, Belgium and France, seemingly unhindered by the European war. He was in Belgium a week before the Battle of Waterloo in 1815.

Harriet and Sophia, William's younger sisters, attended private girls' schools in New York City. A Henry Moscross sent a bill to Hogan in 1814 for their six-month's tuition:

For six months tuition of his two daughters	$32.00
Quills, ink & copy books $3 firewood $4	7.00
2 Murray's grammars .75 cents inkstand .50 cents	1.25
21 Burton's lectures $2 grammar of history .62½	2.62½
Atlas & maps $1.50 History of England $1	2.50
Entrance five dollars each	10.00
	$55.37½

They were also exposed to the refined cultural education required of ladies of the time. Hogan once paid a bill for "lessons to the Misses Hogans, January through June 1812: Forty two lessons $45; *A Favorite Duet* by Clemente $1.50; *The Celebrated Overture* by Haydn $1."

Hogan—or perhaps it was Mrs. Hogan—had cause to be concerned over the health of their eldest daughter, Fanny. Late in 1814 when she was nineteen, Thomas Butler wrote to Hogan in ponderous style, replete with "my dear Sir's," suggesting she be sent to his mother-in-law Madame de Malleveault in Martinique or, " if you should be of opinion or Miss Fanny imagine that a change from the dull society of New York

to the still duller society of our farm [near Philadelphia] can be either agreeable or useful to her, we shall be most happy to receive her...."
In a letter written in French, Madame de Malleveault seconded the invitation for Fanny to visit her in Martinique and inquired warmly after "Madame" Hogan, Harriet and Sophie, as well as William.

Madame Malleveault also described events in Martinique on learning of Napoleon's escape from Elba. She referred to Napoleon as the "disrupter of the peace of mankind" and wanted the "struggle [to] end with the triumph of legitimacy against usurpation," meaning restoration of the monarchy. She applauded the fact that the "Count of Vangiraud, our Governor, ...sent back to France 600 soldiers of our garrison...as these soldiers are a heap of corruption...." She delighted to report that "our generous friends the English, in order to preserve the Colony for our unfortunate King, answered the request of our Governor; 2,000 men, led by Sir James Leith, the commander in chief of the British forces in the West Indies, arrived on the 5th [of June], to take possession of Fort Royal, Fort Bourbon, the stronghold of Bouillé.... Now we can sleep in peace, but before the arrival of the British troops, we were very worried and for good reasons, as the French regiment which was here sympathized with the rest of the Army and they would have taken the first opportunity to devastate our Colony...."

But Fanny did not go to Martinique, which was perhaps just as well, for Thomas Butler and his mother-in-law, Madame de Malleveault, would have a major falling out within a year. Fanny remained physically ill-disposed throughout her life and never married.

Perhaps due to his business problems, Hogan was again suffering from the gout, apparently quite severely. Writing in March 1816, Thomas Butler offered gloomy advice: "I was very much concerned, my dear Sir, to find...that you had been so long confined by the gout. Philosophy is a good, a very good thing, but after all we cannot bring our feelings to be passive under the numberless disappointments and evils with which this transitory life abounds. Let that be it as it may. We must struggle on till it comes to our turn to drop off which comes oftentimes much later than we could be easily reconciled to if we could be indifferent to the feelings of those we should leave behind." However, he did have a new medicine to recommend—*Eau médicinale*, which he claimed "has performed great cures when the directions of the discoverer have been strictly attended to, and I have not heard of a case where it has produced injury when taken as he directs.... I was told by a gentleman of great respectability that the remedy of Pradier was held in the highest estimation in Paris when he was there." Butler claimed that a medical committee established by Napoleon to review all medical discoveries approved *Eau médicinale*, but "would not award the proprietor a sum which he conceived at all adequate to the value of his secret.... The proprietor of the *Eau* went over to England and there disposed of his secret for a large sum.... It is so dear a medicine that it has often been counterfeited. In France it used to sell for 40 sous per bottle, in England now for half a guinea a bottle."

Although there were then hundreds of quack medicines and treatments for the gout, *Eau médicinale* actually contained a chemical with proven therapeutic benefits—colchicum, extracted from the bulb of the meadow saffron. Butler's history of the medicine was roughly correct.[17]

Hogan's gout recurred in 1817. While he was on a business trip in Philadelphia, Frances wrote, "I hope you have found no want of your crutches." Thomas Butler wrote: "My sister was induced to offer [you some pepper] from it's being so superior in strength to any that could be purchased and my father's thinking it beneficial to persons subject to the gout. My father has also found it beneficial applied as a blister to the part in pain which induces my sister to send a second bottle. We hope that it will now find its way to you and wish that it could prolong the relief that you at this moment experience." Unfortunately for Hogan, blistering was an old cure with no benefits.

Thomas Butler had problems of his own. He had met the beautiful Eliza de Malleveault at Ballstown Springs, where the Hogans spent their first summer in 1804 and where they may have met the de Malleveaults about 1812, and married her in Martinique, the home of her widowed mother who had a purse of her own from sugar plantations on that island. Thomas had brought her to Philadelphia where he expected eventually to inherit his father's estates. When Napoleon was at last banished to St. Helena and the Bourbons restored to power, Madame de Malleveault returned to France in 1816, insisting that her daughter and grandchildren accompany her. Thomas meekly went also, to the displeasure of his father who prevailed upon Hogan to write Thomas at Paris: "Your father is really heartbroken to think you should go to France without consulting him. I observe your last son's name is Louis, after his maternal grandfather. I hope the next will be called after your own father and that he will be born in this country."[18] Acting as the friendly intermediary, he also wrote to Madame de Malleveault in January 1817, imploring her to return to the United States with Thomas, principally because "your invaluable son-in-law would inherit an Estate that will otherwise go elsewhere...."

Thomas returned to Philadelphia after only nine months in Paris with two of three children and without his pregnant wife in fear that his father would make good his threat of disinheritance if he did not return.[19] Unpersuaded by Hogan's defense of Major Butler, the infuriated Madame de Malleveault minced no words in telling Hogan what she thought of the major and his son, alleging among other charges that Major Butler "has long been seeking an occasion to disinherit his son [and that] he would have done so before this had he been able to sell his plantation, for then he could have disposed of his property as he chose."

Madame de Malleveault was correct in believing that Major Butler had tried to sell his plantation. In January 1815, before it was known that a peace treaty had been signed, Admiral Cockburn, the one who had torched Washington the previous August, conducted a raid along the Georgia coast where, among other things, he took 138 slaves valued at $61,450 from Butler's Hampton Plantation on St. Simons Island, sending them to Nova Scotia where they were freed. Writing to Hogan in August 1817, Major Butler said: "I have not disposed of my property in Georgia. I am making arrangements for adding to it; by a purchase of Negroes to replace those Admiral Cockburn took from me. I found that those who expressed a desire to purchase [the plantation] expected me to make too great a sacrifice. It is a property I don't like to hold, but I devoted too many years to it to throw it away."[20]

At the end of 1814, apparently expecting an early end to the war, Hogan told Thomas Butler that he was considering resuming life as a merchant at some location in Europe. The opportunity came next year when he heard that the American consul at Cork, Ireland, had died, leaving the post vacant. He may also have been attracted by the possibility of returning to the country of his birth, even though he had shown no sign of attachment to his native land since leaving it at a young age. In October he wrote a letter to Secretary of State James Monroe seeking the appointment, accompanied by letters of recommendation from Henry Brockholst Livingston, one of the judges on the Supreme Court, and Daniel D. Tompkins, Governor of New York. Hogan said that it "would be in my power to procure many such [recommendations] from the finest friends of the Government and the most respectable of the community in all the ports of the U.S., but [I] deem it improper to give you the trouble they would occasion, trusting respectfully to my being in some degree known to you, and to my character bearing the test of inquiry." He explained that "my health and circumstances render it necessary for me to change for a while my place of residence, in the hope of reestablishing the first and repairing the second...." He was straight forward in declaring that "my object is to establish a commercial house of American agency at Cork." Perhaps concerned that Monroe might think his real interest was in returning permanently to his native country, he stressed that "a great desire to preserve my right to citizenship is one of the strongest inducements for soliciting this favor for, although it is desirable to change [my residence] for a time, my attachments and a part of my property will remain here." Livingston's letter of recommendation was gracious and laudatory: "Few men, if any among us, possess more intelligence, greater urbanity, and more mercantile principles and experience than Mr. Hogan."[21]

Michael Hogan received his appointment as consul at Cork in January 1816. On hearing this, Thomas Butler wrote: "I am very much pleased to find that you have succeeded in obtaining the Consulship at [Cork]. At the same time, I think you were more anxious about the success of your application that you need have been...I do not doubt for one moment, my dear Sir, that the duties of the office will be executed creditably for the United States."

Hogan never had a chance to execute the duties of consul at Cork. He may have delayed taking up the Cork post because he was also considering establishing himself at other European locations—he mentioned Liverpool and Bordeaux—or because he had become engaged in several land transactions. In November 1816, he returned the commission to the Department of State; seven months later, he sent a letter formally resigning the Cork position, citing as his only reason that "circumstances prevented me from going there."[22] The probable reason is that either Hogan lost interest or he was told that the position was not going to be filled (in fact, a new consul was not sent to Cork until 1827). It is interesting to note, however, that Hogan returned the commission within a few weeks after Monroe had been elected president (November 5, 1816) and that he penned his resignation letter the day after President Monroe arrived in New York City on his nation-wide tour (June 9, 1817). The first coincidence could be explained by the practice of surrendering offices when a new president comes to office (or on Hogan's assumption that this was the correct protocol); the second by the Monroe's presence in New York when either he or one of his functionaries asked Hogan to send a resignation letter as a matter of form.

No one apparently either recalled or cared about a derogatory letter about Hogan written over ten years previously to then Secretary of State Madison by John Elmslie, the U.S. consul at Cape Town. Hogan had sent a letter to an acquaintance in Cape Town in 1806, probably carried by William Anderson, that he was considering becoming a U.S. citizen. The undisclosed recipient of the letter showed it to Elmslie who thereupon wrote a letter, marked "Private," to Madison in 1806. Elmslie said Hogan's letter "[boasted] of his own growing consequence in America, of the influence which he and his friends were likely to have with the great officers of Government in commercial regulations, and [of] his having repeatedly dined with all of them, except the President whom he makes mention of in the most impudent and indecent terms." Elmslie then wrote that, "having learnt that it is Mr. H.'s intent to become a citizen of the United States, not from any love to America or the Constitution but in order to procure an official appointment under the same, I think it my bounden duty as an officer of the Government to acquaint you in order to guard against his intrigues, that Mr. Hogan is, to my knowledge (however he may get away with his ill got wealth), a person unworthy of any confidential trust."[23]

Elmslie was a British subject, although he had asserted to the British authorities at the Cape that he was truly a U.S. citizen because his U.S. commission said so. Just what Hogan did to incur Elmslie's dislike while both were at the Cape is unknown. Madison's reaction, if any, to Elmslie's letter in 1807 is also unrecorded. Hogan, however, did not have a high opinion of Madison. In a letter written in January 1815, apparently before he had formed a definite idea of seeking a consulship, he commented: "Yet so heart sick am I of being idle and of James the First mode of governing that I am fit to do anything to rid myself of both." Hogan may have been reflecting the general dissatisfaction of Americans over their government during the last year of the War of 1812.

While the Cork post still remained pending, Hogan once again turned his attention to lands in northern New York. He already had some experience with profitable land transactions in Franklin County—the Bombay lands he had sold to the Olivers of Baltimore. His object on this later occasion was lands belonging to the St. Regis Indians, also in northern New York. These lands had originally been occupied by the Seven Nations of Canada, which included the legendary Mohawk Indians, on both sides of the present border. By a 1795 treaty, the State of New York claimed that the Mohawk Indians had ceded all their territory for $1,600, a claim which the latter vigorously disputed. A year later, the State and the Indian Chiefs reached agreement to establish a St. Regis Indian Reservation, originally consisting of Six Mile Square in Franklin County, for which the Indian Tribes were paid £1,230-6-8 in cash with an annuity £213-6-8. In 1802, the New York State Legislature authorized the Indians to lease their lands directly to others, which they did with resulting ill-feelings between white settlers and their Indian landlords. In an attempt to rectify the problem, the State Legislature in 1816 authorized the governor to purchase any part of the reservation the Indians wanted to offer, including the One Mile Square on the Salmon River near what was then called French Mills, so the State would be the landlord rather than Indians. Hogan, who had been appointed land agent by Governor Tompkins, accomplished the first purchase on March 5, 1816. The tract was the One Mile Square and 5,000 acres abutting on the west, for which the Indians were to receive a perpetual annuity of $1,300. The purchase agreement was signed by three Indian chiefs who could not read English. There is a closing paragraph signed by an interpreter stating: "I hereby declare that I have acted as an interpreter in this agreement between M. Hogan and the subscribing Chiefs of the St. Regis Indians to the best of my ability, and that the substance of the same is well understood by them."

The agreement had to be confirmed by a formal treaty between the Indians and the State governor. Hogan must have taken the subscribing chiefs directly to Albany for this purpose, for the necessary treaty was concluded just ten days later. He had no direct pecuniary interest in this particular transaction other than the commission he received.

Shortly after this venture, William returned from his European tour. While Hogan professed the highest regard for his only son and must have been pleased that he had a university diploma and was well traveled and socially acceptable, William at age twenty-four had not succeeded in establishing himself either as an attorney or in commerce. He would have wanted to get his son into some line of permanent but worthy employment. Whether this was the reason or he was himself desperate, he decided to look into acquiring land in northern New York with the help of William, not as speculation but to earn income.

Michael Hogan, suffering from gout, and William visited the area in February and March the next year during one of the coldest periods in many years. The first consequence of this visit was an approach to Robert & John Oliver in Baltimore to try to induce them to sell the Bombay properties back to him. After "observing with concern that your situation is not as good as we expected [and that] you are probably right in your conjecturing that we purchased the Bombay land with a view to serve you," the Olivers told Hogan in June that they accepted his offer to rebuy the properties for $52,000 under a seven percent mortgage, with $6,000 principal to be paid on July 1, 1821, and every year thereafter until the whole debt was discharged.[24] A few days later, Hogan resigned his Cork commission. Acting as though he now had no other choices, he wrote the Butlers that "the die is cast for me to go to the St. Lawrence." Thomas Butler and his father were both aghast, the latter telling Hogan: "I entreat you not to make that decision. I ardently wish you not to make such a determination because it is almost certain death to you. You have suffered and are still suffering for your spring visit to that country. A warmer climate is indispensable for your comfort; nay for your existence. Your life is of the first import to your family. Better is a little [life] with health, than much without." After noting that William had traveled to St. Louis and reported favorably on the climate there, Thomas advised Hogan to go instead to Missouri.

Hogan was interested in more than the Bombay property. On October 20, he leased 144 acres of land and water near what was once called Gray's Mill from the subscribing Chiefs of the St. Regis Indians, for which he agreed to establish and maintain a ferry and to pay $305 annually for ten years. In February the following year, he traveled to Albany in company with John Pintard and Eleazer Williams, a half-breed Caughnawaga Indian whose father was one of the signers of Hogan's 1816 agreement acquiring One Mile Square and who later claimed to be the lost Dauphin of France, the rightful King Louis XVII,[25] to lobby Governor Tompkins to confirm this agreement by treaty, which was done on February 20. He called the area Hogansburgh, a name it bears to this day, but without the final *h*. William, to whom Hogan ultimately assigned the lease and who would reside in Hogansburg for a number of years, visited the site in 1818, probably with his father. The 144 acres were ceded by the Indians back to the State by a release on December 14, 1824, for one dollar and a $305 annuity, which was confirmed by an act of the New York legislature on April 20, 1825. William thereupon acquired the tract outright. Hogansburg also includes part of an 840-acre tract of land sold by the Indians to the State of New York on September 23, 1825, for $2,100 cash. The house that William built, although greatly altered, still stands on Route 37 in Hogansburg. An historical marker that once stood in front of the house attributed the town's name to him, although it was originally his father's doing. The curricle that Michael Hogan imported from England for use in New York City was once stored in Hogansburg and brought out for ceremonial occasions, such as the Fourth of July. In 1918, it was described as "moth-eaten, dismantled and a wreck."[26] It no longer exists.

A century and a half later these lands and others in northern New York and Quebec Province in Canada were to be the cause of legal battles, strikes and even violence by the Indians challenging the original basis for taking their lands.

Hogan had grand visions of what he and his son could do with his northern lands. He had a saw mill and a grist mill built at Hogansburg, based on another agreement with the St. Regis Chiefs signed in July 1816 giving him the right to cut timber on their reservation.[27] As for the Bombay property, he wrote to his uncle's firm, Christopher Richardson & Sons of Limehouse, England, eliciting the response that "we rejoice to find you was [sic] so well as to be able to undertake so long a journey as to Canada and sincerely hope your land there and the timber and ore on and in it will eventually prove a source of great wealth to you and your family. We fear however that the heavy freight on timber to this country will always operate against a favorable importation of it here." The only evidence that the lands produced anything for Hogan at this time was a shipment of some English hares to the Olivers in Baltimore late in 1819 for use as targets for sportsmen.[28]

Figure 5. William Hogan home, Hogansburg, early 20th century Author's Collection.

His apparent obsession with moving to northern New York may have been designed to elicit sympathy and to secure salvation from the depths to which he thought he had descended, due, in his mind, to the deeds and designs of others. He had not given up the possibility of obtaining a consulship in Europe. On May 14, 1818, he wrote another letter to Monroe, this time as president, seeking an appointment at a consular post of his own choosing in England.

The letter began with a flowery introduction that may have been common for the times but completely omitted the purpose of the missive: "I fear much that my taking the liberty of thus addressing what I conceive to be the highest office in the world may be deemed by you improper; imperious necessity compels me to it, and the kind condescension which I have experienced from you encourages me to hope that you will not only forgive but look with a favorable eye to my representation. If vouchers for the correctness of my statement and for character are necessary, I can assure you, Sir, most respectfully that, without the fear of egotism or arrogance being imputable to me, I can procure those of nine-tenths of the first men of the United States who have always and are still my friends and associates, as well as the first of other countries where I have heretofore resided."

Hogan then covered his background in terms that emphasized his accomplishments and blamed his "failures" on the designs of others: "I brought with me in May 1804 to this country Hundred and Thirty Thousand Dollars, the hard earnings of my early life in the worst climates of the Eastern world. The measures of the British Government, under which I was born in Ireland, depriving my ancestor of one of the best inheritances in that country (which ought to be mine) because a Catholic defending his ancient rights (now in the hands of a court favorite) inspired me in early life with a feeling every way unfavorable to oppression and produced an attachment for this country which, though unfortunate in it, has greatly increased by my residence and experience. I became a citizen as soon as the law could permit and was engaged in commerce and largely in the soil of this state. In the first [former] I was one of the sufferers and my interest in the latter was necessarily sacrificed to make up my deficiencies in the first, by which all were paid principal and interest, perhaps the only instance of the kind in this state for the last ten years. It has reduced me to the necessity of determining to remove with my family to the wilderness of Franklin County upon the boundary line near the French Mills.

The state of society there, perhaps the worst in the world, a Siberian winter and the unsafety of a frontier residence are disadvantages too serious for those born in affluence and brought up with tenderness and other expectations."

Only now did he finally get to the point of the matter: "I went to Washington last month with the intention of placing my situation before you and soliciting some employment under Government that might avert the painful necessity of moving to the North."

Since Hogan obviously had not met Monroe on this occasion, one would expect him next to define what employment he desired. But first he needed to emphasize that his claims were "those of a very faithful citizen who has seeded down a heavy sum in the country, the crop collected by others. Other officers could however be called in aid which if necessary would prove my attachment to the Government and show that, if the plan I had submitted to Commodore Decatur in the war had been followed, the burden of that contest would bear altogether on our enemy, that officer would do me the justice to explain it."

Finally, the letter defined the type of appointment Hogan wanted: "I have learnt that, in consequence of the late Commercial Law passed by Congress, it is the intention to appoint consuls or commercial agents at the different great manufacturing towns in England to attend to the requisites of that Law for the benefit of America. If you would be pleased to appoint me as one, giving me a choice of them, I would pledge myself to the most faithful discharge of the duties of the office and of every thing that was for the honor and interest of the United States, and I believe it would be as much in my power to be otherwise useful as in that of any one that could be sent abroad."[29]

To be charitable, the presumed purposes of this letter were to show the president that, though deprived of an inheritance because of the dastardly deed of some unnamed person, Hogan came from good stock, that he had always opposed British oppression, that he amassed wealth through his hard efforts, that his loss of wealth was no fault of his own, that he might be driven to exile in the unforgiving North if not awarded his due by government, and that he defied anyone to say he was not a patriot in the War of 1812, it being well-known that most merchants opposed the war.

Nothing was immediately forthcoming from Hogan's application to President Monroe. He was getting into deeper financial difficulty. By the next year, 1819, he could not keep up payments to the Olivers on the mortgages for either the York House or the Bombay properties.

Fortunately, help at last came from several sources. The first was that his business saviors, the Olivers of Baltimore, once again repurchased the Bombay property. While it is difficult to trace the various land transactions, Hogan could have netted some $17,000 from his original purchases in 1807 and 1809 to the final sale to the Olivers. Then on April 18, William made a fortunate marriage to Sarah Clendening, the daughter of John Clendening, a reasonably prosperous New York merchant. Just two weeks prior to the marriage, the Olivers had appointed William their agent for collecting rents on the Utica property and for its ultimate sale.[30] He also received an appointment a year later from New York Governor DeWitt Clinton to act as State agent in matters relating to the land purchased from the St. Regis Indians.[31]

In June Michael Hogan wrote another letter seeking government employment, this time to Secretary of State John Quincy Adams. The letter began with the claim that President Monroe had suggested to his son William, who must have been in Washington en route to or returning from a visit to Baltimore to see his new employer, the Olivers, that Hogan write directly to Adams: "Not having the honor of being personally known to your Excellency, it may appear improper that I should thus address you without an introduction, but relying on my former situation and present character being well known to the President of the United States, to whom I most respectfully take the liberty of referring you, I have deemed it more proper not to trouble you with letters from others of which I could get many, particularly as the President previous to his departure on his present tour was pleased to say to my son on his coming through Washington, that I should write you stating my views…." While most today would doubt that a president would either recall the name of an occasional letter-writer or take a personal interest in such cases, it was not then unusual for this to happen. Moreover, Monroe was well known for the direct and personal interest he took in government appointments, particularly in the foreign affairs field. In the latter respect, it was often he, rather than his secretary of state, who made appointment decisions.

Apparently believing that a federal statute enacted in March titled "An Act to protect the commerce of the United States and punish the crime of piracy" would lead to the establishment of new offices abroad,[32] Hogan asked to be named as commercial agent in a manufacturing district of England. If such offices were not established, he asked to be appointed as Navy agent at Pensacola, that post presumably becoming available when Spain ratified the recently signed Transcontinental Treaty ceding the rest of Florida to the United States. He made no secret of his wish that the office be one at which he could be compensated from private commercial activity, there being no salary. And, of course, he stressed that he had "so much experience in [commerce] as to feel myself well qualified for the duty that might be imposed upon me."[33]

Hogan soon learned that it had never been the intention to establish new commercial offices as a consequence of the 1819 law and that the Pensacola Navy agent position would likely go to "persons possessing stronger claims than I." Perhaps because no answers were forthcoming to his letters to Monroe and Adams, Hogan decided to visit Washington in mid-August. He called on Adams at his home on the 17th and 18th, accompanied during the first visit by [Thomas] Morris, U.S. marshal for the Southern District of New York,[34] to ask for a consular appointment "at one of the English manufacturing towns or at Marseilles or as Commercial Agent at Havana." He also delivered a letter to Adams dated the 15th, saying that "circumstances in themselves imperious have compelled my adopting another course and having made up my mind to form a commercial establishment at the Havana where the government have not any agent, Mr. Stephenson having died of the fever."[35] He solicited letters of support, which came from John Vaughn of Philadelphia and Stephen Decatur, hero in subduing pirates on the Barbary Coast at Algiers, Tunis and Tripoli. Vaughn's letter was a simple recommendation. Decatur's letter provided a favorable anecdote: "I owe it to him and beg leave to state that, during the late war being under orders for the Indian Ocean, Mr. Hogan waited upon me and gave me such information relative to the trade carried on by the enemy in that part of the world, and such charts of those seas, as would have [been] eminently useful to me had I proceeded on that concern. This information was volunteered by him purely from his good wishes to the cause, for although I had known Hogan to be an eminent merchant of New York, I had not prior to the period spoken of been intimate with him."[36] In his letter to Monroe a year earlier, Hogan had implied that the service he rendered to Decatur during the war was of an immediate military nature, possibly how to escape the British Navy blockade of New York harbor. Perhaps it was; perhaps Decatur, not wishing to have his sailor's knowledge questioned (as Hogan implied in his letter to Monroe), chose to mention only the Indian Ocean matter. Within a few months of writing his letter of support, Decatur would be killed in a duel.

Hogan received his appointment as agent of the United States for commerce and seamen at Havana, Cuba, just a few days later on August 20, 1819. The decision was made by President Monroe, not Adams.[37]

The appointment meant that Hogan could at last avoid the ignominy of moving to the north country, and he could turn over the management and disposal of his Hogansburg lands to his newly married son, now even more in need of a residence and gainful employment. (Later, the Olivers also made William their agent for the Bombay properties.) He could now proceed to Havana where he hoped to earn income from commercial activities, leaving his wife and daughters in New York.

Before assuming his new post, he called on several American merchants in New York and Boston to offer his services in doing business with Havana. This may seem the normal thing for a businessman to do, but to Hogan it was a demeaning experience for which he had to make excuses, although he no doubt hoped that sympathy for his plight would lead to monetary reward. Writing to the Olivers on September 19, he lamented, "It is a late hour of life to become a drummer which in my earliest days I would spurn, but necessity has no law, desperate cases must be met by corresponding remedies." And a little later in another letter, he told the Olivers: "Heretofore, I trusted and depended too much on others. In former times, I managed my own affairs and managed them well, for nothing ever failed through my own hands. I now will do so again and not withstanding all that has befallen me here, which may to the illiberal give the stamp of incapacity or idleness, I hope to prove at least the latter is not a part of my constitution. Those I leave [behind] claim an exertion extraordinary; if I fail they are gone."[38] He also sought help from his friend John Pintard whose cousin, John Marsden Pintard, had "materially injured" him. Writing to his daughter in New Orleans, John Pintard asked that her husband, Richard Davidson, recommend business for Hogan at his new posting: "An opportunity of a good word may possibly occur, which I hope will not be lost, in such case a line from the Doctor [through] my solicitation, will be proof of my regard for my worthy friend Michael Hogan."[39]

The country that laid claim to the largest part of North and South America at the beginning of the nineteenth century was Spain. Within a few years, as the result of revolutionary forces and the culmination of several decades of declining Spanish power, almost all this territory would become independent. The Spanish territory that most directly affected the United States was Florida, and close behind was Cuba. Americans were unanimous in insisting that the remainder of Florida become part of the United States, but negotiations with Spain to achieve that objective had been unsuccessful up to 1818. General Andrew Jackson, the hero of New Orleans, had been dispatched to Florida that year to subdue the Seminole Indians who had attacked white settlers. He not only crushed the weak Seminoles but also forced the Spanish garrisons in several towns to surrender. Jackson's initiative persuaded Spain that it was useless to try to hold on to Florida. After lodging a perfunctory protest, Spain agreed to resume negotiations which led in February 1819 to the Transcontinental Treaty under which Spain ceded not only the remainder of Florida but also all claim to lands to the west as far as the Pacific, excluding portions of present-day Texas, New Mexico, Arizona, Nevada and California. For all this, the U.S. would pay Spain only $5 million. It was a monumental achievement, making possible the further westward expansion of the United States. King Ferdinand II refused at first to ratify the treaty, thus leading to renewed tension.

The successful acquisition of Florida reopened the Cuba question. There were some who wanted to annex the island and others who thought it should become an independent country free from Spain. Laying claim to Florida as a contiguous territory was one thing, but Cuba was in the Caribbean where other countries, chiefly Britain, had an interest. The mutual suspicions between Americans and British that had been such a strong factor leading to the War of 1812 had not abated. The British press, believing the acquisition of Florida confirmed that American war hawks still thirsted for territorial expansion beyond Florida into the Caribbean, had been urging that Britain take immediate possession of Cuba. American newspapers were no less sensational in reporting that Britain and Spain were in secret negotiations which might result in Spain ceding Cuba to the British, and some had raised the cry that the United States should anticipate British designs by seizing Cuba itself. The Anglo-Spanish negotiations concerned only Britain's insistence that Spain terminate the slave trade to Cuba. Nevertheless, suspicions were rampant that Britain had secret designs on Cuba when Hogan sailed for Havana.

Despite the heat that the Cuban question engendered, there was no consensus what policy should be followed. Aside from the hot heads, there were only a few who advocated seizing Cuba—one of them paradoxically was Jefferson, and some other liberals favored independence and close ties with the United States, if not annexation. Many were concerned that Cuba might become another Haiti, whose blacks had established an independent but still violent nation after a bloody revolt against their perceived oppressors in the 1790s. Adams was cautious for another reason. He was concerned that an untimely attempt to annex Cuba would bring the country into conflict with Britain, which seemed to want Cuba for itself, a risk he was unwilling to incur. In this he had the support of American merchants who did not want to risk losing the favorable trade treatment that Ferdinand II had recently granted to foreign vessels and merchants in Cuba. Adams later enunciated a policy of tacit acceptance of Spain's sovereignty until "the ripe fruit" of independence fell into America's lap, and this became the controlling U.S. attitude toward Cuba until the Spanish-American War some seventy years later. Slaveholders in the South were also adamant that Cuba not become independent for they feared that another example of free Negroes would lead to rebellion among their own plantation slaves. They were therefore content with Adam's neutrality policy, although the more reactionary continued to favor annexation, believing that the nearby island would fit conveniently into the growing slave culture of the South.[40]

Hogan was aware of these cross currents when he wrote in one of his letters to the Olivers: "I perceive the removal of the Governor [in Cuba] which I regret. It indicates a hostile disposition to strangers, the other was very indulgent to them. I apprehend our Treaty [with Spain] is to be enforced by the [Vice Rey] or perhaps it is part of the policy of another nation [Britain] in order to procure employment for her refractory [i.e., stubborn] subjects. The whole may end in a general overthrow of the Spanish monarchy which would assure the independence of Cuba in defensive alliance with this country." And later, on the verge of sailing, he wrote: "The ratification of the Treaty, which I hope may prove true, would be of advantage incalculable to me as the next question with that Government would be the acknowledgment of a regular consulate at Havana...." Hogan had cause for being concerned about his official status in Havana. In his second letter to Adams, he had noted that, "under the existing Spanish colonial law, accredited agents are not recognized from any country, and that in consequence masters of vessels in our trade avoid (except in case of real necessity) any application to the agent of our government...."

He was expecting to sail momentarily: "The *Boxer* in which I go is in the stream windbound; perhaps tomorrow she will sail."[41]

On board the ship just before debarking its pilot at Sandy Hook, Hogan dispatched a letter to Adams on November 24 stating that an "apparently intelligent tho' silent respectable-looking man from Canada" who had just boarded the vessel told him he had received a letter from a friend in London reporting that the British Government "are about sending out to America, Halifax and St. Johns in New Brunswick 20,000 men, 5,000 of them to Jamaica, and that ten sails of that line are fitting out, the object believed...to be for taking possession of Cuba, that America being named as the destination is a mask, Cuba being the true object."[42] There is no evidence that the report had any basis in fact. As with his countrymen, Hogan was ready to believe any rumor of British illicit designs, as would soon again be demonstrated.

He arrived in Havana on December 8[43] and stayed only six months, but he quickly became enmeshed in two persistent and interconnected problems. The first was that, as he had anticipated, the Spanish governor refused to recognize his official status, even if it was only as agent for commerce and seamen. The second, consequential problem, which he had also anticipated, was that American ship captains and merchants used this non-recognition as an excuse to evade Hogan's advice and instructions. Hogan surmised that the Spanish authorities objected to having a U.S. consul in Cuba because the "title of Consul [was] in their minds more objectionable than the substance of the duty he has to perform,"[44] but the real reason probably stemmed from increased diplomatic tensions centering around the pending cession of Florida to the United States and fear of revolution in Cuba. As for disrespectful Americans, it is doubtful that they would have been any less so if Hogan's official status had been recognized. Hogan complained frequently to Adams that American captains falsified documents and engaged in other skulduggery to evade customs duties and other legal requirements. In one case, he noted that an American vessel had been hired by the Spanish to deliver ammunition to St. Augustine in Florida,[45] certainly an act contrary to American interests, but in another lengthily reported incident it was the affront to his dignity that was really at issue, however egregious the conduct of the American ship captain in question.

In this incident, Hogan recounted how a Captain Seth Stocking of a ship belonging to a New York merchant, after being accused of mistreating members of the crew, discharged the mate and stabbed him almost to death when he contested unpaid wages. When Hogan sent a note asking the captain to call at his office, Stocking initially refused, reportedly telling the men presenting the note that consuls were only sent abroad as spies. Stocking eventually did appear in Hogan's office. According to an affidavit executed by a sympathetic American ship captain who witnessed the meeting, Stocking threatened to throw Hogan overboard if he came to the ship. Hogan is said to have replied: "There is the door, Sir. Go out! Never enter my office again. I shall represent your conduct to your government whom you have insulted and who I hope will forever prevent your commanding a ship again under the flag you disgrace." Escalating the affair, Stocking threatened to throw Hogan through the office window, or so the witness thought. After more "foul language," Stocking left, leaving Hogan "much mortified, who was at the time very weak and feeble, scarce able to move along with the assistance of a stick, after a severe fit of illness." (The infirmity was probably a return of his persistent gout.)

Hogan wanted Captain Stocking punished in some way because "our national character suffers in the eyes of people of other nations from such [incidents]," but his larger purpose was to press his request that Congress enact legislation "compelling masters of vessels and other citizens trading to ports where commercial agents reside to pay [the same] attention to such officers [as they are required to] do to consuls..., notwithstanding non-recognition of such commercial agents by the authorities of their place of residence." He told Adams that, although there had been "much cause of complaint [from some persons] that the president [has] no right to appoint agents where they [are] not acknowledged by the government of the country to which they were sent..., on showing the law to such [reasonable men], they [are] convinced of their error. Captains and itinerant merchants abroad [however] are great legislators, and forever abusing the makers as well as the executors of the law which they evade by all means that ingenuity will suggest." In a lengthy letter sent as he was waiting to disembark on his return to New York, he told Adams that, "during my six months residence in my unacknowledged situation, I have experienced no difficulties with the authorities and, by conciliating means, have been able to carry many points and surmounted difficulties for our vessels and their people.... But in some instances I have been ill-requited by our own people who have constantly opposed me upon the grounds that, as the office was not recognized by the Spanish Government, they as masters of vessels were not by our laws obliged to regard it otherwise." After asserting that he had been encouraged to pursue this matter by a trustworthy Spanish official, Hogan further said, "I hope you will be pleased to accept my recalling this subject to your consideration and that you will place your views of it [before] the President." Apparently Adams did so, for on the cover of the letter Monroe penned his initials to the following note: "I think that it will be proper to press this recognition, and that the present is a favorable time for it."[46] Nothing immediately came of this endorsement, but Hogan would continue to press for the enactment of legislation according enhanced authority to consular officials, and would live to see a partial fulfillment of his wish.

There was constant speculation about the status of Florida, what King Ferdinand would do with Cuba, and whether the British had designs to acquire the island. Apparently still believing in a British conspiracy, Hogan reported in February 1820 that a British sloop of war had obtained the release of a British major who had been imprisoned on the island. Wondering whether the major had been sent as a spy and "not knowing who to trust," Hogan used his own sources and that "of a private transient acquaintance" (perhaps the same Canadian Hogan met on sailing from New York?) to ascertain the major's real intentions. He reported to Adams that "the major only held the real rank of captain in their Army and was sent and employed here by the opposition in England at the head of which was the Duke of [indecipherable]. His object was information on the political feelings of those in and out of office, the statistical and commercial conditions of the island, of which he had a copy of the best map in the possession of his government.... He thought the whole effort [of conquest] was untenable with a lesser force than 20,000 men...."

Concluding, Hogan said that "those in the interest of England disavow any views toward this Island. I do not believe them. The Spanish authorities are also of that opinion."[47] Shortly after this, Hogan told Adams: "Some of those who feel for their country fear that, in the event of Ferdinand being driven to extremities at home, he may, on condition of promised security, cede this Island to England. If so, it would require a British Army to get possession, and a century of mild government to conquer the hearts of the people who are with [the United States]. If Spain retains her character as a Nation, the cession would be more acceptable, but [Cubans] will not consent to be sold."[48]

Many Creole natives wanted independence from Spain. They were jubilant when they heard in April 1820 that Ferdinand II had been forced to restore constitutional government that would elevate Cuba from a colony to a province of Spain. Hogan noted in a despatch to Adams that news of the King's action was "immediately made publick, and the joy produced by it is not to be described. The officers of the Army [were] more elated than even the classes of persons who suffered most from despotic rule. It is difficult to say who, from the Governor to the lowest, is most happy."[49] A sympathetic Philadelphia newspaper reported that "all the bells were set to ringing in Havana—the people filled the streets shouting 'Viva la Constitution,' and the soldiers joined them.... Pipes of wine, and other good things were freely distributed to the soldiers and to the people and a general jubilee was observed."[50]

Hogan's enthusiasm following the April celebrations was short lived. Just two months later, waiting to disembark on his return to New York, he told Adams that: "Several reports of a disposition on part of many of the inhabitants for total freedom and separation from Spain excited occasional alarms in the minds of those opposed to such a measure...; but while the present Captain General remains in office, his total inability...to rule by any [means] other than the habits [of] fifty years of despotic sway...will produce evils and difficulties among the people...to wean them even from attachment to the Constitution. A stranger to liberty or freedom..., he does the most inconsistent things, always at variance with the code by which he professes to govern. It is thought that on the meeting of the Cortes he will be removed."[51]

Hogan's disillusionment about the prospects for the continuation of constitutional government in Cuba was well based. Real power remained in the hands of the slave-holding landlords who were more interested in preserving slavery than in independence. Both groups saw their hopes dashed when Spain, under pressure from the Holy Alliance of France, Russia, Prussia and Austria and fearful of losing all its colonies in the Americas, revoked its liberal measures in 1823 and reinstituted an iron heel on Cuba.

Hogan had hoped to act as commission agent for American firms, but he had only limited success. He later told Adams that he could earn only $2,500 a year in commerce at Havana.[52] One of his clients was Le Roy Bayard & Company of New York, with the same family as William Bayard with whom Hogan had been in a real estate partnership at Sackets Harbor. On May 13, 1820, the company wrote to Hogan that it would "show to your friend the Baron every attention in our power when he arrives. In the meantime, ... we have effected insurance on the property which he supposes may be shipped on board the *Macedonian*. Of the commission we may be entitled to in this affair as in all others, we shall carry the one third to your credit and should occasions offer from hence to be useful to you, it will afford us much satisfaction by endeavoring to render them so. It will always give us much pleasure to learn that your expectations at...Havana are realized and we hope that the climate may not be found injurious."

The letter also said "business here is more inactive than ever known," a reference to the financial panic that began in 1819, temporarily ending the "era of good feeling." The Baron was probably Kavanaugh, a passenger on the U.S.S. *Macedonian* the preceding year on a voyage from Valparaíso and Lima to the Isthmus of Panama carrying, among other things, $480,000 in specie, part of which was destined for the United States. (It was then common for U.S. Navy ships to carry specie on commercial account for safe keeping.) The nature of Hogan's involvement is unstated, but he probably acted as commission agent.[53]

By the time Hogan received this letter, he had formed a partnership with Jose del Castillo and Francis C. Black and printed a business circular offering their services as commission agents. Although he described the firm as Castillo, Hogan & Company, its official name was listed as Castillo & Company in order to comply with Spanish law that required local ownership. The circular was printed just before Hogan left Havana in June 1820 to be with his family in New York because of "a series of ill health and the impossibility of continuing in Havana during the very sickly summer months." (He named the foregoing Francis Black, who was from Charleston, South Carolina, to act as commercial agent during his absence.) It was the custom for those who were not native to Cuba to find healthier abodes during the hot summer months. Hogan told Adams that he intended to return to Havana in October "taking my family with me for a permanent residence near the town" He initially said he would visit Adams in Washington when he was released from Quarantine Grounds on Staten Island, but on being released and back with his family in New York, he unexplainably said he would defer going to Washington "unless you are pleased to express a wish to see me which I will attend to immediately."[54]

Hogan did visit Washington and even met with President Monroe, but the visit was not about returning to Cuba. By the end of the year, he was looking for a vessel to take him and his family to Valparaíso, Chile.

NINE

AGENT FOR COMMERCE AND SEAMEN VALPARAÍSO

> *My family, thank God, are all well and, although severe sufferers from sea sickness together with the ill consequences of brooding over the causes of this voluntary banishment....*
>
> —Hogan to Olivers, on arrival at Valparaíso

On November 11, 1820, five months after returning to New York from Havana, Secretary of State John Quincy Adams certified that "Michael Hogan of New York has been appointed by the president of the United States as their agent for commerce and seamen at Valparaíso and all the ports on the coast of Chile in South America, with all the privileges and authorities of right appertaining to that appointment." Hogan also received a letter from Secretary of the Navy Smith Thompson stating that "in the event of the United States Ships of War visiting the ports of Chile, you are authorized to act in behalf of this Department, as agent for furnishing such supplies as the Service may require, and for which your draughts upon this Department, in reimbursement, will be duly honored on presentation."

He had strong political backing for his previous appointments to Cork and Havana and was therefore able to rely on the contacts he had made at that time to obtain the Valparaíso appointment.[1] After first saying he would not visit Washington, he finally did, calling on Adams four times and President Monroe once. Adams recorded in his diary that Hogan "wishes...to obtain an appointment...with better prospects [than Havana] of life and health for a family, though also lucrative." He asked for an appointment "at some port on the South Sea, in Chile or Peru," which he then narrowed down to Chile. Almost overnight, Hogan received confirmation in writing of his appointment to Valparaíso. Again, it was Monroe who made the decision. He may have learned this when he met with the president, apparently without Adams present. The only thing known about the meeting is Hogan's later report that Monroe asked him to find a suitable government position for Jeremy Robinson in Chile.[2] The president also asked that Hogan take with him as an assistant the teenage son of a Washingtonian naval surgeon and doctor named John Bullus.[3] Both requests would later give Hogan anguish.

Hogan was a natural selection for the concurrent appointment as Navy agent at Valparaíso based on his background and knowledge that Navy agents had already been posted at some other foreign ports, but not yet on the west coast of South America, where a squadron had been stationed since 1819.

Although American naval traditionalists like to harken back to the exploits of John Paul Jones and other daring commanders during the Revolutionary War, the U.S. Navy was not officially established until 1794 in response to a perceived threat to American merchant vessels off the Barbary Coast. When the War of 1812 broke out, its only warships were those that had been procured in connection with the undeclared naval war with France at the close of the century. Plans were approved to construct nine ships-of-the-line and twelve frigates and to expand the Navy's responsibilities to include the Mediterranean, Caribbean and Pacific Oceans. A Board of Navy Commissioners was established in 1815 responsible for procuring naval stores and materials and constructing and equipping naval vessels. It was attached to the Navy Department which as late as 1842 consisted of only thirty men housed two hundred yards west of the White House in the Southwest Executive Building. There were no departmental branches or offices elsewhere; for this purpose Navy agents were appointed both in the United States and abroad to supply and service U.S. Navy ships. They were subject to direction from the Navy Department but often their only contact was with accountants in the office of the fourth auditor of the treasury which was part of the Treasury Department, although housed in the Navy Department building.[4] Hogan would later have occasion to become painfully acquainted with one particular fourth auditor.

By appointing Hogan as agent for commerce and seamen,[5] rather than consul, Monroe and Adams avoided the necessity of obtaining the advice and consent of the Senate. They probably did this because a formal consular title might have been viewed as a sign of United States recognition of the independence of Chile, a bridge the Monroe Administration was not yet ready to cross.[6] Hogan caused a minor stir when the *New York Gazette,* ten days after the appointment, described it as American "Consul" at Valparaíso. Hogan promptly wrote a letter of apology to Adams swearing he was not responsible for the reporter's gaff.[7] Two years later, when the United States recognized Chile, Hogan became a full consul and there would be no danger of political fallout from publicity.

The consular service was very different in the early nineteenth century from what it is today. Consular officials were on their own, not only in establishing their office but also in how they went about their business. And it was, in many respects, a business. Their main job was to take care of visiting American merchant vessels and seamen. Their reporting responsibilities were minimal. Except for those assigned to the Barbary Coast, consular officers collected no salary; even their transportation expenses, unless they were fortunate enough to secure passage on a U.S. Navy vessel, came out of their own pockets. They were expected to pay their office expenses from income generated from fees charged for the services they were required to render. These rarely provided enough income to meet personal expenses. This stark reality made it necessary for almost all consular representatives to engage in commerce at their posts.

Americans receiving diplomatic appointments as ministers or secretaries received one-time "outfit allowances" and annual salaries, as did special agents, and sometimes consular officers were later able to claim compensation when they performed diplomatic functions. Still, even for the diplomatic corps, the United States was parsimonious in comparison with the benefits bestowed by other countries. It did not begin naming ambassadors until 1893.

During most of the nineteenth century, both consular and diplomatic appointments (and those throughout the entire United States Government, for that matter) were based on political patronage. There was no system of employment standards, much less of examination based on ability or merit. Although a few reforms were introduced from time to time, systems based on merit were not introduced in the domestic Civil Service until 1883 and in the Foreign Service until 1906.

In 1818 the Department of State had only a secretary of state and ten regular clerks, each equivalent to a bureau assistant secretary today. Three more clerks were added by 1827. The Department was housed from 1820 to 1866 in a small building at Fifteenth Street and Pennsylvania Avenue in Washington, D.C., where the Treasury

Department stands today. It did not occupy the old State-War-Navy Building, now part of the Executive Offices of the President, until 1875.[8]

Although there was no salary, consular offices did come with a few perquisites. One of them was the right to don a consular uniform. Hogan ordered his from a London tailor in 1822. The Department of State's 1815 instructions prescribed the uniform:

> Single breast coat of blue cloth, with standing cape or collar, and ten navy buttons in front; one button on each side of the cape; four on each cuff; four under each pocket flap; and one on each hip and in the folds; two on each side of the center; and one on each side of the same at the lower extremity of the skirts.
>
> The front (from the cape down to the lower extremity of skirts), cuffs, cape, and pocket flaps, to be embroidered in gold, representing a vine composed of olive leaves; and the button holes to be worked with gold thread; the button holes corresponding with the width of the embroidery, which is not to exceed two inches in any part.
>
> Vest and small clothes of white, and navy buttons; the former to have ten in front, and four under each pocket flap. With this dress, a cocked hat, small sword, and shoes and buckles are to be worn. The hat to be furnished with gold loop, gold tassels, and black cockade, with gold eagle in the center; added to which, is to be understood that the mountings of the sword, and shoes and knee buckles, are to be of gold, otherwise gilt.

Hogan must have cut a fine figure, dressed in all this regalia, looking more a military figure than a peaceable diplomat. The practice seems hardly in keeping with the democratic American way, supposedly abjuring unnecessary titles and honorifics, but pomp and ceremony in international diplomacy would remain intact for over a century. Diplomatic notes even today begin with the words "I have the honor to refer to your Excellency's note," and it was only some fifty years ago that despatches from American diplomatists abroad to the Department of State ceased using comparable phraseology. How often Hogan wore his uniform in Valparaíso is unknown; only two incidents are recorded.

The independence movement in Spanish America created an entire continent of independent nations (with only a few isolated exceptions), an event not duplicated until decolonization following the Second World War. At its height, the Spanish empire in the New World encompassed Mexico (then called New Spain which included most of the present-day southwest quadrant of the United States), Florida, Cuba, Puerto Rico, Central America and almost all of South America, except Brazil which Portugal claimed. The Spanish territories were ruled either as colonies or as vice royalties, almost separate kingdoms, just as there were several kingdoms in Spain. There were three Spanish vice royalties in South America: New Grenada, encompassing present day Ecuador, Colombia, Venezuela and the Guianas; Peru, which included Bolivia and northern Chile; and La Plata, which is today Argentina, Paraguay, Uruguay, and the southern part of Chile.

Within these territories, antagonism had gradually developed over the centuries between upper-class, land-owning Creoles, often with some Indian blood, and *peninsulares*, who were pure-blooded Spanish either born in or still culturally tied to Spain. Both sought the allegiance—often involuntarily—of native Indians, mestizos, free and slave blacks, and other socially and economically disadvantaged groups. The Creole-*peninsulare* dispute was exacerbated after the Seven Years War when Spain, just as with Britain in North America, attempted to enhance its overseas investment return by reining in its colonialists. There were several local revolts, but it took the unsettling military and political events in Europe during the Napoleonic Wars to arouse a full-scale revolutionary spirit. When Napoleon invaded Spain in 1808, the *peninsulare* governing classes in Spanish America formed provisional juntas to hold local power until King Ferdinand VII could be restored. Creole-backed juntas wanting independence were also formed and in some cases achieved a semblance of control. But when Ferdinand was restored to power in 1814, Spain was able to reassert control for several years before Simón Bolívar liberated Colombia and Venezuela and José de San Martín established the independence of La Plata. In 1817 San Martín and Bernardo O'Higgins, the latter the son of an Irish soldier in the Spanish service, marched with a patriot army across the Andes to defeat a royalist force at Chacabuco in Chile and occupy Santiago. O'Higgins was declared Supreme Director. A year later, on February 12, Chile declared its independence. Much fighting lay ahead, partly in Chile but mostly in Peru where the Spanish Viceroy remained, before all the new nations of Spanish South America were truly free of Spain.

In the early nineteenth century, neither Americans in general nor their government knew much about the events taking place to the south or their implications for the country. Since 1811, the United States had adopted a policy of active sympathy but formal neutrality with regard to the independence movement in Spanish America.[9] But the country could not avoid the area or what was happening there. Although the volume of trade with the area was small, the American merchant marine was looking for new markets, and in the strategic area the United States could not avoid Spain because it continued to control the coveted Florida territory. Since so little was known about the area and its prospects for its future, President Madison dispatched several special agents, sometimes with consular titles, to report on developments so that policy decision could be made.

Joel Roberts Poinsett (after whom the poinsettia flower was named) of South Carolina was sent by Madison in 1810 as consul general to represent the United States at La Plata, Chile and Peru and to survey the situation. Hogan had met Poinsett at Albany in 1806, probably about some real estate matter, and communicated with him by letter for several years in the 1820s. It is possible that, after his return to the United States, Poinsett had a hand in Hogan's consular appointments.[10]

Poinsett was openly sympathetic with the patriots in Chile: he symbolically joined the Chilean patriot army and submitted a proposed constitution, but by 1814 he was out of favor with the ruling Chilean junta and shortly thereafter returned to the United States.[11]

The War of 1812 deferred for a time American interest in and attention to South America, but its conclusion and the end of the Napoleonic Wars in Europe reopened the questions of independence and of commerce with the continent. The chief beneficiary of expanding commercial relations was Britain because of its large Navy and merchant marine, its leading role as producer of manufactured goods and its strength in international finance. The United States was could claim a trade advantage only in agricultural products and perhaps whaling. Another result of these wars was that many soldiers and sailors left unemployed by the war's end sought their livelihood in the armies and navies of South America, sometimes on the side of the patriots but as often with the royalists. Most were English and Irish but there were also some Americans.[12] The area became a haven for adventuresome and often disreputable seamen, merchants and traders, willing to do business with anyone. Several Americans were employed as privateers by Spain or patriots in Latin American waters.

Articles in the American press began to address South American affairs, often portraying what was happening there as similar to the American Revolution. Although this was an inapt comparison, there was political pressure, led by Henry Clay of Kentucky, to recognize the new republics. The Monroe administration was not ready, for good reasons, to take this step, but it needed first-hand information about the situation in South America. It therefore decided to send commissioners on one-time missions to the southern provinces to make recommendations about recognition and other matters. The men selected were Theodorick Bland, Caesar A. Rodney and John Graham, the first to concentrate on Chile.

In 1817 the Monroe administration also resumed the practice of sending special agents to Spanish America. The one principally responsible for Peru and Chile was John Bartow Prevost. He was a stepson of Aaron Burr,[13] had been appointed a judge of the Louisiana Superior Court at New Orleans by Jefferson in 1805,[14] and was probably known to Hogan in New York.[15] William G.D. Worthington was sent to La Plata, Peru and Chile to assist Prevost. but he made the mistake of trying to negotiate agreements on commerce and seamen with both La Plata and Chile and was recalled by Monroe in February 1819, leaving Prevost the only agent in the entire area.[16] A Jeremy Robinson was appointed to Lima in 1817. His appointment was withdrawn but he went to the west coast anyway and attracted considerable attention, as will be seen. The status of special agents was ambiguous both under U.S. law and in the eyes of the host countries. They were considered to be agents of the executive branch of government, not subject to Senate confirmation; as such their status led to friction between Congress and the president at the time and especially in subsequent years. The advantage of naming special agents was that, since they did not have to be formally accredited to a foreign government, their presence did not imply either acceptance of Spain's sovereignty or recognition of independent governments, while leaving them free to perform normal consular and diplomatic functions on an unofficial basis.

By early 1818, Chile was rid of most of the Spanish royalists, but the center of Spanish power on the West coast still flourished at Lima and ports to the south, Spain still controlled the island of Chiloe and the seas, and royalist guerilla forces remained active in the province of Concepción. Chile acquired several ships for its nascent navy, one of them a British East Indiaman at Valparaíso which was renamed *Lautero*, but it had few capable seamen and virtually no officers. It solved the latter problem by hiring a number of foreign naval officers to manage its small fleet. Most of them were British, but there were also several American officers and seamen. Like the United States, Britain had declared itself a neutral in the Spanish American wars of independence and had forbidden its subjects from taking part in the war, but these stances were taken more to avoid giving the Holy Alliance an excuse to intervene in Spanish America on the side of Catholic Spain than out of any conviction or intent to enforce the non-participation edict. The latter certainly did not deter many English, Scot and Irish Navy and Army officers and men from joining patriot forces. There is even evidence that the British Government tacitly consented to these efforts.[17] The American government also found it convenient to look the other way when complaints were made that its citizens were violating U.S. neutrality laws by taking sides in the conflict.

The man Chile hired to lead its fleet was Admiral Thomas Cochrane, a nephew of Admiral Alexander Cochrane, Cockburn's superior in the latter's raid of Georgia and South Carolina in the War of 1812 during which, among other things, Colonel Pierce Butler's slaves were taken to Nova Scotia. Thomas Cochrane had been struck off the British Navy lists in 1814, convicted of stock fraud (though he was probably innocent), and he was an active and energetic opponent of the British government then in power. Unbelievably for an admiral who had fought the French, Cochrane was sympathetic to Napoleon Bonaparte. On his voyage to Chile, accompanied by his wife Kitty (who was considered a beauty) and two children, he planned to stop at St. Helena where he hoped to help Napoleon escape to establish an empire in South America. Fortunately, the world was spared another bout with the scourge of Europe when the ship's captain was ordered not to stop at St. Helena. On his arrival at Valparaíso on November 28, Cochrane was made vice admiral and commander-in-chief of the Naval Forces of the Republic of Chile. In January 1819, he sailed on the 50-gun *O'Higgins* for Lima, accompanied by the *Lautero, San Martín, Chacabuco* and several smaller ships of war. (On board the *Lautero* was an English surgeon, John Styles, who later married one of Hogan's daughters.)[18] This small force spent most of its time over the next four years in Peruvian waters aiding the patriots and achieving several noteworthy victories. But Cochrane's "temper and an intrusion of personal aims," when combined with Latin sensibilities, led to a number of disagreements between the vice admiral and patriot leaders in Peru and Chile.[19]

The problem of protecting American citizens and commerce without incurring unacceptable foreign policy risks had not gone unnoticed in Washington. One step taken was the passage in 1819 of the previously cited "Act to protect the commerce of the United States and punish the crime of piracy" which, among other things, authorized the U.S. Navy to convoy American merchant vessels and to retake vessels "which may have been unlawfully captured upon the high seas." It provided a legal basis for naval actions that were to become increasingly necessary in the Pacific and elsewhere.[20] The other response was to station warships on the west coast of South America to provide continuing protection of American interests.

The U.S.S. *Macedonian*, a 1,325-ton 38-gun frigate that had been captured from the British in the War of 1812, was ordered in May 1818 to prepare for a cruise in the Pacific Ocean under the command of Captain James Downes. The instructions issued to the captain were similar to those later to be given to other commanders sailing for the west coast of South America. He was told "to afford to persons and property of the citizens of the United States protection and security, consistently with the laws of nations, and the respect due to all existing authorities, wherever and whenever such protection may be needed, and can be afforded." The ship was to be "displayed [so as to] produce impressions favorable to the United States," and the captain was to guard "sedulously...against any act that might compromise the United States in any manner, except under the necessity of urging such just claims as may arise out of the detention or interruption of the whaling ships, or others carrying on lawful commerce in that quarter." Lastly, the captain was instructed that, "in all difficult cases, you will advise and consult with John B. Prevost, Esq., United States Agent at Lima."[21]

The *Macedonian* arrived at Valparaíso at the end of January 1819 and for the next two years cruised along the coast as far as Panama, aiding American shipping in the process. Downes refused to accept the legality of the various blockades imposed by either the royalists or Cochrane on behalf of Chile.[22] He also thought the United States should actively protest the seizure of American vessels, whether as contraband or prizes, while Prevost argued that the United States should trust Chilean tribunals to dispense fairness and justice. In this, Prevost had the better of the legal argument because some of the American vessels seized, such as the merchant ships *Montezuma* and *Macedonian* (the latter under Captain Eliphalet Smith), were carrying arms or specie for the Spanish royalist forces at Lima.[23] In a report to Adams, Prevost highlighted the problem of Chilean perception of the United States which haunts it to this day: "There exists a peculiar sensibility to every act emanating from the [U.S.] Government or done by an individual although strictly neutral. [The Chileans] seem to claim a sympathy from us in their struggle that they look for nowhere else, and cannot bear any circumstances that lead to a contrary feeling."[24]

While these events were taking place in South America, political discord in the United States was heating up. The dispatch of the commissioners had temporarily quieted those who were demanding immediate recognition, but in March 1818 Henry Clay challenged the president's constitutional authority in foreign affairs by seeking approval of a Congressional resolution supporting recognition. The resolution failed to pass. The three commissioners returned to the United States that summer and in November submitted lengthy reports about their South American mission. Bland's was the only one that focused on Chile. His report, as well as the others, avoided formal recommendations on recognition. After noting that the "silver and copper of Chile will enable [United States citizens] to extend their enterprise and push their commerce to a greater advantage than ever," he thought "it will not be deemed an exaggeration to set down the commerce of Chile itself as worth to the United States, annually, about two millions of dollars." But, following a line apparently believed then and since to be altruistic, if not realistic, Bland made a point of recalling he had told the Chileans that "the United States wanted no commercial advantage held out to them as an inducement to the acknowledging, or as a compensation for sustaining, the recognition of the independence of Chile."[25] The British, in contrast, later made it clear they expected a commercial quid pro quo for recognition. At Adams' request, Poinsett also submitted a report that was not favorable to recognition but was more realistic about economic policy than Bland's. He noted, with some foresight, that the British were gaining commercial advantages in South America, while the United States stood by doing nothing.[26]

In November, President Monroe told the House of Representatives that "there is good cause to be satisfied" with the independence movement in South America, but he carefully avoided saying anything about recognition. This attitude reflected not only the official stance of American neutrality but the belief of Monroe and Adams, particularly the latter, that the United States should take no steps that might dissuade Spain from forfeiting Florida to the United States. Nor did the Monroe Administration want to provoke European intervention to save the Spanish monarchy in South America. The recollection of the unhappy War of 1812 was still too fresh in memory to warrant any policy other than one of caution.

But a policy of deferring recognition could not continue forever. While Bland, Poinsett and other representatives might express caution and while first-hand reports from South America found increasing fault with the patriots, others were writing about the land to the south, the heroism and patriotism of its leaders in revolting against the Spanish, and—inevitably—the danger of the British gaining an advantage. Clay continued to bedevil the administration by introducing congressional resolutions supporting recognition, some of which were passed by the House but not the Senate and were in any event non-binding.[27] In November 1820, Monroe made a mild suggestion in his message to Congress in favor of recognition, but still avoided a recommendation to that effect. Perhaps Hogan's appointment as agent for commerce and seamen during the same month was an indication of this more forthcoming policy. Then, in February 1821, after a two-year delay, Spain finally agreed to accept the Transcontinental Treaty granting Florida and much of the northwest territory to the United States, thereby removing the main reason for delaying recognition of the new South American countries.

Adams signaled the end of the attempt to cooperate with Britain on the recognition question when, in a speech in Washington celebrating the Fourth of July in 1821, nine days before Hogan arrived at Valparaíso, he denounced England, spoke favorably (if vaguely) of the eventual need to recognize the independence of South American countries, and admonished other nations not to interfere in the hemisphere. It was with this background and in this atmosphere that fifty-four year old Hogan began his new career.

Hogan encountered difficulties in finding passage to Chile. In February 1821 he wrote to Adams suggesting that he be sent in a U.S. Navy vessel because "my arrival there in a man-of-war could not fail of giving my informal station a degree of importance and dignity that would result in advantage to the Publick service, for the lower the office abroad, the more it requires conveyance and support from its own Government and its publick officers, particularly in a Catholic country where there is more show than substance in all their actions."[28] But U.S. Navy transportation was not to be forthcoming. The last Navy ship to sail for the Pacific had been the U.S.S. *Constellation*, leaving New York on July 25 the previous year to take over from the U.S.S. *Macedonian* as the first flagship of the newly created Pacific squadron, and another naval sailing to that part of the world was nowhere in the offing.

In a curious letter sent to Adams about the same time, Hogan reported an article in a Bermuda newspaper announcing the capture of Lima by Lord Cochrane. Hogan apparently intended to use this premature "news" as the lead-in to report that he had received information from an Englishman of two British expeditions being sent to the Pacific, one jointly sponsored by the Houses of Baring and Parish and the other in Liverpool under the direction of John Parish Robertson, as well as a separate venture to the west coast of South America under a Mr. Brown that sailed from London at the end of 1819.[29] Just what this was all about, other than an amateurish attempt to impress Adams, is unknown. The Baring name has long been associated with British investment banking; John Parish Robertson had come to South America in 1808—he and his brother William were prominent British merchants at Buenos Aires and Lima for many years;[30] Brown could have been Thomas Edward Brown, an English merchant who was to be one of Hogan's neighbors at Valparaíso.

Hogan finally found transportation on the merchant vessel *Teaplant*, commanded by Captain Robinson and owned by LeRoy and Bayard.[31] The family boarded the vessel on April 8, 1821, and five days later sailed from New York.[32] With him were Frances and his three daughters, Fanny, Harriet and Sophia, aged 26, 22 and 19. William and his bride Sarah stayed behind in the United States to take up residence at Fort Covington and later Hogansburg in northern New York. Also in the Hogan entourage was the young Bullus. While the *Teaplant* was at Rio de Janeiro, Hogan planned to press the American Minister, Thomas Sumter, Jr., to pay his long neglected bill for transporting him, his family and bed companion on the *Charleston Packet* eleven years earlier, but he found that Sumter had left for the United States just a few weeks earlier. The news persuaded Hogan that he could now pursue his claim against Sumter through courts in the United States; soon thereafter, he wrote to his friend Robert Dickey in New York asking that he find an attorney in Charleston to institute a suit against Sumter.

From Rio, there was the often dangerous passage around Cape Horn. Hogan reported that "no gales to complain of were encountered. We came to the eastward of the Falkland Islands and had Cape Horn, that terrific point, bearing north of us on the 71st day, [at a] distance [of] 75 miles, [where we were] becalmed [but] had fine weather, [it] being the shortest day [of the year] 23rd of June, the meridian [noon] altitude of the sun not more than 8° 30'."[33] It was, just as in Cape Town, winter in the southern hemisphere at the time, the winter solstice being the shortest day of the year. Cape Horn is just 2,300 miles from the South Pole, thus accounting for the low angle of the sun at noon.

When they first sighted land in Chile, Captain Robinson asked Sophia and the other Hogan women, "Well, ladies, would you like a ramble on shore...to get some wild flowers." The delighted Hogan women asked their father for permission to go ashore, but he gave a "most decided refusal [saying] there was always a risk in leaving a ship under weigh." As the ship cleared the headland, the crew sighted a dismasted ship close in shore and some men busy with boats in the water. An American flag was seen being hoisted on a hill. Hogan and Robinson naturally thought shipwrecked American sailors were on shore and were preparing to send a boat to lend assistance. But closer observation by the mate from the rigging revealed cannon being placed in a large cutter and men clothed in red shirts and fur caps and armed with cutlasses. The *Teaplant* promptly set all sails to escape what appeared to be a pirate band.[34] The pirate later proved to be the royalist guerrilla leader Vicente Benavides who had already seized several other ships and either killed their crew or forced them into his service. It would not be for several months that the Hogans learned how fortunate they had been to escape a similar fate.

The *Teaplant* arrived at Valparaíso as night was falling at 6 p.m. on Friday July 13 after a three month's voyage. A British warship, the *Superb*, was in port, as well as an American merchant vessel; the U.S.S. *Constellation* was in Peruvian waters.[35] That night, still feeling it necessary to disparage his new position, Hogan wrote to Robert & John Oliver at Baltimore:[36]

> My family, thank God, are all well and, although severe sufferers from sea sickness together with the ill consequences of brooding over the causes of this voluntary banishment, they have borne the voyage with heroic perseverance and good spirits. My eldest daughter [Fanny] is extremely weak but not more so than myself, for I have been ill all the passage. I hope, however, this climate will regenerate and make me a new man.

He described his illness to another business friend as "a severe fit of the gout." He would continue to be plagued by the disease, despite the temperate Mediterranean-like climate of Valparaíso, which of course could not relieve his distress.

Valparaíso was an important place not only because it served as the port for the capital, Santiago, somewhat inland, but more importantly because it became the principal port on the west coast of South America during the 1820s. It was the first civilized place at which ships could call after rounding Cape Horn and the last port of call before the Cape. Its leading position was also due to the fact that

Callao, the port for Lima, which might otherwise have been in first place, was in the center of the continuing battle for Peruvian independence for several years, as well as to the fact that O'Higgins transferred the central customs house from Santiago to Valparaíso and encouraged foreign businessmen to reside in Chile and become citizens. The port was also used extensively for the transit trade. As a result, the population doubled between 1810 and 1820 to 10,000 and doubled again by 1830, about one-fourth of which were foreigners, principally Spanish, followed by British, Argentines, French and Americans. But foreigners controlled the import-export trade: of the leading forty merchants engaged in this trade in the 1820s, 40 percent were British, 18 percent Argentine, 7 percent Spanish, and 5 percent American, with Chileans accounting for the remainder.[37]

Valparaíso means Valley of Paradise, but the town itself and the port facilities were rudimentary. About a mile to the east was the Almendral, which means Almond Grove, a plain extending from the beach area to the nearby foothills of the towering Andes where most of the merchants and foreigners lived. (Most of the almond trees had disappeared by the time of Hogan's arrival.) Valparaíso was described by Sophia as "very different from any place I had ever seen. There were no piers or docks; the boats were run up on the sandy beach; streets were unpaved, the chief one running along the shore, so narrow that in some places two vehicles could not pass abreast and one had to draw up in spaces cut out of the rock for that purpose. Often when great droves of mules crowded together accidents happened, one or more being pushed over the side of the road onto the beach below." Danger also lurked: "robberies and assassinations were committed in broad daylight; nor was it safe to pass from the port to the Almendral except in parties sufficiently strong to resist the attack of desperados...."[38] Sophia agreed that the "Chilanoes are a violent tempered people, ready to draw the long knife on the slightest provocation," but the local danger was apparently not that great for she later wrote that her sister "Harriet and I often rose at five o'clock and had a good gallop on the broad, hard, sandy beach, attended by a groom followed by a trail of dogs."

Hogan found a second story apartment with a third story and attic in the town. Sophia said that "having brought our furniture from New York, we were quickly settled in our new home—greatly inferior to anything we had been accustomed to." It was not, however, to be the family's permanent residence. He also found office space for an annual rent of $900 and employed a clerk named William Clay at a salary of $1,000 a year.

He had two official responsibilities during his ten-year stay at Valparaíso. As agent for commerce and seamen, and later as consul, he was responsible for encouraging American commerce and protecting American seamen; as Navy agent, he arranged for the supply of U.S. Navy warships stationed in the Pacific. He was not officially responsible for diplomatic relations with Chile, this being the responsibility of Prevost and the American minister at Santiago when he arrived over two and a half years later. But Prevost spent most his time at Lima, leaving Hogan as the only U.S. representative physically present in either Valparaíso or Santiago for over half of this period. Later, after the minister left and even the chargé d'affaires ad interim was sent elsewhere, Hogan was the only American representative in either Valparaíso or Santiago for seventeen months. During these times, he assumed the additional tasks of reporting political and military events in Chile (as well as Peru) and acting, in effect, as diplomatic representative.

In today's world of instant communication, government officials at foreign posts rarely act without detailed instructions from Washington. But during Hogan's stay at Valparaíso, the average time taken for despatches to reach Washington was slightly less than four months, which meant that at least eight months would pass before a reply might be expected.[39] It was therefore unusual for a consular or diplomatic official, at least those as far away as the west coast of South America, to ask for instructions or expect to receive them. If the official felt that action was necessary, he proceeded in whatever direction he thought proper, bearing in mind, but not deterred by, the threat of being reversed or castigated by Washington. Unfortunately, this fact may also have led officials to slant their reporting of events and trends to support the actions they had taken or were about to take.

Hogan found that a local merchant named Horatio Gerauld of Providence, Rhode Island, had been named by Prevost to act as vice consul at Valparaíso after Henry Hill left the post four months before Hogan's arrival.[40] Gerauld was presumably relieved of his temporary assignment. Within a year he would have a falling out with Hogan over some undisclosed incident that led a friend to tell Hogan "by all means...avoid that methodist-looking fellow Gerauld who I think is a snake in the grass."[41]

Hogan's involvement on the political and military side began auspiciously enough. Two days before his arrival at Valparaíso, San Martín had entered Lima and shortly afterwards on July 28 Peruvian independence was declared (somewhat prematurely, it turned out). When a vessel arrived at Valparaíso on August 18 reporting this news, Hogan promptly sent a despatch to Adams:

> I have now the honor to inform you...of the surrender of Lima to General San Martín, and of the inhabitants having sworn to the independence of the place.... The sufferings of the people in Lima for want of bread-stuffs and other food has been great.... It is impossible to say to what extent [the people] had carried their attachment to royalty, or rather their opposition to being conquered by the forces of Chile, whom they had even treated and considered as an inferior people, not entitled to the enjoyment of equal rights with themselves. To expect them to submit tamely to the dictation of this slip of country is, I believe, more than will be realized, although there can never be any doubt of the country of South America facing the Pacific ocean being forever free from the old Government of Spain.

He sent copies of his despatch by two ships sailing the same day for London, with instructions to American Minister Richard Rush there to forward the message to Washington, apparently believing this route would be faster than waiting for a ship on a direct passage.[42] Hogan's message reached Washington before the American naval commander at Callao could send word via Panama, one of the other communications routes sometimes used, and before Prevost's brief message simply enclosing copies of official gazettes sent by a different route three days earlier from Santiago. Even though it took almost eight months (possibly a record) for Hogan's message to reach Washington, it was his report that is recorded in *American State Papers*. There was no question that Prevost was Hogan's superior, and that he normally should have allowed the message to come from him. Although he could defend his action on the ground that there was no time to consult with Prevost at Santiago which, although only 100 miles away by road, was not quickly accessible, it must be wondered whether Hogan deliberately chose to act on his own.

While Hogan may have wished the patriots well in their pursuit of independence and self-government, he had little good to say about them. Some ten months after arrival, he told Adams that "The course this government has pursued for some months past appears calculated to annihilate commerce. They expect to gain an acknowledgment of their independence by coercion [and] commercial restitutions and seizures of property.... Their enmity to our Flag is obvious and, were there no Naval force in this port, I strongly suspect I would very soon be ordered to depart and leave our ships and property in imminent danger.... They are the most vainglorious people on earth, certainly the most ignorant."[43] The reference to "vainglorious people" was one he would repeat on several occasions.

But he was not always negative about Chile and its people. In another despatch, he believed that Chile "would become a strong and happy nation [were] there less vice and more virtue in the few who must ever rule it" because "it is a granary for the [countries] north of it and will continue to be so until California is peopled; its mines are inexhaustible; its climate fine beyond the power of language to describe; [it possesses] some very fine ports to the south with a back country superior to any yet occupied by Europeans in South America; [it is at] ease at home with a full treasury...."[44] The reference to the future settlement of California was prophetic; the discovery of gold there in 1847 also put Chile "on the map" because many gold diggers found their way to California around Cape Horn.

Hogan's despatches to Adams, though tortured in grammar and structure and sometimes difficult to follow, are more interesting and informative—in a folksy sense—than those written by Prevost and other nearby U.S. agents. Whether they were completely accurate, or helpful in developing U.S. policy, is another question. Hogan was ready, perhaps overly so, to characterize the main players as heroes or villains, often in colorful terms. He reported that he was on good terms with Chilean officials. Shortly after arrival, he had told Adams that his "reception from this government was of the most flattering kind: not a cent of duty or any expense charged on my household furniture, an order sent by the Director [O'Higgins] to the Governor of [Valparaíso] to show me every attention, and an exequatur sent me in great form as consul general for all the ports of Chile." But on one occasion early in his tour (and perhaps others that went unreported) he was less than diplomatically circumspect, if not outright insulting, to the highest Chilean officials. Fortunately, his diplomatic acumen improved during his later years at Valparaíso both in quality and accuracy of reporting and in tact.

The fall of Lima did not bring peace or total independence to Peru. The Spanish royalists held the fort at Callao, the port for Lima, other areas of Peru and parts of Chile for another five years. During this period, Chile was heavily involved in Peruvian affairs through its navy under Admiral Cochrane and its armies. British and American naval squadrons were also involved, ostensibly in protecting their trade and merchants but in the process becoming enmeshed in the struggle itself. As agent at the port where U.S. Navy vessels were principally supplied, Hogan's focus was as much on Peru as on Chile during this five-year period.

Present in Callao at the time of Lima's fall was Cochrane's Chilean fleet, as well as several British Navy vessels and the U.S.S. *Constellation*, the flagship of the new United States Navy Pacific squadron under the command of Commodore Charles Goodwin Ridgely.[45] The *Constellation* was a 1,265-ton 38-gun frigate built in 1797 that saw service during the War of 1812.[46] It had arrived at Valparaíso from the United States on February 6 to await the U.S.S. *Macedonian* which was returning to the United States. Proceeding to Callao in June shortly before the fall of Lima, Ridgely ran afoul of Chilean patriots and Cochrane's blockading fleet when he protected several American vessels in Peruvian ports. One of these was Eliphalet Smith's merchantman, the *Macedonian*. Cochrane's forces had seized $70,000 in coined money and silver specie destined for the American vessel, claiming it was Spanish property. Ridgely returned to Valparaíso on August 31 hoping to persuade Prevost to pursue the claims of the American vessels with the Chilean Government, but Prevost was about to sail for Lima and turned the matter over to Hogan. Ridgely, possibly with Hogan in tow, proceeded directly to Santiago where he obtained a promise that the case would be heard before a prize court.[47]

Cochrane's Chilean fleet helped in achieving Peruvian independence and in assuring Chile's future, but Cochrane continued to run afoul of both Peruvian and Chilean officials, and he was heartily disliked by most American officials, including Hogan. The admiral had again run into trouble when he seized some $600,000 belonging to the Peruvian Government to pay back wages to his near-mutinous crew. After Hogan reported this major news item, he added that "his low avarice produced acts of greatest meanness; at one place, after being treated with the greatest kindness, more from fear than love, he took the piano forte from the Lady of the House after playing it to him, and sold it for one hundred dollars to the captain of a vessel." More seriously, in the same despatch Hogan said that, "in a conversation with the Director [O'Higgins], I took the occasion to say that foreign nations could never acknowledge the independence of Chile while such a character [as Cochrane] held the third highest station in its government. It seemed to make a strong impression." O'Higgins was himself jealous of Cochrane, and there would soon be a major falling out which would lead to the admiral's departure.

Hogan's feelings about Cochrane were more than personal. Ridgely was concerned that the admiral's frictions with Peruvian and Chilean officials might lead him to forsake his command of the Chilean Navy and set out on his own, in effect as a pirate. He had already showed some signs of acting as a local potentate, such as by selling licenses for various purposes at several ports. Hogan reported to Adams in November that, at Ridgely's request, he was going to Santiago to call on O'Higgins "to obtain an account of the present standing of Lord Cochrane, whether his acts…are to be recognized by this Government," adding that "in publick estimate Lord Cochrane borders upon a pirate belonging to no nation; it is possible this Government may countenance him till they can get the fleet out of his hands—he is too much for them all—there no longer exists any cause for blockade."[48] There is no record of the results of this meeting—perhaps it did not take place, but in June the following year when Cochrane was in Santiago Hogan reported that "I conceived it my duty to pay him a visit which was received with professions of friendship and respect for the United States. He entered at large into the dispositions of the existing government at Lima when he was invited to land by General San Martín which he replied he never would put his foot in a country not governed by laws."[49]

A presumption of British perfidy in South America persisted in the minds of Americans. Many were convinced that Britain had a grand scheme to support the continuation of Spanish power in the Americas and to obtain preferential treatment to the disadvantage of Americans. There was even concern that Britain still had territorial ambitions in South America. (In fact, Britain did consider sending invading forces on several occasions, but except for Popham's unauthorized seizure of Buenos Aires in 1806, it never implemented any plan and abandoned such ideas completely within two years after the Popham fiasco.) Equally, many Englishmen believed the United States wanted to establish a network of countries in South American sympathetic and in league with it. Both sides were correct that, until about 1823, the United States and Britain had different strategic goals: the United States wanted to recognize and do business with the new countries as soon as politically expedient; England wanted to maintain Spain's authority in the Americas as a counter-weight to the threat of France and the Holy Alliance of Prussia, Russia and Austria and thus to delay recognition as long as necessary to support the first goal. By 1823, it became clear that Spain had lost its Latin American colonies (except Cuba and Puerto Rico) and that the Holy Alliance would not try to intervene or disrupt the European balance of power. From roughly that point on, the political goals of the two countries were not dissimilar and their rivalry would be confined to commerce.[50]

In this area, it would be Britain that would have the upper hand for the remainder of the century. Its Navy reigned supreme, preventing any other outsider from seriously considering intervention and leading most South American countries to realize that it was more important to maintain friendly relations with Britain than with the United States. England's trade and financial resources were far greater than those of the United States, although the balance shifted throughout the century. It succeeded in securing better treatment for its citizens and trade than the United States because it had more to offer and because it was willing to tie recognition to trade concessions, a position which the United States eschewed at the time. Another reason was the lack of experience and small size of the American diplomatic and consular establishment compared with its British counterpart which had been in the business for centuries. An indication of Britain's relatively strong position can be seen from the fact that it managed to maintain friendly relations with Chile even though it delayed formal recognition until 1831, whereas the United States was criticized for waiting as long as 1822 to do so.

These broad considerations did not prevent mutual conjecture of evil intent by local naval commanders, official representatives and merchants of the two countries, nor abate their rivalry, particularly during the period preceding U.S. recognition. Almost all the U.S. special agents and consular representatives sent to Spanish America from 1810 onward reported real or imagined British plans to acquire territory or special position. (At one point, there was even a report—which although true did not reach fruition—that France had designs to establish a monarchy in part of La Plata.)[51] The mutual animosity between Americans and British that prevailed during the War of 1812 was only gradually disappearing. It is possible, however, to detect a sea change in political rivalry as they acquired experience in dealing with the newly independent states. There were numerous incidents of Anglo-American cooperation; for example, when British and American Navy ships came to each other's aid or when one helped the other repair its damaged vessels. Hogan would himself recount incidents of British Navy ships offering protection to American citizens and ships during periods of possible danger. The British position on paper blockades was virtually identical to that of the United States.

Much of Hogan's time, and that of other American representatives during these early years, was spent on cases involving the seizure of American vessels by royalist or patriot forces in Peru or Chile. American seamen were also induced by higher wages or threats of physical violence to join the Chilean Navy or the soon to be formed Peruvian Navy. Some of the ships were seized for alleged violations of the several blockades imposed from time to time or for alleged carriage of arms or specie to the other side. Sometimes, the errant ships were able to escape, either on their own or with the help of U.S. Navy warships, but other cases had to be pursued through the courts or, usually years later, diplomatic channels. Although the official position of the United States was invariably that the ships had done nothing wrong, even when they were carrying arms or contraband to the royalists, as some of them were, it is understandable that Chile felt differently, whatever might have been the niceties of international law. Many of the seizures were made by Benavides, the royalist guerrilla, or by local Chilean officials hoping to line their pockets, and it was these cases that Hogan and other American representatives felt free to wax indignant in their attempts to rectify what amounted to piracy.

One such case involved three ships, the *Ocean*, *Hersilia* and *Hero*, from which the Hogans were to learn what had been happening among the Benavides pirate band on shore while the *Teaplant* was considering sending a boat on a rescue mission. Two months after the Hogans arrived at Valparaíso, a whale boat entered the harbor with the mate of the *Ocean*, William S. Lane, Captain James P. Sheffield of the *Hersilia* and six members of their crews. Lane and Sheffield executed a sworn statement before Hogan recounting their tribulations,[52] but the account of his daughter Sophia is the more detailed and colorful:[53]

[The men] belonged to a small brig [either the *Ocean* or *Hersilia*] which was becalmed off the bay as we had been [in the *Teaplant*], only nearer to the land. Soon two boats filled with armed men boarded the vessel, ordered the crew to go below—who could make no resistance—then closed the hatches and towed the brig to the shore. Each man was now called up separately and asked if he would join a band of freebooters, who enjoyed a happy, careless life, obeyed no laws but their own under a brave chief. If the man replied favorably, he was made to take an oath of obedience. If he refused, he was bound with ropes and thrown into a boat alongside the brig. When all had gone though this ordeal, the captain was called and threatened.... He offered them a large sum of money as ransom and perfect secrecy if they would allow him to live and take his chance on getting away, but his entreaties were unavailing. Seven of the men accepted the terms of the band to save their lives. The others preferred death. Also the cabin boy who boldly said he "would rather die with a good man who loved God, than live with wicked ones like them." One of the ruffians instantly knocked him down with an axe, then threw the insensible lad into the boat with the captain and the two men. Six of the gang then rowed the boat into deeper water and threw the helpless creatures overboard bound as they were....

As one can imagine, these people were all desperate characters, many were Chileans and half-breed Indians, French, Danes, Peruvians, three Americans and two British. Their chief was a very noted brigand who for years had been the terror of the country—Benavides by name. Some weeks after these men had joined the gang, a ship appeared in sight, attracted no doubt by the fires on the hills which were lighted to decoy vessels to approach in belief that there was a town and harbor. The ship proved to be an American whaler [*Hero*]. As [the brigands] were provided with flags of different nations, the American [flag] was hoisted which induced the unsuspicious captain to send a boat on shore, the crew of which were at once secured, a party dispatched to gain possession of the vessel....

The people made a brave resistance but were not well-armed and were overpowered. Several were pitched overboard, the captain and mates first. Some of the men who looked like desperate characters were spared and proved themselves worthy companions of the gang....

Sophia's account continues that "several days of riotous living followed [the pirates'] possession of whiskey, but still a strict watch was kept [on the captured crew], so the poor fellows almost despaired. However, they succeeded in getting a quantity of biscuit and a piece of salt beef which they boiled when cooking their dinners...." Benavides wanted to "refit the [*Ocean*], put a crew of the most trusty men on her, load her with oil and other articles useless to them, go to some port in Peru and sell the cargo and vessel."

It was at this point that the Hogan's *Teaplant* appeared. Sophia reported what the Hogan family then learned about their fortunate escape:

...great was the excitement and rejoicing when [the pirates] saw a possibility of capturing so fine a vessel. Unusual precautions were taken, which made them long in getting their boat off. They were in hopes a boat would be sent from the ship when the flag was hoisted, expressed disappointment when there were no signs of one being lowered.

When almost ready to come off, the wind sprang up, and unconscious of the danger to which we had been exposed, our ship sailed away. Loud were the angry words and abuse of each other for being so long clearing and launching the cutter. One American was cruelly beaten because he was overheard saying to the other, "I saw women on board, I am glad they got away."

Soon after the *Teaplant* incident, four of the captured crew "succeeded one dark night in getting away in the small whale boat; they managed, by keeping close to the shore during the day and at night securing their boat among the rocks, gradually to advance some distance, till feeling safe from pursuit, they ventured out to sea and were fortunate enough in seeing a coasting schooner" which " took them on board and in a few days brought them into Valparaíso." According to Sophia, "on telling their story to [Hogan], they were provided with clothes and money and a good lodging taken for them to rest, for they were weak and much worn by the hardships they had gone through, but very thankful to be free and safe from their hard taskmasters."

Ridgely wanted to send the U.S.S. *Constellation* to free the twenty-three Americans still being held captive by Benavides but his ship was temporarily disabled due to rot in part of a mast. In a sign of Anglo-American cooperation, the British Navy frigate *Conway*, which was also lying at Valparaíso, agreed to make the attempt, partly because some British sailors were also being held captive. Its efforts proved unnecessary because Chilean patriot forces had chased Benavides inland and eventually captured him.[54] Sophia wrote that, "after being hanged, his head was cut off and stuck up over the gate of Mendoza, a town beyond the Cordilleras which had suffered greatly from his depredations. His headless body was placed over one gate of Santiago, and the arms at another."[55] As for the captured American sailors, Sophia reported that "my father, with his usual generosity, rewarded them liberally and secured them good situations in homeward bound ships."

The *Constellation* was still at Valparaíso when, on October 7, the New Bedford whaler *Persia* entered the harbor with news that "11 men and 15 casks of water [from the ship] were kept as hostages for compelling the ship...to carry [some 70 escaped inmates on the prison island of Juan Fernández, most of whom were royalist exiles] to the mainland of Chile." The ship's Captain Latham Cross, who had refused this demand, had come to Valparaíso for help. Hogan "sent the particulars to Captain Ridgely, there [being] no Chilean vessel of war [at Valparaíso]," who transported Chileans troops on the U.S.S. *Constellation* to free the remaining hostages, some having found other means to escape.[56]

The American frigate then sailed for Callao where Prevost asked that the ship go to Guayaquil in present-day Ecuador to free the *Teaplant* which had been detained by local patriots, but the ship on which the Hogans had come from the United States had already been freed by the time Ridgely and Prevost arrived.[57]

The crew of the *Ocean* and its captain had managed to escape from Benavides and his pirate band, and the ship itself was also eventually freed with a new captain, A.B. Pinkham, in command. On February 1 the following year (1822), Hogan received a letter from Pinkam stating that the governor of Concepcíon had imprisoned him on the allegation that he would not surrender 7,000 silver dollars taken on board at Lima. Neither U.S. Navy ships nor Prevost were present in Valparaíso when Hogan received this letter. After waiting three days in the expectation that the new flag ship of the Pacific squadron might arrive, Hogan sent a diplomatic note on the 4th to the Chilean Secretary of State for Foreign Relations Joaquim Echeverría. It began with a bald warning that United States recognition of Chile might be delayed, a threat Hogan had no authority to make. The note then recounted the alleged facts, in straightforward manner. The American vessel *Ocean* had arrived at Talcahuano [Chile] from Lima in ballast. The Government of Concepcíon "resorted to various means" to demand that seven thousand dollars in specie on board the vessel be turned over to the authorities, which the captain "justly" refused to do. He claimed that four thousand belonged to the ship's owner (Richard J. Cleveland) in the United States and three thousand to himself, "being the hard earnings of many years toil and labor as a sea officer." Moreover, the dollars were not on board, having been embarked at Lima through the Customs House.

Hogan then alleged that the captain, "a very respectable citizen of the United States," was taken out of his ship "by a file of soldiers, thrown into a wretched prison in heavy irons, his mate put into a loathsome prison with convicts and his seamen into another prison for no other crime than that of holding faithfully to their duty as true American citizens...."

Concluding the note, Hogan must have felt he had to explain why the president of the United States might act in the manner that Hogan had threatened:

> The president of the United States has in numerous instances given proof of his good disposition toward Chile. It would be painful to suspect that Chile is insensible to those friendly intentions, but the acts of her admiral in seizing upon the cash property of American citizens afloat and on hand for which no satisfactory investigation has yet been obtained forcibly insinuates the belief that the Government of Chile conceives the United States at too great a distance or too little inclined to assert her rights....

The Government of the United States, founded upon pure freedom and equal rights, supported by a union of strength and power, protecting its citizens at home and abroad in their lawful avocations, dispensing equal and impartial justice in its foreign relations, wielded by an energy, if equaled not surpassed, will not submit to indignities to its flag nor to unjust insult or torture of its citizens without ample reparation being made therefor.

The day after Hogan sent this very undiplomatic diplomatic note, the U.S.S. *Franklin* arrived in port to take over command of the Pacific squadron, but it was already too late to change the course of events that Hogan had initiated.

Echeverría relied immediately that the Supreme Director had called for information from Ramón Freire, Governor of Concepción, but in the meantime said that "His Excellency orders me to ask from you…a categorical explanation of [your] reference to the late act of [Chile's] principal general in the second most important post of Chile." Whatever answer Hogan gave is unrecorded for reasons shortly to be addressed, but he must have felt elated because, within a month of his intervention, Supreme Director O'Higgins sent a letter to the authorities at Concepción ordering the release of Captain Pinkham, his crew and the silver dollars.

But the silver specie was not returned immediately because the Chileans discovered at some point that the *Ocean* was not under American flag but owned by a Chilean with American connivance. Just when this information was made known to U.S. officials is not known, but they were still treating the issue as an unwarranted seizure of American property a month after the promised release.[58] Hogan did not report the entire incident to Adams for over almost seven months. During this period, there were two other potentially damaging ship incidents, as well an escalating feud between Jeremy Robinson on the one hand and Prevost and Hogan on the other.

Hogan's first reporting despatch about the *Ocean* in early May was intended to explain why O'Higgins took offense over the insulting note. He said that, when he received the letter that Pinkham was being held in Concepción, he waited three days expecting the arrival of Commodore Stewart on the *Franklin* "to take up the business who could do it with more effect," but "impatient and fearful of being thought neglectful," he then sent the note via a U.S. Navy midshipman who was conversant with the Spanish language. Hogan inferred that the midshipman made an inexact Spanish-language copy of the note, which was the copy that Echeverría read. Since even the English-language version is insulting, Hogan's explanation does not carry much weight. However, Adams may never have known this because the copies that Hogan said were attached to his despatch are not in the National Archives, possibly indicating Hogan may not have forwarded all the correspondence.[59] In his report of the full story three months later, which will be covered shortly, he said he was "aware that my course here has and will bring on me a host of enemies and writers to gentlemen in Valparaíso and of Congress and to editors of newspapers. There are persons of viscous habits who have little else to do than abuse publick servants and envy my possessing any share of the confidence of a country of which I am not a native.... I value not the foul aspersions of the unworthy; a conscious rectitude and the just expectation of being borne out in my duty by my government puts me at ease."[60]

Hogan could not be absolutely certain who his enemies were. There were several possible candidates, including a Henry D. Tracy from Connecticut, but the one he must have been most concerned about was Jeremy Robinson. (Prevost had no doubt that his detractors were specifically Eliphalet Smith, Thomas Ellridge—an alleged privateer, Tracy and Robinson.) As previously noted, he was one of several men who received appointments as special agents in South America in 1817. Monroe almost immediately withdrew his appointment, apparently because of Robinson's overly zealous attempt to form a business partnership with several merchants trading to South America and the Pacific. Robinson went to Lima anyway and from there and Chile sent many letters to Adams and Monroe reporting on developments in Chile and Peru as though he was in fact a special agent. From Hogan's arrival at Valparaíso to Robinson's departure early in 1823, Robinson sent at least 35 letters to Adams and another 16 directly to Monroe from Valparaíso and Santiago, far in excess of the total number of despatches that both Hogan and Prevost sent. Many of them numbered a dozen or more pages, replete with asterisks referring to notes in the margin or letters of the alphabet tied to lengthy endnotes in appendices. Some were marked *Private*. His reporting covered military and political events, character and policy assessments, natural resources, indigenous peoples and even climate.[61] Adams was impressed; in August 1820, he forwarded a Robinson letter to Monroe with the comment that "this man has given us so much valuable information, and sees things with so much more impartiality and therefore accuracy than some others who have been there that I almost wish you would forget his indiscretion by which he forfeited the commission he had obtained and restore him to some subordinate agency."[62] This letter was probably in Monroe's hands when Hogan called on him in November and may have been the basis for his asking Hogan to do what he could for Robinson.

In addition to his reporting, Robinson repeatedly sought an official appointment in Peru or Chile. Prevost had refused to name him vice consul at Concepción in Chile (naming someone else instead) but, according to Robinson, had held out the expectation that he might obtain an appointment for him at some post in Peru. Prevost later denied that he had made such a promise,[63] but he may have led Robinson on as a means of delaying any attack upon him in Washington. As early as January 1821, some four months after returning from his one year's stay at Buenos Aires, Prevost told Adams that "our countrymen generally have not been of a class to claim respect; ...the majority are adventurers who have either been engaged in privateering or in devising some other mode of livelihood alike disgraceful." "I am sorry to say," he continued, "that Mr. Robinson is [one of them]." He recounted that Robinson had accepted $1,000 from the Chilean government to act as its agent in securing a private loan in the United States and that, "with a knowledge of [this], I refused to employ him at Concepción and have thus incurred imputations of which he alone is the author."[64] In fact, Robinson had not yet made directly negative remarks about Prevost to Adams or Monroe, but he had come to Valparaíso in early July just before Hogan's arrival to press Prevost for the necessary credentials of the appointment he thought had been promised and perhaps a showdown.

Four days after Hogan's arrival, Robinson introduced himself to the new consul. Perhaps because he had not yet met Prevost (who was 100 miles away in Santiago) and therefore could not know his views or recent events concerning Robinson, Hogan warmly welcomed the man whom Monroe had mentioned as worthy of an appointment. Robinson promptly wrote to Adams, with a separate letter directly to Monroe, unable to restrain his elation at the apparent change in his fortunes:[65]

[Mr. Hogan] imparted to me, in the most delicate, engaging and friendly manner, the approbation of the President in relation to my having an unofficial correspondence with the government of the United States; and who likewise informed me at the same time of the friendly disposition of the President and yourself toward me....

I had embarked on the ship *Chesapeake* for Baltimore, ...but Mr. Hogan has offered spontaneously to promote my views in so disinterested and obliging a manner as to dissuade me from that determination and to induce me to remain, to wait events, and the further pleasure of the President.

I consider the arrival of Mr. Hogan in this country at this conjuncture an event peculiarly auspicious. Long have the commercial interests and rights of the United States required an important and dignified interposition of an able, experienced, upright and legally authorized civil representative in Chile.

No doubt Hogan regretted the enthusiasm he had displayed when Prevost confided his concerns about Robinson. Both men were in an awkward situation. Prevost must have realized that his previous determination to be rid of the man must be tempered by some caution lest Monroe take offense, while Hogan must have wondered whether he should actively support Prevost because he was his superior or be responsive to the clear wishes of President Monroe. The apparent decision of both was to tell Robinson not to leave Valparaíso and to await a possible appointment. They meant "await an appointment from Washington," but there was no need to make this explicit. Robinson therefore waited, keeping his poison pen mostly stilled, and making repeated formal applications for a position in letters to Adams and Monroe.

The breaking point did not come all at once. Robinson told Adams in October that "neither Mr. Prevost nor Mr. Hogan have done anything for me nor have much expectation that they can or will, but I shall wait their time and for their instructions."[66] In November he heard from Ridgely that Prevost had no intention of giving him an appointment.[67] Robinson turned his attention to Hogan, hoping he would be more sympathetic than Prevost. Finally, Hogan wrote him a letter on January 12, 1822: "You have expected, in consequence of the communication I made to you after my arrival here of the President's good disposition toward you, that I would take measures to be useful to you by appointing you to some one of the ports on this coast of Chile. I do assure you that it would afford me pleasure to do so were there any, but Coquimbo requiring such an appointment, I was then a stranger full of ardent desire as I now am of doing anything that would be acceptable to the President, but I soon learnt obstacles insurmountable to any wish in relation to yourself of which the President was certainly ignorant when he mentioned you to me." The "insurmountable obstacle" was Robinson's alleged refusal to restore to a "dispossessed lady" of Santiago some 18 ounces of gold entrusted to him several years previously in Lima. "The present case would alone destroy all hope," Hogan wrote. Robinson replied denying he was the person responsible for the "dispossessed lady" failing to have her gold returned and swearing his good intentions, innocence, loyalty to the United States and faith in Hogan's fairness. Hogan answered in a brief letter in which he came close to calling Robinson a liar. He then promptly send copies of the correspondence to Adams, noting that "it was not in my power to appoint [Robinson] to some office under me" because they had all been filled and because "I would not compromise the honor of the U.S. by any such appointment. A total destitution of character in him would prevent it. His talent for writing is the only one he possesses...." Hogan "respectfully suggested the propriety of [Adam's] receiving [Robinson's] communications with great caution and many allowances for a distorted mind such as his."[68]

In March, Robinson sent Adams and Monroe a translation of a purported letter from Supreme Director O'Higgins indicating the latter's support of and confidence in him. Then at the end of April he told Adams that, because "Mr. Prevost has not performed his promises to me respecting an appointment," he wanted "to renew my application for an appointment as special or commercial and naval agent of the U.S. for Chile and Peru, including Guayaquil and coast of New Granada and Chiloe," in effect, the entire west coast of South America.[69] (Hogan, as well as Prevost, would have been even more alarmed if they had known that Robinson was asking to take over both their jobs!) In the following several months, several ship incidents (including the *Ocean*) took place in which Hogan, Prevost and Navy officers were variously involved. They provided Robinson new grist for his mill. He told Adams that "Mr. Hogan also acquiesced and displayed more warmth than the case merited in defense of [the *Ocean*] in his correspondence with the government of Chile." He also leveled renewed criticism of Prevost when he told Adams: "Another circumstance has had an influence against our republican institutions, which is that our special agent [Prevost] has always justified and applauded the most oppressive acts, and publicly derided not only our republican institutions and the best patriots and republicans of our nation, including Mr. Jefferson and many others, in the presence of the officers and people of this country and Buenos Aires."[70] (Prevost might be forgiven for thinking ill of Jefferson in light of his role in bringing his stepfather, Aaron Burr, to trial for treason!) Several pages of vituperative attack on Prevost follow. Turning to Hogan, he said that he "came to this country well disposed toward me until his feelings were changed by [Prevost] and his satellites, [and] I will have more to say [about him and Navy commanders] on a future and more fit occasion."

Robinson's attempt to expose Hogan and U.S. Navy officers came in a lengthy letter of August 15. After accusing him of malfeasance in the several shipping cases, he said that "Mr. Hogan has been spoken with upon the subject of [these vessels], but he has suffered them to pursue and continue their traffic unmolested." Then he castigated Prevost for protecting several allegedly shady American merchants in Peru, Chile and Buenos Aires, and lastly Captains Biddle, Downes, Ridgely and Stewart for various infractions.[71] Although some of the charges contain identifiable facts, most of them are stated in general terms, often for deficiencies that are only inferred. When Adams received this letter in November, he called to Monroe's attention a letter written by Robinson in May that was "filled with bitter complaints against all the naval officers of the United States who have commanded in the Pacific since 1817, and against J.B. Prevost, the Agent; whose conduct appears not to have been exactly what it ought to have been, but against whom nothing definite has been proved which required, or would justify, a direct censure upon him."[72]

Ten days later, Robinson penned two apparently separate letters both bearing the same date to Adams. The first two sheets of one of them are missing in official files. The next page contains the following: "British officers and subjects are treated by him with more attention and respect than American officers and citizens. That probability is not surprising; he has been comparatively only a few years, is a short time in the United States, and the causes which induced his domicilitation [i.e., domicile in the United States] are neither honorable nor creditable, if [undecipherable word] speak truth, but a relation of them I will reserve for a future opportunity to be used only in case of a [undecipherable word] necessity." This can only be a reference to Hogan. The charge that Hogan was an Anglophile would be made by several persons in Chile, as will be seen. The more interesting questions are whether the previous pages were removed because they specifically identified Hogan, who removed these pages, and who was the source of information at Valparaíso about Hogan's past. There are no answers.

The letter closes with a feigned apology: "I am mortified and distressed at having become the organ of exposing the misconduct of publick officers and owe you, Sir, and the government an apology for pushing this subject [when I am a candidate for office]."

The other letter with the same date also castigated Hogan:

> Mr. Prevost and Mr. Hogan in close alliance or occasional coalition—inflated with their temporary importance and publick employment, boastful and confident in and elated by the friendship of the President, seem to have forgotten that they are responsible and have [official] obligations to perform.... The President must have been deceived in relation to their character and behavior, and [perhaps] under a delusion, kept up by misrepresentation or he would withdraw his countenance and friendship from them. In addition to what I have stated in my previous letters, I need only refer you Sir to Mr. Albert Morris, a Midshipman in the US Navy, who will acquaint you with the treatment which he received from Mr. Hogan [and] undeceive you with respect to him....

The closing pages of this letter are also not in official archives.[73]

Two days after Robinson wrote these damaging letters, Hogan reported his version of the *Ocean* incident to Adams. The close timing is probably coincidental, but he must have anticipated that Robinson would be writing to Adams with the by then well-known facts concerning these incidents, including possibly the "inexact" Spanish translation of the "undiplomatic" note to Echeverría. (Could Albert Morris have been the midshipman in question?) He began by saying he was bringing the matter again "before you in order to finish an affair that gave me much trouble and great pain because I found myself deceived by the parties entrusted." He explained that, after sending his note to Echeverría, he discovered that the *Ocean* belonged partly to Antonio Sosa, a Lima merchant now resident in Chile and partly to Captain Cleveland, formerly master of the *Beaver* now residing in New Hampshire.[74] He then insisted that the *Ocean* surrender its U.S. papers because it properly should be under Chilean registration. Sosa tried to bribe Hogan through a Valparaíso merchant to overlook this technicality, which Hogan refused. Instead, he demanded that Sosa reimburse him for the cost of his intervention, which Sosa refused. The *Ocean* was then registered under Chilean flag and was no longer Hogan's concern.

Hogan said that the *Ocean* had been originally acquired in France, had come to the Pacific under French flag, had been seized and condemned (presumably by authorities in Lima), bought by Cleveland and operated as a U.S. vessel with "no other papers than a bill of sale which was certified by Mr. [Henry] Hill as consul and also by Captain Downes of the Navy." Hogan did not say whether he thought Hill and Downes acted improperly, but that was the implication.[75]

This finished the *Ocean* incident,[76] satisfactorily to Adams, Hogan no doubt hoped, but he also had to cover another potentially damaging incident. He recounted that the *Flying Fish* had been sold at Lima, supposedly to the previously mentioned Henry D. Tracy of Connecticut but in fact to a Spaniard at Lima. Tracy had "made U.S. papers" for her, and when she was seized, Lt. Commander Connor of the U.S.S. *Dolphin* certified Tracy's protest. "If she comes here, I will deprive her of any American papers given to her by any person whatsoever," Hogan piously told Adams. Now he was in full fettle: "Suffering such proceedings brings our flag into constant disrepute and weakens the efforts for its honor of the faithful representatives. It injures the fair trader and diminishes his national honor."[77] Hogan later received a letter from Tracy "threatening me for a variety of pretended losses he is to suffer in consequence of my sending the papers of the *Flying Fish* to the Treasury Department." Tracy's reputation was probably already known in Washington. Prevost later noted that "the fraud committed by Mr. Tracy upon one of the banks in New York determined [Consul] Forbes while I was at Buenos Aires to deny him access to his house, and I regret to say that his conduct since his arrival on this side of the Andes has not indicated any return to principle."[78]

Robinson's version of the *Ocean* and *Flying Fish* cases was similar to Hogan's but he implied that Hogan knew the facts of real ownership long before he acted.[79] Given Robinson's penchant for unsubstantiated broadsides against so many individuals, Hogan's version may have had more credibility, though it is possible that he would not have taken the scrupulously correct stand that he did had not Robinson (and perhaps others) been determined to find fault with him.

Hogan suspected that Robinson was behind the Tracy complaint, for he had told Adams in the same letter that "it is well understood that Mr. Jeremiah Robinson is one of [Tracy's] adherents.... [Robinson] is now despised by this government, notwithstanding his obsequiousness to them while in their pay, soliciting to be sent as their agent to Washington. Nothing could lessen the dignity of our country more than the anointment of that man to a public situation on this coast of South America where he is universally known as the American spy and called by no other name by the natives."[80] (In fact, Tracy was as much an object of Robinson's venom as was Hogan.) In another despatch, Hogan said Robinson had acquired the name of "double spy." He had, in fact, previously accepted a $1,000 commission to seek a private loan in the United States, but he was not the only American official to be so appointed by Chile and he swore that he had returned the commission.[81] He was an opportunist, willing to accept reward from any quarter. A month later, Hogan opened and read—by mistake, he avowed—a letter he thought had been addressed to him as U.S. commercial agent from the American minister at London, Richard Rush, that was intended for Robinson. He dutifully told Adams that I "read a few lines till came to the part when Mr. Rush informed that he had forwarded to the president the two letters he had enclosed for him with his own recommendation of what he had asked him to do for him." The letters that Rush forwarded to the president were probably ones that Robinson had sent to Rush in March 1822 noting Chilean and Peruvian complaints over the activities of various U.S. Navy commanders.[82] Who can believe that Hogan, or any half-curious individual in similar circumstances, would have stopped reading such a letter after only a few lines? We cannot know whether Rush's letter revealed the target of Robinson's venom, but if this was not evident, Hogan may have feared that he was the target. Perhaps to cover this possibility and recalling that he had earlier promised to provide documentary proof of Robinson's perfidy, he told Adams: "Soon after the Supreme Director came here, Mr. Robinson spent many hours of a night with his aide de camp endeavoring by false representations to injure my publick standing with the Director who ordered it to be made known to me next day. He is much despised by this government, will be of no advantage to any. It is painful to hear the remarks of persons to whom he offers the perusal of his letters to the president and other gentlemen in Congress in the hope of producing some temporary consideration to himself which always vanishes the moment he is by them mentioned to anyone that knows him." Hogan noted that he was not the only one critical of Robinson; Prevost and Captain Ridgely of the U.S.S. *Constellation* were others.[83] In fact, Robinson seems to have held Prevost and U.S. Navy commanders in greater contempt than he did Hogan.

Robinson left Chile to return to the United States sometime between March and June 1823. Hogan was still sufficiently concerned about what Robinson might say about him in Washington, as well about some other unpleasant matters, that on June 25 of that year he wrote an eleven-page letter to President Monroe. This was the third recorded letter that Hogan sent to Monroe. For length, seemingly pointless meandering and obstinacy, it should rank high on any list of letters that, if ever sent, should have first been heavily edited by a neutral observer. But it had never been in Hogan's character to question his own invincibility and judgment.

After recalling that the president "desired I would if possible serve Mr. Jeremiah Robinson..., I met him and, full of anxiety to do any thing pleasing to you, I certainly should have been much gratified were it at the moment in my power to give him any appointment that could serve him.... It was however painful to me to learn very soon from all quarters and particularly from Mr. Prevost of the total destitution of character in that person which forbid my noticing him any more. He was then said to be in the pay of this government and a spy on our actions. The Governor of this place told me soon after that he was actually soliciting the appointment of a publick agent from Chile to Washington. In consequence of my refusal to appoint him vice consul to Concepcion [to replace the man already there], he became one of the enemies that I have [seen] in some of the least worthy of our citizens because of my doing the duty to which my instructions and the laws point out."

There was one other matter Hogan felt he should mention to the president because it involved the 18-year old son of "Doctor Bullus whose family, I understood, expected you would provide for." Hogan had brought the young Bullus with him to Valparaíso where he might "be an acquisition in my office..., and no father was [*sic*] treated a son with more kindness that I did him. Mrs. Hogan was like a mother to him, but he was not more than two months here before he launched into all the vices of the place, setting my [counsels] and remonstrances at defiance, keeping my family up all night anxiously awaiting his safe entry, for murders were frequent almost nightly in fact proving my great error in bringing so very useless a young man 12,000 miles to be a torment rather than a comfort to me. I was obliged to part with him because his conduct was more like that of a wild youth having an estate to spend than one endeavoring to advance by merit. Captain Ridgely, with my approbation and desire, took him as clerk on board the [*Constellation*] and was absent about 5 months. On his return, Mr. Bullus wrote me a most unworthy and scandalous letter which I shewed immediately to Captain Ridgely who turned him out of his ship. Commodore Stewart [commander of the *Franklin*] insisted on my sending it to you in order to keep him out of the publick service, remarking that there were too many spirits like him already agitating the service."

The Bullus letter accused Hogan of misappropriating a 34-gallon cask of rum intended for the U.S. Navy for his private household use. Hogan admitted he had "ordered [the cask] to my house for use," the

Constellation's "spirit rooms being full," but he had "credited the Navy Department with it at the amount charged to the *Constellation*."[84] Bullus may also have provided Robinson with a copy of his letter. In one of the two August 25 letters, Robinson noted that "Mr. Hogan's conduct to the two young gentlemen who accompanied him to this country, Mr. Fletcher and Mr. Bullus, more extremely amiable and interesting young men could not have been found in any country, was exceeded by [several indecipherable words]. He calumniated them in the most shocking [manner] and drove them from his House by slander and ungentlemanly behavior." (There is no mention of Fletcher in any other record.)

Monroe may have seen Hogan's letter by October 8 when he received a note marked *Private* from Robinson datelined Washington which said that "I have important information which I am disposed to communicate personally to the Executive but which from its delicate nature I am at present averse to impart to any other person and…await for an expression of your pleasure when to visit your residence in Virginia or remain in the capital until your return." There is no indication of what Monroe did with either Hogan's or Robinson's letter.[85]

Robinson continued without success to seek a government appointment. As late as 1828, when he was president, Adams wrote in his diary that Robinson had come to "renew his application for employment" and that "the perseverance of this man is proof against any rebuff, and there is so much meekness in his endurance, and so much calmness in his fortitude, that he takes hold of my compassion when he can never recover my esteem." Robinson finally received an appointment, as part of a mission to Cuba in 1832–34 to retrieve certain Florida archives, during the Andrew Jackson administration.[86]

During the period that Hogan thought he was being plagued and discredited by Robinson, he was also involved in several incidents centering around Commodore Charles Stewart, commander of the U.S.S. *Franklin*, flagship of the Pacific squadron, which had arrived at Valparaíso on February 5, 1822, the day after Hogan sent his infamous note to Chile about Captain Pinkham and the *Ocean*. The *Franklin* was one of four ships-of-the-line built during the War of 1812 but finished too late to see service. These 2,243-ton warships carrying 74 guns marked the beginning of the entry of the United States as a world naval power, though it would remain small compared with the British Navy and those of other European powers until the turn of the century when the Great White Fleet, by then ranked third, sailed around the world. Although the Pacific squadron had come into being earlier, President Monroe in his December 1821 annual message to Congress was the first to acknowledge formally that it had been "necessary to maintain a naval force in the Pacific for the protection of our citizens engaged in commerce and the fisheries in that sea." He had been led to take this step by a report of abundant whales and seals off recently discovered Graham Land some 600 miles south of Cape Horn in Antarctica and by pressures from merchants and shipowners for improved naval protection in the Pacific.[87] The *Franklin*, matching the largest and most powerful warships of other navies, would be able to assert its presence more effectively than the smaller *Constellation*. Hogan, who had been told before leaving the United States that the *Franklin* was being dispatched to the Pacific,[88] would have been acutely conscious of this factor from his prior naval and maritime experience.

The *Franklin* had arrived at Valparaíso in company with the U.S.S. *Dolphin*, a newly commissioned schooner captained by Lieutenant David Conner (who had previously been to Valparaíso on the U.S.S. *Ontario* in 1818) and the *Canton*, a merchant vessel owned by Le Roy, Bayard & Company of New York with John O'Sullivan as its master. Mrs. Stewart, her maids and two children were also on board the *Franklin*.[89]

Shortly after the *Canton* arrived at Valparaíso, the Peruvian envoy asked that Chile seize the vessel because he had information that it was carrying firearms for delivery to royalist forces in Peru and had met the U.S.S. *Franklin* at Juan Fernández Island by prior agreement. At 11 p.m. on March 15, Hogan received a note from the Chilean Secretary of State for Foreign Relations Joaquim Echeverría asking for assurances that the arms would not be supplied to royalist forces. Considering that Hogan had addressed his strongly worded note to Echeverría less than five weeks earlier, the latter showed remarkable restraint in the tone of his message:

My Government have just been informed by persons of credit that the American merchant vessels which are now actually at anchor in Valparaíso...have on board (especially the *Canton*) muskets and other implements of war underneath the barrels of flour. They are also informed that the said vessels sailed from the United States before the U.S.S. *Franklin* with whose commander they had agreed to rendezvous in the latitude of Juan Fernández and that their original destination was Callao [Peru] with the view to sell those articles of war to the Government of Lima, supposing that capital was still under the dominion of the arms of Spain.

If those American vessels, being that Lima is joined to the cause of independence, enter in any of the Intermedios ports to sell their armaments to the Spaniards, the consequence would be to prolong for a further term the war with great prejudice to the interests of Peru and Chile.

In this view and you being too sensible of the obligation [empreño] which my Government takes to promote the advancement of the United States of America, I direct myself to you by their orders to the end that you will please to inform me respecting the cargoes and ulterior destination of said vessels, thereby avoiding in all cases those evils which might be produced by their arrival on the enemy's coasts with articles of war.

I hope you will be pleased to give me on those occurrences a favorable answer in order that the His Excellency the Supreme Director may be confirmed in those sentiments which he feels toward the Government of the United States.

Hogan could not deny that the *Canton* was carrying arms, for both he and Commodore Stewart knew it was. His reply note three days later admitted that the *Canton* "has a quantity of muskets on board which were stored with the rest of the cargo, neither secreted under flour nor in any manner hid from publick view," and said that they were intended to be sold in "trade with the natives," by which he presumably meant patriots, along the coast. Fortunately, the Chilean authorities were willing to accept a face-saving solution—the arms were landed and placed in the Customs House.[90] This did not end the affair, however, because Peruvian patriot officials later charged that the arms had been unloaded by the *Canton* at Arica for sale to royalist forces during June. Prevost believed that, "without the knowledge of [the Chilean government] or of Mr. Hogan, with whom some correspondence had taken place on this subject," the arms had been smuggled out of the Valparaíso Customs House to another American vessel named *Pearl* and then either transferred to the *Canton* at sea or unloaded directly from the *Pearl*, which was at Arica at the same time as the *Canton*.[91] Stewart asserted that his ships had searched the American vessels at Arica and found no arms. The truth will never been known, but based on the frequent and widespread smuggling and other skulduggery that occurred during this period in both Peru and Chile involving persons of all nationalities, there may well have been substance to the allegations.

Eliphalet Smith could also have been involved. He had arrived at Valparaíso to plead for Stewart's intercession in obtaining the release of the *Macedonian* and her cargo which had been condemned by a patriot court in Lima as the property of a Spanish company in the Philippines.[92] Hogan reported that: "The answer received from this

Government in November [1821] respecting the seventy thousand dollars taken from Captain Smith of the *Macedonian*..., has not been acted upon. The Director then promised he would have the case tried here by the Prize Court in order to give me an opportunity of showing the illegality of the capture.... The *Franklin's*...appearance is more powerful that the arguments of all the national law writers that ever existed. Force is, and ever will be, the rule or order on this Coast. There is no case, however bad or base, that Spanish law...will not find a palliative for. The royal ordinances are resorted here as formerly when it is convenient to do so in order to defeat just claims, but the law or rule of expediency governs."[93] As Ridgely had done eight months earlier, Stewart sent a letter to O'Higgins in April asking for restitution of property he insisted was American.[94] Despite all these efforts, the case was not finally settled until twenty years later when the owners of the *Macedonian* received only partial compensation.[95] Whatever may have been the true circumstances, Smith was regarded by the patriots as a scoundrel of the worst sort.

Stewart certainly knew that Smith had spent the past three years as a gun runner for the royalists, but he defended him against criticism and ardently supported his claims against both royalist and patriot officials. Smith persuaded Stewart to give him passage on the U.S.S. *Dolphin* so that he could return to Peru. Later, Smith was to spend almost a year aboard the U.S.S. *Franklin*, conducting his business affairs, including the management of the *Canton* which he had chartered from O'Sullivan, from on board the U.S. Navy ship. If the *Canton* was involved in delivering arms at Arica, Smith could have had a hand in the venture.

There is no indication that Hogan played any role in these events, although he was on close terms with O'Sullivan, a fellow Irishman, who in turn often acted as an intermediary in procuring naval supplies from Hogan for the U.S. Navy ships. The *Franklin* left Valparaíso on May 22, 1822, three and a half months after its initial arrival, to cruise mostly in Peruvian waters and did not return until the end of that year. (The *Constellation* was also at Valparaíso from March 28 until May 6, before returning to the United States.)

Hogan's hands were also full with the task of supplying U.S. Navy ships with such items as beef, pork, flour, rice, whisky and rum, candles, paints and oils and other nautical necessities. Some supplies were sent on merchant vessels by Navy agents in Boston and Baltimore; others he procured locally. Inevitably, the question of paying import duties arose, the Customs House insisting they were owed, even though they were to be consumed on American naval ships. Hogan asserted that it was "the courtesy due from one nation to another" that public provisions should be free from such duties, but he lost his appeal; when Prevost refused to back him, he gave up the effort.[96] The question of import duties would arise again several years later. Hogan also found a local oven to bake bread for the ships, using a mixture of local and imported American flour, the former being considered inferior.

An indication of the ethics of American officials of this era can be gleaned from the events surrounding the court martial of Commodore Stewart on his return to the United States over various charges involving his activities along the Peruvian and Chilean coast. The charges came from several sources, including Prevost, but the catalyst was the official complaint made by Peru that Stewart interfered with patriot-declared blockades and allowed American vessels to deliver arms to royalist forces. Stewart was also charged with taking a Spanish spy on board the *Franklin*; in fact, it had been Mrs. Stewart who had allowed a royalist officer to gain passage surreptitiously, much to the commodore's chagrin. Although Stewart was "most fully and most honorably acquitted" in a proceeding that attracted national press attention, the case tells a lot about the mores of the United States Navy at the time, the use of power to protect United States citizens, regardless of their misdeeds, and the attitudes of American officials, naval and civilian alike, toward the royalists and patriots. Hogan was not a conspirator in the alleged misdeeds that led to the court martial, but he was involved in them and may have had knowledge not introduced at the trial. This knowledge might have been helpful to Stewart—he had asked that Hogan be brought back to Washington for the trial but was refused—but equally, as will be seen, it may have redounded to his disadvantage.[97]

The United States Navy had taken many of its customs—both good and bad, from the British Navy. One of these was the carriage aboard U.S. Navy ships of coin and specie owned by American merchants, the justification being that this was the only way to assure the secure carriage of such a valuable commodity in areas threatened by conflict, pirates or privateers. Downes on the *Macedonian* in 1820 was the first to engage in this practice in Pacific waters. Abuses and public complaints led to a detailed Navy Department order in 1823. After stating that, "Our national vessels ought not, and must not, be used for purposes of commercial advantage," commanders were authorized to carry coin or specie only on behalf of American citizens and only between foreign ports or for return to the United States, and they were not to advertize the availability of this service. Although the maximum commission they could charge was set by the Navy Department at a very low level, there is ample evidence that higher levels were common and that several commanders made a great deal of money from the practice.[98] The use of Navy vessels to transport merchandise for private profit had been prohibited since 1800,[99] but Navy commanders were not prohibited from providing supplies to merchant vessels in need, for which a charge could be levied. There were also many opportunities for commanders and pursers (the official accountants on board ships) to fake claims for reimbursement of a variety of expenses incurred by their ship, particularly in foreign waters, despite an elaborate system of receipts and vouchers that were reviewed by the Treasury's fourth auditor attached to the Navy Department in Washington.[100] It was indisputable that captains of ships, both naval and merchant, enjoyed virtually dictatorial power aboard their ships.

As long as these various activities were not pursued with excessive greed or clumsiness, they were tacitly overlooked. But as is so often the case with such unwritten rules of behavior, the bureaucracy must cleanse its soul every so often with a ritualistic in-house trial of a well-known hero in which it is finally determined that there is insufficient evidence and that the defendant is therefore still a hero. Another factor was that, especially since the end of the War of 1812, Navy officers engaged in many bitter disputes over promotions and postings, resorting to charges and counter-charges that often led to courts martial, sometimes at the request of the officer being accused. Guilty verdicts in such cases would impugn the cherished system as much as the defendant. Stewart was brought to trial partly to show that the United States took seriously the Peruvian complaints over his activities, but it also fitted the mold of periodic cleansing and absolution, for he was probably guilty of some of the charges against him. If Hogan had understood all this and acted accordingly, he might have been able to avoid a worse fate several years later at the hands of the United States Navy Department.

The belief that Stewart was probably guilty as charged must be weighed, however, against his mission to protect U.S. citizens and commerce while remaining a neutral. In this, he had at his disposal a powerful naval vessel, the U.S.S. *Franklin*, as well as the smaller U.S.S. *Dolphin*. He also arranged for three small vessels to be refitted in Chile to provide logistical support. This force could not take on Lord

Cochrane's Chilean Navy, but it could deter single war vessels from interceding if Stewart decided to use the threat of his superior firepower to free American ships from detention, which he did on several occasions. As with previous naval commanders, Prevost thought Stewart acted improperly in defying blockades; they had a nasty exchange of letters on the question.[101] Stewart succeeded, however, in asserting a strong American presence in the area and in protecting American commercial interests in the process. In this, he clearly had the support of the Monroe Administration, as evidenced by the fact that Monroe pointedly endorsed his position on the paper blockades in an official rebuke that Adams sent to Prevost.[102]

Whether Stewart served long term American interests is another question. Although the orders he received from the Navy Department before sailing to South America told him that he was to avoid any act that might "in any manner have the appearance or admit the construction of favoring the cause of Spain against [the] struggle [for] liberty and independence," Stewart was more sympathetic to the royalists than the patriots, and he did not keep his views private.[103] Considering the history of Spanish oppression, it may seem difficult now to understand why an American, with the Revolution only half a century old, would align himself with royalists of any country. That Stewart probably found the Spanish royalists more sophisticated and educated than the patriots is easy to understand, and that he found much to condemn among the sometimes ruthless patriots can also be comprehended. But since it was then generally acknowledged that the Spanish hold on South America was ultimately doomed, it did not take keen foresight to appreciate that the United States could not have close and friendly relations with the newly independent countries if it did not take their side from the beginning, at least to the point of not showing sympathy for their enemy. Even today there are those in Chile and elsewhere in South America who attribute the ill-feelings which have marked United States relations in subsequent decades to the first years of independence when the United States was often considered to be unfriendly and arrogant. Stewart was certainly not the only cause of this bad beginning, but he was symptomatic of it.

Hogan must have felt that he was in danger of being recalled or otherwise punished as a consequence of the derogatory reports of Robinson and perhaps other individuals, but in fact there was no reaction whatsoever from Washington. In all other respects, he seems to have enjoyed the friendship and respect of his cohorts—at least to the point that there was no open animosity. His family also found that life for foreigners in Valparaíso was not as lonely as it can be. There was a sizable foreign community in the town, with the British predominating. There were also friendships from unexpected sources. On board the U.S.S. *Franklin* when it arrived in Valparaíso was a twenty-two year midshipman named Charles Wilkes whose father was known to the Hogans when they were in New York. Many years later Wilkes wrote a lengthy autobiography in which he recounted his remarkable career, best known for exploring expeditions and development of naval instruments.[104] The account is effusive in praise of Michael Hogan and his family. Hogan extended an invitation to Wilkes through Commodore Stewart to "come on shore to see [the family]". "Nothing could be kinder," he wrote, "than [their] reception of me and I was at once made at home, to come and go when I pleased, and I passed many happy days and hours under their roof with great pleasure. The girls seemed to me like part of the family although I had not seen them often previous to their leaving [New York]. Yet the tie seemed strong one to me and from the knowledge they had of everybody I knew, brought us very near and through them I heard tidings of her whom I had left behind and who was so dear to me." (Wilkes was referring to his fiancee whom he later married. If he had not already been smitten, perhaps his affection for the Hogan women might have led to a different marriage.) "Mr. Hogan himself was a charming old gentleman, well informed and extremely fond of society. His family, including Mrs. Hogan, were well educated and accomplished ladies, but very taciturn, as Mr. Hogan often remarked. I felt light hearty and contented and was buoyant with Spirit and, as the old Gentleman used to say, always kicked up a row when I came and put spirits in them all. I had reason to esteem them and did what I could to afford them pleasure and gratification. There was always a bed for me and a plate at the Table & to come and go as I pleased. I can never forget their hospitality."

While Wilkes and the *Franklin* were still at Valparaíso, a thirty-seven year old English woman, Maria Dundas Graham, arrived on H.M.S. *Doria*, forlorn that her husband had died on rounding Cape Horn. Captain Ridgely, whose *Constellation* was also in port, brought "Mrs. Hogan and Miss Hogan [on board the *Doria*] to call on her and to offer all the assistance in their power." This plucky woman rented a cottage in the Almendral near the Hogans. She kept a detailed diary, later published,[105] recounting her daily life in which the Hogans are frequently mentioned. Mrs. Graham and the senior Hogans may have traded stories about Calcutta where they both had lived, Graham some fifteen years after the Hogans, or perhaps about Cape Town because Mrs. Graham was of the Dundas family with connections in both London and Cape Town. (Graham had a title, Lady Maria Calcott, which she apparently did not use, perhaps out of deference to her late husband, who was a commoner.) She recounted that she dined with "my good friends Mr. Hogan the American consul and his wife and daughter," that "my friend Miss H [one of the Hogan daughters, probably Sophia] is staying with me and we have had many pleasant walks together," and that upon returning from a trip "I found Mr. Hogan and several other friends waiting to welcome me." Sophia Donnelly loaned her favorite horse, Charlie, to Mrs. Graham for several weeks. Wilkes recounts that he "saw her at the Hogans, who extended to her all the courtesies she was in want of in her affliction." She did not stay in Chile long, leaving in January 1823, two months after a calamitous earthquake.

It was on November 19, 1922, as the Hogans were preparing for bed, that a major earthquake hit the Valparaíso area. Hogan led his family from the apartment house, through damage-littered roads to the waterfront where they were able to board the British vessel *Medway* and gain comparative safety. He reported in graphic terms, if not the best grammar, to Adams:

At 38 minutes past 10 [p.m.], this terrific shock came as sudden as a flash of lightening without preparatory intimation as was usual in the many that we have experienced since I have been here. It lasted about 2½ to 3 minutes, sufficient to destroy most the whole of Valparaíso and the most populous part, the village of Almendral, both said to contain 13,000 inhabitants. The cathedral, church, Governor's place or house and all the rest were either destroyed or rendered uninhabitable with the exception of about twenty that people have got into without fear of crumbling. The consternation, confusion and terror surpassed description. The shrieks and cries and prayers added to the dreadful column of smoke and dirt and heat that arose from the opening of the earth was too awful to be explained. Had it happened at the dead of night, very few would live to see daylight. Then, [the] falling in of houses with their weighty roofs of tiles [would have] have destroyed the sleeping inhabitants who seldom go to rest before midnight because they invariably sleep three hours of an afternoon.

On the first fright, all run into the streets, the natives to the mountains that overhang the town, the foreigners to the sea or on board the ships as fast as boats could be procured.... During the whole time the earth shivering like the spring floor of a great ballroom and opening in giant rents in many parts, no one knowing which way to turn, each family clung to each other ready in tears and screams to resign together their lives whenever the earth opened.... My three daughters were in bed in that dress. I collected them first to one open position in the street, then to another, all equally dangerous, for the earth was jumping up and down, till at length an American sailor informed me of a boat and with the aid of the gentlemen that attached themselves to us got into a yawl half full of water and with two oars 15 of us [including Maria Graham] reached one of the ships, the *Medway* of London, where we were treated with the greatest kindness by Captain Borthwick Wright for ten days. We are now living afloat in the cabin of a ship having neither house nor shelter on shore and the half of our furniture lost or destroyed.

Hogan reported that about 300 people were lost (the correct number was nearer 150), "no Americans but twelve other foreigners." It had not been the worst earthquake disaster of history, but it was one of the six major ones that have hit Valparaíso to date.

The bakery that Hogan had retained to supply bread to U.S. Navy ships had been destroyed. He found other means to continue supplying bread to U.S. Navy ships. The *Franklin* arrived at Valparaíso a month after the earthquake and stayed three months, probably providing some help to the Hogan family, though this is not evident from the frequency of Hogan's complaints.

He had asked Adams to send a "framehouse of dimensions for the climate" because of "dearth of ground and materials which are not procurable locally." But the plea was really an excuse to lay bare once more the difficult circumstances under which he had to operate:[106]

Heretofore, I have [as commercial representative] gone to a greater extent than justice to my family warrants and I am injuring myself daily, being devoted wholly to publick duties that have from a variety of causes multiplied on my hands. No advantage whatever from commerce. No consul that will do his duty so far from home will ever have any. I will do [my duty] fearlessly, find fault who will or complain of me who may.

With their apartment and furniture virtually all destroyed, Hogan engaged a cabin on the English ship *Mary* in Valparaíso harbor, where the family stayed for four months until April 1823 when Hogan found a house that he described as a "barn" to live in for an annual rent of $900 while a new house was being built on the Almendral. Sophia described the new house, or cottage as she called it, as "comfortable and pretty...built around three sides of a square, with wide piazza on front and rear, every bedroom having a door leading to the courtyard. It covered a large extent of ground, being only one story. There were no stairs, nor any chimney, being constructed entirely of timber with shingled roof. Even if a severe earthquake happened, there could not be as much danger as from brick walls and heavy tiles. In front of the house, a flower garden...reached down to the stone wall, with a light fence on top to shut off the road. A trellis of some extent was covered with vines of most delicious grapes. A grass plot, with flowering shrubs, was very attractive to many birds, more especially the lovely, tiny hummingbirds. At the side and back of the house was a vegetable garden, and a variety of fruit trees extending to the foot of another high hill. Kitchen, scullery, bathroom and servants' quarters formed a separate square, while stables and other outbuildings were on one side."

A pencil drawing dated 1825 shows an attractive one-story dwelling surrounded by trees, fences and several outbuildings, though it must have been small by Hogan's New York standards (Figure 6, facing page). The ship *Mary* was shortly thereafter totally lost when a strong gale struck Valparaíso in June 1823 with some of Hogan's furniture still on board. Also on board and totally destroyed were 146 barrels of pork that the Bayard company had entrusted to Hogan for sale.

The storm coming on top of the earthquake led him to include a plea for sympathy in his letter to President Monroe: "My place of residence from being cheap has become one of the dearest and most disagreeable on earth. Earthquakes and the late storm have ruined it. The increase of people, with whose consumption, the cultivation of the country or the increase or care of stock keep no pace, and the total want of good government renders it miserable."

The young Wilkes had also returned to Valparaíso after commanding one of the three tenders built to support the *Franklin*. With Hogan's approval, Commodore Stewart had put him in charge of a merchant ship, the *O'Cain*, whose master had become sick, with orders to return the vessel to Boston. Before this could be effected, however, a Daniel W. Coit from New York arrived with authority to act as supercargo of the *O'Cain* for a venture to Peru. Wilkes recounts how he "determined to buy a lot of goods as I well knew the prices and enhanced value of them on the coast of Peru and the Intermedios." His return to Valparaíso in July "created some little surprise, but on reporting all the circumstances to Mr. Hogan, he approved and justified all I had done." What he had done was to make a tidy profit of $6,000 from engaging in commerce, supposedly while still on official duty, another sign of the naval mores of the times. Wilkes "was welcomed as before at the Hogans, who had moved to their new house at the end of the Almendral where they dispensed their usual hospitality." Before finally leaving

Figure 6. Hogan home on the Almendral, Valparaíso. Author's Collection.

Chile, Wilkes encountered difficulties at the Customs House. He recalled that "Mr. Hogan, who had a great deal of the Irish blood, fully justified me as he had done my conduct with the Customs officers before sailing—at which he laughed heartily. I understood he had had an altercation with the Commandant of the customs house the day before when he learnt they were intending to stop the ship and, in his Irish blood, in his ful[l] uniform, he had drawn his sword and passed it under the officials's nose, telling [him] what would be the consequence and declaring that no money would be paid on any account to permit the vessel's departure which was the object of the plot to extort." These last minute difficulties out of the way, Wilkes "bid adieu to my Pacific home for I could [not] help calling Mr. Hogan's family such...." He was to be involved with Michael Hogan and his family on at least two occasions much later. His praise never wavered.

That autumn, on October 22, Hogan's youngest daughter, twenty-one year old Sophia, married Arthur Donnelly, an Englishman of Irish descent who had come to Valparaíso on business for the East India Company. Since the U.S.S. *Franklin* was then in port, Commodore and Mrs. Stewart probably attended the wedding. Arthur remained in Valparaíso for a little over a year, conducting several business transactions for which his father-in-law stood as surety, but was compelled to return to his place of employment—Calcutta. Sophia stayed behind with her family, apparently without visits from her husband, until August 1830 when she sailed via Manila to join him at Calcutta, taking with her copies of Arthur's account with Hogan showing a debt of some $4,000 (that someone later marked "never paid").

The earthquake marked a transition in Chile and in U.S. relations with that country. Lord Cochrane's role as Admiral of the Chilean Navy came to an end when he left the west coast two months after the earthquake in January 1823 to assume new duties in Brazil. Thereafter, the Chilean Navy, and its Peruvian counterpart, were on their own.

The more important change was that, a few days after Cochrane's departure, O'Higgins surrendered his executive authority as Supreme Director to General Ramón Freire after a dramatic confrontation with a representative group of Santiago citizens. Whatever may have been his shortcomings, O'Higgins was a true patriot and a supporter of friendly relations and intercourse with outside powers; as such he was never fully accepted by the Chilean upper classes or the elite in Santiago, nor by the Catholic clergy. The latter even attributed the earthquake to foreign heretics favored by O'Higgins. The former Supreme Director left for Peru where it was rumored on several occasions that he might mount a campaign to return in triumph to Chile as "The Liberator."

Both Prevost and Hogan were reporting political events at this time, not always consistently. Hogan told Adams that Prevost "would not believe any communication I made to him [about military movements], all of which were well known to me from the parties interested." When Prevost left for Lima on February 16, "it produced remarks unpleasant." He stayed there eight months, squabbling with Commodore Stewart, during which time Hogan was again in charge of political reporting from Chile. He "considered it his duty to call on" Freire, which he did on April 6, reporting to Adams that the Supreme Director believed he was justified in overthrowing the government because of O'Higgins' misrule and lack of authority from the people, and that Freire said his "object was to see established a system of government as much like that of the United States as circumstances would warrant." With considerable foresight, Hogan believed that the "great difficulty is to find any person qualified for the chief magistrate's chair, for they pretend to be republicans without other quality than the name."

Hogan ended his report to Adams with a back-handed compliment for himself: "[Supreme Director] Freire has had the candor to say that, although I made a strong remonstrance against him at first commencement, I was a true representation of my country and to be depended on."[107]

As for Freire's character, Hogan later said (in his letter to President Monroe) that he "is excessively brave, very honest and disinterested, a perfectly laborious field soldier (a gambler)—these are his talents, [but] all are dissatisfied and Freire will not last six months in office." He again had less kind words for the general character of Chileans: "The habitual sluggishness of the natives [is] of the higher order, their little value for time and contempt of improvements [brought in] by foreigners is inconceivable. Neither education nor the arts encouraged, procrastination and a perfect acquaintance with the means by which to defraud the government of its revenue is what the father studies to inculcate in the son from infancy.... In this country of Chile there is no talent, let others say to the contrary that will...."

Among other subjects that Hogan also reported during this period was the suspicion that the French naval squadron on the west coast might intervene to help the Spanish royalists in Peru, where neither side seemed able to win decisive and lasting victory. Although there were in fact French naval plans to act in the Americas if a new war broke out in Europe, the official French position communicated to the British was that France had no intention of using force of arms in Spain's colonies; it was nevertheless content to let Britain believe that it should not consider recognition lest the French intervene.[108]

Prevost returned to Santiago on October 15, explaining to Adams that there was "no subject before me requiring immediate agency and the extreme ill health of Mr. Hogan together with the meeting of the [Chilean Congress] determined me to encounter once more this irksome voyage."[109] His real reason may have been to keep close tabs on Commodore Stewart on the *Franklin* which had also returned to Valparaíso. Then when the *Franklin* left again for Peruvian waters, Prevost followed on January 18, 1824 (though certainly not on the U.S. Navy ship), after giving Hogan instructions to inform any American warships that might come into port of a blockade imposed by the Peruvian authorities.[110] Whether he privately counseled Hogan to tell Navy commanders to respect the blockade is unknown; he had not yet received Adams rebuke on the subject of blockades. After arrival at Lima, he reported to Adams that Supreme Director Freire wanted to give him a departing audience as a "personal compliment," which Prevost on reflection thought he should accept, delivering a warm tribute to Chile in the audience.[111] Whether this indicates that he did not intend to return to Chile must remain unknown. He died in Peru a year later.

During Hogan's first two years at Valparaíso, the question of the United States and other countries recognizing the new South American republics was coming to a conclusion. After word was received that Lima had fallen to San Martín and it seemed that most of Spanish America was now free of Spain (though this was not yet true), Madison sent a message to Congress in March 1822 recommending that the independence of the new republics be acknowledged and that ministers be sent to represent the United States. The Congress agreed that the new republics should be officially recognized; it also appropriated funds to meet the expenses of establishing diplomatic missions. When the news reached Chile in July, there were "ringing of bells and discharge of guns" in Santiago, but the rejoicing was premature because formal recognition did not take place for another five months.[112] Monroe waited because he wanted to be certain European powers would not react adversely. Rumors and conjecture over European intentions were rife; one was similar to the reports that Hogan had sent while he was at Havana that the British had secret designs on Cuba and might obtain it from Spain in return for surrendering Gibraltar; another was that France had designs on Chiloe, a large island off Chile's coast. At a cabinet meeting on November 28, Adams noted that "we had two very different views of [Chile]; one favorable, by Mr. Prevost—the other much otherwise, by Jeremy Robinson; while Commodore Stewart and Mr. Hogan wrote with the utmost disgust and abhorrence of all the leaders and ruling men in [Chile]."[113] Adams may have had in mind Hogan's previously-cited despatch characterizing Chilean leaders as "the most vainglorious people on earth, certainly the most ignorant." Finally, in January Monroe nominated ministers to be sent to Mexico, Columbia, Buenos Aires and Chile. Five of the ten U.S. ministers assigned to various countries in 1824 were in Latin America.[114] Heman Allen from Vermont was confirmed by the Senate as American minister at Santiago on January 27, 1823, and Hogan's appointment as full consul at Valparaíso was confirmed on June 20 (Figure 7, facing page). Allen did not arrive until the following March. Monroe told Adams that he wanted to name Prevost as chargé d'affaires at Peru.[115] This must have surprised Adams for he had just admonished Prevost over the blockade issue with the president's presumed blessing; a diplomatic appointment was in any event premature because Lima did not finally fall for another two years and the Spanish fort at Callao for another year.

While American recognition was a logical progression stemming from developments in the New World, it was also a bold act because it seemed to fly in the face of Europe's clear intention to return to the old order after the Congress of Vienna ended the Napoleonic Wars. France under Louis XVIII invaded Spain in April 1823, and there were suspicions that the Holy Alliance would attempt to restore monarchial order in South America next. Britain, although hardly a champion of revolutionary causes, opposed European intervention in the New World. There was also thought to be a Russian threat. In September 1821, Tsar Alexander I had issued an imperial decree prohibiting foreign vessels from coming within 100 miles of Russian-claimed land north of the fifty-first parallel on the Pacific northwest coast, slightly north of Vancouver but considerably to the south of previous Russian claims. Having recently vied with Spain and Britain over the Pacific northwest, Monroe and Adams were alarmed over the possibility of yet another European intervention. Hogan may have lent credence to these concerns when in September 1822 he reported information he had received that the new Russian frigate *Apollo* was proceeding to the Pacific northwest coast with orders to seize American ships in waters north of the 50° North latitude.[116] The following July Adams told the Russian minister in Washington that the U.S. would contest any Russian territorial possession on the North American continent.

Although Monroe was initially inclined to accept an apparent British offer for joint action or declaration respecting South America, after intense debate he decided that the United States should act alone, perhaps because the country was still not certain of British motives or perhaps because he recognized that the principles involved were ones that the U.S. should decide on its own. He announced what later became known as the Monroe Doctrine in his annual message to

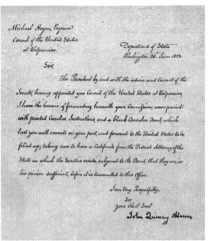

Figure 7. Consular Appointment. Author's Collection.

Congress on December 2, 1823. Miffed that the U.S. had acted unilaterally, Britain tried to discredit the United States in South America. Domestic American reaction was generally favorable. Much has been written interpreting the origins and meaning of this unilateral statement and its subsequent effect on historical events. Some have attributed noble intentions and admirable results to the doctrine, others have seen it as the precursor of attempts to assert American hegemony in the Western Hemisphere, and still others—particularly British sources— have claimed it was entirely dependent on congruent British policy and a strong British Navy. The Monroe Doctrine was more a statement of attitudes than of policy. The doctrine had no immediate practical impact, and it has not been applied (or interpreted) consistently. European moves to intervene in South America (with only a few exceptions) never proceeded beyond speculation; in the decades to come, Europe would focus its energies on industrialization and later on other continents for colonization; the United States remained militarily and economically weak until after the Civil War; and a common interest among all major countries in relatively open trade would lead more often to economic competition than armed conflict.

American recognition, presaging as it did the arrival in Chile of a diplomatic representative, was to change not only Hogan's official status and relationship with his cohorts but also his career and private life.

TEN

AMERICAN CONSUL, VALPARAÍSO

The evening of my life is wearing away in the service and I have never received a dollar of publick money.

—Hogan to Martin Van Buren, March 1830

In the forenoon of March 27, 1824, the U.S.S. *United States,* a 1,576-ton 44-gun frigate, dropped anchor in Valparaíso harbor. Launched twenty-seven years earlier, it had seen service in the undeclared naval war with France, the War of 1812 and off the Barbary coast of North Africa; it was now fondly called the *Old Waggon* because of her sluggish sailing. She was the flagship of Commodore Isaac Hull, victor and hero in the famous sea battle between the U.S.S. *Constitution* and H.M.S. *Guerrière* in the War of 1812. The *United States* had been sent to take over command of the Pacific squadron. The next day, a Sunday, Hull and his entourage came ashore where they were met by Hogan who explained that the *Franklin* was not in port because it had earlier sailed for Callao to protect American shipping when royalist forces again seized Lima. In addition to Hull, the entourage consisted of Heman Allen, the new American minister, his first secretary, Samuel Larned, the wives of Hull and Allen and a sister of the wives. Hogan knew that Allen would be arriving and he may have heard that Larned was coming also, but he must have been not only surprised but confused by the presence of the three women, all sisters. They were Ann Hart Hull, Elizabeth Hart Allen and Harriet Augusta Hart, all from Saybrook, Connecticut, three of the seven beautiful daughters of Captain Elisha Hart. Ann had married Hull in 1813. Elizabeth had met and married Allen in a storybook romance a few months before sailing; she arrived seasick and pregnant. Augusta Hart had come along for the adventure.[1] The Hogan family probably welcomed the Hull and Allen families in expectation of sharing their life and experiences in a foreign land with fellow Americans, but relations would not stay amiable, particularly between the Hogans and the Allens and between Michael Hogan and Commodore Hull.

The first order of official business on Allen's arrival was to arrange for his reception by the Chilean Government. Sophia noted that: "Ours being the first country to [recognize Chile], [Allen] was received with great honors. Every attention was paid: salutes fired from the Fort and frigate [*United States*]; the Governor [of Valparaíso] and suite visited him, a great banquet was given...." Sophia meant that the United States was the first non-South American government to recognize Chile by sending a minister; Peru and Argentina already had ministers in place, and there was also a papal nuncio. Allen was formally received by Foreign Minister Rafael Egaña a month after his arrival. He was offered, but refused, a guard of honor and a house at public expense. The initial reception was replete with mutual assurances of respect and friendly relations. Allen explained the origins of the Monroe Doctrine, emphasizing that the president had decided to act alone when the British foreign secretary, Canning, "grew indifferent to the subject," and that "England should obtain no unmerited applause" in the matter.[2] His Anglophobia was matched by his belief that the Catholic Church was the enemy not only of Protestantism but also of a free and independent Chile.[3] Among the causes that Allen pressed during his tenure was preservation of the right of Protestants to bury their dead in their own churchyard.[4] O'Higgins had made this concession to religious freedom in 1823 when a burial ground for foreigners was established in Valparaíso at an initial cost of $1,136.15. Hogan was one of the contributors, as he was also in 1827 when another $1,017 was raised.[5]

Heman Allen was 45 years old when he came to Chile. A Dartmouth graduate, he practiced law, was chief justice of a Vermont county court, held several political offices in Vermont, and in 1817–18 served one term in the U.S. House of Representatives as a Democrat.[6]

Allen brought with him letters for Hogan, among which was one from DeWitt Clinton, Governor of New York, who said "it will always afford me the highest satisfaction to hear of the welfare of yourself and your family." Clinton also reported that the "political affairs of this country are in a state of great distraction. The contention for the Presidency enters into every great question and is the prevailing topic of agitation. The finale of this controversy is involved in total uncertainty."[7] He was referring to upcoming 1824 election which, although not scheduled for another year, had been the subject of lively debate ever since Monroe began his second term in 1821. John Quincy Adams was an obvious candidate because of his experience at several diplomatic posts and as secretary of state. But other names were put into the ring, including particularly Andrew Jackson, the hero of the Battle of New Orleans in the War of 1812. When no candidate received a majority of the electoral vote, the issue was thrown into the House of Representatives in January 1825. Adams was chosen, accused by Jackson of obtaining the votes of the Henry Clay faction by promising to name him secretary of state, which in fact Adams did. The charge that Adams and Clay conspired to deprive Jackson of the presidency resurfaced during the next presidential campaign in 1828. Showing again his Whig sympathies, Hogan told Larned that the "long vindication by Mr. Clay of his own character against the many charges put forth for the last two years against him...in my opinion acquit him of the whole and leave him as pure as a Diamond of the first grade. It does him Honor and greatly promotes the Election of Mr. Adams."[8] His prophecy proved to be wrong; Jackson won by a landslide in 1828.

Allen also brought with him three instructions from the Department of State. Two dealt with his specific responsibilities in Chile; the other was the standard instruction sent to all ministers at the time.[9] They are of general historical interest in describing how the Department of State and its representatives abroad operated and in shedding light on the attitude of the Department concerning commercial relations between the newly independent South American states and the United States and the role of the U.S. Navy in protecting U.S. interests.

The eight-page general instruction contains several interesting features. One is that ministers were supplied with a "cipher to be used as occasions may require in your correspondence with this Department or with any other of the ministers of the United States abroad." If Allen ever used the cipher, it must have been the practice of the Department of State to keep such papers separate from standard files and eventually destroy them, for there is no record in the National Archives of coded messages from Allen (and possibly from any other diplomatic representative). Since the same cipher was apparently given to all representatives over a period of years, its security is questionable.

Another notable feature concerns the "uniform worn by the ministers of the United States at foreign courts on occasions when full dress is required." Although the instruction emphasized that the uniform is "in no case prescribed by this Government" and that "every Minister of the United States abroad may wear at his discretion any dress comfortable to the customs of the place where he may residence," it enclosed an engraved design for a diplomatic uniform "for the convenience of using the same dress upon all necessary occasions and at every court."

The instruction also shows that ministers received an annual salary of $9,000, a one-time outfit allowance of the same amount and, on being relieved, a "quarters salary" of unspecified amount. In addition, ministers could claim reimbursement for printed materials transmitted to the Department, postage, stationary and "necessary and customary presents to menial attendants of the public functionaries at your presentation and on other established occasions (usually the Christmas and New Year's days)." Notably absent from this limited list are transportation to and from post, office rent and hire of clerks.

Allen's specific instructions concerning his responsibilities in Chile show how much weight the Department of State attached to the settlement of claims by American citizens against Chile and Peru and to the related question of naval protection of U.S. interests and coordination between Navy commanders and American consular and diplomatic representatives.

After some generalizations about overall political relations with the newly independent states of South America, that speak both of welcoming them and of being aware of differences over "religious dogmas, political doctrines and social usages," the instructions drew attention to the fact that Prevost's "views of his duties have so much differed from those of the naval commanders of the United States in the Pacific as to have caused misunderstandings between him and all of them, that he has preferred complaints against them all, while grave complaints have been made against him by several citizens of the United States.... It is highly important...[that] the best understanding should be maintained between Diplomatic and Naval Officers of the United States stationed in [Chilean and Peruvian waters].... It is the President's hope and trust, that there will be, between you and [Hull], and every other officer of the squadron in the Pacific, the most cordial concert and cooperation for the benefit of the public service."

Allen was also instructed to press in particular two cases of claims by U.S. citizens against Chile and Peru. The more contentious one involved the *Macedonian* and the machinations of the vessel's master, Eliphalet Smith. "From the reports of Mr. Hogan..., as well as of those from Mr. Prevost, it is apparent that there has been some irregularity in the commercial transactions of several citizens of the United States in Chile and Peru.... They have signalized by name certain individuals as being concerned in transactions discreditable to the flag of our nation and to the character of our country.... The proof of facts before this Government is not sufficiently clear for pronouncing upon these complaints and recriminations. Circumstances in the conduct of E. Smith, the original captain of the *Macedonian*, have tended to excite suspicions that he had himself failed of doing justice to the interests of his owners.... I have thought it necessary to give you this information, as the interest of his owners is among those which will claim your early and steady attention: that interest being undoubtedly well founded and not justly liable to suffer by his indiscretions or misconduct."

The instructions take specific note of the complaints made against Prevost, but no where is there any negative reference to Hogan. Allen had been asked, however, by President Monroe to look into Hogan's dismissal of Dr. Bullus's son. In his first reporting despatch, Allen told Adams that the "case of young Bullis [*sic*], contained also in a memorandum from the President, has received my attention. He had returned to the United States before my arrival, but I am satisfied his conduct was very irregular and that Mr. Hogan must have been incapable of an unkind act toward him."[10] Six months later, Allen could not have been more effusive in his praise of Hogan: "I owe it to the government, to Mr. Hogan, and to my own feeling to be in testimony to his unvaried attention and devotion to the publick interest as consul to this country. In this expression, I am sustained as well by a careful examination of his correspondence, as by own observation whilst at Valparaíso, and by his communicating with me here, in all of which he appears to have [expended] much labor, inflexible integrity, and the most evident desire to maintain the honor and interest of his country and of her citizens. His duties have certainly been very arduous, not only in resisting the mercenary illegal doings of many of our own countrymen, but in combating many unjust [acts] of this government in which the residence of Mr. Prevost, being primarily in Peru, he could from that source, I understand, desire little or no assistance. Whether in this rigid execution of his duty, Mr. Hogan may have not contracted some enemy, I am unable to determine. It would be strange if he had not. And amongst whom, it is not improbable that a Mr. Bullus, whom I mentioned to you in a former despatch, may be one. From everything which I can learn, in respect to this young man, dissipated habits and improper conduct impelled his separation from the family of Mr. Hogan, where he had been domesticated as a child."[11]

Concluding this glowing report, Allen even urged that Hogan be paid a salary for his efforts: "I take leave to remark that, if my allowance of salary shall be made to any of the consuls of the United States, I do think that the case of Mr. Hogan, whose fees from the little commerce in these ways are trifling, presses hard upon the consideration of the government. For I am at a loss to imagine how with his present means he can afford to support himself and family in this expensive country."

From the time that Prevost had left Chile in January until Allen's arrival two months later, Hogan had sent two despatches to Adams. One of them sarcastically reported that "another constitution [has been] proclaimed by [the Chilean] government with great shew and pomp to which they are now swearing, [it] being Sunday, very little will be attended to.... [A copy] cannot be found although hundreds are swearing to maintain what they absolutely know nothing about, for it has not been read to the multitude; it is sufficient for the few to know there is such a thing without entering into the merits of its provisions—were there one hundred such, the will of the governor is the law of the land and is implicitly obeyed."[12] In the other despatch, after emphasizing that he differed with Prevost, Hogan said that "all the misfortunes of Peru have arisen solely from the inability of those in authority as well as from the incapacity of [General Bolivar]. Had they been honest to themselves and true to [their] country, the coast of Peru would long since be clear of royal authority."[13]

During the first few years after Freire replaced O'Higgins in 1823 as president (abandoning the title of supreme director), Chile remained involved in the liberation of Peru and the remaining Spanish stronghold of the island of Chiloé off Chile's southern coast. When Callao and Chiloé both fell in January 1826, Chile was free from external demands and could have turned its attention to domestic reforms. Instead, there was widespread political chaos, financial and economic disorder and lawlessness. Some thirty governments held office and there were several new constitutions.

Hogan reported political and military events on only three occasions while Allen was in Chile. The first two despatches in January 1825 announced the total defeat of royalist forces in Peru and the impending surrender of Callao to the patriots. Hogan sent the first, datelined 12 o'clock, by "express" to the American consul in Buenos Aires for the first sailing to the United States and then forwarded the information to Allen, who was then still a hundred miles away in Santiago. Simon Bolivar had in fact entered Lima, the patriots had won a decisive victory at Ayacucho, and Peruvian independence was proclaimed, but the fort at Callao did not finally surrender for another twelve months.[14] The third despatch sent in February 1826 gave Hogan's assessment of a Peruvian decree of the previous year threatening to seize Spanish goods on vessels calling at Peruvian ports. In it, Hogan said that "the desire of avoiding collision with the Diplomatic Department [i.e., Allen] has kept me silent even on points that were so purely commercial, that I now rather lament to have been so scrupulous," a pointed dig at Allen for not reporting on the commercial policy implications of the decree.[15]

On July 4, 1826, the United States celebrated its fiftieth anniversary since the signing of the Declaration of Independence. There is no record of how the day was celebrated among Americans in Chile, although when it was later learned that Thomas Jefferson and John Adams had both died on that day, U.S. Navy ships in Valparaíso harbor on November 7 lowered their colors to half mast, other vessels followed suit, and at one p.m. the schooner *Dolphin* "fired twenty-four minute guns [*sic*]."[16] American consuls have traditionally held Fourth of July receptions for resident American citizens and representatives of the foreign government. Hogan wrote a flowery peroration which he presumably delivered to his assembled guests. After acknowledging the significance of the "fiftieth year of the political existence of the United States of America," Hogan spoke about the upcoming Congress of Panama. This was to be a diplomatic conference whose ostensible purpose was to establish a confederation of Latin American states. Hogan's opined that, "whatever may be the degree of [U.S] participation in the...Congress of Panama, the result must induce changes of the most important character in our foreign relations and materially affect our internal national policy. The stupendous revolutions of the southern hemisphere have produced an order of things that could not be anticipated by the Father of his country. We are constrained to depart from his paternal admonitions [to forego entanglements in the affairs of other countries] at a time when the evidences of selfish ambition which are displayed on all sides compel the thought that there now exists but little of that patriotic self devotion which find the breasts of the mothers of revolutionary days." The patriotic theme continued with the sentiment: "Let the [anniversary] be celebrated with demonstrations of heartfelt gratitude for the unexampled prosperity we have hitherto enjoyed, with firm determination to meet the exigencies of the future, whatever they may be, as becomes the first American Republic, and with endeavors to sacrifice to the public good all that is personal."

The speech ended with the following remark: "Would not a general celebration at some convenient and critical point enable us to reserve due honor to the day with more conviction than by [the] mutiny [of] detached parties." The phrase "mutiny of detached parties" would have been understood only by those familiar at the time with the machinations of British Foreign Secretary Canning. Still smarting over Monroe's decision to announce a non-intervention policy unilaterally, Canning believed he could use the Congress to replace the United States as Latin America's protector. Allen tried to persuade Chile not to attend on the grounds that Britain intended to use the conference for its own ends. Chile disregarded the advice, but lack of money prevented attendance of its delegates. Nothing came of the Congress in which only Colombia, Mexico, Central America and Peru were represented, although it is generally conceded that Canning's goal of discrediting the United States was achieved.[17]

Britain did not formally recognize Chile until it finally sent a minister in 1831. It did, however, send a British consul, one Christopher Nugent, who arrived in May 1824, shortly after Allen's arrival. Chile certainly wanted the prestige of formal recognition, but it was more interested in British loans and trade. Knowing this, Britain was prepared to drive a hard bargain by insisting that there were preconditions to recognition, including conclusion of a commercial agreement, a position that the United States eschewed, either out of high mindedness or because it did not have the luxury of leverage.

The personal lives of the Hogans, Allens and Hulls were intertwined in several ways from the very beginning. Shortly after his arrival, Allen found living quarters in Santiago. It was there in August of his first year that Elizabeth Allen gave birth to a stillborn daughter. In January of the following year, Allen "found it necessary to remove [from Santiago] to [Valparaíso] for the benefit of my health and that of my family."[18] Elizabeth Allen suffered physically from the stillbirth and, even though she reportedly recovered from this tragedy, she was never fully healthy thereafter.[19] They made their new home just twelve yards from the Hogans on the Almendral. When Hull returned to Valparaíso on the *United States* on March 22, the Hart sisters, Ann and Augusta, stayed with the Allens for a month. Hogan later alleged that it was during this period that he learned of Commodore Hull's malfeasance involving shipments of naval supplies. But Hogan apparently did not make this allegation public at the time, nor is there any evidence that relations between the Hogans and the Allens and Hulls were yet strained. In fact, the presence in port not only of the *United States* but also of the British Navy sloop-of-war *Eclair* was the occasion for parties hosted by the Allens and Hogans during which a young British Navy friend of the Hogans reported that the atmosphere was convivial. This visit will be covered later.

(It was during the time of Hull's first return visit to Valparaíso that news was received that Prevost had died from a heart attack while traveling in the mountains near Arequipo in Peru. He had by then been discredited in Washington; he would have received orders to return to the United States if he had lived longer.[20])

Hogan may have wondered, however, whether someone had undermined his stature in Washington when in November an American ship brought a letter to Valparaíso addressed to "Daniel Wynn, U.S. Consul, Santiago." Hogan obtained Allen's permission to open the envelope and found it contained a consular commission for a man by that name. He wrote to the new Secretary of State, Henry Clay, calmly but with what must have been consternation, saying he would "take care of it till I have the honor to receive your communication on the subject, in which I respectfully request to know whether it is intended that this commission is in any manner to interfere with my appointment which by the promise of my government before I left Washington was that I should have all the ports of Chile, as will appear by your being pleased to refer to the record of my certificate as agent for commerce and seamen bearing date the 11th day of November 1820...and that of the commission brought me by Mr. Allen [which] was gazetted [in Chile] as consul general for Chile...." Official records do not show that Hogan ever received a reply to his reasonable query, but he presumably later discovered that a commission had in fact been issued to Daniel Wynn of New York as consul at Santiago and that he eventually decided to forego the opportunity. It shows something of the casual attitude of the Department of State that it should name a consul to a post only 100 miles away from one already established. Either the responsible official neglected to look at a map or there was political pressure to give Wynn the appointment he had apparently requested.[21]

The *United States* returned for a second visit to Valparaíso on February 25, 1826, for a month's stay. As before, Ann Hull and Augusta

Hart stayed with their sister Elizabeth at the Allen's home. Elizabeth asked her sisters to stay with her in Valparaíso until Hull returned to the United States, which was expected within a year, but they did not wish to do so. It was during this period that a family feud broke out between the Hogans and the Allens. Frances Hogan and Elizabeth exchanged notes in March in which Frances was "found to have been retailing some gossip about [Hull] to the effect that he spent so much time in Peru because he was making money there." The two women were allegedly not on speaking terms thereafter.

Hull is said to have traced the origin of the rumor to the last visit of the *Peacock* to Valparaíso; specifically to a Lieutenant Ramsay who had run afoul of the commodore for other reasons.[22] This explanation is possible, but it is also possible that Frances Hogan intended to refer to an allegation that her husband would not make public for another year that Hull was engaged in malfeasance involving naval supplies shipped from the United States, not to activities in Peru.[23]

Whatever incident Frances intended by her remarks, the impact on relations between Michael Hogan and Heman Allen was immediate. A few days after the exchange between the wives, Allen wrote to Clay withdrawing the praise he had earlier bestowed on Hogan, without however identifying the incident or incidents that led to his change of mind: "I was certainly on my arrival very favorably impressed with the deportment and publick conduct of our consul, Mr. Hogan.... Subsequent events however have very naturally changed that opinion and imposed on me the necessity of withdrawing all my remarks respecting him, as also a certain Mr. Bullus.... I should regret very much that this course, which duty has impelled me to adopt, should operate in any manner prejudicial to the interests of Mr. Hogan. The remarks referred to were submitted at the time with the best intentions towards him, the government and others, and in the full conviction then that they were just and proper. In retracting that opinion, therefore, I feel no disposition to derogate in the least from the merits of Mr. Hogan. If there have been no complaints against him, those remarks could never have been material to his case and if otherwise everything of that nature will doubtless stand by its own weight on its own merits, unaffected by the representations and withdrawal I have made.[24]

Some six weeks after this retraction, Allen received a diplomatic note from Foreign Minister Francisco R. de Vicuña informing him "of occurrences which have taken place in Valparaíso between the Consul of the United States, Mr. Michael Hogan, on the heads and subalterns of the [Customs] office...." The accompanying letter from the Minister of Finance asked for Hogan's outright removal, but Vicuña merely asked that Allen take steps "to bring [Hogan] back to his duties...in order to prevent in future such occurrences." The specific complaint from the Customs House official was that Hogan's "impetuosity, rude manners and hydrophobia expose us with frequency to very disagreeable occurrences if a stop is not instantly put to his daring haughtiness. He will not confine himself to the course pointed out by law, and with the highest contempt for the supreme disposition and all the officers proceeds solely in conformity with his individual interests without there being any barrier capable of restraining him. He has threatened me and others on various occasions with the ships of war of his nation and with his government because we did not yield to his desires and unjust pretensions." The subject which led Hogan to act in the manner indicated was not stated.

Allen must have gloated that the incidents confirmed his reassessment of Hogan's character but he merely transmitted the complaint to Hogan without comment. He also sent copies of the documents to Clay, carefully noting that "the details of this business do not come properly within the range of my particular duty," presumably because Hogan was acting as agent for the Navy Department, not State Department. However, he did consider it within his range of duty to opine at length why the site of the U.S. Navy agent on the Pacific coast should be moved from Valparaíso to the port of Callao in Peru, the principal location of the Pacific squadron.[25] Allen may have made this argument to back Commodore Hull, who properly complained that the supply system then in place was inefficient, but the removal of Hogan would not have displeased Allen either.

It was at this time that Allen and Hogan began to resort to formal letters to communicate with one another, even though they were next door neighbors. Hogan addressed his letters to His Excellency Heman Allen and began with "I have the honour to...," while Allen would say "I have the honour of receiving your note...."

They had two areas of formal disagreement. The first involved import duties. There had been problems about the customs' treatment of U.S. Navy public stores since the Pacific Squadron first came to the area. Hogan first drew this issue to Allen's attention in April 1825, complaining that as Navy agent he should not have to pay duties when stores were transferred from private vessels to Navy ships or when stores were "deposited" (i.e., held in bond) for a period of time before being taken on board Navy vessels. Allen dutifully made the appropriate arguments to the Ministry of Foreign Affairs, though he reported to Adams that he was not inclined to assign high priority to the matter, which was, "in any case, the responsibility of [Hogan] as Navy agent."[26] In response, Chile issued revised regulations in April 1826 which reduced the duty for supplies transferred from private vessels to Navy ships to two percent (there was no duty if transferred from one public ship to another of the same nation) and established that stores could be "deposited" for no more than eight months without incurring additional duties or charges.[27]

This did not end Hogan's complaints. In June in response to a Hogan request, Allen wrote to the Foreign Ministry complaining that, while the U.S. was obliged to pay an eight percent duty on Chilean products purchased for the U.S. Navy, the British paid only two percent. When the Ministry asked for specifics, Allen eventually ascertained that Hogan was being charged the eight percent because the supplies were being exported for U.S. Navy ships in Peruvian waters, while the British were merely loading local supplies on their ships lying in Valparaíso harbor. In responding to the Foreign Ministry, Allen put all the blame squarely on Hogan, and to Hogan he sarcastically said: "It has seldom fallen to my lot in undertaking to maintain the affirmative of a proposition to be obliged to acknowledge that the evidence adduced to its support emphatically proves the negative."[28]

Hogan asked for Allen's help again in November in obtaining relief from the eight month "deposit" limit in the case of some provisions and cordage that were about to exceed this limit. Allen obtained a three month extension, but told Hogan that arrangements should be adopted to "preclude the necessity of similar applications for indulgences [in the future]." Since the United States was already assured of most-favored-nation treatment and that "it is the undoubted right of every nation to establish municipal regulation as in her opinion are best suited to her interests and convenience; and it is only in case of extreme rigour that other nations pretend to interfere. Considering therefore that the regulation in question does not partake of that character, and that it is already the effect of a lengthy and unpleasant correspondence between the Minister of Foreign Relations and myself, I should not think proper, unless instructed to that purpose, to attempt any innovation of the terms of that instrument."[29]

There was one more import duty incident in which Hogan and Allen were at odds. On January 1827 Hogan had been charged a fee for the purchase of some rum and gin from the Chilean liquor and tobacco monopoly for the *Brandywine* and *Dolphin*, in addition to the two percent transit duty. The monopoly—called *estanco*—had been granted to Portales & Company in August 1824 on the pretext of conserving foreign exchange to pay foreign debts, including a five million dollar British loan. Allen refused to take up the matter with the Chilean Government based on a tortuous argument that there was no legal basis for challenging the action taken. Concluding his despatch to Clay, Allen vented his feelings about Hogan: "I did not think proper to extend [my reasons] to Mr. Hogan because experience has long since taught me the inutility of attempting any reasoning process with him. Indeed, he has already troubled me with so many trifling and unfounded complaints that I have ceased to place much reliance on his representations."[30]

Throughout the business of import duties, Allen took the legalistically correct position that Chile could do whatever it wanted so long as all nations were treated equally. What he failed to acknowledge was that there was no barrier to his asking for changes in Chilean policy that served American interests; it was then the responsibility of other nations to complain if they were not accorded equal treatment. Samuel Larned, who became chargé after Allen left his post on July 31, 1827, was both more responsive to Hogan's pleas and successful with Chilean authorities than the legalistic Allen. After some informal conversations with the vice president at the end of that year, Larned obtained a Chilean extension of the eight month "deposit" period to twelve months and an exemption from various duties and charges amounting to $370 for 100 pounds of salted beef destined for the *Brandywine*.[31] Quiet diplomacy, rather than legalistic argument, proved superior!

The second formal issue over which Hogan and Allen disagreed was the claim of John D'Arcy, Henry Didier, Jr., and Thomas Sheppard of Baltimore for moneys they believe were owed to them for shipments of arms to Chilean rebels in 1816 on the vessels *Savage* and *Clifton* under a contract with the Chilean patriot, General José Miguel de Carrera.[32] (The arms on the latter vessel were never delivered because the Argentine authorities held them at Buenos Aires in order to prevent their use by Carrera who was contending with O'Higgins and Martín for the liberation of Chile. Carrera and two brothers were later executed in Argentina and Uruguay by groups sympathetic with O'Higgins.)

Hogan had been retained by the claimants in 1823 through the good offices of his Baltimore friends Robert and John Oliver to pursue their claim. Apparently believing that Allen could assist in pursuing the claim, Hogan apprized him of the details in an 1826 letter. Allen wrote a response arguing that he could not render assistance because—to summarize his lengthy epistle—the original contract for shipment of contraband by a neutral vessel to rebels in a territory still recognized by the United States as being under Spain's control was an illegal contract. Hogan, somewhat lamely, acknowledged that he had not read the file very carefully on this point, but still felt that a claim against the current Chilean government could properly be pursued on the grounds of "justice and equity," apparently overlooking the fact that Carrera, the instigator of the arms deal, had been *persona non grata* with the O'Higgins faction. Allen delighted in tearing Hogan's "justice and equity" argument to shreds, although he was careful to say that any claim could be pursued privately against Chile, which was what Hogan was doing. A few months after this exchange, Allen received a letter from the Clerk of the State Department, Mr. Brent, requesting that Allen use his "good offices in aid of Mr. Hogan" in prosecuting the claim.[33] He must have been somewhat concerned that he had misjudged the situation, but he replied that, as he had fully reported, "a case more destitute of merit could not well be imagined, ...though I should very cheerfully yield to any instruction to the contrary...." At this point, Hogan advised Oliver that he had "nothing to expect from [Minister Allen]," which led Oliver to decide "it will be best to let the claim on the Government of Chile sleep until Allen is out of the way, and that the best way to get it paid is to agree to give some influential man a part of the sum actually recovered."[34]

There were other instances of the ill-feeling between Hogan and Allen. For example, in January 1827, when a Lieutenant G.D. Brewerton on the U.S.S. *Brandywine* had died, or been killed in a local brawl, a funeral was held for him in Valparaíso. (As a matter of incidental interest, the doctor who attended Brewerton was John Styles, the future husband of Hogan's daughter Harriet—his bill was for $233.50.) The U.S. Navy doctor on board the *Brandywine*, W.S.W. Ruschenberger, wrote an obituary notice for a Santiago newspaper pointedly noting that Minister Allen did not attend the funeral. Allen complained to the secretary of the navy who thereupon admonished the Navy doctor. The doctor, however, was not about to admit error; his reply to the secretary of the navy insinuated that, even if the obituary notice had directly deprecated Allen, neither Chileans nor foreign residents in Valparaíso would have been surprised or thought ill of the United States for the personal transgressions of one man. Hogan, who received copies of this correspondence, fell over backwards in praising the courageous doctor, ending with: "…if opportunity offers, it will be a pleasing part of my duty to represent [my support for your actions] to the secretary [of the navy]. While I regret that you have incurred his displeasure by unguardedly publishing here an expression of highly excited feelings in which you were not alone (for every American felt indignant, and both natives and foreigners of all classes animadverted to the disadvantage of our country), I cannot but regret the absence of magnanimity in our late minister who might, to save the rising bud and preserve the ripening fruit, have coolly, and calmly, as a father and representative, state to you the error, cautioning for the future, thereby avoiding a cause calculated to ruin your future prospects in the service, but I am not surprised by anything from Mr. Allen."

While it is likely that some personal incident or incidents ignited the personal rupture between Allen and Hogan, the nature of which cannot be fully known, it is possible to find more basic causes. One was certainly the fact that they lived so close to one another in the Almendral during 29 of the 42 months that the Allens were in Chile.[35] Close neighbors do not always become friends even under normal circumstances, but when foreigners of the same nationality—and in this case same employer—live near each other in another country, there is an expectation that they should band together. When they cannot, the split can easily become acrimonious.

Another factor could have been the fact that, for some two years, Hogan had been the central American diplomatic kingpin in Chile (Prevost being conveniently no longer in memory), while now he took second place to the better-educated, better-situated and socially-acceptable "Allen-Hull twins," not to mention their beautiful wives. In no way was a proud man who had made his own way in the world going to accept the implication of inferior status. It is the stuff out of which life-long enmities are born and fester.

Lastly, there was the fundamental character of Michael Hogan and, although much less is known about him, of Heman Allen. Hogan, always quick to take offense, could not constitutionally take a measured view of any difficult situation. Once he had crossed the line between civility and censure (or someone else had with him), paranoia tended to replace common sense. Because there cannot be a feud without the involvement of at least two parties, Allen's own character must have come into play. It may say something about Allen to note that, although Hogan became unreasonably incensed over some things that Larned later did when Allen had left (that will be covered later), there is no indication that Larned took the issues personally or tried to berate Hogan, as Allen did. (It must be acknowledged, however, that Larned was better qualified professionally to be a diplomat than Allen, an attribute that may have given him the confidence not to take personally criticism from an amateur such as Hogan.)

Hogan's disputes with Allen did not involve charges on either side of malfeasance. His dispute with Hull did.

By 1824, the Pacific squadron consisted of the flagship, usually a frigate, a sloop and schooner. For a short time, Hull had the continued services of the schooner *Dolphin* under a new captain, "Mad Jack" Percival, but his sloop, the 509-ton *Peacock,* did not arrive until July and two years later was sent to the Marquesas, Tahiti and Hawaii, while Hull was forced to send the *Dolphin* elsewhere in 1825 in an affair that will be covered later. The *United States* was therefore largely on its own during its three years in the Pacific. It spent almost the entire time in Peruvian waters protecting American shipping against both royalists and patriots.

Hogan's difficulties with Hull were affected, if not actually caused, by the way that the *United States* and other U.S. Navy vessels were supplied from Valparaíso. There were three sources of supplies. The main source was naval stores shipped by the Navy Department to Valparaíso in commercial vessels chartered either in whole or in part by the Navy. The two supplementary sources were supplies procured by Hogan directly from imports originally intended for domestic consumption and goods, usually consumables, purchased locally. Because the *United States* spent most of its time at or near Peruvian ports where storage facilities were either not available or threatened by the contending royalist and patriot forces, Hogan had either to store the Navy supplies at Valparaíso to await the arrival of Navy vessels or to transship them in small lots or by charterparty to Peruvian ports. For example, in November 1825, Hogan contracted with the British brig *Hawke* for a charter price of $1,500 to transport 450 barrels of salted and dry provisions and spirits to Callao for the *United States.* These transshipments were expensive and often led to inefficiencies and accusations of mismanagement. In addition, Hull complained about the quantity, timeliness and quality of the bread that Hogan shipped to him in Peru.

In January 1825, Hull wrote to Hogan that he had heard from the Navy agent at Boston, Amos Binney, that two storeships were on their way to Valparaíso with provisions and stores for the squadron. Hogan was therefore to "discontinue baking bread for the squadron and to stop all purchases of provisions and other articles for use of the squadron unless I specially direct it as we shall now have more than we can well dispose of."[36] On March 16 the storeship *Good Hope* arrived at Valparaíso with expected supplies from Boston. Hull arrived on the *United States* six days later. According to an affidavit executed by Hogan two years later, Hull allegedly told him that he wanted him to procure twenty puncheons of New England rum that were on the *Good Hope* as a "private adventure," rather than wait for a larger supply that was to arrive shortly from Washington on the storeship *Eagle*, and to charge the government eighty cents a gallon for this rum. Hogan told Hull he could procure Jamaican rum of superior proof for as low as sixty cents a gallon, but said he would do as the commodore asked if he would sign a statement to that effect, which Hull did. The ship's master, Anthony Kelly, told Hogan "not only then but at several other conversations...that the private cargo of his vessel, of which the rum formed a part, was the property jointly of Mr. Binney, the Navy agent at Boston, and Commodore Hull..., that he Captain Kelly was not to sell any thing until the Commodore was consulted who was to name the price to be received, [and] that his rum cost in Boston thirty-one cents per gallon."[37] Hogan paid for the rum at the price set by Hull (and billed the Navy Department for that amount). He then advised Captain John Percival of the schooner *Dolphin* that supplies were available, including 10,000 gallons of whiskey.[38] Hull himself asked that 3,000 gallons of whiskey be sent to him at Chorillos, as well as thirty or forty thousand pounds of bread, apparently ending his previous instruction to stop sending bread made in Valparaíso.[39]

Navy officers could and did procure alcoholic beverages for their private use on board ship, but the rum and whiskey in the foregoing incident were intended for the consumption of crew members who were still allowed one half pint of distilled liquor per day in the form of grog. It was another of the British customs that had been transplanted in America. (One study shows that Americans consumed more alcoholic beverages per person in the 1790–1830 period than at any other time in their history, including the present.)[40]

The above incident took place a full year before Frances Hogan allegedly spread gossip about Hull's making money in Peru. Moreover, Hogan waited two years after the incident to commit his allegations about Hull to writing. Why the delays?

Perhaps he did not initially intend to make formal charges. Cheating government was not, after all, such a heinous crime, having himself engaged in a scheme to defraud government while at Cape Town, and being aware that officers in both the British and American navies had been known to engage in fraudulent schemes to supplement their pay. But when Hull left the Pacific coast to return to the United States in January 1827 and Allen was known also to want to return—although he did not do so until October, Hogan could have become concerned that both men would speak ill of him when they arrived in Washington, possibly forcing his dismissal. This may have led him to put his evidence in writing.

On August 1, the day after Allen ceased to be U.S. minister to Chile (though he had not yet left the country), Hogan wrote to Joel R. Poinsett, now American minister to Mexico. He accused Allen of "penury, a poverty of mind and ignorance of the common courtesies of life surpassing anything I had ere before witnessed. Inflated with the importance of office, offense has been given to every body, and he has been left to himself." As a result, Hogan asserted, the U.S. no longer "stood highest of any in intercourse with this coast.... No man ever did more for another than I did for him for fifteen months, but when I found him acting with his brother-in-law Commodore Hull a double pact against me (both money savers and money makers), I found myself on that account and also fearful the publick should be confirmed in the opinion that there were no gentlemen amongst us North Americans...."

Turning to his own activities, Hogan pleaded his own innocence and devotion to duty. "I want to go home to state the truth, settle my accounts and, if disapproved, to make my bows, without being a thousand dollars the better for seven years faithful service. In the minds of [Allen and Hull] I am charged with a great crime, that is, I have lived and acted like a gentleman. Men of rank and station of all nations have frequented my house. I was the only publick character here till our Minister arrived. The consequence was that all I made as a merchant was spent as a Consul. The Minister has saved two-thirds of his salary going home sick, has much of it [invested] at 12% interest here, now living at about $1,800 per annum... I hold the lowest office under our

Government abroad, an unpaid (and because I do my duty) an unthanked Consul.... I have experienced [only ingratitude] from our Minister and his brother [sic], both of whom connived that I was to be only a tool in their hands to be made use of. The Minister told me a Consulate was nothing. So far as to pay, he was right, but an honest man that does his duty as well as without pay as others do theirs for large allowances is, in my opinion, entitled to as much respect and consideration as they are and ought not to be imposed [upon] by those to whom he naturally looks for support. The force of untoward circumstances has reversed the order of nature with me but it shall not make me do things unworthy of myself to gratify the poverty of any man's mind."[41]

Then in September of the same year (1827) Hogan received a letter from the Board of Navy Commissioners that questioned some of his actions. He may have thought that Hull was responsible for the letter on his return to the United States, although in fact it was sent before Hull reached New York. Whatever the cause, he lost no time in assuring the Board that he had fully complied with its orders and that, if there was any deficiency, it was due to the unstated but inferentially improper activities of Hull and his brother-in-law Allen. He concluded by saying that he was "extremely anxious to be at Washington to explain to the Department and the Board all that has passed on this coast in what relates to both [Hull and Allen], and soon after Commodore [Jacob] Jones arrives I hope to be able to proceed [on the *Brandywine*], unless I should be prevented by the chargé d'affaires for want of leave from my Government. I applied in June to Mr. Allen who insinuated he would supersede me in the Consulate if I went without that leave, although I expressed to him that I was going especially on Publick Service and that I would appoint a trustworthy substitute."[42]

As can be seen, Hogan's letter did not specifically mention Hull's alleged fraud against government involving the rum and whiskey. He apparently meant to apprize the secretary of the navy personally of this serious charge when he returned to the United States, after—he hoped—whetting the Navy's interest with the vague charges involving the supply of bread and the involvement of Allen.

The first written reference to Hogan's wanting to return to the U.S. is in an earlier June 22 letter to Allen in which he said that "for upwards of a year past it has been my desire to proceed to Washington in order to account to my government for my doings since I landed in this country six years ago, to settle with the Navy Department for my responsibility as its agent, with the Department of State for its disbursements made here in my agency on account of seamen, and to meet and to justify myself against the attacks that I too well know have been unjustly made against me."

Allen's reply two days later said Hogan's returning to the U.S. "must be a matter entirely between yourself and your government," but he pointedly claimed that, "In respect to the appointment of the person who is to perform the temporary duties of the Consulate, I presume you have had reference to your instructions on that subject as well as the usage in such cases. My own instructions are that, in case of any vacancy in the office of Consul..., I am authorized, with the consent of the government of such country, to supply such vacancy, giving immediate notice of it to the Department of State." Then, to confuse matters further, he added that "perhaps your temporary absence may not be such a vacancy as is contemplated by the instruction...; yet I think there can be no doubt that, in whatever manner the appointment is made, the consent of this government should be obtained...."[43]

Two points can be noted. First, the letter exchange took place at the same time that the two were feuding over other issues. Secondly, Allen did not state that he "would supersede me in the Consulate if I went without [government] leave," as Hogan said in his letter to the Navy Board, although he may have left this impression privately.

Hogan did not leave Chile for another four years. His first deferral was probably due to changes in both the naval command of the Pacific squadron and the chief of mission at the legation in Santiago.

When the *United States* left Valparaíso on January 23, 1827, to return to the United States with Hull and two of the Hart sisters on board, the recently built *Brandywine* and *Vincennes*, the two new ships of the Pacific squadron, were already in port. The *Brandywine*, commanded by Commodore Jacob Jones, was a 1708-ton 44-gun frigate that had just completed a journey carrying the Marquis de Lafayette back to France after his visit to commemorate the 50th anniversary of the signing of Declaration of Independence. The *Vincennes* was a 700-ton 18-gun sloop commanded by Captain William Bolton Finch; it would replace the *Peacock* that returned to the United States a few months later. They stayed on Pacific station for two years. The schooner *Dolphin* also remained on station but under new command. Hogan would strike up particularly friendly relations with Finch, as demonstrated by being invited with his family to cruise on the *Vincennes*.

Samuel Larned took over as chargé d'affaires ad interim at the legation on August 1, 1827. He was a thirty-nine year old bachelor who had previously served as American consul at Cadiz. He was obviously well-educated and fluent in Spanish.[44] The contrasts between his lucid, reasoned, grammatical reporting and that of the legalistic, somewhat pompous Allen (not to mention the rambling Hogan) are evident from reading their despatches.[45] He was to stay at Santiago as chargé for a little over two years. In fact, a new minister was not sent to Chile until 1850. One reason may have been that, in February 1828, after his return to the United States, Allen talked with President Adams, who recorded in his diary that "there appears to be no sufficient reason for maintaining a minister plenipotentiary" in Chile.[46] (There is, incidentally, no evidence that Allen said anything to President Adams or then Secretary of State Van Buren, about Hogan, although it is possible he did so privately.)

Except for one minor incident (which Hogan blew out of all proportion to its importance), Hogan and Larned had no serious disputes. By early 1828, not having heard of any repercussions following the return of Hull and Allen to the United States, Hogan must have decided that his plans to return to the United States could safely be deferred. He would continue to stew over the Hull/Allen matter for many years. For example, in a letter to a Navy friend on the *Brandywine* in December 1827, he referred to having "found an enemy in the disguise of friendship," a probable reference to Hull. Five years later he would bring formal charges against Hull, a subject that will be covered in the next chapter.

Unlike Allen, Larned had very little to say about Hogan in his despatches to the Department of State. The only personal reference was in a despatch in which Larned advanced reasons for staying at Santiago, rather than being transferred to Lima: "This capital is distant nearly one hundred miles from Valparaíso, the place of residence of our Consul; the communications are at time tardy and difficult, and besides, the age and infirmity of Mr. Hogan render him incapable, for a great part of the year, of attending to his already numerous duties, as Consul and Agent for the Navy Department, as he labors under periodical and very severe attacks of the gout."[47] Hogan first suffered from gout while in Cape Town and continued in New York. The frequency and seriousness of the attacks increased in Valparaíso and may well have been a factor in his increasing alienation and paranoia. In August 1826, Francis wrote that he had "gout in both hands and other parts." During the latter part of 1828 and early 1829, he was at times so ill that his clerk, William Clay, substituted for him in writing routine correspondence. Shortly before Larned took official notice of his physical condition, Hogan said that he "could only move on crutches."[48] The condition would continue to worsen over the next four years.

Hogan, on the other hand, criticized Larned on several occasions. One was in an 1830 despatch to Van Buren. After expressing his belief that Chile could eventually establish "a republican form" of government, Hogan noted that he differed "with others that held a higher station and who urged, much too early on the people then in power, the adoption of a federal government [and] even wrote pieces in the paper offering plans of revenue, etc."[49]

It was Larned who wrote articles advocating a federal system of government for Chile, but Hogan's criticism was unfair because it had been the Chilean government that had asked Larned to participate in a committee studying the federal system for possible adoption in a new Chilean constitution, and it was Allen who approved his acceptance of the invitation.[50] Whether Larned's apparent belief that the federal system adopted by the United States was suitable for Chile is another question. A constitution based on federal principles was, in fact, adopted in 1826, but a year later it was abrogated after, among other things, a renegade colonel rode on horseback into the halls of congress threatening the representatives with bodily harm if they did not dissolve.

As American consul at Valparaíso, Hogan had to continue to deal with stranded, mutinous or mistreated American seamen and their complaining and sometimes uncooperative captains. Even when it was possible to determine who was at fault, there were few remedies available to the consul given his limited authority and the fact that Chilean law provided few protections for the accused.

A reputable American captain arriving in Valparaíso after a mutinous voyage from Manila wanted the offending members of the crew removed from his vessel and jailed, pending their return to the U.S. for trial. The captain put his request to Hogan who, he said, "was an Irishman with a wooden leg, having lost his leg in the War of 1812."[51] (Did Hogan encourage camouflaging his gouty leg as a wooden one and ascribing a patriotic cause to his limp?) Hogan had to tell him that the earthquake had destroyed the prison and suggested instead shipping the offenders to the United States on the U.S.S. *Franklin* when it ended its tour, a delay the captain was unwilling to endure. The guilty parties eventually shipped out on a whaler.

Because Hogan generally reported ship incidents only where there was trouble, it might be assumed that this was the norm. But there were reputable ship captains who managed to avoid trouble. One of them, a Benjamin Morrell, wrote a book of his adventures in the South Seas in which he had only high praise for the American consul. When his sealer, the *Wasp*, arrived at Valparaiso in July 1823, he recounted that Hogan "received me with that politeness and urbanity of manners which have ever characterized this and other venerable officers" and that he "was universally esteemed as one of the worthiest men in the world." On this occasion Morrell might be excused for some hyperbole because Hogan had advanced him money to repair his vessel and no doubt also waxed eloquently on the burdens of his office and the lack of adequate recognition and just recompense. When Morrell returned on another vessel, the schooner *Tartar*, eighteen months later, he was even more effusive: "…the generous feelings of this truly good man are too prone to run ahead of his limited means, especially in cases where the interests of his countryman are concerned. His life is devoted to acts of usefulness and beneficence, and the emoluments of his office are [not] in comparison with the…good he performs. Few things would afford me greater pleasure that to see this venerable and faithful officer rewarded by his country with some situation under the government where the labors will be lighter and the award more commensurate with his deserts."[52]

Many of the American vessels that came to Valparaíso were whalers manned by officers and crew who led dangerous lives under the most difficult conditions. They were not a peaceable lot—violence, murder and mutiny being common occurrences. When there was trouble, the first port of call was often Valparaíso where Hogan had more than his share of heated and unpleasant incidents, sometimes with physical risk to himself. Larger merchant vessels also sometimes had cruel masters or mutinous seamen. Hogan was often sympathetic with the crew in such situations, perhaps remembering his own days as a British Navy seaman.

One incident, where it was clearly a mutinous crew who were at fault, has been recounted in several books, including Michener's *Rascals in Paradise*. There had been a mutiny aboard the Nantucket whaling ship *Globe* in the mid-Pacific led by Samuel Comstock who may have had visions of establishing his own kingdom on some small Pacific atoll.

He found one but was soon murdered by some fellow conspirators; six of the crewmen absconded with the *Globe* and set off for the coast of South America. After three months of aimless sailing, a Chilean merchant ship spotted the *Globe* and put some hands aboard to see her into Valparaíso harbor in June 1824. Hogan, who initially had no idea what had happened, ordered the six survivors arrested and put in irons below decks on an armed vessel in port, there being no American man-of-war present. After giving them a two-day rest, he took extensive interrogations from each of the survivors over the next three weeks. He refurbished the *Globe* and appointed an American, Captain King, as temporary master with orders to run her around Cape Horn to Nantucket. The vessel sailed on August 15. Four days earlier, Hogan had sent a fifty-page report to Adams, with copies to the collector of customs at Nantucket, the Navy Department and Commodore Hull.[53] News of the bloody mutiny was a sensation in American newspapers. Because hard evidence of criminal wrongdoing was only available from the dead or possibly those left behind in the Mulgraves, no charges were pressed against any of the six survivors.

This was not the end of the matter, however. The owners of the *Globe* and other "oil" interests in New England brought strong pressure to bear on various officials in Washington to rescue the remaining stranded crew. Commodore Hull was instructed to send a vessel to rescue the crew left behind on a Pacific atoll. The task fell to the U.S.S. *Dolphin* with "Mad Jack" Percival in command. It sailed from Peru in August 1825 and eventually found two survivors on one of the Mulgrave Islands, near what is now known as Bikini Atoll. All the others had been killed by natives. When the *Dolphin* arrived at Valparaíso in July 1826, Hogan notified the Connecticut insurance company handling the *Globe's* affairs that "the US schooner *Dolphin* anchored here on the 23rd instant having on board two of the youths belonging to the *Globe* left [at] Mulgrave Islands; William Lay and Cyrus M. Hussey, both grown up fine young men, very much liked by their officers. All the rest were killed by the natives."[54]

Lay and Hussey returned to Nantucket on the U.S.S. *United States* when it left Pacific waters in January 1827 and later wrote a book of their adventure.[55]

Three years later, a seaman named William Comstock allegedly tried to inspire a mutiny on the Newport, Rhode Island, whaling brig *Erie* in waters near Cape Horn. The captain, Henry Adams, brought his vessel to Valparaíso, hoping to persuade Hogan to take Comstock off the ship. Hogan said he could not do that but suggested using a ruse to get the seaman on shore, after which the *Erie* could leave without him, which it did. Comstock sought a berth on the U.S.S. *Dolphin* back to the United States, but when he was interrogated by Hogan at the request of the *Dolphin's* new captain, John P. Zantsinger, Hogan quickly discovered that he was Samuel's brother, the chief mutineer on the *Globe* six years earlier. William would have heard a first-hand account of what happened in the mutiny from the youngest brother in the family, George, who at age sixteen was on the ill-fated ship—one of the few who returned safely to Nantucket in 1824. Based on this information, Zantsinger refused to take Samuel on board. Comstock then wrote a letter to Hogan blaming him for what had happened and claiming his rights as an American citizen had been abridged. Hogan filed a complaint with the Chilean authorities saying that "from the tenor of [Comstock's letter] and other circumstances connected with Comstock, I feel my own life and that of my family [are] in imminent danger while he is at large in this place." Comstock was promptly arrested and imprisoned. It is possible that he really was a dangerous man, but Hogan took pity on him after he wrote several plaintive letters from his miserable prison saying how sorry he was for criticizing Hogan, recounting his extreme poor health, swearing he was a devout Quaker and pleading for a bible. Hogan accepted Comstock's apologies, expressed the hope that he would soon be released (the Chilean authorities were putting pressure on Hogan to get him out of the country), told him that "I hope you will put in practice that cause which you propose [helping his father's business in Newport]," and sent clothing and bedding—but apparently not a bible. After a year's imprisonment, Hogan arranged to place the apparently now contrite and reformed Comstock on board the U.S.S. *Gueriérre*, the flagship of the Pacific squadron at the time.[56]

Another whaleboat incident involved Dennis Covell, captain of the New Bedford brig *Annnawan*, who in 1828 refused to pay the wages of several seamen who wanted to leave the ship at Valparaíso after they thought the captain had deceived them with broken promises of an early return to the United States. Hogan's attempt to intervene with the captain—and force payment of the back wages to the dissatisfied seamen—led to a bitter confrontation. Because Covell claimed to be hard of hearing, Hogan handed him a note that he should pay the seamen. A witness made a sworn statement that "Covell read it and then threw it back on the consul's desk, saying he would not pay for them, and told the consul he might take his vessel and go to hell with her if he liked." Another statement declared that Covell "[said] he would beat the consul of the United States, Michael Hogan, Esquire, before he...left this port, and [he] made use of many indecent, offensive and abusive expressions against the consul...." When Covell finally paid the back wages, Hogan returned the ship's papers that he had demanded as a form of surety, at which point, William Clay, Hogan's consular clerk, attested: "[Covell] said in this office in my presence that he would in future act as he thought proper with sailors, by turning on shore all such as he may have on board his vessel, in any part of the world...and further said that the bill which he had received from the consul for his fees in the case of the [seamen] proved what he had before said, that the consul was a damn scoundrel."

Hogan sent these affidavits to the Department of State two years later in support of the contention he had originally made ten years ago from Havana that the case "pleads loudly in favor of defining by law the extent of the consular duties, its powers and authority."[57]

The life of Hogan and his family at Valparaíso was not all business with its attendant stresses. Acquaintances from all corners of the world could turn up unexpectedly. One was twenty-year-old British Navy lieutenant (later rear admiral) Sir Thomas Sabine Pasley, grandson of the captain of the *Jupiter* when Hogan was on board 44 years earlier, who arrived at Valparaíso on H.M.S. *Eclair* on April 18, 1825, shortly after the contretemps between the Hogan and Allen wives. In his memoirs,[58] later published by his daughter, he recorded: "I managed to go to a dance given by the Consul [Hogan], where we saw the same people nearly, with the addition of a Spanish family of the name Via Real, but the young Senoritas were so monstrously ugly, and so deficient in grace or any attention, that I did not wish to be introduced. Mrs. Allen, of course, was not there, but Commodore and Mrs. Hull were, as the party was given for them. Miss [Augusta] Hart had sprained her ankle, so was obliged to remain on board [the U.S.S. *United States*], much to the disappointment of her numerous admirers. It did not go off so well as the Allens' [party]. The house was ill-adapted to it, and it was got up in a hurry. [As] usual in such cases, the mistress of the house was the one to whom the party was anything but pleasant.... The Hogans...I found most kind and friendly people. He was an Irishman by birth, was once a mid...under my grandfather, when he commanded the *Jupiter*, but left the service before he was made

Lieutenant. After that he commanded an Indiaman, and was a merchant at the Cape, where he married (no, I am wrong there), and made a fortune which he lost at New York, how, I don't exactly know, but I believe for being surety for others who he thought were as honest as himself, but who were not. He then came to Valparaíso as American Consul. His family at Valparaíso consists of his wife and three daughters, the youngest of whom [Sophia] was married. She was the nicest person of them all, and her other sister [Harriet] was a very pleasant, agreeable girl. They were the most kind, hospitable people, and the only people I saw in Valparaíso who did not talk scandal, for of all the places I ever was at, it is the most scandalous. Riding and abusing one another seem to be the only amusements they have."

On being released from the *Eclair* in July, Pasley stayed at Valparaíso five weeks, "spending his time very happily with his friends the Hogans" before boarding another British Navy ship returning to England. His memoir continued with effusive remarks about Michael and Frances Hogan and two of their three daughters: "I found the Hogans so agreeable that I did not feel inclined [to enter Spanish society at Valparaíso]. The *Mersey* arrived the day after I left the *Eclair*, and as they were most of them intimate at the Hogans, we used to escort the ladies on horseback in the mornings (when they rode, that is)—and for the first fortnight I was there every evening but two: [thereafter] I slept at the Hogans, and, in fact, lived there, and made it quite my home. I made myself useful as well as ornamental (ahem!), for I worked in the garden, and put it to rights, which, I believe, was the only use I was of; sketched *at intervals,* rode out now and then, and walked occasionally with Harriet and Mrs. Donnelly; practiced music with Harriet sometimes, and, in fact, walked about the house like a tame cat. Now, being a sort of domestic animal by nature, I enjoyed this life very much, and the time flew very fast—indeed, I do not know what I should have done without this South American *home* of mine, for without anything to do on board, I should most likely have got into all sorts of mischief, etc. Harriet Hogan and Mrs. Donnelly were my companions, and with them I became very intimate; although other people call them stiff and formal, I did not think so, and to me they certainly were not. I found them very agreeable, amiable, quiet creatures…as they would sit upwards of *five* minutes without speaking a word. In short, I liked them very much, and used to call them my South American sisters. Mr. and Mrs. Hogan were extremely kind, and I liked them very much also."

There was another dance given by "old Hogan." Pasley also described an amateur production of Oliver Goldsmith's *She Stoops to Conquer* performed by British Navy officers then in port, with most of Valparaíso's foreign society in attendance. He wrote that he "had the pleasure of spending a quite week with my poor South American sisters, which I was very glad of, as in all probability it was the last I should ever see them of them, in this world at least." Finally, it was time to leave: "I did not leave the Almendral till twelve, and it was with heavy heart that I took leave of them; the poor girls cried as if they were parting from a brother , and I was nearly as much affected.... The old man [Hogan] was very much affected, and said he should always think of me as his own son. I rode Mrs. Donnelly's horse Charley...to the port and...went on board. [The next day about one] we made sail. Harriet and Mrs. Donnelly had come out to watch us on the hill opposite their house three times that day, and as we made sail I watched them with my glass just going in for the last time, and lost sight of them behind the trees perhaps for ever. Such is our sailor's life!"

On his return to England, Pasley married and later became a rear admiral. He was an admirer of Americans and the U.S. Navy. While at Valparaíso, he boarded the U.S.S. *United States* one day and wrote prophetically that "these fellows are getting the upper hand of us. [The *United States*] is in more effective state...than most of our frigates that I have seen on this station; and as to look, her sails are beautifully furled, and you cannot find fault with her rigging. I am a great admirer of the Americans, and had I lived in the year '76, I should have been very much inclined to have turned Yankee myself, but, nevertheless, I should be sorry to see their navy superior to ours, in my time at least, though they are a rising nation, and some day they will be licking us, though I hope I may not live to see it. It seemed to me to be so unnatural the *United States* should be of a different nation when we could hear the duty carried on board her in our own language, and their sentry calling out 'All's well!' and hailing boats, etc., exactly as our own. What a doubly unnatural war a war with them must be! Strange that that war should be carried on with more animosity on our side than any other, but I am happy to say that feeling is becoming less every day, both on their side and ours. Commodore [Hull] was very friendly, offered to lend us any of their artificers, etc., and anything we wanted."

The Hogans were also asked from time to time to help visitors or friends when they came to Chile. Their experience with Dr. Bullus's son had not been a happy one, and so it was also to be with the wayward son of Robert Oliver, named Henry. Substituting for Michael Hogan, Frances told Robert Oliver in August 1826 that "[Mr. Hogan] has for several months past felt much anxiety of mind on account of your son Henry, who has become such a wanderer, and without companion or means attempted a route from Cusco to Buenos Aires through a country of danger and difficulty, but which I hope at last will be safely accomplished.... Mr. Hogan...wrote to his correspondents in Peru and Buenos Aires to dispatch at any expense messengers after him, with the relief he required of money to enable him to pursue his journey, and we are informed...that...he is safe at Buenos Aires or perhaps on his passage home...."[59]

One of the enticements offered by the *Brandywine* was souvenirs made from small, colorful sea shells with silver lid openings on which would be engraved on the outside the name of the U.S.S. *Brandywine* with the American eagle symbol and on the inside whatever name or message was ordered. The Hogan ladies decided to order several such shells. One was engraved "Miss Harriet Hogan 1827" and another "Mr. Donnelly from his affectionate daughter Sophia," the latter intended for Sophia's father-in-law in Ireland.

On January 15, 1828, Hogan and his family were invited by Captain Finch to cruise on the *Vincennes* to Juan Fernández Islands, some 600 miles due west of Valparaíso, the islands that Hogan told Captain White to steer toward on his privateering adventure 26 years earlier. The three islands are now known as Robinson Crusoe Island because Daniel Defoe based his 1719 novel of the same name on the four-year sojourn there of a Scottish mariner named Alexander Selkirk. It had been used by the Spanish and later the Chileans as a penal colony, but in 1827 it had been deserted except for a few stragglers. On arriving, Sophia later recalled that a canoe approached the *Vincennes* with one man aboard "dressed in red shirt; his cap, boots and breeches were made of goat skins, with a cutlass by his side. He was one of a boat's crew left by a sealing vessel from Boston." She recalled a cave "said to be the identical one of Robinson Crusoe's," though it would have been Selkirk's. They spent two weeks on the desolate island, the trip having been designed by Captain Finch "to give full liberty to the men without meeting any harm, for in the seaports they too frequently drank, spent all their money, besides being wounded or even killed in the streets." The *Vincennes* then sailed for Talcahuano, the port for Concepción, where the British Consul, Henry Rouse, entertained the Hogans (they knew one another from Valparaíso) and Captain Finch.

The ship's officers then hosted a party for the British consul and local officials in a "lovely valley" across the bay with a band under a marquee. After admiring the scenery and the many native flowers, trees, bushes and vines, "we were ready for dinner which had been prepared under the direction of one of the officers, and ample justice was done to the abundant supply of delicacies.... The tablecloth was on the grass, with boat cushions around for the ladies and a raised seat for my father as the oldest and honored guest." After dinner, "an active young midshipman requested us to adjourn to the ballroom. We found he had selected a fine greensward among a few trees and had interlaced some of the hanging branches with vines to form a pretty room. The band being ready, soon contredances and waltzes were entered into with great spirit."[60]

Sophia was not enchanted, however, with a visit to a convent at Concepción to witness the somber and, she felt, cruel dedication of a young girl novice to become a sister in the Catholic convent, concluding: "How thankful we should be who have been brought up in the Protestant faith, with the Bible for our guide," forgetting or perhaps never knowing that Michael Hogan had been born a Catholic.

The *Vincennes* returned to Valparaíso on February 8 to cruise with its flagship *Brandywine* in Peruvian and Chilean waters. In July 1829, it sailed from Callao to aid and protect American merchant vessels in the Society and Hawaiian islands and then to circumnavigate the globe, the first U.S. Navy ship to do so. The *Brandywine* also left in 1829, to be replaced by the 44-gun frigate U.S.S. *Guerriére*, one of the warships built during the War of 1812, commanded by Commodore Charles C.B. Thompson. (The recently built 700-ton sloop *St. Louis*, under Captain John Drake Sloat, replaced the *Vincennes*; the schooner *Dolphin* again continued on Pacific station.) When the *Guerriére* first stopped at Valparaíso on June 10, the chaplain on board wrote that "Mr. Hogan...received us with great cordiality... and led the way to the consulate.... I greatly regretted that time did not allow of a walk to the Almendral; which, with its groves of almond and olive trees, had so inviting an appearance from the water. Mr. Hogan, with a hospitality that is proverbial wherever he is known, urged [Commodore Thompson], who came on shore an hour after the first boat, and our whole party to dine with him at the Almendral. But this was determined, under the circumstances, to be impractical. On which, without an intimation to any one, our open hearted friend ordered a repast to be prepared, as speedily as practicable, at the best hotel in the place;

to which, with not any suspicion of the design, we were ushered by him, while on our way, as we thought, to join our own boats. The entertainment, though so hastily provided, was profuse and excellent in kind, and admirably cooked—with a great variety of the finest vegetables, and exquisite fruits. The wines, of superior quality, had been ordered from his own cellar, at the Almendral. The market of Valparaíso is the best on the coast; and whatever may be said of Chile, Mr. Hogan assures us, that she can boast as good eating and drinking as can be found in any part of the world. The climate is at all times fine; and in the winter season, which is now just commencing, not surpassed in any section of the globe.... The warm and cordial manners and intelligent conversation of the venerable consul general—embracing much interesting matter from personal observations, not only along the South American coast, but in Europe, Asia, and Africa, enlivened by anecdotes of all parts if the world, and particularly of the naval service of the United States and of England, in which last he was himself a fellow midshipman and messmate with the Duke of Clarence, heir to the British throne—caused the time to pass rapidly, till we were obliged to take a hasty leave, that the ship might secure an offing before night.[61]

Sixteen months later, the captain of the *Guerriére* would not hold the same favorable impression of Hogan.

Some of the ships that came to Valparaíso were engaged in scientific or navigational studies. One was the British vessel *Adventure* commanded by Philip Parker King, son of Philip Gidley King, governor of Norfolk Island when Hogan visited on the *Marquis Cornwallis* 33 years earlier who later became governor of New South Wales. Hannibal Hawkins Macarthur, who acted as Hogan's agent for his Parramatta properties in Sydney for several years, had married Philip's sister, Anna Maria King, in 1812, thus making Philip Parker King the brother-in-law of Hannibal Hawkins Macarthur. King had been appointed to the *Adventure* in September 1825 to undertake a survey of the southern coast of South America from the Rio Plata around to Chile. It was accompanied on part of its journey by the *Beagle* commanded first by Captain Stokes and, after his death, by Captain Robert Fitzroy. The *Adventure* alone came to Valparaíso on June 22, 1829, remained in port until October 10, and returned briefly the following year.[62] Later, Hogan wrote to Macarthur saying that "the plants and seeds sent to Mrs. [Harriet] King will, I hope, arrive in safety. In a little time, they will increase to such quantities as to supply the whole family, large as it is. I am happy to say [Captain] King left this [place] in fine health and spirits in the expectation of being in London in September [1830], his son the finest boy I ever saw." Hogan heard from Macarthur much later, after he had left Chile, who told him that, "We have heard of the *Beagle's* arrival in England 14th October [1830] and we suppose the *Adventure* will not be far behind. We hope to see King here in all this year. Mrs. King has received the grass seeds, etc., you so kindly forwarded and will I believe acknowledge them by this opportunity." In 1831, the *Beagle* returned to South America, including a stop at Valparaíso, on her famous voyage with Charles Darwin aboard, but by then Hogan had left the country. (His daughter Harriet and her husband, John Styles, who stayed at Valparaíso for several years after Hogan's departure, would have seen the *Beagle*, however.)

Michael Hogan's name appears in a work of historical fiction published 116 years later about the seven Hart sisters of Saybrook. The portion of interest concerns the period during which Commodore Hull, Heman Allen, and three Hart sisters were in South America, when the focus of the book's attention is on the alleged romance and reported marriage between one of the Hart sisters and Simon Bolivar. While the book correctly records the main historical facts about the individuals and incidents involved, it misnames the Hart sister whom Bolivar is said to have romanced and manufactures conversations and other details out of thin air. In September 1826 a Connecticut newspaper reported that Bolivar had become enamored of and married Jeanette Hart. But it was not Jeanette who accompanied Hull and his wife; it was Augusta. The truth appears to be that during mid-1826, when Ann Hull and Augusta Hart rented a house near Lima, Bolivar may have been romantically attracted to Augusta. They most certainly did not marry.

But turning to the book's mention of Hogan, he is described as an Irish redhead, without a "mistress of my home," and with a majordomo named Jaimito. The Allens are said to have lived with Hogan in his house at the Almendral. Various bits of specific conversation are attributed to him. The color of Hogan's hair is unknown; his wife Frances was with him; the Allens did not live with the Hogans but in a separate house twelve yards away; the names of his servants are no where recorded; and the conversations do not even sound authentic.[63]

Larned left Santiago to become chargé d'affaires at Lima in late October 1829, leaving Hogan as the only official U.S. representative in either Santiago or Valparaíso for nineteen months. Although he had no authority from Washington, Hogan acted as though he were in charge of diplomatic relations between the United States and Chile during this period. He signaled his intent in a despatch written to Van Buren a month later: "I asked [Larned] if he had any documents or instructions to leave with me. He replied he had no orders or instructions to leave for me. Presuming, however, that it may be agreeable to the president to be informed of passing events in this country, I shall place before you a situation of what occurs, as opportunity may offer, commencing from the departure of Mr. Larned, when this government was in a state of great confusion."[64]

Hogan had his first taste of diplomatic decorum, or in this case the lack of it, just eight days later when he alleged he was physically attacked while in his consular uniform by a Chilean soldier. Wasting no time, he promptly wrote an impassioned complaint to General Jose Maria Benevente, military governor of Valparaíso: "I am under the painful necessity of representing that about half an hour ago as I was coming into town, I was most grossly insulted by a soldier with a drawn sword who stopped me because my mule was in a gallop arising out of her taking fright from the unloading of cargo further on. I was in the uniform of my station, laid hold of and dragged like the most common peon almost to the ground and otherwise basely used and kept at the door to which I was dragged for half an hour, exposed to insults and the scoff of lookers on. Three officers of foreign ships of war were present, expressing shame and uttering their contempt of such proceedings."

Hogan said that he placed "this matter before your Excellency as well as in point of duty to myself as out of respect to my Government in the hope that, by your interposition in procuring proper redress and granting for the future security against the recurrence of such offence to myself and every member of my family, I may be relieved from the necessity of representing to my Government the insult of which I complain."

Benevente expressed his regrets and said he had referred the incident to the civilian governor to investigate. But this did not satisfy Hogan who felt that his country's honor had been insulted. In a stiff reply to the military governor on the 25th, he said: "It is for the indignities offered to the president of the United States in the gross insult and unparalleled violence committed upon my person as his commercial and only representative in this country that I demand redress." The next day, he wrote to the minister of foreign relations, repeating the indignities to the president and asking that the matter be laid before the vice president of Chile. There is no record what happened next; perhaps Hogan concluded he had done enough.[65]

This incident took place at a time when a rebellion was underway in Chile that would eventually bring some order to the country. General Francisco Pinto had become president in 1828 when another constitution came into effect. He was considered to be a liberal, but the conservatives were gaining strength, led by Diego Portales, a wealthy Valparaíso business man and chief benefactor of the *estanco* tobacco and liquor contract. A year later in September, General Joaquín Prieto, commander of the garrison at Concepcíon, marched north to battle the resummoned Freire, but in April 1830 the latter was forced to concede defeat. Some of the fighting took place at and near Valparaíso.

Hogan and his family were themselves in danger during this perilous time. In December 1829, Hogan reported to Van Buren that "a Sergeant and four of [General Joaquín] Prieto's cavalry accompanied by a gang of robbers attempted to force my gate demanding in the most ferocious and authoritative manner entrance into my house. It was believed I was alone with my family unprepared, but my numbers and arms were equal to a firm defense and it saved us. When they saw my muster for a vigorous defense, their tone softened and after very serious expostulations they retired grumbling at their disappointment. My house has since been a garrison."

Sophia described the incident in colorful detail: "My father's house, being situated at the foot of the hill, where the only road to Santiago crossed, was most exposed to those lawless bands. After one or two alarms it became necessary to take some precautions, and when a report came that a large number were on the road, avowedly to sack the town, several naval officers offered to come to our protection, bringing a party of marines also. A watch was kept all night. Towards dawn a troop drew up on the road in front, demanding admittance, for the gate had been locked and barred. The American flag was flying and Consular Arms were over the door, but these were lawless men who respected no flag. After some parley they attempted to scale the wall, firing as any of our men appeared. At last it became necessary to stop their approach, for hitherto the lieutenant in command had been unwilling to risk firing. Soon shots were flying from both sides...[and] the assailants, who numbered four times our friends, were so active that our defenders could scarcely reload fast enough and I assisted in loading the spare muskets and handing them through the window where the attack was fiercest. This did not last for long, for many of their men seemed severely wounded, lying on the ground. A peon was observed to gallop up with orders for all to join their leader in the town, as the British marines and a large body of sailors from merchant vessels were landed to assist the authorities in driving out these desperados. They were fierce-looking fellows, with their ponchos flying as they galloped furiously away, shouting and vociferating that they would return to the fight and be revenged."

Sophia then recalled that the Hogan ladies, and presumably other non-combatants, were escorted on board H.M.S. *Blonde* "where we remained until tranquility was restored, chiefly through the fear of the British marines and foreign merchants who formed a company to protect their property. Our house was not again molested, as it was believed we had a guard from the frigate." Not all foreigners fared as well as the Hogans during the rebellion; the residence of the French consul was attacked and ravished.

In his report, Hogan praised British Captain Bingham, noting that: "I have frequently experienced the benefit of this good disposition on the part of British ships of war to our commerce in this port and have, as far as was in my power, encouraged the good feeling by civil attention and such little acts of hospitality as I was able to show to publick officers of other nations." He noted that the arrival of the U.S.S. *Guerrière* [Commodore Thompson] on the 17th "puts our citizens at rest as to safety!" and that this and the British and French warships already in port "has brought tranquility to Valparaíso," in contrast to Santiago "where great confusion rages."[66] Five men from the *Guerrière* were sent to protect the Hogan residence at night, making a total of ten under arms.[67]

Hogan refrained from drawing attention to the fact no American warship was in the harbor when the rebellion was most dangerous. However, he had no reluctance in telling Larned at Lima that, "had Commodore Thompson any idea of the necessity of attention to Chile, our situation would be more protected, and our citizens along this coast benefited by a share of that continuing force afforded by our Government. But Commodore Hull's views of the publick interest were always in opposition to naval attention to the coast of Chile, and I fear some of his ideas have guided in the instructions to the present commander."[68] Thompson and others apparently learned of Hogan's remonstrances against the commander. An American merchant in Valparaíso, Charles Bispham, noted in a letter to Larned that "there has been a coolness between the Hogans and Commodore Thompson growing out of some observations I think the old gentleman made against the [U.S.] Government and some of its officers. They have however patched up some kind of a reconciliation, but from what the Commodore says, I conclude they will never be very be warm friends again." Bispham continued: "Mr. Hogan cannot disguise his hatred to Americans, particularly when a little excited and I am confident when Commodore Thompson went there to reside that the old gentleman would soon show the cloven foot. I find he is not particularly fond of you nor would he be of a saint if it came from America. It vexes me to hear him eternally complaining of our Government."[69] The term "cloven foot" means a devilish character.[70] Bispham may have intentionally tried to put Larned at odds with Hogan as a means of enhancing his own interest in taking Hogan's place as American consul, a subject that will covered shortly. The antipathy between Hogan and Thompson, however, was real and would surface again later in 1830.

The perception of some fellow Americans in Chile that Hogan was an Anglophile and anti-American can be discounted on several grounds, including the fact that animosities arising out of the Revolution and War of 1812 were still virulent in some quarters. Insofar as naval protection was involved, the criticism ignored the fact that the British Pacific squadron had been larger than its American counterpart from the beginning and did not hesitate to provide direct protection of its merchants and citizens in time of need; nor was it prohibited, as was the American squadron, from carrying specie for nationals of other countries. All this reflected the undeniable facts that Britain's commercial interests in Chile (and elsewhere in South America) were greater than those of the United States and that it had ample financial and military power to back up its interests.[71]

The immediate result of the rebellion was the installation of a junta with a nominal president and Diego Portales ruling as virtual dictator. When a new constitution was achieved in 1833, General Prieto, whose soldiers had tried to sack Hogan's house, became president. For the next 27 years, conservative forces were in power, dashing the hopes of liberal reformers but bringing a political stability that was uncommon in nineteenth century South America.

During the nineteen month period that Hogan reported on military and diplomatic developments in Chile, he did not involve himself in the main issue in contention between the United States and Chile, namely, the various claims of U.S. citizens against the Chilean government and its citizens. Allen had made virtually no progress in this direction. When Larned became chargé, he concluded—undoubtedly correctly—that a commercial treaty between the two countries was needed to provide a legal and orderly basis for settlement of the claims.[72] Larned had some cold water poured on his initiative when Clay informed him that "it was not expected that [Allen] or you would proceed [to negotiate] without instructions," but allowed that, "if Chile is prepared to proceed, you may...remain in Chile to conclude [the treaty] and the President will send it to the Senate..."[73] The Department's lack of clarity may have been the consequence of confusion over whether Larned should proceed to Lima to become chargé or stay at (or return to) Santiago because another appointment had been made at Lima. In the end, Larned stayed at Lima when the new appointee died en route at Rio. Hogan was presumably aware of Clay's censure of Larned and had no wish to pursue a matter on which he was clearly uninstructed.

Political events in both the United States and Chile were about to change Hogan's official duties and ultimately his position. Andrew Jackson was the easy winner in the presidential elections of 1828, the first president not from Virginia or Massachusetts and the first populist. Whether for ultimate good or bad, Jackson was also the first president to engage in wholesale political house cleaning, bringing with him to Washington a number of friends and supporters who had their own agendas. The new secretary of the navy was John Branch and the new fourth auditor was one Amos Kendall. Forty years old and well-educated with a background in journalism and law, Kendall had supported Jackson and was regarded as a member of his kitchen cabinet. Whether Branch and Kendall were of a joint mind to shake up the Navy Department or were merely dealing with a problem that could no longer be pushed aside, Branch set the course by formally asking Kendall in November 1829 to recommend how the Navy Department could extract itself from "the present confused and unsettled state of [its] fiscal accounts and concerns." Kendall obligingly responded in a letter that was long on complaints but short on solutions, other than to call upon Congress to sort out the mess. Kendall in effect said that the Navy Department had been dispensing money to its employees illegally, particularly in allowing officers a number of allowances that were not sanctioned by the 1809 naval affairs law. He was particularly critical of the Navy's handling of the accounts of naval agents. Branch subsequently recommended several reforms to Congress, but it did nothing.[74] Branch's tenure as navy secretary was short-lived. He and other cabinet members were forced by Jackson to resign when they refused to interfere in their wive's social ostracization of Peggy Eaton, the young, attractive and allegedly promiscuous wife of Jackson's Tennessee friend, secretary of war John Eaton. Jackson was about the only person in Washington who defended Peggy and did not take kindly to men—or their wives—who snubbed her. Amos Kendall, however, remained as fourth auditor long enough to make life miserable for a number of government functionaries, including Michael Hogan.

One of the internal reforms that did not require Congressional authorization was to terminate several of the Navy agents at foreign ports, transferring those responsibilities to pursers. Hogan's agency was one of those to be terminated, as was the one at Lima that had been filled only in 1829.[75] Branch terminated Hogan's appointment as naval agent by letter dated May 12, 1830, which did not reach him until November 27. Although the termination notice explained that it had been "determined to change the mode of procuring supplies for our Naval force in the Pacific by the substitution of pursers for Navy agents," Hogan's suspected that it was "the calumny or undue influence of any person or persons in or out of the Publick Service that might have led to the determination of the change on my removal."

The Navy Department had changed the system of supplying its Pacific squadron because the use of Navy agents was no longer either necessary or efficient, not because it was dissatisfied with Hogan. But Hogan would soon learn, if he did not already suspect, that his accounts were being questioned and that several of his bills would be protested.

On the foreign relations front, the new secretary of state was to be Martin Van Buren from New York, who would become president in 1837. Learning of his appointment in June 1829 and apparently believing Van Buren might be sympathetic to a fellow New Yorker, Hogan sent a letter congratulating him on his appointment but wasting no time in coming to the purpose of the letter: "Would to God my situation was such as to enable me to show my zeal in support of the government of which you form so strong a feature, but such as it is my ardors will not be deficient." With this lead, Hogan expounded in by now familiar refrain: "I have been fourteen years a consul of the United States [apparently counting Cork, Havana and Valparaíso] and so perfectly was everything finished [here] that Mr. Allen had nothing left for him to do; but he will not do me the justice to say so, because I opposed upon principle the course upon which his brother-in-law commenced his command in relation to the expenditure of his squadron, thereby bringing upon myself the enmity and hatred of the whole family. I was so much engaged and so new to the business that I had not time to send to the Department of State one-third of the correspondence that took place in course of my performance of those duties, all of which I have by me, which did not cost the U.S. a dollar...."

He then proceeded to bewail his financial woes and the higher awards bestowed on consuls from other nations: "There are no higher grade from other nations than consuls general, nor are there any necessary. They are paid as follows: The French 50,000 franks [*sic*] a year. The English £2,500 and one percent on sale of shipwrecked property and contingent expenses, such as trips to Santiago or anywhere else on publick service. The Dutch consul 5,600 rix dollars per annum. That nation has very little trade to this coast. The first two are not allowed to trade, but the last is a merchant. The fees received for my consular duties average about $860 per annum for the last eight years, but for the future I do not expect they will yield one-half of that amount, our commerce appearing so much on the decline. For the past four years I have deemed it incompatible with my official situation to have any interest in commerce.[76]

Although it would not affect Hogan, there was a short burst of reform in the Department of State under its new secretary. One was an 1830 circular admonishing consular officers to abjure from including in their communications "epithets of unqualified obloquy and disapprobation" about foreign officials.

Just what gave rise to this injunction is unknown, but it was probably the embarrassment caused when the representatives of some foreign government read in the American press a despatch written by some American consular official with unfavorable comments about his country's leaders. A number of Hogan's despatches could have caused diplomatic incidents if made available to the public, so frequent was his criticism of Chilean officials. He was not, of course, alone in this regard. (Van Buren directly criticized Larned for critical comments he made about Bolivar.)[77] It was common practice then for newspapers to print almost any letter from a foreign place as a way of disseminating foreign news (there were no foreign correspondents). While encryption codes were available to diplomatic chiefs of mission, none were made available to consular officers.[78]

Hogan had last raised the question of consular salaries in his 1823 letter to President Monroe: "I found that in this country the Consulate was made wholly subservient to the interests of a commercial house.

I certainly came with the expectation of establishing one for myself, but with no idea of turning your good intentions to my own advantage by neglecting the publick good in sacrificing the duties of the office you honored me with.... At every session of Congress, the consular [officers] have been [recognized] but remuneration not taken into view. My experience proves to me that, if in the hands of deserving men, the office is both useful and honorable to the country and ought to be placed on a more creditable footing than a painful dependence on fees...."

The Congress and State Department were in fact beginning to take a look at the question of remunerating consular officers. In order to respond to a Senate committee inquiry, Hogan was asked to transmit a list of the fees he charged and any comments he might have on the subject.[79] His list of consular fees ranged from $2 for notarization of documents to $17.25 for drafting, registering and furnishing a protest to a bill of exchange. He said "very few of these fees were ever charged because the opportunity did not offer. The schedule was adopted for general information in compliance with the law." The result of the survey was a State Department recommendation in January 1831 to establish a uniform system of fees based on the tonnage of ships which would produce a fund from which consuls could be paid modest salaries. In his State of the Union address in December 1831, President Jackson called upon Congress to revise the consular laws because "defects and omissions have been discovered in their operation that ought to be remedied and supplied." He also "enjoined on our merchants and navigators strictest obedience to the laws of the countries to which they resort, and a course of conduct to their dealings that may support the character of our nation, and render us respected abroad."[80] Hogan would have been pleased with this official recognition of his oft-made complaint that many American merchants and captains in foreign ports did not respect the American consul or observe foreign laws. Two years later, the Department issued general instructions defining consular duties more precisely than in the past and establishing a partial list of uniform fees. No Congressional action was forthcoming on consular pay, however, until 1856 when an act created two schedules of consular posts. Consuls assigned to the supposedly more important posts would receive salaries ranging from $1,000 to $7,500 and could not engage in commerce. Those assigned to the less important second schedule would receive salaries ranging from $500 to $1,000 and were allowed to engage in commerce. In both cases (with some exceptions), consular fees were to be paid to the U.S. Treasury.[81]

Throughout his ten years at Valparaíso, Hogan professed that his earnings from commerce were insignificant, that his commissions from the Navy did not reflect the work he performed and the expenses he incurred, that his consular fees produced almost no income, and that the State Department should reimburse him for a number of out-of-pocket expenses, such as aiding destitute American seamen. Because there are no records of his private accounts, it is not possible to determine his overall financial position. But some clues are available.

He said that his income from consular fees averaged only about $860 a year, a claim that may be correct. It does not appear that the State Department reimbursed him for any of his expenses, including $872.68 claimed for distressed and disabled seamen over a seven and a half year period.[82]

Consuls were supposed to make ends meet by engaging in commerce. Hogan expected that he could do so when he accepted the Valparaíso assignment.[83] He professed throughout his stay at Valparaíso that his official duties both as consul and Navy agent prevented him from engaging in commerce. Such evidence as exists seems to bear him out, although his claim that he refrained for altruistic reasons is open to question. A controlling factor may have been that for most of the 1820s Chile was overstocked with import goods.[84] (It can be said, however, that none of the charges leveled against Hogan from time to time suggested that he used his position for commercial advantage.) His only recorded business transactions are those in which he acted as agent for others and apparently a few transactions that he concluded on his own account. An example of the latter is an 1825 shipment of 150 quintals (about 7½ tons) of copper to Baltimore on the storeship *Eagle* on its return voyage after bringing the whiskey that Commodore Hull did not want to buy, from which he made a profit of barely $500. He also acted as agent for Robert Oliver in shipping $50,000 worth of copper on the *General Hand* to Baltimore in the same year.[85] Hogan asserted that he did not engage in any commerce after 1825,[86] which may be true, although on leaving Chile in 1831, he had a claim to 400 quintals (about 20 tons) of copper that he wanted to ship to Baltimore.[87]

Hogan was pleased to hear in 1825 from his New York friend Robert Dickey that a jury in Charleston, South Carolina, had awarded him

$2,358 in his suit against Thomas Sumter for non-payment of his passage to Brazil fifteen years previously on the *Charleston Packet*, during which Sumter allegedly attempted to bed the companion of the wife of a fellow passenger.

He also continued to receive income from his properties in New South Wales— on one occasion a sum of £1,200—but this apparently represented several years of back rent or other income. His agent there, the unhappy Hannibal Hawkins Macarthur, urged that he find someone else to handle the vexing matter, but Hogan persuaded him to stay on. Perhaps to appease Macarthur, Hogan said that he "came to [Valparaíso] with the intention of visiting Sydney very soon after my arrival in the expectation of frequent commercial intercourse and some advantageous business to be done, in all which I am disappointed. My unprofitable avocations have been such as to preclude an absence of a few months. I hope however to be able to perform it but God knows when." It is doubtful, as noted previously, that Hogan ever had a serious intention of returning to Australia.

The only firm information about Hogan's income is the amount of money he received from the Navy Department in commissions. He did more than merely collect commissions on the value of stores supplied to the Pacific squadron. He also acted as a conduit for financial transactions involving Navy officers and pursers. For these activities, he received from the Navy Department a 5% commission on the value of supplies and a 2½% fee for negotiated bills of exchange. It may not always have been clear where the dividing line was between the official duties of Navy officers, pursers and agents and their private activities. For example, Commodore Stewart utilized the services of the merchant ship *Canton* to support his squadron; Eliphalet Smith was allowed substantial discretion also to engage the services of the *Canton* and its Captain John O'Sullivan; and Hogan acted as agent for Le Roy Bayard & Company of New York in facilitating some of these transactions.

According to an official audit of the Treasury Department conducted in 1831, he received a total of $48,123.82 in commissions during the entire ten-year period, an average of a little less than $5,000 a year.[88] Although this was then a considerable amount of money (possibly the equivalent of over $75,000 today), Hogan claimed when he left Valparaíso that he was owed much more—an issue that will be addressed in the next chapter. In addition, the Navy Department paid for some of his expenses, including office rent and clerk hire. It was clearly this income that provided his main means of support at Valparaíso.

The position of Navy agent was created by an act of Congress in 1809, but that law applied only to agents stationed domestically in the United States. There was no statutory basis for Hogan's appointment as Navy agent at Valparaíso in 1820, nor for those stationed at a few other foreign ports. It appears that this fact was not drawn publicly to the Navy Department's attention until 1828. Up until that time, the Navy Department and the fourth auditor in the Treasury Department at times treated the Valparaíso agency as though it fell under the 1809 law, while at other times they acted as though Hogan was a private agent without official status under "contract" with the Department. Hogan himself could never make up his mind: he claimed a rate of commission on mercantile grounds while at the same time demanding that his overhead expenses, such as office rent and hire of clerk, be reimbursed by the Navy Department. Today, Hogan's role would be described as a private contractor to the Navy Department that would be subject to normal commercial laws and practices, but in the early 1820s ambiguity suited both the Department and Hogan. Then when Andrew Jackson became president, new faces appeared on the Washington scene determined to leave their mark on the Executive Branch by, among other things, cleaning up malpractices and ferreting out miscreants.

The only instructions that Hogan received from the Navy Department before proceeding to Valparaíso were those in his brief letter of appointment, namely, that "in the event of the United States Ships of War visiting the ports of Chile, you are authorized to act in behalf of this Department, as agent for furnishing such supplies as the Service may require, and for which your draughts upon this Department, in reimbursement, will be duly honored on presentation." A year later, the Board of Navy Commissioners wrote to the Department of State asking "in what character Mr. Hogan proceeded to Valparaíso—if as a commercial agent or consul, and [if] it should be his intention to reside at Valparaíso. [We] propose consigning to him a quantity of provisions for the use of our squadron. The Commissioners also request the Christian name of Mr. Hogan."[89] There is no record of the response to this request for information that should have been in the Navy Department's files. Shortly after this, the Navy agents at Baltimore and New York shipped the first supplies to Hogan consisting of paint, oils, naval stores and four hundred barrels each of pork and flour on the *Armenius* and *Potose*.[90] Hogan continued to receive supplies shipped by the Navy Department, and he also procured supplies locally and from private vessels calling at Valparaíso. As previously noted, he supplied Navy ships with locally baked bread.

The first indication that Hogan's administrative dealings with the Navy would not all be smooth came in April 1823 when he received the Department's letter of the previous November informing him that he would be allowed a commission of two and one-half percent upon all disbursements.[91] Hogan responded immediately, pleading that, given the difficult circumstances pertaining in the area, he should be allowed ten percent but that he would settle for five, the actual amount he had billed the Department in his invoices. The lengthy letter contains the same explanations of actions, concern over what enemies might be saying and proclamations of faithfulness as in letters he wrote to Adams and Monroe about the same time.[92] The Navy Department in fact did allow Hogan a five percent commission on all supplies and two and a half percent on bills of exchange.

There were also bureaucratic difficulties. For example, the Navy Department castigated Hogan for not showing on his invoices the Congressional appropriations under which particular expenses fell, no doubt because the Department was itself being criticized by Congress for not accounting properly for its outlays. The Department said that this requirement was imposed by a notice to Navy agents in 1820, conveniently overlooking the fact it sometimes claimed Hogan was not a Naval agent.[93]

Hogan had been talking about leaving Chile since 1827 (possibly a year earlier) when the Allen and Hull affairs were in their prime. He deferred a final decision when Larned took over at Santiago and new Navy commanders replaced Hull. Possibly because of his close relations with Finch on the *Vincennes*, he planned to return to the United States on that vessel when it was slated to leave in April 1829.[94] This plan was canceled when the *Vincennes* received orders to circumnavigate the globe. Then when Hogan learned in June that Larned was being assigned to Lima,[95] he told Van Buren that "I was prepared to go home in one of our publick ships to settle my account with the Navy Department…, but as Mr. Larned has notified to me that the Legation here is to be discontinued, and that he is going to Lima in his present capacity, I deem it proper to remain at my post in the belief that it is the intention of my government the duty should devolve upon the consul as formerly."[96] What he meant was that he would, once again, be the only American official representative in Chile (other than some vice consuls at far-away ports). He had been informed (perhaps by Captain Sloat on the sloop *St. Louis* when it arrived from the United States several days earlier) that his accounts with the Navy and State Departments were "strictly correct," thus making a voyage home unnecessary.[97] He continued to tell Van Buren, however, of his desire to return home. For example, in March 1830 while once again reporting that an American had threatened "he would have me removed from office," Hogan pleaded that he had given up commerce "years ago" and "done [his consular] duty faithfully and fearfully [for which he had received only] gross abuse...." He wanted to return to Washington "to explain all that I have done here for the last nine years, to submit to its judgment whether it merits that approbation, which has been my pride and my pleasure to deserve, and whether I am to receive for my services such reward as others similarly circumstanced have received. The evening of my life is wearing away in the service and I have never received a dollar of publick money."[98]

It would have been widely known in Valparaíso and Santiago that Hogan wanted to return to the United States—eventually. This knowledge set in train a scramble for the consulship at Valparaíso that could aptly be called "consulate for sale."

Among those aware of Hogan's ultimate intention was Charles Bispham. He was a partner in the firm of Alsop Wetmore & Cryder and head of its Valparaíso office. The senior partner of the firm was Richard Alsop of Philadelphia; it did extensive business with South America where it had offices at several locations. Bispham also had family connections with the Philadelphia trading firm of Archer & Bispham. He wrote to Archer & Bispham seeking their support of his candidacy to become consul and Navy agent at Valparaíso on Hogan's expected departure. Samuel Archer referred the matter to Richard Alsop who in December 1829 wrote a letter to Van Buren recommending Bispham for the post. At that time, Richard Alsop had also been the principal backer of Emanuel West of Illinois who had been named to be the American chargé at Lima. Alsop told Van Buren that he wanted to find a way to help West financially because he could not support himself and his large family solely from his salary. The scheme he advanced was that the first $2,000 that Charles Bispham would earn annually from his Navy commissions at Valparaíso be "paid over to Mr. West." Bispham could do this without financial penalty to himself because—Alsop stated candidly—the Navy agency would be in the capable hands of Alsop Wetmore & Cryder from whom Bispham earned an adequate salary.[99] Nothing came of this scheme because West died en route to Lima and Hogan did not leave Valparaíso for another two years. What it amounted to, of course, was nothing less than a commercial firm buying one consulship, one minister (acting as chargé) and one Navy agency for the bargain price of $2,000 a year. It is even more amazing that Alsop advanced this scheme without the slightest hesitation or apology for its brazenness, at least by any modern concept of what constitutes ethics in government.

Hogan appears to have accepted Bispham as a friend, but Bispham did not return the favor in communications with Larned. His first negative remarks occurred when Hogan berated Commodore Thompson for his inattention in protecting Americans along the Chilean coast during the December 1829 rebellion. Later, when a new chargé d'affaires was expected at Santiago, Bispham told Larned that "Mr.Hogan is an old Granny and completely in his dotage and it appears to me that he is glad of an opportunity of quarreling with anyone. I hope that he will stick to the resolution he has made of returning to the United States, although I should not be surprised if he did not go at all. He says that he is only awaiting the arrival of Mr. Hamm [the expected chargé] and that he shall take passage in the first vessel after his arrival. I shall take care that he does not injure you in the estimation of Mr. Hamm. If that gentleman has any penetration [sic], he will soon discover Mr. Hogan's real character and place little credit in what he may say. I very well know the old gentleman as no friend of yours nor do I believe he is of any American that ever came to the country. He expresses a great deal of friendship for me, but I pass it by as the idle wind. I never have nor never will quarrel with him, but he is a man I have no confidence in whatever."[100]

It was the receipt on November 26, 1830, of the notice terminating his Navy agency that apparently led Hogan at last to leave Valparaíso. His family now consisted of Frances, their thirty-five year old daughter Fanny, still in poor health, and Harriet. On the preceding April 10th, Harriet on her thirty-first birthday had married Dr. John Styles. She was described as "young and blushing" and the groom "as gay as a lark."[101] Styles was one of the Englishmen who had come to Chile in 1818 to join the Chilean Navy under Cochrane. On leaving the Chilean Navy, probably in 1823, he had become a surgeon in Valparaíso where he performed several medical services for American seamen at Hogan's request. (Later, in 1833, he joined several other British doctors in establishing the first hospital in Valparaíso for foreigners.)[102] Four months after the wedding, Sophia journeyed to Calcutta on the British ship *Resolution* to be with her husband after eight years of marriage.

On January 10, 1831, Hogan wrote to Van Buren that "my [Navy] agency...having ceased...and, if ill health permits and opportunity offers, I will proceed to Washington soon after the arrival of the expected chargé d'affaires, leaving the Consulate in trustworthy hands." The new chargé was to be John Hamm of Zannesville, Ohio, whose appointment had been confirmed in June. He could neither read nor speak Spanish.

This despatch also reported another incident, this time involving a ship's captain, its crew and Commodore Charles Thompson of the U.S.S. *Guerriére*. The incident had its origins one Sunday the previous October when Hogan was informed while resting at home that the crew on an American vessel in port, the *Leonides*, appeared to be in danger of their lives at the hands of their captain, George Bugnon of Boston. The consul consented to the intervention of H.M.S. *Tribune*, which took the crew into its protection but subsequently returned them once the immediate threat had passed. Hogan then tried to resolve the dispute, seeming to side with the disaffected crew. Captain Bugnon complained to Thompson, then in Callao, who then wrote to the commander of British Navy forces in the Pacific region demanding an explanation for its intervention. When told that Hogan had requested the intervention, Thompson remon-strated against Hogan. This was too much for Hogan. He told Van Buren that Thompson should have checked with him before impugning the British Navy and that the conduct of Thompson "is of such a character that, were I amenable to a court martial, I would immediately apply for one, but as that is not my situation and that I see myself unjustly attacked by him, I feel bound to appear before my government to explain my conduct and answer to any charge brought by him or any other person against me. I shrink not from but covet investigation, his enmity arises out of my having performed a service in which I saved the Navy Department upward of two thousand dollars. In that act, I merited the approbation, not the reprobation, of a flag officer."[103]

There was another matter that set Hogan on edge in January 1831—the seemingly innocuous matter of the files of the Santiago Legation. When the U.S.S. *St. Louis* arrived at Valparaíso the previous November bringing with it notice of termination of Hogan's Navy agency, Captain Sloat told Hogan that he also had a packet from Larned at Lima containing the files which were to be delivered to Larned's replacement. Then when the *St. Louis* was to leave port on January 9, Hogan learned that Larned had instructed Sloat to hand the packet to Bispham who would give it to Hamm. Hogan wasted no time in telling Bispham that "your chargé has given me a damnable slap in the face by sending you the public papers intended for Mr. Hamm." Bispham tried to calm Hogan by saying he "had no doubt it was an accidental circumstance and that [he] knew [Larned] had the best possible feelings for him," an appeasement that Bispham told Larned "was rather a stretch." His letter again denigrated Hogan by saying "the fact is the old gentleman hates every one unless it is his English friends, and it is now quite impossible to satisfy him...."[104] Hogan immediately penned an indignant letter to Larned, saying "I cannot otherwise view [the incident] than as conveying an injurious reflection upon me who am not aware of having merited it from you either publicly or privately."[105]

Larned may have instructed Sloat to give the files to Bispham because he was displeased with Hogan, but the more likely explanation was that, since he expected Hogan to leave his post in the near future, he put the files in the hands of the man who he had good reason to believe would be named the new consul. There was equally good reason for Hogan to name Bispham vice consul. He might not only have expected that Bispham would be confirmed as full consul but he was himself involved with Alsop Wetmore & Cryder. Hogan's cantankerous reaction was both ill-founded and unnecessary.

On February 4, 1831, Hogan received instructions from the Navy Department to "deliver to...the squadron in the Pacific Ocean the publick stores and slops and all other articles of publick property remaining in your possession as late agent of the United States at Valparaíso," but he had already done this a month earlier, thereby ending his relationship with the U.S. Navy.[106]

Hamm arrived at Valparaíso on May 2. Hogan immediately engaged passage for New York on the merchant vessel *New Orleans* that had arrived from Lima the previous day. Michael Hogan, Frances and daughter Fanny sailed two weeks later during the early evening. On that same day, he wrote two despatches to Van Buren: one simply reporting that he was leaving and naming Bishpam as vice consul; the other a final defense of all he had done during his ten years at Valparaíso. He began the letter by saying that he "had the mortification to [tell Hamm that the Legation files] were placed by Mr. Larned in the hands of a private merchant who would give them to him, consoling myself with the consciousness of having on all occasions discharged with faithfulness every part of the public duty that devolved upon me, and that the slight thus put upon me was unmerited.... If I have expressed myself too strongly to my senior in office (Mr. Larned), I trust an apology for me will be found in the desire of supporting the dignity of our Nation. I do not wish to speak of Mr. Larned's conduct to me in the spirit of complaint, but deem it necessary to place the matter before government in order to meet and, if possible, to prevent the unfavorable impression it is calculated to inspire."

Turning to his entire tenure at Valparaíso, Hogan continued that, "during my residence near this government, I have had (particularly for the first three years) much to contend with in the protection necessary to our commerce; in every case I succeeded. [And] during the late civil war many questions of difficulty arose, the whole of which as related to our flag and the interest of our citizens were adjusted [by me] without loss or expense... I shall have the honor of laying [this performance] before you at an early day, soliciting an examination of their merits or demerits. [Concerning] my standing with the government during the struggle for supremacy, ...I take the liberty of enclosing a newspaper in which the sentiments of the government, and of the people at large, of Chile is exhibited; I would not send it was I not certain it emanated from very high authority.... I sail this evening for New York in a state of health that nothing short of absolute necessity could justify."[107]

Hogan already knew that the Navy Department had protested several of his bills of exchange during the previous December. Before leaving, he deposited with Messrs. Alsop & Company $10,350, which he said was "all the money I possess," to meet protested drafts. He wrote that "I lament the cause taken not only on account of the ruin which it is calculated to bring on me but [also] for the discredit it attaches to the Publick credit of the Nation abroad." He added that, should additional bills not be protested, Alsop should purchase copper at Huasco and ship it him "at the lowest freight possible." In addition, he asked the Alsop firm to sell some 500 barrels of flour and some raisins already in his possession. Additional bills were protested, eventually reaching the considerable amount of $38,254.25.

He would not learn this devastating information until he reached the United States.

ELEVEN

LAST DAYS, WASHINGTON, D.C.

The measures of the late Secretary of the Navy determined my leaving that good climate instantly on the arrival of the Chargé.... They redound so little honor on our country that I do not wish to soil paper that is clean with a repetition of them, but thank God the sin is his own, bolstered by a subordinate who looked for glory by pursuing the drafts of orange and lemon peals.

—Hogan to Poinsett after arrival Washington

Hogan, his wife Frances and their still spinster daughter Fanny arrived in New York on August 28, 1831, after a voyage of three and a half months. He was almost 65 and not in the best of health. While the *New Orleans* was still quarantined, Hogan told Robert Oliver: "This ship has let her anchor go after passage of 104 days from Valparaíso, 19 of them spent at Rio where I thought for the first time I should lay my bones, 52 from that port, 14 of them expended in calms and complying with the force of adverse currents before we rounded Cape Frio [just north of Rio]." Then he added that he had "come to pay my respects to [Secretary of the Navy] Mr. Branch and endeavor to shew that a man ought not to be hung up to publick scorn because he is so unfortunate as to possess common honesty and so much experience as to know his duty. But I am just told there has been a storm at headquarters and that all is gone by the board, except the mainmast. I hope my reporter has made a mistake."[1] He had the report half-correct: John Branch had been replaced by Levi Woodbury as Secretary of the Navy in May, and there were other developments concerning naval accounts about which he would soon learn. He probably heard some of this from his son William whom he met in New York. William, now 39 with a family of eight children and living at Hogansburg in northern New York, also told him that he was a candidate for the House of Representatives in the elections that would be held in two months. But Hogan did not dally long in New York. On the trip to Washington, he stopped at Philadelphia hoping to see Poinsett, probably believing that he could help or give advice about his problems with the new Administration, but Poinsett was not there. He was in Washington by the beginning of fall. During the next eighteen months, his life was consumed by matters relating to his accounts with both the Navy and State Departments and by trying to restore his good name which he was convinced had been tarnished by others, particularly Commodore Hull and Heman Allen.

The United States had changed during the ten years that Hogan had been far away in Chile. The population had increased by a third to almost 13 million. The country was expanding to the West; the East was beginning to industrialize. Railroads were being started and the first telegraph lines would be constructed in the next decade. Domestic politics were reaching a new level of acrimony over such matters as the Bank of the United States and the threat of secession over the related issues of import tariffs and slavery. Andrew Jackson's defenders cited his support of democratic principles and the common man, while the old guard was aghast at what they considered the vulgarity, mediocrity, incompetence and corruption of the new Administration. On his inauguration day in 1829 it is said that 10,000 citizens, many of them seeking government jobs under the spoils system, rampaged the White House. Jackson fought with the old Republicans in Congress, who would soon be called Whigs, and was charged by them with usurping Congressional authority. It would not be the last sea change in the American political scene.

Washington was a very small city that had little to offer other than being the seat of the federal government. The Capitol, White House and other buildings that had been burned during the War of 1812 had been largely rebuilt. Although parts of Pennsylvania Avenue had been macadamized, the surface was mostly crushed rocks that billowed clouds of dust when there was no rain. Farmhouses bordered the avenues and streets, and the summers were unbearable. Michael Hogan, his wife and daughter Fanny made their home at Mrs. Cochrane's, a boarding house on F Street. William, who had won a seat in the House of Representative running as a Jacksonian Democrat from Franklin County, New York, also stayed there during the four to eight months that the Congress was in session each year. Other Representatives at Mrs. Cochrane's were General James Findlay from Cincinnati (with Mrs. Findlay) and James Coke, Jr., of Virginia.[2] A well-known member of the House of Representatives was former secretary of state and president John Quincy Adams.

Hogan may have heard that a man named Heman Allen was also a Congressman, but he would have quickly learned that, although also from Vermont, this Heman Allen was not the same one who had bedeviled him in Chile. The former minister to Chile had become president of the local branch of the Bank of the United States in Burlington, Vermont, a long way from Washington. Hogan's other nemesis, Captain Isaac Hull, was however very much in Washington. After his return to the United States, he sought and obtained an appointment in 1829 as commandant of the Washington Navy Yard. Their paths probably never crossed, but there would be one final twist to the Hogan-Hull affair.

Although there was probably little social life for the Hogans in Washington, they were not inconsequential figures. Frances was invited to attend the 1832 Washington Birthday Night Ball at the Union Hotel in Georgetown where the managers included family names later to become hallmarks in Washington, such as John Mason, Thomas Corcoran and P.W. Magruder. She communicated with the far flung family—Sophia Donnelly, now in Calcutta, and Harriet Styles still in Valparaíso.

Life for Michael Hogan could not have been very happy, given his physical deterioration and his preoccupation with his business affairs, but there were good moments. He visited his friend Robert Oliver in Baltimore on more than one occasion. After a visit in 1832, he wrote that "I want again to see the inside of your house for I have not had anything good to eat since last in it." (The fare at Mrs. Cochrane's must have suffered from the usual deficiencies of boarding houses.) Another welcome time was a visit from his grandson Will, the only living male among William's eight children. William Senior gave his father a small leather-bound booklet with a map of the East Indies on the inside on which he inscribed the following: "These ships' tracks (in red ink) were jotted down by M. Hogan in 1832 to amuse and answer the inquisitions of his grandson W.H., then a boy of ten years." The tracks in red ink show the voyages that Hogan undertook to China, India and New South Wales when he was a youth and later ship's captain and merchant many years ago (Figure 7, facing page). One can picture the grandfather recounting sea tales of mystery and wonder in an area of the world that is still unknown and mysterious to most Americans today and the delight Will must have taken from such treasured times with his

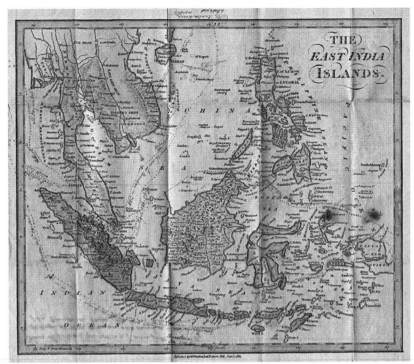

Figure 8. Foldout map of East Indies showing early Hogan voyages. Author's Collection.

grandfather. Twenty-five years later, Will would have occasion to recall these talks when he undertook a voyage to the South Seas on a mission that involved his then deceased grandfather.

Hogan did other things with his "red ink." He went through all his old papers, adding comments in the red ink at several places, comments that have been helpful to the author. He must also have pitched out a number of letters and documents dealing with slave transactions that he believed would place his legacy in a bad light. Curiously, he did not throw out a packet containing his testimony before the Yonge investigation commission on his slave import arrangements with the governor and his aides, perhaps because he was sufficiently parsimonious not to part with documents that had been meticulously prepared by his counsel. He did not know that copies of many of these documents could later be found in various archives and that research could reconstruct many of the incidents he hoped would never be revealed.

A person of Hogan's wide experience and involvement in political happenings at the various places around the world where he had resided could not help but be caught up in the political turmoil that was taking place in the nation's capital during 1832 and 1833. Moreover, he would have met and talked with not only his congressman son William but also other congressmen who lived at or visited Mrs. Cochrane's boarding house. Always eager to show his knowledge of the political scene, he wrote to Robert Oliver on July 10: "You will hear of the rejection of the Bank [of the United States] with the reasoning upon it before the receipt of this. It will be impossible to procure ⅔ of both Houses to act [to override Jackson's veto of a bill extending the bank]. Therefore, nothing can be done this year nor perhaps the next, but there will be sufficient time before the charter is near expiring to form any monied institution the country may desire to have." The letter also said that he "saw Van Buren this morning, fat and very hearty and very glad apparently to meet an old friend. He is at the president's with whom he rode toward the Capitol at one o'clock." Hogan reported that "it is believed [the tariff bill] be finished in the lower House today, but how far it may give general satisfaction is doubtful...." But later in the day he added a P.S.: "The tariff is done, gone to the Senate with the amendments to ensure the duties required, to which if [the Senators] disagree, it must lay over till next session."

Although the BUS charter would not expire until 1836, its supporters believed that Jackson would not dare veto early rechartering legislation during an election year. The extension was enacted on July 3; on the 10th Jackson vetoed the bill. His veto message, which called the BUS unconstitutional, a concentration of private power threatening individual liberty and a vehicle of the monied and aristocratic Eastern establishment, set the stage for a resounding Jackson victory at the national polls in November. He would also have the last laugh on the BUS. He could not revoke its charter, but he could and did arrange to withdraw government funds on deposit at the BUS, which set off another furor with the Whigs in Congress. Finally, during his last year in office in 1836, the charter of the Bank of the United States was not renewed. The United States managed without a national bank until the Federal Reserve System was enacted in 1913.

The tariff issue mentioned in Hogan's letter had its origins in the high import tariffs that had been enacted in 1828 to protect burgeoning industries in the North. The Southern states vehemently opposed the measure because they saw it as supporting the industrial strength of the North and because they feared that other countries (principally Britain) would impose high tariffs in retaliation, thus harming the South whose economic well-being depended on cotton exports. John Calhoun of South Carolina advanced the nullification doctrine, under which states could nullify the applicability of federal laws to their territory. Implicit in this doctrine was that disaffected states might secede from the Union. The tariff act mentioned by Hogan, which passed both houses on July 14, reduced the high 1828 protective tariff levels, but not enough to satisfy the Southerners.

Hogan took note of the threat of nullification and the possibility of a "horrid" civil war in an October 6 letter to Robert Oliver: "My stationary position does not...warrant my expecting to learn much of what goes on. Letters from the South state that the nullifying members are coming to their duty in Congress except General [Robert] Hayne who is expected to be elected Governor [of South Carolina]. I would rather have my own gout than their situation if in the wisdom of Congress a convention of the States may be brought about. A civil war, the most horrid of all wars (the thought of which from the experience I have had makes my blood run cold), may be averted. I do not see any other course by which to save the Union and avoid bloodshed. Such a convention would amend all the doubtful points now charged to the Constitution which by the retention of territory, the increase of population and forces of circumstances the framers could not foresee."

Hogan was in error in his short-term prediction. Southerners did not do "their duty" nor was a convention called to amend the Constitution. After the fall elections, South Carolina nullified both the 1828 and 1832 tariffs. Jackson, although a Southerner and slave-owner, would not abide this threat to the Union. He issued a proclamation in December calling nullification treasonous and warning that he would uphold the law of the land. In January, he asked that Congress enact the Force bill giving him additional powers to enforce the law in the South, and— being a wily politician—also proposed that Congress enact a gradual reduction in tariffs. The carrot and stick approach worked; South Carolina withdrew its nullification of the tariff laws, but, to show it was not conceding the doctrine, nullified the Force Act. Hogan was prescient, however, in the possibility of a civil war over the issues, which stemmed from the South's peculiar institution of slavery. Twenty-eight years later eleven Southern states seceded from the Union and the bloody Civil War followed.

Hogan's disputes with the Navy Department over his accounts held his main attention. The details of these disputes are almost impossible to sort out and need not, in any event, detain the reader. There were two sets of issues. One arose from the bills of exchange that the Navy Department had protested, totaling some $38,000. Hogan petitioned directly to Secretary of the Navy Woodward in January 1832 to make good on these bills. His penchant for finding guilty third parties responsible for his woes and insistence on his unflinching devotion to public duty comes through—once again—from this extract: "Sir, altho' your sense of justice may direct the allowance of my claims, …can you restore to me that commercial credit which has been blasted by the refusal of the [Navy] Department to accept drafts drawn for the public service, …can you compensate for the loss of time so valuable at my age or for the heavy expense to which I am necessarily exposed in bringing home my family a distance of 12,000 miles to vindicate my character and sustain my interests, the one most unjustly impeached, the other most wantonly destroyed by your predecessor in office; or can you or any other power under Heaven heal the deeply wounded feelings of a man whose faithful discharge of duty has provided a cabal which has so far succeeded as to cause great injustice to be practiced toward him. I do not hesitate to affirm and, if such matters could be made the subject of an inquiry and of punishment to the guilty, have no doubt I could prove that the grossest peculation has been attempted and sometimes successfully practiced upon the Government and individuals by some of its officers in the Pacific whose conduct is however an exception to the highly honorable and faithful discharge of duty which has distinguished a great majority of them. Had I lent myself to such schemes of peculation, I have little doubt that I should have retained my office, and in this have amassed an immense fortune, but honor and duty pointed out another course as mine, and I am now before you not to regret that such was my course but to ask you for justice, so far as you can yield it."

The other set of issues involved Hogan's claim that the Navy Department still owed him a large sum of money for services rendered as Navy Agent at Valparaíso. Because the number and nature of these claims kept changing, it is difficult to assign a precise dollar amount to them. The total figures that were mostly used by the parties involved were in the $20,000 to $30,000 range.

Hogan sought Congressional help over both the protested bills and the unpaid claims by petitioning for its intervention and assistance early in 1832. This led to an exchange between Woodbury and the Senate Committee on Naval Affairs, then chaired by the South Carolinian Robert Hayne mentioned in Hogan's October letter to Oliver, the result of which was that most of the protested bills were made good by the Navy Department.

However, the additional claims were another matter. In a March 2, 1832 letter, responding to Hayne's request for a report, Secretary Woodbury claimed that Hogan had been paid more than called for by strict adherence to Navy instructions and precedent, and that additional payment could only be justified if further testimony supported Hogan's claim that his job at Valparaíso was *sui generis*, by which he meant special circumstances. Clearly, the ancient art of passing the buck was known to Secretary Woodbury. He closed his letter by noting that "in either view of the character of his agency [a standard agency or one deserving of additional support due to special circumstances], it gives me pleasure to add as an act of justice to Mr. Hogan that the highest testimonials are before the Department in favour of his general devotion to the duties of his station; ...and that no reasons are known to the Department why he should not receive, if in the opinion of Congress he has not already [received], all [that] the true character of his agency may entitle him to; and even an indemnity and compensation beyond that, if found insufficient, provided Congress choose in all such cases to provide for indemnity and full compensation [i.e., make the necessary appropriations of money]."

But Woodbury was not letting Hogan completely off the hook: "The Department does not, however, as Mr. Hogan seems to suppose, 'require' Congress to settle any principles or confer any 'power' in relation to his accounts; but has been willing to adjust them on such principles as appeared under all the circumstances and the existing laws and usages applicable to the case. The Department neither courts nor shuns the responsibility of adjusting them on any other principles Congress may think proper to have applied."

The Woodbury letter was undoubtedly drafted by Amos Kendall, the man whom Hogan called "a subordinate who looked for glory by pursuing the drafts of orange and lemon peels."[3] As previously noted, Kendall played a leading role in Jackson's house-cleaning campaign. There is no evidence, however, that Hogan was either an important or principal target; he just happened to get caught up in the politics of the time.[4]

Now that it was evident that the Navy Department did not believe (with good cause) that it had the legal authority to satisfy Hogan's claims, William introduced a bill in the House of Representatives in December 1832 to reimburse his father (a compatriot introduced a similar bill in the Senate). The bills were referred to the respective naval committees but no action was immediately take.

Hogan stewed because the attempt to obtain Congressional relief seemed to be getting nowhere. Ever willing to find some hidden cause, he may have come to believe that Isaac Hull had planted derogatory information about him after his return to the United States and that this was the reason for the lack of prompt Congressional action. In fact, Hull had his own financial claims against the Navy Department which he was trying to recover through Congressional bills, with no better success than Hogan. Moreover, they had a common enemy in the ubiquitous Amos Kendall.[5] Whatever the reason, William introduced a resolution in the House of Representatives on January 21, 1833, containing five allegations against Hull, the principal one of which was that Hull had rigged the delivery of whiskey on the *Good Hope* in 1825 for private profit (details of this incident are in the preceding chapter). The other charges were that Hull improperly used deposit money involving the storeship *Jasper*, that he sold Spanish dollars for gold but paid his crew in less valuable currency, that he was paid a sum of money as an inducement to convoy a private vessel in Peruvian waters, and that he wasted government money by long stays in port rather than cruising at sea to protect American vessels. John Etheridge, Hull's long-time secretary, responded three days later to the House Naval Committee denying all the charges. The Naval Committee eventually made a perfunctory report which "was laid on the table," meaning nothing was done.[6]

The dispute with the Navy Department would remain unsettled during Hogan's lifetime. It would be carried forward for another fifteen years by William acting as administrator of his estate, a tale that will be told in the Epilog.

In his dealings with the State Department, Hogan maintained the posture that he would return as consul to Valparaíso after he had settled his accounts with the Navy and State Departments. It is doubtful that he really intended to return, but maintaining the fiction that he would may have helped his cause. Writing to Secretary of State Edward Livingston in January 1832, Hogan claimed compensation as a diplomatic, not consular, officer during the periods that he was the sole U.S. representative in either Valparaíso or Santiago. If his claim were sustained, he would receive a retroactive salary. He first asserted that, "from the date of Prevost's departure 18th September 1821 until the arrival of Mr. Allen 26th March 1824, a period of two years and six months, all the duties of a diplomatic agent devolved on and were discharged by me." In fact, Prevost was absent from Chile during only 16 months of this period,[7] somewhat more than half the time—a large proportion in itself, but hardly the 100 percent that Hogan implied. Hogan also claimed that, when Prevost presented Hogan to O'Higgins in August 1821, "Mr. Prevost informed the Supreme Director that thence forward I would act as the authorized organ of communication between the governments and as charged with the care of all the interests of the United States commercial or political, and in such character I was thereafter considered and treated by the executives of Chile." It is doubtful Prevost would have said this, except possibly as applicable during times he was absent from Chile, but Prevost being no longer of this world and the State Department being unlikely to ask O'Higgins, no one could refute Hogan's recollection.

He was on more solid ground in claiming diplomatic pay status during the 17 months from Larned's departure in October 1829 to Hamm's arrival in May 1831 where there is ample evidence of the diplomatic role that he played. Although he was never authorized to act in this capacity either by the State Department or Larned (and perhaps the latter did not intend or desire that he do so), Hogan gave the Department full opportunity to order him to desist in the first despatch he sent after Larned's departure. Moreover, he had some precedents on his side, which he was quick to draw to Livingston's attention. One was his neighbor consul, William Tudor, in Lima who received pay as a chargé d'affaires during the period from Prevost's death to his departure for another post.

The Department of State consulted with the House Committee of Foreign Relations which wanted further substantiation. Hogan provided it in a second letter to Livingston in April in which he listed thirteen instances of his involvement in "diplomatic" activities prior to Allen's arrival and made general reference to the better documented reporting after Larned's departure. If the State Department ever bothered to compare the interpretations that Hogan attributed to these instances with the actual texts of the original papers it would have found a certain amount of hyperbole. However, perhaps that is to be expected in such situations. It is also instructive to a researcher to note that several of the despatches to the Department listed in his letter are not in the National Archives (or at least not filed where they should be).[8]

The Department replied to the Congressional inquiry ten months later on February 25, 1833, giving Hogan credit for performing diplomatic activities not only during the periods claimed by him but for the entire period prior to Allen's arrival as well as the entire period between Larned's departure and Hamm's arrival.[9] One has to wonder why the Department had become so generous after several decades of seeming disregard of the financial plight of consular officers and of the damage to U.S. interests that resulted when such officers engaged in commerce—with its inevitable potential for conflict of interest—to make ends meet. As previously noted, legislation authorizing pay for consular officers would not be enacted for another 23 years. In the particular case of Hogan, however, the Department of State had to consider the fact that three other representatives in South America who did not hold formal diplomatic titles—Prevost, Tudor and Forbes—had received salaries ranging from $2,000 to $4,500 a year.

The Congress acted quickly. In the general appropriations bill enacted on March 2, 1833, Hogan was awarded $18,122.50 in full payment for diplomatic services rendered in Chile at the rate of $4,500 per annum, the same pay that Prevost received.[10]

When Hogan received this welcome news, his health at the then advanced age of 66 was rapidly declining.[11] He had earlier complained to Robert Oliver about his worsening gout: "I want iron or something to give strength to a deranged stomach and strained old bones, the only support of an active mind and, in spite of difficulties and the intrigues of the fraudulent, one of a cheerful and determined character. Do you think the waters [at York Springs, Pennsylvania] would be useful in restoring strength and dissipating bile." Instead, Hogan took his family to Bedford Springs in the Pennsylvania mountains near the Maryland border in August and September 1832 to find relief from his gout, as well as the heat and humidity of Washington summers. In February 1833 he wrote that he had been become largely immobile: "My limbs are clear of swelling but so weak that I cannot lean any weight on them. I have occupied only one room and one chair since I came here and lived upon hot and cold tea." But he still pined for red meat, telling Oliver: "My only hope was in being able to eat some of your fine venison...but courage failed."

His son William had returned to Hogansburg at the end of the Congressional session on March 2. On the 12th Charles Wilkes, now a lieutenant, arrived in Washington to take charge of the Navy's Depot of Charts and Instruments (that later became the Naval Observatory and Hydrographic Office) and quickly looked up his old friend from Valparaíso. He later wrote that he "had many duties to perform in my new situation, but gave up my time to assist in nursing [Hogan]and passed a part of every night in relieving those who were in attendance on him. From the first he spoke calmly of his end, for he seemed to feel it was approaching altho' he continued to be cheerful and resigned. He was truly a picture of beautiful old age and the impression he made on me at that time remains very strongly as he sat in his great chair, bolstered and pillowed up, in his dressing gown. His white hair, and bearing, and intelligent look, and resignation with his frank and cheerful talk afforded a picture not often seen or heard. He was always glad to see me and I did what I could to amuse and comfort him by my attentions. He felt he could unburthen himself to me and, mixed with his views and thoughts, he drew life characters of many of the officials he had had to transact business with. He was so highly honorable himself he felt greatly the dishonesty and trickery of many he had dealings with, & often cautioned me to beware of certain individuals whom he represented as 'snakes in the grass.' But when he could give praise it was done with heartfelt satisfaction. He continued to grow weaker and finally was unable to arise from his bed and, being affected with the asthma, he required the help of a strong arm and strength to give him ease, and this soon wore his devoted wife and daughter [Fanny] out. The physician endeavored to procure nurses, but at that time in Washington they were unknown and I had no acquaintance on whom to call. We had no idea his end was so rapidly approaching."

But Hogan must have known. There was one last official act he had to perform. On March 21st, he signed a brief note to President Andrew Jackson. It was delivered at the White House the same day:[12]

I feel it incumbent on me to express my Thanks, for your having so long acceded to my request of keeping the Consulate of Chile open for me until I should determine whether to return to the performance of its duties or not. An unfortunate continuance of extreme bad Health obliges me to give up all hope of ever being able to resume the office, and I now beg leave to send in my Resignation.

Five days later, on Tuesday, March 26 1833, Wilkes recorded the final act: "Toward dawn, he suddenly sprang from his bed. I was within his reach and fortunately seized him and, with the aid of his daughter, who at once was awakened, returned him to his bed. This paroxysm exhausted him and he lay for some minutes immovable, and then breathed his last. The physician was near at hand, but too late. For some days before he had been given stimulants to keep him up. His son had been summoned, whom he had requested to see, but before his arrival the old Gentleman had succumbed and all was over."

William arrived at his father's bedside later the same day. He knew that his father had expressed the wish to be buried in Baltimore next to his long-standing friend John Oliver. The next day, William wrote to Oliver: "My friend Mr. Miller communicated to you last night the painful intelligence of my father's death. He has at length fallen the victim of disease, aggravated by a sense of the injustice he has met with from persons so incapable of understanding the feelings and principles which govern the course of an honorable man as of appreciating disinterested integrity of conduct. In life he was most warmly attached to your departed brother and to yourself. In death it was his earnest wish that he might not be separated from that friend who had gone before and from that friend who must follow him, and in obedience to his wish, and the assurance that you will gratify it, I shall set out for Baltimore tomorrow with his remains. We shall arrive on Friday afternoon [March 29], and at such hour on Saturday as you will appoint will pay the last sad service to the father I cannot replace. I think it would have been his wish that Mr. Bathurst, Mr. Tavish, Mr. Isaac McKien, Mr. Gibbs, Mr. Colt, Dr. Bushler, Capt. [Jacob] Jones of the Navy and Mr. Meredith, a gentleman of law he met at Bedford last year, would be his pall bearers. You Sir I was sure will mourn him as a friend and as such, if your own health allows, will accompany his funeral which it is my mother's desire and I believe was equally his should be quite private."

Charles Wilkes noted that "two clergymen of the Episcopal Church had been invited to attend [the funeral], the one whose church the family attended [in Washington], Mr. O[wens], and the other Mr. Hawley who had been very kind and attentive and was the elder of the two…. There were a great many present as Mr. Hogan was, though a stranger, comparatively well respected. Mr. Hawley made a very appropriate and touching address."

The funeral did not, however, proceed smoothly. Wilkes recounted the harrowing details: "When all had gathered for the funeral, the delay of the ceremony was awkward. The clergymen were both present and in an adjoining room. I stepped in to see what was the cause and found, to my astonishment, there was a dispute between them who should perform the Service. I at once took upon myself, in the name of the family, to decide that Mr. Hawley should officiate, and the disagreement was put an end to. The ceremony was performed and then it was found that one of the Pall bearers was absent. He had not been able to serve. I assumed his place. The coffin was a leaden one and the attendant pall [bearers] were unable to lift the corpse. It is the custom in Washington for Pall bearers to carry the coffin to the hearse and afterwards to transport it to the grave. It was immovable with the force we had, Lt. Ramsay and myself being the only able-bodied ones, but by the help of the undertaker & his men this was done through the Narrow entry and safely deposited on the hearse."[13] Hogan would not remain buried in Baltimore; several years later William arranged for the body to be buried in New York City.

At Hogan's death, William was still a resident in Hogansburg, Harriet and Dr. John Styles remained for a while in Valparaíso, and Sophia and Arthur Donnelly were on their way from India to England. By 1836, Harriet Styles and Arthur Donnelly had died and all the rest were in New York City: William with his wife, Sarah, and their seven children on Hudson Street in Manhattan; Frances Hogan, unmarried Fanny, Sophia Donnelly with her two children and John Styles with his five children, all in a house in Richmond on Staten Island. Eventually, most of them went their separate ways, leading normal and, in comparison with Michael Hogan, unadventurous lives.

In romantic sagas, strong personalities such as Michael Hogan leave a legacy and tradition that subsequent generations carry to new heights. Such was not the case with this man. He had hoped his only living son would follow him in commerce, but although William dabbled in real estate, he was happier to act the country gentleman in Hogansburg and Fort Covington in northern New York where his father had bought land, dabbling instead in such professional activities as county judge, congressman and government bureaucrat. Of Hogan's three daughters, only Harriet and Sophia married, both while they were in Valparaíso and both to Englishmen.

In New York State, the towns of Hogansburg and Bombay are reminders of Michael Hogan. A plaque in Grace Church in New York City commemorates him, and in the Trinity Church cemetery at 770 Riverside Drive, now in Harlem, overlooking the Hudson River are the graves and tombstones of Michael Hogan, his wife and 20 of his descendants. His portrait, remembered from the author's childhood, now hangs in his home, but he no longer seems "dark and sullen." There may even be a slight smile in his eyes—perhaps sardonic, as if he wants to say: *I never hesitated to take the bold step—and I made my mark. How many of you can say the same?*

On several occasions throughout his life, Hogan believed he had been wronged by others due to their own misdeeds and intention to harm him. There can be no doubt that he was a man with a chip on his shoulder, perhaps even to the point of clinical paranoia. Manifestations of these traits seem to have begun when he lost his fortune around 1812 and increased in frequency and severity during his later years at Valparaíso. During this latter period, he convinced himself that his troubles were all due to the venality, misbehavior and errors of Minister Allen, Captain Hull and faceless bureaucrats in the Navy Department. Time and again he professed in his letters that the treatment he had been accorded was not worthy of his years of faithful service, the sacrifices he had endured, and his sense of honor. In each of the incidents that led to his state of mind there may have been some element of truth, but he lost the ability to distinguish between those that were minor, petty or best overlooked and those that were intentional acts of unfair, unjust, unnecessary or possibly criminal behavior. Michael Hogan spent the closing years of his life an unhappy and disgruntled man. If he is to be judged by these standards alone, he would rank near the bottom of the scale.

This is, of course, too narrow a standard for judgment. A person's final worth should be measured either by accomplishments in the public sector or by private impact on others, particularly one's own family and friends. In the latter case, Hogan did leave a legacy for his offspring and descendants, a legacy that enshrined him as a romantic adventurer, world traveler, the talk of the town, a charming host, an Irish humorist, and at one time quite rich, even if the truth of some of his activities was hidden from and unknown to his children.

In the public sector, accomplishment today consists of contributing something to society, whether it is a fortune used for peaceful purposes, a scientific discovery or invention, producing goods and services, teaching, governing, healing, defending the innocent, prosecuting the guilty or similar virtuous work and deeds. Fortunately for most, if not all, people in advanced societies, these virtuous accomplishments can be sought without regard to the need for basic survival. This is not to say that modern man is not powerfully influenced to make money, but that his ultimate survival is usually not dependent upon it. During the past hundred years or so, a host of devices have been put in place to sustain human life in adversity: unemployment benefits, workman's compensation insurance, social security, life insurance, pension benefits and medical aid and insurance. In Hogan's time, none of these crutches existed. Unless a man inherited wealth, the only honest way to survive and avoid abject poverty was to make money. Moreover, there did not then exist the means of communication and data compilation that today makes it exceedingly difficult for a person to cheat, whether in taxes, business, government or the professions, although judging from today's media one might think dishonesty is endemic in society. When communication between continents took months and there were no means to cross check information except manually, the fabric of business and commerce had to rest in large part on voluntary adherence to standard procedures and practices. The risk of being caught was so small and the pressure to amass money so great that the temptation to cheat must have been overwhelming, particularly for a man who started with nothing. And it would have been equally important to such a person constantly to deny wrongdoing because the retention of honor—the voluntary adherence to a code of conduct—was all that stood between the only world in which survival could be achieved and banishment from that world and certain death.

In this light, Hogan was no worse a person than many others who acquired wealth. His son William perhaps best captured both the victory and the tragedy of Michael Hogan when he later wrote: "For a time my father reposed from a life of enterprise and adventure and risk, in admiration of the novelties presented by [the United States], a country presenting so many new features to his attention and admiration. With a well invested capital, our unencumbered income exceeding $25,000 a year, it seems strange that he did not rest content. But he was not yet forty years of age; he had ever been, from the crest of life more than twenty years before, eminently successful. He was energetic, impulsive, generous, hopeful and knew no such thought as fail—alas the issue!"

EPILOGUE

Hogan would have been pleased with three events that took place after his death, each of which seemed to validate his worth and character. The first was the outcome of the consulship saga at Valparaíso. Bispham continued to want the post, as did his U.S.-based sponsors. In February 1832, fifteen American citizen merchants in Valparaíso signed a memorial addressed to Secretary of State Edward Livingston recommending that Bispham be named consul. They forwarded it to a New York firm which in turn sent it Richard Alsop at Philadelphia. He could have simply forwarded the memorial to the secretary with his own recommendation, but he did not do so until he heard that Hogan had died. He told Livingston that he had just heard of Hogan's death from Isaac McKim, a leading merchant and industrialist of Baltimore. Alsop wrote: "I have hitherto refrained from doing anything to promote the object of the memorial, [and] indeed have taken the liberty to retain it until now, believing that any application in [Bispham's] behalf, during Mr. Hogan's continuance in office, would be unbecoming as well as offensive to the delicacy of Mr. Bispham who was unadvised of the existence of such a document."[1]

This did not end the squabble. Bispham received letters of support from a dozen or more merchants in Philadelphia, Baltimore and New York. But there was another serious contender for the post, one Thomas S. Russell, who also received many letters of support. On April 13, Jackson penned a note to the Department of State: "I withdraw the appointment of Charles Bispham as consul at Valparaíso and appoint Thomas S. Russell of Massachusetts in his place." Bispham's supporters, principally Richard Alsop, objected to Russell's appointment because, they alleged, he was associated with the London firm of Huth, Gunning & Company and would be in position to favor British commerce from his access to privileged American information. They cited a despatch from Minister Hamm confirming that Russell was a partner in an English firm. Alsop told new Secretary of State John Forsyth that he was not trying to take sides; what was important was to appoint a person who was a naturally born American citizen, American in his feeling and independent of any foreign influence or control. Finally, in May 1834 the Senate revoked its confirmation of Russell's appointment. But Bispham was not the beneficiary; a new consul named George G. Hobson was named to assume the Valparaíso post and was there by the end of the year, thus ending this saga of influence peddling.[2] Perhaps Hogan could draw comfort from his grave that the Valparaíso post was considered so valuable that it attracted spirited lobbying and in-fighting from important American merchants.

The second vindicating event took place on August 14, 1848, fifteen years after Hogan's death when the Congress enacted legislation directing "the Secretary of the Treasury to pay to William Hogan, Administrator of Michael Hogan, deceased, $16,831.87 in full compensation for the services rendered and moneys advanced by Michael Hogan as agent or factor for the Navy Department at Valparaíso."[3]

Hogan's children were probably gratified just to have the money, but perhaps they also tasted the sweet victory of redemption that their father surely would have felt if he had lived to see himself vindicated. It had been a tortuous road.

Hogan had died without a will. For a man with not inconsiderable assets spread in several countries, this would seem surprising, but for Hogan lack of attention to legal details was the norm. William was appointed administrator in New York, which was his father's last legal residence. He made several attempts to recoup the money that the family thought the United States Navy owed the estate. The Senate and House committees considering private bills introduced in 1832 issued reports which might have made passage possible, but the Congress failed to act on the bills over several sessions.[4] They were eventually withdrawn at William's request, either because he had concluded Congressional relief was not to be forthcoming or because he believed a settlement could be reached with the Navy Department. Instead of a settlement, the U.S. Navy brought suit against the estate in 1841 in the Circuit Court of the United States for the Southern District of New York charging that Michael Hogan had reneged on promises allegedly made on October 15, 1832, (just five months before his death) to repay $24,000 in moneys advanced to him while serving as Navy Agent at Valparaíso. No evidence of these "promises" was introduced. The allegation was apparently a legal stratagem to get the case conveniently in court. William filed a counter claim against the Government, based principally on losses Michael Hogan had incurred from flood damage to the bread supplied to the Navy ships at Valparaíso. He retained Samuel L. Southard to handle the case. In documents filed with the court, William said that Southard was a material witness in the case because he was secretary of the navy during most of the time that Michael Hogan was at Valparaíso. However, William's true reason was probably that he hoped Southard would have political influence. He was a senator from New Jersey, an ardent Whig and briefly vice president when John Tyler became president on William Henry Harrison's untimely death in April 1841. But the ascendancy of the Whigs was short-lived, the ailing Southard lost his political clout and died shortly afterwards in June 1842.[5] After at least one postponement, a jury on February 14, 1845, rendered a verdict in favor of Hogan in the amount of $22,539.24.[6] There is no record of a final judicial determination. William Hogan and the Navy Department must have reached an out-of-court settlement which led to the Congressional appropriation of the lesser amount of $16,831.87.

The third and final positive event involved the distribution of Hogan's Australian properties to his children. William had been content to receive the rents from these properties, but at some point the payments ceased and the ownership of the properties was called into question. In 1856 he sent his son Will to Sydney to claim the land and sell it. In an apparent attempt to enhance his credentials, Charles Wilkes, now a captain, executed an affidavit attesting to his knowledge of Michael Hogan and his family and of his property holdings in Sydney, which Wilkes had visited in 1839 on a South Seas and Antarctic surveying and exploring expedition for the U.S. Navy on board the *Vincennes*, the same ship the Hogans had joined as guests in 1828 to visit the Juan Fernández Islands. (Wilkes acquired some renown for this and other accomplishments during his naval career.) Cousin Will, as he was called, found that the occupants of the 400 acres would not accept the Hogan claim, forcing him to bring suit. A lower court found in favor of the Hogan family but the Supreme Court of New South Wales in 1860 reversed the ruling on the ground that the action was barred by the statute of limitations. The case was appealed to the Privy Council in London which a year later restored the original ruling in the Hogan family's favor.[7] The property was then sold, bringing several Hogan descendants a small but certainly welcomed inheritance.

NOTES

The Michael Hogan Family Papers consist of some originals, but mostly copies, of letters, notes and other documents written by, to or relating to Michael Hogan and several of his children and grandchildren dating from 1791 through about 1870. Although the condition of ink and paper in the collection is generally excellent, accurate transcriptions of the sometimes tortured handwriting, inconsistent spelling and poor grammar (sentences often do not begin with capitalized letters or end with periods) have not always been possible. Where words or phrases appearing in the text of this book as quotations from the collection cannot be accurately determined, but the intended meaning seems clear, words or phrases to reflect this meaning have been used. Obvious spelling and grammatical mistakes are corrected, and modern, American spelling usages have been followed, except for a few quaint spellings common at the time, such as *publick* and *compleat.* All editorial additions, corrections, clarifications and comments by the author are in square brackets [ ].

The currencies that appear in this book most frequently are:
- British pound sterling, equivalent then and through World War II to about $5 U.S. Other pounds with differing values, not pounds sterling, were in use in some areas, including some places in the United States even in the early 1800s.
- Indian rupee, worth about 2 shillings or 50 U.S. cents.
- Indian sicca rupee, worth 2 shillings, 3 pence.
- Indian pagoda, a coin worth about 8 shillings or $2 U.S.
- Spanish dollar, an international specie currency of long standing, normally exchangeable at four for one pound sterling and therefore equivalent to about $1.20 U.S.
- Rix dollar (often abbreviated as *Rd*), with subdivisions of six stivers to one skilling and eight skillings to a rix dollar, used at the Cape of Good Hope, denominated as equivalent to 2½ Dutch gulden. In 1797 at the beginning of the first British occupation, one rix dollar was worth about 4 shillings sterling (i.e, one-fifth of a pound or about one U.S. dollar), but its value declined thereafter.
- Chilean dollar, with subdivision of 100 rials. Considered to be equivalent to the U.S. dollar, but exchange transactions usually took place in Spanish silver dollars.
- U.S. dollar, with subdivision of 100 cents, including one-half cents.

No attempt has been made in the text to give equivalent values, except in a few instances where the comparison provides an interesting insight. Although historical price indices are inaccurate and often misleading, multiplying the currency values cited in this book by a factor of fifteen or twenty gives a rough idea of what the same amount might be worth today.

NOTES TO PAGES 5-7

The Bibliography gives full descriptions of primary and secondary works cited more than occasionally in the following Notes, as well as of works providing background not available in standard historical books. Sources cited only occasionally are described in full in the Notes. Citations are usually not given for information in the privately-held Michael Hogan Family Papers (MHFP) or for readily available historical facts.

ABBREVIATIONS USED IN NOTES

AAS	American Antiquarian Society, Worcester, MA
CTG	*Cape Town Gazette and African Advertiser* and
HRA	*Historical Records of Australia*
HRNSW	*Historical Records of New South Wales*
HSP	Historical Society of Pennsylvania, Philadelphia
IRO	India Records Office, British Library, London
KAB	Cape Town Archives Repository, Cape Town
MHFP	Michael Hogan Family Papers, privately held
MHS	Maryland Historical Society, Baltimore, MD
NA	National Archives, Washington, D.C.
NYCA	*New York Commercial Advertiser*
NYHS	New York Historical Society, New York City
PRO	Public Records Office, London
SLNSW	State Library of New South Wales, Sydney

Chapter 1

[1] Details of the secret plan to take territories in Latin America and of the alternative plan to take the Cape of Good Hope are from *Campbell*, vol. 3; *Clowes*, vol. 6; *Alan Frost*, *Harlow*, vol. 1; *Mackesy*; *Rutherford*; L.C.F. Turner, "The Cape of Good Hope and the Anglo-French Rivalry, 1778-1796"; *Historical Studies: Australia and New Zealand* (April 1966), vol. 12; and William B. Wilcox, "The Battle of Porto Praya, 1781," *American Neptune* (1945), 64-78.

[2] *Mackesy*, 373, identifies two such plans. See also *Rutherford*. *Harlow*, 1:105, says that the idea of South Seas conquests originated with Sir Walter Raleigh as far back as 1595.

[3] *Dictionary of National Biography*.

[4] Perhaps not coincidentally, September 29 is St. Michael's Day.

[5] Stonehall was originally built about 1570 by the McClancy (or MacClanchy) family when it was known as Ballynaclough Castle. A Thomas Cullen lived there in 1663. Sir Donough O'Brien of Dromoland (a still partly standing castle near

NOTES TO PAGES 7-10   359

Stonehall), a direct descendant of Brian Boru, acquired the estate sometime after that date from Sir Henry Ingoldsby. He passed it to his son by his second marriage, Henry O'Brien (ca.1680-1724), which family became known as the O'Briens of Stonehall and Stafford. Although the O'Briens apparently retained ownership until modern times, the family did not live there long. (Some O'Briens moved from Stonehall to nearby Cratloe Woods.) After Henry married heiress Sussanah Stafford in 1699, he went to live at her estate, Blatherwyke Park, Northamptonshire, England. Fitzgeralds are recorded as living at Stonehall in 1730 and about 1800 the McMahon family, the last residents before the land was purchased by the Shannon Airport Development Company. Some of the buildings were apparently standing as recently as about 1960 when they were demolished. The ruins are across the local road bordering the prominent Shannon Aerospace Company. The information in this note and the main text about Stonehall, the O'Briens and the Shannon area is based on personal inspection of the Stonehall remains by the author and on James Frost, *The History and Topography of the County Clare* (Dublin, 1843), 403n; Donough O'Brien, *History of the O'Briens from Brian Boroimhe AD.1000 to AD.1945* (London, 1949), 214, 274-7; Grania R. O'Brien, *These My Friends and Forebears: The O'Briens of Dromoland* (Whitegate, Ireland, 1991), 23; *Ordnance Survey of Ireland, 1839*, (plat 51); *Union of Ennis, Valuation of the Several Tenements, County of Clare* (Dublin, 1855), 16; Hugh Weir, *Houses of Clare* (Whitegate, Ireland, 1988), 254; Arthur Young, *A Tour of Ireland in the Years...1776*. (Cambridge, 1925 reprint), 91-94.

[6] The Hogan name appears mostly in Counties Tipperary, Limerick and Clare. Hogan's two brothers, Dennis and Maurice, appear in MHFP and, in Maurice's case, in U.S. census data. Dennis, who may have been married at one time, had four sons, Cornelius, John, Owen and Michael. Maurice married a woman named Mary, also born in 1775. They had two sons, John and William, and a daughter Frances; this is also confirmed by U.S. census data.

[7] Hogan to James Monroe, May 18, 1818, HSP, Joel R. Poinsett Collection.

[8] Samuel Lewis, *A Topographical Dictionary of Ireland* (London, 1837, republished Baltimore, 1984), 2:69.

[9] Quote is from Brian Dinan, *Clare and its People: A Concise History* (Cork, 1987), 85.

[10] *M. A. Lewis*, 152-4.

[11] M.S. Rodney Pasley (ed.), *Private Sea Journals, 1778-1782, Kept by Admiral Sir Thomas Pasley* (London, 1931).

[12] *M. A. Lewis*, 280-1. See also Suzanne J. Stark, *Female Tars: Women Aboard Ship in the Age of Sail* (Annapolis, Maryland, 1996), who attributes the presence of prostitutes on Navy ships in port to the belief of ship commanders that it was better to satisfy the sexual urges of seamen than run the risk that impressed seamen would not return to ship if allowed shore leave. There was apparently a sharp decline in the practice after the Napoleonic Wars when impressment began to be phased out.

[13] William Medows' permanent rank then was Colonel; he became Lieutenant General in October 1793 (*Dictionary of National Biography*).

[14] *Rutherford*, 299n.

[15] The several Johnstone quotes about Pasley and Suffren's intentions are from Johnstone's despatch to Lord Hillsborough, Secretary of State for the Southern Department (of what was soon to become the Foreign Office), which appeared in an extraordinary issue of the *London Gazette* on June 9, 1781, and which is frequently cited in *Rutherford*. Praia, as it is now called, is the capital of independent Cape Verde, perhaps best known as a transit stop for direct flights between the U.S. and South Africa.

[16] Johnstone's report was published in *London Gazette*, October 15, 1781.

[17] *Rutherford*, 301n, states the Colony learned that war had broken out on March 15 and that the British and French squadrons had sailed on May 12. A translation of the journal of a senior officer on the *Middelburg*, which appeared in *Africana Notes and News* 18, no.8 (December 1969), recounts that the five Dutch vessels, which had arrived at Table Bay from the Orient on March 31 on their way to Europe, had been sent to Saldanha Bay on May 16, which was after it was learned that the squadrons had sailed. The author of the journal did not think much of the Governor's decision; nor did Suffren when he arrived on June 21, although the latter did not try to overrule the Governor (*Rutherford*, 302). The likely explanation for sending the kings and princes to Saldanha Bay is therefore that they also were being sent there by the Governor for safekeeping. The journal also mentions that "some convicts" were on the *Middelburg* and were sent ashore on a boat when the British fleet entered the harbor. These were presumably English prisoners. They, as well as the Kings of Ternate and Tidore, are also mentioned in Silas James, *A Narrative of a Voyage to Arabia, India, Etc.* (London, 1797), 36, as follows: "The Dutch at this place are particularly distinguished by their brutality toward prisoners of war. In proof of this, I shall only observe that, in one of their captured ships, they had brought the kings of Ternate and Tidore into distress, similar to that of the two English gentlemen [prisoners on the *Middelburg*]." He then says: "Having rescued these two Asian monarchs, we departed...." James was a sixteen year old sailor on the *Content*, a transport in the fleet; his account of the Porto Praya battle and Saldanha Bay seizures probably drew heavily on Johnstone's published reports in the *London Gazette*.

[18] M. A. Lewis, 318, 330-1.

[19] *Clowes*, 3:359; *Rutherford*, 304.

[20] The *Jupiter's* registers (PRO, ADM/36/8959 & 8960) list Michael Hogan as being on board without interruption from July 1, 1780, until it returned to Deal on July 22, 1783. However, it was common practice to retain names on registers when crewmen were left behind for medical reasons or transferred to other vessels for temporary duty. Hogan probably left the *Jupiter* when it sailed from New York for Boston in mid-September 1782.

[21] The Prince arrived in New York on the *Prince George* on August 24, 1781; transferred to the *Warwick* in spring 1782 for a cruise; was briefly again in New York in November before being transferred to the *Barfleur* which left for Jamaica on November 23; and returned to England in June 1783. Philip Ziegler, *King William IV* (London, 1971), 38-42; Anne Somerset, *The Life and Times of William IV* (London, 1980), 27-31; Percy Hetherington Fitzgerald, *The Life and Times of William IV* (London, 1884) 1:12-21. The only times that the Prince and Hogan could have met would have been November 1782 in New York or during the next six months somewhere in the West Indies.

[22] George Washington to Colonel Mathias Ogden, March 28, 1782, *The Writings of George Washington* (Washington, D.C., 1938) 24:91. The full story is told in Fitzgerald, *ibid.*, 1:12-15.

[23] The quotation is from *Mackesy*, 500, whose book was originally published in 1964. *Parry*, 177, whose work was published seven years later, makes the same point: "The war which began in a leafy village in New England had ended outside a dusty town in South India."

[24] Details of the life of midshipmen are from *M. A. Lewis*.

[25] Lord Charles Cornwallis (1738-1805) was first Vice Treasurer of Ireland 1769-1771, Commander-in-Chief of British forces during the last years of the American Revolution, Governor General of India 1786-1793, and Governor General and Commander-in-Chief of Ireland 1798-1801. Although he fought well for the British in the American Revolution, he disapproved of the British policy which led to the war. According to Franklin & Mary Wickwire, *Cornwallis, the American Adventure* (Boston, 1970), 8 & 39, Cornwallis married for love (not common in those days) and pleaded for the emancipation of Irish Catholics, two factors which may have made him sympathetic to finding a niche for Hogan. Although Irish Catholics were certainly a disadvantaged lot when Hogan was young, their plight was not as bad as it once had been, particularly among those Irish who grew up knowing and speaking English, rather than Gaelic.

[26] Details about Charles O'Hara, his father and Mary Berry are from *Dictionary of National Biography*. It is possible that General O'Hara helped Michael's elder brother, Dennis, obtain a commission as Lieutenant in Ninety-Ninth Regiment of Foot in 1794 or as Adjutant to the Fifty-Fifth (Westmorland) Regiment of Foot in 1797.

[27] The background information in this and the next chapter concerning economics and trade in the East, the East India Company and life in India are from *Aspinall*; *Chatterton*; Sir Evan Cotton, *East Indiamen: The East India Company's Maritime Service* (London, 1949); *Crowhurst*; *Furber*; *Harlow*, vols. 1 & 2; *Keay*; *P. J. Marshall*; *Nightingale*; Parkinson, *Trade in the Eastern Seas* and *Trade Winds*; *Parry*; Philips, *East India Company*; and *Pritchard*.

[28] *M A. Lewis*, 335.

[29] Hogan's listed position on the *Pigot* is in the ship's ledger and pay book (IRO, L/MAR/B/503/0/1 & 2). The claim that he served as executive officer on this vessel and as commanding officer on the *San Antonio* is in notes that his son

William wrote some 40 years later, obviously based on what his father told him. No public reference to the *San Antonio* has been found, which means that it could not have been a Company vessel and was probably engaged in the country trade between India and China. *Chatterton*, 217-8, states that a chief mate had to be 23 years old and have voyaged to India or China in the Company's service as second or third mate, requirements which Hogan did not meet.

[30] The shipyards at Mazagon accommodated the overflow when the Bombay facilities were busy. See Ruttonje Ardeshir Wadia, *The Bombay Dockyard and the Wadia Master Builders* (Bombay, 1955). Although this source does not mention the *Anna*, her name appears in other reference sources as being built at Bombay in 1789-90. The information on Robert Henshaw (1744-1826) is from James Douglas, *Bombay and Western India: A Series of Stray Papers* (London, 1893) 2:17; and *Glimpses of Old Bombay and Western India, with Other Papers* (London, 1900), 220-229. Henshaw may have originally settled in Goa; he was there in 1774 according to Stephen Meredyth Edwardes, *The Rise of Bombay: A Retrospect* (Bombay, 1902), 196.

[31] The Cinderella quote is from *Spear*, 66; the "lived a dull and demoralized life" quote is from *Nightingale*, 14, based on remarks in Maria Graham's *Journal of a Residence in India* (Edinburgh, 1816), cited in *Spear*, 77. Other sources that provided useful background information on Bombay during the late 18th century are the two Douglas books, *ibid.*, and Stephen Meredyth Edwardes, *The Gazetteer of Bombay City and Island* (Bombay, 1909), vol. 1.

[32] He sailed to India on the East India Company ship *Solebay* (IRO, *East India Calendar for 1791*), of which he was then captain (Anthony Farrington, *Catalogue of East India Company Ships' Journals and Logs* (The British Library, 1999), 612.

[33] Boles date of commission as Captain was June 21, 1784 (IRO, *East India Calendar for 1791)*, where he is listed as Burnaby Boles. He later became Colonel and died in England in the early 1800s.

Chapter 2

[1] The descriptions of midshipmen in the British Navy are from *M. A. Lewis*.

[2] MHFP puts the meeting with Cornwallis in late January but the *Crown's* log (PRO, ADM/50/31) shows that the ship did not moor at Bombay until February 25, departing March 25, 1790. Cornwallis was not then an Admiral, as Hogan calls him. Hogan's comment that Cornwallis had broken several of his commanders is borne out by the *Crown's* log. The Lieutenant Moorsom mentioned in Hogan's account was commander of the sloop *Ariel*, one of the ships in Cornwallis's squadron which had left England in February 1789 (*Aspinall*, 201n; *A. Frost*, 147-8). The full text of the last sentence of William's rendition of Hogan's account is: "In a short time, Moorsom was promoted and is now high up in the list of the old Admirals in a place which would have, thus it seems, been filled by my father had not fate doomed him to a warrior's fate and seaman's grave." In this sentence, William changes from quoting his father

to expressing his own thoughts when he transcribed his father's remarks, probably in 1832. The intended meaning of the references to warrior's fate and seaman's grave is unclear; perhaps William meant Michael Hogan fought adversity during his life and would die having only attained the status of ordinary seaman, that is, not an officer.

[3] The quote is from a travel diary written by a Thomas Twining in 1792, the year Hogan first left Calcutta, cited in P. Thankappan Nair, *Calcutta in the 18th Century: Impressions of Travellers* (Calcutta, 1984), 276. The other information about Calcutta is from *P. J. Marshall*, 24-25.

[4] Gillett is called the "eminent shipwright of Calcutta" in a contemporary account. *Hickey* 4:30.

[5] Tonnage of *Netunno* is from PRO, BT/111/1.

[6] Parkinson, *Trade Winds*, 144, 155-156.

[7] The cost is given as 105,000 rupees in *Shipping and Shipbuilding in India, 1736-1839* (IRO, 1995).

[8] *Selections from Calcutta Gazettes...*, 2:73-74. The embargo was revoked a year later on October 29, 1792.

[9] *Spear*, 134, 138.

[10] The original painting dated 1793 signed by Solvyns, which is now in private hands, appears on the cover of Barbara Hall, *A Desperate Set of Villains: The Convicts of the Marquis Cornwallis, Ireland to Botany Bay, 1796*. (Barbara Hall, Australia, 2001). Another version, dated and signed, shows the ship with sails furled; it also is in private hands. Other Solvyns renderings of Bengal boats are in Robert L. Hardgrave, Jr., *Boats of Bengal: Eighteenth Century Portraits by Balthazar Solvyns* (Manohar, New Delhi,2001).

[11] The etchings bear the following inscription: "Published Sept. 1787 by T.F. Harris, N. 3 Seeling's Alley and N. 8 Broad St. London."

[12] According to *Singh*, 9, there were fifteen European agency houses in Calcutta by 1790, most of them British. Perhaps the most prominent was the Fairlie company (in association at one time or another with Ferguson, Reed or Gilmore), closely tied to David Scott in London, and the house with which Hogan did most of his Bengal business for many years.

[13] An indication that this secondary market existed can be found from the fact that in 1791 one private trader brought an accusation that the Calcutta agency houses "had contrived to offer a low rate of exchange [on the China remittance] so that they might be able to lend again to the real [private] traders" at a higher rate. *Singh*, 42-3.

[14] A notice dated November 23, 1791, concerning the China remittance for 1792 appeared in the *Calcutta Gazette* on November 25, as follows (*Selections from Calcutta Gazettes...*, 2:56): "Notice is hereby given that the Governor General in Council has resolved to make a remittance this season to the Hon'ble Company's super-cargoes to China, to an amount not exceeding twenty lakhs of Current

Rupees. The sum is to be advanced here in Promissory Notes, payable according to priority of date, and bearing interest at and after the rate of eight per cent per annum. The payments are to be made into the Canton Treasury, between the 1st of November 1792 and the 31st of January 1793; and the rate of exchange between Current Rupees and Spanish Dollars, at which any person may be desirous of undertaking to make such payment into the Canton Treasury, must be expressed in offers made for this remittance, as well as the amount which any person may be desirous of engaging for, and the securities they would propose for the performance of their engagements.... Sealed proposals for remittance will be received and on Wednesday, the 7th December 1791, the Government will proceed to open all such as may have been received, and determine upon the answers to be communicated to the proposers."

[15] *Harlow* 2:497.

[16] *Harlow* 2:496.

[17] Parkinson, *Trade in the Eastern Seas*, 188; *Furber*, 153-159. Furber conjectures that Robert Charnock may have been related to Job Charnock, one of the founders of British Calcutta a hundred years previously.

[18] See *Popham*, 29-46.

[19] One of these faster ships was the *Anna* which Hogan had helped build in 1790. In 1802, this vessel concluded a voyage from England to India, to China, to India and back to England in just nine months, a voyage that once took over a year. See Parkinson, *Trade in the Eastern Seas*, 364.

[20] Philips, *East India Company*, 106.

[21] *Furber*, 140-1.

[22] P.J. Marshall, 49.

[23] *Furber*, 117.

[24] The notice was published in the *Calcutta Gazette* on February 9, 1792, *Selections from Calcutta Gazettes...*, 2:58.

[25] Cited in Lawrence Freedman, Paul Hayes & Robert O'Neill, eds., *War, Strategy, and International Politics: Essays in Honour of Sir Michael Howard* (Oxford, 1992), 72.

[26] Mary Dorothy George, *London Life in the Eighteenth Century* (London, 1925), 83, states "Covent Gardens acquired its bad reputation as soon as it ceased to be a fashionable district," about 1730. Fanny Hills' residence there is in *Weinreb & Hibbert*.

[27] London characteristics are from *George*, 83, 99-103; quote regarding Limehouse and Bermondsey, 84. The *London Directory for 1799* shows Christopoher Richardson & Son, merchants, at Saw-Mill, Limehouse, or Batson's Coffee House, Cornhill.

[28] The house in Finsbury Square is mentioned in a 1799 letter. Philips, *Correspondence of David Scott* 1:189.

[29] *Weinreb & Hibbert*, 277-8; Sir Walter Besant, *London in the Eighteenth Century* (London, 1902), 374. Finsbury Square was largely destroyed by German bombing during World War II.

[30] *The Times* (London) reported on January 30 that O'Hara had left London for Gibraltar on the preceding day. He sailed from Plymouth on H.M.S. *Assistance* on February 18, two days after the *Netunno* left Deal (*The Times* (London), February 19 & 21).

[31] Hogan was at Ostend on or about January 14, 1793, according to a letter of that date cited in *Hickey* 4:85-90. Since it is confirmed that the *Netunno* sailed from London (on February 16), Hogan probably traveled independently to Ostend beforehand, presumably to work out final details of the ship's voyage with Messrs Robert Charnock & Company or to pick up the new captain.

[32] *The Times* (London), February 16, 1793, shows "remaining at Deal *Il Nutimo*, ____, for India." The February 19 issue shows "came down and sailed [February 17] *Neptune* Scott for Leghorn." The second entry may reflect the way the ship's departure was officially registered with British customs or port authorities. If the Italian name had been given or its destination shown as India, questions might have been raised whether it should be allowed to proceed. The mention of Scott also confirms statements in later Hogan letters that his company was acting as his agent on this voyage, as it would for many years afterwards.

[33] *Hickey* 4:20, 88-90, 98, 105.

[34] Lascars were considered by many ships' officers as more hard working and tractable than European sailors. (Janet J. Ewald, "Crossers of the Sea: Slaves, Freedman, and Other Migrants in the Northwest Indian Ocean, c. 1750-1914", *The American Historical Review*, Feb. 2000, page 76.) They became conspicuous in London beginning about 1783 because they were often discharged there and allowed to sink into desperate conditions. Their plight eventually attracted public attention about 1814. See *George*, 138.

[35] *Calcutta Gazette*, August 8, 1793, in *Selections from Calcutta Gazettes...*, 2:557-563.

[36] Notice of the saltpeter embargo appeared in the *Calcutta Gazette* on June 13, 1793. *Selections from Calcutta Gazettes...*, 2:102-103.

[37] The names shown of merchant houses in India are those that appear most frequently in both the MHFP and *Selections from Calcutta Gazettes...*, vol. 2; *Nightingale*; Parkinson, *Trade in the Eastern Seas*; *Pritchard*; or *Singh*.

[38] Ships could sail to or from Bombay at any time because its good harbor provided protection from storms. Madras was an undesirable port during any season because there was neither a protective harbor nor dock facilities. See *Crowhurst*.

[39] A notice requiring such port clearances was published in the *Calcutta Gazette* on August 22, 1793, while Hogan was in Calcutta. *Selections from Calcutta Gazettes...*, 2:110.

[40] The letter in which the sealed packet is mentioned contains a note added by Hogan in red ink in 1831-33 that the packet included Hogan's will. A will written in 1794, before his family was fully formed, was presumably outdated at his death, which may explain why he died intestate.

[41] The Phoenix Insurance Society had announced in the *Calcutta Gazette* on July 18, 1793, that it had opened for business, offering what appears to be standard life insurance. *Selections from Calcutta Gazettes...*, 2:555-557. Whether this was the *lottery tontine* in which Hogan participated is unknown.

[42] According to *The Times* (London), June 3, 1794, Cornwallis sailed from England for Ostend on June 1.

[43] *Nightingale*, 54.

[44] Details about Scott are from Philips, *East India Company* and *Correspondence of David Scott*, the quotations in his letters from the latter.

[45] Results of loss of monopoly are from *Chatterton*, 242.

[46] Philips, who has delved deeply into Scott's career in his *East India Company* and *Correspondence of David Scott*, had no doubt that Scott, as well as Fairlie, was involved in the illicit trade (see particularly the former work, 99). Other information about Scott's involvement is from *Furber*, 220-4, and *Nightingale*.

[47] *Nightingale*, 158.

[48] Scott corresponded regularly with Louis Barretto (e.g., Philips' *Correspondence of David Scott* 1:123, 178, 199, 201.

[49] Dady Rustomji Banaji, *Slavery in British India* (Bombay, 1944), 3-5, 11-12, 199, 202; Ann M. Pescatello, "The African Presence in Portuguese India," *Journal of Asian History* 11 (1977), 26-48.

[50] Increased demand for silk is from Philips, *East India Company*, 105. An 1825 manual about the Orient trade notes that: "The distance of India is too great to allow speculation [for raw silk] upon contingencies at home [England]"; and that "the greatest care is requisite in packing [Bengal raw silk] for the voyage; if loosely packed, the outside skeins will rub against each other, and the silk will be cut as if by a knife. Silk in this state is of no value whatever." William Milburn, *Oriental Commerce* (London, 1825), 303.

[51] The identity of Mrs. Harwand is unknown. Based on the fact that Hogan said she came from Amiens in France, which is not far from Ostend, and similarity with the name of the British Consul at Ostend (given in *The Times* (London) as Harwald), she might have been his wife.

[52] Registry of *Marquis Cornwallis* is recorded in PRO, BT/111/1.

Chapter 3

[1] There have been a number of recent books about the settlement of Australia, notably *Hughes*, which mentions the *Marquis Cornwallis*, though not the name of its captain. Views differ among historians on the reasons behind the British

policy of transporting convicts to Australia. *Hughes* generally accepts the social undesirability argument, while *A. Frost* and *Harlow* favor the strategic policy viewpoint.

[2] The £10,000 for transport is from PRO, T.I/799 and ADM/108/148. Hogan was paid £32 for each convict carried, in addition to other costs.

[3] William Richardson is shown as ship's "master" in Transport Board accounting of the ship's voyage to New South Wales (PRO, ADM/108/148/PFN/311 and TI/799). He is shown in several records as commander when the ship left New South Wales on its return voyage, but became ill and left the vessel in Calcutta, at which point a John Roberts is shown as commander and Michael Hogan as purser (IRO, L/MAR/B/336A). William is also shown in the charterparty agreement as "master" for the ship's voyage carrying cattle to New South Wales in 1798, even though someone else was clearly captain (see next chapter). As previously noted, William Richardson was shown as master when the *Marquis Cornwallis* was registered in 1794. Although it is impossible to know for certain, there are several possible explanations of the seeming confusion. First, Hogan acted as captain (and is identified as such in several accounts) throughout the New South Wales voyage and return. Second, William Richardson, Sr., may have insisted that he retain legal title to the ship in lieu of Hogan's paying off his debt to him and that William, Jr., be shown as "commander." Writing to Scott from Calcutta on the return voyage in November 1796, Hogan said: "Capt. Richardson will not command her home, but that will make no difference in the [insurance] policy." In a letter to his partner William Fairlie in Calcutta dated March 23, 1795, Scott refers to a "recommending letter in favor of Captain Richardson of the 19th February" (Philip's *Correspondence of David Scott* 1:19). The recommending letter could have come from Hogan or William, Sr.

[4] PRO, ADM/1/4164.

[5] *The Times* (London), August 20, 1795. It is unclear whether the six Defenders mentioned in this article were the same as the nine additional convicts elsewhere reported as boarding at the last minute.

[6] Details regarding the mutiny at sea, which is not mentioned in MHFP, are from *HRA*, series 1, 1:653-661; *HRNSW*, 3:4-5, 102-111; Charles Bateson, *The Convict Ships, 1787-1868* (Sydney, 1959); Con Costello, *Botany Bay* (Dublin, 1987). The incident of Bryan O'Donald at Cork is from MHFP.

[7] Theal, *Records* 1:22; *Keith Papers* 1:210.

[8] Theal, *Records* 1:28; *Keith Papers* 1:213.

[9] For British capture of Cape of Good Hope and the question of its future, see Theal, *History of South Africa*, vol. 1; Turner, "The Cape of Good Hope and the Anglo-French Rivalry, 1778-1796"; *Keith Papers*, 1:215-238; *Cambridge History of the British Empire*, 2:57-59.

[10] *Keith Papers* 1:229.

[11] Elphinstone and Clarke had left the Cape on November 15 bound for India, not Batavia, where Elphinstone was to take the Dutch colony of Ceylon but found this already nearly done by British forces stationed in India. Theal, *Records* 1:265; Parkinson, *War in the Eastern Seas...*, 83-85.

[12] Elphinstone to Dundas, October 10, 1795, Theal, *Records* 1:185.

[13] Theal, *Records* 1:238.

[14] For example, Theal, *Records* 1:237, 254-5, 283-5, 333-7.

[15] War Office to Craig, June 8, 1796, Theal, *Records* 1:385; *Keith Papers* 1:386.

[16] The Army and Navy also argued over housing. Theal, *Records* 1:286-8, 385.

[17] A.G.L. Shaw, *Convicts and the Colonies: A Study of Penal Transportation from Great Britain and Ireland to Australia and Other Parts of the British Empire* (London, 1966), 117.

[18] Surgeon's Certificate of Victualling is from *HRNSW* 3:34; also PRO, CO/201/13. A more generous Certificate, also in *HRNSW* 3:33-34, was executed on the same day by Ensign John Brabyn of the New South Wales Corps. He reported that the troops "had fresh provisions served them several days during the passage, and every other indulgence shown them by the said Mr. Hogan, such as giving the sick tea and sugar and many little comforts not provided by Government, and that I never knew Mr. Hogan to use a soldier ill, or that he suffered an officer, seaman, or other person to do so."

[19] *HRA*, series 1, 1:556.

[20] Collins and Balmain to Hunter, April 30, 1796, *HRA*, series 1, 1:653.

[21] Hunter to Duke of Portland, May 2, 1796, *HRA*, series 1, 1:569.

[22] *HRA*, series 1, 1:653.

[23] Portland to Hunter, August 30, 1797, *HRNSW*, 3:291n.

[24] David Collins, *An Account of the English Colony in New South Wales*, (London, 1798 & 1802, reprint edition, Sydney, 1975), 1:398.

[25] Cornwallis Estate (or plain Cornwallis) is shown on maps in Bobbie Hardy, *Early Hawkesbury Settlers*, (Kenthurst, Australia, 1985) and Windsor Municipal Council, *Historic Hawkesbury* (5th edition, 1980). Cornwallis Road now connects the area with the town of Windsor, which received its name in 1810. According to D.G. Bowd, *Municipality of Windsor: Origin of Names of Streets, Parks and Features*, (Windsor, 1973), Cornwallis Road was named after Lord Cornwallis of Yorktown fame, which seems correct, but it was Hogan who imported the name. Brabyn Street in Windsor was named after the Ensign John Brabyn (later a captain) who commanded the military contingent on the *Marquis Cornwallis*. The author has not found Rowan Farm named in any source other than MHFP.

[26] Hunter to King, April 30, 1796, *HRA*, series 1, 1:565-6.

[27] The most authoritative source about the tenants and ownership of Cornwallis is the record of a law suit brought by Hogan heirs in 1856 concerning the property. Philip Tully and John Riley remained tenants until their deaths in

1835 and 1847, respectfully. William Cox acquired a lease to the property from Michael Hogan in 1832. Cox died in 1837, but John and Mary Hand and Alfred Norris continued in possession until the Hogan family legal challenge was decided in the family favor in 1861. (Edmund Fitz Moore, *Reports of Cases Heard and Determined by the Judicial Committee and the Lords of Her Majesty's Most Honorable Privy Council*, 14 (London, 1861):310-328.) Bobbie Hardy, *Early Hawkesbury Settlers*, (Kenthurst, Australia, 1985), lists the following as the original tenants from the *Marquis Cornwallis*: Connolly, Dennis McCarty, Patrick Partland, John Riley , Philip Tully. Other later tenants mentioned are: Thomas Biggers (ca. 1806), William & Jane Ezzy (1797-1827?), Forrester (ca. 1820), Patrick Hand (ca. 1803-10) and son John Hand (1830?-1861).

[28] King to Earl Camden, April 30, 1805, *HRA*, series 1, 5:10, 453. Other references to the rent of Cornwallis Farm are in *HRA*, series 1, 4:80, 90, 307, 480, 496, 613.

[29] Grant of six acre plot to Hogan is confirmed in Australian land grant records, 1788-1809, Mitchell Library, Ref. 4/Q333.16/3.

[30] Bennelong Point was named after an Australian tribesman. He was the first native to learn English, sent to England in 1792 where he was feted as a Noble Savage, and returned in 1795 neither English nor native. *Hughes*, 11n.

[31] Hogan's plan to return to Port Jackson is mentioned in a June 8, 1796, letter from William Neate Chapman, Storekeeper at Phillipsburg, Norfolk Island, to his mother (SLNSW, A1974 (CY866)). There are also allusions to returning in letters written by Hogan in the 1820s (MHFP).

[32] The existence of Mary Ryan Hogan and her parentage came to the author's attention, through a series of fortuitous circumstances, from her great great great granddaughter, Janine Bell, who lives in Mackay, Australia. Michael Hogan's paternity is in the register of St. John's Parramatta, Church of England, showing that Mary, daughter of "Michl. Hogan" and Ann Ryan, born May 1, 1796, was baptized March 24, 1799, by the Reverend Samuel Marsden (*New South Wales Register of Births, Deaths and Marriages*, 242, vol: 148).

[33] Collins' "family" is from Mollie Gillen, *The Founders of Australia: A Biographical Dictionary of the Third Fleet*, (Sydney, 1989), 397; information on his voyage to England from *Australian Dictionary of Biography, 1788-1850*, (Melbourne, 1966). Hogan received Collins' letter at Cape Town in April 1797 on his return voyage to England. Collins arrived in London in June, in time to meet Hogan before he left for the Cape of Good Hope in November, but there is no record of nor reference to this possibility.

[34] Letter dated February 9, 1797, PRO, ADM/108/148.

[35] M. H. Ellis, *John Macarthur*, (Sydney, 1955), 139; Lennard Beckel, *Australia's First Lady: The Story of Elizabeth Macarthur*, (Sydney, 1991), 58.

[36] Sarah Whitelam, her husband John Coen Walsh and their three sons. Siân Rees, *The Floating Brothel: The Extraordinary True Story of an Eighteenth-Century Ship and Its Cargo of Female Convicts* (New York, 2002), 212.

37 Collins to King, May 14, 1796, SLNSW, CY 891 (C187).

38 Supplies had also been brought to Norfolk Island on April 4, 1796, on H.M.S. *Supply*. King to Secretary of Treasury, June 9, 1796 (SLNSW, CY891 (C187)), who pointedly contrasted the Island's situation with the "abundant supplies that have arrived at Port Jackson."

39 Trading wages and future harvests for spirits are from Daniel Paine, *The Journal of Daniel Paine, 1794–1796* (Sydney, 1983), xvi.

40 Prices paid for goods and King's letter to Treasury are in SLNSW, CY891 (c187).

41 Daniel Paine, *The Journal of Daniel Paine, 1794–1796* (Sydney, 1983), xvi.

42 King to Duke of Portland, June 8, 1796, SLNSW, CY891 (C187), 344.

43 The amount of clothing imported and Chapman's commission rates are from a June 8, 1796, letter that Chapman wrote to this mother in England in which, among things, Chapman saw a great future for himself because of his appointment as sales agent by Hogan whom he expected to return to New South Wales "to reside there." (SLNSW, CY 866 (A1974), 48-51). However, John Macarthur later told Hogan in an October 28, 1798, letter: "You inquire whether I have ever heard from Captain Chapman any thing respecting your Norfolk Island speculation. He came over here a few months since in a wretched boat built at Norfolk Island commissioned by Townson to inquire what the Devil we were doing here, that we neither sent them news or supplies. They were most shamefully neglected, it is true, but I will not say anything of politics in this letter. Mr. Chapman does not speak to me on the subject of your joint concerns and I did not feel myself at liberty to begin it with him. I have however reason to think from report that he has remitted on your account the proceeds of that business." (MHFP).

44 Margin note May 1796 from Hunter to King in Collins to King letter, May 14, 1796, SLNSW, CY891 (c187).

45 SLNSW, CY891 (c187).

46 SLNSW, A81 (FM4/1752).

47 SLNSW, CY891 (c187).

48 Marnie Bassett, *The Governor's Lady: Mrs. Philip Gidley King*, (Oxford, 1956), 114-7. King's illegitimate sons are not mentioned in a biography written by King descendants (Jonathan & John King, *Philip Gidley King: A Biography of the Third Governor of New South Wales*, Methuen, Australia, 1981).

49 The tracks taken by *Marquis Cornwallis* are marked on three maritime charts, now in MHFP, which Hogan probably obtained while in Sydney. The shortest route through Endeavour (now Torres) Strait between Guinea and the Australian continent was the most dangerous to navigate in the 18th century.

50 Parkinson, *War in the Eastern Seas...*, 94-95, 100-101.

[51] *Register of Ships* establishes that *Fort William* sailed from England on July 9, 1795, on an Orient voyage, returning December 19, 1797. Its master is shown as Captain Simson, not Simpson as in MHFP; the correct spelling seems to be Simson. *Europa* sailed from England May 17, 1796, and returned February 4, 1798; its captain was Charles Jones.

[52] The 1796 struggle with the East India Company is reported in Philips, *East India Company*, 86-87.

[53] SLNSW, CY3005/335-340.

[54] *Clowes* 4:502-503; Parkinson, *War in the Eastern Seas...*, 101-106. Sercey was finally driven from the East Indies by a Captain Charles Lennox in the Straits of Malacca who in January 1797 bluffed Sercey into believing that the poorly armed British East India Company vessels Lennox was escorting were large British Navy warships (*ibid.*, 106). Hogan's wish that "Sir George" [King George III] would take Batavia was not fulfilled until 1811, although there were tentative plans to do so as early as 1797.

[55] *Calcutta Gazette*, December 29, 1796. *Selections from Calcutta Gazettes ...*, 2:459-460. One of the captured British schooners was the *Cornwallis*, no relation to Hogan's *Marquis Cornwallis*. Previously in January 1796, the famous French corsair captain, Robert Surcouf, had captured two British merchant ships in the Bay of Bengal under similar circumstances (*Austen*, 78-79).

[56] Details about the voyage from Calcutta to England, including the names of crew and passengers, are in IRO/MAR/B/336A.

[57] Parkinson, *War in the Eastern Seas...*, 85-87.

[58] Edward Macarthur's destination is in MHFP; Norfolk King's in Marnie Bassett, *The Governors's Lady: Mrs. Philip Gidley King*, (Oxford, 1956), 114.

[59] *The Times* (London), July 24 & 25, 1797.

[60] Payments in specie were not resumed for twenty-four years, well after the Napoleonic Wars, during which time Britain did not succumb to financial ruin, as advocates of specie-based currency insisted would happen.

[61] *VOC* stood for Vereenigde Oostindische Compagnie. The company was formally dissolved in 1795.

[62] *Cambridge History of the British Empire*, 8:179-180. This system essentially paralleled that in effect under Dutch rule.

[63] Alexander Farquhar, who was soon thereafter appointed Navy Victualler at the Cape, was the intermediary who delivered Scott's letters to the Dutch authorities and apparently received their replies in June 1795. Theal, *Records* 1:45, 58.

[64] A scribbled note of William Hogan in MHFP reads: "1794: Sittingbourne, an afternoon with William Pitt and what of it." Two other notes are: "1794, Sittingbourne, Kent" and "Again in London in June [1794]. The meeting at Sittingbourne." Sittingbourne is a town southeast of London. William Hogan probably wrote these notes in 1831-33 when his father, then in his closing years, was recounting his life and career. Of course, Hogan may only have been trying

to impress his son by telling him that he attended a social occasion at Sittingbourne at which Pitt was present; hence William's "and what of it" comment. The author has been unable to verify any meeting that Pitt attended at Sittingbourne during the times in question.

[65] Letter of introduction from William Huskisson, London, to Macartney, October 31, 1797, University of the Witatersrand Library, Gubbins Collection of Africana, Earl of Macartney Papers, which contain no other similar letters of introduction. The clerk mentioned, Peter Thomas Richardson, was probably a son of Peter Richardson, a brother-in-law of Michael Hogan and thus a nephew, but his name does not appear in MHFP.

[66] The *London Directory for 1799* lists Clealand, White & Company, merchants, at 33 Finsbury Square.

[67] *The Times* (London), August 15, 1797, shows only one stock, listed as "3 per c. Red" having a low price of 52 the day before.

[68] Clive Emsley, *British Society and the French Wars, 1793-1815* (Totawa, New Jersey, 1979), 57-58.

[69] PRO, ADM/108/148.

[70] Hogan to Duke of Portland, September 23, 1797, *HRNSW* 3:299-300.

[71] *HRNSW* 3:300. King to Secretary of Treasury, July 7, 1800, states the price paid was £37, although Hogan originally offered them at £35 a head (*HRA*, series 1, 2:524).

[72] *Harbinger* was built in Quebec, commissioned on July 24, 1797 (*HRNSW* 5:469) and registered in London on October 16, 1797 (PRO, BT/111/1).

[73] Details regarding the convoy are from MHFP and *The Times* (London), November 8, 1797.

[74] Scott's acquaintanceship with Ross is based on the fact that Ross was one of the two recipients (Scott was the other) of the letters that the Dutch authorities at the Cape sent in reply to Scott in June 1795 (Theal, *Records* 1:45), and on a Scott to Ross letter of May 1, 1796, which also refers to Charnock supplying transports for the Cape (Philips, *Correspondence of David Scott* 1:69).

[75] Christian had sailed from Portsmouth on *La Virginie* several days after Hogan left that port on the *Anna* (Theal, *Records* 2:201; *The Times* (London), November 22, 1797). It was apparently while they were both at Portsmouth that Christian gave his "promise" to Hogan. Christian arrived at the Cape on January 28, 1798, took over command of the White Fleet in April and died in November. He gave Hogan a silver gravy boat engraved with his family's coat of arms which is still in the possession of a Hogan descendant.

Chapter 4

[1] *Arkin*, 201.

[2] Alan Frederick Hattersley, *An Illustrated Social History of South Africa* (Cape Town, 1973), 62.

[3] John Turnbull, *A Voyage Round the World in the Years 1800, 1801, 1802, 1803, and 1804* (London, 1813, 2nd edition), 62.

[4] *Ibid.*, 62

[5] The unidentified coffee house established after the arrival of the British is from *Laidler*, 116; the one called Commercial Coffee House is named frequently in *CTG* during 1800 and 1801. Sociological background about Cape Town and its residents, not separately noted, is from Trewhella Cameron & S.B. Spies, *An Illustrated History of South Africa* (Johannesburg, 1991), 61-62, 75-78.

[6] John Pringle brought the first thoroughbred mare to the Colony with the occupying forces inn 1795 and the Turf Club was established in June 1796 by the 34th Regiment (Roger Longrigg, *The History of Horse Racing* (New York, 1972), 249). *CTG* October 25, 1800, lists the spring races in1800 which featured three days of racing, with typical purses, including a Ladies' Purse, of 100 pagodas. Most of the horse owners were British owners and officials.

[7] See, for example, *CTG*, September 20, 1800.

[8] *Laidler*, 204.

[9] A survey of advertisements (other than those involving real property, estates and government transactions) in the first sixty issued of *CTG* from August 16, 1800, to October 3, 1801, shows the following frequencies: Walker & Robertson—51; Hogan—31; Bray & Venables—27; Thomas Haines—23; Strombom—22. The number of advertisements of all Dutch (and German) merchants and individuals taken together was much higher than of all British merchants, but the frequency per individual was much lower. The fact that Walker & Robertson lead the tabulation does not necessarily mean they were the most important merchants since these partners owned the newspaper. Haines was declared insolvent in 1802, and hence is not listed in the text. Alexander Farquhar, who was also victualing agent for the British Navy, died on September24, 1800 (*CTG*, September 27, 1800), The quote about commercial and financial connections is from *Elphick & Giliomee*, 328, who list only Tennant, Hogan and Murray as the British traders.

[10] *Freund*, 85.

[11] Macartney to Henry Dundas, July 10, 1797, Theal, *Records* 2:118.

[12] Macartney to Henry Dundas, November 26 & 27, 1797, Theal, *Records* 2:205-6.

[13] War Office to Macartney, January 26, 1798, Theal, *Records* 2:226-7.

[14] Theal, *Records* 2:283-4.

[15] Macartney reported by letter to Henry Dundas on September 18, 1798, that commercial intercourse had progressed so much that the silver dollar was then at a par with the paper money exchange rate and that merchants were beginning to speculate thereon. Theal, *Records* 2:286.

16 See *Arkin* for an analysis of the role played by the East India Company. The quote is *ibid.*, 205.

17 Eric Rosenthal, *Cape Directory, 1800* (Cape Town, 1969).

18 Hogan's properties are described in KAB, A/2151 and J/37.

19 Anne Barnard in a letter to Henry Dundas of February 17, 1801, cited in *Fairbridge*, wrote: "Let me tell you a little news of your friends here. Your adorer Mrs. Hippisely has given the world another little one, as has...Mrs. Hogan...." John, however, died at least two months earlier sometime between November 7 and December 5, 1800.

20 KAB, BO/ 113.

21 Hunter's comments and the 1800 decision to breed cattle are in *HRA*, series 1, vol.2.

22 KAB, BO/112. *La Union* was captured in Montevideo on February 19, 1798, and brought to the Cape Colony by the *Indispensable* (Macartney to Henry Dundas, May 1, 1798, Theal, *Records* 2:251).

23 KAB, BO/115. Hogan advertized the sale of a brig called the *William* in the *CTG* on October 25, 1800, but it was reported in the *CTG* of November 29, 1800, as having been "totally wrecked on Robben Island." However, Hogan offered in *CTG* of August 29, 1801, freight to London or Surinam on a ship named *William* (Captain Colborne), the vessel having arrived from England on the 26th (*CTG*, September 26, 1801). Whether these are all the same vessel or different ones is unknown.

24 Macarthur, in a October 28, 1798, letter to Hogan, said he would not have joined in the complaints against John Cameron, Captain of the *Barwell*, over his prices had Cameron not added insult to injury by telling the complainants: "You do not seem to like it; with this I will accommodate you and what you now do not approve of at two pounds, you shall hereafter pay fifty shillings (£2½) for."

25 Timber approval in Dundas to Hogan, December 20, 1798, Theal, *Records* 2:315. The permission was conditioned: "provided...no piece goods or manufactures of India...are to be put on board [in India]." This prohibition was to protect the East India Company's monopoly on trade to the East. Pringle's report to the East India Company in London, January 24, 1799, is in IRO, G/9/6. Barnard's January 25, 1799, letter in *Fairbridge*, 87.

26 *Freund*, 40-48

27 Data on slaves at the Cape are from *Elphick & Giliomee*, 120-121 & 337-338; Nigel Worden, *Slavery in Dutch South Africa* (Cambridge, 1985), 6.

28 James Duffy, *Portuguese Africa* (Cambridge, MA, 1961), 145-147; *Haight*, 86-91, 145-149. According to latter, there was also a substantial export of slaves from Mozambique to Île de France in French ships. *Hamm*, 192-199, records American ship *Don Galvos* (Captain Gray of Newport) engaged in this trade in 1793-4.

29   Hogan and Tennant probably preferred to import their slaves from Mozambique because they could be procured there more cheaply than from the much more competitive West Coast markets. A contemporary noted that, "in the long, cold and stormy passage around the Cape of Good Hope, many more of the slaves died, than even in the passage from the coast of Guinea to the West Indies; yet their cheapness at Mozambique fully compensated for their increased mortality." *Donnan* 2:618n. The Portuguese difficulty in obtaining goods to trade for slaves is noted in *ibid.*, xviii.

30   Craig to Henry Dundas, January 14, 1797, Theal, *Records* 2:39-40.

31   Theal, *Records* 1:272.

32   Burgher Senate to Dundas, February 25, 1799, Theal, *Records* 2:372-4. According to this letter, the two Burger Senate requests to Macartney were dated November 27, 1797, and January 30, 1798, and Macartney's two rejections November 2, 1797 [*sic*] and February 10, 1798.

33   The number 605 is in *Elphick & Gilomee*, 120. In a January 14, 1797, letter to Henry Dundas, General Craig stated that no slaves had been imported since 1793, in consequence of which he had allowed a Portuguese vessel from Mozambique to land and sell 350 slaves from which 100,000 rix dollars were collected (Theal, *Records* 2:39-40). There is a subsequent reference in *ibid.*, 2:206, to H.M.S. *Crescent* bringing in a Spanish brig (possibly the *Ascension*) on November 16, 1797, with an unspecified number of slaves from Mozambique.

34   Tennant's background and reputation are in Theal, *Records*, vol.3, and Philip, *British Residents*, 416-417.

35   Details of Trail's career are principally from Michael Flynn, *The Second Fleet; Britain's Grim Convict Armada of 1790*, Sydney, 1993. The quote about him is from a Anne Barnard letter of July 10, 1797, cited in Philip, *British Residents*. His departure from the Cape Colony is also noted in a Pringle letter of May 18, 1799, in IRO, G/9/6.

36   Tennant to Macartney, March 20, 1798, questions of same date by Macartney, Tennant's replies March 21, University of the Witatersrand Library, Gubbins Collection of Africana, Earl of Macartney Papers.

37   Macartney's original authorization of May 22, 1798, is in KAB, BO/93; Hogan & Tennant's reply to Hercules Ross of May 30 in KAB, BO/90.

38   *Fairbridge*, 76.

39   Admiral Pringle to Admiralty, January 24, 1797, Theal, *Records* 2 :48, editor's summary of enclosures. In his summary of events (Theal, 5:29), he refers to an incident in which, after slaves from Mozambique were landed from a Portuguese vessel, it had been found out that the French had a scheme to send ships carrying slaves from Mozambique, but falsely flying Portuguese or Danish colors, into Table Bay pretending to be bound for Brazil and in distress. Using the plea of distress, the slaves would be allowed to be sold; grain was then purchased to supply Île de France. Theal presumably based this on Pringle's above-cited letter. *Fairbridge*, 173n, cites the same incident.

[40] Questions of Macartney to Tennant, March 20, 1798, University of the Witatersrand Library, Gubbins Collection of Africana, Earl of Macartney Papers.

[41] Theal, *Records* 2:372-4.

[42] Dundas to Messrs Hogan & Tennant, March 2, 1799, KAB, BO/153; Theal, *Records* 2:377. Hogan & Tennant had to clarify the terms of the permission in a March 5 letter to Dundas (KAB, BO/90; Theal, *Records* 2:378-9).

[43] Dundas to Henry Dundas, April 6, 1799, Theal, *Records* 2:416-7; PRO, CO/49.

[44] Hogan & Tennant to Dundas, March 5, 1799, Theal, *Records* 2:378.

[45] Dundas to Hogan, June 14, 1799, KAB, BO/153.

[46] The *Collector* incident is described in detail in the Report of the Commission Appointed to Investigate Certain Charges Against Sir George Yonge, reprinted in Theal, *Records* 4:221-273, and various documents in KAB, VAC/1 & BO/90.

[47] The evidence of their early relationship is a March 26, 1798, record of a power of attorney executed by Smart, Captain of the *Bombay Castle*, authorizing Hogan to act on his behalf (KAB, NCD 1/12, no. 660). A Pringle letter of May 19, 1798, also refers to him as commander of the *Bombay Castle* (IRO, G/9/1).

[48] The 48 slaves from *La Rose* were sold on December 19, 1799, for 21,979 rix dollars, an average of 458 each (PRO, HCA/49/31/8).

[49] The practice of privateering was finally prohibited by European powers by the 1856 Declaration of Paris following the Crimean War. Although the U. S. did not formally adhere to this provision, it did so in practice.

[50] *Harriet's* letters of marque are in KAB, BO/92, and her departure from the Cape is in KAB, BO/115.

[51] An embargo on Danish, as well as Russian and Swedish, ships from using ports in the Cape Colony, accompanied by instructions to British Navy ships to bring in all such vessels, was announced in *CTG*, April 25, 1801, more than a year and a half after the *Holger Danske* was seized; moreover, the notice did not authorize private seizure of Danish vessels. (Hogan and White could also not have known of British Orders in Council, one issued June 4, 1800, and another on January 28, 1801, the latter noticed in *CTG* on May 2, providing that detained goods from Russian, Danish or Swedish ships not belonging to subjects of these countries were to be restored to the owners.)

[52] Illicit trade by Danes and Americans is noted in *Arkin*, 200. *Haight*, 146, and Parkinson, *War in the Eastern Seas*..., 18, 46-47, record the lure of low prices at Île de France. The American consul at Île de France is from *Smith*, 93, and a full listing of American ships calling there 1786-1810 is in Auguste Touissant, *Early American Trade with Mauritius* (Port Louis, Mauritius, 1954).

[53] Seizure of the *Christianus Septimus* and sale of its cargo are in Theal, *Records*, vols. 2 & 3; IRO, G/9/1 & 6; *Arkin*, 202n. Tennant was agent for the supercargo on the ship when he sold the cargo at auction in April 1800, the cargo then being exported to England on the *Young Nicholas*. The *Christianus*

Septimus was apparently released because it is recorded as having arrived again at the Cape Colony on December 25, 1799, from Copenhagen (Theal, *Records*, vol.3). Hogan purchased the hull of the ship on August 3, 1800, for 3,975 rix dollars (*CTG*, August 16, 1800). He had previously on March 28 purchased a one-third share in the ship from F.C. Loos (possibly Casper Loos) of Cape Town for 3,500 rix dollars to increase his share to two-thirds (MHFP). "Teak pieces and planks lately broken off from the ship *Christianus Septimus*" were advertised for sale at Simon's Bay on October 4 (*CTG*, October 4, 1800). A ship called *Christianus Septimus* was subsequently reported as having been detained at the Cape on arrival from Tranquebar by H.M.S. *Rattlesnake* in 1801 (Theal, *Records*, vol.4; *CTG*, September 26, 1801). Whether this was the same ship or the record is incomplete or incorrect is unknown.

[54] The intercepted letter is in University of the Witatersrand Library, Gubbins Collection of Africana, Earl of Macartney Papers.

[55] Cited in *Furber*, 111.

[56] An August 27, 1799, letter from the War Office to Dundas answered some of the points Dundas had earlier raised and said the other issues (i.e., including the slave question) had been laid before the King. Theal, *Records* 2:477. There is no further mention of the matter in Theal.

[57] Anne Barnard in her *Cape Diaries*, 2:230, called Yonge "a twaddling old fool." Sir George Yonge (1731-1812), from Honiton in Devon, sat in the House of Commons 1754-1761 and 1763-1796 and was a lord of the Admiralty 1776-1770, secretary of war 1782-1794 and master of the Mint 1794-1799. No biography about him apparently exists. Residents of Toronto, Canada, will know his name from Yonge Street in their city, originally laid out in 1794.

[58] All references and quotations concerning Hogan's involvement with Yonge, Blake, Cockburn and others in obtaining preferential treatment in the slave business that are attributable to Hogan are taken from "Communications made to the Secret Committee at the Cape of Good Hope relative to Sir George Yonge," previously noted.

[59] Anne Barnard was told that Mrs. Blake was an in-law of Yonge, not his niece, *Diaries*, 2:165.

[60] Proclamation of February 1, 1800, Theal, *Records* 3:32-33.

[61] Yonge appointed Cockburn Deputy Barrack-Master General on December 31, 1799, and promoted him to Lieutenant Colonel on March 29, 2000. Barnard *Diaries*, 1-341.

[62] Yonge's February 15, 1800, letter is in KAB, VAC/1.

[63] Barnard *Diaries*, 1:71.

[64] Mrs. King's diary is in SLNSW. The author is indebted to Mrs Dee Nash for the extract. Mrs. King's visit to Cape Town (but not the reference to Hogan) is described in Marnie Bassett, *The Governor's Lady: Mrs. Philip Gidley King* (Oxford, 1956), 48-51.

[65] Barnard *Diaries*, 2:46, 49.

[66] KAB, BO/114 & BO/153.

[67] *Arkin*, 202.

[68] IRO, G/9/6.

[69] Complaint of Royal Navy Captains was dated March 7, 1800; Green replied on March 8. Theal, *Records* 3:79; *Fairbridge*, 175.

[70] Barnard *Diaries*, 2:60, 63-64, 95.

[71] Theal, *Records* 2:237.

[72] KAB, BO/90.

[73] Yonge to Henry Dundas, March 29, 1800, Theal, *Records* 3:93.

[74] The 250 slaves on *L'Auguste* is from PRO, HCA/49.

[75] Barnard *Diaries*, 2:94-95.

[76] Barnard *Diaries*, 2:101-103. Because it is often not clear whether particular events take place on the day recorded or previously, the exact chronology of Andrew Barnard's involvement concerning *Collector* up to April 15 is uncertain.

[77] Theal, *Records* 3:121-2.

[78] Hogan's intercession with Yonge over the *Collector* incident is in KAB, BO/116. There is an inference that Justice John Holland of the Vice Court of Admiralty may have tried to assist Hogan's defense. Anne Barnard recorded on April 18, while the court inquiry was underway, that she observed Hogan, Holland and several others in "busy consultation," with "anxiety" on Hogan's face. Barnard *Diaries*, 2:107.

[79] Barnard *Dairies*, 2:123-125.

[80] Barnard *Diaries*, 1:152-153, 282.

[81] Barnard *Diaries*, 2:280.

[82] *CTG* December 20, 1800, which also reported that the 82 slaves on board the *St. Josea DeIndiana* were bound for Lisbon.

[83] The quote about Duckitt is from *CTG*, August 23, 1800; his date of arrival (September 11, 1800) is from *CTG*, September 27, 1800, and Eric A. Nobbs, "William Duckitt's Diary," *Archives Yearbook for South African History* 2 (1942):73-89.

[84] *CTG* January 10, 1801. The slaves were also advertised for sale in *CTG* January 24, 1801.

[85] *CTG*, August 22, 1801.

[86] *CTG* September 27, 1800.

[87] *CTG*, February 14, 1801.

[88] Barnard to Green, April 8, 1800, KAB, BO/155.

[89] *CTG*, March 6 & 13, 1802.

NOTES TO PAGES 117-122 379

[90] The total of 2,000 slaves is from *Elphick & Gilomee*, 120.

[91] Hogan's contract to supply lumber for British troops and overheard conversation are in Theal, *Records* 4:243.

[92] Barnard *Diaries*, 2:248.

[93] Noted in Philip, *British Residents*, 349.

[94] *CTG* December 20, 1800, April 18 & May 30, 1801.

[95] Hogan's role as agent for the *Young Nicholas* and the monthly charter figures are from Hogan to Barnard, April 22, 1801, KAB, BO/125. The ship was released from government service by Dundas in November (Hamilton Ross to Hogan, November 20, 1801, KAB, BO/157).

[96] The May 1800 permission for *Sir George Yonge* to go to India is in KAB, BO/117. It is not known whether the 1801 voyage of *Sir George Yonge*, recorded in MHFP, was pursuant to the December 20, 1798, permission granted by Dundas (Theal, *Records* 2:315) or some subsequent authorization.

[97] The reference to Hogan being only a shareholder in the *Sir George Yonge* transaction is in his letter to Anderson of April 10, 1802, in which he states: "I have no letters from Bengal but Adamson informs me of the recovery on the *Sir George Yonge* [insurance] policy. I have written them fully by a Dane [ship] and directed my shares in the office to be sold out."

[98] Theal, *Records* 3:211-2; PRO, CO/49.

[99] The barrack's contract incident is in Theal, *Records* 4:255.

[100] Hogan to Dundas, April 30, 1802, KAB, BO/128. The "different" Hogan document noted later is in MHFP.

[101] The criticisms from London are War Office to Yonge, April 28, 1800, Theal, *Records* 3:123; War Office to Yonge, July 28, 1800, *ibid.* 3:199-206; War Office to Yonge, September 26, 1800, *ibid.* 3:300-1. Examples of Yonge's complaints and rejoinders are Yonge to Henry Dundas, May 15, 1800, *ibid.* 3:182; Yonge to Henry Dundas, October 22, 1800 (5 letters), *ibid.* 3:318-341.

[102] *CTG* November 1, 1800.

[103] Tucker's not returning to Cape is from Philip, *British Residents*, 430.

[104] April 4, 1801, issue.

[105] Yonge's letter is in KAB, BO/85.

[106] *CTG*, May 30 & September 12, 1801.

[107] Yonge to Henry Dundas, February 19, 1801, Theal, *Records* 3:429; Yonge to Henry Dundas, April 16, 1801, *ibid.* 3:467.

[108] The three rice contracts are in Theal, *Records* 4:142-216, and also noticed in *CTG*, March 7 and 21, 1801. *Fanny* sailed from Table Bay on March 16, 1801 (*CTG*, March 21, 1801).

[109] Pringle to East India Company, London, January 3 & March 9, 1802, IRO, G/9/6; Theal, *Records* 4:212-3.

110 On September 8, 1798, Black wrote from Sydney to his father that he had "laid in an investment at the Cape for this place" (*HRNSW*, 3:729-730).

111 *CTG*, August 23, 1800.

112 *CTG* August 16, 1800.

113 There are several related stories that a "gigantic" Danish sailor named Jorgen Jorgenson, who had a varied and adventurous life and is the subject of several books, was involved in one or more of Hogan's ventures. The principal story is that he sailed with Black on the *Harbinger* or H.M.S. *Lady Nelson* to New South Wales. Both vessels left the Cape of Good Hope within a month of one another in 1800. Other "stories" involve Hogan's *Fanny* and *Harriet*. While there is probably some truth in several of the stories, it is unlikely that all the facts are today ascertainable. The fullest account is Dan Sprod, *The Usurper: Jorgen Jorgenson and His Turbulent Life in Iceland and Van Diemen's Land, 1780-1841* (Blubber Head Press, Tasmania, 2001), 7-21.

114 The government commission of the *Harbinger* is in KAB, BO/115; its letters of marque in KAB, BO/92; Hogan's instructions to Black to proceed to Brazil in MHFP; its capture of two Spanish vessels and disposition of prizes in *CTG*, August 16 and 23, 1800; its encounter with the *Lady Nelson* in *Grant*, 34; the alleged third prize vessel in *CTG* October 11, 1800; its departure from Table Bay in *CTG* November 8, 1800; and its arrival at Port Jackson and navigational voyages and purchase by Australian government in *A. Frost*, 162; *HRA*, series I, 4:305-307, 354n, 669n, 829; *HRNSW* 4:469.

115 The *Harriet's* capture is in *CTG*, September 20, 1800; the report of an American captain in *CTG*, October 18, 1800. Although many captures are mentioned in *Austen*, the *Harriet's* is not one of them.

116 Advertisements in *CTG* of December 27, 1800, January 3 & 10, 1801, offer goods for sale imported in the ship *Chance* from London. Hogan presumably acquired the ship sometime after this.

117 *Essex Institute Historical Collections*, "Extract of Captain E. Preble's Journal on Board the Essex," 10, part III (Salem, Mass., 1870), 63-69.

118 Cited in *Arkin*, 200.

119 *A. Frost*, 165, infers that the authorities in New South Wales encouraged privateering, but his only evidence of this is a statement in a single 1799 letter from Sydney (*HRNSW* 3:717) that several whalers, "animated by the hopes of privateering to advantage on the coast of Peru, have been furnished with letters of marque here, and have gone over to that coast." No doubt, however, the authorities were not adverse to privateering, so long as it did not deplete the Colony's meager shipping resources.

120 *CTG*, February 28, 1801

121 Date of arrival at and departure from Port Jackson and details of cargo from *HRNSW* 4:470, 472.

NOTES TO PAGES 126-131

[122] Black left New South Wales after October 1801 but returned to Port Jackson from Bengal sometime in 1802, according to a letter Hogan wrote to Anderson on November 28, 1802.

[123] *HRA*, series 1, 3:594.

[124] *The Times* (London), February 24, 1802; also cited in *Statham*, 333-336.

[125] *CTG*, December 12, 1801.

[126] Hogan's power of attorney was recorded at the Cape on July 17, 1802 (KAB, NCD 8/15, no.6503).

[127] *Campbell* 7:223.

[128] For example, the *Pitt* (Captain John Sewell) owned by Henry Wildman of London. Hogan procured letters of marque for *Pitt's* voyage to Jamaica early in 1801. KAB, BO/92.

[129] *Salamander's* prizes, its condemnation and Hogan's sales are in *CTG*, April 11, 18 & 25, 1801, and Theal, *Records* 4:189; October 1, 1801, letter to Dundas in KAB, BO/ 122; the Commissioners denial of the appeal in Theal, *Records* 4:205; Mellish's involvement in MHFP; *Salamander's* letters of marque, issued in London on December 29, 1799, in PRO, ADM/7/328. Mellish may have been William Mellish, described as a wealthy wholesale butcher and long-time whaleship owner in Granville Allen Mawer, *Ahab's Trade: The Saga of South Seas Whaling* (New York, 1999), 284.

[130] *CTG*, October 18, 1800; PRO, HCA/49/31/8.

[131] Another possibility is the previously-mentioned Spanish prize *La Union* whose cargo of candles and tallow Hogan shipped to New South Wales in May 1798.

[132] *Union's recapture* and the advertisements are in *CTG* October 11, 18, 25, November 22, 1800. A Spanish vessel with the same name was reported as seized by H.M.S. *L'Oiseau* in *CTG* January 23, 1802; whether it was the same vessel is unknown.

[133] Quote is from a December 20, 1800, notice in *CTG*. The inspection by seven persons declared the *Union* seaworthy.

[134] Information about the Egyptian campaign, not otherwise separately noted, is from *Cambridge History of the British Empire* 2:70-76; 5:326-329; Shafik Ghorbal, *The Beginnings of the Egyptian Question and the Rise of Mehemet Ali* (Routledge, Vermont, 1928); IRO, G/9/6; Piers Mackesy, *British Victory in Egypt*, 1801 (London, 1995); Alan Moorehead, *The Blue Nile* (New York, 1962), 55-140; Parkinson, *War in the Eastern Seas...*, 132-155, 173-183; and *Popham*, 86-89. Details about the Red Sea campaign in these sources are sketchy and sometimes inconsistent.

[135] Hogan's involvement in the *Hope* is in KAB, NCD 1/13, no. 1065. The government order is in War Office to Macartney, June 18, 1798, Theal, *Records* 2:261-4, 284.

[136] Theal, *Records* 2:333.

[137] Date of *Regulus* arrival is in *CTG* February 7, 1801; prize status of *Sea Nymph* from PRO, HCA/49/3, and *CTG*, October 18, 1800; its sale at auction on January 3 and 22, 1801, in *CTG* January 3 and 17, 1801; the origin, status, tonnage and captains of both vessels in KAB, BO/92. The *Montgomery* was seized in 1800 by H.M.S. *Etienne* (Captain George Losack) according to PRO, HCA/49/16, but by Losack on H.M.S. *Jupiter* according to *CTG* of August 16, 1800 (which reported the ship's arrival at Simon's Bay on July 29, 1800) and *CTG* of January 10, 1801, which advertised the ship's sale.

[138] Hogan gave Adamson a power of attorney for this purpose dated June 17, 1800. KAB, NCD 1/14, no. 1273.

[139] IRO, G/9/6; Theal, 4:3, 17, 56, 69-71, 77; *CTG*, August 18, 1801.

[140] Hogan offered the *Fanny* and its stores for sale in *CTG* September 19, 1801. He transferred ownership to Walker & Robertson on October 16, 1801 (KAB, NCD 1/42, no. 892). The subsequent history of the *Fanny* comes from MHFP.

[141] The British authorities accepted Elmslie's letters patent issued at Philadelphia on February 22, 1799, over two years later in a notice dated April 28, 1801, which appeared in *CTG* May 2, 1801. See also Theal, *Records* 3:478. According to records in NA, T-191/T-1, Barnard originally accepted Elmslie's appointment as of March 15, 1800, on the understanding that Elmslie remained a British citizen. Elmslie maintained, however, that he had become a U.S. citizen as the result of his letters patent. It was apparently this disagreement that delayed the formal acceptance until April 1801, with the citizenship issues apparently left unsettled.

[142] There is a reference in KAB, BO/206, to a November 7, 1801, letter sent by Hogan to the Cape Town authorities applying for clearance for *Montgomery*, possibly meaning the vessel did not leave the Cape for India, and from there sail to the Red Sea, until then.

[143] Popham's vigorous denial of any wrong doing and his claim that he was charged for political reasons is ably documented in *Popham*, 103-107, 109-110.

[144] The *Sea Nymph* first sailed sometime earlier, but had to return to Table Bay for ballast. *CTG*, March 7, 1800, gives the date of her return as March 5, but Richard Renshaw, *Voyage to the Cape of Good Hope and up the Red Sea, with Travels in Egypt, Etc.* (third edition, Manchester, 1821), 73, gives the first date of sailing as March 18. Theal, *Records* 3:463, states that troops were embarked on the *Sea Nymph* on February 24. All sources agree that the final date of sailing was March 30.

[145] Theal, *Records* 3:496.

[146] Most of the ships apparently reached Cossier by June, but the *Sea Nymph* did not get there until July 24, according to *Renshaw op.cit.*

Chapter 5

[1] Hobart to Dundas, May 2, 1801, Theal, *Records* 3:484-7.

[2] Barnard's *South Africa a Century Ago...*, 11. The several letters of the Barnards to Dundas and Macartney are in this edition, as well as in two later editions: Dorothea Fairbridge, *Lady Anne Bernard at the Cape of Good Hope, 1797-1802* (Oxford, 1924) and A.M. Robinson, ed., *The Letters of Lady Anne Bernard to Henry Dundas from the cape and Elsewhere, 1793-1803* (Cape Town, 1973).

[3] Theal, *Records* 4:85-6.

[4] Theal, *Records* 4:121, 221, 276. The full report, on which the account in the text is based, is in *ibid.* 4:221-274.

[5] Hogan to Dundas, April 30, 1802, KAB, BO/128.

[6] KAB, BO/126, 138, 139.

[7] The Preliminary Peace Articles were published in an extraordinary issue of *CTG*, December 16, 1801. The speculation about a free port was in *CTG*, December 19, 1801.

[8] Background on Fowkes is from Mollie Gillen, *The Founders of Australia: A Biographical Dictionary of the First Fleet* (Sydney, 1989), 132, and KAB, BO/196.

[9] There is no record when Anderson arrived in the Cape Colony but it would have had to be after 1796. According to Philip, *British Residents*, 7, he was born in Auchterarder, Pertshire, Scotland, and had a son born in Scotland in 1796 named William, Jr. Except for a reference to his brother John in England and an unnamed mother in Scotland, there is no information about him in MHFP. His wife and son were therefore presumably not with him at the Cape during Hogan's stay there.

[10] Hogan requested permission to land a "slave boy" from H.M.S. *L'Oiseau* on August 1, 1799 (KAB, BO/90).

[11] Hugh Thomas, *The Slave Trade: The Story of the Atlantic Slave Trade: 1440-1870* (New York, 1997), 706.

[12] Hogan gave Monteiro a general power of attorney to act on his behalf in Mozambique. It was recorded on May 13, 1800 (KAB, NCD 1/14, no. 1238) but was undoubtedly originally executed before that date.

[13] KAB, BO/92.

[14] Date of *Regulus* arrival at the Cape is in *CTG*, November 28, 1801, and sale of its Red Sea cargo at Cape Town in *CTG*, December 5, 1801.

[15] This is the explanation given in the December 1, 1801, letter from the Mozambique Governor to former Governor Yonge.

[16] Application of Samuel Peckham, Chief Mate, and W. Banger, Second Mate, to Andrew Barnard, April 5, 1802, asking permission to land three slaves purchased at Mozambique with their pay, which permission Dundas granted on the 9th (KAB, BO/91, 29). Peckham is presumably the same person as Puckham, referred to in a Hogan letter as steward on the *Sea Nymph*.

17 The statement that "the Captain and Mate [of the *Sea Nymph*] are dead" appears in a Hogan letter dated April 10, 1802. The subsequent quoted statement indicating McKellar was alive appears in a Hogan letter dated January 14, 1803. McKellar would have been seen at Mozambique in November, or possibly earlier.

18 Date of *Ninfa do Mar* (aka *Sea Nymph*) arrival at Cape and number of slaves on board are in *CTG*, April 3, 1802.

19 KAB, BO/158, 31. The letter was received on January 26, possibly by the *Joaquim* which arrived on the 21st with 450 slaves bound for Rio de Janeiro (*CTG*, January 23, 1802). The retiring Governor also sent a letter to Dundas while the ship was lying at Simon's Bay that he wanted to pay his respects (KAB, BO/158, 69).

20 Simao Joze de Barros to Dundas, April 1 and 7, 1802, KAB, BO/91, 27, 31.

21 Theal, *Records* 5:157, where the vessel is listed as *Sea Nymph*.

22 *CTG*, January 19, 1802.

23 Guezzi to Dundas (in French), January 27, 1802, KAB, BO/126, no. 120.

24 Governor's letter of December 1, 1801, KAB, BO/122.

25 Governor to Yonge (translation from Portuguese), December 1, 1801, KAB, BO/122, no. 70b.

26 H. Ross to G. F. Goetz and Messrs Walker & Robertson, February 6, 1802, KAB, BO/157, no. 445; Guezzi to Dundas (in French), January 27, 1802, KAB, BO/126, no.121.

27 Barnard to Collector of Customs Greene, March 12, 1802, KAB, BO/157, no. 510.

28 H. Ross to Messrs Robertson & Walker, February 2, 1802, KAB, BO/157, no. 437.

29 A notarized copy of Guezzi's account current with Hogan covering transactions in 1802 is in KAB, NCD 20/7, no.414.

30 The full text of Hogan's statement in a letter dated November 28, 1802, to Anderson about the gold is: "I have just delivered to our friend [Lt. William] Munro a lump of pure gold weighed by [William] Ballantine [a watchmaker at Cape Town] 46 ounces 19 pennyweight to be given to you. It was given to me by Mr. [Paul] Roux in payment for the £200 bill negotiated in the Coast of Brazil. I beg you will sell it immediately and inform me of its product that I may debit Mr. Roux with any loss on final settlement. It cost him (for the convenience of smuggling) 850 Spanish dollars and, as I may be in receipt of gold and silver money from the same quarter, I wish to be informed particularly as to the value of bullion and all coins in London." This amount of gold was probably then worth about £200 (it would today bring at least ten times that much). Hogan's reference to the cost of smuggling being 850 Spanish dollars must have been in error because this amount would itself be equivalent to a little over £200.

[31] Such evidence that exists about the *Holger Danske* mystery is from MHFP; KAB, BO/120, 121, 122, 127; PRO, HCA/49; *CTG*, November 7 & 14, 1801, February 27, 1802.

[32] *Castle of Good Hope* later traded with New South Wales. It is shown as arriving at Port Jackson on February 14, 1803, with live stock and general merchandise from Calcutta, registered at Cape of Good Hope, 1,000 tons, owned by Scott & Company and under command of A. McAskill, departing on March 21 in ballast for Calcutta. *HRNSW* 5:165, 270.

[33] Scott & Company to Cottam, May 7, 1801, quoted in September 20, 1801, deposition by Cottom to Vice Admiralty Court. PRO, HCA/49/17.

[34] Philips, *Correspondence of David Scott*, makes no mention of the circumstances of the financial difficulties of the House, nor of the reasons for Lennox's death. The quote is from a Scott letter dated October 4, 1802 (*ibid.* 2:406). Scott was not well at the time. His wife died a year later on March 23.

[35] *The Times* (London), February 16, 1802, reported the death of William Lennox, Esq., "of Broad Street buildings" at his house at Hornsey.

[36] Ponterdant's dismissal is in Theal, *Records* 3:174-5; his expulsion from Cape of Good Hope in *Barnard*, 286-7; *Fairbridge*, 203; *Robinson*, 243; IRO, G/9/1; the quote from *Robinson*, 243. Jessup's suspension is in KAB, BO/128; Theal *Records* 3:152. Arkin, 204n, states both Mosse and Jessup were expelled, but this is in error with regard to the latter who did not leave the Colony until the British evacuated in 1803 (Theal, *Records* 5:167). Philip, *British Residents*, 328, states that Ponterdant "was descended from a French Protestant family which had settled in London." He returned to the Cape Colony in 1806 where he again served with the Vice Admiralty Court, and died in London in 1825.

[37] Ponterdant to Hobart, April 21, 1802, Theal, *Records* 4:282.

[38] There is no evidence that David Scott or his associates were directly involved in the *Holger Danske* trading mission to Batavia. The David Scott company (though not necessarily David Scott himself) and, for that matter, many other British agents, both in England and India, had been extensively involved in the illicit trade between the Orient and Europe and England. Scott's company had a close relationship with the Deconnick company and, according to Philips (*Correspondence of David Scott*, 1:xix), it had given the Duntzfeldt company "more help than was prudent." This trade was illicit only because it violated the East India Company's monopoly. An issue during the war years was Englishmen trading with the enemy, either directly or more likely indirectly through ships of neutrals. But they may have seen little difference between the two because in both cases the same instruments were used (usually Danish and American ships) and the same origins and destinations of cargo were involved. The only real difference was that the Netherlands (now Batavia) was now an enemy.

[39] Rex's true parentage is established in Patricia Storrar, *George Rex: Death of a Legend* (Johannesburg, 1974).

⁴⁰ The *Lapwing* (Captain Clapp) sailed from Batavia on Jul 10, 1800, under the protection of the U.S.S. *Essex*; she lost her masts in a gale on August 12; and arrived at Table Bay on September 9 (with coffee and pepper) where her masts were presumably repaired. *CTG*, September 13, 1800. According to MHFP, she sailed for New York in December.

⁴¹ *Joseph Harvey* (Captain R. Paddock) left Bombay on September 28, 1800, and arrived at Table Bay on December 7 bound for New York. *CTG*, December 20, 1800.

⁴² Letters in MHFP show that, at some point in 1801 or 1802, possibly on a later voyage, the *Fanny* had to return to Kedgeree on the Hooghly River near Calcutta after encountering a gale, its Captain Thompson dying there. The ship subsequently came to an end at one of the places called Padang in Indonesia where it was declared on survey to be "completely rotten and consequently not seaworthy." This *Fanny* is not to be confused with the one by the same name on which Hogan imported slaves from Mozambique and attempted to fulfill a contract to send supplies to the Red Sea in 1800-01, which vessel was later sold to Walker & Robertson.

⁴³ The charter of the *Harriet* to government is in Barnard to Hogan, April 7, 1802, KAB, BO/158; its loss at Algoa Bay in *CTG*, May 29, 1802, and MHFP. The seizure by H.M.S. *Penguin* and request for reimbursement is in Hogan to Dundas, November 17, 1802, KAB, BO/129.

Chapter 6

¹ *Arkin*, 207.

² Hogan's gout was mild compared with that of Wittenoon who, Hogan reported on July 7, "has had the gout for three months in his head, eyes, legs and body and in fact is reduced to a mere skeleton." (MHFP.)

³ IRO, G/9/1. Theal, *Records* 4:450-3 & 5:158, also lists the *Henry Dundas* with 251 troops.

⁴ *CTG*, January 2, 1802.

⁵ White must have left for Mozambique sometime between March, when Anderson left the Cape for London, and mid-July, when Hogan wrote to Anderson in London describing White's venture.

⁶ KAB, BO/91.

⁷ Details on the return of Dutch governance are from Theal, *Records* 4:474-491.

⁸ *Cambridge History of the British Empire* 8:191. However, vol. 2:87-88 attributes the decision as much as to Napoleon's interference in Swiss affairs as to Pitt's intercession, though "probably in the end, [Addington] acted on Pitt's advice."

⁹ *Cambridge History of the British Empire* 2:89-90. The incident is also in Theal, *Records* 4:486-7, 491.

[10] Details about the slaves landed from the *Felis Eugenia* are in KAB, BR/536; and *CTG*, February 5 & 19 and March 12, 19 & 26, 1803.

[11] *Cambridge History of the British Empire* 8:191.

[12] The history recorded here of the *Limeno/Felis Eugenia/Favorite* is based on several pieces of evidence. A note of William Hogan states that his father renamed the *Limeno* as the *Favorite*. KAB, BR/536, confirms that the *Felis Eugenia* and *Favorite* must have been the same ship. Thus, the only explanation must be that Hogan first transferred the *Limeno* to Portuguese owners, possibly to facilitate his trade in slaves with Portuguese territories and possibly under an understanding that the real owner remained Hogan, that she was then called *Felis Eugenia*, and that Hogan took the ship back early in 1803, renaming her the *Favorite*. To add to this convoluted history, a ship named *Favorite* of 271 tons was registered in London on January 29, 1801 by William Richardson, Jr., probably Hogan's brother-in-law. She is shown as built in Northumberland, England, in 1788, taken by enemy, repurchased, re-registered and decommissioned in 1803. If this is also the same ship, the history of the vessel before her seizure by the *Chance* must have been that Richardson first registered her as the *Favorite* in London in January 1801, she was soon seized by the Spanish and named *Limeno*, which was the ship White seized on the *Chance* in September 1801. The difficulty with the latter history is that Hogan's *Favorite* was still in service in late 1804 when MHFP shows her ready to sail from England to New York. Such conundrums abound, due either to incomplete information available to the author, faulty recollections by Hogan and his descendants or errors in recording information in contemporary records or making transcriptions thereof.

[13] The *Favorite* parted company with the British Navy squadron under Admiral Curtis on May 27, proceeding to Spithead. Theal, *Records* 5:190.

[14] *CTG* of December 25, 1802, contained an advertizement involving the *Carteret*, offering it for "sale or charter or on freight for England, may be ready for sea by 1 February [1803]."

[15] 80,000 florin or gulden (guilder) was equivalent to about £7,000. Pringle is reported in *Arkin*, 206, as paying 80,000 guilders for his residence at Cape Town, thus showing that Hogan's sales price was not unusual. However, KAB, A/2151, records that Hogan sold his residence to Johan Fred. (not Andries, as in another source) Veyl for only £1,847, which seems too low, possibly showing Veyl's intent to evade tax on a higher valuation. Hogan's business offices were sold to Cloete & Cruywagen for a reported £750. If the official records are correct, which is doubtful, the total amount Hogan received for selling his properties at the Cape was only £4,847. If the ratio 7000:1847 is applied to 4847, the total and more likely correct figure would about £18,000, still a considerable amount.

[16] The George Grand story is from *Freund*, 185. The story of Catherine Werlée is told in Annette Joelson, *Courtesan Princess* (New York, 1964).

[17] *Rose*, 131.

[18] *Cambridge History of the British Empire* 2:89-90.

[19] *Freund*, 192-3.

[20] *Rose*, 130.

[21] *Freund*, 241, 248-249.

[22] The report that he was friendly with Janssens came from his son William many years later. De Mist, who was supposed to be senior to Janssens, was opposed to the war, the VOC and, at least in principle, slavery. He tried to impose various reforms at the Colony but without much success. Janssens assumed increasing power as de Mist's influence waned. Disillusioned, de Mist left the Cape Colony on February 24, 1805, leaving Janssens solely in charge for the remaining year before the British again occupied the Colony. *Freund*, 154-179.

[23] According to *CTG*, June 11, 1803, the *Maria*, Captain Beyer, sailed from Simon's Bay on June 4 for Madagascar. Hogan was issued a travel permit on June 2 authorizing him to travel to Mozambique on the Dutch ship *Maria*, Captain Benjamin Beast (KAB, BR/584). "Beyer" and "Beast" were probably the same person, transcripts of names in official records not always being accurate.

[24] A notice appearing in *CTG*, May 7, 1803, noted the intention of Francis Fowke [*sic*] and Edward Lewis of leaving the Colony.

[25] *NYCA*, October 25, 1803.

[26] *Freund*, 394.

[27] *Freund*, 152.

[28] The request to sign the oath was announced in *CTG*, November 12, 1803; text with Hogan's signature in KAB, BR/506. According to Theal, *Records* 5:191, the Batavian authorities demanded the oath as early as June 24, 1803, when only about 60 to 70 British residents signed.

[29] *CTG* of November 12 has the date of sailing from Table Bay as October 10, not 19th as in Hogan's letter, but KAB, BR/536, confirms the October 19 date and other facts in MHFP.

[30] KAB, NCD 9/13, no.46. After Hogan left the Colony, McClure transferred his power of attorney on May 9, 1804, to Cloete & Cruywagen (KAB, NCD 20/35, no.718).

[31] *Charleston Courier*, July 12, 1804. Alexander McClure is shown as the captain of the ship, although its operating captain seems to have been James B. Marston. The slaves and the ship's non-human cargo, consisting of "65 leaguers of Cape wine, Batavian arrack, Chinese sugar candy, tamarinds, aloes and colombo root," were advertised for sale in subsequent issues of the *Charleston Courier*. The newspaper also contained the following account: "The *Horizon* left Mozambique with 549 slaves [and] made her passage from the Cape of Good Hope in 51 days. The *Horizon* had put into Simon's Bay where, while lying at anchor, she was taken possession of by a French national corvette then in port under pretense of being a British vessel with American papers. The Dutch governor, with proper spirit, immediately interfered, but the Frenchman, refusing to give her up and

threatening to take her off to the Île of France, he ordered two seventy-fours to watch her motions and, in the event of their attempting to put to sea, to take possession of the ships. Things remained in this state for nearly a month, during which time, through the neglect of the Frenchmen in not paying proper attention to the Negroes, nearly 300 of the them died." KAB, BR/536, shows the *Horizon* (Captain James B. Marston) sailing from Mozambique on March 18, arriving at Simon's Bay April 19, and departing there for America with 310 slaves on April 29. A detailed account of the seizure of the *Horizon* in Simon's Bay on suspicion of being English with false papers and the involvement of the French corvette *Le Belier* is in KAB, BR/35, 82-88. McClure and Marston were detained on the French ship while the *Horizon* was subjected to a thorough search. The ship was cleared of suspicion and allowed to proceed on her journey after taking on water. Contrary to the account in the Charleston newspaper, the *Horizon* was detained only ten days.

[32] *Charleston Courier*, December 4, 1804. This departure is not listed in *Donnan*, vol. 4, which otherwise appears to be a thorough analysis of the Charleston slave trade 1804-1807. The *Horizon* was lost May 20, 1807, near Brest on a voyage from London to Lisbon and Lima (*Charleston Courier*, August 14 and September 18, 1807).

[33] Cited in *Mannix*, 188.

[34] Ships intending to import slaves legally at Charleston first had to lay over ten days at Sullivan's Island in quarantine where they were incarcerated in a "pest house" while a doctor inspected for smallpox or other contagious diseases. *Hamm*, 263.

[35] *NYCA*, January 12, 1804. The Captain is shown therein as James, not Francisco Louis Madeiro, as appears in Hogan's letter to Anderson, but the letter also states that the ship "has two excellent English officers and chiefly English seamen."

[36] Ports in Georgia had been legally closed to the slave trade from October 1, 1798 (*Donnan* 4:244); Northern and Mid-Atlantic ports had also been closed for some years.

[37] A notice in *Columbia Museum & Savannah Advertizer* on March 17 inserted by Beggs & Groves read: "All persons having business with the ship *Excellentissimo Augusta* are requested to hand them [over] on or before Saturday next in order to close her accounts."

[38] Anderson may have had a hand in the plans of the *Perseverance* and *Louisa*, but not the cases of the *Surprize* (because it left Philadelphia before Anderson arrived in the U.S.), the *Juno* (which came to the Cape from Île de France) or *Silenius* (which came from the Netherlands). The dates of departure and arrival of these vessels are from NA, U.S. Customs Records of Foreign Ship Arrivals and Departures; KAB; *NYCA*; and *CTG*.

[39] Advertised for sale in *CTG*, November 19, 1803.

⁴⁰ The *Juno* had arrived at Table Bay on November 11 from Île de France, from which it had departed on October 22, with a cargo of coffee, sugar and cotton (*CTG*, November 12, 1803).

⁴¹ The Dutch proclamation was dated February 7, 1804; it appeared in *CTG*, February 11. Its non-enforcement is in Theal, *Records* 5:135. The proclamation was issued, in its own words, "as a result of the scandalous breach of faith involved in the theft of the prize ship *Mary* and to ensure the safety of the Colony." The *Mary* was a British whaler captured by the Dutch in Simon's Bay. Its crew escaped from custody while on board another vessel lying in anchor on February 4, retook the whaler and sailed out of the harbor (Theal, *Records* 5:206-208).

Chapter 7

¹ The quotations are from *Scoville* whose recollections about old merchants in New York were published in 1866. Because Scoville was born in 1815 and did not become a merchant in New York City until 1837 when he was 22 years old, his reports about Hogan must have been based on the recollections of other persons. Many of the books and newspaper articles which mention Hogan's New York residence draw on Scoville as a source, thus repeating his errors. (The latest is Leo Hershkowitz, "The Irish and the Emerging City: Settlement to 1844," *The New York Irish*, ed. Ronald H. Bayor & Timothy J. Meagher (Baltimore, 1996), 19).

² The $430,000 figure is given in Hogan to Monroe dated May 14, 1818, HSP, Joel R. Poinsett Collection. William later wrote that his father brought with him to New York half a million dollars, but this information would have come from his father. Although MHFP contain several papers reciting Hogan's assets as he was leaving the Cape of Good Hope, it is not possible to construct a complete or accurate account from them. For example, a letter to Anderson dated April 17, 1803, seems to show a total of 154,000 rix dollars in cash, accounts receivable and unsold property at the Cape of Good Hope (thus excluding accounts held in London and elsewhere); and an 1805 accounting shows he paid 103,458 rix dollars for coffee, sugar and pepper purchased from the Dutch authorities before his departure. These amounts do not include his profits from the sale of slaves on the *Excellentissimo Augusta*, which would have been at least $40,000— considerably more if, as Hogan seems to say in one letter, he procured the slaves to clear a debt owed him at Mozambique. Nor do these amounts include his profits from the sale of goods on the four vessels on which he shipped goods to New York, Boston, Philadelphia and Baltimore and two others that followed soon thereafter. Using optimistic assumptions for other transactions, Hogan would still have had to make an average profit of at least $50,000 from each of these six ships to have acquired net assets of $430,000 which, while not impossible, seems unlikely. Quite possibly, therefore, $430,000 was not a net amount under modern accounting standards. There is no question, however, that the total value of Hogan's transactions was large. Anderson's account with Hogan, which in September 1803 showed total debits and credits of £21,282, by December 1804 had increased to £91,370, and this represented only business transacted with

London.

[3] *Haswell*, 38-39; Isaac Newton Phelps Stokes, *The Iconography of Manhattan Island, 1498–1909* (New York, 1928), 3:510-511; William Earl Dodge, *Old New York: A Lecture* (New York, 1880).

[4] Burr used the alias "R. King" during his flight, a name that has puzzled historians. Possibly it was Butler who suggested this alias believing that using the name of a real person connected with Burr's destination (Roswell King was the overseer of his Georgia plantation) would dispel suspicion.

[5] These contacts and associations are developed subsequently. The arresting officer whose son later married a Hogan granddaughter was (then Lieutenant, later General) Edmund Pendleton Gaines (James Wesley Silver, *Edmund Pendleton Gaines: Frontier General*, (Louisiana State University, 1949)).

[6] The travel permit issued to Hogan by the Dutch authorities on March 7, 1804 (KAB, BR/548) shows the number of Hogan slaves and their names somewhat differently: Christian, Lodewyk, Charles, Rainissa, Vennissa and Charlotte. Charlotte was, however, sold to Mistress Venables for 400 rix dollars on March 7, instead of Hogan's "two old slaves called September and Silvia," who by an earlier instrument of March 5 were to be transferred to Venables on condition that they were not to be "sold, transferred or otherwise disposed of as slaves, but that...by the said Mistress Venables leaving the Colony or after her decease shall be set free." (KAB, NCD 20/27, nos. 245 & 246.) What finally happened to September and Silvia is unrecorded. The notice of arrival of the *Silenius* in New York that appeared in *NYCA* on May 5 states that Hogan was accompanied by his "lady, three children and ten servants." William Hogan, Jr., Hogan's grandson, later wrote that "when grandpa first came to New York..., he brought 13 slaves from the Cape"; another descendant said the number was 12. Whichever account is correct, the numbers of servants and slaves in Hogan's entourage was not unusual.

[7] KAB, NCD 20/7, no. 415.

[8] The total census data are cited in Leon F. Litwack, *North of Slavery: The Negro in the Free States, 1790–1860* (Chicago, 1961), 3, 14; the New York City data in David T. Gilchrist (ed.), *The Growth of Seaport Cities, 1790-1825* (Charlottesville, Va., 1967), 34.

[9] The laws are in William Edward Du Bois, *The Suppression of the African Slave-Trade to the United States* (New York, 1873), 240; Shane White, *Somewhat Independent: The End of Slavery in New York City, 1770-1810* (Athens, Georgia, 1990), 38; Arthur Zilversmit, *The First Emancipation: The Abolition of Slavery in the North* (Chicago, 1967), 149, 150, 182, 208, 213. The 1799 law allowed masters to abandon their slaves, making them wards of the state, a thinly veiled method of compensating slave owners, according to *ibid*, 182.

[10] See, for example, *NYCA* for August 31, 1804.

[11] Dennis Hogan's tract is noted in *Bibliotheca Britannica* 4:1824.

[12] *Philadelphia Evening Post*, May 31, 1804. *Surprize* is recorded in NA, U.S. Customs Records of Foreign Ship Arrivals, as sailing from Philadelphia under the command of Daniel McLoud on October 1, 1803, bound for the Cape of Good Hope. Its captain on the return voyage, Richard Renshaw (but also shown in the newspaper article as John Renshaw), was not the Richard Renshaw, a Royal Artillery gunner, who sailed in Hogan's *Sea Nymph* to the Red Sea in 1801 and wrote the previously-cited *Voyage to the Cape of Good Hope and Up the Red Sea, with Travels in Egypt Etc.*

[13] Several newspapers (*New York Post*, May 4; *NYCA*, May 7; *Philadelphia Evening Post*, May 4) confirm that the *Silenius* and *Perseverance* both sailed from Table Bay on March 8 and the *Louisa* on March 9. It was a busy three days at the Cape: the *Betsey* sailed for Salem on March 7 and the *Magistrate* for London on March 9, neither apparently a Hogan ship. Dates of arrival of *Perseverance* and *Louisa* are confirmed in NA, U.S. Customs Records of Foreign Ship Arrivals.

[14] *NYCA*, February 27, 1805. The ship appears to have had a difficult passage, receiving "needed provisions from the Brig *Hope* (Riley) of Portsmouth, New Hampshire, on February 20 at Latitude 35° N, Longitude 70° W."

[15] Quoted by *Scoville*, 117.

[16] Robert Lenox's background is from *Scoville*, 148; *Mott*, 316; *New York Genealogical and Biographical Record* 61:365; *"Letters from John Pintard...."* 1:229-232.

[17] *Freund*, 152, 193-194.

[18] De Mist left the Cape of Good Hope on February 25 on the *Silenius*, the same ship Hogan and family had taken a year earlier. Theal, *Records* 5:102, 126; *Freund*, 154 (who mistakenly states the American ship took de Mist to Philadelphia).

[19] *NYCA*, July 23, 1804.

[20] After being shipwrecked on the *Hercules* 500 miles northeast of Cape Town in 1796, Stout proposed that the U.S. establish a colony on the African east coast. Clarence Clemens Clendenen & Peter Duignan, *Americans in Black Africa up to 1865*, (Hoover Institute, 1964), 24-25; Eric Rosenthal, *Stars and Stripes in Africa: Being a History of American Achievements in Africa by Explorers, Missionaries, Pirates....* (Cape Town, 1968) 34, 67-68.

[21] New York departure date, *NYCA*, September 8, 1804; Cape Town arrival date, *CTG*, December 22, 1804.

[22] Table Bay departure, *CTG*, February 2, 1805 (where she is mistakenly shown as bound for Boston); New York arrival, *NYCA*, April 3, 1805.

[23] *Philadelphia Evening Post* of April 17, 1804, reported the *Industry* (Millrea) from Savannah passing Charleston bar on April 2, bound for the Cape of Good Hope.

[24] *Charleston Courier*, November 7, 1804; advertisements in issues from November 13 though December 27.

[25] *Charleston Courier* for January 8, 1805, reported the departure of the *Industry* (Millrea) for New York; *NYCA* for January 18 reported the arrival of the *Industry* (Ray) from Charleston in 7 days. The two were clearly the same vessel.

[26] *Poulson's American Daily Advertiser* (Philadelphia), August 18, 1804. The *Ganges* traded with China and Île de France, as well as the Cape of Good Hope.

[27] *CTG*, November 17, 1804.

[28] A copy of the Pendleton-Boston-Lord agreement is in MHFP. The full and correct story of the incidents is impossible to determine because the several contemporary sources of information had ample reasons to obfuscate their involvement. The saga appears in Edmund Fanning, *Voyages and Discoveries in the South Seas, 1792-1832* (New York, 1833, reprint edition, New York, 1989), 230-241; Gordon Greenwood, *Early American-Australian Relations From the Arrival of the Spaniards in America to the Close of 1830* (Melbourne, 1944), 92-96, 134-138; David Roger Hainsworth, ed., *Builders and Adventurers: The Traders and the Emergence of the Colony, 1788-1821* (Casell Australia, 1968), 107-108; Hainsworth, *The Sydney Traders: Simeon Lord and His Contemporaries, 1780-1821* (Cassell Australia, 1972), 132, 165-6; HRA, series 1, 5:167-169, 720-739, 809-811.

[29] According to *Mannix*, 243, slaves from the east coast of Africa had been sent to the U.S. as far back as 1678 by the Royal African Company, but this trade seems to have stopped sometime during the 18th century. Mannix cites the 1804 *Horizon* incident, recorded in the previous chapter, as evidence of slaves being imported into the U.S. from the east coast of Africa at the beginning of the 19th century. As will be seen, there is evidence of substantial slave shipments from Mozambique to both the U.S. on American ships and on both American and Portuguese ships to South America at about this time. Later from about 1819, there was a sizeable American trade from the slave dens of Zanzibar, mostly to Brazil.

[30] John M. Ehrick is shown in *South Carolina Historical and Genealogical Magazine*, 49 (1948):156, as dying in New York on March 18, 1822, having lived there the last seven years, previously "many years a resident of Charleston." He had a business relationship with Hogan in 1809-10, as will be seen.

[31] Adam Gilchrist (1760-1816) is shown as a merchant in the 1806 *Charleston City Directory*. Unsigned and undated papers in "Gibbs-Gilchrist Collection," SCHS, describe him as "a merchant in successful business. Had a reputation of wealth. One of the founders of the [Charleston] Chamber of Commerce and president of the branch bank of the Bank of the United States in present [Charleston] City Hall. He was involved in business with his brother Robert in New York. In the War of 1812, the British captured an East Indiaman belonging to him and caused his failure. This also involved his brother Adam [presumably means Robert] and caused his failure and resulted a few years later (1816) in his death." The same source describes Robert Gilchrist as follows: "Robert settled in

New York as a merchant, married Elizabeth Roosevelt July 14, 1789.... The capture of his East Indiaman by the British off Sandy Hook in the War of 1812 caused his notes to go to protest. He immediately assigned all his property to Robert Livingston for the benefit of his creditors; his property consisted of valuable real estate in New York City, at Castle Hill and the Adirondacks and he retired to the country in the mountains near Weavertown, Warren County, with his family [where he died at age 54, Livingston having paid off his debts] at 100 cents on the dollar." Robert Gilchrist's marriage to Elizabeth Roosevelt is confirmed in Charles Barney Whittelsey, *The Roosevelt Genealogy, 1649-1902* (Hartford, Conn., 1902), 19.

[32] There is a listing for "Depau & Fountain, merchants," in the 1806 *Charleston City Directory*, and a Francis Depau of Charleston is shown as marrying Sylvia De Grasse, daughter of the late Count De Grasse" on January 31, 1798 (*South Carolina Historical and Genealogical Magazine*, 25 (1924):38). This Francis Depau is undoubtedly the same as Francis Depau of New York, described by one author as a well known businessman, son-in-law of Admiral de Grasse and founder of the first line of Le Havre packets in 1822 (Robert Greenhalgh Albion, *The Rise of New York Port, 1815-1860* (New York, 1984), 239). He was elsewhere described as "a Frenchman. He died worth $700,000—a large sum in his day. He lived on the west side of Broadway, between Leonard and Franklin streets, until he built Depau Row at the southeast corner of Bleeker Street and Depau Place, a structure now [1892] occupied by the Five Points class" (George W. Sheldon, "Old Shipping Merchants of New York," *Harper's New Monthly Magazine* 84 (Feb. 1892):464-5. Hogan's grandson, William Hogan, Jr., many years later penciled a note which mentions "Depaw who built Bleeker Inn, or some of his family" as one of the men responsible for Hogan's financial downfall, a subject that will be covered later. Depau (first name not given) is mentioned as a tenant of Claremont in *The Mail and Express* (New York), April 3, 1897.

[33] Hogan may have been led to Butler by William Anderson when he was in Philadelphia late in 1803 or Robert Lenox after Hogan's arrival in New York. Hogan's involvement with Butler is known because MHFP contain a series of letters to and from the major and his family in the 1810s. None of these letters mentions or hints at the slave trade but their presence in an otherwise bleak period in the MHFP is mysterious. The records of Roswell King, manager of Butler's Hampton Plantation on Simons Island in Georgia (at HSP) contain no mention of any arrival of slaves, which they surely would have if the almost 300 slaves on the *Excellentissimo Augusta* had been sent to Butler's plantation. It is still possible that these slaves were landed at any one of the many plantations along the coast or on the many islands offshore Georgia, and that Butler had a hand in recommending such a destination in 1803. Of course, the Butler letters might have been retained by a descendant (others having clearly been destroyed) only because a subsequent resident at Hampton Plantation was Fanny Kemble, a flamboyant British actress whose messy divorce in 1849 from the major's grandson attracted public attention in both the U.S. and England. Butler's background and that of his descendants are told in *Bell*; colorful details are in Bessie Lewis, *King's Retreat Plantation* (St. Simon's Island, Georgia 1980);

Patriarchial Plantations of St. Simons Island (St. Simons Island, Georgia, 1974); *They Called Their Town Darien* (Darien, Georgia, 1975).

[34] Stuart Weems Bruchey (ed.), *Cotton and the Growth of the American Economy: 1790-1860* (New York, 1967), 7. The other principal cotton growers were India, the West Indies, Arabia and Asia Minor (*ibid.*, 43). Bruchey states there is no direct evidence that the production costs of American cotton were less than elsewhere in the world, but believes this must have been the case. The importance of the West Indies as a cotton supplier may have declined because, unlike the American government, the British were increasingly effective in prohibiting slavery and the slave trade in their colonies after the Napoleonic Wars. American textile production prior to the War of 1812 was negligible, but by 1853 U.S. mills were using one-third of domestically grown cotton (*ibid.*, 46).

[35] *Donnan* 4:525.

[36] Patrick S. Brady, "The Slave Trade and Sectionalism in South Carolina, 1787-1808," *The Journal of Southern History* 38 (November 1972):616; *Hamm*, 114.

[37] *Mannix*, 194-202. By 1825, a prime field hand was worth $1,500 and in 1860 $2,500.

[38] *Mannix*, 188-9.

[39] *NYCA*, March 26, 1806.

[40] This interpretation of the basis of the British decision is based on *Turner*, "The Cape of Good Hope and the Anglo-French Conflict, 1797-1806."

[41] *Young Adam's* departure date from Charleston, its cargo and its arrival date at Cape Town with "passenger W. Henderson (English)" are recorded in KAB, CO/6083. The Henderson mentioned must have been Anderson. According to Philip, *British Residents*, 7, William Anderson was given permission to reside in the Cape Colony on October 21, 1806, with P.L. Cloete and J.F. Reitz giving security. His wife was apparently with him on the occasion of his second residence at the Cape, though she may have arrived separately from England. The departure date of the *Young Adam* from Charleston, its captain and the ship's local agent are confirmed in *Charleston Courier*, May 9, 1806. The *Dolphin's* departure date, the last name of its captain and the ship's local agent are in *Charleston Courier*, May 10, 1806; its arrival at the Cape is from KAB, CO/6083. The latter references give Ross's first name as Andrew, which is presumably correct. However, *Charleston City Directory* for 1806 shows a Thomas Ross as the only possible resident and *South Carolina Historical and Genealogical Magazine*, 20 (1919):261 records a Captain Thomas Ross of Charleston marrying Nancy Mortimer on February 8, 1787. *Charleston Courier*, December 1, 1806, reported that the *Dolphin* had been sighted at Table Bay on August 30 and that its destination was Mozambique. *Hamm*'s exhaustive list of ships engaged in the African slave trade does not mention either the *Dolphin* or *Young Adam*, nor the *Horizon*, presumably because he believed these were not American ships, the subject of his dissertation. He also excluded several Depau ships, presumably based on Depau's French citizenship (*ibid.*, 101).

[42] There was a dispute in August involving the cargo of the *Augusta* between General Baird and a British Navy officer, which may have made it easier to obtain permission to land the cargoes of the *Young Adam* and *Dolphin* (Theal, *Records* 6:20-21). In a letter to London dated September 11, General Baird reported that, with the arrival of several vessels from India, America and England, "we are most plentifully provisioned for a considerable time" (Theal, *Records* 6:20-21, 37-38). Whether Baird intended to include the *Young Adam* or *Dolphin* in his reference to American vessels is unknown.

[43] KAB, NCD 20/35; KAB, CO/6100A.

[44] Ponterdant's presence at the Cape is confirmed by a list of British government expenditures showing that in 1806 he was paid 625 Rds "for his legal opinion on different subjects." Theal, *Records* 6:78.

[45] The departure of *Young Adam* for Mozambique on October 4 is in KAB, CO/6083. It was earlier sighted on September 26 at the Cape of Good Hope (*Charleston Courier*, January 14, 1807).

[46] *Haight*, 89n. The date of the receipt is shown here as "11 April 1806," but this is not possible because the ship was then at Charleston. The date must have been recorded in Mozambique records as 11/4/1806, which Haight, being British, assumed was entered in European style.

[47] The expected arrivals at the Cape were reported in *Charleston Courier*, September 14, 1807. Since Cape archives do not show the presence of either vessel at the Cape during the period in question, it is likely they avoided stopping there out of fear of being detained or seized, either because of their slave cargoes or because all American ships were then in potential jeopardy from the British Navy. Cape archives show that the American brig *Ann of Bristol* was detained at the Cape on March 28, 1807, having been taken a prize on the River Plate with 160 slaves, as was the American ship *Juno* on May 21, 1807, also a prize at Montevideo with assorted cargo. The Portuguese *General Izedro* was detained at the Cape on December 20, 1806, with 420 slaves from Mozambique.

[48] *Charleston Courier* for December 19, 1807, reports the arrival of 120 slaves from Mozambique, but the *Young Adam* and *Dolphin* would have arrived considerably earlier, about August or September.

[49] The number of other ships for which Gilchrist and Depau acted as agents is from *Donnan* 4:516, 521–524. Gilchrist's name also appears in *Charleston Courier* advertisements offering goods "suited to the African trade." (*Donnan* 4:515.)

[50] These totals are from *Donnan* 4:521–525.

[51] One piece of evidence that slaves continued to be landed illegally in South Carolina is the following item in *The City Gazette & Daily Advertiser* (Charleston) of July 21, 1806: "A brig from the Coast has been disposing of her slaves to the southward. The Customs House officers at Savannah seized upon a pilot boat attempting to land them; but being on the Carolina side, they were given up again."

⁵² Paul Finkelman (ed.), *Slave Trade and Migration, Domestic and Foreign,* vol. 2 of *Articles on American Slavery* (New York, 1989), 180. *Louisiana Gazette* for 1806 and 1807 does not show any arrivals for the *Young Adam* or *Dolphin,* but it does not seem to show arrivals of any identifiable slave ships, except possibly the *Agent,* one of Francis Depau's slave ships which arrived at New Orleans on January 29, 1808, after clearing Charleston on December 13, 1807, with 120 slaves from Mozambique.

⁵³ *Charleston Courier,* April 20, 1806. According to Charles Lyon Chandler, "United States Merchant Ships in the River de la Plate (1801-1808), As Shown by Early Newspapers", *The Hispanic American Historical Review* 2 (1919):26-54, at least forty American ships visited the River Plate in 1806 and 1807, but he does not distinguish between those trading with the U.S. and those coming from Africa, i.e., with slaves, although a number clearly came from there, including some identified as calling at the Cape of Good Hope.

⁵⁴ KAB, CO/6067. The "short period" is from a notice Anderson placed in *CTG* on September 24, 1808. Anderson's notice to Governor Caledon reads: "... the state of my health rendering it absolutely necessary that I should immediately try the sea air and a change of climate, by the advice of my physicians, I have taken passage on the brig *Jeune Laure* that sails in a few days for the coast of Brazil" (KAB, CO/11). Anderson presumably returned to the Cape and died there sometime prior to 1818, because, according to Philip, *British Residents,* 7, his widow took out a license in that year to sell vegetables in Simon's Town.

⁵⁵ Although there is ample reason to believe that illegal imports of slaves into the U.S. continued up to the Civil War (see *Mannix,* 194-202; *Du Bois,* 109-112), there is no firm statistical evidence of the volume of this trade. Philip D. Curtin, *The Atlantic Slave Trade: A Consensus* (Madison, Wisconsin, 1969), 234, whose estimates of the trans-Atlantic slave trade are perhaps the most thorough, simply guesses that the level was 10,000 during each of the five decades from 1811 to 1860, about one-third of the average level during the previous century.

⁵⁶ KAB, CO/6083 & 6084.

⁵⁷ The owners of the fishery and other details are in P.D. Shaughnessy, *Investigational Report 127: Historical Population Levels of Seals and Seabirds on Islands off Southern Africa, with Special Reference to Seal Island, False Bay* (Sea Fisheries Research Institute, Cape Town, 1984), 14-17, for which the author is indebted to Mrs. Dee Nash. Notices in *CTG* of October 17, 1807, and August 20, 1808, warned persons not to land on the islands.

⁵⁸ Miranda first sought American assistance through Alexander Hamilton and Rufus King in January 1798 but President Adams opposed the idea. Miranda was again in New York in November 1805 where he met William Steuben Smith and Samuel G. Ogden. They offered to send the *Leander* which sailed in February 1806 and provided some minimal assistance. Both Spain and France objected to this private activity; Smith and Ogden were tried but acquitted. Bernard Moses, *Spain's Declining Power in South America, 1730-1806* (Berkeley, 1919), 331-333; Henry Adams, *History of the United States...During Jefferson,* 733-738.

[59] The little-known British occupation of Buenos Aires, as well as Montevideo, is described in Frederick Alexander Kirkpatrick, *A History of the Argentine Republic* (Cambridge, 1931), 46-58; Ricardo Levene, *A History of Argentina*, translated by William Spence Robertson (New York, 1965), 191-202; Bernard Moses, *op. cit.*, 341-371.

[60] The *Rolla*'s arrival at Île de France from New York on July 27, 1805, and from Calcutta on December 31, 1805, are in Auguste Touissant, *Early American Trade with Mauritius* (Port Louis, Mauritius, 1954). Its arrival at New York on June 4, 1806, is in *NYCA*, June 4, 1806.

[61] A vessel listed as *Rollo* is shown in KAB, CO/6083, as arriving at Table Bay on February 21, 1806, "French, from coast of Africa (2 months) to the Cape. A captured brig fitted as a man of war by Adm. Linois." This is probably our *Rolla*. There was also a British Navy brig *Rolla* that is shown in KAB, CO/6083, as being at the Cape as early as August 13, 1806, and sailing with the British fleet for the River Plate on August 22. This could not have been the *Rolla* that left New York bound for Montevideo on July 5 (*NYCA*, July 5, 1806). It was presumably this latter *Rolla* that was seen at Montevideo on October 25 and November 26, having arrived about September 10 (*Georgia Republican*, January 20, 1807; *Chandler, op. cit.*, 37, 39). The coincidence of two ships named *Rolla* being at Montevideo at the same time leads naturally to conjecture that they were the same ship, but this is a digression.

[62] It is certain that Hogan acquired the property in 1806, but from whom and how is described differently in several sources. Theodosia Burr Alston (and/or her husband Joseph Alston) is reported to have been a previous title holder in *Mott*, 26, and Samuel Wandell, *Aaron Burr: A Biography...* (New York, 1925), 1:222. *Mott* and *Old Buildings of New York City*, 131, also say that Hogan acquired Monte Alto from John Marsden Pintard, whose name will reoccur in this account. *New York Times* much later (July 18, 1949) claimed that Theodosia and Joseph Alston lived at Claremont after their marriage in February 2, 1801, but Burr's leading biographer (Milton Lomask, *Aaron Burr: The Years from Princeton to Vice President, 1756-1805*, (New York, 1979), 286) confirms that Theodosia lived with her father in a mansion called Richmond Hill in New York City prior to her marriage and for a month thereafter before moving to South Carolina. Perhaps the *Times* mixed up Richmond Hill and Claremont.

[63] Isaac Newton Phelps Stokes, *The Iconography of Manhattan Island, 1498–1909* (New York, 1928), 1:404.

[64] The names sometimes appears as "Clermont," probably because the mansion is confused with Fulton's famous steam boat *Clermont*.

[65] *New York City Guide* (New York, 1939), 288, claimed that Claremont was built by George Pollock in 1893, and *New York Times*, July 18, 1949, said that Hogan merely moved it to a new location. The name of the original builder is probably correct, but it is unlikely that Hogan physically moved the edifice. Architectural drawings prepared for Hogan by a New York builder in 1806 show a plan to add a second story to Claremont and to improve Monte Alto. (There

is also a drawing for elaborate entrance gates, which apparently were not installed.) The drawing for Claremont is shown as Figure 3. A painting of 1814 in which Claremont appears in the distance (John Punnett Peters, *Annals of St. Michael's: Being the History of St. Michael's Protestant Episcopal Church, New York, for One Hundred Years, 1807–1907* (New York, 1907), 375) shows no detail. Figure 4 (ca. 1860) and an ink drawing in an 1870s book (*Lossing*, 385) of "Jone's Claremont Hotel" show a substantial addition, but the addition does not appear in a turn-of-the-century photograph (*Old Buildings of New York City*, 128). All depictions show the wood facing.

[66] Details about occupants of Claremont are variously from *Haswell*, 25; *Lossing*, 387-388; *Mott*, *Peterson*; *The Mail and Express* (New York), April 3, 1897; *New York Times*, December 26, 1909; *Old Buildings of New York City*, 129-137; *New York City Guide* (1939), 288. These sources are not consistent in all cases.

[67] The estate was earlier known as Strawberry Hill (*Old Buildings of New York City*, 129-30). Margaret Clendening Lawrence, a Hogan granddaughter, told (*Mott*, 26) that Prince William once visited with Hogan in the U.S. Mott thereupon erroneously wrote that the Prince "visited [Hogan] at his town house in Greenwich Street," although he did have correct the year of the visit—1782. The author has found four separate locations at which the Prince is reported to have stayed or been a guest in 1782: (1) Hanover Square at Sloat Lane (later Beaver Street), *Mott*, 346, *Historic New York* (1897, reprint edition 1969), series 1, 2:314, Percy Hetherington Fitzgerald, *The Life and Times of William IV*, (London, 1884) 1:15; (2) the Walton House on old Franklin Square (junction of Pearl and Cherry Streets) near Peck Slip, *Lossing*, 421; (3) the Van Courtlandt Mansion, still standing at 246nd Street and Broadway in the Bronx, Martha J. Lamb, *History of the City of New York* (New York, 1877), 3:807 and Frank Bergen Kelley, *Historical Guide to the City of New York* (New York, 1913), 64; (4) the Kreuzer-Pelton House, 1268 Richmond Terrace (foot of Pelton Avenue), Richmond, Staten Island, *New York City Guide* (1939), 620. It was from the Hanover Square location that the Prince was to be kidnaped in 1782 (see Chapter One). Hogan lived on Franklin Square for a brief period but nowhere near the other locations.

[68] Fulton had earlier tried, unsuccessfully, to convince the British, and then the French, of the practicality of an under-sea, steam-powered boat. While in Paris, he met the American Minister, Robert R. Livingston, who agreed to back Fulton's idea for an American steamboat. (Experimental steamboats had already been built in Europe.) In 1797, the New York State Assembly, amid shouts of laughter, enacted a bill granting Livingston a perpetual right to navigate inland waters. The venture became known as *Fulton's Folly*. The steamboat was named after the Livingstone's family estate some 40 miles south of Albany. The *Clermont* was not the first steamboat to operate successfully in the U. S., but earlier ventures were not pursued to fruition. Fulton and Livingston enjoyed their steamship monopoly on the Hudson for thirty years until a court declared it invalid. Details are in Henry Collins Brown, *The Story of Old New York* (New York, 1934), 350-357.

[69] Although not fully known until later, Jackson spent an estimated £700 to support editorials and letters to the editors of Federalist newspapers sympathetic to the British cause. Josephine Fisher, "Francis James Jackson and Newspaper Propaganda in the United States, 1809–1810," *Maryland Historical Magazine*, 30 (June 1935):93-113. Financially supported editorials and news stories—from both foreign and domestic sources—were quite common at the time.

[70] Jackson's arrival and departure dates are from Henry Adams, *History of the United States During...Madison*; the quote on p. 152. *Lossing*, 388, says Jackson resided at Hogan's summer mansion Claremont for a short time.

[71] Courtenay's parentage, title and parliamentary position are in *Dictionary of National Biography*; the quote on his character from *Lossing*, 388; the reason for his departure from England from both *Lossing*, 387, and *Haswell*, 25. Both the latter put Courtenay at Claremont before 1812 and say that he returned to England when the War of 1812 broke out. There is a confirming record of this in the form of an income statement of Courtenay dated Bloomingdale April 20, 1812, at HSNY. There is other evidence (*Mail and Express* (New York), April 3, 1897) that Courtenay did not go back to England in 1812 but only to Poughkeepsie, later returning to Claremont where he may have been in 1819. Several scraps written by Hogan grandchildren in MHFP also state that Courtenay was at Claremont in the late 1810s. The truth here, as in other old stories of New York, is elusive.

[72] It was Margaret Clendening Lawrence, a Hogan granddaughter, who "always understood that the monument...was erected by [Hogan]" (*Mail and Express* (New York), April 3, 1897). Another grandchild, William Hogan, Jr., opined that Hogan was "interested in the child's grave, enough to build a monument," because Hogan's son William and the "amiable child" were both born in 1792.

[73] Other depictions of Claremont are in *Claremont of History and To-Day* (New York 1907) and Eric K. Washington, *Manhattanville: Old Heart of West Harlem* (Arcadia Publishing, 2002), 98, 107, 122, 126.

[74] *New York City Guide* (1939), 288.

[75] *New York Times*, July 18, 1949.

[76] Michael Hogan and family are listed among "aliens authorized to purchase real estate in New York State" in 1806 in Carl Boyer (ed.), *Ship Passenger Lists, New York and New Jersey (1600-1825)* (Newhall, California, 1978), 188.

[77] A settlement of accounts of June 1819 and a 14-year lease of December 20 of the same year show that Hogan, Bayard and Ray jointly owned land in Sackets Harbor itself and the nearby town of Hounsfield (Cornell University Library, Elisha Camp Papers).

[78] *Seaver*, 185; *Donovan*, 52.

[79] Details about Thomas Sumter, Jr. (1768–1840) and his wife, Natalie, are from Robert D. Bass, *Gamecock: The Life and Campaigns of General Thomas Sumter* (New York, 1961); M. Ignatia Gavaghan, *Nathalie De Lage Sumter: A Dedicated Life of Faith* (Sumter, S.C., 1983); Anne King Gregorie, *Thomas Sumter*

(Columbia, South Carolina, 1931); and Mary Virginia Saunders White, *Fifteen Letters of Nathalie Sumter* (Columbia, S.C., 1942). These sources do not mention Hogan, the shipboard incident or the law suit, but they do establish that Thomas, Jr., lacked the attributes that made his father a hero.

[80] Barnard *Diaries,* 1:178.

[81] The quote citing nine famous Irish residents of New York is from Michael Jospeh O'Brien, *In Old New York: The Irish Dead in Trinity and St. Paul's Churchyards* (New York, 1928), who also wrote that a number of Catholics attended Trinity Church.

[82] Hogan's church affiliations are principally from William Rhinelander Stewart, *Grace Church and Old New York* (New York, 1924), 82-86, 99, 120, 299, 453. Other background on the churches he attended is from Carl Lamson Carmer, *The Years of Grace, 1808-1958* (New York, 1958); Jonathan Greenleaf, *A History of the Churches of All Denominations in the City of New York from the First Settlement to the Year 1846* (New York, 1846); Clifford Phelps Morehouse, *Trinity: Mother of Churches: An Informal History of Trinity Parish in the City of New York* (New York, 1973), and *Peters, op. cit.* The latter includes the story (p. 377) that Hogan "seems to have become so familiar with [New York's] waters that he was commissioned to bring a French prize which his ship had captured into this port without a pilot." The author cannot even guess where this clearly untrue story came from. The quote about Grace Church is from *Carmer, ibid.*

Chapter 8

[1] Hogan to Monroe, May 14, 1818, HSP, Joel R. Poinsett Collection.

[2] *Wilkes,* 297-298.

[3] Hogan's date of American citizenship is in Scott Kenneth (ed.), *Early New York Naturalizations, 1792-1840* (Baltimore, 1981). Under the law as it then existed, Hogan's wife and his three children automatically acquired U.S. citizenship when he did.

[4] *Smith,* 207. A search of despatches from Madeira in the NA reveals virtually none signed by John Marsden; he may have resided in the more comfortable Portuguese capital of Lisbon.

[5] *Columbia Museum & Savannah Advertizer,* March 12, 1806. A notice on March 29 read: "*Minerva* (Nathaniel Franklin) will sail from Charleston and arrive Savannah 4 days later. For freight or passage, apply to John M. Pintard at Capt. Spellman's or to Captain on board." On April 5, John M. Pintard was listed as one of the persons for whom there was undelivered mail at the Savannah post office. Another possible indirect connection with Hogan can be gleaned from letters published in *ibid.* on March 17, 1807, showing that Pintard was interrogated in connection with the search for Aaron Burr (preceding his arrest and trial) while he was on a journey from Louisiana to New York in company with (among others) the "little son" of Aaron Burr's son-in-law, John Bartow Prevost. There are indications in MHFP that Prevost was known to Hogan at this

time; they were certainly closely acquainted when both were in Valparaíso, Chile, fifteen years later. See also next chapter.

[6] Information about John Pintard and his cousin John Marsden Pintard and the quotations from John Pintard's letters are from "Letters from John Pintard...." 1:108, 231; 3:264, 273. John Pintard is mentioned frequently in Edwin G. Burrows & Mike Wallace, *Gotham: A History of New York City to 1898* (Oxford Univ. Press, 1999).

[7] *Stokes*, 1:403.

[8] Hogan to Monroe, May 14, 1818, HSP, Joel R. Poinsett Collection.

[9] The Oliver business history is recounted in Stuart Weems Bruchey, *Robert Oliver, Merchant of Baltimore, 1783–1819*, The Johns Hopkins University Studies in Historical and Political Science, series 74, no. 1 (1956), which does not mention Michael or William Hogan.

[10] *Donovan*, 52, 204; *Seaver*, 185.

[11] Joseph's residence at Claremont is from *Mott*, 26; *Peterson*, 99; Rufus Rockwell Wilson, *New York Old and New: Its Story, Streets and Landmarks* (Philadelphia, 1902), 1:315; and *New York Times*, December 26, 1909. The story of his U.S. ventures is from William Chapman White, *Adirondack Country* (New York, 1967), 181-185.

[12] Elizabeth Cilman Brown, *Outline History of Utica and Vicinity* (Utica, 1900), 66.

[13] MHS, Robert Oliver Papers, MS 626.

[14] *Congressional Record, House of Representatives*, December 23, 1818.

[15] *U.S. Statutes-at-Large*, 15th Congress, 2nd Session.

[16] John Wells (c.1770-1823), who became an attorney in New York in 1791, "was a man of much ability and possessed characteristics that made him greatly beloved." *Dictionary of American Biography* 10:642-3.

[17] Roy Porter & G.S. Rousseau, *Gout: The Patrician Malady* (Yale Univ. Press, 1998), 132-135.

[18] Cited in *Bell*, 240.

[19] When Major Butler died in 1822, Thomas Butler was bequeathed $20,000 but the bulk of his estate went to his sister Frances. *Bell*, 220.

[20] In 1826, the British agreed to pay over a million dollars in satisfaction of all claims for slaves and other property seized in the Georgia raid, of which the Butler estate received "something in excess of $7,000, far below expectations." The full story of the seizure of Butler's slaves and the consequences is told in *Bell*, 170-191.

[21] Hogan to Monroe, October 24, 1815, Livingston to Monroe, August 12, 1815, NA, RG 59, M 438. Tompkins letter (supposedly enclosed with Hogan's) is not in the file.

[22] Hogan to Richard Rush, June 10, 1817, NA, RG 59, T 196, vol. 1.

23 Elmsie to Madison, October 15, 1806, NA, RG 59, T 191, vol. 1.

24 Robert & John Oliver to Hogan, June 6, 1817, MHS, Robert Oliver Papers, MS 626.

25 Williams presence on the trip is in "Letters from John Pintard...," 1:108. His father Thomas Williams was an Indian chief, although probably a white man who married an Indian woman. Eleazer Williams opened a school for Indian children in Hogansburg or St. Regis in 1850 and allegedly built a church at Hogansburg, but the later claim has been shown to be incorrect (*Seaver*, 680). His claim to be the lost Dauphin of France who should have been Louis XVII of France gained national attention in 1853 with an article in *Putnam's Magazine*, followed in 1901 by a best-selling novel, *Lazarre*, by Mary Hartwell Catherwood. The story is regarded as a complete fabrication (*Seaver*, 677-695).

26 Hogan's land transactions with St. Regis Indians are from *Donovan*, *Hough* and *Seaver*. The quote about the curricle is from the latter, 187.

27 Agreement between Michael Hogan and St. Regis Chiefs, July 27, 1816, miscellaneous manuscripts, 1819-1981, Special Collections & Archives, St. Lawrence University Libraries.

28 Hogan to Robert Oliver, September 18, 1819, MHS, Robert Oliver Papers, MS 626.

29 Hogan to Monroe, May 14, 1818, HSP, Joel R. Poinsett Collection.

30 Robert & John Oliver to William Hogan, April 5, 1819, MHS, Robert Oliver Papers, MS 626.

31 Clinton to William Hogan, February 19, 1820, miscellaneous manuscripts, 1819-1981, Special Collections & Archives, St. Lawrence University Libraries.

32 *Annals of Congress*, 15 Congress, 2nd Session, 2:2523-2524.

33 Hogan to Adams, June 14, 1819, NA, RG 59, M 439, vol. 9.

34 Thomas Morris (1771-1849) was the son of Robert Morris, "financier" of the Revolution. He served in the House of Representatives (1801-03), practiced law in New York City and was appointed U.S. marshal for the Southern District of New York in 1816, 1820, 1825 and 1829. *Biographic Directory of the American Congress, 1774-1996*, Washington, D.C., 1997. There is no other mention of him in connection with Michael Hogan than the one entry in John Quincy Adams, *Diary* (see note 37 below).

35 Hogan to Adams, August 15, 1819, NA, RG 59, M 439, vol. 9.

36 Vaughn to Adams, August 14, 1819, Decatur to Adams, August 16, 1819, NA, RG 59, M 439, vol. 9.

37 Hogan's two calls on Adams in August 1819 are recorded in John Quincy Adams, *Diary*, The Adams Family Papers, reel 34, microfilm copy, Library of Congress. The diary entries note that Hogan made much of his Irish origins and the fortune he brought to the U.S. and "lost" due to his "misplaced confidence in others."

[38] Hogan to Robert & John Oliver, September 18 & November 23, 1819, MHS, Robert Oliver Papers, MS 626.

[39] Pintard to daughter, October 5, 1819, "Letters from John Pintard...," 1:231. It is not known whether Pintard referred to his son-in-law, Richard Davidson, as "doctor" because he was a doctor of medicine or as a sign of respect.

[40] For U.S. policy toward Cuba, see Foner. *La fruta Madurai* (ripe fruit) policy is a term adopted by Cubans scornful of this U.S. policy; *ibid.*, 145.

[41] Hogan to Robert & John Oliver, September 18 & November 23, 1819, MHS, Robert Oliver Papers, MS 626. The vessel is not to be confused with the U.S.S. *Boxer*, a U.S. Navy brig that was lost two years earlier.

[42] Hogan to Adams, November 24, 1819, NA, RG 59, T 20, vol. 3.

[43] Hogan to Adams, December 14, 1819, NA, RG 59, T 20, vol. 3.

[44] Hogan to Adams, December 14, 1819, NA, RG 59, T 20, vol. 3.

[45] Hogan to Adams, February 19, 1820, NA, RG 59, T 20, vol. 3.

[46] The Stocking incident is in Hogan (at New York Quarantine Grounds) to Adams, June 24, 1820, NA, RG 59, M 146, vol. 1. The call for legislation is in Hogan to Adams, March 2, 1820, NA, RG 59, M 146, vol. The Monroe endorsement is in Hogan (at Staten Island) to Adams, June 15, 1820, NA, RG 59, T 20, vol. 3.

[47] Hogan to Adams, February 3, 1920, NA, RG 59, T 20, vol. 3. The conjecture that one of Hogan's sources wasthe Canadian he met on sailing from New York is based on the facts that the Canadian was also destined for Havana and that the two reports on British invasion plans were remarkably similar.

[48] Hogan to Adams, February 18, 1820, NA, RG 59, T 20, vol. 3.

[49] Hogan to Adams, April 15, 1820, NA, RG 59, T 20, vol. 3.

[50] Cited in *Foner*, 100.

[51] Hogan (at Staten Island) to Adams, June 15, 1820, NA, RG 59, T 20, vol. 3.

[52] November 3, 1820, entry in John Quincy Adams, *Diary*, The Adams Family Papers, reel 34, microfilm copy, Library of Congress.

[53] *Billingsley*, 106. Kavanaugh may have come to Havana from Panama or, more likely, he communicated with Hogan by letter from Panama. Several of the U.S.S. *Macedonia's* crew who were ill were sent home from Panama, including Lieutenant John Percival (whom Hogan was to meet again later in Valparaíso). Percival arrived in Havana from Chagres (present-day Colon) in Panama on the *Gulph* on the 12th. He had "been very ill and on the point of death," but recovered and sailed for Baltimore on the 24th (see Hogan to Adams, February 18, 1820, NA, RG 59, T 20, vol. 3).

[54] Hogan (at Staten Island) to Adams, June 15, 1820, NA, RG 59, T 20, vol. 3. His deferred visit is in Hogan (at New York) to Adams, June 24, 1820, NA, RG 59, M 146, vol. 1.

Chapter 9

[1] There are no letters of recommendation in NA for Hogan in 1820. He may have political support supplied privately, possibly by Martin Van Buren, future president. By 1820 Van Buren had become firmly established in New York Republican politics, holding the position of chairman of a committee on appointments in the Assembly, and in 1821 he became a U.S. senator. When Van Buren became secretary of state in 1829, Hogan wrote to him in terms that inferred a kinship, although admittedly it may have been only that they were both New York residents. The other possibility is Joel Roberts Poinsett—see note 10 below.

[2] Hogan's calls on Adams and Monroe's decision are recorded in entries for November 3, 4, 10 and 11, 1820, in John Quincy Adams, *Diary*, The Adams Family Papers, reel 34, microfilm copy, Library of Congress. There is no independent record of Hogan's meeting with Monroe.

[3] The author's belief that the Bullus matter was also raised in Hogan's meeting with Monroe is based on the fact that Hogan felt it necessary to explain directly to Monroe in 1823 why he had turned young Bullus out of his home. Before Heman Allen left Washington in 1824, Monroe asked him to look into the Bullus matter which Allen did and then reported the results to Monroe. Hogan spelled the Bullus name as "Bullis." However, the person was undoubtedly Dr. John Bullus, a naval surgeon in Washington in the early 1800s who operated a small apothecary at 7th and L Streets, S.E. (*The Sunday Star*, April 29, 1934). Another source states that Bullus was Stephen Decatur's "old business partner" in 1814 (James Tertius de Kay, *Chronicles of the Frigate Macedonian, 1809-1922* (New York, 1995), 98). When mentioning the young Bullus in his 1823 letter to Monroe, Hogan refers to "Doctor Bullis whose family, I understood, expected you would provide for." The inference is that Dr. Bullus was deceased and that the young Bullus was a ward or protege of Monroe. The author has been unable to determine when Dr. Bullus died, but because he is not listed in the 1822 directory of Washington residents (the earliest of such listings), it is possible that he was dead in 1820.

[4] Charles Oscar Paullin, "Naval Administration Under the Navy Commissioners, 1815-1842, *Proceedings of the United States Naval Institute*, XXXIII (1907), 611-614.

[5] Agents for commerce and seamen were created by an act of Congress in 1796 for the protection of American seamen in foreign ports. *Pine*, 73.

[6] Three persons served as vice consuls at Valparaíso and/or Santiago before Hogan's arrival, but all were local merchants appointed by special agents. They were: (1) Matthew Hoevel, a Swedish citizen who became a naturalized American and later Chilean citizen, appointed by Poinsett but dismissed by him in 1814; (2) Henry Hill appointed by Worthington in 1818 on Prevost's advice; (3) Horatio Gerauld (sometimes spelled Jerauld) appointed by Prevost on Hill's departure in 1821. There were also locally appointed vice consuls at some lesser ports in Chile. Hogan was the first to receive a full, lawfully recognized consular

appointment from Washington.

[7] Hogan (at New York) to Adams, November 11, 1820, NA, RG 59, M 146, vol. 1.

[8] Accurate information about the early Department of State is surprisingly sparse. The treatment here relies principally on *Hunt* and *Kennedy*.

[9] The policy was reflected in a joint resolution of Congress on December 10, 1811 (*Sherman*, 11) and several neutrality acts (*Pine*, 8-51).

[10] Four Hogan letters to Poinsett with dates from 1827 to 1831 are at HSP, Joel R. Poinsett Papers, as is his May 14, 1818, letter to Monroe. Monroe or Adams may have given that letter to Poinsett as part of a file to make recommendations on appointments to posts in Latin America. Although Poinsett had returned to the U.S. in 1814, he remained involved in South America matters. In October 1818, Adams asked him to submit a report on South America to complement those provided by the three commissioners (*Pine*, 304).

[11] *Sherman*, 11-12; *Whitaker*, 71, 79; *Pine* 174-195.

[12] *Neumann*, provides details of American participation in both ships and men in Chile.

[13] In 1782, Burr married Mrs. Theodosia (Bartow) Prevost, ten years his senior, widow of Colonel James A. Prevost, British Army officer, by whom she had three daughters and two sons, James Augustine Frederick Prevost and John Bartow Prevost. Both stepsons were devoted to Burr, as was his own daughter, Theodosia (1783–1813), who in February 1801 married Joseph Alston (1779–1816), later Governor of South Carolina (1812–14). Theodosia met a tragic death when the ship on which she was traveling from South Carolina to New York to meet her father was lost at sea. Although numerous books have been written about Burr, his daughter Theodosia and others with whom they came in contact, information about Burr's stepchildren is sketchy. John Bartow Prevost (known to his family by his middle name Bartow) was born in 1766, married Frances Ann Smith, daughter of Princeton president, Samuel Stanhope Smith, in 1799. They had four children: Marcus (died young); Stanhope Prevost (married with children, died in Lima, Peru); Frances (married William L. Breckenridge of Kentucky, one son and two daughters); and Theodosia (born 1801, unmarried, died 1864). In addition to his judicial appointment, Prevost was secretary of Legation at Paris when Monroe was minister from 1794-96 and served as member of New York legislature in 1799. Information about Prevost is mainly from Evelyn Pierrepont Bartow, *Bartow Genealogy* (Baltimore, 1878), 61; Anna Key Bartow Cumyn, *The Bartow Family: A Genealogy* (Montreal, 1984), 100-103; and Milton Lomask, *Aaron Burr: The Years from Princeton to Vice President, 1756-1805* (New York, 1979). Prevost's Paris appointment, which was sought by Burr for his stepson, is in Harry Ammon, *James Monroe: The Quest for National Identity* (Charlottesville, 1990), 114.

[14] According to Adams, *History of the United States...Thomas Jefferson*, 450, Jefferson appointed Prevost to this position to conciliate Vice President Burr whose opposition to the impeachment of Supreme Court Justice Chase in

1804/05 was feared. Caesar Rodney, one of Monroe's South American commissioners in 1817, was also involved as manager of Chase's trial.

[15] Prevost was with Thomas Sumter, Jr., and his wife Natalie in Washington, D.C., on their trip from South Carolina to New York in October and November 1809 to sail on Hogan's *Charleston Packet* to Rio de Janeiro (shipboard incident described in preceding chapter). Thomas Butler, in a July 27, 1817, letter to Hogan at New York, asked: "Pray what has become to my friend, J. B. Prevost, Esquire. Upon my return to Philadelphia I addressed a letter to him, as before, Greenwich Street, New York, but have not had a line from him. What has become of his daughter?" Prevost received his appointment the same month this letter was written.

[16] *Pine*, 378.

[17] Eric Lambert, "Los Legionarios Britanicos," *Bello y Londres: Segundo Congreso del Bicentenario* (Caracas 1980), 1:364. See also Alfred Hasbrouck, *Foreign Legionaires in the Liberation of Spanish South America* (New York, 1928).

[18] John Styles was examined, passed and became a member of the Royal College of Surgeons of England on April 5, 1816 (letter from the College to author). Shortly thereafter, he went to Chile. J. Styles is shown as a surgeon in an 1818 Chilean Navy list in Charles F. Hillman, *"Old Timers" British and Americans in Chile* (Santiago, 1901), 49; and his name appears as surgeon on *Lautero* in an 1822 list in Luis Uribe y Orrego, *Nuestra marina militar* (Valparaíso, 1910), 387.

[19] Warren Tute, *Cochrane: A Life of Admiral the Earl of Dundonald* (London, 1965), 176. The quote about Cochrane's temper is from British historian F. A. Kirkpatrick, cited *Billingsley*, 61.

[20] *Whitaker*, 286.

[21] *Billingsley*, 81.

[22] Under generally accepted rules of international law, a belligerent could declare a blockade of an enemy port or ports and oblige neutral nations to respect the blockade. This general rule was subject to caveats and exceptions—some generally accepted, others not—and was ultimately negated when the neutral had superior power and was prepared to enforce its will. The U.S. had already had its share of involvement with both the theory and practice of blockades prior to the War of 1812. One of the major caveats adopted by countries having naval strength, including the U.S., was that a blockade should be respected only if it could be and was effectively enforced, otherwise it was considered to be an unlawful paper blockade. In the case of Peru and Chile, the Spanish (and later the patriot) blockades were usually paper blockades, which served as an excuse for U.S. Navy vessels often to take aggressive roles.

[23] Details of *Macedonian* incidents, as well as Downes's letter to O'Higgins and Prevost's purported comments, are in *Billingsley*, 111-120.

[24] *Billingsley*, 97.

[25] *Manning* 2:1004-5.

[26] *Manning* 2:1005-1019.

[27] *Pine*, 37-39.

[28] Hogan to Adams, February 14, 1821, NA, RG 59, M 146, vol. 1.

[29] Hogan (at New York) to Adams, February 2, 1821, NA, RG 59, M 146, vol. 1. The letter is dated February 2, 1820, but this is in error because Hogan was then in Havana. He sent a second letter to Adams on February 9 (this time clearly dated 1821) reporting on developments in Cuba since his departure. Both letters may have been intended to assure Adams that he was taking care to continue to report on Cuban matters, having left the island with the intention of returning, pending the appointment of a new American representative.

[30] Robert Arthur Humphreys, "British Merchants and South American Independence," *Proceedings of the British Academy* (London, 1965), 51:167-170. The Robertsons negotiated a loan with Barings for the government at Buenos Aires in 1824; it was one of many ventured in 1820s between newly independent countries in South America and Britain, almost all of which turned out badly for creditors.

[31] Richard J. Cleveland, who will appear again, stated in his memoirs that, "after my return [to the U.S. in 1820], in an adventure to Peru in the ship *Tea-Plant*, with Messrs LeRoy and Bayard, I made eight thousand dollars." *Voyages and Commercial Enterprises of the Sons of New England* (New York, 1968, reprint of original two volume 1842 edition), 403.

[32] Hogan to Adams, March 31, 1821, and July 13, 1821, NA, RG 59, M 146, vol. 1.

[33] Hogan to Robert & John Oliver, July 13, 1821, MHS, Robert Oliver Papers, MS 626.

[34] Details of piracy threat to *Teaplant* are from Sophia Donnelly, *Memories of Former Days*, recounting her life in Valparaíso and Calcutta between 1821 and 1831. The manuscript was written in long hand some fifty years later in Stuttgart, which a relative had typed. The stories contain few dates or names but are a treasure trove of first hand reports of several events in Hogan's career and of life and customs in Chile and India.

[35] Hogan to Adams, July 13, 1821, NA, RG 59, M 146, vol. 1.

[36] Hogan to Robert & John Oliver, July 13, 1821, MHS, Robert Oliver Papers, MS 626.

[37] Population data for Valparaíso and size business community are in *Rector*, 63-65, 253. By the time Hogan arrived at Valparaíso, its population was reported by Prevost to be 15,000 (*Manning* 2:1073).

[38] James M. Gillis, *Chile: Its Geography, Climate, Earthquakes, Government...* (Washington, 1855), 1:226.

[39] The average time for the 46 Hogan despatches on which a receipt date is shown was 118 days (3.9 months); the longest time 237 days (7.8 months); the shortest 76 days (2.5 months). The U.S. Navy sometimes sent despatches via

Panama, a route that required an overland messenger on the Isthmus. The Navy claimed the transit time was much less than around Cape Horn, but this was apparently not always the case. See Robert Erwin Johnson, *Thence Around Cape Horn: The Story of U.S. Naval Forces on Pacific Station, 1818-1923* (Annapolis, 1963), 8.

[40] Prevost, Santiago, to Adams, March 10, 1821, NA, RG 59, M 37, vol. 7.

[41] John O'Sullivan (Captain of *Canton*) to Hogan, December 10, 1822, MHFP. In a subsequent letter of February 20, 1823, O'Sullivan tells Hogan: "I spoke to Captain Mathewson [captain of *Mercury*] but he appears to be much in favor of that Gerauld. Captain M has a very different opinion of you to mine, though I have partly convinced him. He says you paid more attention to the English than the Americans. I did all in my power to convince him. This I mention to put you on your guard." Gerauld was apparently an American businessman, possibly retained at one time by the firm of Alsop Wetmore & Cryder. Several of his letters to Larned in *Larned Family Papers, 1753-1859*, American Antiquarian Society, Worcester, Massachusetts, speak of unidentified "thems" and "others" seeking to defame Larned.

[42] Hogan's August 18, 1821, despatch is in *Manning* 2:1055, and *ASP, Foreign Relations* 4:827. Prevost's despatch is also in *Manning* 2:1055.

[43] Hogan to Adams, May 6, 1822, *Manning* 2:1062.

[44] Hogan to Adams, January 15, 1822, *Manning* 2:1061-62.

[45] The U.S. Navy did not authorize the rank of admiral until after the Civil War. Commodore was a courtesy title applied to commanders of naval squadrons, the equivalent today of admirals. *McKee*, 29.

[46] The recently overhauled *Constellation* that now attracts tourists in Baltimore harbor is not the original vessel, despite earlier claims to the contrary. The original frigate was dismantled in 1853; construction of the second *Constellation* began a year later. *Washington Post*, July 3, 1999.

[47] *Billingsley*, 139.

[48] Hogan's report of his meeting with O'Higgins, his comments about Cochrane and his plea for consul general title are in Hogan to Adams, October 9, 1821, and November 4, 1821 (*Manning* 2:1058-1060). Hogan was not, of course, consul general, much less consul, a distinction of which the Chileans must have been aware. Perhaps to cover any inference that he had misled the Chileans, he added that "I hope you will be pleased to send me that commission when the independence of the country is acknowledged by the president." He may also have been concerned that there were other candidates for the job. Prevost later recommended a Valparaíso resident, Edward McCall, son of Archibald McCall of Philadelphia, for a consulate, presumably at Valparaíso (Prevost to Adams, November 15, 1822, *Manning* 2:1072).

[49] Hogan to Adams, June 5, 1822, NA, RG 59, M 146, vol. 1.

50 These considerations are addressed in James Fred Ripley, *Rivalry of the United States and Great Britain over Latin America, 1808-1830* (Baltimore, 1929).

51 *Pine*, 440-444.

52 Hogan to Adams, October 9, 1821, NA, RG 59, M 146, vol. 1.

53 Sophia Donnelly's account does not name vessels involved, except for *Teaplant*, but her rendition matches in its main points *Billingsley*, 126, 129, 139-140.

54 *Billingsley*, 129, 139-140.

55 Hogan reported that Benavides had been captured near Concepción, sent to Santiago where he was hanged, his body burned and his head and arms returned to Concepción where they were fixed on a pole. Hogan to Adams, May 5, 1822, NA, RG 59, M 146, vol. 1.

56 Hogan to Adams, October 9, 1821, NA, RG 59, M 146, vol. 1; *Billingsley*, 142-3.

57 Prevost, Lima, to Adams, February 6, 1822, NA, RG 59, M 37, vol. 7; *Billingsley*, 143.

58 Commodore Charles Stewart to O'Higgins, April 16, 1822. *ASP, Naval Affairs*, 2:568-569.

59 Hogan to Adams, May 6, 1822, NA, RG 59, M 146, vol. 1.

60 Hogan to Adams, August 27, 1822, NA, RG 59, M 146, vol. 1.

61 These letters are in both Department of State (NA, RG 59, M 37, vol. 5) and Navy Department records (RG 45, T 829, vol. 434).

62 Adams to Monroe, August 26, 1820, *Writings of John Quincy Adams*, ed. Worthington Chauncey Ford (New York, 1917) 7:68.

63 "I never promised you an appointment." Prevost to Robinson, June 14, 1822, enclosed with Prevost, Santiago, to Adams, August 22, 1822, NA , RG 59, M 37, vol. 5.

64 Prevost, Santiago, to Adams, January 6, 1821, NA, RG 59, M 37, vol. 5. Robinson claimed he had a receipt showing he had returned the commission (Prevost, Santiago, to Adams, May 21, 1822, NA, RG 59, M 37, vol. 5). It is not clear whether this alleged loan incident was the one did take place in 1819 or subsequently.

65 Robinson, Valparaíso, to Adams, July 18, 1821, NA, RG 59, M 37, vol. 5.

66 Robinson, Valparaíso, to Adams, October 8, 1821, NA, RG 59, M 37, vol. 5.

67 Robinson, Valparaíso, to Adams, November 4, 1821, NA, RG 59, M 37, vol.5.

68 Hogan to Adams, January 20, 1822, NA, RG 59, M 146, vol. 1.

69 Robinson, Valparaíso, to Adams, April 29, 1822, NA, RG 45, T 829, vol. 434.

70 Robinson, Santiago, to Adams, May 25, 1822, NA 45, T 829, vol. 434.

[71] Robinson, Valparaíso, to Adams, August 15, 1822, NA, RG 59, M 37, vol. 5.

[72] Adams note refers to a May 15, 1822, letter from Robinson. The author could not find any Robinson letter with that specific date in NA.

[73] The first letter is in Department of State records (Robinson, Valparaíso, to Adams, August 25, 1822, NA, RG 59, M 37, vol. 5. The second is in Navy records (Robinson, Valparaíso, to Adams, August 25, 1822, NA, RG 45, T 829, vol. 434).

[74] Cleveland was actively involved in several American ships trading along the west coast of South America from 1817 to 1820. These included the *Canton* and *Ocean* which returned to these familiar waters during Hogan's stay at Valparaíso. Cleveland makes no mention of any continuing involvement with any of these vessels after he returned to the U.S. in 1820.

[75] Hogan to Adams, August 27, 1822, NA, RG 59, M 146, vol. 1. Hill in a December 31, 1818, letter to Adams, had asked whether a consul may provide U.S. papers for foreign vessels purchased by U.S. citizens at a foreign port and whether a Department Circular to Consuls dated July 12, 1805, on the subject remained applicable (NA, RG 59, M 78, vol. 1). Adams answer of July 11, 1820, received as Hill was about to leave Chile, supported the action he had taken with respect to a vessel (not the *Ocean*) and confirmed that the 1805 circular was still in force (NA, RG 59, M 78, vol. 1). Henry Hill had a colorful background. He came to Valparaíso in 1817 as supercargo on the American vessel *Savage* carrying arms for the Chilean patriots The *Savage* incident is described in Henry Hill, *Incidents in Chile, 1817-21* (unpublished memorial, 1889); and Roberto C. Hernandez, *Valparaíso en 1827: una rešena histórico local, con motivo del Centenario de "El Mercurio"* (Valparaíso, 1927), 158.

[76] On April 25, 1831, the State Department asked Hogan whether he still had the money that was allegedly due to the cook on the *Ocean* when that vessel was sold at Valparaíso by its crew (NA, RG 59, M 78, vol. 3). There is no way of knowing whether this was the same vessel as in the 1822 incident. The date of the sale and the nature of Hogan's reply are also unknown.

[77] Hogan to Adams, August 27, 1822, NA, RG 59, M 146, vol. 1.

[78] Prevost, Lima, to Stewart, May 12, 1823, *ASP, Naval Affairs* 2:564.

[79] In his August 15 letter to Adams, Robinson alleged that "Mr. Hogan is well acquainted with the character and circumstances of the *Ocean*. Yet he allowed that ship to fly the American flag nine months after he assumed his official function at Valparaíso where she was lying at the time and for three months after and finally irritated and abused the government of Chile for having seized the ship and captain at Talcuhana. The real owner then came forward, claimed the asset, took the oath of allegiance, became a citizen of Chile and put the ship under Chile flag for a second time and which flag she now bears." Robinson said that the *Ocean* had supplied arms to the Royalist pirate Benavides, but this would have had to be before the specie incident.

80 Hogan to Adams, November 2, 1822, NA, RG 59, M 146, vol. 1. Prevost's views about Tracy are in Prevost to Stewart, January 24, 1823, *ASP, Naval Affairs*, 2:564. Prevost reported similar information about Tracy in despatches to Adams of April 24, 1823 and May 1, 1823 (NA, RG 59, M 37, vol. 7). One American official who continued to think well of Tracy was Henry Hill. In letter sent to Hogan on September 12, 1831, after Hogan's return to U.S., Hill referred to his "friend Mr. Tracy of New York."

81 Robinson received the $1,000 commission in 1819, following one awarded to Worthington the previous year (*Neumann*, 218). Prevost in effect acknowledged that Robinson had returned the money in a postscript to a May 21, 1821, letter to Adams (NA, RG 59, M 37, vol. 5).

82 NA, RG 45, T 829, vol. 434.

83 Hogan to Adams, December 13, 1822, NA, RG 59, M 146, vol. 1.

84 Hogan to Monroe, June 25, 1823, NA, RG 59, M 146, vol. 1. Adams diary entry for January 27, 1824 (*Memoirs* 6:239-240), speaks of urging Monroe to support Congressional resolution dealing with Astoria "on occasion of receiving a letter from Mr. Hogan...mentioning that an American vessel had met a British one carrying supplies to the British establishment at Astoria." No Hogan letter on this subject can be found at NA, but if there had been one it would have been sent about the same time as his June 25, 1823, letter to Monroe. Perhaps he sent another letter marked Confidential that was withheld from official records.

85 Robinson, Washington, to Monroe, September 21, 1823, NA, RG 59, M 37, vol. 5.

86 Adams *Memoirs* 7:494. Also appointed at that time was Richard Cleveland, the same one involved with the *Beaver, Ocean* and *Canton* in the 1820s.

87 *Whitaker*, 295-298. Adams brought a Jeremy Robinson letter of 1819 on this matter to Monroe's attention (Adams to Monroe, August 26, 1820, *Writings of John Quincy Adams*, ed. Worthington Chauncey Ford (New York, 1917), 7:67.

88 The British naval commander in Valparaíso port when Hogan arrived there reported that Hogan told him "an American ship-of-the-line and a schooner are coming to the Pacific, the American government being excessively displeased at the conduct of the Chilean admiral [Cochrane] toward some American vessels." *The Navy and South America, 1807-1823: Correspondence of the Commander-in-Chief on the South American States* (Edward Gerald Sandford Graham & R.A. Humphreys, eds., Publications of the Navy Records Society, 1962), 104.343.

89 Navy regulations prohibited the carriage of women on board ship without permission of the Navy Department or the squadron commander. *McKee*, 440. According to *Billingsley*, 151, Stewart had the approval of the Secretary of the Navy to carry his wife on board the *Franklin*.

90 *Canton* incident is described in *Billingsley*, 159-192. Echeverría's note and several of O'Sullivan's letters are in MHFP. Hogan's reply note is in NA, RG 59, M 146, vol. 1.

[91] Prevost to Stewart, January 26, 1823, *ASP, Naval Affairs,* 2:654. In NA, RG 59, M 37, vol. 5, there is an undated, unsigned paper purporting to be a memorandum by John Boston, quartermaster on the *Franklin* and at the time master of the Stewart-commandeered schooner *Peruvian,* stating that "arms were landed in the *Canton's* boats while lying at Arica under the protection of the *Franklin* and that one or two guns were landed from the *Canton* in the night about the same time...."

[92] The several episodes involving Eliphalet Smith are described in *Billingsley.*

[93] Hogan to Adams, January 15, 1822, *Manning* 2:1061.

[94] Stewart to O'Higgins, April 16, 1822, *ASP, Naval Affairs,* 2:568-569.

[95] *Sherman,* 40.

[96] Hogan to Adams, November 2, 1822, NA, RG 59, M 146, vol. 1.

[97] Stewart's court martial and the incidents leading to it are covered in *Billingsley,* 169, 185-193.

[98] The applicable Navy orders dated February 17, 1820, and December 24, 1823, are in *New American State Papers, Naval Affairs,* 6:72, 74. The original legislative authorization stemmed from the 1800 "Act for the Better Government of the Navy of the United States." The maximum commission was set at 0.5% for the first $10,000 and 0.25% thereafter. *McKee,* 338-41; *Whitaker,* 300-310.

[99] *McKee,* 172.

[100] *McKee,* 375-391, who notes that the Auditor's office was twice as large as that of the rest of the Navy Department.

[101] *ASP, Naval Affairs,* 2:562-565.

[102] Adams to Prevost, December 16, 1823, *ASP, Naval Affairs,* 2:557.

[103] *Whitaker,* 311.

[104] All quotations attributed to Wilkes are from *Wilkes.*

[105] Maria Dundas Graham's, *Journal of a Residence in Chile....*

[106] Hogan to Adams, December 16, 1822, NA, RG 59, M 146, vol. 1.

[107] Hogan to Adams, January 31 & April 7, 1823, *Manning* 2:1079, 1080-1083.

[108] William Spence Robertson, *France and Latin American Independence* (Baltimore, 1939), 269, 341.

[109] Prevost, Santiago, to Adams, October 28, 1823, *Manning* 2:1087-1088.

[110] Prevost, Santiago, to Hogan, December 13, 1823, *Manning* 2:1090.

[111] Prevost, Lima, to Adams, January 10, 1824, NA, RG 59, M 37, vol. 7.

[112] Prevost to Adams, July 24 & August 22, 1922, NA, RG 59, M 37, vols. 5 & 7 (also *Manning* 2:1066).

[113] Adams *Memoirs* 6:110-113.

[114] *Whitaker,* 553.

[115] Adams *Memoirs*, 6:122.

[116] Hogan to Adams, September 3, 1822, NA, RG 59, M 146, vol. 1, received December 19, 1822.

Chapter 10

[1] The seven Hart sisters of Saybrook have attracted considerable attention from writers, perhaps because Elisha Hart came from an old colonial family that had amassed some wealth, because the sisters were all reputed to be beautiful, and because Simon Bolivar supposedly became enamored over one of them. Their full story is told in Marion Hepburn Grant, *The Hart Dynasty of Saybrook* (West Hartford, Connecticut, 1981), a work that unfortunately contains no citation of sources and misnames one of the Hart sisters who accompanied Hull. The correct identification is in *Maloney*,

[2] Allen to Adams, April 29, 1824, *Manning* 2:1091-95; NA, RG 59, M 10, vol. 1. Before leaving for his post, Allen called on Monroe at the president's request to discuss South American issues, which probably included the reasoning behind the Monroe Doctrine that the president had announced the previous December (Adams *Memoirs* 6:204).

[3] See, for example, Allen to Adams, May 26, 1824, NA, RG 59, M 10, vol. 1., in which Allen reported his attempt to persuade the presumably sympathetic future Chilean minister to Washington (Campino) to oppose the acceptance of Catholicism as the state religion of Chile in its constitution. Also, Allen to Clay, September 1, 1825, *Manning* 2:1104.

[4] *Evans*, 36.

[5] Charles F. Hillman, *"Old Timers" British and Americans in Chile* (Santiago, 1901), 37-38; Benjamin Viçuna Mackenna, *The First Britons in Valparaíso, 1817-1827* (Valparaíso, 1884), 43.

[6] *Who Was Who in America: Historical Volume, 1607-1896* (1967), 87.

[7] Clinton to Hogan, November 6, 1823, Misc. Mss. Clinton, DeWitt, NYHS.

[8] Hogan to Larned, June 3, 1828, AAS, Larned Family Papers.

[9] The three instructions are: No. 1, Adams to Allen, November 23, 1823; No. 2, Adams to Allen, November 30, 1823; No. 3, Adams to Allen, November 30, 1823. NA, RG 59, M 77, vol. 10. An extract from No. 3 is in *Manning* 1:213.

[10] Allen to Adams, April 29, 1824, NA, RG 59, M 10, vol. 1.

[11] Allen to Adams, October 22, 1824, NA, RG 59, M 10, vol. 1.

[12] Hogan to Adams, January 19, 1824, *Manning* 2:1091.

[13] Hogan to Adams, March 12, 1824, NA, RG 59, M 146, vol. 1.

[14] Hogan to Adams, January 9 & 27, 1825, *Manning* 2:1100-1101.

[15] Hogan to Clay, February 4, 1826, NA, RG 59, M 146, vol. 1.

[16] Allen to Clay, November 15, 1826, NA, RG 56, M 10, vol. 2.

[17] *Evans*, 40; *Webster*, 1:51-52.

[18] Allen to Adams, January 24, 1825, NA, RG 59, M 10, vol. 1.

[19] *Maloney*, 392, is the source of the recovery information, but there are references in Allen's despatches to Elizabeth's continuing ill health.

[20] Prevost's last recorded despatch (to Adams) was dated January 10, 1825, from Lima: "I have asked Captain Hull a passage on the *Dolphin* as far as Quilca in order to proceed from there to Arequipo and Cusco. It appeared to me that it might be interesting to our government to have some view of the interior and of its commerce and this I hope to offer in my next [despatch] to bear date from the decayed capital of the Incas." (NA, RG 59, M 37, vol. 7.) After receiving Adam's rebuke on the blockade issue (Adams to Prevost, December 16, 1823, NA, RG 59, M 78, vol. 2), a separate demand that he explain his accounts (Adams to Prevost, November 16, 1823, *ibid.*), and a protest by American citizens in Callao and Lima (Adams to Prevost, December 24, 1823, *ibid.*), Prevost sought to defend himself against the charges and the enemies he was certain were behind them. After one explanation, he said: "I may have erred, Sir, in the discretion reposed in me and I may have erred in the grounds assumed to attain to the object of those claiming redress, but Never! Never!, Sir, has a representation been made to me of the infringement of a right, that I have not taken the earlier occasion for its correction and none, Sir, have occurred that have not been submitted in due course in my correspondence." He then asked that the secretary of state "acquaint [the president] of my determination to retire as soon as a successor can arrive to relieve me." (Prevost, Truxillo, to Adams, June 9, 1824, NA, RG 59, M 37, vol. 7.) The Department of State waited some four months after receiving this letter to advise Prevost (who was by then dead) that his letter "would have required special notice with regard to erroneous impressions on your mind contained in it, but for the determination of the President [Adams] to consent that you should immediately return to the United States. This is desirable as well to enable you to give such explanation of your own conduct as may be thought expedient [and] that you may be present to give such testimony as may be required upon the intended trial of Capt. Charles Stewart by court martial." (Clay to Prevost, July 20, 1825, NA, RG 59, M 78, vol. 2.) Prevost's son, Stanhope Prevost, acted as vice consul at Lima for a while and later as consul as late as 1848 and was associated with the house of McCall & Prevost. It is not known whether Stanhope's wife or children were with him in South America. He apparently died in Lima (note 13 of previous chapter). L.V. Prevost is shown in John H. Morgan, *The Foreign Service of the United States* (1961) as dying at Guayaquil on May 23, 1867, possibly one of Stanhope's children.

[21] Hogan to Clay, November 16, 1825, NA, RG 59, M 146, vol. 1; Wynn to Clay, June 25 & October 4, 1825, May 8, 1826, NA, RG 59, M 531. On the cover of one of Wynn's letters, a State Department clerk has written: "Wishes his consular commission for Chile." This is followed by "Send it to him. [A scribbled initial that is presumably Clay's]. Sent 7th October 1825." However, Hogan had a paper that he described as a commission for Wynn in his hands by November 3 on a ship that left New York on May 2. Possibly Hogan had a letter announcing the

commission, rather than the commission itself. Further evidence is that Wynn's name continued to appear on lists of consuls until 1834 when a subsequent consul at Valparaíso drew the anomaly to the State Department's attention, commenting that a separate consul at Santiago was hardly necessary (Thomas S. Russell to Secretary of State Louis McLane, January 1, 1834, NA, RG 59, M 146).

[22] Frances Hogan to Elizabeth Allen, March 15, 1826; Elizabeth Allen to Frances Hogan, March 16, 1826. The letters are in a private collection, cited in *Maloney*, 401.

[23] *Maloney*, 401-2, correctly notes that Hull did not have any business ventures in Peru, other than commissions he received for transporting specie, which was not an illegal activity. Hull netted about $10,000 from this activity.

[24] Allen to Clay, March 20, 1826, NA, RG 59, M 10, vol. 1

[25] Hogan's altercations with the Customs House and Allen's views on the proper location of the Navy agent are all in Allen to Clay, May 4, 1826, with enclosures, NA, RG 59, M 10, vol. 2.

[26] Hogan to Allen, April 20, 1825, enclosure to Allen to Adams, Sept. 1, 1825; Allen to Adams, September 16, 1825; NA, RG 59, M 10, vol. 1.

[27] Allen to Clay, May 4, 1826, with enclosures, NA, RG 59, M 10, vol. 2.

[28] Allen to Clay, August 1, 1826, with enclosures, NA, RG 59, M 10, vol. 2.

[29] Allen to Clay, November 19, 1826, with enclosures, NA 59, M 10, vol. 2.

[30] Allen to Clay, June 14, 1827, with enclosures, NA 59, M 10, vol. 2.

[31] Larned to Clay, October 25 & December 15, 1827, NA, RG 59, M 10, vol. 2. At Hogan's behest, Larned also obtained an exemption from duties for supplies loaded on the *Brandywine* and *Vincennes* on their departure from Chilean waters (Larned to Clay, June 5, 1829, NA, RG 59, M 10, vol. 3).

[32] The delivery of arms and ammunition to Chilean patriots by the *Savage* and several other American vessels in 1817 is covered in *Neumann*, 216-217. The Carrera episode and its relationship to Baltimore is in Laura Bornholdt, *Baltimore and Early Pan Americanism: A Study in the Background of the Monroe Doctrine* (Northampton, Mass., 1949) 57-80.

[33] Brent to Allen, July 18, 1826, NA, RG 59, M 77, vol. 11; Allen to Clay, December 22, 1826, NA, RG 59, M 10, vol. 2.

[34] Oliver to Hogan, September 10, 1826, MHS, Robert Oliver Papers, MSS 626.1, Box 20. An October 6, 1828, letter from Oliver to Hogan gives Oliver's opinion that the claimants might have to accept stock, not cash, in settlement.

[35] Based on the origin of all of Allen's despatches to the Department of State in NA, RG 59, M 10, he was in Santiago for nine months from April 10, 1824 (shortly after his arrival in Chile on March 27) to sometime in January 1825 and again from mid-March until July 31, 1827, a total of 13 months. The remaining 29 months (until his final departure on September 25, 1827) were spent in Valparaíso. Both Hogan and Allen in their letters and despatches refer to their neighbor status at that place.

[36] Hull to Hogan, January 24, 1825, MHFP, and Naval History Society Collection, Isaac Hull Letterbook, 1834-27, NYHS.

[37] Affidavit of Hogan dated May 7, 1827, MHFP. According to a statement added by him to this document at a later date, Hogan was unaware that Hull had laid claim to the 20 puncheons of rum at the Valparaíso Customs House until Kelly appeared demanding payment at the price stipulated by Hull. The rum was transferred to the *United States* on April 10 and paid for by Hogan on the 16th.

[38] Hogan to Percival, May 7, 1825, MHFP.

[39] Hull at Chorillos to Hogan, June 10, 1825, Naval History Society Collection, Isaac Hull Letterbook, 1823-27, NYHS.

[40] *McKee*, 221, 452.

[41] Hogan to Poinsett, August 1, 1827, HSP, Joel R. Poinsett Collection.

[42] Hogan to Commodore William Bainbridge, President, Board of Navy Commissioners, September 22, 1827, MHFP. Hull arrived in New York on April 24, a month after Bainbridge's letter to Hogan.

[43] Allen to Clay, July 18, 1827, with enclosed exchange between Hogan and Allen, NA, RG 59, M 10, vol. 2.

[44] *The Learned Family*, compiled by William Law Learned, 2nd edition (Albany, 1898), 203. Larned spoke of his upbringing abroad in Larned to Van Buren, July 8, 1829, NA, RG 59, M 10, vol. 3.

[45] An example is Larned to Clay, August 30, 1827, RG 59, M 10, vol. 2, in which Larned lucidly analyzed the difficulties in obtaining relief from Chile for the several claims of American citizens which he estimated totaled $160,000.

[46] Adams *Memoirs* 7:456.

[47] Larned to secretary of state, June 9, 1829, NA, RG 59, M 10, vol. 3.

[48] Clay to Larned, July 16 & September 15, 1828; Hogan to Larned, January 9, 1829, AAS, Larned Family Papers. Frances Hogan to Oliver, August 30, 1826, MHS, Papers of Robert Oliver, MSS-626, Box 2.

[49] Hogan to Van Buren, June 17, 1830, NA, RG 59, M 146, vol. 2.

[50] Allen to Clay, July 10, 1826, Larned to Clay, August 25 & November 10, 1826, October 25, 1827, April 11, 1828, NA, RG 59, M 10, vol. 2.

[51] The incident took place in early 1824. Charles Tyng, *Before the Wind: The Memoir of an American Sea Captain, 1808-1833* (Viking Penguin, 1999), 109.

[52] Benjamin Morrell, *A Narrative of Four Voyages to the South Sea, North and South Pacific Ocean, Chinese Sea...* (New York, 1832), 108, 173-4.

[53] Hogan to Adams, August 11, 1824(NA, RG 59, M 146, vol. 1).

[54] Hogan to William Coffin, President, Union M. Insurance Company, Nantucket, July 30, 1826, reprinted in *Savannah Georgian*, November 11, 1826. The *Dolphin's* rescue mission is in David F. Long, *"Mad Jack": The Biography of Captain John Percival, USN, 1779-1862* (Westport, Conn., 1993), 57-63, as

well as in Gibson and Heffernan, *op. cit.*

[55] William Lay & Cyrus Hussey, *A Narrative of the Mutiny on Board the Ship "Globe" of Nantucket, in the Pacific Ocean, January, 1824...*(New London, Conn., 1828).

[56] Hogan to Van Buren, with enclosures, November 12, 1830, NA, RG 59, M 146, vol. 2. William Comstock later wrote two books, *Voyage to the Pacific Descriptive of the Customs, Usages and Sufferings on Board Nantucket Whale Ships* (Boston, 1838) and *The Life of Samuel Comstock, the Terrible Whaleman* (Boston, 1840). The first is a work of fiction; the second is based on what George Comstock told his brother about Samuels' mutiny. It does not mention William's 1830 episode in Valparaíso.

[57] Hogan to Van Buren, November 12, 1830, with enclosures, NA, RG 59, M 146, vol. 2.

[58] Louise M. Sabine (ed.), *Memoir of Admiral Sir Thomas Sabine Pasley* (London, 1900), 52-57.

[59] Frances Hogan to Oliver, August 30, 1826, MHS, Papers of Robert Oliver, MSS-626, Box 2.

[60] The voyage to Juan Fernández Islands and Concepción is mentioned in *A Private Journal Kept by Mdn. Stephen C. Rowan Aboard the Vincennes, August 27, 1826-January 2, 1828* (NA, RG 45, M-180), but the festivities in which Navy personnel joined is not.

[61] C. S. Stewart, *A Visit to the South Seas in the U.S. Ship Vincennes During the Years 1829 and 1830* (New York, 1831), 1:130-135.

[62] *Narrative of the Surveying Voyages of His Majesty's Ships Adventure and Beagle Between the Years 1826 and 1836, Describing their Examination of the Southern Shore of South America* (London, 1839), vol. 1 (1826-1830).

[63] The historical novel is Marguerite Allis, *The Splendor Stays: An Historic Novel Based on the Lives of the Seven Hart Sisters of Saybrook, Connecticut* (New York, 1942). The romance of Jeanette Hart with Bolivar is repeated in Allen's *Commodore Hull...Papers*; Bruce Grant, *Isaac Hull, Captain of Old Ironsides: The Life and Times of Isaac Hull and the U.S. Constitution* (Chicago, 1947); and Marion Hepburn Grant, *The Hart Dynasty of Saybrook* (West Hartford, 1981). *Maloney*, 405, identifies the correct sister.

[64] Hogan to Van Buren, November 15, 1929, NA, RG 59, M 146, vol. 2.

[65] Filed under dates indicated in NA, RG 59, M 146, vol. 2, but without covering despatch from Hogan to Department of State.

[66] Hogan to Van Buren, December 26, 1829, NA, RG 59, M 146, vol. 2. Hogan's report said the family was taken to the British ship *Thetis*, not *Blonde*, as Sophia wrote.

[67] Hogan to Larned, January 27, 1830, AAS, Larned Family Papers.

[68] Hogan to Larned, December 10, 1829, AAS, Larned Family Papers.

69 Bispham to Larned, January 20, 1830, AAS, Larned Family Papers.

70 Webster's unabridged *New International Dictionary* (1958) defines "cloven foot" as "the sign of devilish character, Satan being often represented, like Pan, as cloven hoofed."

71 See for example *Rector*, 122-28.

72 Larned to Clay, May 10, 1828, *Manning* 2:1128-30. Larned argued for the commercial treaty even before Allen left (Larned to Clay, October 12, 1825, NA, RG 59, M 10, vol. 1).

73 Clay to Larned, January 29, 1829, NA, RG 59, M 77, vol. 12. A commercial treaty was finally concluded by chargé John Hamm on May 16, 1832; it was terminated by Chile in 1858.

74 Branch to Kendall, November 10, 1829 (mistakenly shown as 1820), & Kendall to Branch, November 30, 1829, *ASP, Naval Affairs* 3:375-381; *American Secretaries of the Navy*, ed. Paolo E. Coletta (Annapolis, 1980), 1:146-149. The Board of Navy Commissioners had earlier (May 28, 1828) promulgated regulations concerning the accounts of Navy agents but they applied only to the twelve domestic agents (*ASP, Naval Affairs* 3:370).

75 Although there had been a number of Navy agents located domestically within the U. S., a Treasury Department report of Hogan affair said there were only two others stationed at foreign locations—the American Consul at Barcelona, later Gibraltar, appointed in 1815 to supply the Mediterranean squadron, and the agent appointed in 1828 to Lima. The system was terminated in 1830.

76 Hogan to Van Buren, June 27, 1829, NA, RG 59, M 146, vol. 2. British Consul Nugent's salary was actually £2,000 plus £700 for expenses (*Webster*, 1:351).

77 Van Buren to Larned, June 2, 1830, NA, RG 59, M 77, vol. 14.

78 Letters were also intercepted by various parties, a practice made possible because there was usually no way to send international mail except through private channels. British Consul Nugent reported in 1825 that Parish Robertson & Company of Buenos Aires intercepted official correspondence "by bribery" (*Webster*, 1:357).

79 Circular instruction, June 9, 1830, NA 59, M 78, vol. 3.

80 *Journal of the Senate*, December 6, 1831, pages 13-14.

81 *Kennedy*, 73-78, 83-84.

82 Hogan to Van Buren, June 27, 1829, NA, RG 59, M 146, vol. 2. Hogan should have had no reason to expect the Department would reimburse him for handouts to seamen. Some other consuls established funds to which American ships contributed for the care of distressed and disabled seamen.

83 While waiting in New York for passage to Valparaíso, Hogan had asked Senator Rufus King, a fellow New Yorker, about U.S. duties applicable to imports from the Cape of Good Hope and Mauritius, an indication that he might have been thinking of trade with those areas. Rufus King to Hogan, December 21, 1820, Rufus King Papers, NYHS.

84 *Rector*, 50, 92.

85 Oliver to Hogan, April 28, 1825, MHS, Papers of Robert Oliver, MS-626.1, Box 20.

86 Hogan said in two letters written in 1829 that he had not engaged in commerce of any sort for the last four years. Hogan to Van Buren, June 27, 1829, NA, RG 59, M 146, vol. 2. Hogan to Board of Naval Commissioners, August 22, 1829, NA, RG 45, Naval Records Collection of the Office of Naval Records and Library, Board of Naval Commissioners, 1815-1842, Letters Received from Navy Agents, Sept. 1814-July 1842, vol. 30.

87 Hogan (at New York) to Oliver, August 28, 1831, Papers of Robert Oliver, MS-626, Box 2.

88 Audit signed by Kendall, March 2, 1831, *ASP, Naval Affairs*, 4:882-3.

89 John Rodgers to Department of State, October 8, 1821, NA, RG 59, M 179.

90 James Beatty, Navy agent, Baltimore, to Hogan, November 14, 1821; Robert Swarthout, Navy agent, New York, to February 24, 1822; MHFP.

91 Smith Thompson, Secretary of the Navy, to Hogan, November 16, 1822, *ASP, Naval Affairs*, 4:881.

92 Hogan to Thompson, *ASP, Naval Affairs*, 4:882.

93 "Regulations for the Naval Service" issued April 10, 1818, do not specify that requisitions from Navy agents must show the appropriation under which an expense falls (*ASP, Naval Affairs*, 1:532-3). This omission was apparently corrected in a notice of May 11, 1820, to Navy agents (*The New American State Papers: Naval Affairs*, 6:73).

94 Hogan announced his intention to Larned by letter of March 10, 1829, which Larned answered on March 12, noting Hogan would appoint William Clay in charge. AAS, Larned Family Papers. The cancellation is noted in Larned to Clay, March 20, 1829, NA, RG 59, M 10, vol. 3.

95 Larned to secretary of state, June 9, 1829, NA, RG 59, M 10, vol. 3.

96 Hogan to Van Buren, June 27, 1829, NA, RG 59, M 146, vol. 2.

97 Hogan to Larned, June 7 & 9, 1829, AAS, Larned Family Papers.

98 Hogan to Van Buren, March 6, 1830, NA, RG 59, M 146, vol. 2.

99 Richard Alsop, Philadelphia, to Van Buren, December 19, 1829, NA, RG 59, M 639. The information about Archer & Bispham comes from the Samuel Archer entry in *Dictionary of American Biography*.

100 Bispham to Larned, April 9, 1831, AAS, Larned Family Papers.

101 Bispham to Larned, April 13, 1830, AAS, Larned Family Papers.

102 J. Styles appears in an 1822 Chilean Navy list but not one in 1823, indicating he probably left the naval service that year, the same year Cochrane terminated his association with the Chilean Navy (Luis Uribe y Orrego, *Nuestra marina militar* (Valparaíso, 1910), 387, 426). John Styles contributed in 1833 to the first

hospital in Valparaíso and in 1835 contributed to earthquake relief (Charles F. Hillman, *Old Timers: British and Americans in Chile* (Santiago, 1901), 427, 429). Several sources mention the "English hospital" in Valparaíso, founded by a "British surgeon" (see, for example, Frederick Walpole, *Four Years in the Pacific in Her Majesty's Ship "Collingwood" from 1844 to 1848* (London, 1850), 1:101). The Styleses remained in Valparaíso until 1836 when they journeyed to the U.S. to live with Frances Hogan and other family members.

[103] Hogan to Van Buren, January 10, 1831, NA, RG 59, M 146, vol. 2.

[104] Bispham to Larned, January 11, 1831, AAS, Larned Family Papers. Bispham also told Larned that "there will be a row between Commodore Thompson and Mr. Hogan..., as the old man has done several things lately that will have to be noticed by the Commodore."

[105] Hogan to Larned, January 8, 1831, enclosure to Hogan to Van Buren, May 16, 1831, NA, RG 59, M 146, vol. 2. Larned's instructions appointing him to the Lima position told him that he should "carefully place [the Legation files] under seal and deposit them with some trustworthy officer or citizen of the United States if such an [*sic*] one is found, and, if not, you will carry them also with you to Lima to be hereafter returned to this Department." (Clay to Larned, January 1, 1829, NA, RG 59, M 77, vol. 12.) Hamm's instructions said that, because Larned had not informed the Department what he did with the files, Hamm was to demand them from Hogan or whoever had possession. (Van Buren to Hamm, October 15, 1830, NA, RG 59, M 77, vol. 14.)

[106] John Branch to Hogan, May 12, 1830, & September 28, 1830, MHFP.

[107] Hogan to Van Buren, May 16, 1831, NA, RG 59, M 146, vol. 2.

Chapter 11

[1] The Hogan to Oliver letters quoted in this chapter are dated August 28, 1831, July 10, 1832, October 6, 1832 & February 8, 1833, all in MHS, Robert Oliver Papers, MS 626, Box 2.

[2] *Congressional Directory of the Second Session of the 22nd Congress*, Washington, 1832.

[3] Quote is in Hogan to Poinsett, November 18, 1831, HSP, Joel R. Poinsett Collection. Although Southard and Kendall were both from New Hampshire, they were not always political allies (Donald B. Cole, *Jacksonian Democracy in New Hampshire, 1800-1851* (Cambridge, MA, 1970), 95-97).

[4] In his autobiography, Kendall boasts "how an end has been put to many abuses, frauds and corruptions, which consumed [the Navy's] means and cankered [its] morals and honor," but never mentions Hogan. William Stickney (ed.), *Autobiography of Amos Kendall* (Boston, 1872), 299.

[5] *Maloney*, 430.

[6] Allen, *Commodore Hull...Papers*, 64-67.

⁷ Specifically, Prevost was absent from Chile from September 18, 1821, to May 22, 1822, again from February 16 to October 15, 1823, and lastly from January 18, 1824. During the times that he was in Santiago, he reported frequently on political and military developments in Chile, as well as Peru.

⁸ The two letters are Hogan to Livingston, January 30 & April 5, 1832, NA, RG 59, M 146, vol. 2.

⁹ Livingston to James M. Wayne, Chairman, House Committee on Foreign Affairs, February 25, 1833, NA, RG 59, M 40, vol. 18.

¹⁰ *ASP, Naval Affairs* 4:881. The amount of salary could be considered generous ($4,500 would today be worth over $67,000), but consular and diplomatic representatives were not then reimbursed for most official expenses, including transportation, hiring of clerks and other direct operating costs, nor did they receive entertainment allowances.

¹¹ The exact cause of Hogan's death is unknown. A cholera epidemic, the first in North America, hit many American cities in summer 1832 (Washington in September). Hogan took note of the cholera threat, but without further comment, in his July 10, 1832, letter to Oliver.

¹² Hogan to Andrew Jackson, March 21, 1833, NA, RG 59 M 146, vol. 2.

¹³ The several Wilkes' quotes are in *Wilkes,* 296-298.

Epilogue

¹ Richard Alsop, Philadelphia, to Edward Livingston, February 30, 1833, NA, RG 59, M 639. The correct date must have been March or even April 30 because Hogan did not die until March 26.

² The many letters written to the secretary of state and president by private parties and Congress concerning Bispham and Russell and Jackson's note are in NA, RG 59, M 639. Russell's and Hobson's arrivals in Valparaíso are in NA, RG 59, M 146.

³ *9 U.S. Statutes-at-Large 742.*

⁴ The committee reports, including several enclosures, are in *ASP, Naval Affairs,* 4:536-538, 880-883.

⁵ Michael Birkner, *Samuel L. Southard: Jeffersonian Whig* (Cranbury, NJ, 1984), 196-199.

⁶ U.S. vs. William Hogan, NA, Northeast Region, Bayonne, NJ.

⁷ Edmund Fitz Moore, *Reports of Cases Heard and Determined by the Judicial Committee and the Lords of Her Majesty's Most Honorable Privy Council,* 14 (London, 1861):310-328

BIBLIOGRAPHY

PRIMARY SOURCES

Archives

American Antiquarian Society, Worcester, Massachusetts. Larned Family Papers, 1753–1859.
Cape Town Archives Repository, Cape Town, South Africa.
Congressional Records. 1831–1837.
Cornell University Library, Ithaca, New York. Elisha Camp, 1786–1866, Papers.
Historical Society of Pennsylvania, Philadelphia. Joel R. Poinsett Papers.
India Records Office, London.
Library of Congress, Manuscript Division, Washington, DC. The Adams Family Papers.
Maryland Historical Society, Baltimore. Robert Oliver Papers.
Michael Hogan Family Papers, privately held.
National Archives, Washington, DC.
New York Historical Society, New York City.
Public Records Office, London, England.
South Carolina Historical Society, Charleston, SC.
State Library of New South Wales, Sydney.
St. Lawrence University Libraries, Special Collections & Archives.
University of the Witwatersrand Library. Gubbins Collection of Africana, Earl of Macartney Papers. Catalogued by Anna M. Cunningham, *The Earl of Macartney Papers*, University of Witwatersrand, Johannesburg, 1977.

Newspapers

Cape Town Gazette and African Advertiser. Published in English and Dutch beginning August 1800 and in Dutch only as *Kaapsche Courant* beginning April 1803. The issues from August 16, 1800, to October 19, 1801 are published in *The Cape Town Gazette and African Advertiser*, The South African Library, Cape Town, 1982.
Charleston Courier.
New York Commercial Advertiser.
Selections from the Calcutta Gazette of the Years 1784–1823. Vols. 1–3, edited by W.S. Seton-Karr; Vols. 4 & 5, edited by H.D. Sandeman. Calcutta, 1864–69.

Published Collections

Allen, Gardner Weld (ed.). *Commodore Hull: Papers of Isaac Hull.* Boston, 1929.
American State Papers, 1831–1836, Foreign Affairs, Vol. 4; *Naval Affairs*, Vols. 1–4.

Donnan, Elizabeth (ed.). *Documents Illustrative of the Slave Trade in America*. 4 vols. New York, 1965.
Historical Records of Australia. Series 1, vols. 1, 2, 3, 4 & 5. Sydney, 1914.
Historical Records of New South Wales. Vols. 3, 4, 5 & 6. Sydney, 1895.
The Keith Papers. Publications of the Navy Records Society. Vol. 1. London.
Manning, William Ray (ed.). *Diplomatic Correspondence of the United States Concerning the Independence of Latin American Nations*. 3 vols. New York, 1925.
Register of Ships Employed in the Services of the Honorable the United East India Company. London, 1835.
Theal, George McCall (ed.). *Records of the Cape Colony*. Vol. 2 (1796–1799), vol. 3 (1800–1801), vol. 4 (1801–1803), vol. 5 (1803–1806). Cape Town, 1898–99.
Webster, Charles Kingsley. *Britain and the Independence of Latin America, 1812–30: Selected Documents* .... 2 vols. London, 1938; New York 1970.

Published Diaries, Letters and Journals

Adams, John Quincy. *Memoirs of John Quincy Adams*. 12 vols. Edited by Charles Francis Adams. Freeport, New York, 1969.
Barnard, Lady Anne. *South Africa a Century Ago: Letters Written from the Cape of Good Hope (1797–1801) by Lady Anne Barnard*. London, 1901.
Fairbridge, Dorthea (ed.). *Lady Anne Barnard at the Cape of Good Hope: Extracts from Letters from Andrew Barnard to Lord Macartney*. Oxford, 1924.
Graham, Maria Dundas (Lady Maria Calcott). *Journal of a Residence in Chile During the Year 1822....* London, 1824 (reprinted New York 1969).
Lenta, Margaret & Basil Le Cordeur (eds.). *The Cape Diaries of Lady Anne Barndard, 1799–1800*. 2 volumes. Van Riebeeck Society, Cape Town, 1999.
"Letters from John Pintard to His Daughter, Eliza Noel Pintard Davidson, 1816–1833." *Collections of the New York Historical Society for the Year 1937*. Vols. 1 & 3. New York, 1940.
Pasley, M.S. Rodney (ed.). *Private Sea Journals, 1778–1782, Kept by Admiral Sir Thomas Pasley*. London, 1931.
Philips, Cyril Henry (ed.). *The Correspondence of David Scott*. 2 vols. London, 1951.
Robinson, A. M. (ed.). *The Letters of Lady Anne Barnard to Henry Dundas from the Cape and Elsewhere, 1793–1803*. Cape Town, 1973.

SECONDARY SOURCES

Adams, Henry. *History of the United States of America During the Administrations of Thomas Jefferson. 1801–1809*. Library of America edition. New York, 1986.
_____. *History of the United States of America During the Administrations of James Madison, 1809–1817*. Library of America edition. New York, 1986.
Arkin, Marcus. "John Company at the Cape: A History of the Agency under Pringle (1794–1815)." *Archives Yearbook for South African History* 23 vol. 2 (1961).
Aspinall, A. *Cornwallis in Bengal*. New Delhi, 1987.

BIBLIOGRAPHY 425

Austen, Harold Cholmby. *Sea Fights and Corsairs of the Indian Ocean, Being the Naval History of Mauritius from 1715 to 1810*. Port Louis, Mauritius, 1935.

Bell, Malcolm, Jr. *Major Butler's Legacy: Five Generations of a Slaveholding Family*. Athens, GA, 1987.

Billingsley, Edward Baxter. *In Defense of Neutral Rights: The United States Navy and the Wars of Independence of Chile and Peru*. Chapel Hill, NC, 1967.

Biographical Directory of the United States Congress, 1774–1989. Bicentennial Edition. Washington, DC, 1989.

Cambridge History of the British Empire. Vol. 2 (The New Empire, 1783–1870), vol. 8 (South Africa). Cambridge, 1929.

Cambridge History of India. Vol. 5 (British India 1497–1858). Cambridge, 1929.

Campbell, John. *The Naval History of Great Britain*. Vols. 3, 6, 7. London, 1813.

Chatterton, Edward Keble. *The Old East Indiamen*. London, 1971.

Clowes, William Laird. *The Royal Navy*. Vols. 3, 4 & 6. London 1899.

Crowhurst, Patrick. *The Defence of British Trade, 1689–1815*. London, 1977.

Dictionary of American Biography. New York.

Dictionary of National Biography. London.

Donnelly, Sophia. *Memories of Former Days, By a Grandmother*. Unpublished MS, Stuttgart, 1873.

Donovan, Herbert D.A. *Fort Covington and Her Neighbors: A History of Three Towns*. New York, 1963.

Elphick, Richard & Hermann Giliomee (eds.). *The Shaping of South African Society, 1652–1840*. Middleton, CN, 1989.

Evans, Henry Clay, Jr. *Chile and Its Relations with the United States*. Durham, NC, 1927.

Foner, Philip Sheldon. *A History of Cuba and its Relations with the United States*. 2 vols. New York, 1962–3.

Freund, William Mark. "Society and Government in Dutch South Africa: The Cape and the Batavians, 1803–6." Unpublished Ph.D. dissertation. Yale University, 1971.

Frost, Alan. *Convicts and Empire: A Naval Question, 1776–1811*. Melbourne, 1980.

Furber, Holden. *The John Company at Work: A Study of European Expansion in India in the Late Eighteenth Century*. 1948.

Haight, Mabel V. Jackson. *European Powers and South-East Africa: A Study of International Relations on the South-East Coast of Africa, 1796–1856*. London, 1942 (1967 edition).

Hamm, Tommy Todd. "The American Slave Trade with Africa, 1620–1807." Unpublished Ph.D. dissertation, Indiana University, 1975.

Harlow, Victor Todd. *The Founding of the Second British Empire, 1763–1793*. 2 vols. London, 1952.

Haswell, Charles H. *Reminiscences of an Octogenarian of the City of New York, 1816–1860*. New York, 1896.

Hickey, William. *Memoirs of William Hickey*. Edited by Alfred Spencer. Vol. 4. New York, 1925.

Hough, Franklin B. *A History of St. Lawrence and Franklin Counties, New York, from the Earliest Period to the Present Time.* Albany, N.Y.,1853.

Hughes, Robert. *The Fatal Shore.* New York, 1987.

Hunt, Gaillard. *The Department of State of the United States: Its History and Functions.* New Haven, 1914.

Keay, John. *The Honourable Company: A History of the English East India Company.* New York, 1994.

Kennedy, Charles Stuart. *The American Consul: A History of the U.S. Consular Service, 1776–1914.* New York, 1990.

Laidler, Percy Ward. *A Tavern of the Ocean.* Cape Town, 1926.

Lewis, Michael Arthur. *A Social History of the British Navy, 1793–1815.* London, 1960.

Lossing, Benson J. *The Hudson from the Wilderness to the Sea.* Troy, N.Y., 187?.

Mackesy, Piers. *The War for America, 1775–1783.* Cambridge, MA, 1964.

Maloney, Linda M. *The Captain from Connecticut: The Life and Naval Times of Isaac Hull.* Boston, 1986.

Mannix, Daniel Pratt & Malcolm Cowley. *Black Cargoes: A History of the Atlantic Slave Trade, 1518–1865.* New York, 1976.

Marshall, Peter James. *East Indian Fortunes: The British in Bengal in the Eighteenth Century.* Oxford, 1976.

McKee, Christopher. *A Gentlemanly and Honorable Profession: The Creation of the U.S. Naval Officer Corps, 1794–1815.* Annapolis, MD, 1991.

Michener, James A. & A. Grove Day. *Rascals in Paradise.* New York, 1957.

Mott, Hopper Striker. *The New York of Yesterday: A Descriptive Narrative of Old Bloomingdale.* New York, 1908.

National Cyclopaedia.

Neumann, William L. "United States Aid to the Chilean Wars of Independence." *Hispanic American Historical Review* 27, no. 2 (May 1947):204–219.

Nightingale, Pamela. *Trade and Empire in Western India, 1784–1806.* Cambridge, 1970.

Old Buildings of New York City. New York, 1907.

Parkinson, Cyril Northcote. *Trade in the Eastern Seas, 1793–1813.* New York, 1966.

_____ (ed.). *The Trade Winds, a Study of British Overseas Trade During the French Wars, 1793–1815.* London, 1948.

_____. *War in the Eastern Seas, 1793–1815.* London, 1954.

Parry, J.H. *Trade and Dominion: European Overseas Empires in the 18th Century.* Newark, NJ, 1971.

Pasley, Sir Thomas Sabine. *Memoir of Admiral Sir Thomas Sabine Pasley.* Edited by Louise Maria Sabine Pasley. London, 1900.

Peterson, A. Everett (ed.). *Landmarks of New York: A Historical Guide to the Metropolis.* 1923.

Philip, Peter. *British Residents at the Cape of Good Hope. 1795–1819.* Cape Town, 1981.

Philips, Cyril Henry. *The East India Company, 1784–1834.* Manchester, 1940.

BIBLIOGRAPHY 427

Pine, John Crane. *The Role of United States Special Agents in the Development of a Spanish American Policy, 1810–1822.* Unpublished Ph.D. thesis, University of Colorado, 1955.

Popham, Hugh. *A Damned Cunning Fellow: The Eventful Life of Rear-Admiral Sir Home Popham, 1762–1820.* Cornwall, 1991.

Pritchard, Earl Hampton. *Crucial Years of Early Anglo-Chinese Relations, 1750–1800.* Vol. 1. Research Studies of the State College of Washington, Pullman, WA, 1936.

Rector, John L. *Merchants, Trade and Commercial Policy in Chile, 1810–1840.* Unpublished Ph.D. dissertation, Indiana University, 1976.

Rose, J. Holland. "The French East-India Expedition at the Cape in 1803." *English Historical Review* 15 no. 57 (1900):29–132.

Rutherford, G. "Sidelights on Commodore Johnstone's Expedition to the Cape." Parts 1 & 2. *The Mariner's Mirror: Journal of the Society for Nautical Research* 28 (1942):189-212, 290-308.

Scoville, Joseph Alfred (Walter Barrett, pseud.). *The Old Merchants of New York City.* Fourth Series. New York, 1866.

Seaver, Frederick Joel. *Historical Sketches of Franklin County and Its Several Towns with Many Short Biographies.* Albany, N.Y., 1918. Separate index by Walter C. Smallman, *Genealogical Index to Seaver's Historical Sketches of Franklin County*, 1983.

Sherman, William Roderick. *The Diplomatic and Commercial Relations of the United States and Chile, 1820–1914.* New York, 1973.

Singh, S.B. *European Agency Houses in Bengal, 1783–1833.* Calcutta, 1966.

Smith, Walter Burges. *America's Diplomats and Consuls of 1776–1865: A Geographic and Biographic Directory of the Foreign Service from the Declaration of Independence to the End of the Civil War.* Washington, DC, 1986.

Spear, Thomas George Percival. *The Nabobs: A Study of the Social Life of the English in Eighteenth Century India.* London, 1932.

Stokes, Isaac Newton Phelps. *The Iconography of Manhattan Island, 1498–1909.* New York, 1928.

Theal, George McCall. *History of South Africa from 1795 to 1872.* Vol.1: *The Cape Colony from 1795 to 1828.* London, 1891.

Turner, L.C.F. "The Cape of Good Hope and the Anglo-French Conflict, 1797–1806." *Historical Studies: Australia and New Zealand* 9 (May 1961), Melbourne.

_____. "The Cape of Good Hope and the Anglo-French Rivalry, 1778–1796." *Historical Studies: Australia and New Zealand* 12 (April 1966), Melbourne.

U.S. Navy Department. *Dictionary of American Naval Fighting Ships.* 8 vols. Washington, DC, 1981.

Weinreb, Ben and Christopher Hibbert (eds.). *The London Encyclopedia.* Bethesda, MD, 1986.

Whitaker, Arthur Preston. *The United States and the Independence of Latin America, 1800–1830.* New York, 1962.

Wilkes, Charles. *Autobiography of Rear Admiral Charles Wilkes, 1798–1877.* Edited by William James Morgan and others. Washington, DC, 1978.

INDEX OF NAMES

Only names of persons, companies and ships are shown. Names of presidents, prime ministers, kings, queens and other national leaders are not shown unless there is a connection with Michael Hogan or persons with whom he was closely associated. Because Michael Hogan's name appears on almost all pages, his name is not indexed.

Adams, John Quincy, 228-230, 237-239
Adamson, Alexander, 47, 48, 131
Allen, Elizabeth Hart, 289, 296, 298, 314, 320
Allen, Heman, 286, 289-291, 293-303, 306-310, 314, 320, 324, 326, 332, 339
Alsop Wetmore & Cryder, 333, 334, 336, 337
Alsop, Richard, 333, 334, 354
Anderson, William, 140, 141, 144, 146, 147, 149-151, 154-158, 160-162, 166, 167, 169, 171, 180-182, 192, 222

Baird, David, Gen., 191
Balmain, William, 63
Banks, Joseph, 71, 74
Baretto & Co., 48
Baring, Sir Francis, 58
Barnard, Andrew, 91, 105, 110-112, 121, 135
Barnard, Lady Anne, 91, 108, 110, 111, 114, 118, 135, 137
Bayard, William, 201, 236
Beard, David, Gen., 133
Benavides, Vincente, 250, 258-261
Biddle, James, Capt., 267
Binney, Amos, 305
Bispham, Charles, 333, 336, 354, 355
Black, Francis C., 237
Black, John, 122, 123, 125

Blake, Richard, 106, 107, 110-112, 115-119, 121, 136, 138, 146
Bland, Theodorick, 244, 247
Blankett, John, Commodore, 57, 58, 60
Boles, Barnaby, Capt., 25, 28-30, 40, 44
Bolivar, Simon, 242, 294, 295, 320, 327
Boston, John, 187
Brabyn, John, Ensign, 55-57, 63
Branch, John, 325, 326, 338
Brewerton, G.D., Lieut., 302
Brown, Thomas Edward, 249
Bugnon, George, Capt., 335
Bullus, John, Dr., 239, 249, 271, 293, 298, 316
Burr, Aaron, 176, 197, 201, 244, 266
Butler, Pierce, 176, 189, 205, 215, 216, 220, 224
Butler, Thomas, 205, 217-221, 224

Campbell & Co., 46
Campbell, Donald, Port Capt., 111, 112, 135, 137
Chapman, Morton, Capt., 86
Chapman, William Neate, 70
Christian, Sir Hugh, Adm., 87, 88
Clarke, Sir Alured, Maj. Gen., 58
Clay, Henry, 243, 247, 248, 291, 297
Clay, William, 252, 310, 314
Clendening, Sarah, 228, 249, 351
Cleveland, Richard Jeffry, 261, 268
Clinton, DeWitt, Gov., 216, 228, 290

INDEX

Cloete & Cruywagen, 92, 94, 164, 185, 188, 192, 194
Cochrane, Thomas, Adm., 245, 246, 249, 254-256, 334
Cockburn, James, Major, 107, 113, 116, 119, 136, 138, 146
Cockburn, Sir George, Rear Adm., 213, 220, 245
Collins, David, 63, 67, 76, 108
Comstock, Samuel, 311, 313
Comstock, William, 312, 313
Cornwallis, Charles, Lord, 16, 19, 24, 27, 37, 46
Cornwallis, William, Commodore, 27
Costa, F.J., Capt., 157
Cottam, Bartholemew, 129, 144, 145
Covell, Dennis, 313, 314
Craig, Sir James Henry, Gen., 57, 60, 76, 93
Curtis, Sir Roger, Vice Adm., 88, 125, 126, 139, 155

D'Arcy, John, 301
David Scott & Co., 40, 46-48, 51, 59, 61, 74, 78-80, 82, 87, 105, 131, 144, 147, 149-152
Davidson & Maxwell & Co., 42
de Grasse, Adm., 6, 17
de Lacey, Anna Maria, 25, 141
de Malleveault, Madame, 217-220
de Mist, Jacobus Abraham, Gen., 159, 164, 184
de Suffren, Pierre Andre, Adm., 10, 12
de Waal, Arend, 135, 137
Decatur, Stephen, Commodore, 213, 227, 229
Deconnick & Co., 105, 144, 148, 150
Depau, Francis, 189, 192, 193, 207-209
Dickey, Robert, 207, 209, 216, 249, 329
Didier, Henry, Jr., 301
Digby, Robert, Adm., 17
Donnelly, Arthur, 283, 351

Downes, James, Capt., 246, 267, 268, 276
Duckitt, William, 115
Duncan, James, 83, 84
Dundas, Francis, Maj. Gen., 76, 88, 93, 100, 105, 109, 120, 121, 134-136, 138, 142, 143, 145, 159, 160
Dundas, Henry, 58, 76, 78, 79, 88, 93, 106, 114, 120, 130, 134, 135
Duntzfeldt & Co., 144, 145, 150
Dutch East India Company, 12, 13, 89

East India Company, 5, 6, 10, 21, 23, 24, 31, 32, 34, 35, 37, 38, 43, 44, 46, 47, 50, 51, 53, 58-60, 67, 74, 75, 77, 78, 81, 82, 86, 92, 95, 109, 145, 147, 149, 155, 164, 211, 283
Echeverria, Joaquim, 261, 262, 268, 273
Ehrick, John Mathias, 189, 202
Ellis, Sgt., 55-57
Elmslie, John, 131, 222
Elphinstone, Sir George Keith, Rear Adm., 57-60, 72, 76
Erskine, Henry, Major, 135, 137
Evarts, William Maxwell, 207

Fairlie Gilore & Co., 131
Fairlie Reid & Co., 43, 45, 47
Fanning & Co., 187, 188
Finch, William Bolton, Capt., 308, 317, 332
Flood, Mark, 65, 85, 94, 126
Forbes Sheppard & Co., 30
Fowkes, Francis, 140, 166
Franklin Robertson & Co., 170
Freire, Ramon, Gen., 284, 285, 294, 322

Gaffney, Lawrence, Private, 57, 63
Gerauld, Horatio, 252

Gilchrist, Adam, 189, 192, 193
Gillett Lambert & Ross & Co., 29, 31
Gilmore, Mungo, Capt., 80, 86
Goetz, George Frederik, 143
Gordon, Robert Jacob, Col., 79
Graham, Maria Dundas, 279, 281
Grand, George Francis, 163
Grant, James, Capt., 122
Green, John Hooke, 109, 112
Guezzi, Charles Joseph, 143, 159, 166

Hamm, John, 334-336, 347, 354
Harris, John, Dr., 127
Hart, Harriet Augusta, 289, 296, 298, 308, 314, 320
Henshaw, Robert, 23
Hill, Henry, 252, 268
Hines, Patrick, 56
Hogan, Cornelius, 7, 8
Hogan, Dennis, 7, 8, 85, 146, 151, 181
Hogan, Fanny, 50, 86, 88, 209, 217, 218, 249, 250, 334, 338, 339, 349, 351
Hogan, Frances, 29, 30, 37, 45, 49, 54, 85, 86, 88, 94, 108, 109, 114, 115, 155, 162, 173, 209, 215, 217, 219, 249, 271, 279, 298, 306, 315, 317, 320, 334, 338-340, 351
Hogan, Harriet, 94, 217, 249, 251, 302, 315, 316, 320, 334, 340, 351
Hogan, John, 94
Hogan, Mary, 7, 19, 20, 28, 31, 40, 66, 67, 108
Hogan, Maurice, 7, 8, 202
Hogan, Sophia, 94, 140, 162, 179, 217, 249-251, 258-260, 280, 281, 283, 284, 290, 315-317, 322, 323, 335, 340, 351
Hogan, William, 38, 86, 88, 140, 146, 162, 171, 180, 199, 202, 206, 215-217, 223-225, 228, 230, 249, 338-340, 346, 349-351, 353, 355, 356
Hogan, William, Jr., 206, 340, 356
Holland, John, 103, 105, 149, 151
Hull, Isaac, Commodore, 289, 290, 296, 298, 299, 303-309, 312, 314, 320, 323, 329, 332, 339, 340, 346, 352
Hunter, John, Gov., 62, 63, 65, 69, 70, 94

Jackson, Samuel, 64
Jackson, William James, 173, 197
Janssens, Jan Willem, Gen., 159, 166, 171
Jessup, Henry James, 149
John Ferguson & Co., 43
John Forbes & Co., 43
Johnstone, George, Commodore, 7, 9, 11-13, 15, 16
Jones, Jacob, Commodore, 308, 350

Kendall, Amos, 325, 326, 345
Kenyon, William, 151, 152, 184
King, Anna Josepha, 71
King, Joseph, Capt., 171
King, Philip Gidley, Gov., 68-72, 108, 187
King, Philip Parker, Commander, 108, 319
Larned, Samuel, 289, 291, 301, 304, 309, 310, 320, 323, 325, 327, 332, 334, 336, 347, 348
Le Roy Bayard & Co., 236
Leadan, John, 103
Lennox, William, 47, 82, 84, 144, 145, 147, 148, 150, 151
Lenox, Robert, 151, 152, 170, 172, 182, 184, 188, 189, 206, 207, 209
Leroy Bayard & Co., 236, 249, 273, 282, 330
Lewis, Edward, 140, 156, 170, 182, 188

INDEX

Livingston, Henry Brockholst, Judge, 220, 221
Lord, Simeon, 126, 187

Macarthur, Edward, 68, 76
Macarthur, Hannibal Hawkins, 319, 330
Macarthur, John, 65, 67, 94
Macartney, George, Lord, 32, 79, 88, 93, 98, 104, 108, 111, 120, 135, 154
Macomb, Alexander, 201, 214
Madison, James, 211, 222
McClure, Alexander, 168, 170, 185, 189
McKellar, Archibald, Capt., 116, 131, 141, 142
Medows, William, Gen., 11-14, 26
Mellish, William, 128, 151
Michell Amos & Bowden & Co., 31
Monroe, James, 206, 213, 220, 221, 226-230, 237-239, 270, 272, 282, 285, 293, 327
Monteiro, Joaquim do Rosario, 141, 142, 166
Moore, William, Ensign, 57, 63
Morrell, Benjamin, 311
Mosse, Peter, 149
Munn, Charles, Capt., 84, 95

Nelson, Sir Horatio, Adm., 19, 139
Nugent, Christopher, 296, 327

O'Donald, Bryan, 54
O'Hara, Charles, Gen., 19, 20, 28, 40, 50
O'Higgins, Bernardo, 242, 251, 254, 255, 262, 266, 275, 284, 290, 294, 301, 302, 347
O'Sullivan, John, Capt., 273, 275, 330
Oliver, John & Robert, 214-216, 222, 224, 225, 227, 228, 230, 232, 250, 302, 317, 329, 338, 340, 342, 343, 345, 348, 350

Osborne, John, Capt., 109

Palmer, John, 65, 126, 127
Parish & Co., 49, 249
Pasley, Sir Thomas Sabine, Lieut., 314, 316
Pasley, Thomas, Capt., 7, 9-13, 15, 16, 314
Pendleton, Isaac, 187
Percival, John, Capt., 304, 305, 312
Pigot, Hugh, Adm., 17
Pinkham, A.B., Capt., 261, 262, 272
Pintard, John, 184, 207, 208, 224, 230
Pintard, John Marsden, 177, 201, 207, 208, 230
Pinto, Francisco, Gen., 322
Pitt, William (The Younger), 79
Poinsett, Joel Roberts, 243, 247, 306, 339
Ponterdant, David, 149, 150, 192
Popham, Sir Home Riggs, Capt., 35, 131, 132, 141, 191, 195, 256
Portales, Diego, 301, 322, 324
Preble, Edward, Capt., 125
Prevost, John Bartow, 178, 201, 244, 246, 252, 253, 255, 260-267, 269-271, 274, 276, 278, 284-286, 294, 297, 303, 347, 348
Prieto, Joaquin, Gen., 322, 324
Pringle, John, 59, 76, 77, 86, 87, 93, 105, 109, 121, 125, 131, 136, 154, 156

Renshaw, Richard, Capt., 171, 182
Rex, George, 151
Richardson, Christopher, 25, 39, 205, 225
Richardson, Frances, 25, 26
Richardson, Jane, 25
Richardson, Peter Thomas, 79, 132
Richardson, Rowland, 25
Richardson, William, 25, 29, 36, 37, 39, 40, 44, 80, 81, 140

Richardson, William, Jr., 53, 55, 57, 141, 205
Ridgely, Charles Goodwin, Commodore, 255, 260, 265, 267, 270, 271, 275, 279
Riley, John, 65
Robert Charnock & Co., 31, 34, 36, 37, 39-41, 46, 49
Robertson, John Parish, 249
Robinson, Jeremy, 239, 244, 262-265, 267, 269, 270, 272, 278, 286
Ross, Hercules, 87, 139
Roux, Paul, 144
Ruschenberger, W.S.W., Dr., 302
Rush, Richard, 253, 270
Ryan, Ann, 66, 67, 109

Sharpe, Nathaniel, 43, 48, 49
Sheppard, Thomas, 301
Ships, British Navy
    Adventure, 319, 320
    America, 58, 59
    Arrogant, 75
    Crown, 27
    Diomede, 128
    Eclair, 297, 314, 315
    Isis, 12
    Jupiter, 7, 9, 11-17, 20, 314
    Lady Nelson, 122
    Romney, 7, 13, 14, 131, 256
    Ruby, 59
    Sirius, 71
    Tremendous, 109, 155, 162
    Tribune, 335
    Victorius, 75
Ships, Chilean Navy
    Chacabuco, 245
    Lautero, 244, 245
    San Martin, 245
Ships, French Navy
    Annibal, 10-12
    Cybele, 75
Ships, merchant
    Adventura, 131
    Amiable Maria, 126, 156

Angelique, 109
Annawan, 313
Asenath, 188
Augusta, 192
Barwell, 86, 95
Beagle, 319, 320
Beaver, 268
Belvedere, 86
Boa Caetana, 115, 116
Bombay Anna, 23, 28, 79, 86, 93
Bombay Castle, 102
Boxer, 233
Britannia, 67
Calypso, 143, 144
Canton, 273-275, 330
Carron, 86
Carteret, 162
Castle of Good Hope, 144
Chance, 123, 125, 126, 187
Charleston Packet, 201, 202, 209, 249, 330
Charlotte, 128, 182
Christianus Septimus, 104
Clermont, 197
Clifton, 301
Collector, 102, 111, 113, 114, 116, 134, 137, 138, 141, 142, 148, 150, 155, 170
De Drie Broeders, 118
Diana, 100
Dispatch, 119-121, 138
Dolphin, 191, 192, 201, 207
Dublin, 72
Eagle, 305, 329
Europa, 74
Excellentissimo Augusta, 167-169, 186, 190, 192
Fair American, 187
Fanny, 116, 122, 131
Favorite, 182
Felis Eugenia, 157, 160, 161, 165
Flying Fish, 269
Fort William, 74
Friendship, 140
Ganges, 186

INDEX 433

General Hand, 329
Globe, 311-313
Good Hope, 305, 346
Harbinger, 86, 100, 103, 122, 123, 126, 187
Harriet, 103, 113, 123, 145, 150, 152
Hero, 258, 259
Hersilia, 258
Holger Danske, 103, 105, 109, 111, 113, 123, 140, 144, 145, 147-150, 170
Hope, 130, 188
Horizon, 168
Il Netunno, 31, 34, 37, 38, 40, 45, 46, 48, 49, 60
Il Triomfo, 42
Industry, 185
Joaquim, 100, 101, 107-110, 113, 117, 135, 141, 144
Joseph Harvey, 151
Juno, 169, 170, 181
L'Africana, 102, 111
L'Auguste, 111, 112
La Rose, 102, 111
La Union, 95, 122
Lady Shore, 122
Lady Yonge, 118, 121
Lapwing, 151, 184
Leonides, 335
Limeno, 126, 127, 157
Louisa, 169, 171, 182
Louisa, Portuguese, 143, 144
Macedonian, 237, 246, 255, 274, 292
Manhattan, 156
Maria, 166, 170
Marquis Cornwallis, 49, 51, 53, 55, 58, 61-63, 67, 72, 74, 75, 77, 80, 81, 84, 94, 95, 99, 151, 319
Mary, 282
Matilda, 122
Milford, 156
Montgomery, 132
Mountain, 113
Myrtle, 30, 48

Neptune, 99
New Orleans, 336, 338
New Triumph, 29, 77
Nossa Senhora del Carmen, 122
Nossa Senhora del Rosario, 122
Numero Seite, 128
O'Cain, 282
Ocean, 258, 259, 261, 262, 266, 268, 272
Octavia, 184-186, 208
Orb, 202
Perseverance, 169, 171, 182, 186
Persia, 260
Phoenix, 153, 156
Pigot, 23
President, 156
Regulus, 131, 132, 141, 151, 157
Rolla, 196
Salamander, 128
San Antonio, 23, 47
Santa Rosa, 116
Savage, 268, 301
Sea Nymph, 131, 132, 141, 142, 151
Serah, 159, 161
Silenius, 169, 182
St. Antonio de Ballena, 128
St. Josea DeIndiana, 115
St. Josea Escabre, 128
Surat Castle, 86, 93
Surprize, 169, 171, 182
Tartar, 311
Teaplant, 249, 250, 258-260
Tremendous, 131
Union, 128, 182, 187
Wasp, 311
Young Adam, 191, 192, 195, 201, 207
Young Nicholas, 118
Young William, 95
Ships, U.S. Navy
    Brandywine, 301, 302, 307, 308, 317, 318

Constellation, 248, 250, 255, 260, 270, 271, 273, 275, 279
Dolphin, 269, 273, 275, 277, 295, 301, 304, 305, 308, 312, 313, 318
Essex, 125
Franklin, 262, 271, 272, 275, 277, 279, 281, 283, 285, 289, 310
Guerriere, 318, 319, 323, 335
Macedonian, 237
Ontario, 273
Peacock, 213, 298, 304, 308
St. Louis, 318, 335
United States, 289, 296, 297, 304, 308, 312, 314, 316
Vincennes, 308, 317, 332, 356
Sibbald, James, 47
Simson, George, Commodore, 74
Sloat, John Drake, Capt., 318, 333, 336
Smart, David, Capt., 102, 111-114, 137
Smit, Hans Laurens, Capt., 111, 145, 149, 150
Smith Eliphalet, Capt., 246, 263, 274, 275, 292, 330
Solvyns, Balthazar, 31
Southard, Samuel L., 356
Stewart, Charles, Commodore, 262, 267, 271, 272, 274-278, 282-284, 286, 330
Stocking, Seth, Capt., 233, 234
Stogdell, John, 65
Strombom, Isaac, 92, 98
Studdent, Thomas, 84
Styles, John, Dr., 245, 302, 320, 351
Sumter, Thomas, Jr., 177, 201, 202, 249, 330

Tate, James, 47, 48

Tennant, Alexander, 29, 77, 92, 94, 99, 100, 117, 137, 164
Tewajusett, Pondoosett, 29, 44
Thompson, C.B., Commodore, 318, 323, 324, 334, 335
Thompson, Smith, 238
Thrale, Hester, 25
Tompkins, Daniel D., Gov., 220, 223, 224
Tracy, Henry D., 263, 269
Trail, Donald, 99, 128, 182
Tucker, John Gouston, Capt., 119, 120, 139
Tully, Philip, 65

Van Ryneveld, Willem Stephanus, 92, 112, 114, 136, 164
Vaughn, John, 229
Vicuna, Francisco R., 298
von Pfister, Alexander, 217

Walker & Robertson & Co., 92, 118, 131, 143
White, William, Capt., 103, 123-125, 127, 145, 150, 156-158, 160, 161
Wilkes, Charles, Adm., 206, 279, 282, 349, 350, 356
William Henry, Prince, 17, 197, 319
Williams, Eleazer, 224
Wittenoon, Thomas, 149
Woodbury, Levi, 338, 345
Worthington, William G.D., 244
Wynn, Daniel, 297

Yonge, Sir George, 99, 105, 107, 110, 112, 115, 117, 119, 121, 125, 134-140, 142, 143, 146, 341

Zantsinger, John P., Capt., 313

About the author...

Michael Styles is a retired foreign service officer who served in several capacities abroad and in the State Department, including economic officer at the American Embassy in Tokyo and director of the office dealing with international civil aviation issues. After government service, he served as a consultant in the latter field. A history buff, he teaches history courses at the Learning in Retirement Institute at George Mason University. He was inspired to write this book because he is in possession of the letters and other memorabilia of Michael Hogan, his triple great grandfather, and found many others in archives around the world. The author makes his home in Fairfax Station, Virginia, with his wife Page and nearby children and grandchildren.